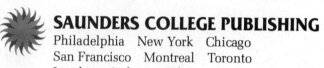 **SAUNDERS COLLEGE PUBLISHING**
Philadelphia   New York   Chicago
San Francisco   Montreal   Toronto
London   Sydney   Tokyo   Mexico City
Rio de Janeiro   Madrid

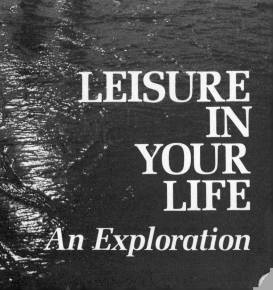

# Geoffrey Godbey

Recreation and Parks Program
The Pennsylvania State University

# LEISURE IN YOUR LIFE

## An Exploration

**Address Orders to:** 383 Madison Ave.
New York, NY 10017
**Address Editorial correspondence to:**
West Washington Square
Philadelphia, PA 19105

This book was set in Melior by Caledonia Composition, Inc.
The editors were John Butler, Carol Field, and Louise Robinson.
The art director and cover designer was Nancy E. J. Grossman.
The cover and title page photo, "A family enjoys an early morning
  walk in the splashing waves" (Wildwood, N.J.) by Ken Kasper,
  ©1980.
The text design was done by North 7 Atelier Ltd.
The production manager was Tom O'Connor.
R. R. Donnelley and Sons was printer and binder.

**LIBRARY OF CONGRESS
CATALOG CARD NO.: 80-53929**

Godbey, Geoffrey
Leisure in your life: An exploration.
Philadelphia, Pa.: Saunders College
352 p.
8101        801010

LEISURE IN YOUR LIFE: AN EXPLORATION                    ISBN   0—03—057673—3

1234 39 987654321

**CBS COLLEGE PUBLISHING**
Saunders College Publishing
Holt, Rinehart and Winston
The Dryden Press

# Preface

Writing about leisure is a lot like throwing stones at the wind—it's hard to know when you've hit the target. Nevertheless, this book is about leisure. The attempt here will be to do three things: (1) provide an elementary base of information about leisure from a historical, behavioral, and philosophical perspective; (2) help to clarify your values concerning various aspects of leisure; and (3) expand your awareness of leisure as it relates to your life and those of others. Attempting these three objectives is rather ambitious, if not downright foolhardy. In order for these objectives to be met, I'll need your help. You will have to *participate* in this undertaking—you will have to read carefully and thoughtfully, and you will have to respond honestly to the leisure exercises. Also, it will constantly be necessary to try to compare what you read on these pages to what you observe in the "real world." Actually, I hope you will become convinced that what appears in this book *is* part of the real world.

Much of this writing, and many of the exercises contained here, are the result of having taught courses dealing with leisure behavior to over 1,000 university students. The material covered here has been revised many times, based upon classroom experience.

In 1966 Dr. Stanley Parker of the British Office of Population Censuses and Surveys and I collaborated on a book entitled *Leisure Studies and Services: An Overview*. Although the writing here was originally conceived as a revision of that book, the project evolved in purpose. Dr. Parker, realizing that I wanted to follow my classroom approach more closely in revising the book (and would keep returning to it like the firehouse horse), suggested that I write the new book by myself. His further writing has included *The Sociology of Leisure* (published by George Allen and Unwin, 1976). I have continued to benefit from Dr. Parker's counsel and friendship.

Thanks to Dr. Douglas Sessoms, Dr. Larry Williams, Dr. Gerald Fain, Dr. Rick Bunch, and Dr. Thomas Damron for critiquing this manuscript and suggesting needed changes. Thanks also to Mr. John Butler, Health, Physical Education and Recreation editor at Saunders College Publishing, for his expert assistance from the beginning of this project to its completion.

GEOFFREY GODBEY

# Contents

# chapter 1

# Why study leisure?

**T**o have leisure is the oldest dream of human beings—to be free from an endless round of labor, free to pursue what one wants, to spend time in voluntary, pleasurable ways, free to find and accept one's place in the world, free of the tyranny of nature and of other human beings, free to exist in a state of grace. Living life on your own terms, being free to do what you choose, is a central ideal of Western society and, quite probably, of you as an individual.

In spite of this, the study of leisure and related notions of recreation and play is not often undertaken. Perhaps this is because many in our society still think of recreation and leisure as being merely time which is "left over" after the important activities which we must attend to—"work"—have taken place. Perhaps also it is because it is difficult to examine leisure in any systematic manner. Leisure is not neatly confined to any one part of our lives, or to any one social institution. You may find leisure by yourself, at school, church, clubs, shopping centers, in automobiles, tents, caves, in front of a television, behind home plate, in the formations of drifting clouds, and in many other circumstances. Consequently, when we study leisure, we must try to examine many different parts of the human condition in ways which are sometimes difficult to do, or which require many kinds of diverse knowledge. We must also try to clarify some of our values about what role leisure can and should play in our lives, both at the individual and societal levels.

Despite these difficulties, in a society where the potential for leisure continues to increase, it is essential that we reach some understanding about recreation and leisure in order to shape both our individual lives and our

1

society more intelligently. Various questions must be considered. What are recreation and leisure? What roles have they played in other societies? Is a life of leisure desirable? How do people use leisure? Are some leisure activities better than others? How does leisure behavior relate to our work, education, economy, religious beliefs, and so forth?

In answering these and related questions, it will be the assumption of this book that whenever possible our examination must begin with the life of you, the reader, and then expand to consider society at large. This approach asks more of the reader in some ways, since you will be asked to think about your own values and behavior. You will be asked to clarify your values concerning leisure, make some judgments on a personal level about how you spend your time, and speculate about what kind of work-leisure model you would find pleasing. Briefly, you will be asked to examine your own leisure life and then to compare your own behavior and values to those of others.

To do this, it will not be assumed that you should be led to certain beliefs or certain ways of behaving, but that you should examine alternatives and understand more clearly your current position in regard to leisure. While the author admits to some biases (I love poetry, tennis, parties, "rooting" in the yard), at the end of this book you should be a little closer to formulating and

**FIGURE 1-1** You will be asked to clarify your values concerning leisure, make some judgments about how you spend your time, and speculate on what kind of work-leisure model you would find pleasing. (Courtesy of Springfield College)

understanding your leisure ideals rather than adopting mine. You should also be a little more knowledgeable regarding the role leisure plays and can play in our own society.

Before we review various concepts of recreation and leisure, stop a minute and think about these terms. In the first Leisure Exercise of this book you will be asked to define these terms as you understand them.

# Leisure Exercise 1·1

## Your Definitions of Recreation and Leisure

"Recreation" and "leisure" are similar to lots of other broad concepts in that it's difficult to state exactly what they mean. In spite of this, most of us know whether or not a certain situation is "recreation" or "leisure" for us. The following questions may help you clarify your own ideas about these concepts. Answer them in terms of your definitions, not those of the book.

**1.** Describe some situations in which you experience recreation. What makes it recreation?

**2.** Could any activity potentially be recreation for you? Why or why not?

**3.** Are certain activities always recreation? Why or why not?

**4.** Can recreation be physically painful? Why or why not?

**5.** Is recreation always fun? Why or why not?

**6.** What functions does recreation serve?

**7.** Is leisure different from recreation? If so, how?

**8.** How is leisure related to time, if at all?

## WHAT IS LEISURE?

Like most important words—"love," "education," "work"—the term "leisure" has many shades of meaning and, in fact, has some meanings which are almost entirely distinct from each other. If you stopped someone on the street and asked them to define leisure, what would they say? The answer might well be "free time," and they might also say "relaxing" or "doing what you want." Free time is also sometimes referred to as "spare time"; this seems to imply that individuals may have time which is left over after they have done everything they have to do.

If we examine definitions of leisure by categorizing them, we find that leisure has been conceptualized in three basic contexts: "time, activities or a state of mind."[1]

### Leisure Defined as Time

When we think of leisure in terms of time, it usually refers to some portion of our lives in which we have comparatively greater freedom to do what we want. Aristotle called this available time.[2] Such time may be thought of as something negative; Veblen did this at the turn of this century, when he bemoaned the emergence of a new leisure class which consumed time unproductively.[3] Another way of conceptualizing such time is "the time surplus remaining after the practical necessities of life have been attended to."[4]

Defining leisure as "free time" or the like raises a number of issues. First we must determine what constitutes free time. Some definitions of free time say it is time which the individual doesn't sell for economic gain, but some of us freely and voluntarily choose to do certain things for which we are paid money. In our own culture it is often difficult to draw the line between obligated and unobligated time. Is going to church or synagogue obligated? For some cultures it may be, but not for others. Is eating obligated in all instances, and is sleeping? In a society where only a small fraction of the population starves, it is not always easy to define what *must* be done. And, in a complex society such as ours, no time is free of the constraints of norms of behavior. We still have certain social rules to follow.

For some in our society it is particularly difficult to determine what is free time and what is not. What is free time for the retired person, the student, the homemaker, the unemployed, the bedridden, the artist, the professor, or the hobo? If we assume that "free time" is primarily time when we aren't involved in an activity for which we receive money, then the definition has no meaning to many in our society who do not do such work. Furthermore, we are compelled to do many things that don't involve money. We may sometimes feel compelled to attend a wedding, polish the car, jog to lose weight, or do a number of other things which use our time but which we are compelled to do for reasons other than economic ones. In other words, many different factors may keep our time from being free; these are not only economic but also include social, psychological, spiritual, and political reasons. An individual may have time which is not related to economic survival but may not be politically free to travel or indulge in self-expression. One may also be prevented from having free time due to spiritual emptiness or psychological injury suffered during work. Thus, the things which place limitations upon our free time differ for us as individuals and as members of different cultures and subcultures.

When leisure is defined as "free time," Kaplan identified five different kinds of free time which have emerged in our society. These include the "permanent, voluntary leisure of the rich, temporary, involuntary leisure of the unemployed, regularly allocated voluntary leisure of the employed on holidays or vacations, and the temporary incapacity of the employed, permanent incapacity of the disabled, and the voluntary retirement of the aged."[5] A fifth type is the free time of unemployed old people and the disabled. As you can see, these kinds of "free time" have very different consequences for those who have them. A holiday differs in meaning from retirement in fundamental ways.

## Leisure Defined as Activity

Leisure has also been defined as certain types of activities. The ancient Greek word for leisure, *schole*, means "serious activity without the pressure of necessity."[6] This term does not imply a strict distinction from work, nor is it

**FIGURE 1-2** Leisure may be thought of as serious activity undertaken without the pressure of necessity. (Courtesy of the National Park Service)

**FIGURE 1-3** Pieper believed leisure was a sense of celebration based on accepting your place in the world with joy. (Courtesy of the Bureau of Land Management)

synonymous with the term "recreation," since the Greeks had another term meaning "playful amusement to pass the time." The English word "school" is derived from the Greek word for leisure.[7] This conception of leisure as activity has been broadened to include "a number of occupations in which the individual may indulge of his own free will—either to rest, to amuse himself, to add to his knowledge or improve his skills disinterestedly or to increase his voluntary participation in the life of the community after discharging his professional, family and social duties."[8] When leisure is defined as activities or occupations it quickly becomes apparent that, while no activity can always be said to serve as leisure for the participant, many activities are typically undertaken in the role of leisure. Playing softball, for instance, is typically undertaken more or less voluntarily during non-work time and is pleasurable for the participant. There are exceptions. A few people play softball to earn money. Some may feel that they have to play the game to protect their jobs or to win the friendship of those who are important to them. For most people, however, playing softball is leisure activity.

## Leisure Defined as a State of Existence

If leisure is defined as a state of existence it is, as Aristotle said, the "absence of the necessity of being occupied."[2] This state has also been thought of as "a mood of contemplation."[9] Thus, leisure is often used as an adjective to mean unhurried, tranquil, or without regard to time. Leisure defined as a state of existence may also be tied to religious celebration. Pieper believed that leisure was a sense of celebration which characterized the lives of some people who accepted the world and their place in the world with joy.[10] Leisure was therefore a state of grace bestowed upon those capable of spiritual celebration.

## Proposing a Definition

From the preceding it is evident that while leisure varies in meaning, some areas of agreement exist. Foremost among these is the notion of freedom on an individual level. No single definition, however, can incorporate all definitions into one without sacrificing some elements of the term. In spite of this, I propose the following:

> Leisure is living in relative freedom from the external compulsive forces of one's culture and physical environment so as to be able to act from internal compulsion in ways which are personally pleasing and intuitively worthwhile.

Several ideas here need to be expanded. The term "relative freedom" is used because there are always some constraints on us and on our behavior. Such constraints are imposed by our social roles, time, weather, money, and so forth. For some people, however, these constraints are minimized. Also, for some portions of our lives or daily routines these constraints are minimized, and under such conditions our potential for leisure is great. At some times, for instance, there are few things which we *must* do, such as when we have enough money, the right weather, and friends who want to pursue a mutually enjoyed activity.

Leisure requires that we "act" in the sense that it requires us to choose to do and choose to act in ways that are personally pleasing. Such "acts" may not be physically demanding. We may sit, for instance, and contemplate the way trees move in the wind; we have chosen behavior and, thus, acted. Such behavior must be personally pleasing and intuitively worthwhile. We often cannot explain why we are pleased by some behavior. We may know we like to play the guitar, but may not be sure why. As we will see later, the attempts of researchers to examine what attracts individuals to various leisure activities always fall short of providing satisfying answers. Leisure involves acting with some degree of internal compulsion, and we never perfectly understand the sources of such compulsion. While it is often said that leisure is "voluntary," it might be more accurate to say that leisure is behavior which draws us to something. This magnetic attraction, which is pleasurable for us, is an inward compulsion. There is a sense of mystery about why certain of our behaviors please us, and it probably makes more sense to try to explain the mystery in spiritual rather than psychological terms. Leisure activity is uplifting, and we feel right about participating without needing to know why fully.

## Recreation

While words like "recreation," "leisure," and "play" are sometimes used interchangeably, the term "recreation" is often used in a more specific and limited sense. Recreation has traditionally been defined as activity done in opposition to work which refreshes and restores the individual. Margaret Mead has said that recreation represents a "whole attitude of conditional joy in which the delights of both work and play are tied together in a tight sequence. Neither one may be considered by itself, but man must work, then weary and 'take some recreation' so he may work again."[9] Recreation, in other words, is dependent upon work for its meaning and function. Work comes first, then recreation, and then more work. If we think of leisure in the sense of "free time," then it may be said that recreation is "any activity pursued during leisure, either individual or collective, that is free and pleasurable, having its own immediate appeal, not impelled by a delayed reward beyond itself."[11]

In popular usage recreation may be thought of as activity which isn't serious—that is, "fun and games." Recreation may also refer to sports and related athletic activities. We often expect to find only sports and games at "recreation centers."

Sometimes definitions of recreation limit the term to leisure time activities that are "morally sound, mentally and physically upbuilding, respectful of the rights of others, voluntarily motivated, and [which] provide a sense of pleasure and achievement."[12] If recreation is limited to morally sound activities, we are faced with the question of who decides what is morally sound. Society may reach a consensus regarding the moral soundness of some activities, but there are many others where no such agreement exists. Another way of looking at this question would be to say that recreation activity has great potential for good or for harm, but the definition should not be limited to those instances in which the goodness is achieved.

Recreation in our own society is often thought of as a given set of activities which are somehow inherently recreational. Such activities may be designated in the following categories: Amusements, Arts and Crafts, Dance, Drama, Games and Sports, Hobbies, Music, Outdoor Recreation, Reading, Writing, and Speaking; Social Recreation; Spectating, Special Events and Voluntary Service.[13] While we may commonly think of recreation in these terms, nearly any activity has the potential to be recreation. That is, it may be undertaken voluntarily, during leisure time, and provide pleasure. Some people earn their livings as carpenters while others undertake similar activity for recreation. Some ride bicycles to get to work; others ride as recreation. Thus, in an absolute sense, we can't limit our definition to a list of specific activities.

Gray and Greben have suggested that recreation, rather than being a set of activities, is an emotional condition. They define recreation as follows:

> an emotional condition within an individual human being that flows from a feeling of well-being and self-satisfaction. It is characterized by feelings of mastery, achievement, exhilaration, acceptance, success, personal worth and pleasure. It reinforces a positive self-image. Recreation is a response to aesthetic experience, achievement of personal goals or positive feedback from others. It is independent of activity, leisure or personal acceptance.[14]

This definition stresses the response to activity rather than the activity itself. In fact, we don't always experience feelings of well-being from participation in activities commonly thought of as recreational. According to this definition we might play volleyball during our leisure but still not be able to define it as recreation if we are playing poorly and are unhappy about it. Also, since the definition states that the emotional condition of recreation is independent of leisure, we might experience recreation as a job for which we are being paid. This is a major difference from most previous definitions.

As you can see, a number of disagreements exist among various definitions of recreation. These are concerned with whether or not recreation is a means to an end (such as achievement) or an end in itself, whether or not it should be limited to "moral" activity, whether or not it must refresh the individual for work, and whether or not it is determined primarily by the nature of the activity, the attitude of the respondent toward the activity, or the respondent's psychological state during the activity.

## LEISURE PAST AND PRESENT

Leisure has differed historically in different societies, both in quantity and quality. The forces which shaped leisure—food supply, religious beliefs, political systems, wars, weather, rate and type of learning, playfulness, amount of industrialism, and other factors—are so varied that it is difficult to make meaningful generalizations. Although the following section is certainly not comprehensive, it will illustrate some of the major differences in leisure within different societies and different ages.

Let's start with three broad statements: (1) It is not always correct to say that societies continue to have more and more leisure time. Rather, it is more correct to say that the quantity and quality of leisure has varied greatly within different periods of history and within different societies. (2) As societies become more urbanized and industrialized, work and leisure have become more highly separated than previously. (3) What is satisfying and worthwhile during leisure varies greatly from culture to culture and reflects the values and conditions of that culture.

## Amounts of Leisure

Do societies continue to have more and more leisure? Many people seem to believe that we have progressively more leisure, and that this is essentially a product of technology. As Joffre Dumazedier, the French leisure sociologist, stated

> First of all, leisure time is obviously the result of the application of discoveries in technical science. This progress has come about by a double play: that of the trade unions, which insist on salary increases and shorter working hours, and that of businesses which need to extend the time of consumption in order to use up their products (the consumer must consume vast quantities and it takes time to consume).
>
> However, this technological-economical component does not explain everything: a socio-ethical component must come into it, and I call this a decline in institutional control over individuals. This means that society's fundamental institutions (family, socio-religious, socio-political) control time less and that free time is used especially in leisure activities. This decline is related to the youth and feminist movements against the all-important family and conjugal duties, to religious movements which insist on lay responsibility, and to citizen's movements against totalitarian politics.
>
> Leisure has been introduced by means of a profound mutation of the being which means that a new relationship is established between the individual and his or her exterior nature, and the individual and his or her inner being. This results in leisure becoming the framework of a kind of cultural revolution.[15]

In other words, Dumazedier believes that more leisure results from both increased technology and more individual freedom from large social institutions.

**Arguments For Increasing Leisure.**  Perhaps, in our own society, we could point to the following arguments as to why leisure is increasing.

1.  *The increased production of material goods through the application of technology.* This increased productivity, often 2 to 3 per cent per year during the last half-century, has meant that the worker has the potential for more leisure if the material standard of living is kept the same.*

2.  *The creation of labor-saving devices for household maintenance and other essential duties.* Labor-saving devices for maintaining households and other living spaces have meant that if the level of maintenance required stays the same and it takes less time to achieve that level, more time is available for leisure. Sometimes, however, the result of this has been an increase in the desired level of maintenance.
3.  *The decline of the influence of social institutions such as the church and the family in establishing predetermined roles for individuals in all aspects of life.* This has, in effect, produced more individual dis-

---

*In the last few years, however, such increases have been almost halted.

cretion in the selection of activities. Changes in religious beliefs concerning man's relationship to the macrocosm and the decline of the influence of secular religion in the twentieth century have made man exercise his will to a greater extent than before, since fewer usable guidelines for behavior exist which are based upon religious doctrine.

4. *Differences in attitudes toward pleasure.* It appears that contemporary society has become a pleasure-seeking one. The Puritans' distrust of pleasure and the Christian belief in original sin have both declined in popularity, thus diminishing many individuals' needs to justify their lives. As de Grazia mentioned, the "leisure kind," who have existed in small numbers in every society, have not felt the need to justify their lives and have, therefore, devoted most of their energies to pursuing what *they* wanted to do rather than what someone else wanted them to do. It is evident that this attitude is far more prevalent today than it was in the past.

5. *Substantial increase in the education level of individuals.* Valuing certain leisure activities is usually a product of exposure. For instance, an individual may not value reading novels until he has been exposed to several and been taught about them. The increased education of the average citizen has caused an expansion of interest in various activities which, coupled with the rise in disposable income, has brought about greater interest in obtaining leisure and a greater diversity of interests during leisure.

6. *Lack of physical fatigue associated with many forms of employment.* In most pre-industrial societies, which were primarily agrarian or hunter-gatherer societies, work was physically exhausting. Because of this, recreation or leisure was synonymous with resting or relaxing, but little else. The exhausting demands of work prevented life away from work from realizing its potential. Today many forms of work involve a minimum of physical energy and therefore leave the individual in a position to enjoy a variety of leisure activities that require intensive energy.

7. *An increase in discretionary income.* While some leisure activities cost the participant nothing in terms of money, most today have some cost associated with them. Because of this, the rise in personal disposable income during the last three decades has resulted in a generally proportionate rise in leisure spending and thus in the potential to participate in many activities. Certainly, however, this rise has at least temporarily ended due to prolonged inflation and energy scarcity. Whether discretionary income will continue to decrease may be directly related to energy cost and availability.

**Arguments Against Increasing Leisure.**   Unfortunately, these same societal conditions that have created the increased *potential* for recreation and leisure have also created a number of other factors that have either negated this potential or altered the meaning of leisure in our society. Among such factors are the following:

1. *Limitless materialism.* Many people in our society today have an inability to satiate their material desires. The acceleration of consumption has found no limits, even though we have no societal justification for it. The acquisition, maintenance, and use of the vast number of material goods which we increasingly want takes time and increases the amount of work we are compelled to undertake in order to sustain our lifestyle.*

2. *Increased societal complexity and change.* Coping with the increased complexity and accelerated rate of change within our society has blunted our leisure potential in a number of ways. Decisions have become more complicated and time-consuming in a society where planning and regulation by government are increasingly necessary and where citizens expect a greater role in that process. The average individual is being forced to absorb more and more information, often of a complex technical nature, at an increasingly accelerated rate. Some scientists believe that much of the pathological behavior evidenced in most industrialized societies is due to "brain overloading"—a condition brought about by the constant mental strain resulting from the increased tempo of everyday life and the political, technical, and moral changes to which man must adapt.

3. *The increasing demands of service occupations.* While the amount of time spent at work has doubtlessly decreased since the turn of the century, evidence is contradictory concerning whether there has been any further decrease in the amount of work activities since World War II. Many statistics argue against any decrease. There has been a 70 per cent increase in the number of people employed in service occupations during the last decade, while the percentage of those producing goods has decreased. Services are devourers of time because live performance and personal contact are involved, service workers are less efficient, and capital cannot be substituted for labor. The amount of overtime done by wage earners has also been increasing, and the amount of dual job holding has increased. In addition, the percentage of adult women employed in the labor force has now increased to almost 50 per cent. Almost 20 per cent of full-time workers in our society work 48 hours a week or more.

4. *The carryover of "work values" into leisure.* Many of the goals, methods, and styles of our work institutions are increasingly spilling over into our leisure institutions. In much of our "leisure" activity, no less than in our "work" activity, we place a high value on ad-

---

*Perhaps the notion of limitless materialism will be controlled in the next decade not by individuals desiring less but by an increased scarcity and cost of material goods due to inflation.

vanced planning and goal setting, competition, incremental improvement through the mastery of special knowledge and technique, the efficient utilization of time, and winning. What has emerged is a situation in which one worries about doing the activity sufficiently well regardless of whether it is work or leisure. This seriousness of approach has led to the decline of many forms of pleasure.

 5. *Prolonged unemployment for some who seek work.* All democratic industrial societies continue to be faced with the problem of chronic unemployment of from 5 to over 20 per cent of those who seek work. While those who are unemployed may have more time for leisure, they often lack the financial, educational, and social resources for meaningful leisure experience.

In summary, while our potential for leisure has increased, we are nowhere near the society of leisure about which so much has been written.

## Leisure as a Mirror of Culture

The leisure activities of a culture reflect the existing conditions and values of that culture. This point may be illustrated by the theater of fourteenth century Europe, where life on earth was made uncertain by plagues which caused large parts of the population to die horrible deaths. Ceaseless, savage fighting took place between and within kingdoms, from which no one was safe. It was a time in which life on earth was merely endured as a prelude to eternal life in heaven and when even the church, highly corrupt and divided on many issues, was part of the general malaise.

Consequently, it is not surprising that much of the recreation and leisure of the time was characterized by violence, excess, fatalism, and spectacle. Theatrical productions demonstrated these tendencies; miracle plays and mysteries tried to achieve spectacular realism. Jesus was resurrected from the tomb using a system of weights and pulleys to ascend to a ceiling of clouds. Devils and angels magically appeared through trap doors. When Noah's flood was depicted, the stage was actually flooded with water by casks of water overturned backstage. "More completely than any other medium," Tuchman wrote, "the stage mirrored medieval life."[16] Drama, once characterized by liturgical plays performed at the church door, left the church for the street. Acting guilds on wheeled platforms, with different scenes drawn along in succession, traveled from town to town performing to audiences from all walks of life.

While the subject matter of such plays was religious, its presentation was for entertainment and was "irreverent, bloody and bawdy."[16] Nero was depicted slitting his mother's belly to see where he came from, complete with gory entrails supplied by the local butcher. Catastrophe, the agony of hell, miracles performed by the Holy Virgin, and a large helping of sex and violence were standard fare and reflected the culture of the time.

## Leisure In Non-Industrial Cultures

If we examine non-industrial cultures we may begin to wonder whether technology has really given us more or better leisure. While it is certainly true that many pre-industrial cultures were characterized by long hours of toil, some were not. Additionally, the line between labor and leisure is not so distinct. Primitive people tend to approach a great many of their daily activities as if they were play. Anthropologists who have studied the daily routines of agrarian and hunter-gather societies report a pattern of work and leisure that is much more integrated than that of a modern industrial society. Thus, anthropologists Stumpf and Cozens reported of the Maori culture that every aspect of their economic life was characterized by an element of recreation. "Whether engaging in fishing, bird-snaring, cultivation of the fields, or building a house or canoe, the occasion was marked by activities which we could definitely classify as recreational."[17] These activities— singing, loud talking, laughing—are also features of the cooperative work parties which are to be found in many parts of Africa.

Not only was there an element of recreation in the economic activities of some pre-industrial cultures but, in some, the amount of time available for leisure appears to have been as great or greater than our own. Anthropologists Allen and Orna Johnson studied the Machiguenga Indians of Peru for 18 months and found this to be the case. These Indians survive by growing food in gardens, hunting, fishing, and collecting wild foods. "They are self-sufficient; almost everything they consume is produced by their own labors using materials that are found close at hand."[18] When the Johnsons divided the time of the Machiguenga into production time (work), consumption time (using consumer goods for pleasure, eating), and free time (idleness, rest, sleep, chatting), and then compared these time expenditures to those in current French society, they discovered that French men and women (both working and housewives) spent more time in production activities than the Machiguenga. The French also spent from three to five times more hours in the consumption of goods than the Indians. The Machiguenga's free time, however, was found to surpass that of the French by more than 4 hours a day. The Johnsons argued that while technological progress has provided us with more goods, it has not resulted in more free time for most people living in industrial society. They also pointed out that the pace of life for the Peruvian Indians was leisurely; daily activities never seemed hurried or desperate. "Each task was allotted its full measure of time, and free time is not felt to be boring or lost but is accepted as being entirely natural."[18] (We will discuss this time speedup in the pace of life shortly.)

These findings agree with those of Sahlins, who found that many hunter-gatherer societies, such as the Australian aborigines and the San of South Africa, require only 3 or 4 hours of work per day to provide the material requirements for their simple way of life.[19] Thus, as Sahlins pointed out, there are two ways to reach affluence: our own way, which is to produce more, or what Sahlins called the Buddhist way, which is to be satisfied with less.

We can also conclude that the existence of large amounts of free time doesn't necessarily lead to what we think of as higher forms of civilization. It was once believed that, by producing large food surpluses, people would automatically experiment with various activities thought to characterize "higher" civilizations, such as art, mathematics, and written language. This, however, has frequently not been so.

In terms of amount of leisure, the Roman passion for free time reached its climax in the fourth century, when there were 175 holidays per year. Whatever the work schedules of slaves and women, leisure for the ruling class, for administrators and professionals, would never again be so abundant. In France and England, from the late Middle Ages to about 1800, the trend in manual occupations was toward longer hours. By the mid-nineteenth century the work week of factory workers in these countries and in America reached 70 or more hours. Farm workers were exceptions to this trend; estimates suggest that they worked very long hours during the whole period, with some reduction only in the twentieth century.

## Industrialization

The decline of leisure from the end of the Middle Ages to the height of the Industrial Revolution is not, however, to be measured only by the increase in work hours. In pre-industrial society, work was incorporated into everyday life, and leisure time was not separate. Work was carried on in the fields within sight of home or within the home itself, accompanied by friendly conversations and the business of village life. It was only when work came to be done in a particular place, at a special, separate time and under certain conditions that leisure came to be demanded as a right. More precisely, "time-off work" was demanded, since there was no way that the intimate, pre-industrial relationship between leisure and life could be restored in the factory towns of the nineteenth century.

Industrialization and urbanization during the Industrial Revolution brought about a greater separation between work and leisure and reduced the amount of leisure enjoyed by the ordinary citizen, at least in its initial stages. Thus, work came to be scheduled first, to suit those who owned the means of production. Leisure became leftover time.

The transition from pre-industrial to industrial society brought with it a speeding up of the pace of life. This occurred partly because of the demands made upon factory workers by their employers, upon whom they were almost completely dependent. It also took place because technology enabled a worker to produce more in a given period and, thus, his time increased in value. As his time increased in value it became more scarce, like most economically valuable commodities. The increased scarcity of time also came about because the individual in an industrial society had more options available in terms of what could be done. For instance, opportunities for travel were broadened. Also, many minds were awakened to the potential of leisure as formal and informal education increased. Interests were stimulated regarding many forms of activity about which individuals were previously unaware or did not appreciate.

Industrialism also began to produce more material goods for the common people, and the desire to acquire goods became incorporated into a materialistic style of life. The acquisition, use, and maintenance of a progressively greater number of material goods further contributed to the speedup in the pace of life.

## Time Deepening

In concert with these changes people began, however imperfectly, to deal with this faster pace of life. Results of a study of people's use of time in 12 nations seem to confirm this: ". . . the more a person is part of an industrial society with a very high density of communication, and the more educated the person, the more he is likely to do a number of activities simultaneously."[20] This phenomenon, called "time deepening," actually has three related aspects: undertaking an activity more quickly or satisfying some need through an activity more quickly, undertaking more than one activity simultaneously, and using time more precisely.

Many activities are performed more quickly nowadays than they were previously, including leisure activities as well as work. You can paint by number, learn to play the guitar in three easy lessons, tour Europe in a week, or play a new "time-deepened" game like racquetball, where people get lots of exercise in a short period of time and can begin playing "instantly." Years ago, going to the zoo was an all-day trip—packing a lunch in the early morning,

**FIGURE 1-4** As "time deepening" occurs, people do things more quickly, combine activities, and schedule activities more precisely. (Courtesy of Air France)

traveling to the zoo, strolling leisurely from place to place, having lunch and a nap, with the kids perhaps playing tag for awhile, going back to see your favorite animals, and then, as the kids started to get tired and quarrelsome, returning home for dinner. Today the same trip may consist of tossing the kids into the station wagon and speeding down the freeway to a new kind of zoo, Animal Safari, where, for seven dollars apiece, you can drive through and never get out of the car, snap instant cameras through the rolled-up windows, and be through and back on the freeway in 45 minutes.

Activities are also increasingly done in combination in our time-deepened society. Increasingly television appears to be viewed while doing something else, such as eating or talking to friends. People knit at meetings, do business while playing golf, read, eat, and listen to music or watch movies while flying in a plane. Contemplation, idleness, doing nothing are, for many people, extremely rare.

The third aspect of time deepening, using time more precisely, could be illustrated in a number of ways. The best example I can think of is a university class schedule at Penn State which requires that certain classes be scheduled from 3:55 to 5:10 P.M. In regard to leisure activity, many activities are scheduled with great precision, such as indoor tennis. Players may have the court for one hour, not a minute more or less. Vacation travel schedules may be as precise as work travel schedules.

Time deepening has meant that we can do more in our leisure, have more experiences, and possibly derive more pleasure. It has often, however, made us rushed, anxious, and unable to let go. Perhaps it makes sense to say that we have become "unleisurely" in our leisure.

## A Leisure Democracy

If our leisure behavior reflects a rushed lifestyle for many, it also increasingly reflects advances in the "democratization" of leisure. Compared to a few decades ago, or other eras of history, the average citizen today has a far greater range of alternatives available during leisure. It is hard for us to understand that, at the turn of the century, leisure and its use were often reserved for the elite. One of the more important concepts of leisure in this country was developed by Veblen, who believed that a leisure class had emerged in society who, having both the time and money, used leisure activity to set themselves apart from common people.[3] Such leisure activity, which was characterized by conspicuous display, contributed little to society. It was, as Veblen stated, unproductive. Using leisure to display wealth and privilege to the common people whom they economically victimized, the leisure class, Veblen believed, was an intolerable blight upon society.

This suspicion of leisure as being (1) unproductive, (2) springing from undeserved privilege, and (3) used in ways of little value or of harm to society at large has been deep-rooted in our culture. Certainly this belief has some basis in fact.

Today leisure is more widely available to the average person, regardless of income. As a matter of fact, little relationship is evident today between income level and work hours: people with high incomes are not more likely to have shorter working hours than those with low incomes. Additionally, the range of activity available to individuals of modest means has increased dramatically. Foreign travel is no longer limited to the rich, and neither is tennis, drinking good wine, nor owning a sophisticated camera.

The combination of decreased working hours and increased discretionary income evident since the turn of the century have greatly helped to democratize leisure and broaden the functions of leisure from diversion, fun, and refreshment after toil to include voluntary learning, self-expression and creativity, social bonding, physical fitness, sensory pleasure, political expression, and many others. As these functions of leisure have broadened, how we use leisure has become an increasingly important clue to who we are; perhaps it is the single most important clue.

Why study leisure? Leisure has become increasingly the arena for both the search for pleasure and the exercise of freedom. It is what happens when we control the situation, when we do what our individual will compels us to do rather than what outside circumstances dictate. The ability to use leisure intelligently, as Bertrand Russell observed, is the final test of a civilization.[21] The possibility that human beings can use technology in ways that meet their physical needs in harmony with nature is a real one. As that happens, and it already has for a few, the question of human purpose will begin to be answered.

**FIGURE 1-5** Some musical instruments are designed so that you can begin playing them almost instantly. (Courtesy of H. Armstrong Roberts)

**FIGURE 1-6** Leisure is a vehicle for discovering who you are. (Courtesy of the Bureau of Land Management)

By studying your leisure values and activities, as well as those of others, you may determine how much freedom you have and how you have chosen to use it. You may also gain a heightened consciousness concerning the importance of leisure in your life, and how much leisure defines who you are. Why study leisure? Because it is the central challenge of a privileged society.

In studying leisure and recreation, there are a number of written resources to draw on. In the final exercise of this chapter you will be asked to help identify such resources.

# Leisure Exercise 1·2

The purpose of this exercise is to identify as many periodicals as possible which could be used by a student at your college or university in studying leisure.

Below is a list of periodicals directly concerned with various aspects of leisure. There are others you may find which I haven't listed. Keep in mind that the magazine, journal, newsletter, etc. should be devoted *primarily* to leisure or recreation and not just occasionally contain relevant articles.

To complete this exercise, divide into teams with equal numbers of students on each team. Decide if your search should be limited to your college or university library, or if it should include other library facilities. Each team should attempt to identify as many leisure periodicals as it can in a one-week period. To show that you have identified a leisure periodical, record its name, where you locate it, and a one-paragraph review of an article from a current issue. The team turning in the largest number of periodicals wins. By the way, if you find your school library doesn't have most of these periodicals, get going and find out why not. How can they be ordered?

*Recreation Research Review*
Ontario Research Council on Leisure
400 University Avenue, 23rd floor
Toronto, Ontario M7A 1H9
Canada

*Society and Leisure*
University of Quebec at Three Rivers
C.P. 500, Three Rivers
Quebec G9A 5H7
Canada

*Tourism Management Review*
Centre for Research in Tourism Development
P. O. Box 599, Station A
Montreal, Quebec H3C 2T6
Canada

*Words on Wilderness*
School of Forestry
University of Montana
Missoula, MT 59812

*Journal of Sport and Social Issues*
ARENA
Virginia Wesleyan College
Norfolk, VA 23502

*Sport and Recreation*
British Sports Council
70 Brompton Road
London, England SW3 15X

*Leisure Today*
American Alliance of Health, Physical Education, and Recreation
1201 16th Street, N.W.
Washington, D.C. 20036

*Outdoor Recreation Action*
Heritage Conservation and Recreation Service
U. S. Department of the Interior
U. S. Government Printing Office
Washington, D.C. 20402

*Leisure Information Newsletter*
The Leisure Institute
145 East 92nd Street
New York, NY 10028

*World Leisure and Recreation Association Bulletin*
WLRA
345 East 46th Street
New York, NY 10017

*Journal of Leisurability*
Box 281, Station A
Ottawa, Ontario K1N 8V2
Canada

*Recreation Canada*
Canadian Parks and Recreation Association
333 River Road
Vanier City, Ontario K1L 8B9
Canada

*Loisir Plus* (French Language)
Le Magazine Quebeçois Du Loisir
1415 rue Jarry est
Montreal, Quebec H2D 2Z7
Canada

*Parks and Recreation; Journal of Leisure Research; Therapeutic*
  *Recreation Journal*
National Recreation and Park Association
1601 N. Kent Street
Arlington, VA 22209

*Leisure Sciences—An Interdisciplinary Journal*
Crane, Russak and Company
347 Madison Avenue
New York, NY 10017

*Review of Sport and Leisure*
Governors State University
Park Forest South, IL 60466

*Journal of Outdoor Education*
Northern Illinois University
Dekalb, IL 60115

*Annals of Tourism Research*
Department of Habitational Resources
University of Wisconsin—STOUT
Menomonie, WI 54751

*Rural Recreation and Tourism Abstracts*
Commonwealth Agricultural Bureau
Farnham Royal, Slough SL2 3BN
United Kingdom

# STUDY QUESTIONS

1. Is it possible to find consistent differences in definitions of "recreation" and "leisure"? Can you identify any differences?

2. Analyze the definition of "leisure" I have proposed. On what basis can you agree or disagree with it?

3. Overall, can it be said that tribal societies distinguished work from leisure? Why or why not?

4. In what sense is leisure a by-product of our country becoming an industrial nation?

5. Do you think the study of leisure will be as important to you as other subjects you are currently studying? Why or why not?

## REFERENCES

1. Meyersohn, Rolf B. "Americans Off Duty," in Donahue, Wilma, et al. (eds.), *Free Time—Challenge to Later Maturity*. Ann Arbor: University of Michigan Press, 1958, p 46.
2. Aristotle, quoted by de Grazia, Sebastian. *Of Time, Work and Leisure*. New York: The Twentieth Century Fund, 1961, p. 19.
3. Veblen, Thorstein. *The Theory of the Leisure Class*. New York: B. W. Heubsch, 1899, p. 40.
4. May, Herbert L., and Petgen, Dorothy. *Leisure and Its Uses*. New York: A. S. Barnes, 1928, p. 3.
5. Kaplan, Max. *Leisure In America*. New York: John Wiley and Sons, 1960, p. 21.
6. Goodman, Paul. "Leisure: Purposeful or Purposeless," in Madow, Pauline, (ed.), *Recreation in America*. New York: H. W. Wilson Company, 1965, p. 31.
7. Larrabee, Eric, and Meyersohn, Rolf, (eds.). *Mass Leisure*. Glencoe, Ill.: The Free Press, 1958, p. 2.
8. Dumazedier, Joffre. "Current Problems of the Sociology of Leisure," *International Social Science Journal*, Vol. XII, Winter, 1960, p. 526.
9. Mead, Margaret. "The Pattern of Leisure in Contemporary American Culture," in Larrabee, Eric, and Meyersohn, Rolf, (eds.), *Mass Leisure*. Glencoe, Ill.: The Free Press, 1958, pp. 11–12.
10. Pieper, Joseph. *Leisure the Basis of Culture*. New York: New American Library, 1952, p. 40.
11. Fairchild, Henry (ed.). *Dictionary of Sociology*. New York: Philosophical Library, 1944, pp. 251–252.
12. Doell, Charles, and Fitzgerald, Gerald. *A Brief History of Parks and Recreation in the United States*. Chicago: The Athletic Institute, 1954, p. 127.
13. Hovis, Watson B., and Wagner, Frederick W. *Leisure Information Retrieval System—City-Wide Recreation Project*. Seattle: Leisure Services, Inc., 1972, pp. 17–18.
14. Gray, David E., and Greben, Seymour. "Future Perspectives," *Parks and Recreation*, Vol. 61, July, 1974, p. 49.

15. Dumazedier, Joffre. "Prominent Recreationist Defines Leisure," *Loisir Plus* (Quebec); reprinted in *Recreation Canada*, No. 32/5/74, p. 55.

16. Tuchman, Barbara W. *A Distant Mirror—The Calamitous Fourteenth Century.* New York: Alfred Knopf, 1978, p. 312.

17. Stumpf, F., and Cozens, F. W. "Some Aspects of the Role of Games, Sports, and Recreational Activities in the Culture of Modern Primitive People," *Research Quarterly*, Vol. XVIII, 1947, pp. 104-108.

18. Johnson, Allen. "In Search of the Affluent Society," *Human Nature*, September, 1978, pp. 50-59.

19. Sahlins, Marshall. *Stone Age Economics.* New York: Aldine Atherton, 1972, p. 72.

20. Scheuch, Erwin. "The Time Budget Interview," *in* Szalai, Alexander (ed.), *The Use of Time—Daily Activities of Urban and Suburban Populations.* The Hague, Netherlands: Mouton, 1972, p. 77.

21. Russell, Bertrand. Quoted by Godbey, Geoffrey, and Parker, Stanley, in *Leisure Studies and Services: An Overview.* Philadelphia: W. B. Saunders, 1976. p. 175.

# chapter 2

# What we do with our time-

## And (maybe) why

**I**'ll Make You A Deal You Might Refuse.   Here's the deal. For the next 24 hours, beginning tomorrow morning when you wake up, you can do whatever you want. I'll see to it that any responsibilities you have are taken care of. Also, I will give you enough money to get you through the day. You will have no responsibility to anyone unless you choose it and no penalties later, since I will take care of your responsibilities. Will you accept my offer of doing what you want for one day?

For those of you who took the first offer, allow me to raise the ante. I'll make you the same deal and put enough money in the bank to support you in the manner to which you are presently accustomed to living. You can do what you want and I will see to it that any obligations you have, such as taking tests or working a part-time job, are taken care of. You can do your own thing for a week. Whatever you want. Is it a deal?

If you are still with me, let's make the offer for a month. All the same rules apply. Do whatever you wish. How about it?

By now many of you have decided not to accept my offer but, if it still sounds good to you, how about an offer of one year, beginning tomorrow, of doing exactly what you want? I will deposit enough money in the bank each month to support you to the tune of, oh, let's see, $20,000 a year. You don't have to do anything for the money. Sound good?

If you are still playing "let's make a deal," you are ready for the ultimate question. Beginning tomorrow, for the rest of your life, you will have financial independence and can do whatever you like, where and with whom you please. Eat and sleep when you want and choose your own lifestyle, no strings attached. Do you accept?

Later in this chapter you will be asked to respond formally to these questions. A number of thoughts may have occurred to you when you were considering my offer. You may have thought that, since it is possible to do whatever you choose, you could continue to do just what you are presently doing. But, it would not be necessary since you would be financially independent and, if you desired, socially independent. You may have found it very easy to envision what you would do with one free day but more difficult to imagine how a whole year might be spent. Many of the activities in which you now participate when a free hour occurs might not be satisfying if done over a whole year. Imagine a whole year of watching television—daytime TV, quiz shows, reruns of *I Love Lucy*. For that matter, imagine a whole year of camping or bowling or going to parties. Many of these activities are satisfying when they are a break from an obligated routine, when they are done on "special occasions." As the central activities of our lives, however, they might become boring or meaningless. You might decide to travel or just to wander and that, too, might have its limits. Some of you might even, perish the thought, return to school. Whatever is done, the responsibility for designing your life would fall more directly upon you, and this responsibility might prove to be a mixed blessing.

An exercise has been prepared to help you clarify your own feelings about such a life. What is being discussed here is, in some ways, a modern version of the life of leisure in the Golden Age of Greece. But let's do the exercise now. We can think about what leisure meant to the ancient Greeks, and to many other people, later in the book.

# Leisure Exercise 2·1

Beginning tomorrow, I will make you financially independent for as long as you like. It will be possible to do whatever you want, and with all duties taken care of so there will be no penalties when and if you return to your present life. Financial obligations will be met by money being deposited in a bank account for you that will average $20,000 a year.

**1.** Will you accept my life of leisure offer?

_____ Not at all

_____ For one day

_____ For one week

_____ For one month

_____ For one year

_____ For the rest of your life

**2.** What opportunities and problems are there in such an offer?

**3.** If the offer were accepted, what would you do? Why?

**4.** If this offer were going to be accepted for the rest of your life, would any special educational preparation be needed? Why?

**5.** Would you be happier leading the life of leisure offered to you? Why?

**6.** Do you think most people would accept this offer for the rest of their lives? Why?

Now that we've discussed whether you would like to be free to spend your time as you please, let's return to reality and discuss how people actually do spend their time, and what we might learn about leisure from such a determination.

## MEASURING LEISURE AS TIME

Time is one of the most complex ideas in our language, and one of the most important. According to leisure educator James Murphy, there are essentially three kinds of time: cyclical or natural time, mechanical or clock time, and personal or psychological time.[1] Each of these time perspectives conditions the individual to behave in a certain way and affects his/her understanding of others' movements in space. Cyclical time consists of the daily, monthly, and seasonal rhythms of the natural universe. The rising and setting of the sun, the fluctuations of tides, the moon's stages, and seasonal changes were the measures of time around which tribal life was based. This view of time was circular: spring will come again; the sun will rise again. Time could not be "lost" under such a concept, because it would come again.

Mechanical time, which has been measured by clocks since the thirteenth century, arose as society became more complex and people began to earn their living in ways other than farming and hunting. Mechanical time is linear, a straight line of minutes and hours without beginning or end which has no organic connection to nature. Mechanical time is a reflection of our industrial society where people and machines must interact precisely. Time in this sense could be lost or gained and was always limited, since a given hour or minute was never going to come again. Mechanical time allowed the splitting of the day into work and leisure.

Psychological, or inner, time is concerned not with the specificity of quantitative time, but rather with quality. It is our perception or inner sense of the passage of events. In this sense, time can only be judged in terms of personal meaning.

Most methods of measuring leisure have concentrated on recording amounts of time devoted to various activities classified as either leisure or non-leisure. Time has been measured in the following ways: "(a) the chronological sequence, 1-2-3 o'clock, (b) the attitudes or meanings about time held by the person, or his perception of the sequential relations of events, and (c) institutionalized segments, such as holidays, hours for work, hours for sleep, etc., as passed on through the generations."[2]

## Time Budgets

A research tool known as the time budget is often used to determine people's daily leisure patterns. A time budget is a structured diary in which people record what they do at certain regular intervals during their waking hours. Usually the day is recorded in periods of one hour or less. In determining which of the recorded activities are really leisure pursuits, some researchers have excluded such non-leisure activities as "sleep, paid work, care of household and children, care of self, transportation, and other items which the record indicates are primarily instrumental or incidental to the other activities rather than ends in themselves."[3] Leisure includes all other activities. However, many human activities are not easily distinguishable as leisure or non-leisure pursuits. Therefore, some time budgets have sought to specify some middle category to include semi-leisurely activities, as in Table 2-1.[4] Some members of society, such as homemakers, might record the majority of their time in the "highly committed" category in this time budget classification.

One major advantage of the time budget is that it allows different categorizations of leisure and non-leisure activity to be made while using the

**TABLE 2-1  A LEISURE MODEL***

| FULLY COMMITTED | | PARTLY COMMITTED | |
|---|---|---|---|
| *Essential* | *Highly Committed* | *Optional* | *Leisure* |
| Sleeping | Essential sleep | | Relaxing |
| Personal care and exercise | Health and hygiene | | Sport and active play |
| Eating | Eating | | Drinking and dining out |
| Shopping | Essential shopping | Optional shopping | |
| Work | Primary work | Overtime and secondary work | |
| Housework | Essential housework and cooking | House repairs and car maintenance | Do-it-yourself projects, gardening |
| Education | Schooling | Further education and homework | |
| Cultural and communication (non-travel) | | | TV, radio, reading, theater, hobbies, and passive play |
| Social activities | | Child-raising, religion, and politics | Talking, parties, etc. |
| Travel | Travel to work/school | | Walking, driving for pleasure |

*SOURCE: R. Maw, "Construction of a Leisure Model, Official Architecture and Planning, August, 1969," in I. Cosgrove and R. Jackson (eds.), *The Geography of Recreation and Leisure.* London: Hutchinson University Library, 1972, p. 14.

same data. The time budget, however, presents many problems for the researcher. Many people, for instance, are not willing to participate in such a study, the refusal rate sometimes being as high as 90 per cent. Additionally, time budgets are dependent upon the memory of the individual involved. People are likely to remember some leisure activities longer than they remember others, especially those that were most enjoyable, and to underestimate the amount of time spent in activities that they consider to be of "low status." Illegal activities, or those considered immoral, are likely to be omitted as well. Another problem is the actual recording of the activities. Right now, for instance, you might say that you are reading a book, doing homework, or learning about leisure. You might also have the television on and be eating an apple while you are reading. How would you describe this situation? Some studies have attempted to make the respondent's record both primary and secondary activities undertaken simultaneously in order to solve this problem. Time budget data are often unable to represent more than a few days in the lives of the respondents, and people's activity patterns are different for different days of the week, months of the year, and so forth. In spite of these problems, time budget studies have contributed much to our knowledge about people's activity patterns. One study was *The Use of Time,* a cross-national comparative study of how people spend their time in East and West Germany, Russia, the United States, Bulgaria, Czechoslovakia, Hungary, Poland, Yugoslavia, Belgium, France, and Peru.[5] The study sought to determine how much time is spent sleeping, commuting, doing paid and unpaid work, shopping, playing with the children, reading books or watching television, listening to music, making conversations, pursuing hobbies, or participating in civic activities. It also explored how these activity patterns varied according to sex, age, size of family, education, type of employment, and socioeconomic status.

## Measuring Work Time Segments

A second way of attempting to measure leisure is to total that part of an individual's time spent in work or work-related activity, and to consider leisure as the remainder. The most frequently cited statistic in such a measurement is the length of the work week. Many other kinds of information are also used in analyses of work time, including percentage of individuals in the labor force, percentage of those holding two or more jobs (moonlighting), the age of entry and retirement from the labor force in relation to life expectancy, the rate of unemployment, the number of vacations and holidays, and time spent traveling to and from one's job (commuting). Table 2-2 reflects an attempt to measure the increase in non-work time during the life cycle from 1900 to 1960.[6] It shows the inadequacy of using data concerning workweek length alone as a means of estimating leisure time increases.

Segments of time such as vacations, commuting time, and job-related

TABLE 2-2   REDUCTIONS IN PER CAPITA WORK TIME, U.S. MALES,
1900–1960*

|  | 1900 | 1960 |
|---|---|---|
| (1)  Hours of work per week† | 58.5 | 41.0 |
| (2)  Total years of life, expected at birth‡ | 48.2 | 66.6 |
| (3)  Years in labor force, expected at birth‡ | 32.1 | 41.4 |
| (4)  Years out of labor force, expected at birth‡ | 16.1 | 25.2 |
| (5)  Proportion of week spent in market employment: (1)/168 | 0.348 | 0.245 |
| (6)  Proportion of life spent in labor force: (3)/(2) | 0.666 | 0.622 |
| (7)  Proportion of life spent at work: (5) × (6) | 0.234 | 0.152 |

*SOURCE: J. D. Owen, *The Price of Leisure.* Rotterdam: Rotterdam University Press, 1969, p. 11.
†SOURCE: Owen, *loc. cit.,* p. 67.
‡SOURCE: Seymour Wolfbein, *Changing Patterns of Working Life.* Quoted by J. D. Owen.

homework are typically not included in the measurement of an average workweek. Some studies, however, have shown that when the length of the workweek shortens, many workers take a second job. A study by Swados, for instance, found that employees in an Akron, Ohio, rubber factory that had cut back to a 36-hour workweek took second full-time jobs in 20 per cent of the cases.[7] Another 40 per cent engaged in part-time work. Swados concluded that the initial workweek length was extremely misleading. Workweek length does, however, provide an important clue as to what potential an individual has for leisure.

## Measuring Leisure Time Segments

Studies of leisure time segments ask people to report what activities they undertake away from their place of work, or to report the frequency and duration of participation in preselected leisure activity categories. Such research is often useful in predicting future participation rates. These studies are sometimes conducted by governmental agencies to aid in planning leisure services for the public.

In some studies of leisure time segments, people are asked about their attitudes toward various activities and their meanings for the individual's life. When this is done a more complete picture is obtained because the individual's perception of the activity is defined by him/her, rather than by the researcher. Many studies have shown that people's attitudes toward various leisure activities are not always those which might be expected. A study of business executives, for instance, found that much of their work is characterized by qualities which would ordinarily be associated with leisure.[8] Conversely, about one-third of the executives said that they considered their involvement in church and charity activities that bettered the community as "work" that helped to advance their careers. Because of findings such as these, there is increasing agreement among social scientists who study leisure that the individual's own perception of leisure time and activity should be given more attention in leisure-related research.

## HOW WE SPEND OUR TIME*

Now that we have examined some methods to tell us how we as individuals spend our time, and discussed the measurement of leisure as time, let's look at how our society spends its time.

As our lives have become more complicated during the last century, our power over the environment has increased; as we have adopted a style of living in which we depend more and more upon each other, time has become an increasingly important "resource." While we used to speak of "passing" the time, today we "spend" time, "gain" or "lose" it, "save" it, or even "make" it. As time and money are equated, we begin to see ourselves as consumers of experience just as we formerly saw ourselves as consumers of material goods. Time, therefore, is an increasingly important medium of exchange for those who have reached an income level that meets their basic material needs. Such a shift in scarcities profoundly alters our behavior. Thus, we may choose to donate our money rather than our time to worthy causes. People in old age homes may have access to sophisticated medical machinery, but they suffer acute loneliness. The word "instant" on almost any product or service causes us to investigate it further. We eat in "fast food" restaurants, buy appliances which claim to make household chores disappear more quickly, and seek "short cuts" when we travel. We often establish a social pecking order based upon whose time is believed to be most important. We see a doctor when the doctor has time; housewives are expected to be home whenever it suits a workman or repairman, who usually doesn't specify a precise time of arrival.

Our current leisure activity patterns also demonstrate this desire to save time even if the quality of the experience suffers. As mentioned earlier, you can paint by number, tour an entire country in three days, skydive and jump your first time up, play the guitar in only three easy lessons, or visit a number of commercial zoos and animal habitats without even getting out of your car.

While time is increasingly important to us, surprisingly few studies have examined how Americans organize their everyday lives. For economic purposes the U.S.S.R. undertook extensive studies of how citizens spend their time as early as the 1920s, but in the United States few time diary studies had been undertaken until 1965, when the U.S. participated with 11 other

---

*Dr. John Robinson helped me write this section. John is a researcher who was involved in the United States portion of the largest international time budget study ever undertaken, which was mentioned earlier.[10]

nations* in a study sponsored by UNESCO.⁵ From the results of this study, and subsequent related research, the first comprehensive glimpse of how Americans spend their time in their everyday lives can be determined.† These studies used time budgets in which respondents were asked to reconstruct how they spent all their time during the day in question. The time budget provides a special kind of insight into our lives since it provides a highly reliable answer to the question, "What do you do?" This question is one of the first we ask when meeting a stranger, since we assume it is the easiest way to find out about the person. Time budgets show us if managers really spend their time managing, if we really "hardly ever" watch television, or how often we play with our children. University students who have kept time diaries as a class assignment have occasionally been so surprised by the results that they have made radical changes in their behavior, in one case even quitting school.

From the new time budget studies, a number of interesting highlights have emerged concerning our work and leisure. The rest of this section presents several findings.

*While we may think of daily lives as being divided into 8 hours for work, 8 for sleep, and 8 for leisure, the study found both men and women average only about 5 hours of leisure activity a day.* Furthermore, there was a steady decline in the amount of leisure per day of about one hour from adolescence up to retirement. Perhaps to paraphrase, leisure, like youth, is wasted on the young.

*With regard to leisure activities, we seem to be emerging into a "leisure democracy."* That is, what people do during their free time is determined less by status or station in life than by personality, individual interests, or lifestyle. Satisfaction derived from activities, for instance, was a primary determinant of how much time was devoted to such activities. For instance, people who said they derived "great" satisfaction from watching TV spent almost five times as many hours in viewing as those who derived "little" or "no" satisfaction. The differences that do emerge between the more or less affluent or between the more or less educated are not in how much free time they have but in what activities they take part. Our common rhythm of life is indicated by the fact that it is simply not possible to find consistent, systematic, or significant differences in time usage between different regions of the country, between urban and rural locations, or even by weather and seasons. Thorstein Veblen, who at the turn of the century condemned a

---

*Belgium, Bulgaria, Czechoslovakia, East Germany, France, Hungary, Peru, Poland, U.S.S.R., West Germany, Yugoslavia, and U.S.A.

†This study utilized separate data from a national sample and from the single city of Jackson, Michigan. A follow-up study was undertaken in 1975 in Jackson. Jackson, Michigan, was chosen for its convenience and similarity in sociological structure to the urban industrial European sites in the multinational study. Time usage results from Jackson and the national sample were extremely similar.

predatory leisure class in America who spent its time unproductively, might have great difficulty today identifying who was excluded from such a class.[9] While it may be argued that the quality of life or leisure experience varies by income or education, it appears senseless to argue that one economic, educational, or occupational class has leisure at the expense of another.

*Television has reshaped the way we spend time like nothing else in our society.* It is our most time-consuming leisure activity, using about one-third of our free time. Time spent viewing television has replaced not only some of the time formerly spent listening to radio or going to the movies, but also time previously spent in other leisure activities, such as visiting and gardening, as well as time spent sleeping.

Overall, Americans spend more total time with the mass media than people in any of the other countries surveyed. Americans spend more time watching television than any other nation, and spend an average of at least five minutes a day more reading newspapers than any other country. They spend the least time of any surveyed country, however, in reading books. Perhaps we spend less time with books because, in our rush for leisure experiences, books simply take too long, in spite of the advent of "speed reading."

We should note that the actual amount of TV viewed per day—between 2 and 2½ hours—is much less than that reported by TV rating services and other polls of mass media consumption. Furthermore, roughly one-fourth of those 2 to 2½ hours is "secondary" viewing, where television viewing is combined with another activity which the participant feels is more important. It may be that television will go through a transition similar to radio, becoming an activity which is used in combination with other activities.

*Participation in sports and outdoor recreation activity, while an im-*

**FIGURE 2-1** Television has reshaped the way we spend time like nothing else in our society. (Courtesy of H. Armstrong Roberts)

*portant part of our leisure lives, represents relatively minor expenditures of our free time.* Outdoor recreation activity consumes less than 1 per cent of our free time while active sports consumes 3 per cent of the free time of employed men, 2 per cent for employed women, and 1 per cent for housewives. To put these figures into international perspective, however, it should be noted that Americans spend *more* time in active sport participation than any of the other 11 nations surveyed and *less* time in outdoor recreation than any of the other 11 nations.

There are many conflicting figures available concerning which sport is most popular in our country. The survey found that bowling was more popular than all other sports combined during the non-summer months. While some other sports such as swimming may have more participants, bowlers apparently spend the most time.

*The importance of time spent in recreation and leisure in contributing to individual happiness is increasingly evident.* The study found a relation between a person's satisfaction with leisure activities and satisfaction with life as a whole. This relationship was even stronger than the relation between life satisfaction and satisfaction with the job. The kind of activities one engaged in during leisure didn't seem to determine whether or not his or her leisure life was satisfactory. Those who are more active in their leisure, participate more in voluntary organizations or adult education, or make use of the outdoors are no more likely to be satisfied with their spare time than those who do not. As the song says, "It ain't what you do but the way that you do it." What does appear to be an important determinant of spare time satisfaction, according to Robinson's time budget research, is the number of friends the respondent believes he or she has.[10]

*Household chores are still "for women only."* Over 80 per cent of all time spent in household chores is spent by women, and this doesn't change much even if the housewife takes a full-time job or has young children. In fact, husbands whose wives are in the labor force have more time for leisure activities than those whose wives stay home. Results of other research found that the total time devoted to household chores has not changed much in the last two decades.[11] In spite of this, married women in this survey generally did not want more help from their husbands; less than 25 per cent expressed such a desire. While employed women or those with young children are far more likely to report feeling "rushed to do the things you have to do," they reported no less overall satisfaction with their lives than other women. The home-making role is so pervasive for women that unmarried women were found to spend almost as much time in housework as did married ones.

*Many Americans feel they are racing through their lives.* One out of four respondents said they "always feel rushed." Time on our hands is a fictitious problem for most Americans; only one respondent out of ten said they sometimes experienced the feeling of unwanted time. It may be the more affluent in our society who feel most rushed. They spend more total time in

**FIGURE 2-2** While the situation is changing, women still spend four times as many hours on housework as men. (Courtesy of H. Armstrong Roberts)

travel than do others, more time in adult education courses, in formal organizations, in recreation and entertainment away from the home, with less time resting. Economic affluence, in short, may be associated with increasing the range of activities in which the individual is interested, as well as increasing the means necessary to undertake such activities. This increased potential for leisure, ironically, may cause people to lead a very rushed (unleisurely) lifestyle.

Such an overstimulated lifestyle may produce boredom as surely as understimulation. Let us make an economic analogy. The usefulness (marginal utility) of material goods lessens as we acquire more so that, for instance, owning seven television sets is only a little more useful than owning six, but two is considerably more useful than owning one. In similar fashion, the usefulness (satisfaction) from leisure activities may diminish as more are added. The popularity today of "high risk" leisure experiences such as hang-gliding, rock climbing, or white water canoeing may represent an attempt to find satisfaction on the part of those for whom satisfaction from more conventional leisure activities has declined.

A preliminary look at the results of the 1975 data indicates several major changes in time usage, including a startling 20 per cent drop from 1965 in time

**FIGURE 2-3**   Hang-gliding, for some, provides a thrill and excitement worth the risk. (Courtesy of the National Park Service)

spent in family care, which includes housework, child care, and shopping. This unparalleled decline has come about mainly because of less time spent in routine housecleaning and upkeep. On a per child basis, child care time was actually higher in 1975 than it was in 1965.[10]

An additional preliminary finding of great significance is a gain in non-work time of about 10 per cent. This is of particular importance since, contrary to popular belief, there was little evidence of a gain in non-work time from 1940 to 1965. From 1965 to 1975 time spent in working for pay dropped from 51.3 to 47.4 hours a week for married men, and from 51.4 to 40.0 hours for single men. Among employed women the drop was from 38.4 to 30.1 hours a week for married women, and 39.8 hours for single women. The leisure activities that gained in popularity during this period were the use of television and other mass media, adult education, and recreation activities, such as sports and walking or driving for pleasure. In contrast, there was a notable drop in visiting and other informal social life.[10]

Regardless of how these findings are interpreted, it appears certain that leisure, and how we use it, is increasingly important in defining who we are. It may be that the greater bureaucratization of the work place increasingly constrains our self-expression. It may also be that we have raised our expectations and complicated our lives to realize three fundamental values more fully: freedom, accomplishment, and pleasure.

# Leisure Exercise 2·2

It should be obvious to you by now that to many in our society time is a scarce resource. Probably, as a result of thinking about time and a few time-oriented exercises we will do, you may become a little more time-conscious. Sorry. The object here is not to bring about a change in the way you use your time but merely to create a little more awareness of how you "pass" or "use" your time.

Speaking of time-related exercises, let's take a look at how you spend your time.

## TIME BUDGET

The purpose of this exercise is to gain a better understanding of your usage of time and, in particular, your leisure time use. Additionally, the exercise will provide a basis for comparison of your leisure time usage with other students.

To complete the assignment, refer to the seven Time Budget Sheets and the Time Budget Activity Summary. A Time Budget Sheet should be completed for each of the following days: Saturday, _____
_____. For each of these days, your primary activities should be recorded in your own words as precisely as possible. For example:

This record should be kept for all your waking hours (except if you believe reporting some activity would be an invasion of your privacy). Do not report any illegal activities. Fill out your Time Budget just before going to bed.

| Activity | Where | With Whom | Time Began | Ended |
|---|---|---|---|---|
| Woke up, showered (and shaved) | Home | — — | 7:45 | 8:15 |
| Ate breakfast | Home | Wife and two daughters | 8:15 | 8:45 |
| Drove to work | Rec hall | — — | 8:45 | 9:00 |
| Attended meeting | Rec hall | Professors | 9:00 | 10:30 |

After recording your activities for each of the days in question, fill out the Time Budget Activity Summary by recording the total minutes spent for each day in each of the categories of leisure activity. If your Time Budget has listed "played basketball 4:30–5:00," for instance, you would enter that 30 minutes in line 14 under active sports (participating). Complete the Time Budgets and the Summary, staple them together with the Time Budget Summary on top, and submit them.

The Time Budgets and Summary are due on _____.

# TIME BUDGET

## SUNDAY

Name: _____

ID Number: _____

| Activity | Where | With Whom | Time Began | Time Ended |
|---|---|---|---|---|
| | | | | |
| | | | | |
| | | | | |
| | | | | |
| | | | | |
| | | | | |
| | | | | |
| | | | | |
| | | | | |
| | | | | |
| | | | | |
| | | | | |
| | | | | |
| | | | | |
| | | | | |
| | | | | |
| | | | | |
| | | | | |

# TIME BUDGET

## MONDAY

Name: _____

ID Number: _____

| Activity | Where | With Whom | Time | |
|---|---|---|---|---|
| | | | Began | Ended |
| | | | | |
| | | | | |
| | | | | |
| | | | | |
| | | | | |
| | | | | |
| | | | | |
| | | | | |
| | | | | |
| | | | | |
| | | | | |
| | | | | |
| | | | | |
| | | | | |
| | | | | |
| | | | | |

# TIME BUDGET

## TUESDAY

Name: _____

ID Number: _____

| Activity | Where | With Whom | Time Began | Time Ended |
|---|---|---|---|---|
|  |  |  |  |  |
|  |  |  |  |  |
|  |  |  |  |  |
|  |  |  |  |  |
|  |  |  |  |  |
|  |  |  |  |  |
|  |  |  |  |  |
|  |  |  |  |  |
|  |  |  |  |  |
|  |  |  |  |  |
|  |  |  |  |  |
|  |  |  |  |  |
|  |  |  |  |  |
|  |  |  |  |  |
|  |  |  |  |  |
|  |  |  |  |  |
|  |  |  |  |  |
|  |  |  |  |  |
|  |  |  |  |  |

# TIME BUDGET

WEDNESDAY  Name: _____

ID Number: _____

| Activity | Where | With Whom | Time | |
|---|---|---|---|---|
| | | | Began | Ended |
| | | | | |
| | | | | |
| | | | | |
| | | | | |
| | | | | |
| | | | | |
| | | | | |
| | | | | |
| | | | | |
| | | | | |
| | | | | |
| | | | | |
| | | | | |
| | | | | |
| | | | | |
| | | | | |
| | | | | |

# TIME BUDGET

THURSDAY  Name: _____

ID Number: _____

| Activity | Where | With Whom | Time | |
|---|---|---|---|---|
| | | | Began | Ended |
| | | | | |
| | | | | |
| | | | | |
| | | | | |
| | | | | |
| | | | | |
| | | | | |
| | | | | |
| | | | | |
| | | | | |
| | | | | |
| | | | | |
| | | | | |
| | | | | |
| | | | | |
| | | | | |
| | | | | |
| | | | | |
| | | | | |
| | | | | |
| | | | | |
| | | | | |
| | | | | |

# TIME BUDGET

## FRIDAY

Name: _____

ID Number: _____

| Activity | Where | With Whom | Time Began | Time Ended |
|----------|-------|-----------|------------|------------|
|          |       |           |            |            |
|          |       |           |            |            |
|          |       |           |            |            |
|          |       |           |            |            |
|          |       |           |            |            |
|          |       |           |            |            |
|          |       |           |            |            |
|          |       |           |            |            |
|          |       |           |            |            |
|          |       |           |            |            |
|          |       |           |            |            |
|          |       |           |            |            |
|          |       |           |            |            |
|          |       |           |            |            |
|          |       |           |            |            |
|          |       |           |            |            |
|          |       |           |            |            |

**TIME BUDGET**

SATURDAY  Name: _____

ID Number: _____

| Activity | Where | With Whom | Time |  |
|---|---|---|---|---|
|  |  |  | Began | Ended |
|  |  |  |  |  |
|  |  |  |  |  |
|  |  |  |  |  |
|  |  |  |  |  |
|  |  |  |  |  |
|  |  |  |  |  |
|  |  |  |  |  |
|  |  |  |  |  |
|  |  |  |  |  |
|  |  |  |  |  |
|  |  |  |  |  |
|  |  |  |  |  |
|  |  |  |  |  |
|  |  |  |  |  |
|  |  |  |  |  |
|  |  |  |  |  |

Name: _____

## Time Budget Activity Summary
### Record in "Minutes" of Activity

| Primary Activity | Sunday | Monday | Tuesday | Wednesday | Thursday | Friday | Saturday | Total Minutes |
|---|---|---|---|---|---|---|---|---|
| 1. Leisure travel | | | | | | | | |
| 2. Religion | | | | | | | | |
| 3. Organizations (voluntary) | | | | | | | | |
| 4. Radio | | | | | | | | |
| 5. Television (home) | | | | | | | | |
| 6. Television (away) | | | | | | | | |
| 7. Read paper | | | | | | | | |
| 8. Read magazine | | | | | | | | |
| 9. Read books | | | | | | | | |
| 10. Movies | | | | | | | | |
| 11. Social. (home) | | | | | | | | |
| 12. Social (away) | | | | | | | | |
| 13. Telephone conversation | | | | | | | | |
| 14. Active sports (partici-pating) | | | | | | | | |

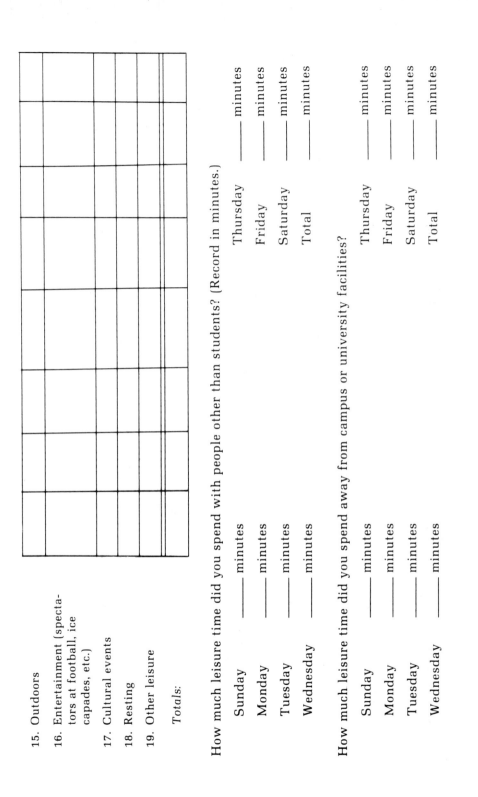

15. Outdoors

16. Entertainment (spectators at football, ice capades, etc.)

17. Cultural events

18. Resting

19. Other leisure

Totals:

How much leisure time did you spend with people other than students? (Record in minutes.)

Sunday ———— minutes  Thursday ———— minutes

Monday ———— minutes  Friday ———— minutes

Tuesday ———— minutes  Saturday ———— minutes

Wednesday ———— minutes  Total ———— minutes

How much leisure time did you spend away from campus or university facilities?

Sunday ———— minutes  Thursday ———— minutes

Monday ———— minutes  Friday ———— minutes

Tuesday ———— minutes  Saturday ———— minutes

Wednesday ———— minutes  Total ———— minutes

It may have occurred to you in completing your time budget study that the particular week for which you kept a diary was not typical. Actually, it is very hard to imagine a "typical" day of the week, week of the month, month of the year, or year of your life. What you did during this week was affected by many factors, from weather conditions to personal health to your schoolwork to what was on television. Results of the time budget exercise will give you some insight into a single week of your life, and greater insight as to how you spend your time while at your college or university. We will see later that these patterns are likely to change quite a bit as you get older.

## Some Other Time Budget Findings

To help put your classes' time expenditures into perspective, here are two tables from the 12-nation time budget study which show the percentage of "free time" devoted to various leisure pursuits, and the average hours spent per day in these "free time" activities.[5] As you can see in Table 2-3, housewives spend an average of 25 per cent of their free time watching television (24 per cent watching at home and 1 per cent watching away from home). How does this compare with the percentage of free time you spend viewing TV? In Table 2-4, you can see that employed males in the two different United States samples have 3.8 and 3.9 hours of "free time" on weekdays. I'll bet you have more. Notice that for most of the countries men and women spend more time in "free time" activities on a Sunday than on a Saturday. How about you?

## SATISFACTION WITH TIME SPENT IN LEISURE ACTIVITIES

You may have noticed that time spent in different activities is not qualitatively comparable. A minute spent kissing your boyfriend or girlfriend isn't the same as a minute spent reading this book (no clever comments, please). Thirty minutes watching television is different from the same amount of time spent camping in the wilderness. We don't always spend greater amounts of our time on activities we find very satisfying than on those which are less satisfying. Table 2-5 shows activity satisfaction scores from the U. S. sample of the 12-nation time budget study.[10] You can see that some activities which might not be considered leisure are more satisfying to people than some activities which are considered leisure. Thus, we can't think of work or "obligated" activities as being worthless or worth less than recreation or leisure activities in terms of satisfaction. What kinds of leisure activities are satisfying to you? Let's see if the leisure activities you find most satisfying are those in which you spend the most time.

**TABLE 2-3   PERCENTAGE OF FREE TIME ALLOCATED TO VARIOUS LEISURE ACTIVITIES (AVERAGE ACROSS SURVEY SITES; BECAUSE OF ROUNDING, PERCENTAGES DO NOT ADD UP TO EXACTLY 100 PER CENT)**

|  | Employed Men | Employed Women | Housewives |
|---|---|---|---|
| Education | 6 | 4 | 1 |
| Religion | 1 | 2 | 2 |
| Organization | 2 | 2 | 1 |
| Study-participation | 9 | 8 | 4 |
| Radio | 4 | 3 | 3 |
| TV (home) | 23 | 22 | 24 |
| TV (away) | 1 | 1 | 1 |
| Newspaper | 8 | 4 | 4 |
| Magazines | 1 | 2 | 2 |
| Books | 4 | 5 | 4 |
| Movies | 2 | 3 | 1 |
| Mass media | 43 | 40 | 39 |
| Social (home) | 5 | 6 | 6 |
| Social (away) | 9 | 9 | 9 |
| Conversation | 6 | 6 | 7 |
| Sports | 1 | 1 | † |
| Outdoors | 7 | 5 | 6 |
| Entertainment | 2 | 2 | 1 |
| Culture | † | 1 | * |
| Resting | 8 | 9 | 11 |
| Other leisure | 3 | 8 | 13 |
| Leisure | 7 | 7 | 5 |
| Other leisure | 48 | 54 | 58 |
|  | 100% | 100% | 100% |
| Total average minutes of free time | 272 | 206 | 263 |

*SOURCE: A. Szalai (ed.), *The Use of Time: Daily Activities of Urban and Suburban Populations in Twelve Countries.* The Hague, Netherlands: Mouton and Company, 1972, p. 132.
†Less than 0.5 per cent.

**TABLE 2-4  FREE TIME AS A FUNCTION OF DAY OF THE WEEK AND EDUCATIONAL LEVEL (IN HOURS PER DAY; DATA ARE WEIGHTED TO ENSURE EQUALITY OF DAYS OF THE WEEK AND ELIGIBLE RESPONDENTS PER HOUSEHOLD)***

| | Belgium | Kazanlik, Bulgaria | Olomone, Czechoslovakia | Six cities, France | 100 electoral districts, Fed. Rep. Germany | Osnabruck, Fed. Rep. Germany | Hoyerswerda, German Dem. Rep. | Györ, Hungary | Lima-Callao, Peru | Torun, Poland | Forty-four cities, USA | Jackson, USA | Pskov, USSR | Kragujevac, Yugoslavia | Maribor, Yugoslavia |
|---|---|---|---|---|---|---|---|---|---|---|---|---|---|---|---|
| Employed men, weekdays | 3.7 | 2.3 | 3.7 | 3.0 | 3.4 | 3.8 | 3.4 | 3.0 | 3.9 | 3.9 | 3.8 | 3.9 | 4.2 | 4.2 | 3.5 |
| Saturday | 5.7 | 4.4 | 4.9 | 4.8 | 5.7 | 6.4 | 6.2 | 3.7 | 4.6 | 4.9 | 6.2 | 6.2 | 5.0 | 4.8 | 4.3 |
| Sunday | 9.3 | 6.6 | 7.8 | 7.5 | 8.6 | 8.5 | 7.6 | 7.5 | 7.3† | 8.5 | 8.3 | 8.9 | 8.2 | 9.2 | 8.0 |
| Employed men, all days | 4.8 | 3.8 | 4.5 | 4.1 | 4.4 | 5.0 | 4.4 | 3.8 | 4.5 | 4.8 | 4.8 | 5.2 | 5.1 | 5.1 | 4.2 |
| primary education | 5.1 | 3.5 | 4.2 | 4.0 | 4.3 | 5.0 | 4.3 | 3.4 | 3.9 | 4.6 | 4.7 | 5.0 | 4.4 | 4.6 | 3.6 |
| secondary and higher | 4.7 | 4.3 | 4.7 | 4.2 | 4.8 | 5.0 | 4.9 | 4.9 | 5.4 | 5.0 | 4.8 | 5.3 | 5.2 | 5.4 | 4.9 |
| Employed women, weekdays | 3.0 | 2.5 | 2.4 | 2.2 | 2.6 | 3.1 | 2.5 | 6.0 | 3.3 | 2.8 | 3.2 | 3.3 | 2.6 | 3.2 | 2.1 |
| Saturday | 4.7 | 3.3 | 3.9 | 3.3 | 3.8 | 5.6 | 4.3 | 6.0 | 2.8† | 3.4 | 5.6 | 4.5† | 3.0 | 3.6 | 2.3 |
| Sunday | 7.7 | 5.2 | 5.1 | 6.3 | 5.8 | 7.7 | 4.9 | 4.9 | 7.0† | 6.5 | 7.0 | 7.1 | 5.6 | 6.6 | 4.5 |
| Employed women, all days | 3.8 | 3.2 | 2.9 | 3.0 | 3.3 | 4.3 | 3.1 | 2.5 | 3.6 | 3.5 | 4.1 | 4.3 | 3.5 | 3.9 | 2.4 |
| primary education | 3.7 | 3.0 | 2.9 | 3.0 | 3.2 | 4.0 | 3.1 | 2.2 | 3.2 | 3.1 | 5.6 | 4.2 | 2.6 | 3.5 | 2.0 |
| secondary and higher | 3.8 | 3.3 | 3.0 | 3.0 | 4.3 | 4.9 | 3.8 | 3.3 | 4.2 | 3.9 | 4.1 | 4.3 | 3.5 | 4.7 | 3.2 |
| Housewives, weekdays | 4.4 | 3.8 | 3.6 | 3.7 | 4.0 | 4.2 | 3.7 | 2.4 | 4.6 | 3.6 | 5.1 | 5.3 | 3.9 | 5.5 | 2.2 |
| Saturday | 5.1 | 4.4† | 4.6 | 4.1 | 5.0 | 5.5 | 4.4 | 2.7 | 4.4† | 4.1 | 6.2 | 6.1 | 5.2 | 5.6 | 2.3 |
| Sunday | 7.5 | 7.1† | 4.6 | 5.7 | 7.0 | 7.0 | 5.5† | 5.0 | 6.2 | 7.0 | 8.3 | 7.1† | 6.4 | 6.3 | 4.4 |
| Housewives, all days | 5.0 | 4.4 | 3.9 | 4.1 | 4.6 | 4.9 | 4.0 | 2.8 | 3.5 | 4.2 | 5.7 | 5.6 | 4.3 | 5.7 | 2.6 |
| primary education | 5.0 | 3.9 | 4.0 | 4.1 | 4.6 | 4.7 | 4.1 | 2.8 | 4.3 | 4.1 | 6.0 | 5.8 | 4.1 | 5.7 | 2.5 |
| secondary and higher | 5.1 | 5.8† | 3.6 | 4.2 | 5.4 | 5.6 | 3.5† | 5.0† | 6.6† | 4.6 | 5.5 | 5.5 | 4.7† | 5.4 | 3.5† |
| Distance to city center all people, all days | | | | | | | | | | | | | | | |
| 0–2 kilometers | 5.0 | 4.1 | 4.2 | 4.2 | NA | 5.2 | 3.9 | 3.9 | 4.8 | 4.4 | 5.6 | 5.4 | 4.4 | 5.2 | 4.3 |
| 2–10 kilometers | 5.1 | 2.9 | 3.6 | 4.0 | NA | 4.9 | — | 3.1 | 5.3 | 4.2 | 5.1 | 5.1 | 3.5 | 4.8 | 3.2 |
| over 10 kilometers | 4.4 | 3.3 | 3.4 | 4.1† | NA | — | — | 2.7 | 4.5 | — | 4.9 | 5.0 | 3.2 | 2.3† | 2.2 |

*SOURCE: A. Szalai (ed.), *The Use of Time: Daily Activities of Urban and Suburban Populations in Twelve Countries*. The Hague, Netherlands: Mouton and Company, 1972, p. 133.
†N between 10 and 29.
‡N between 4 and 9.
—N less than 4.
NA Data not available for this variable.

**TABLE 2-5  ACTIVITY SATISFACTION ITEMS AND RESPONSES IN THE 1965–1966 STUDY (PER CENT EXPRESSING SATISFACTION ON A FIVE-POINT SCALE)***

| | 5. Great | 4. Much | 3. Some | 2. Little | 1. None | Total | Average Score Men | Average Score Women |
|---|---|---|---|---|---|---|---|---|
| Watching TV | 17 | 24 | 46 | 11 | 2 | 100 | 3.5 | 3.4 |
| Sports or games | 26 | 22 | 22 | 13 | 17 | 100 | 4.0 | 2.8 |
| Your house (or apartment) | 40 | 38 | 15 | 6 | 1 | 100 | 4.1 | 4.1 |
| Shopping, except for groceries | 17 | 25 | 26 | 20 | 12 | 100 | 2.5 | 3.7 |
| Religion | 34 | 28 | 24 | 9 | 5 | 100 | 3.5 | 4.0 |
| Reading | 32 | 30 | 23 | 10 | 5 | 100 | 3.6 | 3.8 |
| Following politics or voting | 9 | 16 | 33 | 26 | 16 | 100 | 3.0 | 2.7 |
| Your (house)work | 25 | 35 | 25 | 9 | 6 | 100 | 3.7 | 3.6 |
| Preparing or cooking food | 23 | 26 | 21 | 13 | 17 | 100 | 2.5 | 3.7 |
| Making or fixing things | 27 | 31 | 23 | 13 | 6 | 100 | 3.5 | 3.7 |
| Your children† | 79 | 16 | 3 | — | 2 | 100 | 4.6 | 4.8 |
| Your car† | 25 | 29 | 27 | 12 | 7 | 100 | 3.6 | 3.5 |
| Relaxing, sitting around | 24 | 29 | 27 | 14 | 6 | 100 | 3.7 | 3.4 |
| Helping others | 33 | 44 | 21 | 2 | — | 100 | 3.9 | 4.2 |
| Being with relatives | 27 | 37 | 27 | 7 | 2 | 100 | 3.6 | 4.0 |
| Being with friends | 33 | 46 | 18 | 2 | 1 | 100 | 4.0 | 4.2 |
| Clubs you belong to | 13 | 21 | 21 | 10 | 35 | 100 | 2.7 | 2.6 |
| Your marriage | 75 | 18 | 4 | 1 | 2 | 100 | 4.7 | 4.6 |

*source: John Robinson, How Americans Use Time: A Socio-Psychological Analysis of Everyday Behavior. New York: Praeger, 1977, p. 117; compiled by Robinson from his Study of Americans' Use of Time (1965–1966).

†If respondent has.

‡A dash indicates less than 0.5 per cent.

Note: The following question was asked: "Some ways of spending spare time are very satisfying to one person, while another may not enjoy them at all. I'd like to ask how much satisfaction you get out of some of these different things (hand card). Take watching TV, for example. All in all would you say you get great satisfaction, much satisfaction, some satisfaction, little satisfaction, or no satisfaction from watching TV?"

NAME _____

DATE _____

# Leisure Exercise 2·3

For each of the following activities, please check in the appropriate place to indicate whether your participation in the activity produces great satisfaction, much satisfaction, some satisfaction, little satisfaction, or no satisfaction.

|  | Amount of satisfaction | | | | |
|---|---|---|---|---|---|
|  | Great | Much | Some | Little | None |
| Leisure travel | ___ | ___ | ___ | ___ | ___ |
| Religion | ___ | ___ | ___ | ___ | ___ |
| Organizations (voluntary) | ___ | ___ | ___ | ___ | ___ |
| Radio | ___ | ___ | ___ | ___ | ___ |
| Television | ___ | ___ | ___ | ___ | ___ |
| Reading papers | ___ | ___ | ___ | ___ | ___ |
| Reading magazines | ___ | ___ | ___ | ___ | ___ |
| Reading books | ___ | ___ | ___ | ___ | ___ |
| Movies | ___ | ___ | ___ | ___ | ___ |
| Social activities | ___ | ___ | ___ | ___ | ___ |
| Telephone conversation | ___ | ___ | ___ | ___ | ___ |
| Active sports (participating) | ___ | ___ | ___ | ___ | ___ |
| Outdoors | ___ | ___ | ___ | ___ | ___ |
| Entertainment | ___ | ___ | ___ | ___ | ___ |
| Cultural events | ___ | ___ | ___ | ___ | ___ |
| Resting | ___ | ___ | ___ | ___ | ___ |

How often do you feel rushed to complete your day's activities?

_____ I always feel rushed.

_____ I only sometimes feel rushed.

_____ I almost never feel rushed.

After you have done this, you can compare this information with the results obtained in your time budget study to see if there is a relation between how much time you spend in a given leisure activity and how much satisfaction you derive from it.

# Why Do People Spend Time in Leisure Activities?

The best answer may be that no one knows. "Why?" is a tough question in the social sciences; some scholars believe that we can't give definitive causal answers to why we undertake certain activities, or that we have to trace the question back past the limits of science to God or to macrocosmic sources.

If we ask people why they participate in various leisure activities, a number of things may happen. First, the person may not know why he participates in the activity, or the reason may be too complex to answer simply. A number of reasons may come to mind. The individual also may not be willing to tell you, for instance, that he goes to discos to "pick up girls." Rather, he may say he goes because he enjoys dancing and being with friends.

In spite of these complications, several studies have dealt with why people participate in leisure activities. Havighurst concluded from his studies that different age, sex, and social class groups can derive similar values from different leisure activities.[12] The principal reasons for involvement in a person's favorite leisure activity were, in order of frequency, just for the pleasure of doing it, as a welcome change from work, encouraging contact with friends, giving new experience, making the time pass, and providing a feeling of creativeness.

Notice how many of these answers just beg for another "Why?" question. If one collects coins "just for the pleasure of doing it," why it is pleasurable? A study by Lundberg *et al.* of high school students found that students' statements concerning why an activity was enjoyable could be classified as follows: (1) new experience; (2) thrill and excitement; (3) friends and fellowship; (4) personal achievement; (5) good food; (6) beauty of nature; (7) freedom from home and school routine; and (8) music, singing, etc.[3]

While different leisure activities may have similar sources of satisfaction for people or meet similar needs, they may also be different in regard to the extent to which they meet needs. A study by Tinsley and colleagues, for example, examined the need-satisfying characteristics of five common leisure activities: watching TV; attending plays, concerts and lectures; bicycling; and drinking and socializing.[13] They found great variation in the extent to which people said each of the five activities met a list of 45 needs. In fact, 42 of the 45 needs varied significantly among the activities. Table 2-6 shows the six needs that had the greatest variation among the five activities. The need for understanding, for instance, was more highly associated with attending plays and reading than with drinking, and more highly associated with drinking than with TV and bicycling. The need for sex was more highly associated with drinking than with the other four activities.

While a given leisure activity may be highly associated with certain motivations or sources of satisfaction, the range of motivations associated with an individual activity is often surprisingly broad. A study by Kathy Golden and I examined the sources of satisfaction associated with the game of handball in both pick-up games and in organized tournament play.[14] When respondents were asked to list the most important reasons for their participation in handball, the resulting list was enormous (Table 2-7). These sources of

**TABLE 2-6  SIGNIFICANT DIFFERENCES AMONG LEISURE ACTIVITY GROUPS FOR NEED DIMENSIONS ASSOCIATED WITH AN OMEGA-SQUARED GREATER THAN .20***

| Need dimension | Leisure activities | | | | |
|---|---|---|---|---|---|
| Sex | [Reading TV Bicycling Plays] | | | | [Drinking] |
| Catharsis | [TV Plays Reading] | | [Drinking] | | [Bicycling] |
| Independence | [Drinking Plays] | [TV] | [Bicycling Reading] | | |
| Understanding | [TV Bicycling] | [Drinking] | [Plays Reading] | | |
| Getting along with others | [Reading TV] | [Bicycling Plays] | [Drinking] | | |
| Affiliation | [TV Reading Bicycling] | [Plays] | [Drinking] | | |

*source: Howard Tinsley et al., Leisure Activity and Need Satisfaction," *Journal of Leisure Research*, Vol. 9, No. 2, 1977, p. 118.

Note: The brackets group together activities which did not differ significantly on the need dimension.

satisfaction, which we sorted into five domains, show tremendous variation. Answers were as diverse as "to make social contacts which will help me in the future" to "to be physically exhausted in a short period of time."

Part of the appeal of leisure activity is the same as that of play, in that the individual doesn't know or can't explain why he or she likes the activity. As Huizinga said, the element of "fun" can't be broken down into sub-categories.[15] Something is either "fun" or it isn't. Leisure activity ultimately resists rational analysis. We can learn some things but not everything by logical inquiry about leisure.

If you ask me why I liked to sit and watch the waves at twilight on Lake Simcoe, Ontario, I would have to answer you with a poem instead of survey results.

*Waves—Lake Simcoe*

Dream signals
in love with the far
wash of waters.

Breaking on shore
like pods of sleep.

Nomads.
Nuns of the deep.

Ghost breakers.
Sound of time's cleansing.

Caravan.
Constant reaching.

## TABLE 2-7   MEANING STATEMENTS BY CATEGORY*

### Psychological

To develop new strategies
To show others my ability
To look forward to something
To play with little consideration of losing
To relax
To feel skillful
To feel refreshed
To win
To enjoy the excitement of other players
To take my mind off studies or work
To relieve frustrations
To clear my mind
To enjoy the mental and physical skills of others
To change the everyday routine
To feel powerful
To feel temporarily uninhibited while playing
To compete as hard as I can
To satisfy my urge to compete
To enjoy physical exhilaration
To feel tough
To feel healthier
To feel that winning depends upon me or me and my partner
To release hostilities
To be challenged
To be mentally stimulated
To feel fulfilled

### Social

To have fun playing with others
To have comradeship beyond work and study relationships
To joke and kid with friends
To be with friends
To enjoy team spirit
To meet people
To play with opponents of similar skills
To promote the unity of my group
To enjoy social interaction
To compare my skills with the skills of others
To interact with a small number of people
To share the company of other males
To make social contacts which will help me in the future
To contribute to my group
To socialize in the activities associated with the game
To make my team better than other teams
To respond to urging from my peers to play
To share a common bond with others like me

(continued)

## TABLE 2-7  MEANING STATEMENTS BY CATEGORY* (continued)

### Physical

To improve my coordination
To use both sides of my body
To feel the physical exhaustion of activity
To improve my physical condition
To stay in shape
To be physically active
To burn up energy
To control weight
To be physically exhausted in a short period of time
To participate in intense activity
To develop quick reflexes

### Incidental

To have to get together only a few players
To pass time in an agreeable way
To do something to use up time
To fill a need for a player
To play a sport I already know
To play a year-round sport
To play an inexpensive sport.
To play a lifetime sport
To participate in an activity which is conveniently organized
To play because the facilities are available
To use my leisure wisely

### Learning

To improve by learning from others
To learn a new sport
To round out my education
To develop skills which carry over into later life.

*SOURCE: Kathy Golden, "The Meaning of Participation in Handball at Two Structural Levels," Unpublished Master's Thesis, Pennsylvania State University, 1979.

# Leisure Exercise 2·4

## A Peak Leisure Experience

In this exercise you are asked to describe one of your most memorable leisure experiences to a few of your classmates in groups of three or four. Each person in the group will share a peak leisure experience with the others. To prepare for this exercise, you should answer the questions in the spaces provided below.

1. Describe the activity and the circumstances surrounding your participation.

2. What role, if any, did other people play in the activity?

3. Describe your attitude and emotional state.

**4.** Were there elements of pain or work involved?

**5.** What role did the activity play in your life?

**6.** What needs or sources of satisfaction did the activity provide?

**7.** Did the activity progress as expected?

**8.** Did your participation in the activity have any lasting effects on you?

After each group member has related his/her peak leisure experience to the others, see if you can find any common elements in your peak leisure experiences. If you can, what are they?

## STUDY QUESTIONS

1. Define and discuss some different ways of conceptualizing time. Do you operate under more than one of these concepts in your personal life? Why or why not?

2. In terms of the entire life span, is it accurate to say that people today are likely to spend a smaller portion of their life at work than they did in 1900?

3. What does the term "leisure democracy" mean?

4. Compared to other uses of leisure time, are time expenditures for sport and outdoor recreation major time expenditures?

5. Discuss why people participate in various forms of leisure activity. Do individual leisure activities tend to have a common source of satisfaction for all participants? Why or why not?

**REFERENCES**

1. Murphy, James F. *Concepts of Leisure: Philosophical Implications.* Englewood Clitts, N.J.: Prentice-Hall, 1974, pp. 5-7.
2. Kaplan, Max. *Leisure in America: A Social Inquiry.* New York: John Wiley and Sons, 1960, p. 264.
3. Lundberg, A. M., Komarovsky, M., and McInervy, M. *Leisure: A Suburban Study.* New York: Columbia University Press, 1934, p. 73.
4. Maw, R. "Construction of a Leisure Model, Official Architecture and Planning, August, 1969" in Cosgrove, I., and Jackson, R. (eds.). *The Geography of Recreation and Leisure.* London: Hutchinson University Library, 1972, p. 14.
5. Szalai, A. (ed.). *The Use of Time: Daily Activities of Urban and Suburban Populations in Twelve Countries.* The Hague, Netherlands: Mouton and Company, 1972, pp. 132, 135.
6. Owen, J. *The Price of Leisure.* Rotterdam: Rotterdam University Press, 1969, p. 11.
7. Swados, Harvey. "Less Work—Less Leisure," *The Nation,* February 22, 1958, pp. 155-160.
8. Heckscher, A., and de Grazia, S. "Problems of Executive Leisure," *Harvard Business Review,* Vol. XXXVII, July-August, 1959, pp. 6-10, 146-154.
9. Veblen, Thorstein. *The Theory of the Leisure Class.* New York: Viking Press, 1899, pp. 1-207.
10. Robinson, John. *Changes in Americans' Use of Time: 1965-1975—A Progress Report.* Cleveland: Cleveland State University, 1977, pp. 4-6.
11. Walker, Katherine. "Homemaking Still Takes Time," *Journal of Home Economics,* Vol. 56, 1969, pp. 621-625.

12. Havighurst, Robert. "The Nature and Values of Meaningful Free Time Activity," *in Aging and Leisure.* New York: Oxford University Press, 1961, pp. 309–344.

13. Tinsley, Howard, et al. "Leisure Activity and Need Satisfaction," *Journal of Leisure Research.* Vol. 9, No. 2, 1977, pp. 110–120.

14. Golden, Kathy, and Godbey, Geoffrey. "The Meaning of Participation in a Leisure Activity at Two Structural Levels," unpublished. University Park, Pa.: Penn State University, 1977, pp. 1–89.

15. Huizinga, Johan. *Homo Ludens.* London: Paladin Books, 1970, p. 31.

# Spending money for leisure-

## The best things in life are free (or fee)

**L**eisure doesn't have to cost money. Children's games—hopscotch, climbing trees, running—cost little or nothing. So, too, do leisure activities such as contemplation, political dialogue, writing poetry, voluntary community service, and other activities which the ancient Greeks considered to be leisure.

Hobos who rode the rails to wherever the trains took them had leisure but no money and, even if they stole, it was usually just something to keep them going to the next place. When most people long for leisure, de Grazia stated, what they really want is free time with ease and abundance.[1] What most of us want costs money, however, and money costs us work, which in turn costs us time.

# Leisure Exercise 3·1

Stop and think about your own recreation and leisure activities for a minute. Do you participate in leisure activities which don't cost any money? Think about this a minute before you answer. List any leisure activities which qualify in the space provided here and be prepared to report them or write them on the board if requested by your instructor.

I participate in the following leisure activities which have no monetary costs.

1. T.U. —(free because of scholarship)

2. Talk

3. Walk

4. read

5. music

71

6.

7.

8.

9.

10.

# HOW MUCH MONEY IS SPENT FOR LEISURE? Difficult to determine because a.) business b.) illegal

It is difficult to determine how much money we spend for leisure. Many things we buy have some connection to our work as well as to our leisure. I might, for instance, buy a sports car to drive to work as well as to drive in road rallies during my leisure. Some "sports" clothing is also worn to work. The entertainment of business clients may be partly a leisure experience as well as work. Another reason for uncertainty about how much money we spend for leisure is that many expenditures are illegal and thus are never reported. We can only estimate how much money people spend on prostitution, drugs, or gambling, since much of such behavior is illegal. (It may be argued that compulsive drug use or gambling doesn't represent leisure behavior at all.) Table 3-1 shows products and services with significant though varying degrees of usage in leisure time. Note the wide variety of uses to which many of these products can be put.

Finally, it's tough to estimate what part of government expenditures go to further leisure activity. What part of the expenditure of the United States Forest Service, for instance, is counted as a leisure expenditure? In spite of these difficulties, we can obtain a reasonable estimation of your own leisure spending and get a rough estimation of leisure spending in the United States. Let's start by getting some idea of how much money you spend for leisure activity and what you spend it for.

## TABLE 3-1   LEISURE-RELATED PRODUCTS AND SERVICES*

| Admissions | Boats and motors | Camping equipment | Facilities |
|---|---|---|---|
| (a) Movies | (a) Sailboats | (a) Tents | (a) Swimming pools |
| (b) Plays, concerts, museums, etc. | (b) Canoes | (b) Sleeping bags | (b) Tennis courts |
| (c) Sports events, circuses, bingo, etc. | (c) Pleasure boats | (c) Coolers, stoves, lanterns, etc. | (c) Skating & curling rinks |
| | (d) Motors | | (d) Bowling alleys |
| | | | (e) Parks, playgrounds, gymnasiums |
| | | | (f) Stadia, tracks, etc. |

*(continued)*

*what are* 2

*Examples*

## TABLE 3-1   LEISURE-RELATED PRODUCTS AND SERVICES* *(continued)*

| Food and drink | Hobbies and hand-crafts | Electronic home entertainment | Information publications |
|---|---|---|---|
| (a) Beer, liquor, wine | (a) Craft supplies | (a) Phonographs | (a) Books |
| (b) Soft drinks | (b) Musical instru-ments | (b) Records and tapes | (b) Magazines |
| (c) Meals in eating places other than work or school | (c) Other hobbies | (c) Television | (c) Newspapers |
| | | (d) Radios | |
| | | (e) Tape recorders | |
| | | (f) Combinations | |

| Photographic equip-ment & supplies | Power tools and lawn care | Sporting goods | Sports clothing and footwear |
|---|---|---|---|
| (a) Cameras | (a) Power tools for home workshop | (a) Swimming pools | (a) Jerseys, sweat suits, etc. |
| (b) Projectors | (b) Garden tools | (b) Bicycles | (b) Athletic foot-wear |
| (c) Film | (c) Lawn mowers & snowblowers | (c) Fishing | |
| (d) Flash cubes, etc. | (d) Garden supplies, seeds, etc. | (d) Hunting | |
| | | (e) Team sports equipment | |
| | | (f) Gymnasium equipment | |
| | | (g) Other sports equipment | |

| Tourism | Toys and games | Vehicles | Miscellaneous |
|---|---|---|---|
| (a) Package holiday trips | (a) Children's toys and games | (a) Automobiles | (a) Jewelry |
| (b) Beyond city transportation | (b) Tricycles, wagons | (b) Motorcycles | (b) Lottery tickets |
| (c) Luggage | (c) Wading pools | (c) Powercycles & scooters | (c) Pets and pet care |
| (d) Other holiday expenses | (d) Sleds and toboggans | (d) Snowmobiles | |
| | | (e) Camping trailers & vacation homes | |

*SOURCE: Jiri Zuzanek, *The Determinants of Leisure Demand and the Prospects for Leisure.* Ottawa: Department of Industry, Trade and Commerce, 1976, p. 33.

# Leisure Exercise 3·2

The purpose of this exercise is to gain a better understanding of your own leisure monetary spending patterns and the relationship of such expenditures to your leisure time and leisure activity patterns, and to compare such information with similar data from other students.

To complete the assignment, refer to the leisure monetary expenditure sheet in the course outline. Each student will be asked to keep a record of his/her leisure monetary expenditures for a one-week period beginning on Monday, _____ and ending Sunday, _____ (seven-day total). In keeping this record, each student should observe the following rules:

1. Record only those expenditures you actually make during the period or expenditures you agree to make—e.g., charging the cost of a pair of skis.

2. Record all items you purchase whether or not they are for your own use—e.g., record the cost of a toy you bought for your little sister.

3. Do not record the cost of a leisure item which was bought for you—e.g., your boyfriend pays your way to the movies.

4. Do not "prorate" any expenditure but leisure travel—e.g., if you receive a daily newspaper, but have a subscription which you have not paid for during the seven-day period, don't record any portion of it. If you have paid for the subscription during the seven-day period, however, record the entire amount. All leisure travel in an automobile you own or have financial responsibility for should be prorated at 25 cents per mile traveled.

In regard to expenditure categories, please note the following. Sporting goods and clothing should include all clothing purchases used primarily for a leisure activity, even if there is some *limited* use for everyday wear—e.g., tennis shoes which you occasionally wear to class. Food should not include any expenditure for your normal breakfast, lunch, and dinner. Only dining out where the meal constitutes a leisure experience and a break from routine and snack food (soft ice cream, pretzels, hoagies) should be recorded. Licenses and dues refer to any payment you have made to be eligible for participation in a leisure activity—e.g., hunting, ham radio operator—or have paid to become

**75**

a member of a club which will further your leisure interests—e.g., dues to an outing club. Fees and admissions refer to payment for tickets, cover charges, and other payments you have made to be a spectator or participant in a leisure activity not covered under licenses and dues. Reading refers to all reading matter of your own choosing which you purchased during the seven-day period. Leisure travel and vehicles include all payments for travel which was undertaken by choice during the period and not made necessary by your status as a student or by other obligations. Prorate car travel expenditures at 25 cents per mile, and record the amount of bus, train, air, or taxi fare. Also include the cost of any leisure vehicles such as snowmobiles, motorcycles, or other travel vehicles used *primarily* for leisure activity. Do not include any automobile costs other than the 25 cents per mile expenditure.

## Leisure Spending Today

Today expenditures for recreation goods and services total $160 billion, according to a study by Elizabeth Owen, of the U. S. Department of Commerce.[3] This represents almost triple the amount spent in 1965: $58.3 billion. To put this amount in perspective, it far exceeds the amount spent annually for home construction or for national defense. Similarly, in Canada, it has been estimated that 12 cents of every consumer dollar is spent for leisure.[2] This amount reflects spending on all forms of leisure pursuits, from admission to sports events and movies to phonograph records, sporting goods, vacation homes, ski lift tickets, and all the expenses associated with travel for pleasure.

The private recreation sector today employs over five million people.[4] While there are no comprehensive employment figures for the public sector, the government probably hires no more than 200,000 individuals. With the exception of vacation homes, the leisure industries appear to be healthy. According to Owen, a doubling of leisure expenditures every eight or nine years is to be expected, based upon past trends.[3]

A number of reasons account for the good growth prospects of leisure commodities. The shifting of the U. S. population to the South and West will generate more spending since people are more active where the weather is conducive to outdoor recreation and, in non-metropolitan areas, the land needed for many forms of recreation is more abundant and more easily accessible. By 1990, the South is expected to increase its population by 20 per cent, the Mountain States by 24 per cent, the Southwest by 25 per cent and the West by 18 per cent.[5] The large eastern and midwestern population centers will grow more slowly or even decline. Another reason for such expected growth is that the number of people aged 25 to 34 will increase by 35 per cent in the next ten years.[5] This age group is a prime target for sales of commodities related to active sports and outdoor recreation.

The changing role of women has also resulted in increased leisure

# LEISURE MONETARY EXPENDITURES

Record only those costs you personally paid for or charged during the period under study. Any item bought by someone else is not to be recorded.

NAME: _____

FROM: _____   TO: _____

| Date | Games, Toys | Radio, TV, Phono, Tapes, Musical Instruments | Sporting Goods, Clothing | Food | Licenses, Dues | Pets, Pet Food | Photo | Fees, Admissions | Hobbies | Alcohol, Tobacco | Travel, Vacations, Vehicles | Reading | Other |
|------|-------------|-----------------------------------------------|--------------------------|------|----------------|----------------|-------|------------------|---------|------------------|------------------------------|---------|-------|
|      |             |                                               |                          |      |                |                |       |                  |         |                  |                              |         |       |
|      |             |                                               |                          |      |                |                |       |                  |         |                  |                              |         |       |
|      |             |                                               |                          |      |                |                |       |                  |         |                  |                              |         |       |
|      |             |                                               |                          |      |                |                |       |                  |         |                  |                              |         |       |
|      |             |                                               |                          |      |                |                |       |                  |         |                  |                              |         |       |
|      |             |                                               |                          |      |                |                |       |                  |         |                  |                              |         |       |
|      |             |                                               |                          |      |                |                |       |                  |         |                  |                              |         |       |
|      |             |                                               |                          |      |                |                |       |                  |         |                  |                              |         |       |
|      |             |                                               |                          |      |                |                |       |                  |         |                  |                              |         |       |
|      |             |                                               |                          |      |                |                |       |                  |         |                  |                              |         |       |
|      |             |                                               |                          |      |                |                |       |                  |         |                  |                              |         |       |
|      |             |                                               |                          |      |                |                |       |                  |         |                  |                              |         |       |
| TOTALS |           |                                               |                          |      |                |                |       |                  |         |                  |                              |         |       |

**FIGURE 3-1** Tourism has become a major source of leisure spending. (Courtesy of AAHPERD)

spending. Spurred on by Title IX of the Educational Amendments passed by Congress in 1972, which required schools receiving federal aid to provide equal equipment, facilities, and opportunities for women, spending for women's sports and athletics has risen sharply.

*Big scale business to make money*

## COMMERCIAL LEISURE SERVICE ORGANIZATIONS

If you think about your own community for a minute, you can probably identify several organizations which are "in business"—that is, directly related to recreation and leisure. The leisure service industry is primarily a twentieth century phenomenon which is growing and will continue to grow. These organizations have undergone tremendous structural differentiation during the last few decades and are now often quite specialized. One company, for instance, may manufacture only A-frame houses while another specializes in bowling equipment. The Wham-O Company specializes in leisure products of a "fad" nature, such as hula hoops, slingshots, plastic flying saucers, and the Superball. While some huge conglomerates such as AMF now own many subsidiary companies specializing in various kinds of leisure equipment, 90 per cent of all commercial recreation ventures are small businesses.[4]

It is difficult to categorize all commercial leisure service operations, but Karl Munson, who has studied the subject thoroughly, came up with the following listing: hotels, motels, and restaurants; sports tracks and arenas; golf courses; tennis clubs; health clubs; theaters; theme parks (such as Disneyland); swimming pools; private lakes for swimming; boating clubs and marinas; riding stables; fee fishing places; charter fishing boats; nature trails;

caves and caverns; sightseeing excursions; hunting guides; shooting preserves; pool halls; bowling centers; ski resorts; ice-skating arenas; vacation
farms and dude ranches; vacation camps; camping areas; adventure trips and
picnicking areas.[4] Additionally, those who provide consulting, booking,
management, and listing services, as well as those who manufacture,
distribute, and retail recreation supplies such as athletic equipment, would be
considered as being in the leisure industries. Let's look at a few of these areas
in a bit more detail.

## Resorts

*What are some examples of resorts?*
*Are resorts important commercial organizations?*

At present from 30–35 per cent of all receipts in the lodging industry come
from pleasure travel.[4] This situation has not only contributed to the success of
well-known resorts such as Sun Valley in Idaho, the Greenbrier in West
Virginia, and French Lick Springs Hotel in Indiana, but it has also caused
many hotel/motel operators to add such features to their properties as
electronic games and pinball centers, tennis, handball, or racquetball courts,
and arrangements with nearby golf courses, ski areas, or theaters. For many
urban dwellers, hotels and resorts increasingly are offering specific "programs" or "packages," such as get-away weekends for families. "Singles"
weekends, where the opportunity to meet members of the opposite sex and
participate in various recreation activities is more important than the room
itself, are flourishing.

Resorts are also managed by the public sector. The Kentucky State
Parks, for instance, now operate resort-type parks which have many of the
features found in resorts in the private sector.

## Theme Parks

Theme parks, such as Disneyland and Disney World, Busch Gardens, Six
Flags Over Texas, and many others are a fairly recent form of recreation. In
1976 such parks attracted more than 76 million visitors, more than professional baseball, football, and basketball combined.[4] Disneyland and Disney
World, by themselves, grossed more than $68 million, a 19 per cent increase
over 1974. Most theme parks represent diversified recreational opportunities
which are oriented toward the family, including carnival-type rides and
"thrill" rides, zoos and animal habitats, theatrical performances and ap-
pearances by celebrities, restaurants and concessions, educational tours and
exhibits, and so forth.

## Sport Facilities

Commercial enterprises which offer specialized sport facilities are becoming
increasingly popular. In some cases, such as bowling, the commercial sector is
almost the sole provider of opportunity while in others, such as tennis, the

**FIGURE 3-2** Theme parks are an important segment of the leisure industries. (Courtesy of Scholastic Photography Awards sponsored by Eastman Kodak Company)

commercial sector sometimes overlaps the public and private non-profit sectors or may provide more specialized, elaborate facilities for the true tennis "nut" who is willing and able to pay for superior resources. Such operations may include swimming pools, tennis courts, fee fishing ponds and lakes, hunting preserves, golf courses, marinas, bowling lanes, skateboard centers, billiard parlors, ski centers, ice-skating rinks, racquetball centers, and many others. In some cases, such as racquetball, the phenomenal growth of interest in the sport has brought about a boom in the growth of commercial facilities almost overnight.

## Vacation Homes

More and more people today are buying a second home to use as a vacation or leisure home. Well over 2 million Americans currently own such homes and over 9,000 companies are in the second home business.[5] Many large corporations are now getting involved in recreation real estate, not merely developing the land but also offering the leisure amenities which have become necessary to make a success of such complexes. Ski trails, tennis courts, golf courses, swimming pools, and riding stables must be developed, as well as boutiques, night clubs, hotels, lodges, and other amenities. The developer typically is not interested in offering these facilities himself. His object is to raise the value of the surrounding land so that houses or condominiums may be built and sold at a profit. Some well-known recreation real estate developments, such as Sun

Valley, Idaho, Sea Pines Plantation, South Carolina, New Seabury on Cape Cod, Massachusetts, and Big Sky in Montana are not nearly as large as those that are currently being planned. Challenges to these new undertakings by organizations concerned with the environment, however, may temporarily or even permanently block them.

## Pleasure Travel

Travel and tourism, once reserved for society's privileged few, have today become available to a much wider segment of society. International tourism receipts amounted to $2.4 billion in the United States in 1971.[6] In some countries, international tourism is a much more important component of the economy than it is in the United States. In Canada, for instance, with one-tenth of the population of the United States, half as many international tourism dollars are generated; a sizable portion of the tourists are Americans. Spain, with a population of 33 million, had 24.1 million tourists visit in 1970, and will have an estimated 50 million per year by the end of the decade.[7]

To gather some idea of the size of the travel and tourism industries, consider that 50 million Americans took at least one trip of ten days' duration or more in 1972.[5] Since it is estimated that as many as 90 per cent of all vacation and other recreational journeys are made by automobile, widespread automobile ownership has been the key to the tourism explosion. (This has also meant that the recent gasoline shortages have had a profound effect on the travel and tourism industries.) Travel and tourism have also been aided by the advent of the jumbo jet, seating as many as 400 people. This has allowed airlines to cut their fares by one-third during the last ten years. Jets of even larger size could further reduce costs.

The recreation vehicle industry has also contributed to the travel and tourism boom. The manufacture and sale of such "campers" grew to $5 billion a year in the early 1970s.[8] "Fancy camping," using camping-type vehicles, is a whole new style of travel. Campsites for people traveling in such vehicles are beginning to include facilities such as swimming pools, babysitting services, golf courses, kennels, cocktail lounges, restaurants, and tennis courts. Some hotels and convention centers are establishing nearby campsites for campers who want to sleep in their camper but use other facilities of the hotel or convention center.

Other forms of travel are becoming popular both as leisure activities themselves and as methods of travel to other leisure activities. Americans spend $1 billion a year taking vacations at sea.[6] Over 60,000 workers are employed in the $3 billion-a-year motorcycle industry. Over 500,000 snowmobiles are sold every year. More bicycles were sold in 1972 than automobiles, 11.5 million,[7] although by 1979 the sales boom had peaked.

The popularity of all these forms of travel is heavily dependent upon the cost and availability of fuel. It is almost impossible to determine whether electric and alcohol-burning cars will become a practical reality in the next few years, although General Motors plans to introduce electric cars during the mid-1980s. Similarly, it is not known whether synthetic fuels will be a significant source of energy during the next decade.

Herman Kahn, Director of the Hudson Institute, believes that no prolonged energy shortages will exist among the industrial nations, and that the future of travel and tourism is bright. Pleasure travel is expected to continue its growth through the end of the century, with new technology changing the experience markedly. During this era, travel agents will increasingly serve as counselors who aid in planning experiences as well as make actual travel arrangements. New modes of travel will make tourism less costly and more convenient, in spite of rising energy costs.

## LEISURE COMPONENTS OF BUSINESS AND COMMERCE

In addition to the previously mentioned forms of commercial recreation, many businesses and commercial ventures may be said to have an important leisure component. These are discussed in the following sections.

**FIGURE 3-3** Tourism is no longer just for the rich. Wanderlust has been institutionalized. (Courtesy of AAHPERD)

# Mass Media and Other Spectator Activities

The communications media have become among the most important leisure activities in industrial societies, from the standpoints both of time spent with them and of importance. The majority of adults in Western societies now come in contact with one or more of the communications media on a daily basis. Radio, television, books, magazines, and newspapers probably account for more than half of our leisure time expenditures. As early as 1964, Wilensky stated that the mass media had become the core of American leisure activity and that television had become the core of such exposure.[9] A 12-nation time budget study found that 40 per cent of the leisure time of adults in the United States is devoted to television viewing.[10] Even among the busy members of the labor force, the study found an average viewing time of 90 minutes per day when television was a primary activity, and an additional 30 minutes per day when television viewing constituted a secondary activity. A study by A. C. Nielson found that television viewing during the winter months of 1973 averaged an incredible seven hours per day per American household.[11] The reasons for this extraordinary rate were thought to be the public's growing interest in football and other televised sports, a rise in daytime viewing on weekends, and bad winter weather in urban areas. It has been estimated that many children spend more time with the television set than with their mothers. While there have been some small declines in the amount of time spent viewing television during the last few years, television continues to be the most typical way in which Americans spend their leisure time.

While mass media functions previously included primarily observation of the environment, correlation between different parts of the environment, and transmission of cultural heritage, entertainment today has become the primary function of the media, necessary to fulfill their other purposes. Now, even news shows are expected to be entertaining as well as informative. Newspapers have also changed during the last decade so as to become more entertaining.

The tremendous impact of television on our society is not yet understood. From a time standpoint, watching television is undoubtedly the most popular leisure activity in North America. Part of the appeal of television has to be due to its relative inexpensiveness. A study by Andresen and Company found that the direct cost of watching television came to about three cents per hour, and listening to the radio cost only one cent per hour.[12] It should be recognized, of course, that we indirectly pay much more by subsidizing advertising through purchasing products whose price is higher owing to television or radio advertising costs. We would pay such costs, however, whether we used the television or not. Television viewing, I believe, is also quite popular for many segments of the population because it offers the opportunity to escape the complexity and anxiety of modern society. Television viewing is often escapist behavior, which provides a sense of catharsis—that is, a sense of recreation, refreshment, or restoration, not of a fatigued body but of a fatigued psyche. What happens when one watches television is usually predictable, relatively pleasant, and involves little real choice or investment of self. The activity is perhaps not really freely chosen, but it is acceptable.

Regarding the actual amounts of time spent with mass media, Szalai found that participants in time budget studies in the United States spent an average of 8 minutes per day listening to the radio, 84 minutes watching television, 16 minutes reading the newspaper, 5 minutes reading magazines, 14 minutes reading books, and 4 minutes watching movies.[11] As secondary activities, the participants spent an additional 72 minutes with the radio on, 10 minutes with the television on, 9 minutes with the newspaper, 2 minutes with magazines, and 5 minutes with books. As may be observed, listening to the radio has become, for the most part, a secondary activity that typically consists of listening to music or the news. Television viewing rates appear to affect participation in other communications media. The more time people spend watching television, the less time they spend listening to the radio and reading books, newspapers, and magazines.

The study by Andresen and Company found that the average American working adult spends the following percentages of his/her leisure time with the mass media: television, 45 per cent; radio, 34 per cent; newspaper reading, 8 per cent; magazine reading, 6 per cent; listening to records and tapes, 2.6 per cent; attending movies, 0.4 per cent; reading books, 0.2 per cent.[12]

A number of studies have concluded that the significance of educational levels on television viewing habits is not very great, although there is some evidence that those with low educational status view television for more hours than those with higher education. It is also estimated that blacks constitute approximately 20 per cent of the average television-viewing public even though they represent only 12 per cent of the population. Differences in the use of print media among people of varying education attainments are generally much greater than corresponding differences in the use of radio and television. Szalai found that in the United States, the percentage of those with a college education who had read a "serious" book the previous day was 5.8 per cent, compared with 0.9 per cent among those who had not finished high school.[10] In regard to time spent reading, the college-educated group spent an average of 36 minutes during the previous day reading magazines, books and reports, whereas the group that had not completed high school spent an average of 9 minutes. Newspaper reading accounted for about 80 per cent of the reading time of the less educated group, but only 48 per cent of the reading time of the college graduates.

It remains to be seen whether the mass media's ability to occupy a major portion of people's leisure time will continue. Many studies of people's leisure patterns and their attitudes toward these patterns find that they do not desire to spend any more time watching television than they currently do, but would like to spend more time in many other leisure activities.

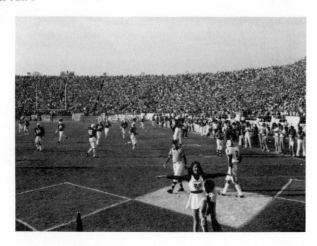

**FIGURE 3-4** College football has been a popular way to spend an autumn afternoon for many decades. (Courtesy of Leesa Massey)

In addition to television and other mass media, people in your community also patronize a number of forms of sport, entertainment, and cultural events. While the generalization is often made that spectators at such activities are more likely to be lower-middle or working-class people rather than upper class, there is considerable variation in the clientele that attends various sporting events, concerts, ballet, burlesque, theater, and so on.

While attendance at sporting events has consistently been a popular pastime during the last 50 years, it is only recently that attendance at cultural events has reached similar levels. Government subsidies, more discretionary income, and higher education levels have all contributed to this rise in attendance. A study conducted by Statistics Canada dramatically illustrates this point. It found that more Canadians paid to go to the theater, opera, ballet, and concerts than paid admission prices for sports events.[13]

**FIGURE 3-5** For many, "tailgating" is an important aspect of being a football spectator. (Courtesy of Leesa Massey)

# Gambling

Gambling, in both legal and illegal forms, takes place in nearly every American community. The amount and scope of gambling in the United States is staggering. A study by Li and Smith, with the help of the Gallup Organization, indicated that gambling is "the major American business."[14] The President's Commission on Law Enforcement and Administration's lowest estimate on illegal gambling profits was $6 billion per year.[14] One out of every three American adults gambles at least once a month. The Gallup Survey of individual gambling habits showed that card games account for more than half the total money wagered, with sporting events and horse racing accounting for an additional 22 per cent.[14]

While individuals of upper and lower social classes gamble more extensively than those of the middle class, the rise of televised sports such as football and basketball has brought an upswing in the amount of gambling activity in the middle and upper-middle classes. It is estimated that 90 per cent of the business done by bookies relates to betting on team sports, not on horse racing.[15]

Many forms of gambling behavior are legal in the United States. Church bingo, raffles for charity, and contests requiring an entry fee have long been popular. Government sponsorship of gambling has increased greatly during the last decade and will probably continue to increase. One reason for this increase is the liberalization of attitudes toward gambling. Another is the realization that gambling laws are unenforceable and that the government's refusal to be involved means that profits are made by the underworld with no taxes paid to the government. Legal gambling already pays for 40 per cent of the Nevada state budget.[14] The successful introduction of casino gambling in Atlantic City, New Jersey, in 1978 has caused many other communities which depend upon revenue from tourists, such as Miami Beach, Florida, and the Pocono resorts, to consider introducing it. Parimutuel betting is allowed in 28 states. New York State has legalized off-track betting and Pennsylvania and Connecticut plan to follow suit, with other states expected to do so shortly. Many states sponsor lotteries. Since gambling is the main source of income for the American underworld, government sponsorship of gambling could affect organized crime significantly. However, Li and Smith found that most gambling is done through an informal system of friends and relatives, and that an individual is not necessarily more likely to gamble in areas where gambling has been legalized.[14]

The widespread introduction of government-sponsored gambling puts the moral status of gambling in an awkward position. If the state believes that gambling is immoral and prosecutes people for engaging in it, how can the state justify encouraging the same activity under its own sponsorship?

It appears that monetary reward is not always the major reason for the attraction to gambling. The "high" produced from "the action" of gambling

**FIGURE 3-6** Gambling has been described as the major American business. (Courtesy of Resorts International Hotel Casino, Atlantic City, New Jersey)

may explain why, according to Gamblers Anonymous, there are an estimated 10 million compulsive gamblers in the United States.

## Eating

Naturally, eating food cannot always be considered leisure activity, since some food consumption is necessary for survival. Our eating habits, though, often reflect elements of leisure behavior. We eat more than we need to for survival purposes, we eat "fun" foods and other foods that we choose because of taste or attractiveness rather than nutrition, we eat in leisure environments, we eat as a part of a leisure experience such as a vacation, and we eat meals with friends and associates as a leisure experience in itself.

Americans spend over $30 billion a year eating in restaurants and hotels.[16] Many of these dining facilities provide a programmed eating environment, which may include a motif in keeping with the kind of food served, music or accompanying entertainment, a pleasant view, wine and liquor, as well as food that is eaten as a treat or only on special occasions. The fastest growing kinds of restaurants are the franchised fast food or pop food establishments. Chains such as McDonald's, Kentucky Fried Chicken, and Dairy Queen account for one-fifth of all the revenue spent in United States restaurants.[16] Such restaurants demonstrate the mobility of the American public. They serve bland food in bright, usually clean surroundings that make use of a myth built up by advertising, such as Ronald McDonald or Dennis the Menace. They also, however, demonstrate the unleisurely pace at which many Americans live. Meals are served instantly and are often eaten in 20 minutes or less. Food is also eaten in the car, sometimes while the driver is hurriedly driving somewhere else.

Many foods we buy to eat at home are attractively packaged, quick and easy to prepare, full of sugar, and designed to free the cook for some other activity. Food preparation, however, is sometimes a leisure activity in itself for both men and women. Renewed interest in gourmet cooking, wine making, gardening, and natural foods has resulted in increased leisure activity related to food.

Children's breakfast cereal, until manufacturers began to fortify it artificially, had almost been removed as a source of nutrition, but has now become a source of play. Today, children's cereal may be chocolate flavored, come in all colors of the rainbow, contain prizes or have games and puzzles on the back of the box, have a funny name, such as "Cap'n Crunch," and have a mythology associated with it which promotes the cereal in advertising. As Toffler[17] would say, the psychological component of cereal and other food has become increasingly important, and we can no longer assume that food has only one use.

## Use of Alcohol and Other Drugs

Many Americans choose to spend their leisure consuming various forms of drugs such as marijuana, hallucinogens (such as LSD), cocaine, sedatives (such as Quaaludes or sleeping pills), tranquilizers, heroin, stimulants (amphetamines), alcohol, tobacco, and caffeine.[18] While the economic impact of the use of such drugs is enormous, it is difficult to estimate, since much of such drug use is illegal. When you consider the following illustrations, however, the economic impact of the recreational use of drugs is staggering: one out of twelve Americans says that he/she "regularly" uses marijuana, 93 million Americans drink alcohol, and 65 million Americans smoke tobacco.

**FIGURE 3-7** The cost of drug use in our society is truly staggering. (Courtesy of H. Armstrong Roberts)

Cocaine, an increasingly popular "recreational" drug, costs upwards of $100 a gram, which two people can easily use in one evening. The 5.5 million heroin users in this country must often turn to robbery or prostitution to earn sufficient funds to support their habit.

The use of drugs also creates industries to promote their use. Look around your community and you'll find some: taverns and saloons, "head" shops, cigar stores, "drug" stores. Additionally, the production of such drugs, government regulation, law enforcement and prosecution of illegal drug users, rehabilitation of addicts, and other expenses make the cost of drug use in our society truly staggering.

## CHALLENGES TO COMMERCIAL RECREATION

Commercial recreation is not without problems for those who own and manage such operations. The rate of failure for such ventures, according to Owen, is higher than for any other small business.[3] One reason for this is that private investors frequently neglect to measure the demand and profit potential for such services before investing. It is often hard to obtain financing for commercial recreation projects due to these factors.

Many commercial recreation operations deal with activities which may prove to be "fads." It is difficult to predict, for example, how long interest in skateboarding will be great enough to keep skateboard parks profitable. Because of the uncertainty of many recreation activities provided by the commercial sector, an attempt is often made to combine many activities or services as a hedge against changing interests. For example, swimming, tennis, racquetball, saunas, and exercise rooms may be combined at one location to broaden the appeal to the potential client. Other problem areas of commercial recreation are identified by Munson as liability, financing, seasonal characteristics, vandalism and theft, and the energy shortage.[4]

Of these problems, perhaps the availability of energy will have the greatest impact on people's use of commercial recreation, as well as of other forms of leisure.

Most forms of commercial recreation, as well as other leisure experiences, will be greatly affected by the current energy situation for at least three reasons:

1. Most forms of commercial recreation require some travel on the part of the user.
2. Many forms of commercial recreation, such as motorboating, consume fuel during the leisure experience itself.
3. Most forms of commercial recreation utilize facilities and equipment which consume extensive amounts of energy in their manufacturing, maintenance, and operation.

A golf course, for example, consumes considerable energy in each of these three ways. Most people drive to a golf course. Once there, many people go through the entire 18-hole course by riding in an electric golf cart. Golf clubs, bags, and shoes are expensive to manufacture, as are golf balls, which are often lost or destroyed in the process of playing (as well as an occasional broken club or golf bag thrown in a water hazard). Golf courses need extensive maintenance, such as watering and grass cutting, which also utilizes much energy.

The availability of alternatives to rapidly depleting fossil fuels will have a tremendous impact on what we do during our leisure. In recent national surveys undertaken by the Heritage Conservation and Recreation Service, both the general public and users of federal outdoor recreation areas were asked several questions about the impact of gasoline prices on their outdoor recreation behavior. The following results were obtained:[19]

|  | Yes | No | No Opinion |
|---|---|---|---|
| Has the present price of gasoline caused you to take fewer trips than you normally would for outdoor recreation activities? | 47 | 50 | 3 |
| Has the present price of gasoline caused you to take shorter trips than you normally would for outdoor recreation activities? | 49 | 47 | 4 |
| Has the present price of gasoline caused you to use public transportation more often than you normally would for outdoor recreation activities? | 15 | 81 | 4 |
| If the price of gasoline doubled within the next six months, would this be likely to limit or curtail the number of trips you might take by automobile for outdoor recreation activities? | 80 | 16 | 4 |

As these results show, leisure patterns are shaped by the cost of gasoline very directly. The availability of gasoline and other energy sources will continue to affect commercial leisure services for the next few decades. A continuing tight energy situation is likely to bring about a greater concentration on home entertainment centers, complete with oversize television screens on the wall, video cassettes, computer games, and laser-operated stereo equipment. Additionally, commercial enterprises such as sport centers and theme parks are likely to diversify their operations so that individuals or families can travel directly from home to the facility and home again, with no side trips. Some United States' sport centers will begin to look more like those in Britain, where such centers are likely to include supervised baby-sitting facilities, sauna baths, swimming, a restaurant, gymnasium, areas for judo, squash, outdoor tennis courts, athletic fields, and even a pub. Commercial leisure services will also work increasingly with public transportation authorities to make their facilities easier to reach via public transportation.

## LEISURE AND MATERIALISM

How shall we judge the materialistic lifestyle reflected by the leisure behavior of many of us? While on the one hand we may be distressed by the commercialism of much of our leisure experiences, the overwhelming evidence is that we prefer it that way, although these preferences have been molded by advertising.

The ability of the common person to obtain increasingly higher amounts of disposable income during the last century has triggered multiple revolutions, dealing with expectations as well as behavior. A primary change has been the ability of the (mythical) average citizen to participate in activities which were once reserved exclusively for the rich. Many sports and physical recreation activities, such as golf, tennis, sailing, tourism, roller skating, and bicycling, were the almost exclusive province of the rich less than 150 years ago. Bicycles, for instance, cost from $100 to $125 in 1880, when that amount of money represented a small fortune.

Diversity of leisure experience is also a consequence of increased discretionary income during the last century. The range of leisure experiences available to us has increased dramatically. Because of this, we are experientially richer than we would be otherwise. My 11-year-old and 8-year-old daughters, for instance, have been to England on vacation and already have some understanding about how our culture differs from our British neighbors, which couldn't have been obtained without the trip.

A third benefit has been the quality of certain leisure experiences. If you hear or play the same song on a Martin guitar which you previously heard on an inexpensive one, you can tell the difference. Some high culture art forms, such as opera, cannot be produced without lots of money. But money doesn't automatically improve the quality of a leisure experience, and a person with very little money may lead a rich leisure life—take Socrates, for example. If we are to delight in the world rather than devour it, then many leisure pursuits are free, or nearly so: singing, walking through a forest, running, writing stories or telling them to children, talking with a friend, watching the moon climb over tall buildings, or just resting.

Our materialistic lifestyle has hurt our leisure experiences in many ways. Our desire for *things* has made us, often, live in an unleisurely manner, or trade away opportunities for leisure for more money. Materialism has also sometimes caused us to equate leisure with a time for the consumption of products at the expense of our own imagination and inner resourcefulness. The desire to sell leisure goods and services has led to the creation of artificial needs. Children are sold endless toys on Saturday morning television. Adults become convinced that their game of tennis is inadequate without expensive equipment and accessories. Further, those who are poor are often taught to believe that they cannot use their leisure in satisfying ways because of their limited incomes. Leisure products and services may serve to distract us from that which is important, may complicate our lives, and may ruin any chance for inner peace or serenity.

In spite of all this, materialism appeals to most of us and, given a chance, there is considerable evidence that it appeals to much of the rest of the world.

## STUDY QUESTIONS

1. Why is it difficult to determine how much money is spent for leisure?

2. Discuss some trends in our use of the mass media.

3. Why is the operation of many forms of commercial recreation more financially risky than other businesses?

4. Is it accurate to say that our leisure behavior reflects a "materialistic" lifestyle? Why or why not?

5. What was your reaction to the results of the monetary spending exercise? Were you surprised? Why or why not?

## REFERENCES

1. de Grazia, Sebastian. *Of Time, Work and Leisure.* New York: Twentieth Century Fund, 1962, pp. 58-83.
2. Zuzanek, Jiri. *The Determinants of Leisure Demand and the Prospects for Leisure.* Ottawa: Department of Industry, Trade and Commerce, 1976, p. 33.
3. Owen, Elizabeth. "Recreation and Business—The American Connection," *Commerce America,* September 12, 1977, p. 67.
4. Munson, Karl. "Commercial and Member-Owned Recreation Forms," in Godbey, Geoffrey (ed.), *Recreation, Park and Leisure Services: Foundations, Organization, Administration.* Philadelphia: W.B. Saunders, 1978, pp. 133-175.
5. "Good Times In the Playtime Field," *Nation's Business,* March, 1973, p. 62.
6. *International Tourism Quarterly,* No. 4, 1972, p. 62.
7. *International Tourism Quarterly,* No. 2, 1972, p. 80.
8. Kahn, Herman. "Leading Futurist Traces Next Half Century in Travel," *Travel Trade News Edition,* January 31, 1979, p. 1.
9. Wilensky, H. "Mass Society and Mass Culture: Interdependence or Independence," *American Sociological Review,* Vol. XXIX, 1964, pp. 173-197.
10. Szalai, A. (ed.). *The Use of Time: Daily Activities of Urban and Suburban Populations in Twelve Countries.* The Hague, Netherlands: Mouton and Company, 1973, p. 206.
11. Nielson, A. "Nation of Video Freaks," *Week-End Magazine,* April, 1973.
12. Buckley, W., Jr. "On Our Leisure Time," *National Review,* Vol. 25, September 14, 1973, pp. 10-15.
13. "Ottawa Studying Cultural Aid," *Kitchner-Waterloo Record* (CP), March 22, 1973, p. 62.
14. "Gambling As Business and Sport," *Intellect,* Vol. 51, November, 1972, p. 48.
15. "Everybody Wants A Piece of the Action," *Newsweek,* April 10, 1972, p. 48.
16. Morgenstern, J. "The Roadside Gourmet: Pop Goes the Food," *Newsweek,* September 25, 1972, p. 76.
17. Toffler, Alvin. *Future Shock.* New York: Bantam Books, 1970, pp. 219-234.
18. Harris, Art. "Drug Use on the Increase," *Washington Post,* July 30, 1978, p. A7.
19. *National Outdoor Recreation Survey.* Washington, D.C.: Heritage Conservation and Recreation Service, U.S. Department of the Interior, 1978, p. 5.

# chapter 4

# Work and leisure and work and leisure

**A**s we noted previously, the industrial revolution changed our methods of work so that it became more centralized in factories. The proportion of people engaged in agricultural occupations diminished, and the cities grew. One effect of industrialization was to divide work and the rest of life into separate spheres. By work we mean "disciplined and persistent activity devoted to achieving a goal, with the actual activity only instrumental to the accomplishment of the final goal of this activity."[1] We add to this definition that work is activity which is externally compelled rather than internally compelled; it is activity you undertake because other people require you to do it or because circumstances, such as lack of food, require you to do it. This definition of work fits most factory workers very well—work is what you have to do, and leisure is what is left over. The whistle blows and you begin working; the whistle blows again and you stop. People who run a drill press all day, or mine coal, or sort vegetables on a conveyor belt have little doubt about when they are at work and when they are not. For them, the line of demarcation between work and leisure is very rigid.

It is hard for us to understand life in primitive societies, where work and leisure were inextricably related. Hunter-gatherer and agrarian societies involved a continuous fusion of work and leisure—the notion of being "at work" would be lost on a Bushman. So, too, the line between work and leisure is meaningless for the artist and craftsman. Acording to C. Wright Mills, the simple self-expression of play and the creation of the ulterior value of work are combined in work-as-craftsmanship.[2] The artist is at work and at play in the same act.

One reason for this fusion of work and leisure in the activity of the artist and craftsman is that the same activity which satisfies an *inner* compulsion also satisfies *external* compulsions, such as the need for food and shelter. That is, the same activity which satisfies an unexplicable inner urge to, say, create a painting also produces a painting which can be sold in some cases for money to buy food. Such fortunate circumstances, in which an individual can "earn" a living for an activity which he or she would "do for free," is historically a rare circumstance and one that, perhaps, would be extended to everyone in an ideal society.

Another set of traditions has made a distinction between work and leisure in terms of the relative worthiness of work or leisure. The ancient Greeks, as mentioned earlier, insisted that work could have nothing to do with leisure. Work was a necessary material evil to them to be avoided by the leisure elite. Only a fool would choose to work, and the only real justification for work would be to obtain leisure.

These traditions, however, are not really our own. The Puritan Protestants who came to America from England had little of the fatalism and other worldly asceticism which had been associated with Roman Catholicism since medieval times. Indeed, the hard life of these settlers meant that their very survival was dependent upon an ethic which admired work and distrusted idleness. As the sociologist Max Weber has pointed out, Calvinism was the Protestant sect which was most responsible for the formulation of a work ethic.[3] The Calvinists believed that people were predestined to heaven or to hell; those going to heaven would show some sign that they were among those selected while they were still on earth. By hard work, frugality, and accumulation of capital, an individual might show that he or she was saved from eternal hell. Hard work and material possessions could literally buy one's salvation. Thus, a harsh physical environment, economic necessity, and religious belief combined to produce an ethic of salvation through work. Recreation and leisure were suspect in such circumstances. Even though they were never stamped out by the Puritans, who nevertheless kept trying long after any economic justification for doing so was gone, leisure and recreation were suspect and considered to be inferior to work.

## WORK AND LEISURE TODAY

If we take the two variables of (1) priority for work or leisure and (2) separation of work and leisure or their joining together, it quickly becomes apparent that our own society is comprised of individuals in many situations involving each variable.

Let's consider separation of work and leisure. If we find that our leisure and work are fused together, or that they are split apart at opposite poles, this will affect the role leisure plays in our lives. These two corresponding functions of leisure have been labeled by Harold Wilensky as "spillover" and "compensation."[4] Work may be said to spill over into leisure to the extent that leisure is the continuation of work experiences and attitudes; leisure is compensatory if it seeks to make up for dissatisfaction felt in work.

Stanley Parker has carried the analysis of these two types of relationships further, and has added a third.[5] He distinguished between extension (spillover), opposition (compensatory), and neutrality. With the *extension* pattern the similarity of at least some work and leisure activities and the lack of demarcation between work and leisure are the key characteristics. This pattern is typically shown by social workers, successful businessmen (perhaps they are successful because they have little or no time for leisure), doctors, teachers, and those engaged in similar occupations. The main aspects of the *opposition* pattern are the intentional dissimilarity of work and leisure and the strong demarcation between the two spheres. People with demanding physical jobs, such as miners and oil rig workers, may either hate their work so much that any reminder of it in their off duty time is unpleasant, or they may have a love-hate attitude toward it. The third pattern, that of *neutrality*, can be partly defined by a "usually different" content of work and leisure and an "average" demarcation of spheres. But it is *not* the intermediate pattern between the other two, because it denotes detachment from work rather than either positive or negative attachment. It often goes along with jobs that Peter Berger has called "gray"—neither fulfilling nor oppressive.[6] People in such jobs tend to be as passive and uninvolved in their leisure as they are in their work.

Parker used results of other research to suggest that each of the three patterns of the work-leisure relationship is associated with a number of other work and non-work variables.[5] People with high autonomy in their work are likely to reflect the extension pattern, while those with low autonomy show the neutrality pattern. (The effect of autonomy upon the opposition pattern is not clear.) Extension is usually accompanied by a feeling of being stretched by the work, neutrality by being bored with it, and opposition by being damaged by it. The likelihood of having some work colleagues among one's close friends seems to be high among those with the extension pattern and low among the neutrality group. The level of education apparently plays no significant role in differentiating groups with the extension, neutrality, and opposition patterns. These and other conclusions about the three patterns are tentative, however, and remain to be verified or modified by subsequent research.

Another approach to work-leisure relationships is found in the functional tradition of sociological theory. Briefly this theory, whose foremost exponent is Talcott Parsons, is concerned with the types of problems that have to be solved in order for society to survive and evolve.[7] These problems, and the subsystems of society that face them, are adaptation (the economy), goal attainment (the political system), integration (family or ethnic groups), and latency (the cultural system). Edward Gross has applied this theory to leisure and work.[8] He noted the following: *adaptation* functions of recreation and creative leisure in compensating for the fatiguing or deadening effect of some forms of work; the *goal attainment* functions that are served by assigning differential access to leisure opportunities; the *integration* functions of sociability and horseplay at work; and the *latency* functions of colleague groups of "mutually trusting equals who drink coffee or play cards together."[8] This theory may be criticized as a somewhat strained attempt to put leisure behavior into four convenient boxes, and it is questionable whether it adds very much to our understanding of the relationship between leisure and work.

## Questioning the Work-Leisure Relationship

Some researchers have begun to question whether one's work role is related at all to leisure roles. After studying an English New Town, for instance, William Bacon concluded that there was little evidence to suggest that alienating work was associated with particularly passive or deviant forms of social behavior.[9] He postulated that, to a considerable extent, what people did in their free time was unrelated to the nature of their occupational experiences.

Similarly, studies by Kenneth Roberts and his coworkers of employed males in Liverpool, England, led to the following conclusion: "In particular, we question the utility of conceptualizing leisure as a part of life mainly ancillary to work, to be understood in terms of the degree to which it is complementary to, the opposite of, or an extension of occupational life. While this perspective contains some validity, we are skeptical of efforts to treat it as of central importance in the study of leisure behavior."[10]

While this warning makes sense—leisure *has* become a separate sphere of life for many—there are still some relations that are worth examining and, as you might have guessed, we are going to start by examining your work-leisure relations. Most of you reading this book are students who don't "work" for monetary compensation at all, or only work part-time. Many of you, however, consider some of your college or university activities as work, as well as things you are obligated to do to maintain yourselves, your living quarters, and so forth.

# Leisure Exercise 4·1

The purpose of this exercise is to examine your work activity and the relation between your work and your leisure. In this exercise we will consider work to be "disciplined and persistent activity devoted to achieving a goal with the actual activity only instrumental to the accomplishment of the final goal of the activity." It is activity which is externally compelled rather than internally compelled, and undertaken because people or circumstances require you to do it.

**1.** List some current activities in which you are involved which you consider to be work.

**2.** Look at your time budget for the week you kept it. How many hours of work did you do that week?

**3.** What was your most time-consuming work activity?

99

4. Using Parker's conceptualization of work-leisure relations as extension, opposition, and neutrality, which work-leisure relationship do you think most closely describes you, or do you see no relationship at all between your work and leisure? Why?

5. What kinds of work do you expect to do when you leave this college or university?

6. What relationship do you think your work and leisure will have in that job, if any? Why?

7. Do you think you could be happy if your primary opportunity for self-expression and achievement comes during your leisure and not from your work? Explain.

## Who Works, and for How Long?

Given our previous definition of work, it can be said that everyone does some work. In our own society we could attempt to measure the amount of such work with a time budget study, as was done earlier. In our own and other industrialized nations, work is usually considered to have another element: you get money for doing it. Much of the discussion in the mass media about how long we work or how much leisure we have is based upon information concerning the amount of time spent in paid work or in work-related activities. The most frequently cited statistic is workweek length. Many other types of information are used in analyses of work time, including percentage of the population in the labor force, percentage of those who hold two or more jobs (moonlighting), age of entry and retirement from the labor force in relation to life expectancy, unemployment rate, number of vacations and holidays, and time spent in continuing job-related education. Table 4-1 reflects an attempt to measure the increase in non-work time during the life cycle from 1900 to 1960. While the chart shows the inadequacy of using only workweek length, it may also be considered inadequate as an indicator of free time in our society since it deals only with men (the percentage of women who work for money is now approaching 50 per cent), and because it doesn't include commuting time to and from work and other necessary work-related data, such as "take home" paperwork, business entertainment, and additional job training and educational upgrading. Table 4-2 shows the hours of work of full-time workers in the U. S. and gives a somewhat different picture, in that 34 per cent worked 41 hours a week or more and over one out of five worked 49 hours a week or more in 1974 and 1975.

There seems to be fairly widespread agreement that there has been relatively little change in workweek length since the 1940s. The growing number of women and students employed part-time has obscured the fact,

**TABLE 4-1   REDUCTIONS IN PER CAPITA WORK TIME, U.S. MALES, 1900–1960***

| U.S. Males | 1900 | 1960 |
|---|---|---|
| Hours of work per week† | 58.5 | 41.0 |
| Total years of life, expected at birth‡ | 48.2 | 66.6 |
| Years in labor force, expected at birth‡ | 32.1 | 41.4 |
| Years out of labor force, expected at birth‡ | 16.1 | 25.2 |
| Proportion of week spent in market employment: (1)/168 | 0.348 | 0.245 |
| Proportion of life spent in labor force: (3)/(2) | 0.666 | 0.622 |
| Proportion of life spent at work: (5)×(6) | 0.234 | 0.152 |

*SOURCE: J. D. Owen, *The Price of Leisure*, Rotterdam: Rotterdan University Press, 1969, p. 11.
†SOURCE: J. D. Owen, *The Price of Leisure*, Rotterdam: Rotterdam University Press, p. 67.
‡SOURCE: Seymour Wolfbein, *Changing Patterns of Working Life*, p. 10.

TABLE 4-2  PERCENTAGE DISTRIBUTION OF HOURS WORKED BY FULL-TIME WORKERS; SELECTED YEARS 1955 to 1975*

| | | Hours of Work | | | | | |
|---|---|---|---|---|---|---|---|
| Year | Number of Workers | Total | 35–39 | 40 | 41–48 | 49–59 | 59 and over |
| 1955 | 51,008 | 100 | 7 | 49 | 21 | (23)† | |
| 1960 | 52,723 | 100 | 7 | 52 | 17 | (23)† | |
| 1965 | 56,528 | 100 | 8 | 51 | 17 | 12 | 11 |
| 1967 | 57,839 | 100 | 8 | 51 | 17 | 12 | 11 |
| 1969 | 58,679 | 100 | 9 | 52 | 16 | 12 | 12 |
| 1970 | 58,360 | 100 | 9 | 53 | 15 | 12 | 11 |
| 1971 | 58,444 | 100 | 9 | 54 | 15 | 11 | 11 |
| 1972 | 60,285 | 100 | 9 | 54 | 15 | 11 | 10 |
| 1973 | 62,250 | 100 | 10 | 52 | 15 | 12 | 11 |
| 1974 | 63,557 | 100 | 9 | 54 | 14 | 12 | 10 |
| 1975 | 61,335 | 100 | 10 | 55 | 13 | 11 | 10 |

*SOURCE: Geoffrey Moore, and Janice Hedges, "Trends in Labor and Leisure," *Monthly Labor Review*, February, 1971. Reprint 2714. Updated with recent data from the Bureau of Labor Statistics.
†Percentage with workweeks of 49 hours and over.

according to Owen, that over the past 25 years the average male non-student workweek has remained about 43 hours.[11] There have been gains in non-work time in some other categories, however. The average number of years a person can expect to live after retirement has increased dramatically. These extra years certainly represent a gain in leisure, thus creating new opportunities and problems. The percentage of people holding two or more jobs has also declined by roughly 1 per cent from 1956 (5.5 per cent) to 1975 (4.7 per cent).[12] Moonlighting figures are somewhat inaccurate, however, since many people working second jobs do not report them to avoid paying income taxes.

It is in the area of vacations and holidays that a significant gain in non-work time is occurring. The average worker's vacation length increased from 1.3 to 1.7 weeks from 1960 to 1969 and, as may be seen in Table 4-3, the amount of paid vacation time in more recent collective bargaining agreements has continued to increase dramatically.[12] By 1973, almost half these agreements involved maximum vacations of at least 5 weeks. This trend shows the increasing preference for larger blocks of time off the job, as opposed to a shorter workweek. The 4-day workweek has been another attempt to gain a larger block of time for leisure. Under such an arrangement a worker would work 4 days during a workweek, for a period of 10 hours or less a day. Thus, the 3-day weekend, with greater opportunity for leisure travel or sustained leisure activity, has become a reality for some. To date, however, 98 out of every 100 full-time employees work a 5-day week. While the 4-day workweek has many advantages, it is ill-suited for working women (and men) with young school-age children, since it is likely to mean that the parent will be working after the children return home from school.

Leisure activity that occurs on weekday evenings after work or school overwhelmingly takes place at home. Many forms of leisure activity can't be undertaken until the weekend, holidays, or vacation because they involve travel and other special preparation. Thus it is not surprising for people to feel

**TABLE 4-3 MAXIMUM VACATION ALLOWANCES IN SELECTED COLLECTIVE BARGAINING AGREEMENTS; SELECTED YEARS, 1949-1973***

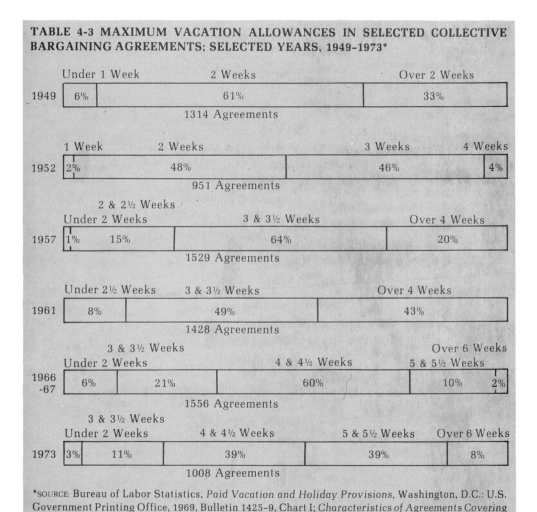

**1949** — Under 1 Week 6% | 2 Weeks 61% | Over 2 Weeks 33% — 1314 Agreements

**1952** — 1 Week 2% | 2 Weeks 48% | 3 Weeks 46% | 4 Weeks 4% — 951 Agreements

**1957** — Under 2 Weeks 1% | 2 & 2½ Weeks 15% | 3 & 3½ Weeks 64% | Over 4 Weeks 20% — 1529 Agreements

**1961** — Under 2½ Weeks 8% | 3 & 3½ Weeks 49% | Over 4 Weeks 43% — 1428 Agreements

**1966-67** — Under 2 Weeks 6% | 3 & 3½ Weeks 21% | 4 & 4½ Weeks 60% | 5 & 5½ Weeks 10% | Over 6 Weeks 2% — 1556 Agreements

**1973** — Under 2 Weeks 3% | 3 & 3½ Weeks 11% | 4 & 4½ Weeks 39% | 5 & 5½ Weeks 39% | Over 6 Weeks 8% — 1008 Agreements

*SOURCE: Bureau of Labor Statistics, *Paid Vacation and Holiday Provisions*, Washington, D.C.: U.S. Government Printing Office, 1969, Bulletin 1425-9, Chart I; *Characteristics of Agreements Covering 1000 or More Workers, July 1, 1973*, Washington, D.C.: U.S. Government Printing Office, 1974, Bulletin 1822, Table 49.

that having leisure time during holidays or vacations is far preferable to a few hours after dinner. The gains in non-work time that are taking place for full-time employees reflect this desire.

The weekend, holidays, or vacation opens up new opportunities. Leisure activity confined to the evening is often of a routine nature. A Gallup Poll found that Americans' favorite way of spending an evening was watching television—30 per cent, reading—15 per cent; movies or theater—6 per cent; listening to radio or records—4 per cent, and visiting friends—4 per cent. Other responses accounted for less than 1 per cent each.

## Changing Definitions of Who Should be a Worker

In most pre-industrial societies everyone had some work role: children, old people, sick people—everyone contributed. Those of you raised on a farm are aware that this situation still exists on family-run farms. The idea that a child could or should do nothing productive is a rather recent one. The industrial revolution changed all this. Work became specialized, and when and how the work was done was planned to suit the needs of those who owned the means of production. Children at first worked incredibly long hours in the factories, right along with adults, but gradually the inflexible work schedules and intolerably hard working conditions changed when child labor laws were passed. Similarly, peonage laws were enacted to protect the mentally retarded, emotionally disturbed, and others confined to institutions from being forced to perform what amounted to slave labor. During the 1930s, the retirement ages of 65 for males and 60 for females were selected by the federal government to serve as a base for paying social security. These ages were chosen for political expediency to curb unemployment among younger workers.

All these situations, combined with the continuing attitude that a woman's place was in the home and that those engaged in specialized technical work had to have specialized training, restricted those who worked for money to adult males under the age of 65 and a small percentage of women. A common life cycle was legislated. One went to school, by law, during the first two decades of life, worked full-time the next four (or became a homemaker), and then retired for the next decade. This "linear life pattern," as it has been called by Best and Stern, has had profound implications for the pattern of leisure (recreation is probably a better term, since this activity was tied to and dependent upon a work-recreation-work cycle).[13] Recreation on weekday evenings, weekends, holidays, or vacations was the reward for the worker who had earned the chance for refreshment.

Today, this linear life pattern is breaking up, for various reasons. Among these are the changing role of women, the changing age composition of our society, expanding continued education, changes in attitudes toward work, and many other factors. Today almost one in six employees works voluntarily part-time. Often such workers are homemakers, students, or those who have "retired" from a full-time job. "Flexitime," the use of flexible hours for employees, allows many part-time workers to plan their work schedules so as to accommodate other duties, rather than the reverse. Thus, a mother with school-age children might put in her 30 hours a week by selecting to work from 9 to 3 daily so she can return home when her children do. The changing role of women is also breaking up this linear progressive. Almost 50 per cent of adult women are now employed outside the home, and the number enrolled in higher education continues to rise.

## Changing Attitudes Toward Work and Leisure

Our attitudes toward work and its role in our lives appear to be in the process of change, as the nature of work also changes. Today more workers are involved in the production of services (teachers, lawyers, salespersons) than are involved in the production of material goods (welders, bakers, automobile assembly line workers). While the number of people providing goods has increased only slightly in the last 20 years, the number employed in services has increased 70 per cent. (At Penn State I have taught this class to about 1,000 students and have found less than ten who planned a career involved in the production of goods. How about you?)

In terms of the ways in which individuals perceive the relationship between work and leisure in their own lives, we may distinguish three patterns: (1) priority of work; (2) priority of leisure; and (3) equality of work and leisure.[14] One way of surveying these patterns is to ask people about their "central life interest," a term coined by Robert Dubin to refer to a significant area of social experience.[15] Assuming that participation in certain activities may be necessary but not important to an individual, Dubin classified replies to a series of three-choice questions as job-oriented, non-oriented, or indifferent. Work was found not to be a central life interest for industrial workers by a margin of three to one. However, Louis Orzack gave an amended version of Dubin's questionnaire to a sample of professional nurses, and confirmed the hypothesis that work *would* be a central life interest to them.[16]

These and other studies suggest that people will identify more strongly either with work or non-work depending, to a large extent, upon how fulfilling their work is. People who say that work is the most important interesting thing in their lives are not necessarily saying that their lives are devoid of leisure-like experiences. Perhaps they are able to get some of the satisfactions from work which other people derive from leisure. Also, there may be cultural influences operating to produce a change in people's attitudes over a rather short period of time. A Japanese study in 1967 showed that more than half those polled gave priority to work, while one-third gave equal priority to work and leisure.[17] A similar study in 1971, only 4 years later, showed that the "equal priority" view was then held by 89 per cent. We may conclude that both the type of work and type of culture affect the relative importance accorded to leisure in the life pattern.

Another clue to the relative importance attached to work and leisure is the choice that people make between having more income or more leisure. Given the separation between work and leisure, which requires one to work "for a living," how much should one work so as to have both time and money for leisure? Some economists have argued that after people receive a comfortable margin over what they consider to be necessary, they will not seek additional work. This is no doubt true of most simpler non-industrial societies, but evidence shows that among the economically advanced nations of the world more people prefer additional work or a second job to more leisure. In 1969 two out of five "moonlighters" interviewed in the United States claimed a need for additional income for regular household expenses.[12]

A study of 1,322 randomly selected U. S. respondents to determine whether they would like to work more hours a week at their jobs and be paid for it, or work less hours with a proportionate salary reduction, found that 34 per cent would work more, 10 per cent would work less, and 56 per cent would work the same number of hours as they did then.[18]

Best *et al.*, after reviewing studies dealing with income-time tradeoffs, concluded that workers still attached a greater importance to more income than to more time off, but that the gap between them was narrowing. "A review of attitudinal data suggests that the desire for free time among workers has been increasing. The evidence is mixed, however, about whether workers would be willing to give up some of their income in order to get more free time."[12]

## Satisfaction With Work

There appear to be a number of indications that people are less satisfied with their work than in the past. One reason for this may simply be that workers have higher expectations than they previously had. To a generation which went through the Great Depression, the chance to achieve a subsistence income was very often enough to satisfy a worker. To a generation raised in a period of economic affluence, however, a subsistence wage is often not enough.

Parker, from a review of related research, found six main themes concerning work satisfaction.[5] These include (1) creating something—a feeling that one has put something of oneself into a product, (2) using skill—whether the skill is manual or not, (3) working wholeheartedly and not being arbitrarily slowed down, (4) using initiative and having responsibility—freedom to make decisions, (5) mixing with people—social contact, and (6) working with people who know their job—competent bosses and associates. Work was not satisfying when the following five themes were in evidence: (1) doing a repetitive job, (2) making only a small part of something—making the worker an appendage of the machine, (3) doing useless tasks, (4) feeling a sense of insecurity, (5) being too closely supervised.

For factory workers and others in blue collar trades, sociologist Robert Schrank has argued that the opportunity to socialize on the job (he calls it *schmoozing*, which is Yiddish for chatting or gossiping) is more important to the happiness of workers than the satisfaction of accomplishment.[19] Schrank, who worked for many years as a mechanic in an auto plant, argued that the repetitive tasks of a factory or assembly line can't be made creative. Workers can, however, be given more opportunity to socialize: desks can be turned so they face each other, CB radios can be installed in company trucks, telephones can be made available to assembly line workers, and machines can be positioned so that people working at them can talk with each other. Such moves, Schrank contended, may increase rather than decrease productivity, since workers will be less likely to feel "stuck" in the factory. While *schmoozing* may take a little of the workers' time, Schrank said that most workers don't work as hard as they can anyway. Also, "Standing around not working is a lot duller than doing the work."[19]

One reason for increasing dissatisfaction with jobs may be the higher educational level reached by employees. Quinn and Mandilovitch re-examined nine national surveys of the American labor force, and found only a small increase in job satisfaction between those with a college degree and those without one. Even these small differences were provided mostly by the intervening effects of the quality of employment. "Education appeared to have little effect upon job satisfaction, but rather served to provide workers with generally better and hence more satisfying jobs."[20]

While better educated employees have fewer problems with their physical work environment, they have increased difficulty with working hours and excessive workloads. Also, as education level increases, the importance of challenge increases and there is a decline in the importance of comfort, financial rewards, and resource adequacy. Additionally, it was found that workers are satisfied to the extent that their educational attainments match the educational requirements of their jobs. The most dissatisfied workers are those who are too highly educated for their jobs.

All this information we have reviewed would seem to be directly applicable to many of you. Perhaps you perceive yourself as preparing not for a job, but for a "career," in which you will have increasingly high levels of responsibility in a professional capacity. The college you attend may be encouraging you to seek self-expression, primarily through your job—but what if it doesn't work out that way? The job "mix" today doesn't match the educational and training "mix." Suppose you find that, upon graduation, the only offer you have is to work as a salesperson in a large department store. This, as you have guessed, brings us to Leisure Exercise 4-2. When completing it remember that, according to the U. S. Department of Labor's *Occupational Outlook Handbook,* the vast majority of the 46 million jobs that will open up in the next half-dozen or so years will require less than 4 years of college.[21]

# Leisure Exercise 4·2

The object of this exercise is to examine your reaction to having a job which might cause a "neutrality" or even "opposition" work-leisure relationship for you.

Assume that after 6 months of searching for a job after graduation, you can find only a salesperson's job in a large department store. You accept the job.

**1.** Do you believe your leisure patterns would change from what they currently are? Why?

**2.** Do you believe you could find adequate means for self-expression and fulfillment during your leisure? Why?

**109**

**3.** Do you think any of your leisure activities could make a meaningful contribution to society? Why?

**4.** Could you be a "success" in the eyes of your friends and family with such a job? Why?

**5.** What kind of leisure behavior, if any, do you think would be denied you because of such a job? Why?

**6.** Could you be happy with leisure as a central life interest instead of work? Why?

## Leisure as Compensation for Unsatisfying Work

Sociologists and psychologists who have studied the modern work experience generally conclude that there are fewer opportunities today than in the past for feelings of self-expression and creativity through work. Some critics want to amend the content, organization, and environment of work itself to solve this problem. To date this has taken a number of forms, such as flexible working hours, profit-sharing plans, job rotation, increasing employee decision-making in how a job should be done, and other techniques. In experiments undertaken by Volvo, for instance, workers were allowed to organize into teams and decide among themselves the allocation of tasks for building automobiles, as long as the production quota was met. The importance of such experiments has been underscored by increasing union demands for "humanization of the workplace."

Many have suggested that leisure can be used as compensation for unchallenging work. To some extent, the previous research dealt with this issue. Aside from the question of whether the spread of dehumanized labor is inevitable, we can take note of what has been concluded about the compensation theory. The evidence that has been gathered does not, in general, support its validity. From his study of alienation in various forms of work, Robert Blauner concluded that the problem with the leisure solution is that it

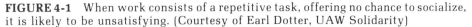

**FIGURE 4-1** When work consists of a repetitive task, offering no chance to socialize, it is likely to be unsatisfying. (Courtesy of Earl Dotter, UAW Solidarity)

underestimates the fact that work remains the single most important activity for most people in terms of time and energy.[22] The leisure solution ignores the subtle ways in which the quality of one's work life affects the quality of one's leisure. Furthermore, emphasizing leisure as a solution to work problems involves a basic inequality—a division of society into one section of consumers who are creative in their leisure time but have meaningless work, and a second segment capable of self-realization in both spheres of life.

The organization theorist Chris Argyris has reviewed a number of studies of work and leisure from the standpoint of personality and organization theory.[23] He is critical of the idea that leisure can be used as compensation for work, or that there is a kind of tradeoff between the two spheres. The model of man used in personality and organization theory would require that the compensation theory be rejected. The logic is as follows. If individuals tend to experience dependence, submission, frustration, conflict, and short time perspective at work, and if they adapt to these conditions by psychological withdrawal, apathy, indifference, and a decrease in the importance of their worth as human beings, these adaptive activities become more important in the person's life and will guide his/her leisure behavior outside the workplace. Individuals will seek leisure activities that are consonant with the adaptive activities.

Another relevant study was conducted by Bishop and Ikeda, who examined 32 leisure activities of people in 18 occupations.[24] They concluded that the active leisure of those in high prestige occupations might indicate a compensatory leisure mechanism for the sedentary life of many such occupations. But people in more traditionally masculine occupations tend to participate in masculine-oriented leisure, while those in traditionally feminine occupations tend to choose feminine-oriented leisure activities. Beyond these two patterns, the researchers suggested a third: work and leisure may be different in terms of their energy requirements, but similar in terms of their sociability requirements. In other words, compensation may be a more physical process, and spillover a more mental process.

A final piece of evidence for the greater effect of spillover comes from John Anderson's study of a small town.[25] He found that employed persons over 65 were superior to retired persons in the same age bracket in the intensity and scope of their leisure time activities. Many books have been written about how to prepare for a life of leisure in retirement, but it would seem that the best way to get the most out of retirement is to retain some connection with the world of work.

While this evidence is somewhat pessimistic regarding the ability of leisure to compensate for dehumanizing work, keep in mind the previous research of Roberts et al.[10] and Bacon,[9] which doubts the importance of the relation between work and leisure. Perhaps, as leisure becomes more independent from work, its potential to shape human behavior will increase.

An indication of this is the finding by John Robinson, from a large sample of adults, that a greater relation exists between satisfaction with leisure activities and overall life satisfaction than between satisfaction with work and life satisfaction.[26] For many, leisure, not work, is becoming a primary determinant of life satisfaction.

Finally, job dissatisfaction may have implications for education. Quinn and Mandilovitch recommended the following changes for the role of education in preparing people for careers: (1) requirements for jobs should be realistically based upon skills, rather than degrees earned; (2) job content should be altered as far as possible through job enrichment to help satisfy more highly educated workers; (3) less emphasis should be placed upon career-oriented skills and more upon general abilities in primary and secondary education.[20] The occupational payoff, they stressed, should not be used as a means of justifying learning experiences.

## Work Role and Leisure Participation

One's work role is often related to participation in leisure behavior. This is not to say that one's work role *causes* one to perform certain activities, although sometimes this happens, but that the likelihood or probability is greater that people with certain work roles will participate in certain leisure activities. Since work role is related to other socioeconomic variables, such as income, educational level, and age, some of these variables may help explain differences associated with work role more than the actual work role itself.

The first distinction we can make is that occupational status—student, unemployed, full-time worker, part-time worker, retired—has a significant relation to how free time is used, as well as to the amount of free time itself (if you are willing to define "free time" as the amount of time spent in various recreation and leisure activities). Robinson found that employed females average about 2 hours of leisure a day less than those unemployed, while employed males average over 4½ hours less than unemployed males.[26]

Several studies have sought to establish a relationship between type of occupation and choice of leisure activity. Leonard Reissman found that people in higher level positions were more active and diverse in their social and leisure participation than those in lower positions.[27] Saxon Graham concluded that the proportion of professional workers participating in strenuous exercise was nearly twice that of unskilled workers.[28] Sometimes occupational prestige is taken to be the variable, as demonstrated by the studies of Clarke[29] and Burdge.[30] The general conclusion is that those in higher prestige occupations participate in a greater variety of leisure activities than do those in lower positions although a few pursuits, such as bowling and gardening, are more favored by the lower classes. Nevertheless, one wonders if more specific occupational differences may be linked with characteristic forms of leisure behavior.

In an article entitled "The Long Arm of the Job" Martin Meissner

**FIGURE 4-2** Being unemployed has a profound impact upon one's leisure. (Courtesy of H. Armstrong Roberts)

considered the effect of work on leisure.[31] He was particularly interested in three dimensions of both work and leisure: (1) the amount of choice or discretion that is possible or demanded; (2) the extent to which the activity is either purpose-directed or carried out for its own sake (instrumental or expressive); and (3) the amount of social interaction involved. He concluded that when choice of action is suppressed by the constraints of the work process, the worker's capacity for meeting the demands of spare time activities that require discretion is reduced; the worker engages less in those activities that necessitate planning, coordination, and purposeful action, but more in sociable and expressive activities. Lack of opportunity to talk on the job is associated with greatly reduced rates of participation in associations—that is, in activities commonly believed to help integrate individuals into the community.

The examples of work's influence on leisure thus far considered have been taken from American and British studies, but the cross-cultural nature of these influences is illustrated by Ezra Vogel's study of middle-class Japan.[32]

The Japanese businessman, like his American counterpart, finds it difficult to distinguish working time from leisure time, and often entertains clients with a trip to a golf course or a party with geishas. Like successful businessmen, doctors rarely make a sharp separation between work and leisure, partly because working hours are determined by the arrival of patients. It is the salaried worker who makes the sharpest distinction between working time and free time. He generally has inflexible working hours, thus permitting him to plan certain hours of the day and certain days of the week for himself and his family.

Within various kinds of occupations we can see pronounced differences in participation. Table 4-4 shows differences in participation in various outdoor recreation activities associated with various types of occupations and occupational status. This table is based upon data from a national survey of over 4,000 individuals undertaken as part of the *1978 National Outdoor Recreation Survey*.[33] As you can see, there are some pronounced differences in the percentage of various groups participating in these activities. Take a look at the student category (and you thought you were always at work). Students are more likely to participate in most of these activities and in some, such as tennis, bicycling, ice-skating outdoors, and other outdoor sports and games, they have a far higher participation rate than any other category. How do you account for this? (We will examine this idea a bit further in Chapter 7.) Farmers, housewives, and the retired generally have lower rates of participation, while professionals and managers usually have higher rates.

## A HOLISTIC APPROACH TO WORK AND LEISURE

Much has been written about the need for a "holistic" approach to work and leisure as we make the transition from an industrial to a post-industrial society. As Parker stated:

> In this fusion, work may lose its present characteristic feature of constraint and gain the creativity now associated mainly with leisure, while leisure may lose its opposition to work and gain the status—now associated mainly with the product of work—of a resource worthy of planning to provide the greatest possible human satisfaction.[5]

I raised this issue from a bit different perspective earlier by saying that, in an ideal society, the activities that we are externally compelled to do would be the ones which we are also internally compelled to do.

Such a holistic approach would seem to imply a concept of leisure as a state of mind rather than as a period of time after work. Our work would be more like our leisure, and vice versa. This integration of work and leisure is widely advocated by leisure theorists. Let's think critically about this idea for a minute before we accept it, and also examine its practicality.

**TABLE 4-4 PERCENTAGE OF POPULATION ENGAGED IN OUTDOOR RECREATION ACTIVITIES ONE OR MORE TIMES DURING 1978***

| | Professional | Manager | Clerical, Sales | Craftsman, Operator | Service, Laborers | Farmer | Student | Retired | Housewife | Unemployed |
|---|---|---|---|---|---|---|---|---|---|---|
| Camping in developed area | 39 | 41 | 33 | 36 | 28 | 24 | 41 | 11 | 26 | 24 |
| Camping in primitive area | 26 | 26 | 20 | 29 | 26 | 22 | 29 | 6 | 14 | 21 |
| Canoeing, kayaking, river-running | 22 | 13 | 14 | 16 | 16 | 9 | 28 | 4 | 12 | 13 |
| Sailing | 19 | 14 | 14 | 8 | 6 | 0 | 20 | 3 | 7 | 13 |
| Water-skiing | 21 | 17 | 23 | 21 | 18 | 11 | 25 | 0 | 8 | 9 |
| Fishing | 51 | 64 | 47 | 68 | 56 | 54 | 67 | 37 | 46 | 52 |
| Other boating | 40 | 46 | 39 | 39 | 31 | 8 | 43 | 18 | 27 | 27 |
| Outdoor pool, swimming, sunbathing | 78 | 69 | 76 | 60 | 60 | 29 | 90 | 23 | 59 | 53 |
| Other outdoor swimming and sunbathing | 56 | 52 | 54 | 49 | 47 | 18 | 63 | 15 | 44 | 28 |
| Walking to observe nature, bird watching | 66 | 49 | 47 | 47 | 46 | 56 | 57 | 35 | 54 | 48 |
| Hiking or backpacking | 43 | 32 | 28 | 30 | 29 | 20 | 42 | 10 | 20 | 23 |
| Other walking or jogging for pleasure | 76 | 66 | 67 | 60 | 64 | 39 | 88 | 54 | 71 | 61 |
| Bicycling | 53 | 41 | 49 | 44 | 53 | 27 | 87 | 32 | 41 | 40 |

| | 21 | 12 | 15 | 18 | 13 | 14 | 25 | 0 | 12 | 16 |
|---|---|---|---|---|---|---|---|---|---|---|
| Horseback riding | 21 | 12 | 15 | 18 | 13 | 14 | 25 | 0 | 12 | 16 |
| Driving vehicles or motorcycles off-road | 27 | 26 | 25 | 38 | 31 | 24 | 40 | 4 | 18 | 24 |
| Hunting | 17 | 23 | 15 | 38 | 24 | 40 | 20 | 10 | 9 | 21 |
| Picnicking | 83 | 79 | 77 | 75 | 68 | 66 | 77 | 49 | 76 | 76 |
| Golf | 28 | 28 | 14 | 14 | 11 | 7 | 22 | 10 | 11 | 13 |
| Tennis outdoors | 46 | 34 | 37 | 27 | 27 | 12 | 67 | 4 | 24 | 26 |
| Cross-country skiing | 7 | 2 | 2 | 1 | 2 | 3 | 6 | 0 | 1 | 1 |
| Downhill skiing | 12 | 7 | 9 | 7 | 7 | 1 | 15 | 0 | 3 | 1 |
| Ice-skating outdoors | 19 | 15 | 19 | 16 | 14 | 9 | 32 | 2 | 14 | 10 |
| Sledding | 22 | 16 | 19 | 22 | 20 | 20 | 43 | 2 | 19 | 10 |
| Snowmobiling | 8 | 12 | 7 | 12 | 10 | 17 | 12 | 1 | 7 | 2 |
| Other outdoor sports and games | 63 | 56 | 55 | 59 | 65 | 49 | 88 | 19 | 48 | 42 |
| Sightseeing at historical sites or natural wonders | 79 | 75 | 65 | 62 | 54 | 50 | 62 | 47 | 63 | 60 |
| Driving for pleasure | 77 | 81 | 76 | 78 | 70 | 70 | 58 | 50 | 74 | 70 |
| Visiting zoos, amusement parks, fairs, carnivals | 83 | 73 | 77 | 80 | 76 | 56 | 85 | 42 | 71 | 68 |
| Attend outdoor sports events | 73 | 72 | 69 | 70 | 61 | 47 | 82 | 54 | 48 | 46 |
| Attend outdoor dances, concerts, or plays | 55 | 39 | 42 | 43 | 44 | 35 | 59 | 17 | 33 | 40 |

*SOURCE: Heritage Conservation and Recreation Service, 1978 National Outdoor Recreation Survey. Washington, D.C.: U.S. Department of the Interior, 1980.

It has often been argued that we are better off if we live our lives as unified beings, with the same set of values, behaviors, and beliefs evident in our work, play, and learning. This consistent or integrated response to experience, it is supposed, makes us better, freer, no longer in need of many masks to wear or roles to play. It is also often assumed that the individual, free of fragmentation, is more capable of experiencing religion, more able to celebrate and affirm the universe.

Interestingly enough, this idea of holism negates many chances for playfulness. That is, if our lives are segmented, we play different roles in different situations. We may invent different selves or at least playfully stress different aspects of ourselves in various situations. You, for instance, probably present yourself differently and act differently around the professor who teaches this course than you do around your roommates or friends (maybe not). In most of our roles, we are one-eyed jacks or one image in a kaleidoscope. This variation in being may actually be very functional to society; it allows us to reconcile different expectations we have about each other. Our grandparents, for instance, may want their teenage grandchildren to use no foul language, so that the teenager will present himself/herself that way when around them. It may be argued that segmented behavior such as this is undesirable since, ideally, we should be able to accept each other's differences and perhaps even appreciate them. Historically, however, we have little reason to believe that we can function collectively without being somewhat segmented in our different roles.

While a characteristic trait of most types of work is "constraint," we have a lot to learn from such constraints that we cannot learn during leisure. This is not to argue that we must suffer "pain" to experience pleasure, but only that we are complex, multifaceted beings with only partial understanding of ourselves. Work and its constraints may teach us about what is important to us or show us our limits. The constraints of work may sometimes cause us to learn when we otherwise might not. To be constrained is to be limited, and we are limited by time, by our imagination's limits, and by the capacity of our environment. To be without constraints would mean we were God-like, and I still hope that a God exists other than ourselves.

This, of course, is not to say that we should always live under the constraints of work. We need the freedom of leisure, the removal of constraints (or, more properly, the changing of one set of constraints for another). We do not need, however, to remain the same in terms of our behavior in all situations, nor do we need to remain under the same constraints. While it is doubtful that we can be slaves at work and simultaneously be happy during our leisure, it is possible to act differently at work than at leisure and still be happy.

In the near future it looks as though many of the jobs available are going to be those which "constrain" many aspects of the individual, which do not provide for "self-actualization"—whatever that is. This may increase our tendency to be segmented or polarized in our work-leisure relations.

Various jobs, of course, are not inherently more satisfying than others. To some extent, the work assumes the worth brought to it by the individual. I remember an old man in Boothbay Harbor, Maine, who sold hot dogs from a bicycle which had a steam cabinet on two wheels in front. His bicycle was absolutely clean, he was neatly dressed, and he presented himself with dignity. His hot dogs were great, served with spicy brown mustard and homemade relish on bakery buns fresh from the steam cabinet. No one, apparently, had told the old man that selling hot dogs was unimportant. The way he did his job and the care he took made the job important. He did what he did well, and the community recognized and benefited from it as surely as we benefit from a first rate bus driver, secretary, or baker. Students in college today, I believe, are often being conned into believing that they can only be happy or successful in a handful of jobs. This can become a kind of self-fulfilling prophecy. Thus, for example, a student may begin to believe that it is worthwhile to become a guidance counselor but not a baker. Which of these two profit society more? I find it a tough question to answer. Both jobs involve "constraints," as most jobs do, and both have the potential to enrich our lives. While some jobs may be more clearly integrated into the rest of our lives than others, the very separateness of a job from the rest of our lives may be beneficial. Jobs which allow for a "holistic" approach to living are jobs which are *never done*. No matter how satisfying the job is, there are times when it is comforting to escape from it. This is much easier to do when the job is a distinct, well-defined, limited part of our lives.

Conversely, play is separate and distinct from the rest of life. As Huizinga pointed out, all play is limited in time and space and understood by the players to be separate from "real life."[34] It has its own rules, which players voluntarily agree to follow. While play-like behavior is evidenced in many parts of our life, play itself remains distinct and separate. Play, as it turns out, also has constraints. Although we may bring some of the play spirit into many realms of our lives, play itself is worthwhile in part because it is separate and distinct, outside ordinary life. To combine it with work would be to destroy it in much the same way that keeping a wild bird in a cage will destroy it. While it is hard to argue against "creativeness" in our work as well as in our leisure, such creativeness will be constrained in different ways from our leisure and there is no reason to believe that this is bad.

Perhaps we need "holism" only in a spiritual sense—that is, that we are a meaningful part of a larger scheme and integrated into it. If this is true, then a holistic approach to work and leisure may be more a matter of integrating our work and leisure lives through faith than through changing the constraints of work and making it more like leisure.

## STUDY QUESTIONS

1. Describe the extension, opposition, and neutrality relationships between work and leisure.

2. What is a linear life pattern? What is causing the breakup of this life pattern?

3. What generalization can be made about workers' preferences for more free time as opposed to more money? Do you think continued inflation is likely to change this?

4. What is *schmoozing*? Why is it important to workers?

5. What, in your opinion, are the advantages and disadvantages to a holistic approach to work and leisure?

## REFERENCES

1. Theodorson, George A. and Achilles G. *Modern Dictionary of Sociology*. New York: Thomas Y. Crowell, 1969, p. 466.
2. Mills, C. Wright. *White Collar*. New York: Oxford University Press, 1956, p. 222.
3. Weber, Max. *The Protestant Ethic and the Spirit of Capitalism*. New York: Charles Scribner's Sons, 1958.
4. Wilensky, Harold. "Work, Careers and Social Integration," *International Social Science Journal*, Vol. XII, 1960, pp. 543–560.
5. Parker, Stanley R. *The Future of Work and Leisure*. New York: Praeger, 1972, ch. 8.
6. Berger, Peter (ed.). *The Human Shape of Work*. New York: Macmillan, 1964, pp. 218–219.

7.  Parsons, Talcott. Quoted by Godbey, Geoffrey, and Parker, Stanley, *in Leisure Studies and Services: An Overview.* Philadelphia: W.B. Saunders, 1976, p. 37.

8.  Gross, Edward. "A Functional Approach To Leisure Analysis," *Social Problems,* Vol. IX, 1961, pp. 2-9.

9.  Bacon, William. "Leisure and the Alienated Worker: A Critical Reassessment of Three Radical Theories of Work and Leisure," *Journal of Leisure Research,* Vol. 7, No. 3, 1975, pp. 179-190.

10. Roberts, Kenneth, Clark, S.C., Cook, F.G., and Semeonoff, E. "On the Relationship Between Work and Leisure: A Skeptical Note," University of Liverpool: Department of Sociology, 1976, p. 29.

11. Owen, I. *The Price of Leisure.* Rotterdam: Rotterdam University Press, 1969, p. 11.

12. Best, Fred, Bosserman, Phillip, and Stern, Barry. "Income-Free Time Trade Preferences of U.S. Workers—A Review of Literature and Indicators." Washington, D.C.: Department of Health, Education and Welfare, 1977, pp. 14, 24, 29.

13. Best, Fred, and Stern, Barry. "Lifetime Distribution of Education, Work and Leisure— Research, Speculations and Policy Implications of Changing Life Patterns." Edited transcript of presentation sponsored by Institute for Educational Leadership.

14. Godbey, Geoffrey, and Parker, Stanley R. *Leisure Studies and Services: An Overview.* Philadelphia: W.B. Saunders, 1976, pp. 29-41.

15. Dubin, Robert. "Industrial Workers World," *Social Problems,* Vol. III, 1956, pp. 131-143.

16. Orzack, Louis. "Work As A Central Life Interest of Professionals," *Social Problems,* Vol. VII, 1959, pp. 32-41.

17. Cited by Best, Fred, Bosserman, Phillip, and Stern, Barry. *In* "Income-Free Time Trade Preferences of U.S. Workers-A Review of Literature and Indicators." Abridged updated summary. Washington, D.C.: Department of Health, Education, and Welfare, 1977, pp. 1-42.

18. *Ibid.,* p. 27.

19. Schrank, Robert. "Schmoozing with Robert Schrank," *Successful Business,* Spring, 1979. pp. 40-44.

20. Quinn, Robert P. and Martha S. Baldi de Mandilovitch, "Education Not the Key to a Satisfying Job," *ISR Newsletter,* Spring 1976, Vol. 4, No. 2, p.5.

21. *Occupational Outlook Handbook.* U.S. Department of Labor. Quoted in *Parade,* June 11, 1978, p. 12.

22. Blauner, Robert. *Alienation and Freedom: The Factory Worker and His Industry.* Chicago: University of Chicago Press, 1964, p. 183.

23. Argyris, Chris. "Personality and Organization Theory Revisited," *Administrative Science Quarterly,* Vol. XVIII, 1973, pp. 141-167.

24. Bishop, Doyle, and Ikeda, M. "Status and Role Factors in the Leisure Behavior of Different Occupations," *Sociology and Social Research,* Vol. LIV, 1970, pp. 190-209.

25. Anderson, John. "The Use of Free Time and Energy," *in* Birren, J. (ed.), *Handbook of Aging and the Individual.* Chicago: University of Chicago Press, 1960, p. 792.

26. Robinson, John. *How Americans Use Time: A Socio-Psychological Analysis of Everyday Behavior.* New York: Praeger, 1977, pp. 1-209.

27. Reissman, Leonard. "Class, Leisure and Social Participation," *American Sociological Review,* Vol. XIX, 1954, pp. 76-84.

28. Graham, Saxon. "Social Correlates of Adult Leisure Time Behavior," *in* Sussman, M.B. (ed.), *Community Structure and Analysis.* New York: Thomas Y. Crowell, 1959, p. 347.

29. Clarke, Alfred. "The Use of Leisure and Its Relation to Levels of Occupational Prestige," *American Sociological Review,* Vol. XXI, 1956, p. 301.

30. Burdge, Rabel. "Levels of Occupational Prestige and Leisure Activity," *Journal of Leisure Research,* Vol. III, 1969, pp. 262-274.

31. Meissner, Martin. "The Long Arm of the Job," *Industrial Relations,* Vol. X, 1971, pp. 239-261.

32. Vogel, Ezra. *Japan's New Middle Class: The Salary Man and His Family in a Tokyo Suburb.* Berkeley: University of California Press, 1963, p. 21.

33. Heritage Conservation and Recreation Service. *1978 National Outdoor Recreation Survey.* Washington, D.C.: U.S. Department of the Interior, 1980.

34. Huizinga, Johan. *Homo Ludens—A Study of the Play Element in Culture.* Boston: Beacon Books, 1962, p. 13.

# chapter 5

# Culture as shaper of leisure-
## And leisure as shaper of culture

**T**he idea of "culture" is one that traditionally has made students uneasy, since they suspect it really doesn't have much to do with the real world. Actually it does, but the concept is broad enough so that "culture" often ends up being thought of as everything that exists because a social group exists. It has been defined as "the way of life of a social group; the group's total man-made environment, including all the material and non-material products of group life that are transmitted from one generation to the next."[1] Tylor's classic definition is "that complex whole which includes knowledge, belief, art, morals, law, custom and any other capabilities and habits acquired by man as a member of society.[1] In addition we often speak of subcultures, which are merely "the culture of an identifiable segment of a society."[1] Therefore, we might speak of a college student subculture.

## WHAT AFFECTS OUR CULTURE'S LEISURE?

Our leisure is a product of our culture, and to some extent, our culture is a product of our leisure. The philosopher Josef Pieper has argued that leisure, in the Western World, is the basis of our culture. Pieper used the term culture to mean

> the quintessence of all the natural goods of the world and of those gifts and qualities which, while belonging to man, lie beyond the immediate sphere of his

**123**

needs and wants. All that is good in this sense, all man's gifts and faculties are
not necessarily useful in a practical way; though there is no denying that they belong to a truly human life, not strictly speaking necessary, even though he could
not do without them.[2]

Culture in this sense is not possible without leisure, and leisure in a special
sense:

> Leisure is a form of silence, of that silence which is the prerequisite of the
> apprehension of reality; only the silent hear and those who do not remain silent
> do not hear. Silence, as it is used in this context, does not mean "dumbness" or
> "noiselessness"; it means more nearly that the soul's power to "answer" to the
> reality of the world is left undisturbed. For leisure is a receptive attitude of mind,
> a contemplative attitude and it is not only the occasion but also the capacity for
> steeping ourselves in the whole of creation.[2]

Thus culture, which makes us distinctly human, is not possible without
contemplation and celebration of the divine. Our culture, then, is dependent
upon a receptiveness to religious experience in the broadest sense of the word.
The inability to celebrate the universe and one's place in it would greatly harm
our culture. It is easy to argue that some signs of this are evident today: boredom in literature, meaninglessness in the arts. It may be said that leisure as
used by Pieper might refer to a celebration of man rather than a celebration of
the divine. Indeed, many countries today worship or celebrate the state,
rather than the divine, but almost inevitably they do not value leisure as
receptive contemplation. Leisure, or more accurately recreation, must be
justified in terms of its benefit to the state.

## Culture and Play

A related theory is that of Huizinga, who saw the following connection
between play and culture:

> . . . culture arises in the form of play, . . . [that] it is played from the very
> beginning. Even those activities which aim at the immediate satisfaction of vital
> needs—hunting, for instance—tend, in archaic society, to take on the play form.
> Social life is endured with supra-biological forms, in the shape of play, which
> enhance its values. It is through this playing that society expresses its interpre-
> tation of life and the world. By this we do not mean that play turns into culture,
> rather that in its earliest phases culture has the play-character, that it proceeds
> in the shape and mood of play. In the twin union of play and culture, play is
> primary.[3]

Here it is argued that a social group's way of life and the important features of
that group—its law, language, poetry, even its way of fighting—emerge from
play. Remember that play, according to Huizinga, was

> A free activity standing quite consciously outside "ordinary" life as being "not
> serious," but at the same time absorbing the player intensely and utterly. It is an
> activity connected with no material interest, and no profit can be gained by it. It

proceeds within its own proper boundaries of time and space according to fixed rules and in an orderly manner. It promotes the formation of social groupings which tend to surround themselves with secrecy and to stress their difference from the common world by disguise or other means.[3]

The playfulness of a culture may change. We can see how the play spirit rises and falls over time with regard to certain human activities, such as war. Cavemen did not "play" at war or battle; their fighting had no rules, nor was it limited in time and space. If you could squash your enemy with a rock, you did so. Material interest was quite important: if you killed an opponent, you took his possessions—no playfulness here. We can find many playful elements in war or battle in other epochs. The jousting of knights in the Middle Ages, with its elaborate rules, was sometimes done for honor rather than material gain. Duels between offended parties with swords or pistols, in which combatants willingly agreed to follow rules, limit their fighting to a dueling area, and seek only to "draw first blood" rather than to kill their opponents, were playful. The British, accustomed to fighting on a battleground in symmetrical formations after the beginning of the battle was formally announced, thought that the American Indians were barbarians because they preferred to fight from behind trees and to sneak up on their enemy. Both had different ways of playing at war.

Today much of our war shows little playfulness. In Vietnam, for instance, war was not limited to combatants; civilians were often killed. There was no agreed-upon battlefield; war was waged for territory, not honor, and there were few rules. If you could kill your opponent with sharpened sticks, jellied gasoline, or any other means you did. War was different from that of the cavemen only in that it was technologically more advanced.

## Cultural Pluralism

Our leisure behavior and values are also dependent upon the extent to which our culture is pluralistic—that is, the extent to which it is shaped by many ethnic and minority groups who have a common culture and maintain their identity, rather than assimilate completely and become the same as their neighbors in values and behavior. The United States historically has represented a model of cultural pluralism; this has been due not only to its historic ties with Britain, Europe, Spain, and Africa, but also to immigration policies which continued the immigration of new groups. Canada has also experienced a more pluralistic culture during the last few decades, as immigrants from Europe, Asia, the Caribbean Islands, and the United States have transformed the country from one which was dominated by the English, French and, to a lesser extent, Canadian Indians to a multicultural nation.

The effects of cultural pluralism upon the leisure behavior of a post-industrial society are illustrated in Table 5-1, which shows the features in a mass culture that moves toward having even more things in common,

## TABLE 5-1    LEISURE IN SINGULAR AND PLURAL CULTURE SOCIETIES

|  | Plural Culture Society | Single Culture Society |
|---|---|---|
| Concept | Leisure is anything the individual chooses to do which he/she finds pleasurable; leisure is unlimited, an end in itself. | Leisure is a set of identifiable experiences which the individual is taught to enjoy; leisure is limited, a means to an end. |
| Variation in behavior | Range of acceptable behavior wide. | Range of acceptable behavior narrow. |
| Standards to judge behavior | Laws set limits; no universally accepted mores by which to judge leisure behavior. | Mores and folkways set limits of behavior; universal standards for leisure based upon perceived cultural necessity. |
| Role | Individual and subcultural identity linked to leisure behavior. | National identity linked to leisure behavior. |
| Role problems | Difficult to judge leisure ethically; dispute over leisure values; lack of meaning. | Lack of experimentation or alternatives; persecution of that which is foreign; easy to use leisure as a means of social control. |
| Government's role | Identification of recreation needs difficult; may provide only selected kinds of services or serve certain subcultures or groups disproportionately. | Identification of recreation needs easy; may provide services which act as a common denominator. |
| Commercial organization's role | Commercial sector has more diverse opportunities; can cater to individual or subculture's tastes; easier to create needs. | Commercial sector has more limited opportunities; more difficult to create needs or cater to individual or subculture's tastes. |
| Mass media's role | Limited in its ability to reflect culture; diversion and entertainment function. | Less limited in its ability to reflect culture; transmission of culture function. |

primarily due to the emergence of the mass media. Mass culture may be defined as

> Elements of culture that develop in a large, heterogeneous society as a result of common exposure to and experience of the mass media. . . . The emergence of mass culture is a part of the process of the development of common unifying cultural values and attitudes in the new and vast population of modern national social units.[4]

Cultural pluralism emphasizes the role of leisure as anything the individual chooses to do for pleasure. The limits of such behavior are defined only by laws, with activity representing an expression of personal interest, or "lifestyle," rather than one's culture. Fads and created leisure needs may cause more innovation, a speeding up of the consumption of leisure experience with a corresponding questioning of what is worth doing. One resolution to this uncertainty is to try to do nothing, but a more prevalent reaction is to try to do everything.

## Rural vs. Urban Society

A related variable is the extent to which a society is rural or urban. In Table 5-2 Kaplan has shown how characteristics of leisure might vary in rural and urban societies using the ideal type *Gemeinschaft-Gesellschaft* devised by the German sociologist Tonnies.[5] This division distinguishes between societies which are rural and simple in their social organization, and those which are socially complex and urban. Notice how these characteristics can still be distinguished within rural and urban areas of your state. Can you think of some leisure "fads" which are popular in urban areas which aren't acceptable in more conservative rural areas?

## Other Cultural Determinants of Our Leisure

We have seen that our culture's leisure, like any other, is affected by the extent to which we are rural or urban and the extent to which we are a singular or pluralistic culture. Two other aspects of our culture profoundly influence our leisure lives—democratic government and a modified capitalist economic system.

### Democracy

Leisure has always been closely interwoven with political belief and political systems. Our freedom to do what we want is shaped by many factors, and the systems by which humans exercise power directly influence the quantity and quality of our leisure experience. The original notion of leisure, born in the Golden Age of Greece, was directly formed by a political system which confirmed citizenship on a minority of its residents, made their participation in the decision-making process of the state mandatory, and promoted the ideal of cultivation of self through the existence of an extensive slave system, thus freeing the citizen from the necessity of being occupied with mundane work. Our own democracy, unlike that of the ancient Greeks, was constructed around two key ideas: individual freedom and equality under the law. Over 100 years ago de Tocqueville wrote

> When men living in a democratic state of society are enlightened, they readily
> discover that they are not confined and fixed by any limits which constrain them

### TABLE 5-2   CHARACTERISTICS OF LEISURE*

| Gemeinschaft | Gesellschaft |
|---|---|
| *Outdoor* | *Indoor* |
| More use of large yards, streams; outdoor games. | More use of special buildings or rooms in the home; indoor games. |
| *Participation* | *Observation* |
| More self-reliance in leisure; more talk and visiting. | More reliance on entertainers; more mass media; more reading. |
| *Noncommercial* | *Commercial* |
| More activities in schools, homes, and community buildings. | Willingness to pay for entertainment; theaters and other establishments. |
| *Group-centered* | *Individual-centered* |
| Family activity; church groups; leisure close to group norms. | Tolerance of individuality; less dominance by family. |
| *Few choices* | *Many choices* |
| Relatively small range of interests among residents. | Larger variety of interests and types of persons. |
| *Generalized activities* | *Specialized activities* |
| Less opportunity to develop or use special play skills. | More specialized training and outlets. |
| *Utilitarian-orientation* | *"Cultural" orientation* |
| Leisure as outgrowth of household or work skills. | Wider interest in artistic activities. |
| *Spontaneous* | *Organized* |
| Little need for formal organization of play-life. | Dependence on recreational specialists. |
| *Body-centered* | *Mind-centered* |
| Games of strength; play in setting of physical work (communal home building or harvesting). | More reading; creative activity. |
| *Classless* | *Classbound* |
| Activities cut across social stratification. | Leisure as symbol of status. |
| *Conservative* | *Faddish* |
| Slow to change play-ways. | Follows newest fads and crazes. |

*SOURCE: Max Kaplan, *Leisure in America: A Social Inquiry.* New York: John Wiley and Sons, 1960, pp. 113–115.

to take up with their present fortune. They all, therefore, conceive the idea of increasing it—if they are free, they will attempt it; but all do not succeed in the same manner.[6]

Thus, differences in our fortunes were more closely linked to our efforts, to our ability to compete, to our level of aspiration, and to our level of need or greed. Among those things we have pursued competitively is "happiness," which can include the acquisition of experiences as well as the acquisition of objects. Having been historically in a situation where the acquisition of material goods was a perpetual struggle for most, pursuing happiness may at first have been an economic matter—instrumental activities—but it gradually became also a matter of individual self-expression—expressive activities.

Democracy with its ideas of individual freedom of choice, voluntary action, and the notion of technological capitalism, in which emphasis was placed upon maximizing profit and production divorced from identified need, have combined to change what is "voluntary" or "freely chosen." Since leisure is usually thought of as a freely chosen activity, this change is important.

In the traditional sense "voluntary" means a choice from among many alternatives which is freely and agreeably made by the individual and is not externally compelled. Inherent in this notion is the idea of giving up several alternatives to gain the most satisfying one; sacrifice, in short, goes hand in hand with pleasure. To choose to go on a picnic, for example, means that one gives up reading a book. This sacrificing of second and third best alternatives to select the single best one is in keeping with the rationalism which produced industrialism and, like it, is becoming obsolete.

Leisure activity today often seems to avoid the process by which alternatives are sacrificed, seeking instead to experience all choices—do it all, see it all, and do it and see it now. It is not surprising that, on a recent *Nationwide Outdoor Recreation Survey* (1978) undertaken by the Heritage Conservation and Recreation Service, respondents listed "time" more frequently than anything else as the factor limiting their participation in outdoor recreation[7]—not money, not transportation, not crowding or health problems, but time. In one sense this might appear to be a statement of our system's success. Imagine a former generation saying that the main limitation on their leisure was not money or transportation but merely enough time. Time budget research by Robinson found that approximately one of four adults said they *always* felt rushed.[8] This rush to experience seems to indicate that, in some sense, democracy is succeeding, since people can do more and more activities they have chosen. In terms of the unwillingness to give up one activity for another, the rush to do it all, the democratic notion of free choice is in trouble.

## Post-Industrial Capitalism

As Daniel Bell observed, our post-industrial society, where more people are involved in the production of services (teachers, salespersons, lawyers) than in the production of goods (farmers, carpenters, automobile assembly line workers) is characterized not by an absence of scarcity, although certain traditional forms of material scarcities such as food and shelter have been eliminated for the majority, but by new forms of scarcity.[9] Such costs or scarcities include the cost of information, the cost of coordination, and the cost of time.

Learning is mandatory in our society, and the rate at which we are bombarded with information increases daily. Every new social or political movement speaks of the need to "educate the people." The new consumer activist movement, for instance, is based upon providing more and more accurate information to the consumer so as to insure a logical choice on his/her part. This movement's success, however, is dependent upon individuals internalizing huge amounts of information, processing it in a logical way, and then making calculated decisions (not unlike a computer). To buy a tennis racket intelligently, therefore, one would need to have reliable data concerning comparative price, durability, flexibility of head, throat, and shaft, weight and weight distribution, head shape; size of sweet spot, racket head torque, vibration, stringing pattern, grip size, grip composition, string type, string tension, etc., etc. Such an approach ensures that the individual pays for the racket not only with money but with time, energy, and added complexity to his/her life. In many ways the consumer movement is an apology for materialism—which doesn't usually question the need for products but just gives the potential buyer instructions on how best to do so.

Similarly, our society is characterized by new costs of coordination. As society becomes more complex, as we become more interdependent, and as our ability to harm each other increases, planning and regulating our society becomes more important and more difficult. Additionally, the necessity of interacting with increasing numbers of people and a greater number of social situations is necessary and, to facilitate that, more travel is needed. Such coordination is not the prerogative of an elite but is necessary for everyone so that we are not killed by our own cars, chemicals, or radioactive wastes.

Finally, of course, is the factor of time, the ultimate scarcity for those who wish to consume and experience at an historically unprecedented rate. How shall we view this ironic situation? What an extraordinary luxury to have, as a problem, a perceived scarcity of time not tied to economic production. The desire to experience all things pleasurable, to be needed and involved in as many sets of human experiences as possible is, in many respects, the ultimate greed, the greed of a small frog who tries to swallow the sun. Two things must be said about this greed for experience. First, it springs directly from the mentality and processes of economic capitalism, where competition for goods and the production process are divorced from need. It is natural that this progression has taken place. Capitalism may be defined as

> an economic system based upon the accumulation and investment of capital by private individuals who then become the owners of the means of production and distribution of goods and services. Capitalism is also characterized by economic motivation through private profit, competition, the determination of prices and wages primarily through supply and demand, an extensive system of credit, freedom of contract and a free labor market.

In similar terms, the accumulation and investment of time by individuals in diverse pleasurable activity has taken place as a means of self-actualization.

**FIGURE 5-1** Time is the ultimate scarcity for those who wish to consume and experience at an unprecedented rate. (Courtesy of AAHPERD)

It has become a competition, with time the scarce resource, to find out who we are—literally, to re-create ourselves, experientially.

Capitalism also sowed the seeds of our experiencing everything by saturating us with unneeded material objects. As the ability of our economic system to create needs for new material products begins to find limits, the creation of needs is transferred to another realm: leisure experiences. People are sold the experiences of gambling, traveling through Europe, viewing other people's sexual activities, going down a wild river on a rubber raft, learning tennis from a Zen Buddhist perspective, changing personal relationships through a multitude of therapies, making wine, and any others they will buy. What is produced is a wanderlust, not for other places but for other lives.

## HIGH CULTURE AND POPULAR CULTURE

In most cultures, particularly those which are more pluralistic, certain leisure activities are considered better or more important than others. Kando said that the notion of high culture has been used in at least four different ways: (1) as the culture of the social elite—for example, that of Veblen's leisure class; (2) as culture that is exploratory, creative, revolutionary; (3) as the repository of a society's great cultural tradition (the "classics"); and (4) as

**FIGURE 5-2**   High culture, such as opera, has traditionally been associated with the socially elite. (Courtesy of Metropolitan Opera Association, Inc.)

excellent culture.[10] While these definitions vary, Kando gave a practical definition, as "the recreational, cultural and artistic activities traditionally not included in mass culture, such as theater, ballet, classical music, and the fine arts." Mass culture, of course, is transmitted by the printing press, electronic media, and other means of mass communication.

While these definitions are not completely clear, most of us understand which activities are regarded by society at large as high culture. Going to the opera is high culture, while watching a soap opera such as "The Edge of Night" on television is not. Playing Mozart on a flute is high culture, while throwing a frisbee is not.

If you look back at the second and fourth of Kando's definitions, however, it may occur to you that there is some dispute over which activities contribute to an "excellent" culture or which are exploratory, creative, or revolutionary. For some, however, no such dispute exists. Let's examine leisure activities in terms of what you consider good and bad culture.

# Leisure Exercise 5·1

1. Name some leisure activities in which you participate that contribute to or are part of an "excellent" culture.

   What is it about your participation in these activities which makes you believe they are part of an "excellent" culture?

2. Name some leisure activities in which you participate that are exploratory, creative, or revolutionary.

What is it about your participation in these activities which makes you believe they are exploratory, creative, or revolutionary?

3. Name some leisure activities in which you participate that are part of a bad or poor culture.

What is it about your participation in these activities which makes you believe this?

4. Name some leisure activities in which you participate that are in no way creative, exploratory, or revolutionary.

What is it about your participation in these activities which makes you believe this?

## Classifying Activities as High Culture

It is often assumed that leisure activities can be classified as high culture simply by assuming that the activity does or does not fulfill a certain function. The classification of leisure activity developed by Winthrop assumes that there are four major ways in which leisure is used: rest, relaxation, recreation, and renewal ("developmental leisure").[11] Rest refers to the recovery from fatigue. Relaxation is considered to be the free time used to escape boredom. Recreation is the purposeless use of free time, activity done for its own sake, such as sports, games, hobbies, play, and socialization. Renewal is time used for the expansion of intellectual, spiritual, and cultural horizons, which might tax the energy of the individual but still help develop potential and expand the appreciation of life. In providing this classification, Winthrop assumed that some consensus on a definition of "the good life" could be achieved through basic categories of experience, such as aesthetic, intellectual, social, religious, and spiritual. He further believed that developmental leisure activities can help realize these aims through a better individual understanding of culture in regard to the good life.

Developmental leisure includes such activities as the following: attending classical concerts, museums, art galleries, the opera, and lectures of an intellectual nature; adult education classes of an intellectual, artistic, or literary nature; amateur astronomy; or unpaid civic functions requiring planning, developmental activity, and unpaid teaching experience. Examples of leisure as relaxation activity include playing cards, checkers, or chess, attending burlesque or striptease shows, drinking in bars and taverns, and attending the circus. The rest or recuperative function of leisure includes such activities as taking steam baths, sunbathing, taking drugs, and feeding birds. Leisure as recreation includes do-it-yourself activities, sailing, doing cross-word puzzles, ballroom dancing, and attending rock concerts.

The above categorization may be criticized by claiming that it prejudges activity in regard to the motivation for undertaking it, its meaning to the individual participant, and its potential intellectual merit. Might not a crossword puzzle serve in some instances as developmental leisure activity? Could attending a classical concert be a form of rest or recuperation? This typology seems to assume that all people derive similar meanings and learn similar things from an activity such as, say, sailing boats—I would contend that they do not.

## Participation In High Culture

During the last few decades there has been a growing belief that participation in high culture activities has increased greatly, due to increasing leisure and affluence. Many of these assumptions have come from the mass media, which have portrayed a "cultural boom" in the United States. In spite of such a line of reasoning, a good case can be made that participation in high culture activities is not increasing, and that such participation involves only a tiny fraction of the public/at least in terms of "regular" participation. In terms of time spent, for instance, Robinson found that in 1965 and 1966 less than 0.1 hour per week was spent attending theater, opera, and symphonies.[12] Time spent producing art, sculpture, painting, and writing also averaged less than 0.1 hour per week, while an additional 0.1 hour per week was spent practicing music, dance, and singing. Thus, only about 18 minutes a week of 35 hours of "free time" per week were spent in high culture activities. When Robinson repeated the survey in 1975 the average amount of free time for U.S. adults had increased to 38 hours per week, but the amount of time devoted to high culture remained unchanged, although television viewing time increased.[8] How did your class time budget data concerning culture compare to the national adult average of 18 minutes per week?

In regard to literature, a 1978 study commissioned by a book industry study group found that nearly one-half the American people *never* read a book—either hardback or paperback.[13] The most popular non-fiction categories were biographies and autobiographies, followed by cookbooks, history, religion, instruction, current events, sports, psychology, and self-help texts. In the fiction category the most popular books were action and adventure stories followed by historical novels, mysteries, short stories, modern dramatic novels, and romances.

Similarly, a Ford Foundation survey found that less than one per cent of the public reported attending the theater, ballet, or concerts during a one-week period.[14] From this and other evidence, Zuzanek concluded that in spite of the growth of the total amounts of leisure time during the last decade, this increase has been translated mostly into mass media consumption and has had little effect upon the amounts of time spent in attending the arts.[15]

## Leisure Subcultures

We can examine leisure subcultures either by studying the leisure behavior of specific subcultures, such as college students, migrant workers, or retired business people, or we can examine the "culture" which is built up around a particular activity or activities. Schaffer has distinguished the following subdivisions of leisure culture:

> *Recreation Culture:* Parks, Beaches, Conservation and Recreational Areas . . .
> *Physical Culture:* Competitive Sport, Individual Sport, Gymnastics, Track and Field . . .
> *Media Culture:* Publishing, Radio, Television, Film and Libraries . . .
> *Artistic Culture:* Performing Arts, Exhibiting Arts and Crafts, Writing . . .
> *Multiculture:* Language, Linguistics, Folk Arts, Ethnic and Native Expression . . .
> *Environmental Culture:* Aesthetics of Urban Design, Cultural Facilities, Landscape, Architecture, Historic Sites. . .[16]

This conception of leisure culture concerns subdivisions of activities that are enjoyed by people but are not necessarily higher or lower on a scale of moral superiority of worth. Both as individuals and members of societal subgroups, however, we each make such value judgments to some degree.

Different leisure subcultures are often associated with a particular lifestyle or set of life circumstances. McKechnie, for example, has analyzed leisure behavior from a psychological standpoint through factor analysis of 121 different leisure activities.[17] By relating these to demographic variables and scores on an Environmental Response Inventory, he found that the people who were highly identified with individual factors had the following characteristics:

Mechanical: Typically a mechanically-minded male who likes to work with his hands, enjoys the out-of-doors and getting away from his home now and then.

Crafts: Likely to be a woman who enjoys doing things at home, making clothes, decorating the home and making it a cozy place to live.

Intellectual: Typically from a privileged background. Enjoys and tries to protect the natural environment. Involved in civic and community work.

Slow Living: Usually a person for whom home is a refuge from his white collar job and commuting. Likes to relax on the patio and enjoy passive leisure activity.

Sports: Likely to be a young, well-educated male who enjoys the outdoors as long as a playing field is nearby and a game going on.

Glamor Sports: Typically a well-educated male who enjoys the intense stimulation that such outdoor activities as motorcycling, water-skiing and sailing provide. Uses sports equipment as a means of stimulating environmental experience.[17]

Although this analysis is not comprehensive, it does demonstrate how individual leisure activities form constellations that appear to make up components of a leisure subculture, but the reasons for participating in these different constellations of activity are quite different. Because of this, it is not surprising that individuals who participate in a given leisure activity have socioeconomic characteristics that are markedly different from those of the population at large. Romsa, for example, using a sample of Quebec residents, found that there were a number of differences between those who participated in swimming and those who did not.[18] Compared to non-swimmers, swimmers were more likely to come from large urban centers, be younger, have a higher income, live in less dense housing areas, be Protestant, and so on.

## Popular Culture

It is difficult to get the "flavor" of popular culture from what has been said so far. Kando has pointed out another way of looking at popular culture: "popular culture . . . refers to the study of certain artifacts, folkways and institutions which have been overlooked by sociologists in the past. For example, the telephone, the bicycle, TV dinners, roadside restaurants, or any other element in America's everyday life."[10] Perhaps by discussing two examples we may better understand popular culture in our own society; I have chosen the bicycle and disco dancing.

**Bicycles.**   Since ancient times man has dreamed of building a vehicle driven by the strength of his own muscles. While it is difficult to determine where the bicycle began, the Celerifère, conceived in France in 1670 by Count Mede de Sivrac, was demonstrated before Marie Antoinette by aristocrats in the palace courtyard at Versailles. Like many other important forms of leisure expression in those days, the bicycle started out as a plaything, a diversion of the elite.[19] The celeripede subsequently was modified by the addition of a steering device in 1816 and, in 1869, a crank, pedals on the front wheel, and a chain-driven transmission. In the late 1800s bicycles were found in England, France, Germany, and the United States. Many of these were "bone shakers," made of steel tubes and wheels, iron rims, and hard rubber wheels. The first pneumatic tire was developed in 1886.

As bicycle clubs formed in the United States, bicycling shaped our culture in two important ways. The League of American Wheelmen became a major force in pushing for improvements to public roads. Their efforts were instrumental in bringing about road construction laws in 16 states between 1891 and 1894, and in the creation of state highway departments. Additionally, as bicycles improved in design and more and more people rode them, women's fashions began to change to suit the bicycle. Part of the freedom of dress which women enjoy today is directly attributable to the bicycle. The bicycle also led directly to the perfection of motorized wheeled vehicles, such as the motorcycle and automobile.

Bicycling was, perhaps, the most spectacular leisure craze at the turn of the century. Clubs were organized in almost every town throughout the land. According to Dulles, it was "the era of impressive bicycle parades, competitive club drills, hill-climbing contests, and race meetings."[20] Initially women rode large tricycles, but these vehicles were not considered inferior since they were almost as fast as bicycles. In 1890 the record for the mile was 2.33 minutes for the tricycle and 2 minutes 29 seconds for the bicycle. Unlike the horse, a bicycle didn't need daily cleaning and didn't eat or need an expensive harness. It opened up types of activities which changed our behavior—young boys and girls, for instance, could now drive out into the country together, much to the displeasure of their elders.

Bicycling experienced a new "boom" in 1971 to 1974 when there were an estimated 59 million bikes in use, up from 33 million in 1970.[21] United States manufacturers were making more bicycles than automobiles. Much of the boom was attributable to the expansion of sales to those 15 and over who, with a greater awareness of the energy crisis, and with greater concern for physical fitness, began to purchase bikes in record numbers. With this growth came increasing product differentiation: high-rise bikes with "banana" seats for kids, dirt bikes and scramblers modeled after motorcycles for juveniles, lightweight, highly sophisticated ten-speeds for the serious cyclist, and three-speed lightweights for the casual and adult rider. Certainly the ten-speed bike was one reason for the bicycle boom since it made it easier to climb hills, thus helping to create the adult market.

The "demographics" of bicycling look somewhat similar to those for many other outdoor activities. That is, participation in bicycling decreases progressively with age, increases with higher levels of education and income, and is participated in by more males than females, although this difference is much less than for many other outdoor recreation activities. Today most people use bicycles for commuting, touring, racing, or just enjoyment. Its immense popularity is due to the fact that the activity is socially acceptable to both sexes, it is a self-regulating activity, it can be done alone or with a group of people, it usually doesn't require traveling somewhere to do it, and equipment costs are relatively minor. Additionally, the tremendous variety of bicycles available and new marketing techniques have helped introduce the bicycle to millions. The bicycle boom has produced a major wave of bicycle thefts and countless accidents, helped build suburban bike trails and create a Bikecentennial, become the first serious, self-operated mode of transportation for children, and provided an important form of exercise for older adults. Bicycles are part of our everyday life.

**Disco Dancing.**    Dance has always been a special form of play. Huizinga, in his searching and exhaustive study of play, said of dance:

**FIGURE 5-3** Bicycling has become part of our popular culture. (Courtesy of the National Park Service)

> Whether we think of the sacred or magical dances of savages, or of the Greek ritual dances or of the dancing of King David before the Ark of the Covenant, or of the dance simply as part of a festival, it is always at all periods and with all people pure play, the purest and most perfect form of play that exists.[3]

Dance has been described by Huizinga as follows:

> It is musical and plastic at once: musical since rhythm and movement are its chief elements, plastic because inevitably bound to matter. Its execution depends on the human body with its limited maneuverability, and its beauty is that of the moving body itself. Dancing is a plastic creation like sculpture, but for a moment only. In common with the music which accompanies it and is its necessary condition, it lives from its capacity for repetition.[3]

Human beings have always danced, and the way they danced reflected their culture and their life situations. Thus, it is not surprising that Dulles described the dancing of Nebraska settlers in the 1800s, where life was physically exhausting and pleasures simple, as follows:

> They danced the scamperdown double shuffle, western swing, and half-moon:
> > Grab your honies, don't let'em fall,
> > Shake your hoofs and balance all.
> A deep pull from the little round jug; the men would swing their partners until they kicked the ceiling—if there was a ceiling. Faster, faster, the old fiddler would sway over his precious instrument, and heavy boots stamp on the hard ground floor. Receptions, and assemblies, and cotillions were just over the horizon. This was still the frontier. Another swig from the little brown jug; call out the numbers:
> > Ringtailed coons in the trees at play;
> > Grab your pardners and all run away.[20]

Social dancing in America was heavily influenced by the dances of Europe, which settlers brought with them. English folk dances were particularly influential, although inevitably they were adapted to suit the lifestyle of the settlers. Gradually the United States began to develop forms of social dance which were not European imitations. The two-step, made popular in the 1890s, was one of the first of such forms. It became a national craze, as was the cakewalk a few years later. Prior to World War I, Vernon and Irene Castle, who went to London looking for work, became overnight dancing sensations quite by chance. On their return to America, they were instrumental in introducing new dance forms and in refining social dance. During this era,

> New social dances of significance were the turkey trot (1911), bunny hug (1911), tango (1912), one-step (1912), castle walk (1912), Brazilian maxixe (1913), hesitation waltz (1913), fox trot (1913), and toddle (1915). The "Flapper Era" of the twenties saw a strong Negro influence in the advent of the shimmy (1920), Charleston (1923), dance contests (1923), black bottom (1926), and varsity drag (1927). The Depression of the thirties fathered the rumba (1930), big apple

(1936), truckin' (1936), Susy Q (1937), shag (1938), lindy hop (1938), conga (1939) and samba (1939).[22]

As dance fads and crazes continued to gain popularity in the 1940s, it was estimated that five times as many people took dancing lessons as enrolled in college.

While the 1940s produced few new dance crazes other than the mambo, the 1950s produced the bunny hop (1953), merengue (1954), bop (1955), cha cha (1955), calypso (1958), and madison (1959). The television program *American Bandstand* with Dick Clark helped introduce these dances to millions of teenagers. Dances of the 1960s and 1970s included, in quick succession, the twist, mashed potato (1961), watusi (1963), swim (1964), monkey (1964), pony (1964), jerk (1965), shaggy dog (1966), skate (1967), bus stop (1969), rope (1969), bump (1970), roach (1971), Latin hustle (1974), Spanish hustle (1974) and, in 1977, disco dancing.

Disco dancing, which represents one more in a series of social dance fads, became popular in somewhat the same way as the twist in the 1960s. The twist, a dance in which partners twist their hips, arms, and shoulders but never touch, was created by and for teenagers but soon became popular with cafe society. Certain singers, such as Chubby Checker and Joey Dee, became associated with the dance, and the Peppermint Lounge in New York City became the Mecca of twist. This rather mechanical dance, which created a national outbreak of back problems for middle-aged twisters, captured the attention of the mass media. The dance, however, died out as suddenly as it sprang up.

Discotheques, dance halls with strobe light displays where disc jockeys played a kind of music which was generally a straight soulless 4/4 time, with few subtle inner rhythms or counterpoint, were popular in Europe in the 1960s. In Europe discotheques may have represented a somewhat revolutionary expression of change in values but, in the United States, coming on the heels of the rapid value changes and widespread protest movements of the late 1960s and early 1970s, disco might be characterized as purposely mindless.[23]

While the music of the Supremes may have laid the groundwork for much of the disco music, the music itself was born in New York from a combination of black and Latin music. At its worst, the music was mindless escapism. The hit song "Disco Duck," by Rick Dees and his Cast of Idiots, endlessly repeated the words "disco, disco duck" in Donald Duck voices. The tremendous popularity of discos may have been due in great part to the extraordinary success of the film *Saturday Night Fever* starring John Travolta, with music by the Bee Gees. This film not only exposed millions to the talented dancing of John Travolta, but also gave an inside look at the disco scene.

Discos are characterized as "unreal" places which serve as escapism for the participant. Their decor often features technologically sophisticated sound systems and lighting effects. While the dress style of those who attend may vary widely, what is worn is quite important. As many social critics have pointed out, discos are narcissistic, places for the celebration of self. They are for exhibitionism: in dress, dance style, and sexual behavior. They are places where homosexual and heterosexual, black and white, young and middle-aged live and let live, stay cool.

Among the new sensibilities of the 1960s, only those regarding sex and race have retained their influence.[24] These sensibilities are expressed in disco and, perhaps, in new attitudes toward drugs, or at least cocaine. If disco dancing has little meaning other than pleasure-seeking through dance, social contact, the use of alcohol and other drugs, and sexual expression, it certainly is nothing new. While disco is different in style from the union hall dances, sock hops, and roadhouse dances of former eras, it has much in common with them. Important to all are the opportunity for play and the display of human movement, the mingling of the sexes, escape from the ordinary world and, at its best, celebration. The fad of discos represents one more variation on a theme. Disco, like so many social dance forms before it, is temporary. No one can predict what will replace it.

**FIGURE 5-4** Roller disco dancing, a variation of the disco craze, will eventually be replaced by another popular dance fad. (Courtesy of H. Armstrong Roberts)

## Popular Culture Activity Life Cycles

As you can see from the previous examples, many forms of popular culture have a "life cycle" all their own. From the time I write this chapter until the time you read it, for example, disco dancing may have declined tremendously in popularity or have been replaced largely by disco roller skating. The twist met a similar fate several years ago. Many activities that are part of popular culture appear to go through an entire life cycle and then, after disappearing for awhile, begin a new life cycle. The recreational use of bicycling, for instance, underwent a dramatic increase at the turn of the century and then slowly declined, only to return again in the early 1970s. The leisure behavior that makes up our popular culture is always in a state of change. While advertising and many other factors may influence trends in popular culture, predicting which activities will become or remain a part of our popular culture is almost impossible. Changes in tastes, interests, and styles influence such activities and such changes are often, like play itself, not rational.

## STUDY QUESTIONS

1. In what sense may it be said that leisure is the basis of culture?

2. What is a plural culture society? How does leisure behavior vary in such a society from a single culture society?

3. What are some of the major ways in which capitalism has shaped our leisure behavior?

4. What is "developmental leisure"? Do you agree with the idea that certain activities can be classified as "developmental"? Why or why not?

5. What are some forms of dancing which are "popular" culture? What are some forms which are "high" culture? On what basis can they be distinguished?

## REFERENCES

1. Tylor, E. B. *Primitive Culture*, Vol. 1. London: John Murray, 1871, p. 17.
2. Pieper, Josef. *Leisure: The Basis of Culture*. New York: New American Library, 1952, pp. 11, 41.
3. Huizinga, Johan. *Homo Ludens*. London: Paladin Books, 1970, pp. 13, 46, 164, 166.
4. Theodorson, George A., and Theodorson, Achilles G. *Modern Dictionary of Sociology*. New York: Thomas Crowell, 1969, p. 245.
5. Kaplan, Max. *Leisure In America: A Social Inquiry*. New York: John Wiley and Sons, 1960, pp. 113–115.
6. de Tocqueville, Alexis. *Democracy In America*. New York: Mentor Books, 1956, p. 161.
7. Heritage Conservation and Recreation Service. *Report on the 1977 National Outdoor Recreation Surveys*. Washington, D.C.: U.S. Department of the Interior, November, 1978, p. 7.
8. Robinson, John. *Changes In America's Use of Time—1965-1975*. Cleveland: Communication Research Center, 1977, pp. 1–209.
9. Bell, Daniel. "The End of Scarcity," *Saturday Review of the Society*, May, 1973, pp. 49–52.
10. Kando, Thomas. *Leisure and Popular Culture in Transition*. St. Louis: C. V. Mosby, 1975, pp. 19, 42.
11. Winthrop, H. "The Meaning and Measurement of Developmental Leisure Time," *Sociologia Internationalis*, Vol. VII, 1972, pp. 15–18.
12. Robinson, John. *How Americans Use Time: A Socio-Psychological Analysis of Everyday Behavior*. New York: Praeger, 1977, pp. 1–209.
13. Mitgang, Herbert. "Study Finds Nearly Half of U.S. Do Not Read Books," *New York Times*, November 14, 1978, p. c13.
14. *Finances of the Performing Arts*, Vols. 1–11. New York: The Ford Foundation, 1974, p. 000.
15. Zuzanek, Jiri. "Cultural Boom: Myth and Reality." Paper presented at the International Conference on Leisure and the Urban Society. Manchester, England, Sept. 23–25, 1977, p. 5.

16. Meisel, J. "Political Culture and the Politics of Culture." Speech to Canadian Political Science Association, Ontario, Canada, June 5, 1974.
17. McKechnie, George. "The Psychological Structure of Leisure Past Behavior," *Journal of Leisure Research,* Vol. 5, Fall, 1973, pp. 28-41.
18. Romsa, G. "A Method of Deriving Recreational Activity Packages." *Journal of Leisure Research,* Vol. 5, Fall, 1979, pp. 35-46.
19. Stimson, Judy. *"Bicycling."* Term paper, Pennsylvania State University, 1978, pp. 1-35.
20. Dulles, Foster Rhea. *A History of Recreation: America Learns to Play.* New York: Appleton-Century-Crofts, 1965, p. 195.
21. "U.S. Bicycle Market Statistics—1895-1976," *Schwinn Reporter* (Chicago, Schwinn Bicycle Company), February 1977, pp. 17-18.
22. Young, J. G. *Social Dance.* Pacific Palisades, Calif.: Goodyear Publishing, 1969, p. 45.
23. Foley, Patrick. "The Historical Development of Recreational Social Dances of the 20th Century." Term paper, Pennsylvania State University, Fall, 1978, pp. 1-18.
24. "Disco Survival System," *Mademoiselle,* Vol. 83, Nov. 1977, pp. 178-179.

# chapter 6

# Holy days, holidays, and celebrations

**R**eligion and leisure have always been related in ways which may not be readily apparent. Before considering these, let's examine a conventional definition of religion:

> Concern over what exists beyond the visible world, differentiated from philosophy in that it operates through faith or intuition rather than reason, and generally including the idea of the existence of a single being, a group of beings, an eternal principle, or a transcendent spiritual entity that has created the world, that governs it, that controls its destinies, or that intervenes occasionally in the natural course of its history, as well as the idea that ritual, prayer, spiritual exercises, certain principles of everyday conduct, etc., are expedient, due, or spiritually rewarding or arise naturally out of an inner need as a human response to the belief in such a being, principle, etc.[1]

From this definition, religion is seen as an attempt to make sense of the world in matters which are beyond our observation, proof, or understanding. In this sense we all have religion, since we all have shown concern for what exists beyond the visible world in a number of ways. Each of us has addressed the question "Why?" to the universe. Each of us has also considered the beliefs of a body of people with a similar set of beliefs. Whether or not we are members of an organized religion, we have been influenced by their beliefs and are likely to have given them serious consideration at some point in our lives.

# SIMILARITIES BETWEEN LEISURE AND RELIGION

How we attempt to make sense of the universe and our part in it will shape our leisure values, behavior, and the extent to which we experience leisure as a state of mind. In considering these relationships, perhaps we should begin by examining some ways in which religion and leisure are similar, or share characteristics.

## Celebration

Of all the links between leisure and religion, the common root of celebration is most important. Religious belief leads to a sense of celebration of the universe and one's place in it, and celebration also springs from religion in more formal ways. Christmas, for instance, celebrates the birth of Christ, although it also serves as a time for celebration which is not connected with Christianity. "To hold a celebration," stated the Swiss Catholic philosopher Josef Pieper, "means to affirm the basic meaningfulness of the universe and a sense of oneness with it, of inclusion within it."[2] This sense of celebration, then, means that we accept our very lives and our places in the universe with joy. Such a sense of celebration, Pieper believed, is at the heart of true leisure. "Leisure, it must be clearly understood, is a mental and spiritual attitude—it is not simply the result of external factors, it is not the inevitable result of spare time, a holiday, a week-end or a vacation. It is, in the first place, an attitude of the mind, a condition of the soul. . . ."[2]

Leisure occurs, in other words, only when and if we are capable of spiritual celebration. We cannot "force" leisure to happen any more than we can force ourselves to have religious faith. The celebration which is necessary for leisure and religious expression can't be brought about by "working" at it. For example, think of those times when you have gone out to celebrate, even planned and prepared for it carefully, but not found such a feeling within yourself. The most careful planning for a party, the most frantic fun-seeking, according to Pieper, will not automatically result in leisure. At certain times, and in some lives, the ability to accept and celebrate our lives in the greater scheme of things is simply lacking. Leisure, according to this conceptualization, is something that occurs from the inside out. Pieper believed that we cannot "force" this sense of celebration to occur; we cannot experience leisure just because we wish to. The state of leisure, however, is more likely to be attained by those who are quietly contemplative, those who are open to experience. Individuals who quietly observe what the world has to teach them are more likely to obtain leisure—not because they gain power over the world, but because they delight in it.

## Free Will

Both religious belief and practice and leisure behavior and values spring from the individual will. As Charles Brightbill has stated, "Each places us at the center of our own destiny and each recognizes the supreme worth of the individual."[3] In matters of religious faith, as well as the use of leisure, there are no experts. While some individuals may study religion or leisure behavior all their lives, they cannot determine what you should believe or how you should use your leisure. You cannot be advised successfully as to what you should put your faith in, or how your leisure should be spent. This is not to say that our religious beliefs and leisure values and behavior are not influenced by many different forces in society, but only that without individual acceptance or selection neither religion nor leisure come about. A person cannot be forced to have faith any more than he or she can be forced to engage in pleasurable activity voluntarily.

## Integration

Religion and leisure, in a broad sense, are both integrative and inclusive. Gordon Dahl has referred to leisure as "man's synthesizing factor in a component civilization."[4] Leisure can provide an opportunity to express the whole self rather than only one part or facet. Leisure activity may also serve the same integrative function as religion. Recreation, which is often used as a

**FIGURE 6-1** Religion is an attempt to make sense of the world in matters which are beyond our observation, proof, or understanding. (Courtesy of H. Armstrong Roberts)

synonym for leisure, may be considered as "re-creation," a therapeutic process of repairing the wear and tear resulting from work and its processes. Thus, by recreation we mean to restore, to re-establish, to return to an original or ideal state. In other words, recreation may serve to make us whole again.

In some cases we may not believe that a recreation or leisure activity can be integrative, since we are often taught that such activities are secondary in importance. It is individual faith and perception, however, that determine such things rather than the characteristics of the specific activity. Recently, for instance, a man visited me who was interested in finding ways to make tennis more accessible to older people who had never played before. The man, who was in his sixties himself, had been an excellent player all his life but was now hesitant to devote his energies to a game when there were so many "serious" problems in the world. After giving the matter much thought, however, he concluded that any activity can be the mechanism which gives meaning to a person's life or serves as an integrating mechanism. What is important, in the end, is "faith" in the activity.

Certainly, those who have found a sense of wholeness or integration in specific recreation or leisure activities exhibit an attitude toward the activity that could easily be identified as religious. Many people "believe" in camping or rock climbing or gardening or smoking grass as an integrating experience which transcends everyday life and is worthy of celebration.

## Personal Well-Being and Self-Realization

Both religion and leisure also express the desire for personal well-being and self-realization if we make certain assumptions. Leisure here is considered as a state of mind or as the opportunity to engage in worthwhile activities. Its function is that of personal development. In our present society, which contains increasing numbers of people who are concerned with how leisure is spent, religious thinkers of many faiths tend to accept free time as a period of potential spiritual growth. The spirit of leisure, according to Robert Lee, is the spirit of learning, of self-cultivation. "Leisure is the occasion for the development of broader and deeper perspective," Lee wrote, "and for renewing the body, mind and spirit. . . . Leisure provides the occasion for learning and freedom for growth and expression, for rest and restoration, for rediscovering life in its entirety."[5] Such a conception of leisure brings it close to a conception of the religious life in both its active and contemplative aspects.

## HOLY DAYS AND HOLIDAYS

Special days of celebration are nothing new; they are found in all cultures, and do not always have a religious basis. In 321 A.D., for instance,

**FIGURE 6-2** Many people "believe" in camping as an activity worthy of celebration. (Courtesy of the National Park Service)

Constantine the Great ordered Sunday to be a public holiday, but not in reference to Christianity.[6] While some holidays originated as religious ceremonies, others came about as festivals celebrating spring or the harvest. In primitive cultures it was believed that gods manifested themselves in many ways through weather or the forces of nature or the success or failure of crops. Holidays in such cultures were often used to observe various "taboos" or restrictions which, it was believed, would insure good treatment from the gods, or at least appease their anger.

   In medieval Europe, however, holidays became increasingly associated with religion. The Catholic church declared about one day in three to be a holy day of some kind, but many of those days which honored a saint were abandoned after the Reformation. As civilization became more complex and more urbanized, empires arose and, along with them, feelings of patriotism and national ties. Holidays then took on the added function of celebrating military victories, honoring military and religious leaders, or marking important events in the development of the nation. In urban areas holidays began generally to be less a celebration of a specific event than a termination of work and an opportunity to play.

Holidays in the United States and Canada have evolved from a variety of sources and have changed greatly in their meanings and how they are celebrated. Such holidays may be considered either patriotic (Washington's Birthday or Dominion Day in Canada), seasonal (New Year's Day), or religious (Christmas). In addition to these there are unofficial holidays, such as Super Bowl Sunday and local or regional holidays which sometimes have official recognition in certain areas. Gentle Thursday at Penn State University, for example, is a holiday for many students who ignore classes and celebrate the coming of spring by playing, dancing, drinking beer, smoking marijuana, and throwing frisbees in a giant outdoor gathering. The first day of deer hunting season is also a holiday in some parts of central Pennsylvania— public school is let out in some areas, and many employers don't expect their employees to report for work. Think about your own region and local area for a minute. Are there any holidays unique to them? How do you suppose they came about?

For many holidays in North America, the occasion is increasingly marked by celebrations which have little relation to the origins of the holiday. There is also the feeling that Americans don't give sufficient attention to such holidays, but this is by no means new. In 1876 President Grover Cleveland observed, "The American people are but little given to the observance of public holidays."[7] While many people feel that Christmas is too much devoted to Santa Claus, presents, and parties, Thanksgiving to eating, and New Year's Eve to drinking, a holiday in a democracy provides the choice of celebrating or not, as well as choosing how one will celebrate. In some totalitarian countries, such as the Union of Soviet Socialist Republics, a holiday such as May Day *must* be observed by the public.

The observance of holidays in the United States also varies tremendously because of our diverse ethnic and experiential backgrounds. It is not surprising that Leif Ericson Day (October 9) is more likely to be celebrated by Norwegian-Americans than by Italian-Americans, that Rosh Hashonah is a New Year's celebration for those of the Jewish faith but not for others, and that Veterans' Day may mean more to the American Legion or the Veterans of Foreign Wars than to others.

While there are many holidays recognized by various groups in our society, Congress has declared nine federal legal public holidays: New Year's Day, Washington's Birthday, Memorial Day, Independence Day, Labor Day, Columbus Day, Veteran's Day, Thanksgiving Day, and Christmas Day. Since

January, 1971, five of these have been officially celebrated on Mondays (Washington's Birthday, Memorial Day, Labor Day, Columbus Day, and Veteran's Day), thus creating 3-day weekends for millions of federal employees and others.

Many holidays have been transformed from their original significance as religious holy days to holidays with little or no religious meaning. Groundhog Day (February 2), for instance, is the American version of Candlemas Day, which originated in Europe as a religious observance centered around the purification of the Virgin Mary. The belief that if Candlemas Day were sunny winter would continue was somehow brought to this country and changed to involve the shadow of a groundhog.[7]

A number of other minor holidays have fluctuated in popularity, including the birthdays of Martin Luther King, Robert E. Lee, Jefferson Davis, and others. Other minor holidays include Inauguration Day (January 20, the day of the President's inauguration), National Freedom Day (February 1, celebrating the Emancipation Proclamation), Alamo Day (March 6, celebrating the standoff at the Alamo by Davy Crockett's boys), Pan American Day (April 14, to foster intercontinental solidarity and cooperation among members of the Organization of American States), Patriot's Day (third Monday in April, to celebrate the American Colonies breaking free from the British), Loyalty Day (May 1, to stimulate patriotic displays in the United States to counter May Day celebrations in the Soviet Union), Cinco de Mayo (May 5, to commemorate the efforts of Mexicans to retain their national independence), Armed Forces Day (third Saturday in May, a chance for the Armed Forces to display their readiness), Bunker Hill Day (June 17, a celebration of the American colonists' victory in that famous battle), Citizenship Day (September 17, a celebration of the immigration of foreign citizens to the United States), American Indian Day (fourth Friday in September, in honor of "native" Americans), United Nations Day (October 24, to honor the United Nations), Election Day (Tuesday after first Monday in November, a day for casting a vote), Bill of Rights Day (December 15, a day to reaffirm our national purpose, proclaimed by President Franklin Roosevelt in 1941), and Forefather's Day (December 21, in celebration of our founding fathers). In addition to these holidays manufacturers and special interest groups have promoted a huge number of "special" days, such as National Cheese Day or Aviation Day.

In summary, holidays, like the rest of leisure in our society, are characterized by diversity and change.

## Vacations

A vacation is an extended paid holiday which may be used as the vacationer sees fit. As discussed in Chapter 4, paid vacations are an increasingly common "benefit" of formal employment. While vacations don't always involve travel and unique activity, a giant industry has grown up around transporting, lodging, feeding, entertaining, and otherwise catering to those who take vacations.

Not everyone, of course, takes vacations. Travel Research International has estimated that, of all people eligible for vacations, one out of every six refuses to take one. "While your first guess might be that lack of money would be the biggest reason preventing people from leaving work and taking vacations, a higher percentage of those with incomes in the twenties refuse to take vacations than those with lower incomes."[8]

There are many reasons for not taking vacations other than lack of money. A national insurance company characterizes those who refuse to take vacations as follows: the Victim—wants a vacation but remains imprisoned in the office by his or her boss; the Mouse—hounded by constant fear of being replaced at his or her job while on vacation; the Follower—work is much easier than planning a vacation; the Spendthrift—will never save or spend money for a vacation; and even the Crook—an embezzler who must work 52 weeks a year to cover his thievery.[8]

Some people, of course, just prefer to keep their normal routine or lack interest in many of the activities typically associated with a vacation. The following describes how I have sometimes felt on vacation:

> A woman walks into water
> slowly, like a final act.
>
> I am drinking gin
> almost as if by decree.
>
> A vacation is a little time
> without a dream.
>
> In place of imagination
> there is the sea.

Although only about five per cent of all U.S. corporations require their employees to take vacations, many physicians believe that vacations often play an important role in relieving work-related tension. Such tension may cause headaches, insomnia, irritability, family conflict, alcoholism, etc.

While the use of a vacation for tourism may explore new environments and pursue unique experiences, many vacationers prefer their experiences and surroundings to remain familiar. Cohen has characterized tourists according to how much novelty and familiarity the tourist desires in vacation travel.[9] The organized mass tourist is the least adventurous and remains largely confined to an "environmental bubble" throughout the trip; the stops on the tour are planned in advance and guided. This tourist buys a package tour in much the same way as purchasing a radio. The individual mass tourist still uses a package tour but in this case the tour isn't entirely planned, and the tourist may occasionally venture out of the "environmental bubble." The "explorer" arranges the trip alone and tries to experience novel environments, but still retains some of the basic routines and comforts of his/her way of life. The fourth type of tourist, who Cohen has called "the drifter," is furthest removed from his/her accustomed ways of living.[9] He/she tends to make it alone, living among the people and taking odd jobs to keep going. The drifter has no fixed itinerary or timetable and is almost totally involved with the host culture.

Each of these types of tourist is increasingly less plugged into the commercial tourist trade. The fourth type, the drifter, may in many ways be said to be closest to many of the leisure ideals of the ancient Greeks. That is, he/she is most likely to have an absence of the necessity of being occupied. The term "bumming around" conveys what many in our society think of those who wish to see the world on its own terms. For the drifter (or bum) work is secondary to wandering, and people for whom work is secondary are suspicious to many in our society. College students who do such drifting can justify it for a little while as a break from routine, but when it affects the rest of their lives they, too, are just "bumming around" in the eyes of many.

## Sunday or the Sabbath

Sunday in our society serves as a day of Christian religious observance and also as a day of leisure for most of us. However, the concept of a special day for rest and religious observance is a tradition that predates Christianity. The Jewish Sabbath evolved as a special day, to be set aside from other days as a sign of the covenant between God and Israel. No work was to be done on that day, travel and business transactions were not allowed and even food had to be prepared on the preceding day. Even though these regulations were restrictive, the Jews regarded the Sabbath with joy and pleasure.[5] This holiday affirmed Israel's faith in God.

For early Christians the origin of Sunday was obvious: Sunday, the first day of the week, was the day of Christ's resurrection from the dead. For some time, however, these Christians continued to celebrate the Jewish Sabbath. The actual designation of Sunday as a day of worship and rest evolved gradually. The New Testament in no way provided any authority for such a designation, nor is there any indication that either Jesus or the early Christian leaders thought of Sunday as a continuation of the Jewish Sabbath simply continued to another day. It was not until the Puritan movement of the sixteenth century that the Lord's Day began to be referred to as the Sabbath, and laws were enacted to make it a day of rest, quiet, and religious observance.

During the fifteenth century the disagreement between Puritans and non-Puritans concerning appropriate behavior on Sunday grew quite bitter in England. Compulsory church attendance was the rule in early seventeenth century England, and it was not of the Puritans' doing. However, the rest of the day was given over to sports, dancing and other forms of recreation. The Puritans objected to this, believing that no recreation whatsoever was appropriate on Sunday. Such attitudes were based upon the Old Testament interpretation of the Sabbath which King James challenged by issuing a pronouncement, the *Book of Sports*, in 1618. It was the King's pleasure, the pronouncement stated:

> that after the end of Divine Worship, our good people not be disturbed, letted or discouraged from any lawful Recreation, such as dancing, either men or women, archeries for men, leaping, vaulting, or other harmless Recreation, nor from having of May-games, Whitson Ales, and Morris dances, and the setting up of Maypoles and other sports therewith . . .[10]

Unlawful pastimes, however, such as bull- or bear-baiting, were prohibited, as were "interludes."

The bitterness of the dispute in England concerning Sunday recreation was so great that, when the Puritans took power, they had the Book of Sports burned by the public hangman. The Puritans took this attitude of intolerance to America, and continued to try to prohibit all forms of recreation on Sunday. While attitudes toward Sunday recreation slowly changed, the issue was widely debated; change did not come without bitter fighting. Rural areas were slower to change such customs than urban ones. In South Carolina, for instance, church attendance was compulsory until 1885.[10] While some members of the clergy began to support Sunday recreation, others preached against it. "You cannot serve God and skylark on a bicycle," one minister told his congregation.[10] A number of "blue laws" were enacted by local governments which specifically forbade individuals from participating in a wide range of leisure activities, made it illegal for movie theaters, dance halls, taverns, and other places of amusement to open, and tried to enforce a general halt to pleasure-seeking.

In spite of such ordinances Sunday gradually became a day devoted to social and recreational activities as well as to worship. As commercial recreation opportunities expanded, Sunday blue laws began to have a negative effect on the local economy as well as on people's enjoyment. Today, although some blue laws continue to exist, few are enforced. The extent to which Sunday is differentiated from other days varies in different regions of the United States. While the "Sabbath" is less a day of rest than formerly, it continues to be a day away from paid employment for most people, as well as one of religious observance for many. Nowadays Sunday is somewhere between a holy day and a holiday.

## LEISURE AND ORGANIZED RELIGION

Organized religion shapes leisure behavior in a number of ways. The ideals and beliefs of the religion define, to some extent, the relation of humans to a supreme being and delineate those human qualities and behavior which are worthy and those which are sinful. All these beliefs will shape the leisure values and behavior of followers of the religion. Additionally, organized religion usually addresses the question of what forms of pleasure are worthwhile.

Established religions are also able to exert a restrictive influence on the ways in which the general public is able to spend its leisure, although this influence is generally less today than it was in the past. One example is restrictive Sunday legislation, which has affected people in many countries during many periods in history. In England, for instance, the Lord's Day Observance Act of 1780, drawn up by the Bishop of London, severely limited Sunday trade.[6] All places of commercial entertainment were to be closed. Subsequent legislation closed public houses on Sunday and prohibited the sale of newspapers, tobacco, and even implements for shaving.

A very different example of religious influence on leisure patterns may be seen in the Mexican institution of bullfighting. Kluckholn and Strodbeck have described the typical Mexican's passive dependence upon the saints and his/her submissive and accepting attitude toward the super-natural.[11] These attitudes are reflected in many of their leisure pursuits, such as bullfighting. The domination of the bull by the matador and the submissive behavior the matador expects from his assistants may be said to stress the attitudes of fatalism and submission.

In America and Europe the Church's traditional attitude toward games has been one of condemning them outright, or at least controlling them, with the strongest opposition usually reserved for games of chance. Kaplan has argued that this is because, in such games, one's luck is uncontrollable whereas, according to the church, God is not at all fickle; He establishes an order with cause and effect.[12] Religious belief, based upon reward for good behavior and punishment for bad, cannot permit luck to become viewed as a powerful factor.

In specific terms, then, organized religious institutions have sought to ban some forms of leisure behavior and to promote others. While it is impossible to generalize about these forms of leisure behavior, those activities which historically have been condemned most widely include (1) theatrical productions, (2) consumption of alcohol or other drugs, (3) games of chance and gambling, (4) dancing, (5) sexually related activity, (6) idleness, and (7) violence or cruelty.

The Puritans who settled in America were opposed to most forms of recreation, and even today not all of their attitudes have disappeared. We have come to use the term "puritan" to describe someone who is against pleasure, who is a prude. The Puritan attitude toward leisure and recreation actually came about for a number of reasons. Part of the Puritan distrust of pleasure resulted from dissent against the Anglican Church—the Catholic Church which, in fourteenth century England, had become increasingly worldly.[10] True spiritual values, the Puritans believed, could only be realized if one refused the pleasures of the world.

There was also a reflection of class conflict in the behavior of the Puritans. These people, who were from the lower classes, resented the pleasures of the rich, which they could not afford. Resentment towards the privileged "leisure class" easily led to a condemnation of the pleasures of which they partook. As Dulles has pointed out, "These two influences, spiritual reform and economic envy, can never be disentangled."[10] Additionally, the Puritans who settled in New England had little time for pleasure, as they were struggling to exist in a hostile land. The work ethic and their disdain for pleasure and idleness were, to some extent, necessary to help insure survival. Those who wish to improve themselves economically often take on some of the traits we associate with Puritanism. The Chinese, under Mao, adopted many ways of behaving similar to Puritanism in order to make the "great leap forward" economically. In times of economic plenty, Puritanism has nearly always declined.

Many of the Puritans who settled in North America believed in original sin. "In Adam's fall, we sinned all." Believing that mankind was inherently sinful, and maintaining an Old Testament attitude toward sin, the conclusion was logical that man was in need of punishment. They believed that as humans we were not worthy of pleasure. Belief in original sin may have been the biggest religious barrier to the pleasurable use of leisure in North America and, perhaps, in other countries as well.

The notion of predestination was also subscribed to by many Puritans. It was believed to be predetermined at birth that some people would go to heaven, while others would not. Those who were among the "elect" would show some sign of their good fortune while on earth, and such a sign was usually economic well-being. The Puritans worked tirelessly to get ahead to try to achieve this economic well-being and thus show that they were going to heaven.

It would be incorrect, however, to assume that the Puritans were successful in halting recreation and leisure activity. The rules of conduct were so strict for church members that only 4,000 out of 16,000 arrivals at Massachusetts Bay Colony belonged to the Church.[10] Taverns sprang up in New England, and drinking became an outlet for many. As Dulles has stated, regarding the Massachusetts Bay Colony as being devoid of all amusement ignores the fact that large numbers of its settlers were not sympathetic to Puritanism and could not be convinced to equate pleasure with sin. "Puritanism failed to eradicate the early Americans' natural urge for play. It brought on the inevitable revolt against attempted suppression of human impulses."[10]

While organized religion continued to exert pressure for prohibiting certain forms of recreation and leisure, it also gradually came to promote many forms of such activity. Slowly the Church came to understand that objecting to idleness or drinking did little good if the substitute was always more work. Since factory workers were usually working 10 to 12 hours a day, the Church's warnings against strong drink and idleness often fell on deaf ears.

Gradually the Church began to realize that it could not impose its will upon an increasingly urban population without some accommodation to prevailing conditions. If the Church disapproved of commercial recreation, it had to provide some alternatives. As the Northwestern Christian Advocate stated: "If amusing young people aids to save them, then the work is fully and gloriously worthy of the church."[10] During the close of the nineteenth century the churches made increasing provision for recreation and social activities. Libraries, gymnasiums, auditoriums, and other facilities became part of the facilities at churches. Activities such as pot luck suppers, strawberry festivals, raffles, charades, fairs, and athletic events have become standard offerings of many churches.

Religious reformers of this era were also responsible for the development of formal organizations "which purported to provide wholesome, moral and character-building experiences that would prevent the evils of the adult world from tempting young people into partaking of sinful pleasures."[13] Such organizations as the Young Men's Christian Association, Young Women's Christian Association, Young Men's Hebrew Association, Young Women's Hebrew Association, Catholic Youth Organization, Salvation Army, B'nai B'rith, and the Christian Service Brigade/Pioneer Girls are examples of groups which evolved as alternatives to saloons, pool halls, and idleness.

Today, agencies affiliated with major religious orders are among the most active voluntary organizations addressing leisure needs. The "Y," for example, has assumed a large responsibility in many communities for meeting public recreation needs. In a number of smaller cities and towns, it provides the best facilities for indoor sports and games, physical fitness activities, and social and cultural programs. These agencies are more and more inclusive in terms of who may participate.

## LEISURE EXPERIENCE AS RELIGION

Much of the dissatisfaction with religious institutions today centers around the great extent to which they have become rational, serious bureaucracies devoid of celebration. Congregations are often bored, and churches have become filled with a commercial spirit. The sense of mystery, so necessary for faith, is gone for many. Ceremony and ritual are sometimes missing, or are reflections of past cultures to which we can barely relate. To the extent that spiritual expression is nearly lacking or unsatisfying in existing organized religion, three kinds of alternatives have emerged to try to fill the void.

First has been the return to fundamental Christianity, and to ways of practicing religion associated with former times. If modern religion has lost its way, then for many the solution has been to return to religion as it was practiced in previous times, when it had more meaning. Such religious practice is characterized by a new emphasis upon the importance of faith, a greater dedication to the teachings of Christ, a missionary approach to non-believers, and emotional celebrative worship. Along with these beliefs has been an attempt to re-emphasize the concept of sin, as well as that of religious joy.

A second approach to finding new meaning in spiritual terms has been widespread interest in new cults, such as Reverend Moon's Reunification Church or the Hare Krishna sects. Such groups, which require total dedication from their members, are characterized by secrecy, individual devotion to and dependence upon other members of the group, and personal sacrifice for the goals of the organization. Such behavior may serve to shield the individual from the meaninglessness of society at large.

A third approach in seeking more satisfying spiritual expression is to use some leisure experience or activity as a means of finding satisfaction. While any leisure activity may serve as the means for such spiritual expression, certain activities such as wilderness camping, growing plants, taking drugs, and jogging seem to be more obvious in their contributions to some individuals' spiritual needs. In wilderness camping and other outdoor recreation activities which isolate the individual from others, as opposed to mass outdoor recreation, one may gain, according to Aldo Leopold, "the perception of the natural processes by which the land and the living things upon it have achieved their characteristic forms (evolution) and by which they maintain their existence (ecology)."[14]

Another leisure experience which has served as a religious experience for many is jogging. One survey of joggers, for instance, found that over one-half of the respondents reported experiencing a spiritual high while running. Higdon saw the following parallel between the born-again Christian and the "born-again" runner:

> There is the phenomenon of the born-again runner, akin to the born-again Christian; the individual, often-middle-aged who might have been active athletically in youth, but then lapsed into sinful ways; eating too much, drinking too much. . . . allowing the body, described by the scriptures as the "temple of the spirit" to degenerate to the point where the temple appeared threatened by destruction (i.e., occluded coronary arteries).
>
> When that person decides to run, it is a form of spiritual as well as a physical awakening, a conversion to a new discipline which will result in a rebirth of the spirit.[15]

Running may represent the form by which many practice their religious beliefs. Running itself is for many no less an act of purification than prayer or confession. Running expert George Sheehan has said that the runner's spiritual experience occurs in what he calls the "transpersonal stage" of

**FIGURE 6-3** For the "born again" runner, running is an expression of religious belief. (Courtesy of the American Heart Association)

running. According to Sheehan, this stage often comes after 30 minutes into the run when "meditation becomes contemplation: what has been a measure of things become awareness of the sacred."[16] For the jogger, running can become a mystical experience which transports the normal ego into deeper transpersonal spaces. For the transpersonal runner, life may begin to revolve around running, which represents an encounter with the sacred.

In Britain, sociologists Edgell and Jary have shown that the game of soccer has many features similar to a religion. A soccer field can possess the aura of a church.[17] A sports writer expressed an almost religious feeling when he said, "Whenever I arrive at any football (soccer) ground, or merely pass close to one when it is silent, I experience a unique altering of the senses. The movement evokes my past in an instantaneous rapport which is more certain, more secret than memory."[17] Professional soccer players have reported a similar sense of awe. Soccer fans, when giving traditional cheers and responses, participate in ritual and ceremony. Edgell and Jary concluded that an argument for soccer as a form of religion stresses not only its function in providing identification with a particular group or nation, but also its capacity to generate a wider, more universal sense of shared humanity, or what may be called "the ultimate."

## Stages of Participation

Regardless of the leisure activity which serves as religious experience, it is likely that a given leisure activity will provide such experience only after the individual has gone through a series of stages of participation. Sociologist Hobson Bryan has characterized these stages as follows:

1. Newcomers to the activity are interested in getting results, any results. The individual who has just begun hiking, for instance, may merely want to get from point A to point B in relative comfort. The beginning tennis player may seek merely to hit the ball across the net.

2. As the leisure activity becomes established behavior, the participant becomes more competent and seeks to show that competence with a number of successes or by operating in settings which provide greater challenges. The hiker may choose longer trails or more rugged terrain. The tennis player may win a match with one opponent and then seek to win a match against several other players or against tougher opponents.

3. After the "generalist" stage, above, the participant is likely to become more specialized. The tennis player, for instance, may become a "clay court" specialist or play a certain strategy, such as "serve and volley." A fisherman may become a fly fisherman or specialize in trout fishing. A photographer may become interested in all kinds of gadgets and specialized equipment.

4. Finally, according to Bryan, there are those participants who place the greatest emphasis upon doing the activity for its own sake, for whom the quality of the experience is most important.

Comprised in this category are the "artist photographers" who view the camera as a means to creative expression. Here too are found the hunter who minimizes the importance of the kill, the hiker who seeks the challenge of unguided journeys, and the "free-climber" who enjoys the form, the process of the activity. These are the core members of leisure social worlds. They sometimes center much of their lives and identities around their sports or hobbies.[18]

The fourth category is where we are likely to find those for whom participation in a given leisure activity takes on spiritual qualities. Here the participant begins to value the activity for its own sake, meaning that participation is undertaken based upon faith in the activity, an intuitive belief in its worth. All of us have met people who "believe" in some leisure activity. At this stage, leisure becomes a pleasurable compulsion. It is, as Pieper has stated, celebration, and such celebration is the highest form of religious expression.

To conclude this chapter, you will be asked to examine your leisure activities as they relate to religious experience.

# Leisure Exercise 6·1

## Leisure As Religious Participation

1. Think about your own leisure activities in relation to Bryan's four stages of participation. Is there any leisure activity in which you participate in which you have reached the fourth and final stage? If "no," why do you think you have not?

2. If "yes," what is the activity or one such activity? Describe how you moved from Stage 1 of participation in the activity through Stage 4.

3. Does participation in the activity fulfill any spiritual or religious need for you? Describe any religious or spiritual aspects of your participation.

**163**

## STUDY QUESTIONS

1. What makes celebration a common link between religion and leisure?

2. Do "holy days" ever become holidays? Give an example and discuss how the change took place.

3. Discuss the four different kinds of tourist identified by Cohen. Which type are you likely to be? Why?

4. How did the tradition of observing Sunday come about? How has its observance changed?

5. What are some major ways in which organized religion shapes leisure behavior in our society?

## REFERENCES

1. Stein, Jess. (ed.), *The Random House Dictionary of the English Language.* New York: Random House, 1966, p. 1212.
2. Pieper, Josef. *Leisure—The Basis of Culture.* New York: New American Library, 1952, pp. 43–45.
3. Brightbill, Charles K. *The Challenge of Leisure.* Englewood Cliffs, N.J.: Prentice-Hall, 1960, p. 38.
4. Dahl, Gordon. *Work, Play, and Worship in a Leisure-Oriented Society.* Minneapolis: Augsburg Publishing, 1972, p. 74.
5. Lee, Robert. *Religion and Leisure In America.* New York: Abingdon Press, 1964, p. 33.
6. Godbey, Geoffrey, and Parker, Stanley. *Leisure Studies and Services: An Overview.* Philadelphia: W. B. Saunders, 1976, p. 52.
7. Greif, Martin. *The Holiday Book: America's Festivals and Celebrations.* New York: Universe Books, 1978, pp. 1–255.
8. Rakstis, Ted. "Why You Need a Vacation," *Today's Health,* August, 1969, p. 25.
9. Cohen, Eric. "Toward a Sociology of Internal Tourism," *Social Research,* Vol. 39, Spring, 1972, pp. 164–182.
10. Dulles, Rhea Foster. *A History of Recreation: America Learns to Play.* New York: Appleton-Century-Crofts, 1965, p. 151.
11. Kluckholn, F., and Strodbeck, F. *Variations In Value Orientations.* New York: Row and Peterson, 1961, p. 235.
12. Kaplan, Max. *Leisure In America.* New York: John Wiley and Sons, 1960, p. 150.

13. Farrell, Patricia. "Recreation Youth-Serving Agencies," in Godbey, Geoffrey, *Recreation, Park, and Leisure Services: Foundations, Organization, Administration.* Philadelphia: W. B. Saunders, 1978, p. 188.

14. Leopold, Aldo. *A Sand County Almanac.* New York: Oxford University Press, 1949, p. 19.

15. Higdon, Hal. "Running and the Mind," *Runner's World,* January, 1978, p. 36.

16. Sheehan, George. "Dr. Sheehan on Running," *Runner's World,* May, 1979, p. 35.

17. Edgell, S., and Jary, D. "Football: A Sociological Eulogy," in Smith, M. A., et al. (eds.), *Leisure and Society in Britain.* London: Allen Lane, 1974, pp. 74-82.

18. Bryan, Hobson. "Conflict in the Great Outdoors," University, Alabama: University of Alabama, Bureau of Public Administration, 1979, p. 87-88.

# chapter 7

# Leisure throughout the life cycle

**M**any leisure activities which did not interest you as a child are now important to you. It is sometimes difficult for us to understand the pleasure that those in different stages of the life cycle derive from certain leisure activities. During the journey from birth to death the activities which we find pleasurable, what we do voluntarily, and the economic and social constraints on our free time, health, and work roles are in a state of change, and these changes affect our leisure attitudes and behavior.

Many changes which take place in regard to our leisure behavior throughout the life cycle are due more to changes in social situation which may be associated with different ages. For instance, it may be more important that a married couple's children have all left home, in terms of impact on their leisure patterns, than that the couple has advanced from the age of 40 to 50. Leaving high school may change recreation and leisure patterns more than the passage of years from 15 to 20. Kelly has found the family life cycle was a better predictor of participation in outdoor recreation than age.[1] Being a parent of a preschooler, for instance, may be more relevant than age in decreasing participation in activities, such as golf and tennis, but increasing the use of swimming pools in order to take the children swimming.

In attempting to divide the life cycle into stages, there is little agreement

**167**

among social scientists concerning what the precise age limits should be for each stage. Age stages, of course, can't be thought of as fixed and absolute. We don't all make the same major life transitions, such as marriage, at the same age and, indeed, some don't make them at all. While marriage has a profound impact upon the leisure behavior of individuals, some today will not marry, marry at different ages, marry more than once, or live unmarried with their mates. Thus, life stages are overlapping and subject to wide individual variation. Consequently, although we can't make absolute divisions, Levinson has divided life into the following stages: (1) childhood—0 to 12 years; (2) adolescence—13 to 21 years; (3) early adulthood—21 to 40 years; (4) middle adulthood—40 to 65 years; (5) late adulthood—65 to 75 years; (6) old age—75 and over.[2]

If we view life from a "developmental" or "life stage" standpoint, then we believe that we continue to change and evolve and to do so by stages which have some similarities for most people. Table 7-1 shows various stages of the life cycle as well as those who serve as the most important references for the individual in decision-making.[3] The model is meant to apply to those who are contemporary, urban, middle-class Americans. It identifies major "themes" in regard to values at a particular stage of life, as well as dilemmas between major value themes. These value conflicts are of differing intensity for different individuals. For example, in early adolescence, acceptance by one's peers may conflict with achievement in school to the extent that working to achieve good grades doesn't help or actually hurts the extent to which one is accepted by one's peers. Thus, the challenge of achieving good grades might conflict with the security provided by peer acceptance. In early-maturity, the desire to succeed in one's career may involve taking risks which threaten one's stability. These changing values and attempts to integrate conflicting values directly shape the role of leisure in our lives, as well as where and with whom it occurs.

## LIFE STAGES AND LEISURE'S FUNCTIONS

If we examine various life stages, it quickly becomes apparent that leisure fulfills different social functions. There are some leisure activities one typically does alone, some done only with members of the same (or opposite) sex, some done only with one's peers (others whose status is roughly equal to ours), and some which are usually done with one's parents, spouse, children, or relatives.

As Cheek and Burch have pointed out, many leisure activities are undertaken not because of an individual personal preference or because a particular leisure activity is uniquely appealing.[4] Rather, they are undertaken because they permit the strengthening or maintenance of social bonds with friends, neighbors, or kin. Thus, while at an individual level, an adult male or

TABLE 7-1   HUMAN LIFE CYCLE: ROLES AND VALUES*

| Life-Cycle Stage; Approximate Ages or Timing | Most Significant Others | Major dilemma of value-theme differentiation and integration | | |
|---|---|---|---|---|
| | | Security | vs. | Challenge |
| I. Infancy 0–12 months | Mothering one | Affective gratification | vs. | Sensorimotor experiencing |
| II. Early childhood ~~1~~5 years | Mother, father | Compliance | vs. | Self-control |
| III. ~~Oedipal period~~ ~~3 years~~ | Father, mother, siblings, playmates | Expressivity | vs. | Instrumentality |
| IV. Later childhood 6–11 years | Parents, same-sex peers, teachers | Peer relationships | vs. | Evaluated abilities |
| V. Early adolescence 12–18 years | Parents, same-sex peers, opposite-sex peers, teachers | Acceptance | vs. | Achievement |
| VI. ~~Later adolescence~~ ~~16–18/20 years~~ | Opposite-sex peers, same-sex peers, parents, teachers, lover(s), husband, wife, employers | Intimacy | vs. | Autonomy |
| VII. Young adulthood or youth 19/21– 20–29 years | Lover(s), wife or husband, children, employers, friends | Connection | vs. | Self-determination |
| VIII. ~~Early~~ maturity ~~30–45~~ years  30– Retirement | Wife or husband, lover(s), children, superiors, colleagues, friends, parents | Stability | vs. | Accomplishment |
| IX. Full maturity 45 to age of retirement | Wife or husband, lover(s), grown children, colleagues, friends, younger associates | Dignity | vs. | Control |
| X. Retirement retirement age to onset of severe illness | Remaining family, lover(s), long-term friends, neighbors | Meaningful integration | vs. | Autonomy |
| XI. Disability onset of severe illness to death | Remaining family, friends, medical professionals, caregivers | Survival | vs. | Acceptance of death |

*SOURCE: Chad Gordon, Charles Gaitz, and Judith Scott, "Leisure and Lives: Personal Expressivity Across the Life Span," in Binstock, R., and Shanas, E. (eds.), Handbook of Aging and the Social Sciences. New York: Van Nostrand Reinhold, 1976, p. 317.

female might prefer a game of tennis to Monopoly, the family's group decision may be to play Monopoly in order to be with one another, enjoy each other's company, or show each other respect.

After studying leisure behavior patterns and motivations for participating in them, Kelly has concluded that participation in various leisure activities can be explained in terms of the extent to which they correspond to one of the following:

1. Unconditional leisure. Such activities are relatively unconstrained by one's family and social roles and are chosen primarily because the activity is satisfying in and of itself. Examples might include pleasure reading or learning pottery-making.
2. Compensatory and recuperative leisure. These activities are chosen because of what the activity is expected to do for the individual. It is a desirable contrast from the constraints and conditions of work. It may be negatively conditioned by employment, such as the need to relax, or it may be a need for stimulation or excitement. Watching television or going to the movies are examples.
3. Relational leisure. Such activities are not undertaken because the individual feels their role requires it, but because of the positive values of building and maintaining personal relationships. Activities such as entertaining at home, marital affection, and playing with children are chosen primarily because the companionship is enriching.
4. Role-determined leisure. These activities also are ones in which social relationships are central to the decision to participate, but there is in addition a strong component of responding to role expectations of those who have the greatest influence upon an individual's self-evaluation, especially family. Playing golf with your boss or taking the children to an amusement park could be examples.[5]

Kelly found that, while with most leisure activities there was considerable mixing of reasons, many activities were undertaken mainly within one of these categories. Sports, for example, were highly likely to be unconditional while family activities were disproportionately relational.

The extent to which leisure activity is undertaken with these various motivations appears to vary throughout the life cycle. In regard to participation in voluntary associations, for instance, Babchuk and Booth have indicated that children tend to affiliate and participate in organizations and activities which might be classified as "unconditional leisure."[6] Among adults, particularly males, such participation is more likely to become compensatory-recuperative, relational, or role-determined. When an individual reaches old age, involvement once again is likely to become unconditional.

Thus, the motivations and satisfactions associated with leisure activity may vary according to our stage in the life cycle. Let's examine how leisure patterns change throughout the life cycle.

## Childhood

For preschool children it may not make sense to use the term "leisure," since there is little division between work and leisure for children. Their freedom to choose what they want to do (or know how to do) is greatly restricted by lack of money, transportation, parental control, and their lack of experience in the world. Children are involved in the magical world of play. We may attempt to explain play in a number of ways. Play is distinct from work in that it involves the child's internal reality (fantasy) rather than external reality. It is self-motivated behavior—you cannot force a child to play. Huizinga has defined characteristics of play as follows: (1) voluntary behavior; (2) a stepping outside of ordinary life; (3) secluded and limited in time and space; (4) not serious but absorbs the player intensely; (5) bounded by rules; (6) promotes formation of social groups which surround themselves with secrecy.[7] When at play, Huizinga said, children know they are playing and, even though deeply absorbed in what they are doing, understand that play is not like the rest of life. Play, he contended, is irrational; it is done for its own sake and can't be understood in purely rational, scientific terms. Children play because they want to, because it is fun.

Even though play may not be done for any purpose outside itself, many social scientists believe that play serves as a way in which the child takes on the culture he or she is born into. It is also sometimes considered to be a way for the child to resolve conflicts without serious consequence. Sutton-Smith has suggested that through play a child may "test out" his/her curiosities without experiencing repercussions in the event of failure.[8]

Play has more recently been conceptualized as arousal-seeking behavior by Berlyne, who believed play is caused by the need to find some optimum level of arousal for the individual.[9] Finding this optimum level causes the individual to interact with the environment or self to increase his/her level of interest or stimulation. Stimuli which cause this arousal involve novelty, complexity, or the transmission of new information. Because the optimum level of arousal is different for different individuals, some play activities may be satisfying for some individuals but not for others. Arousal-seeking is a theory which fits equally well for work and play and, in fact, questions the validity of separating work and play.

White has sought to explain play in terms of a need to show the ability to control or produce effects upon the environment.[10] An example might be putting together a puzzle even though there is no reward for it, or tossing a ball of wadded paper into a trash can from a long distance. Such behavior is a form of mastering the environment, even though it is not done for external reward.

**FIGURE 7-1** Children play because they want to. Because it is fun. (Courtesy of Liselott Diem)

These theories have a close relation since producing an effect in the environment may be thought of as a kind of arousal-seeking. Play theorist and researcher Michael Ellis has integrated existing play theory in the following extraordinary paragraph:

> The formulations of play as caused by arousal-seeking and learning and the cognitive dynamics of development can be integrated in this way. The arousal-seeking model explains the mechanism driving the individual into engagement with the environment in ways surplus to the need of immediate survival. The consequences of such behavior come, via learning, to condition the content of the behavior so motivated. The accumulative effect of such learning interacts with the arousal-seeking motive to produce an upward spiral in the complexity of the interactions. Similarities in that developmental path have led to the separation of the continuous process of growth into developmental stages where growing individuals are seen to move through similar phases at approximately the same time.[11]

In other words, play occurs because the individual seeks arousal in ways beyond immediate survival. What happens to the individual because of this play behavior shapes the future play so that, combined with continuing desire for arousal, the play becomes more complex. The development of more and more complex levels of play happens in most children at approximately the same age.

## Playgrounds

Because play increases in complexity as it evolves, many public playgrounds are not really appropriate places for children to play, because most play equipment has a single static use which does not increase in complexity. We may remember that, as children, we often tried to increase the complexity of our play in playgrounds by walking up the sliding board backwards, standing up on the swings or swinging sideways, suddenly jumping off seesaws, and acting in ways which adults thought were inappropriate. Perhaps if the playground provided for a progression of increasing complexity, the child would not have to "invent" it. Certainly many playgrounds are underused or used for only a short period of time. A study of playgrounds in Philadelphia by Wade, for instance, found that children stayed an average of play 15 minutes at the playground and made practically no use of play equipment which could not be manipulated.[12]

The "Adventure" playground movement, which has migrated from Europe to the United States, advocates play areas in which children have greater freedom to play at increasing levels of complexity, stimulation, and risk. Adventure playgrounds give the child a greater role in determining what forms of play and uses of equipment are proper. They provide the child with more opportunity to select or construct the equipment with which he/she wishes to play, but have often been criticized for being dangerous.

## Shapers of Children's Play

Several variables are important in helping to shape children's play patterns, including the child's sex, age, social class, style of upbringing, and the culture in which the child is raised. The social class of a child's parents, for instance, may greatly determine how much space a child has in which to play. In an apartment, particularly a high-rise, parents may not let the child play on the grounds surrounding the building since they cannot watch the child as they could in a detached house. Parents' style of upbringing will also affect play. Many of you, for instance, were taught as a child that play was worthwhile, but only after your chores had been done. "Sure, you can go out and play. But first—clean your room." Thus, you were taught the importance or, more precisely, the centrality, of work. Other children may not have been taught this, and were left more or less free to do what they wanted. Those who have been taught to do their work first are better prepared to function in an industrial society where work is of prime importance.

The culture in which a child is brought up will also influence play. In societies which stress individual success as a goal children are more likely to play physical skill games and to use success in these games to relieve their anxiety about achievement. Failure, of course, will increase that anxiety, as I recall from my Little League days. In a society such as that of the Hopi Indians, however, children play games which imitate the activities of adults in a non-

**FIGURE 7-2** Children's play patterns are influenced by available play space. (Courtesy of Leesa Massey)

competitive way; little achievement anxiety is instilled.[13] In our own highly competitive society, parents often look for an "end product" from children's play which demonstrates achievement or success; therefore, parents structure play to achieve these aims. Beauty pageants or competitive swimming meets for young girls or Cub Scout merit badges for young boys are examples. Perhaps it can be said that all societies demonstrate important aspects of their culture by the ways in which their young play.

## Adolescence

It was not until recently in the Western World that adolescents or "teenagers" achieved a separate status from adults and children. The term "teenager" did not appear in the American vocabulary until the 1930s. It has been argued that increased technology, urbanization, and specialization of society have produced problems which are either exclusive to this age group or more intense than in others. Perhaps because of this, as sociologist James Coleman has observed, "There are few periods of life in which associations are so strong, intimate, and all-encompassing as those that develop during adolescence."[14]

Teenagers experience a great confusion of values. While there is a strong trend toward social conformity with their peer group, there is also a shifting back and forth from childish to more adult behavior. In some ways, teenagers suffer from the same lack of clearly defined roles as do the elderly in our society. As Bennett Berger has stated,

> The well-publicized conflicts and tensions of the teen-age "transitional stage" stem from the combination of an acceleration in the individual's physical and cultural growth with the continued refusal by society to grant to adolescents many of the rights and opportunities of adults: when sexual desires are more powerful than they ever will be, sexual opportunities are fewest; obedience and submission are asked of adolescents at precisely the time when their strength, energy, and desire for autonomy are ascendant; responsible participation in the major social institutions is denied or discouraged at the moment when their interest in the world has been poignantly awakened.[15]

Many of these situations serve to bring teenagers closer to each other, as in gangs or social groups who develop leisure activity patterns which are not accepted by the rest of society. The high crime rate among teenagers, prevalent use of drugs, and high rate of auto accidents may all, to some extent, reflect this situation.

As children enter adolescence, they begin to increase their independence from their parents and are affected more by the influence of others their own

**FIGURE 7-3** Where a child plays is largely determined by social class. (Courtesy of the National Park Service)

ages. Some take part-time jobs, their mobility often increases, and thus they begin to have a greater range of options in regard to the use of leisure. Rapoport and Rapoport have used the term "preoccupation" to explain what motivates adolescents to pursue particular leisure patterns.[16] Preoccupation, a kind of mental absorption, arises from psychological and biological development interacting with social and environmental conditions. These preoccupations change at various stages of life, and the changes can be partly attributed to changes in the social roles one occupies throughout the life cycle. The Rapoports have indicated that the major preoccupations of adolescents grow out of the need for identity.[16] You may remember as a teenager "trying out" different roles or forms of behavior to see what they were like and whether or not they "fit" you. Table 7-2 shows the major preoccupations of adolescence, and the interests and examples of activities that emerge from such interests. As you might expect, not everyone develops

**TABLE 7-2   LEISURE IN ADOLESCENCE\***

| Preoccupations | Interests | Examples of Activities |
|---|---|---|
| Autonomy | Variety | Arts and crafts |
| Stimulation/boredom | Doing one's own thing | Dancing |
| Work | Rapidly changing activities and situations | Mountaineering |
| Sociability | | Music—listening and |
| Physical maturation | Brightness and noise | playing |
| Mental development | Work prospects | Going to class |
| Environmental experience | Bodily: sex play and fashion | Rock festivals |
| | | Travel |
| Moral sensitivity | Experience | Sports—football, soccer, |
| Balance | Acquiring knowledge | etc. |
| | Exploring, feeling, seeing life | Biking |
| | | Visiting with friends |
| | Religion, politics | |
| | Novelty | |

| Sex and class differences\* | | |
|---|---|---|
| | **Boys** | **Girls** |
| Middle class | Go out more often | Go out less |
| | | More leisure time |
| Working class | Less leisure | Go out less |
| | | Less leisure |

| **Both** | | |
|---|---|---|
| Physical activity | | |

\*SOURCE: Adapted from Rhona and Robert Rapoport, *Leisure and the Family Life Cycle.* Boston: Routledge, 1975, by Barbara A. Wood, *in* "Leisure Patterns Throughout the Life Cycle: Policy Implications For Providers of Leisure Services." Term paper, Pennsylvania State University, 1978. p. 7.

all these preoccupations, nor do they always lead to the same interests and activities. They do, however, provide a useful guide to the concerns of adolescents. While these activities are not the only ones engaged in, those activities which are undertaken are likely to be done to satisfy the preoccupations mentioned.

In adolescence, the individual must internalize the knowledge and attitudes appropriate to certain adult roles. Most adolescents in our culture, for instance, must learn the appropriate driving rules and regulations to pass a state driving examination. Similarly, he or she must learn safe and legal driving techniques or risk fines, injury, or even death.

During this period the individual is also going through small successive shifts in status and role which often make the juvenile uncertain as to how he or she should behave. With increasing age and education, generally, comes increasing freedom and access to resources. Adolescents also appear to have more time for leisure and higher participation rates in leisure activities than their older counterparts. As may be seen in Table 7-3, teenagers are more likely to participate in most forms of outdoor recreation than those who are older, unless an automobile is involved.

It is often argued that at this stage of the life cycle a separate "youth culture" emerges, complete with separate values, music, clothing, hair styles, social concerns, language, attitudes, and sexual mores. Members of such a culture are, in some ways, segregated from the rest of society, particularly in the case of male adolescents. Hanging out on street corners, in cars, or at the local amusement arcade, teenagers often appear to withdraw into a separate society which has neither the status of children nor of adults.

# Adulthood

Becoming an adult in our society is something that doesn't happen all at once at a given age. With regard to one's use of leisure, also, one finds certain options open at different ages: being eligible to drive for pleasure at one age, enter a nightclub at another, buy a snowmobile on credit at another. In one sense, when teenagers long for adulthood in our society, they are longing for leisure—freedom to do what they want when they want.

Rather than considering adulthood as a single period, it makes more sense to envision it as several periods with different preoccupations, interests, and changing patterns of leisure. The Rapoports have divided these periods into early adulthood, middle adulthood, and late adulthood or retirement.

## Early Adulthood

During the years of young adulthood, ages sixteen through the early twenties, the leisure pattern which an individual adopts depends upon the life style he or she assumes. The Rapoports have characterized such styles as straight and conforming, student, involuntarily unemployed, and alterna-

## TABLE 7-3 PERCENTAGE OF RESPONDENTS PARTICIPATING IN OUTDOOR RECREATION ACTIVITIES DURING 1977*

| Activity | Age Category | | | | | | |
|---|---|---|---|---|---|---|---|
| | 12-17 | 18-24 | 25-34 | 35-44 | 45-54 | 55-64 | 65 and over |
| Camping in developed area | 40 | 45 | 38 | 36 | 23 | 21 | 8 |
| Camping in primitive area | 31 | 36 | 27 | 24 | 13 | 7 | 5 |
| Canoeing, kayaking, or river-running | 29 | 27 | 19 | 14 | 14 | 3 | 2 |
| Sailing | 19 | 17 | 13 | 12 | 8 | 4 | 2 |
| Water-skiing | 23 | 31 | 21 | 17 | 9 | 3 | 0 |
| Fishing | 72 | 60 | 57 | 56 | 52 | 46 | 30 |
| Other boating | 48 | 39 | 41 | 37 | 31 | 19 | 17 |
| Outdoor pool swimming | 90 | 82 | 78 | 73 | 51 | 41 | 19 |
| Other outdoor swimming | 64 | 61 | 61 | 51 | 37 | 24 | 11 |
| Hiking or backpacking | 41 | 40 | 38 | 32 | 19 | 14 | 7 |
| Other walking or jogging | 87 | 79 | 78 | 62 | 57 | 53 | 53 |
| Bicycling | 89 | 67 | 59 | 46 | 32 | 16 | 10 |
| Horseback riding | 30 | 27 | 20 | 15 | 9 | 2 | 1 |
| Driving vehicles or motorcycles off-road | 43 | 46 | 31 | 28 | 15 | 11 | 2 |
| Tennis outdoors | 65 | 53 | 43 | 34 | 18 | 7 | 2 |
| Cross-country skiing | 5 | 4 | 3 | 3 | 1 | 1 | 0 |
| Downhill skiing | 13 | 14 | 8 | 7 | 4 | 1 | 0 |
| Ice-skating outdoors | 33 | 22 | 22 | 18 | 10 | 4 | 1 |
| Sledding | 46 | 31 | 28 | 28 | 10 | 4 | 2 |
| Snowmobiling | 14 | 15 | 10 | 6 | 5 | 4 | 1 |
| Other outdoor sports and games | 87 | 73 | 69 | 62 | 45 | 30 | 15 |
| Golf | 21 | 18 | 17 | 15 | 14 | 19 | 8 |
| Driving for pleasure | 52 | 83 | 80 | 79 | 67 | 66 | 51 |
| Visiting zoos, outdoor aquariums, fairs, etc. | 86 | 87 | 87 | 80 | 66 | 53 | 38 |
| Attending outdoor sports events | 82 | 74 | 66 | 67 | 59 | 49 | 30 |
| Attending outdoor dances, concerts, plays, etc. | 57 | 62 | 45 | 36 | 36 | 31 | 18 |
| Walking to observe nature | 54 | 47 | 60 | 62 | 48 | 43 | 33 |
| Hunting | 24 | 25 | 18 | 27 | 17 | 15 | 8 |
| Picnicking | 77 | 74 | 84 | 81 | 75 | 64 | 47 |
| Sightseeing at historical sites or natural wonders | 61 | 63 | 70 | 73 | 64 | 59 | 44 |

*SOURCE: Heritage Conservation and Recreation Service, *National Outdoor Recreation Survey*. Washington, D.C.: U.S. Department of the Interior, 1978.

tive lifestyles.[16] The major interests of individuals in all four of these lifestyles are the same but they are expressed differently.

The major preoccupations at this stage of life, according to the Rapoports, are identification with social institutions, intimacy and commitment. The commitment at this stage of life may be to a beginning career or to a marriage in the conforming lifestyle, a given field of study, certain leisure activities, or a social cause for students, a social club or gang for the involuntarily unemployed, and for those in the alternative lifestyle it may be finding a way of life which relies little upon industrial technology or pursuing some art form. Preparing for marriage at this stage of life is (still) a major commitment for many women as well as many men.

There is some "squeezing out" of interests at this stage of life, according to Lowenthal,[17] who found that high school boys began to see work as central to their lives, while high school girls viewed marriage and family as central.[17] In leisure pursuits, young men emphasized "play" or physical activity while women emphasized sociability. Newlywed men were heavily involved in preparing for their life's work, while newlywed women helped their husbands get started.

As more and more women assume careers outside the home, this stage of life is increasingly characterized by both males and females preparing for a career, often living together but not married. In an increasing number of cases, there is tension in the relationship of young couples concerning whether living arrangements should accommodate the man's or woman's career. A common characteristic of this stage of life is a constriction of leisure activities as young people focus on one major interest, such as occupation, finding a mate, or friendship with peers. Table 7-4 illustrates the preoccupations, interests, and activities of young adults.

Before proceeding further, let's examine your preoccupations, interests, and leisure activities.

**TABLE 7-4   LEISURE PATTERNS OF YOUNG ADULTHOOD***

| Preoccupations | Interests | Examples of Activities | Sex Differences | |
| --- | --- | --- | --- | --- |
| | | | Men | Women |
| Identification with social institutions | Occupational Forming relations with opposite sex | Pubs, bars, discos Movies | Play/ physical activity | Sociability Plan for marriage |
| Intimacy | Parental-familial | Dancing | | |
| Commitment | relationships | Buying clothes | | |
| | Friendships | Sports | | |
| | | Visiting with friends, family | | |
| | | Pop concerts | | |

*SOURCE: Op. cit., Wood, Table 7-2, p. 8.

# Leisure Exercise 7·1

## Preoccupations, Interests, and Leisure

1. Examine the preoccupations and interests of adolescence and young adulthood in Tables 7-2 and 7-3 (check Tables 7-4 or 7-5 if you're older). Which of the preoccupations and interests listed would you identify as your major preoccupations and interests? Do you have any which are not listed?

*My major preoccupations*

_____

_____

_____

_____

_____

*My major interests*

_____

_____

_____

_____

_____

2. Discuss the relationship of your use of leisure to these preoccupations and interests. How does your choice of leisure activities, your style of participation, the people with whom you participate, and the satisfactions you seek relate to your preoccupations and interests?

### Middle Adulthood

This phase of life stretches from the middle twenties until retirement and may, itself, be divided into three stages: early establishment, mid-establishment, and late establishment. During middle adulthood, people typically work, raise children, and pursue leisure activities. Today, compared with a decade ago, fewer children, on average, are raised within each family, and the likelihood is increasingly greater that both male and female will be employed outside the home. There is also a greater probability that the person in the middle adult stage will live alone, as compared to a decade ago. Table 7-5 shows the three subphases of middle adulthood.

**Early Establishment** In this subphase, when the couple has preschool children, their interests are likely to be home-centered. Watching television becomes a standard part of weekday evening behavior for many. Men and

**TABLE 7-5    LEISURE PATTERNS OF MIDDLE ADULTHOOD***

| Subphase | Preoccupations | Interests | Examples of Activities |
|---|---|---|---|
| Early establishment (preschool children) | Productivity: choices and plans | Home-centered | Men: do-it-yourself decorating, home improvements, fixing car<br>Women: crafts, hobbies, knitting<br>Both: TV viewing |
| Mid-establishment (children in school) | Performance: effectiveness, competence at what is chosen | Family-centered activities at home and outside; sensory and sexual gratification; competitive events | TV<br>Gardening<br>Vacations<br>Trips<br>Boating<br>Camping<br>Viewing sporting events<br>Visiting friends |
| Late establishment (children out of school) | Evaluation: meaningfulness of commitments | Things to do as couple if marriage still intact | Golf<br>Exercise<br>TV<br>Hobbies<br>Travel<br>Adult education classes |

*SOURCE: *Op. cit.,* Wood, Table 7-2, p. 10.

women may become involved during leisure in activities which have a useful end product, such as knitting, home improvements, crafts, or fixing the car.[16]

Leisure activity during this period usually becomes less spontaneous and more highly regimented and planned. For many parents of preschool children, leisure must be arranged around both work and the needs of the young children. A formerly casual trip to the movies must now be carefully planned. A babysitter must be obtained and, perhaps, picked up and returned home. The baby's feeding schedule and husband's and wife's work schedules have to be considered.

**Mid-Establishment** In this subphase, when the children are in school, the preoccupation becomes competence at what the individual has chosen to do—that is, effectiveness. This is a stage of life at which men and women are likely to be highly competitive in their careers, and leisure interests may include competitive activities as well as family-centered activities inside and outside the home. Additionally, activities providing sensory and sexual gratification are prominent. For many, this period of life produces a greater tendency toward a consumer model of leisure behavior—planned vacations, buying a boat or mobile home, dining out, etc. For those in the middle and upper social classes, the range of leisure activities undertaken may increase during this phase, both because of the children being in school and becoming more independent as well as an increase in discretionary time.

**Late Establishment** When children leave home the recreation and leisure interests of married couples, now in the late establishment subphase, center more on activities which can be done together. New interests must be developed if the couple is to withstand the strain of marriage during this stage. In many cases the demands of a career are refocused toward hobbies or other voluntary activities. Adjustment to this phase of life varies greatly: some individuals feel revitalized, able to pursue new interests and challenges for the first time; others become passive, homebound, heavy users of television—they feel old, finished, and useless.

This is not to imply that older adults and the elderly live in isolation from their children. One study of three industrial nations, including the United States, found that 84 per cent of the sample of elderly adults lived within one hour of at least one child.[17] Over three-fifths of the elderly had seen at least one child the day of the interview or the previous day.

One critical aspect of how adults adjust to this phase may be the extent to which they have recognized and planned for children leaving home. For the woman who has been a homemaker and taken primary responsibility for raising the children, this period may be especially difficult. While less attention has been paid to "retirement" from this role than to "retirement" from paid work, it is still retirement. While children don't usually cease to be in contact with their parents after leaving home, the change is great for the

**FIGURE 7-4**   Leisure activities often become more family-centered as children enter school. (Courtesy of H. Armstrong Roberts)

woman (or man) who has had primary responsibility for raising the children. Living under the same roof with one's children, sharing their daily joys and sorrows, taking responsibility for what they eat and wear, shaping how they behave is an awesome task. It involves a kind of personal sacrifice that may be difficult for many to understand. When this period of life comes to a close, the woman who has been a full-time mother and homemaker may experience a feeling of uselessness. In the late establishment subphase, the Rapaports have stated, couples are preoccupied with the meaningfulness of the commitments they have made so far in life.[16] For the homemaker, this period may actually be adjustment to retirement from the major role of her or his life.

During this period of life, men and women often change in different ways. According to Gutmann, women may become more aggressive and interested in achievement, while men become more passive.[18] This may be due to the fact that, during the early stages of parenthood, sex role distinctions are established in which women need to suppress their aggressive impulses in order to care for their children, while men need to suppress their impulses for close affiliation with the family in order to succeed as economic providers. When children grow up these suppressed elements of personality can be expressed, so that men and women move in opposite directions, but both move toward the "normal unisex of later life."[18] As older men become more tender and sensual about the world—interested in pleasant food, sights, sounds, and associations—women become more managerial, less sentimental, and less interested in communion. The husband, during post-parental years, becomes more dependent upon the wife, who becomes something of an authority to him.

Consider the extraordinary implications of this situation: women whose children have left home, seeking achievement, seeking to find ways of shaping the world which their traditional role of "primary" parent denied them; middle-aged, often with little "practice" at being aggressive in the outside world, often needing but lacking formal educational skills; and perhaps, finding that their children, especially the males, who have been socialized into patterns in which aggressive pursuit of career is important, do not seem to appreciate the mother's sacrifice. In families of lower social class career may not be important, but male children may have been socialized into the "macho" tradition, where the expression of feeling is suspect. According to psychiatrist Kathleen Mogul:

> In order to change her lifestyle during her middle years without either too much guilt and inhibition or too much angry repudiation of her former life, a woman has the psychological task of testing and making room for new identities and new self-perceptions without entirely discarding old ones that had gathered gratifications and grounds for previous self-regard. It is helpful to have social and family support for these changes and also to have denied solid gratifications from the previous roles.[19]

For women whose primary commitment has been to a career, awareness of limited time left for childbearing or mixed emotions about not having had children may produce psychological problems. It appears that for all women who formed their identity and sense of self in their youth entirely around finding a suitable mate and around motherhood, the potential for crisis is great in the middle years. When such women become "underoccupied and less needed by children who grow up and by husbands whose interests are in their careers and elsewhere, these women are very prone to depression, and they are sometimes very hard to help: the props of their previous identity have crumbled, and they had laid little groundwork for any other."[19]

While the mid-life crisis of females may revolve around work and identity, for the male the crisis may be described as follows:

> . . . the hormone production levels are dropping, the head is balding, the sexual vigor is diminishing, the stress is unending, the children are leaving, the parents are dying, the friends are having their first heart attacks, the past floats by in a fog of hopes not realized, opportunities not grasped, women not bedded, potentials not fulfilled, and the future is a confrontation with one's own mortality.[18]

Certainly, however, some of these problems are also shared by women.

A blue-collar male at middle age may find that the mid-life crisis involves feeling trapped in a job with reduced opportunities for better employment. He may question whether to stick with his job or marriage, but have no one with whom to discuss his problems. According to Gutmann, the male mid-life crisis is made worse because our culture does not readily accept the more passive, receptive, sensitive aspects of the older male.[18]

The post-parental stage of life, for all its trials, is often viewed by couples as more rewarding than the preceding stages. One study of a middle-class neighborhood found that 22 of 49 older couples considered the post-parental period of life to be "better" than the previous one, while only three said it was worse.[20] Those who said it was better mentioned the absence of certain responsibilities which allowed them new freedoms. Many families at the post-parental stage are also at a period of life in which their economic resources are greater than they have been previously, thus providing opportunities for new and more leisure experiences such as travel.

In summary, it is difficult to generalize about the satisfaction couples experience during this period. Their age group, according to time budget studies by Robinson, doesn't show much increase in the amount of leisure time they have.[21] The major resources that help or hinder the older family may include physical and emotional health and economic and social resources, such as family and friends. To the extent that these resources are in accord with the desired goals of the couple, their leisure lives may be satisfying.

## Later Adulthood and Retirement

This period of life is one which is characterized by the male, and increasingly the female, ceasing full-time employment. The Rapoports have divided later adulthood into three stages: pre-retirement, retirement, and old age (see Table 7-6).[16] The very term "retiree" indicates the centrality of work in our society. It also indicates how much we take our self-definition from our work role. If a person describes him-/herself as "retired" it only identifies the role they don't have, and says nothing of the roles they do have. In our culture retirement brings a preoccupation with realigning commitments but need not bring a retirement *from* commitments. From the standpoint of leisure, this period of life brings change rather than retirement.

TABLE 7-6  LEISURE IN LATER ADULTHOOD*

| Subphase | Preoccupation | Interests | Examples of Activities |
|---|---|---|---|
| Pre-retirement (55–65 years) | Anticipation of retirement | Women: Job, grand-children<br>Men: Anxiety over loss of work role<br>Both: Prepare to develop new interests, cement marital relationship | Recurrent or adult education<br>Pre-retirement courses |
| Retirement (65–75 years) | Realignment of commitments | Social and kin relations<br>Meaningful life interests<br>Disengagement vs. engagement | Inventing and upgrading social roles<br>A population "at risk"<br>Walking<br>Visiting parks |
| Old age (75+) | Life before death | Tendency to be alone | Age-segregated vs. age-integrated facilities |

*SOURCE: Op. cit., Wood, Table 7-2, p. 14.

There is a great tendency to misjudge the situation of retirees. The majority of those 65 years of age or older live as a dyad (husband and wife) in their own home—79 per cent of men and 59 per cent of women. Only 4 per cent of those aged 65 and older reside in institutions, such as homes for the elderly. Most elderly continue to live where they did before they retired. Less than one out of five has an income below poverty level.[22] Thus, for many retired people, the potential to use leisure in meaningful ways is great.

Among those who retire, however, meaningful work may be even more important than leisure or recreation. Consider the viewpoint of Alexander Comfort, as he advised elderly people:

> Leisure is a con. It should mean time when you do what you yourself want to do. It gets sold, as part of the unperson package, as time in which you are expected to do trivial things for which you have to pay money. . . . People only need leisure if they do dull, resented or exploited work, and even they don't need the Coney Island-Retirement Village package which makes them into permanent children; this is good for an afternoon, not for a life-style. What the retired need, what the unemployed need and what more and more of us shall need as commercial rationalization pushes us out of participant living, isn't leisure, it's occupation.

> Leisure supplied as a package is something to chuck right back at the suppliers, unless you want to buy the whole phony aging package along with it. Get occupation first. Leisure in the right sense will follow, if you have time for it.[23]

What Comfort rages against here is the tendency of our culture not to take old people seriously and, therefore, to try to "fill up" their empty time with childish, unimportant recreation. Since retirement is, for many, a "roleless" state, it is easy for recreation to become harmless diversion which is not suitable for anything but special occasions: bingo, for instance, is fun for special occasions, but imagine playing it every day. When such behavior becomes planned as the central focus of an older person's existence, it is society's way of saying that such people have little value to society. Organizations and institutions which plan recreation activity for the aged often seem guilty of this.

Let's investigate this a little further in the exercise on the following page.

# Leisure Exercise 7·2

## Recreation Programs For the Elderly

The purpose of this exercise is to observe a recreation program for the elderly sponsored by a public or private nonprofit leisure service agency. Such a program might be found at a local senior citizens' club, recreation center, public high school, etc. The program could be sponsored by a church, municipal or county recreation and park department, service club, or other organization.

Identify such a program and request permission from the sponsoring agency to observe it. After securing permission, attend and observe the program; keep your eyes and ears open. After attending the program answer the following questions in the space provided:

**1.** What organization sponsored the program?

**2.** What was the nature of the program?

**3.** Why do you think the organization sponsored this program?

**4.** Describe what happened from the time the participants began to arrive until they left.

**5.** In your judgment, did the program have meaning for the participants? Was the program trivial? Did it fully utilize the talents of the participants? Were they involved in planning the program? Were they treated as individuals? How could the program have been made more meaningful to the elderly participants?

Share your answers with classmates in small groups.

In terms of the impact of old age upon leisure behavior, it has often been said that age is a "false" variable—that is, it is not so much age as such which causes changes in leisure behavior but some other conditions which are sometimes, but not always, associated with growing older. Those who are elderly are more likely than their younger counterparts to live in urban areas, to be in poor health, to have lower levels of formal education, and to possess low income. These conditions, rather than old age itself, shape and limit leisure behavior. Those among the elderly who are not in these circumstances behave much differently than those who do. A study by Godbey et al. for instance, found that urban elderly who are poor and have low levels of formal education are considerably more likely to be prevented from using public parks and recreation centers due to fear of crime than those with higher income and education.[24]

Old age is associated with a decline in participation in some kinds of leisure activities, particularly those which involve high levels of physical exertion. In some cases, though, it is difficult to tell if this decline in participation is due to the physical changes which take place during old age or the fact that many elderly people, in their youth, established sedentary patterns of leisure or were not taught to value physical fitness. As today's young people grow older they may continue to be active in a wider variety of leisure activities, due to greater exposure to them in their youth.

Studies which show that participation in many forms of leisure behavior declines with age are in keeping with the belief that older individuals change their orientation to some degree, from the outer world to the inner world. Older people, as Neugarten has said, "put their store of memories in order."[25] They also contemplate or meditate. Thus, if we see an elderly person sitting on a park bench, it is probably incorrect to assume that they are doing nothing; they may be doing "nothing" in the outer world but may be actively and, perhaps, pleasurably involved in the inner world.

A major question concerning the elderly is whether declining participation in the world about them is inevitable. Disengagement theory, developed by Cumming and Henry after extensive research with the elderly, assumes the following: "Disengagement is an inevitable process in which many of the relationships between a person and other members of society are severed, and those remaining are altered in quality."[26] Because of individual differences it is assumed that some people will disengage before retirement, others will begin the process after retirement, and others will not do so at all. The key idea here (although later revised by the authors) is that the process of withdrawing from society is unavoidable. While studies show us that many older people participate less in certain forms of recreation and leisure, many others do not. If some people "naturally" become less involved in society in old age, the implication seems to be to let them do so—don't fight the tendency. (Table 7-3, p. 178, shows that as people get older they are less likely to participate in most forms of outdoor recreation.)

Another theory applicable to the aged, however, assumes that older people should remain active in social roles for as long as they can. "Activity" theory is based on the belief that old people benefit from staying active and that, when the time comes to give up certain activities and relationships, it is important to find substitutes to replace those activities and relations which were surrendered.[27]

The fact that participation in many forms of leisure behavior declines with age doesn't necessarily lend support to the idea of disengagement. Let's examine some circumstances surrounding the decline in participation in sport associated with age.

**Sport In An Aging Society.** The young participate in nearly all sports to a greater extent than the old, and in many cases this difference is pronounced. What ages are most of the players you see on softball diamonds, tennis courts, jogging paths, or basketball courts? As may be seen from Table 7-3 (p. 178) and Table 7-7 (below), both taken from national surveys, as people get older they are progressively less likely to participate in sport or to exercise. We may believe that this decline with age is somehow "natural," but before accepting this viewpoint let's look at some of the factors which may account for declining participation.

**Physical Ability.** The physical ability to participate in many sports is highest in late adolescence and thereafter declines. Aerobic capacity, the

**TABLE 7-7  A LOGICAL PROGRESSION BY DECADES: ILLUSTRATIVE ONLY, NOT TO BE CONSIDERED COMPREHENSIVE\***

| Decade | Highly Recommended | Worth Investigating | Demanding But Possible |
|--------|--------------------|--------------------|------------------------|
| 5–15 | Walking<br>Swimming<br>Tennis | Baseball<br>Basketball<br>Soccer<br>Skiing<br>Boating<br>Bicycling | Track and field<br>Football (not before age 11)<br>Hockey (not before age 10)<br>Golf (not before age 9) |
| 15–25 | Walking<br>Swimming<br>Tennis<br>Golf<br>Baseball<br>Basketball | Soccer<br>Skiing<br>Boating<br>Bicycling | Football (last decade)<br>Track and field<br>Hockey<br>Rodeo<br>Handball<br>Squash |

*(continued)*

TABLE 7-7   A LOGICAL PROGRESSION BY DECADES ILLUSTRATIVE ONLY,
NOT TO BE CONSIDERED COMPREHENSIVE* (continued)

| Decade | Highly Recommended | Worth Investigating | Demanding But Possible |
|---|---|---|---|
| 25–35 | This is the crucial decade, because what happens here may determine the quality of subsequent life. Unusual attention must be paid to making an orderly transition into lifetime sports, if this has not already been done. | | |
| | Walking | Softball | Track and field (last decade) |
| | Swimming | Volleyball | Baseball (last decade) |
| | Tennis | Bowling | Basketball (last decade) |
| | Golf | Skiing | Hockey (last decade) |
| | Boating | Soccer | Handball |
| | | Bicycling | Squash |
| | | | Rodeo |
| 35–45 | Walking | Bowling | Rodeo (last decade) |
| | Swimming | Volleyball | Soccer (last decade) |
| | Tennis | Fishing | Handball |
| | Golf | Skiing | Squash |
| | Boating | Horseshoes | Softball |
| | | Bicycling | Volleyball |
| 45–55 | Walking | Bowling | Handball (last decade) |
| | Swimming | Bowling on green | Squash (last decade) |
| | Tennis | Fishing | Volleyball (last decade) |
| | Golf | Skiing | Softball (last decade) |
| | Boating | Shuffleboard | |
| | | Horseshoes | |
| | | Bicycling | |
| 55–65 | Walking | Shuffleboard | Skiing (last decade) |
| | Swimming | Bowling | |
| | Tennis | Horseshoes | |
| | Golf | Bicycling | |
| | Boating | | |
| | Fishing | | |
| | Bowling on green | | |
| 65–75 | Walking | Shuffleboard | Tennis (last decade) |
| | Swimming | Horseshoes | Golf |
| | Boating | | Bowling (last decade) |
| | Fishing | | Bicycling (last decade) |
| | Bowling on green | | |
| 75–85 | Walking | Shuffleboard | Golf |
| | Boating | Horseshoes | |
| | Fishing | Swimming | |
| | Bowling on green | | |

*SOURCE: James Michener, *Sports In America*. New York: Random House, 1976, pp. 274–275.

ability to take in and use oxygen, is one of the best overall measurements of athletic capacity, and it is highest around age 19 or 20.[28] Aerobic capacity begins to decline slowly and then increasingly quickly after that. Michener has quoted the following ages at which male athletes reach their peak ability: basketball—24; football—28; ice hockey—27; boxing—26; tennis—27; bowling—32; golf—30; and pistol shooting—27.[28] Thus we are likely to be "best" at these sports during the first half of our lives. Certainly we can find many individual exceptions to this generalization. Ken Rosenwall played successfully against the best tennis players in the world well into his forties; Sam Snead remained a world class golfer into his sixties; Al Oerter is an Olympic-caliber discus thrower at 40.

The fact that sport ability declines with age, however, only puts the participant at a competitive disadvantage if he or she is competing against those who are younger. Since we nearly always age-segregate sports for younger athletes in our country—Little League, junior tennis and golf tournaments, peewee soccer—age-segregating sport participation for older people so that they compete against their physiological equals would also seem to make sense.

**"Lifetime Sports."** Many of the sports emphasized for youth are not "lifetime" sports. Baseball, football, wrestling, gymnastics, hockey, most track and field events, lacrosse, soccer, and some other sports which are often stressed in elementary and secondary schools have very little carry-over value to later life. Although some schools have initiated lifetime sports programs which stress carry-over sports, such as golf, tennis, bowling, archery, swimming, badminton, and others, many other schools continue to emphasize traditional sports which receive most of the funding. When this happens, those who have been football, baseball, and basketball players may, in later life, become spectators of these same games but no longer active athletes.

**Role Models.** Older people don't often see appropriate role models of older athletes on television or in the newspapers. Most sports which are viewed and covered by the mass media—baseball, basketball, football, ice hockey—are those which are played by young males. Older people don't see themselves in these sport situations, and may begin to think they are too old to participate.

**The Role of Institutions.** Institutions which organize and administer sport for people of all ages don't often cater to older people. While many organizers of sport, such as public recreation and park departments, don't purposely discriminate against older people, most don't modify their programs in ways which will encourage older athletes. As an example, such agencies will often provide a youth baseball league with (1) an age-segregated format for youth within a 4-year age span, such as 8 to 12, (2) a scaled-down baseball diamond, (3) balls, bats, and other equipment modified for young players, and (4) modifications in rules—number of innings played, base-

**FIGURE 7-5** Is this the only "sport" in which the elderly can participate? (Courtesy of AAHPERD)

stealing rules, etc. In many cases older people would benefit from rule modifications, changes of equipment (lighter balls, bats, racquets), and specialized playing areas (shorter basketball courts, softer tennis courts, etc.). However, because there is often a tendency to assume that *all* athletes from the age of 18 on are "adult" participants, these modifications usually aren't made for older athletes.

Many of our sport facilities are consciously or unconsciously geared to youth. Look at many public and commercial swimming pools. Often they are ugly, rectangular concrete bathtubs with high diving boards and competition lanes painted on the bottom of the pool. These pools are designed to cater to the swimming patterns of younger people.

In summary, older people will participate in sport to a greater extent, and exercise more, when society tries harder to make sports participation more appropriate for them. Michener has suggested in Table 7-7 that certain sports are appropriate for people in particular age groups.

## CONCLUSIONS

While one's stage in the life cycle is an important determinant of leisure attitudes and behavior, we should remember that different generations of those in the same life stage will often behave differently. Those who are retired now, for instance, are likely to behave differently from retirees of a previous generation. Those who reach retirement in the next generation will likely differ from those now retired. Because those in the middle stages of life are more likely to participate in sport than the last generation of middle-agers, it is likely that they will also participate at higher rates during retirement.

As human beings we are constantly evolving. Not only do the values and preoccupations which shape our leisure behavior change throughout various stages of life, the impact of these stages changes from generation to generation. What being a teenager meant to your parents is different from what it meant (or means) to you. Thus, the forces which limit and shape our leisure are not only our life stage but also the unique conditions of the generation with which we share that stage.

It would also be wrong for us to conclude that people are happier during their youth than in middle and old age. Bernice Neugarten, a scholar of adult development, has summarized three important generalizations concerning the development of adults:

1. It makes no more sense to think of middle age or old age primarily in terms of "problems" or "losses" than it does for youth.
2. As lives grow longer, and we make more choices and commitments, lives grow more unique, more different from each other. Most people do not lose this uniqueness until their death.
3. Most people who have reached the ages of 40, 50, or 60 do not wish to be young again. Instead, they wish to grow old with the assurance that they have had a full measure of life's experience.[25]

These conclusions would seem to indicate the wisdom of an old adage: every age has its rewards.

## STUDY QUESTIONS

1. Briefly describe a leisure activity in which you participate which is unconditional leisure, one which is compensatory or recuperative leisure, one which is relational leisure, and one which is role-determined leisure.

2. What does it mean to say that play is "arousal-seeking" behavior?

3. Why is one's stage in the life cycle an important factor in shaping leisure behavior?

4. What does it mean that, according to Comfort, leisure for the aged is a "con"?

5. Are younger people "happier" than middle-aged or old people? Why or why not?

## REFERENCES

1. Kelly, John. *Outdoor Recreation Prediction: A Comparative Analysis.* Urbana-Champaign, Ill.: University of Illinois, 1978, pp. 1–22.
2. Levinson, Daniel J. *The Seasons Of A Man's Life.* New York: Alfred Knopf, 1978, p. 000.
3. Gordan, Chad, Gaitz, Charles, and Scott, Judith. "Leisure and Lives: Personal Expressivity Across the Life Span," in Binstock, R., and Shanas, E. (eds.), *Handbook Of Aging And The Social Sciences.* New York: Van Nostrand Reinhold, 1976, p. 317.
4. Cheek, Neil, and Burch, William. *The Organization Of Leisure In Human Society.* New York: Harper and Row, 1976, pp. 1–283.
5. Kelly, John. "Leisure Styles And Choices In Three Environments," *Pacific Sociological Review,* Vol. 21, April, 1978, pp. 187–207.
6. Babchuk, N., and Booth, A. "Voluntary Association Membership," *American Sociological Review,* Vol. 34, 1963, pp. 31–45.
7. Huizinga, Johan. *Homo Ludens—A Study Of The Play Element In Culture.* Boston: The Beacon Press, 1962, p. 13.
8. Sutton-Smith, B. "Children At Play," *Natural History,* Vol. 80, No. 1, January, 1971, p. 55.
9. Berlyne, D. E. "Laughter, Humor and Play," in Lindzey, G., and Aronson, E. (eds.), *Handbook Of Social Psychology.* New York: Addison-Wesley, 1968, p. 67.
10. White, R. W. "Motivation Reconsidered: The Concept of Competence," *Psychological Review,* Vol. 66, 1959, pp. 297–333.
11. Ellis, Michael. *Why People Play.* Englewood Cliffs, N.J.: Prentice-Hall, 1973, p. 118.
12. Wade, Glenn. "A Study of Free-Time Patterns of Elementary School-Aged Children in Playground Equipment Areas." Master's Thesis, Pennsylvania State University, 1968, p. 000.
13. Queen, S., and Habenstein, R. *The Family In Various Cultures.* Philadelphia: J. B. Lippincott, 1974, p. 59.
14. Coleman, James S. "The Teen Agers," *Newsweek,* Vol. LXVII, March 21, 1966, p. 58.
15. Berger, Bennett M. "Teen Agers Are An American Invention," *The New York Times Magazine.* June 13, 1965, p. 47.

16. Rapoport, Rhona, and Rapoport, Robert. *Leisure And The Family Life Cycle.* Boston: Routledge, 1975.

17. Lowenthal, Marjorie F., et al. *Four Stages Of Life.* San Francisco: Jossey-Bass, 1975, p. 144.

18. Guttman, David. "Individual Adaptation in the Middle Years: Developmental Issues in the Masculine Mid-Life Crisis," *Journal of Geriatric Psychiatry,* Vol. 9, 1976, pp. 41-57.

19. Mogul, Kathleen M. "Women In Mid-Life: Decisions, Rewards, And Conflicts Related To Work And Careers," *American Psychiatric Journal,* Vol. 136, No. 9, September, 1979, p. 1,142.

20. Sussman, Marvin. "The Family Life Of Old People," *in* Binstock, R., and Shanas, E. (eds.), *Handbook Of Aging And The Social Sciences.* New York: Van Nostrand Reinhold, 1976, p. 47.

21. Robinson, John. *How Americans Use Time: A Social Psychological Analysis Of Everyday Behavior.* New York: Praeger, 1977, pp. 1-209.

22. Flint, Jerry. "Early Retirement Is Growing In U.S.," *New York Times,* July 10, 1977, pp. 1, 22.

23. Comfort, Alexander. *A Good Age.* New York: Crown Publishing, 1976, p. 124.

24. Godbey, Geoffrey, Patterson, Arthur, and Brown, Laura. *Crime And Fear Of Crime Among The Elderly—Relationships To Leisure Behavior.* Washington, D.C.: American Association of Retired Persons, 1979, p. 3.

25. Neugarten, Bernice. "Time, Age And the Life Cycle," *American Psychiatric Journal,* Vol. 136, No. 7, July, 1979, p. 891. *10*

26. Cumming, E., and Henry, W. *Growing Old.* New York: Basic Books, 1961, p. 14.

27. Maddox, G. L. "Persistence Of Life Style Among The Elderly," *in* Palmore, E. (ed.), *Normal Aging.* Durham, North Carolina: Duke University Press, 1970, p. 174.

28. Michener, James. *Sports In America.* New York: Random House, 1976, pp. 274-275.

# chapter 8
# Education and leisure

In this chapter we will examine the relationships between leisure and education. Among the more important ways that this can be done are the following: (1) the relation between the kind and amount of education and leisure patterns and values; (2) the purposes and qualities of formal education in society (are individuals educated only for a vocation? is the education process pleasurable and voluntary?); (3) learning as a use of one's leisure.

## LEVEL OF EDUCATION AND LEISURE BEHAVIOR

What people do during their leisure and the leisure values they have are influenced by the level of their education. Education serves not only to stimulate interests in many forms of leisure activity, but also to enable participation in some forms of leisure by providing necessary skills and developing appreciation. Many leisure activities cannot be enjoyed without some skills which are gained through formal education. Additionally, formal education develops appreciation for many forms of leisure expression which may not be instantly appreciated, such as many forms of "high culture"—poetry, opera, ballet—whose enjoyment is enhanced through repeated exposure. The same may be said of fly fishing.

Because higher levels of education tend to stimulate participation in leisure activities, it is not surprising that many studies have found a broader range of participation in leisure activities among those with higher income

**201**

levels.[1] Also, those with higher education are more likely to participate in most forms of outdoor recreation, sports, high culture, tourism, continuing education, reading, and volunteer activities. While part of this greater participation reflects the fact that those with higher education levels are likely to have higher incomes and be younger than their counterparts with less education, education itself often has a distinct bearing on such participation, even after the effect of income and age are taken into account.

Within given types of leisure experience, such as sports or outdoor recreation, certain activities are strongly associated with low education or high education groups. Stone, for instance, found that wrestling is favored more by less educated individuals with low status jobs; one survey showed that those who identified themselves as wrestling fans had relatively little education.[2] As Table 8-1 shows, hunting is the only activity where participation systematically decreases as education level increases.[3] For other activities, such as camping in primitive areas, those with higher education are predominant.

## EDUCATION FOR LEISURE

The educational needs of a society reflect the situations and conditions under which its members live. While the ancient Greeks, with their slave culture, assumed that educating for leisure was imperative if the free man was to avoid disaster, our own formal education systems have been centered around work, both in respect to teaching methods and the use made of various areas of study. Until we reach our mid-teens, schools are places we attend because we are obligated by law, where we do school "work." Students usually attend colleges or universities to aid them in the pursuit of a career (although their reasons for going are, of course, diverse and complex). Although education for leisure has been one of the seven aims of the National Education Association, it is only recently that work has begun to achieve this goal.[4]

In the following sections we will examine some different conceptualizations of education for leisure.

### Stressing Leisure-Related Content

If education for leisure is the responsibility of the schools, just what does that imply that the schools should do, if anything, that they are not currently doing? One simple answer might be that the schools must devote considerable attention to the "liberal" arts as well as to the "servile" arts. The servile arts deal with those skills that are related to work and to survival, to those activities which are primarily means to economic ends. If one wishes to be a computer programmer, carpenter, accountant, or nurse there are skills that

**TABLE 8-1   PARTICIPATION IN OUTDOOR RECREATION ACTIVITIES ONE OR MORE TIMES DURING LAST YEAR BY VARIOUS EDUCATION LEVELS\***

| | Years of Formal Education | | | | | |
|---|---|---|---|---|---|---|
| | 0–8 | 9–11 | 12 | 13–15 | 16 | 17 or more |
| Camping in Developed Area | 9% | 23% | 33% | 37% | 30% | 33% |
| Camping in Primitive Area | 5 | 14 | 22 | 27 | 22 | 25 |
| Canoeing, Kayaking, River Running | 3 | 7 | 15 | 20 | 21 | 22 |
| Sailing | 2 | 3 | 8 | 15 | 24 | 24 |
| Water Skiing | 2 | 6 | 16 | 23 | 19 | 21 |
| Fishing | 47 | 49 | 53 | 58 | 47 | 43 |
| Other Boating | 15 | 24 | 32 | 43 | 40 | 40 |
| Outdoor Pool Swimming and Sun-bathing | 25 | 43 | 63 | 74 | 74 | 77 |
| Other Outdoor Swimming and Sun-bathing | 26 | 31 | 45 | 58 | 55 | 57 |
| Walking to Observe Nature, Bird-watching | 29 | 38 | 51 | 59 | 60 | 70 |
| Hiking or Backpacking | 8 | 14 | 27 | 36 | 36 | 45 |
| Other Walking or Jogging for Pleasure | 48 | 61 | 65 | 75 | 76 | 77 |
| Bicycling | 15 | 27 | 43 | 55 | 52 | 48 |
| Horseback Riding | 4 | 8 | 14 | 18 | 15 | 19 |
| Driving Vehicles or Motorcycles Off Road | 9 | 24 | 27 | 28 | 20 | 17 |
| Hunting | 22 | 15 | 20 | 20 | 13 | 11 |
| Picnicking | 52 | 69 | 74 | 78 | 77 | 82 |
| Golf | 3 | 8 | 14 | 23 | 25 | 28 |
| Tennis Outdoors | 6 | 16 | 18 | 40 | 45 | 48 |
| Cross-Country Skiing | 0 | 0 | 2 | 3 | 3 | 8 |
| Downhill Skiing | 2 | 1 | 5 | 10 | 11 | 14 |
| Iceskating Outdoors | 3 | 7 | 16 | 18 | 17 | 18 |
| Sledding | 7 | 6 | 21 | 22 | 19 | 19 |
| Snowmobile Riding | 3 | 6 | 9 | 9 | 6 | 5 |
| Other Outdoor Sports and Games | 24 | 47 | 54 | 63 | 57 | 60 |
| Sightseeing at Historical Sites or Natural Wonders | 37 | 49 | 64 | 72 | 81 | 84 |
| Driving for Pleasure | 46 | 69 | 76 | 77 | 75 | 76 |
| Visiting Zoos, Amusement Parks, Fairs, Carnivals | 39 | 63 | 76 | 77 | 78 | 79 |
| Attending Outdoor Sports Events | 27 | 49 | 63 | 67 | 66 | 70 |
| Attending Outdoor Dances, Concerts and Plays | 17 | 31 | 40 | 47 | 49 | 59 |

\*SOURCE: Heritage Conservation and Recreation Service, National Outdoor Recreation Survey. Washington, D.C.: U.S. Department of the Interior, 1978.

must be learned to perform these occupations. The liberal arts, however, deal with areas of human endeavor which are not, strictly speaking, necessary for survival or for work but which help to define and fulfill us as human beings. Such areas of study might include a range of activities, including drawing, singing, playing tennis, writing short stories, and studying history. In short, the school curriculum should reflect a balance between those subjects which are useful to us in an economic sense and those which are intellectually, physically, and aesthetically "useful."

Charles K. Brightbill, an American scholar of recreation and leisure, has been influential in developing a concept of education for leisure which is based upon exposure to leisure activities.[5] He has begun by inviting us to think of education not in the narrow, fact-cramming, diploma-directed sense, but rather in its deepest and best meaning—the thinking and learning processes. If we are to have a flood of leisure, we must educate people for it. If we do not learn how to use the new leisure in wholesome, uplifting, decent, and creative ways, said Brightbill, we shall not live at all. This does not mean that leisure should be regimented. It is not as important that people use parks, beaches, and libraries as it is that they learn to use their leisure time in personally satisfying and creative ways, either with or without society's organized resources.

Brightbill has stated that "education for leisure" means exposing people early and long—in the home, the school, and the community—to experiences that will help them develop appreciations and skills to use in their increasingly available leisure time.[5] He stressed that education for leisure is a slow, steady process, involving the imparting of skills and the readiness to exercise them. Leisure can contribute to the aims of education: comprehending the world, attaining health and emotional stability, appreciating and expressing beauty. In this sense leisure is not an escape from the toil of education; it is a revitalizing element in the process of education itself. Brightbill was optimistic about the possibilities of educating for leisure, but thought that "the school will have to drop its traditional policy of isolating leisure education on the island of extracurricular activities and bring it into the mainland of the school curriculum itself."[5]

The views of the British educator James Simpson on leisure are, on the whole, less optimistic than those of Brightbill.[6] He has attached importance to the function of education in enriching leisure by widening horizons of interest and enjoyment, and he has written about changing the curriculum in the schools to include leisure subjects. But he pointed to three "dangers and difficulties" which beset the concept of education for leisure. The first is the practice of putting new labels on old bottles: the repackaging of existing curricula as "education for life" or "for maturity" without much change in the subject matter or the practice of educators. The second danger lies in paying too much attention to what surveys of leisure behavior reveal, which tends to reduce education for leisure to facilitate mass trends that are often dictated by irresponsible interests. Thirdly, we must beware of calling upon education to solve the "problem of leisure."[6] Contrary to forecasts, the problem is not likely to be one of vast amounts of free time to fill, and those who worry about the quality of other people's leisure may simply be expressing their disappointment in this, and so consider leisure trivial, escapist, or stultifying.

Recreational activities now occupy an accepted place in the curriculum of nearly all educational institutions. Subjects and activities of a recreational nature were initially incorporated into school life because it was believed that healthy recreation could produce beneficial moral effects, and because some influence over pupils' recreation made it easier to control their behavior. Today, however, recreation is recognized as being desirable for its own sake, and most schools employ specialists to deal with this increasingly broad aspect of the curriculum. Apart from learning sports, pupils can be introduced to literature, art, different types of music, handicrafts, and various other potentially satisfying leisure activities.

## Making the Educational Process More Leisurely

A second way of regarding education for leisure is to view it in terms of the educational process rather than the academic content. If a school is to reflect a leisure ethic and prepare students to live in a society with such an ethic, the school must do this by example. The school, for instance, should not look like a factory. Students should have some experience with high autonomy situations in which they "practice" exercising freedom. There should be periods of time which are not rigidly scheduled, during which contemplation can take place. There should also be times to play, to celebrate, to volunteer, even to loaf. Now, all this is easier said than done but certainly some changes can be made, both in the physical layout and design of a school, in procedures of instruction, and in other factors involved in teaching.

Let's take a single example of this—a classroom. Classrooms are often pathetically ugly, devoid of color, decoration, and any attempt at warmth, cheerfulness, or personality. In some cases chairs are actually fastened to the floor so the placement of the students is established in advance. If there is any furniture or equipment in the room, it is likely to be standardized; such furniture is justified as being "functional" as a means to an end. The room is eminently forgettable, an environment to be "endured."

If classrooms are to be more in keeping with a leisure ethic, they should not be standardized. Works of art, plants, fish, music, warm colors, sunlight wherever possible, displays and exhibits, and many other things could be used to make the classroom more leisurely. Such changes, however, would still be suspect in many schools.

Many of you reading this book (in fact, probably everyone but my wife and parents) are students enrolled in a college or university. If you are, this book is used in connection with a course you are taking which is probably held in a classroom. If so, let's try a short exercise dealing with your particular classroom.

# Leisure Exercise 8·1

1. Name three specific physical changes which could be made to provide your classroom with a more "leisurely" atmosphere for learning, and explain why each suggestion would improve the leisure quality of the environment.

   a.

   b.

   c.

2. If your suggestions were undertaken, would there be any negative consequences in making these changes?

3. Do you think your college or university would be receptive to making these changes if your class suggested them? Why or why not?

## Leisure Counseling

A third way of thinking about education for leisure might be called "consciousness expanding." That is, the student would be presented with information about such matters as recreation and leisure in our society, its relation to work, its importance in relation to life, satisfaction, leisure opportunities in the community or society at large, and the consequences of leisure behavior.

Brightbill, Simpson, and others have agreed that education does and should have a role to play in helping people make better use of their leisure. The difficult question is how far educators should go in telling people what kind of leisure is good for them. Brightbill is typical of the more confident, convinced, and moralistic school of thought which appeals to a consensus (one is tempted to say a silent majority) on the subject of what is "good" leisure.[5] Simpson is more concerned with exposing the bases of our moral judgments, and tends to be skeptical about how far we can truly "forge out our own values."[6] Both views are fundamentally democratic, although Brightbill has emphasized the provision of public services and voluntary contributions, while Simpson has focused on the linking of policies for improvement with the welfare and happiness of people, individually and as a community. We should be thankful that there is open debate on this problem, insisting on no single or easy answer.

One of the major difficulties in framing leisure education policy lies in deciding how to make the content of the courses relevant to the lives and interests of the students while preserving, and if possible enhancing, values that ultimately will be thought worthwhile by all concerned. Richard Kraus has stated that "if education is to be concerned with the recreational lives of students, it should prepare people to use their time wisely and constructively. . . . [and] there should be a direct concern with exploring the role of leisure in one's life. Schools should offer learning experiences in a wide variety of skills and interests useful in enriching lifelong recreational pursuits."[7] Few would disagree with such a wide, varied, and long-term policy, but we need to beware of words such as "wisely" and "constructively." How are we to say what is wise for someone else to do during leisure, and does not "constructive" usually refer to work rather than to leisure?

Again, a cautionary view should be set against some of the excesses of optimism and self-confident certainty. Peterson has stated that "we must admit that in the very assumption that education for leisure should take the form of arousing interest leading to enjoyment both in the arts and in sports, we are already involved in a value judgment. . . . If people prefer to work double shifts and buy a third television set for the bathroom, rather than to work single shifts and play string quartets or go sailing in their time off, have we any right as educators to try to change this pattern?[8] The answer is that educators do not have any such right but they will no doubt continue to behave as if they did, because mankind has a long and sometimes noble history of efforts to "improve" other people.

Some precepts that are derived from general educational principles apply in specific forms to leisure. There is, of course, a need to develop sound judgment and good taste. However, it is possible to believe that the cultivation of judgment and taste is desirable and still allow individuals to disagree about the soundness of particular judgments and the goodness of particular tastes. Of course, this raises the question of uniformity in education generally, and education for leisure in particular. Robert Frederick has traced the status of leisure time (extracurricular) activities in American public schools through at least four stages of development.[9] During the Colonial period an attitude of abstinence prevailed; children were expected to attend to their lessons. With the lessening of formal religious influence in different parts of the country, there was tolerance of children organizing their own dances, parties, and so on. Early in the twentieth century, schools developed their own extracurricular programs, with expanded plants and staff. The contemporary period, actually an extension of the third, is one of formalization, including the assigning of academic credit to leisure subjects.

Ronald Corwin has criticized some of the effects of the formalization. Certain leisure activities have become standard features of schooling, while others have been ignored.[10] Struggles for favored status have developed between the teachers responsible for various activities. The band director who needs new uniforms and instruments complains that the athletic team is receiving too much money for its uniforms, or that the drama coach's sets are too expensive. Under these circumstances, students also have become involved in many bitter struggles with the sponsors of activities, whose prestige depends upon the number and caliber of students they attract. While these activities ostensibly exist for the students, once the activity is formalized students sometimes are recruited simply to fill a quota. A prestige hierarchy of leisure time activities develops from interdepartmental struggles, and from this hierarchy children learn which leisure activities are "good"—that is, approved—and which are not. Perhaps the most serious criticism of the present system is that formalization of leisure encourages children to participate only in uniform, faculty-approved activities rather than to explore the multitude of alternative available uses and conceptions of leisure. This uniformity leads people to prefer organized leisure activities in later life, and to use leisure to escape from solitude and from themselves.

The way in which leisure subjects are taught in school has also been attacked. There is a lack of teacher-training courses that include the implications of leisure for education. Those who defend the present content of teacher-training courses point out that material on education for leisure is included in other courses. But Corbin and Tait have claimed that "emphasis in such courses has been placed upon perfection of performance rather than upon enjoyment of performance. When graduates of such courses enter the field of teaching, their methods are bound to be directed toward perfection rather than enjoyment."[11] In music, art, and dramatics, particularly, Corbin and Tait have felt that teaching should demonstrate that these activities are fun and that everyone, not just a talented few, can take part.

Jean Mundy, a leisure educator who has been instrumental in promoting education for leisure, has conceptualized it through a series of statements concerning what it is and what it is not. While all these statements do not fall into one of the three conceptualizations mentioned, you can see the strong emphasis upon the consciousness-expanding and value clarification aspect.

LEISURE EDUCATION IS *NOT*:

A new name for recreation or recreation services.

Just using leisure content as examples in class.

A watered-down, simplified version of a recreation and parks professional preparation program.

Attempting to replace an individual's set of leisure values with our set of leisure values.

A focus on the value of recreation or the recreation profession.

Imparting standards of what is "good" or "bad" use of leisure.

A focus on getting people to participate in more recreation activities.

Only teaching skills and providing recreation programs.

A program to undermine the work ethic.

Advocating a leisure lifestyle for everyone.

Restricted to the American educational system.

Relating every school subject to leisure.

A course or series of courses.

A subject to be taught.

Restricted to what educators should do but not leisure service personnel.

LEISURE EDUCATION *IS*:

A total movement to enable an individual to enhance the quality of his/her life in leisure.

A process to enable the individual to identify and clarify his/her own leisure values and goals.

An approach to enable an individual to enhance the quality of his/her life during leisure.

Deciding for oneself what place leisure has in his/her life.

Coming to know oneself in relation to leisure.

A lifelong, continuous process encompassing pre-kindergarten through retirement years.

Relating to one's own needs, values, and capabilities of leisure experiences.

Increasing the individual's options for satisfying quality experiences in leisure.

A process whereby the individual determines his/her own leisure behavior and evaluates the long- and short-range outcomes of his/her behavior in relation to his/her goals.

A movement in which a multiplicity of disciplines and service systems have a role and responsibility.[12]

These statements provide a very broad conception for leisure education. In fact, if we made parallel statements about work and combined the two sets of statements, we would be talking about the education of a free person in an industrial society.

If we attempt to make some of these statements operational, however, we would have tremendous disagreement concerning what educational process would bring them about. "Deciding for oneself what place leisure has in his/her life," for example, might mean to some that an individual first perform full-time "work" in order to experience the satisfactions derived from it. Others might feel it necessary only to experience a wide range of leisure activities first, and others might say that meeting the *people* involved in certain leisure activities are necessary to understand the place of leisure in one's life. Then, too, when can one logically decide? How long does one have to decide—for the rest of his or her life? Such questions do not have precise answers.

### Objectives of Leisure Counseling

Leisure counseling has been viewed in a number of ways. According to McLellan and Pellet:

The object of leisure counseling is to determine the patient's leisure interest and then to assist in locating activities in the home community to meet their interest. The leisure counselor also helps the patients to examine the feasibility of their activity choices in terms of cost, accessibility and personal skills and capabilities. Many different techniques are used in leisure counseling. These include individual or group counseling, the use of interest-measuring instruments and referral services to community resources.[13]

Dickason has stressed that leisure counseling must focus upon the feasibility of participating in an activity. Feasibility variables include (1) financial resources, (2) social, physical, and mental abilities, (3) accessibility, and (4) related background experience.[14] Counseling programs could include (1) community field trips to gather information concerning available activities, (2) individual and group discussion programs about what is available in the community, (3) referral services where counselor and individual clients discuss and decide what type of introductory procedure would best help the client become acquainted with the services of a particular leisure service agency, (4) follow-up programs in which clients report individually or in a group on their involvements in avocational activities within the community, and (5) family counseling where a leisure education program involves relations of the client to better provide the client with support.[14]

Basically, leisure counseling appears to be aimed at two groups: (1) those who are institutionalized and/or have a special disability, such as the emotionally disturbed, physically handicapped, prisoners, etc.; and (2) the general public. In regard to leisure counseling with psychiatric patients, for instance, O'Morrow has defined leisure counseling as:

> . . . the technique in the rehabilitation process whereby a professional person uses all information gathered about a patient prior to discharge to further explore interests and attitudes, with respect to leisure, recreation, and social relationships, in order to enable the patient to identify, locate and use recreation resources within the community.[15]

In all these conceptualizations, leisure counseling seems to be (1) expanding consciousness and clarifying values, (2) providing information about leisure resources and otherwise "enabling" the client, and/or (3) changing values.

A number of leisure counseling projects have been initiated during the last few years which have sought to expand consciousness, clarify values, and provide information about leisure. The Milwaukee leisure counseling model, for instance, evolved through the Milwaukee Public Schools' Division of Municipal Recreation and Adult Education.[16] Its basic components include (1) an understanding counselor, (2) the use of an interest finder, and (3) an inventory of locally available projects. "The Mirenda Leisure Interest Finder is an assessment tool used to help adults determine interest levels in a wide variety of leisure-time pursuits."[16] This counseling project is available to three distinct populations:

> For individuals in the mainstream of society it "opens doors" to the abundance of leisure activities available within the community. While readjusting to "mainstream" life, the drug addict, alcoholic, prison inmate, and others in a "halfway" or sheltered population will find leisure counseling helpful in assessing personal potential and having assistance by counselors who can easily refer them to activities. The special population, the aged, ill, handicapped, and culturally disadvantaged, can also benefit through rediscovering personal worth via meaningful activity involvement.[16]

Such counseling is available to all for a nominal fee.

It is in regard to changing values that I have doubts about leisure counseling. McDowell, for instance, has referred to a leisure counseling technique in which those being counseled are asked to consider whether in their leisure (he calls it "leisure life space," whatever that is) he or she is a person who makes things happen, a person who watches things happen, or a person who doesn't know what's happened. "This technique centers on the conviction that a person who makes things happen in his leisure time is in a healthy leisure mode."[17]

Similarly, a leisure counseling technique described by Hitzhusen asks individuals to record their use of time during a 24-hour day. "The person who says 'I don't have the time' may find that he really does, but that he is misusing it."[18] Contrast these assumptions about the wise use of leisure with those of the philosopher Josef Pieper:

> Leisure is not the attitude of mind of those who actively interview, but of those who are open to everything; not of those who grab and grab hold, but of those who leave the reins loose and who are free and easy themselves—almost like a man falling asleep, for one can only fall asleep by "letting oneself go." Sleeplessness and the incapacity for leisure are really related to one another in a special sense, and a man at leisure is not unlike a man asleep.[19]

A man at leisure, then, might be one who watches things happen or who, if asleep, doesn't know what's happened (in some sense). One begins to see the problem here immediately. Who is to say that people should try to cram as many leisure activities into 24 hours as possible? Robert Bly's poem *Driving to Town Late to Mail a Letter* shows us what a beautiful experience wasting time can be:

> It is a cold and windy night. The main street is deserted.
> The only things moving are swirls of snow.
> As I lift the mailbox door, I feel its cold iron.
> There is a privacy I love in this snowy night.
> Driving around, I will waste more time.[20]

Who is to say what leisure should be in a multiculture society such as our own? The leisure counselor must assume that his/her own values are superior to those of the person being counseled; this would often seem to require some unwarranted assumptions on the counselor's part. Certainly we can find some extremes in values where counseling would be warranted, such as cases where people break the law during their leisure, but generally such counseling is suspect. If this function of leisure counseling is proselytizing (seeking to convert others to your values), then we find a huge number of counseling "sources" in our society: parents, schools, commercial advertising, the scouting movement, Trout Unlimited, the lyrics of rock songs, the Bible, and many other sources. Perhaps leisure counseling which seeks to change values is best done by organizations which seek to change behavior. It is doubtful that public recreation, park, or leisure service organizations can undertake such a function or that they should undertake it even if they could, since such organizations must seek to reflect the current leisure values of their clientele, which are often quite diverse.

There does, however, seem to be great value to helping individuals seek to clarify their values concerning recreation and leisure, and in giving them ideas and information about what they could do in their own communities.

Many people haven't thought much about their leisure activities, or even considered what they seek during leisure. Similarly, people are often unaware of things they can do and places they can go which are often right under their noses. If leisure counseling can help people examine themselves in terms of their leisure activities and values it may aid self-understanding. If leisure counseling can identify those leisure resources which people desire, then it may increase happiness.

If leisure counseling can play a role in the adjustment of a prisoner who is being released into the community, it can benefit both society and individuals. But, if leisure counseling is merely one more way of trying to sell a given leisure lifestyle which the leisure counselor happens to prefer, it is of limited use and has no place in public projects. We have all been counseled about our leisure, even if we did not recognize it as such. As a teenager I was counseled by a policeman about my use of leisure to race cars. My experiences as a leisure counselee have also included advice from teachers, girlfriends, poolroom proprietors, a tennis coach, poets, parents, salespeople, and many

**FIGURE 8-1**  We have all had leisure counseling, even if we did not recognize it as such. (Courtesy of H. Armstrong Roberts)

others. Leisure counseling is the most difficult to give wisely, since it involves guiding another person's freedom in ways which (hopefully) result in their increased happiness. What an extraordinary responsibility! Perhaps we ultimately counsel by example.

## A HOLISTIC VIEW OF EDUCATION FOR LEISURE

Some scholars of educational policy have sought to promote leisure in the educational process in form, content, and purpose. In examining education for leisure from the standpoint of educational policy, the education consultant Robert Bundy stated that the modern problem of leisure has been defined in two quite different ways.[21] The modern or industrial notion for creating a leisure society is to increase free time activities and keep people occupied constructively. The post-modern view, however, is that people must be helped to find self-defined work so that they can find leisure as a state of existence. Today's educational policy, Bundy believed, has concentrated more on the former version. In formal education today, young people are segregated from society and have practically no responsibility for the welfare of others. In school the intellect is trained to control the emotions and only pathways to knowledge that involve hard work are considered legitimate. Quantitative measurement and "useful" learning are stressed; job preparation and manpower planning dominate; little money is spent on the arts and humanities; knowledge is fragmented into specialized areas.

For educational policy to help create a society of leisure in the post-modern sense, educational policy would need to undergo many changes. "There would be a strong emphasis on the long-term educational objective of helping people find a self-defined work to do in life as well as a strong case for style and craft in one's work."[21] The arts and humanities would occupy a central place in the curriculum. Learning would seek to interrelate different fields of knowledge. The basic thrust of education would be to fully develop the senses, the emotions, intellect, the psychic and spiritual. There would be a reduction on quantitative measures of evaluation. "More play, spontaneity, and festivity, and the capacity to be enchanted would be evident in the schools."[21] The notion of free time would make no sense. These changes are beginning to come about, Bundy has stated, both because public education can no longer afford our present methods of operation but also because the Eastern and Western Worlds are drawing closer together, bringing a desire to synthesize knowledge in new ways.

## WHO SHOULD EDUCATE FOR LEISURE?

We have discussed education for leisure so far primarily in terms of the role of the school. Actually, the public schools may not be the most important agents for education for leisure. Research by Kelly has found that youngsters were initiated into leisure activities more often by their parents and by their friends than through the schools.[22]

The schools, as Ken Roberts has pointed out, have a number of limitations that make it difficult for them to have an impact on their student's future lives.

> Many forms of recreation cannot be fully appreciated until people have attained physical, emotional or social maturity. Developing an appreciation of literature among children, for instance, is extremely difficult. It is not easy for the educational system to impart a set of values that pupils will use continuously to structure their leisure lives as they mature into adulthood. Technological and social developments are continuously modifying the range of available leisure activities, making it difficult for the schools to prepare young people for their future leisure lives. Schools tend to emphasize organized competitive team games, but few adult leisure activities are of this kind. Finally, just as industrial recreation is shunned by many employees because it reminds them of work, so are extracurricular activities shunned by many students (particularly the less successful ones) because they remind them of school.[23]

These limitations are rather important, particularly the one dealing with changes in people's leisure interests associated with age. Our leisure values change with age. This limits the schools not only in their ability to provide leisure experiences which can serve as models for the future years, but also in their ability to provide leisure counseling. In regard to the first point, I can remember as a child watching my father grow a vegetable garden year after year. I had not the slightest interest in it. Now, however, in my middle thirties, I have become interested enough to have a large garden, complete with parsnips, a compost pile, and an occasional Japanese beetle. I doubt that school could have interested me in gardening at the age of 14—I was a different person. In regard to the second point, leisure counseling in the public schools is limited to the extent that it deals with specific values or activities, since the individual is likely to change leisure values and some activities as maturity is reached. (These problems are not unique to leisure, of course. Vocational counseling has the same problems. Students change their ideas about what careers they want to pursue and what they want to do with their lives.)

Because of these limitations, it may be appropriate to consider giving many other kinds of organizations responsibility for education for leisure. I made such a suggestion to educational critic John Holt (author of *Freedom and Beyond*), when he wrote an article in *Harper's* deploring the limited role schools play in the cultural life of the community.

> In "The Little Red Prison," much of the discussion seemed actually to center around the lack of community resources for the leisure needs and interests of its citizens. Although avoiding the term "leisure," Holt frequently dealt with it in the classical Greek sense: serious activity undertaken without the pressure of necessity. Since the Greek word for leisure, *schole*, is the term from which our

**FIGURE 8-2** Since our interests change with age, it is difficult for public schools to prepare students for leisure throughout the lifespan. (Courtesy of H. Armstrong Roberts)

"school" derives, Holt really wants to deschool society by returning it to this ancient concept.

If such a return is desired, a coordinated community effort will be necessary among those institutions and agencies that people seek out in their leisure. Perhaps foremost among such organizations should be municipal recreation and park departments. Even as presently structured, many such departments could provide the opportunities Holt desires for citizens, including singing or playing musical instruments, participating in unsupervised sports, using potter's equipment, hearing and participating in discussions of topics of interest, and voicing requests for a number of kinds of learning equipment and facilities.

Perhaps the most important qualification municipal recreation and park agencies can contribute to Holt's vision is their considerable experience in dealing with people of all ages and socioeconomic levels in the provision of activity where the external obligations to participate are minimal.[24]

John Holt replied:

Mr. Godbey's suggestion is excellent. I must remember, when young people say to me that they want to work with young people, or in education, but don't like schools, to suggest that they consider working in parks and recreation programs. There are many ways, in addition to working in and for a school, of being a true teacher.[24]

It seems amazing to me how automatically people associate a kind of educational need with the public schools. Many kinds of local leisure service agencies, from municipal recreation and parks departments to voluntary youth-serving agencies to commercial operations, are involved in education for leisure. Such educational undertakings include (1) formal instruction in a leisure skill such as oil painting, golf, or flower arranging, (2) providing information about available community resources for leisure, (3) lectures, exhibits, seminars, displays, trips, festivals, and other methods which provide new ideas, information, and experiences, (4) research findings about what people do in the community and what they want to do, such as special populations' leisure needs, etc., (5) unique learning in programs such as urban gardening, camping, cultural exchange programs, and "outward bound"-type experiences.

In all these ways and others, leisure service organizations are involved in leisure education.

## Adult Education

Both formal and informal learning continue in most industrial societies after the completion of high school and college. Johnstone and Rivera have stated that three out of five adult Americans reported engaging in some aspect of adult education after the conclusion of their formal schooling.[25] The United States Office of Education reported that one out of every eight people, age 17 or over, was enrolled part-time in a formal adult education activity.[26] They further reported that if educational activities were counted where no enrollment is necessary, about one out of four adults participated during the last year. Within colleges and universities in the early 1970s, Gordon Godbey pointed out, more adults were registered as part-time students than there were full-time students.[27]

The increased involvement of the public in various forms of adult education is explainable in a number of ways. A primary reason would seem to be that our level of formal education is increasing, and that those with higher levels of formal education are more likely to value and participate in continuing adult education. The rapid rate of technological change has meant that many adults must continue their formal learning to remain competent to perform their jobs or advance in their careers. Godbey has identified three goals that rank high among those involved in adult education as "improving job skills, finding a more desirable job, or becoming better informed."[27] A survey undertaken by Bergsten of Swedish adults, however, found that the most prevalent reasons given for participation were to learn more about (my) work and to learn more concerning (my) use of leisure time.[28] Other reasons given in order of frequency included to learn more about (my) rights and obligations as a citizen, to become a better parent, personal development, and to get a new job.

Another reason for increased participation in adult education is the heightened leisure potential which many in our society have. As discussed in Chapter 1, this heightened potential means more opportunity for many in our society in terms of new leisure experience, and often this experience brings about learning. Such learning may be a specific leisure skill, such as flower arranging or tennis, or a subject whose study is undertaken as an end in itself, such as the history of ancient Egypt.

The increasing convenience of participating in many forms of adult education may also have spurred participation. Early morning television classes have enabled many to study without leaving home, and such factors as the low cost of many non-credit courses offered through public schools, and weekend learning retreats have brought adult education to millions who otherwise would not participate.

A final factor influencing the growth of adult education is the age characteristics of our population. As our population ages, we will have proportionately less of our population in elementary and secondary schools.

Adult education is sponsored by a diverse array of organizations which may be identified as public and private school systems, colleges, community groups, recreation departments, correspondence courses, tutors and others. However, the greatest participation is through state school systems. To this listing Gordon Godbey has added prisons, libraries, hospitals, and adult education centers such as the Chautauqua School, which has operated for over 100 years in western New York State.[27] The range of such sponsors appears to be widening.

While adult education will continue to serve the changing vocational needs of our society it is in the area of education for leisure—lifelong education—that the greatest advances may take place.

## STUDY QUESTIONS

1. What generalizations can be made about the relationship between leisure and educational level?

2. What are some various meanings of "education for leisure"?

3. Do you think leisure counseling is a good idea? Why or why not?

4. What agencies and individuals should be involved in "education for leisure"?

5. Will participation in adult education increase during the next 20 years? Why or why not?

## REFERENCES

1. See, for instance, Terence White: "The Relative Importance of Education and Income as Predictors in Outdoor Recreation Participation," *Journal of Leisure Research.* 1975, Vol. 7, pp. 29–37.
2. Stone, Gregory. "Wrestling—The Great American Passion Play,"*in* Dunning, E. (ed.), *The Sociology of Sport.* Cass, 1971, p. 45.
3. Heritage Conservation and Recreation Service. *National Recreation Survey.* Washington, D.C.: U.S. Department of the Interior, 1980, p. 18.
4. National Education Association. Cited by Godbey, Geoffrey, and Parker, Stanley, *in Leisure Studies and Services: An Overview.* Philadelphia: W. B. Saunders, 1976, p. 151.
5. Brightbill, Charles K, *The Challenge of Leisure.* Englewood Cliffs, N.J.: Prentice-Hall, 1960, p. 32.
6. Simpson, James. "Education for Leisure," *in* Smith, M.A., *et al.* (eds.), *Leisure and Society in Britain.* London: Allen Lane, 1974. p. 14.
7. Kraus, Richard. *Recreation and Leisure in Modern Society.* New York: Appleton-Century-Crofts, 1971, p. 15.
8. Peterson, A. *The Future of Education.* London: Cresset, 1968, p. 18.
9. Frederick, Robert. *The Third Curriculum.* New York: Appleton-Century-Crofts, 1959, p. 72.
10. Corwin, Ronald. *A Society of Education.* New York: Appleton-Century-Crofts, 1965, p. 86.
11. Corbin, H., and Tait, W. *Education for Leisure.* Englewood Cliffs, N.J.: Prentice-Hall, 1973, pp. 61, 156.
12. Mundy, Jean, and Odum, Linda. *Leisure Education—Theory and Policy.* New York: John Wiley and Sons, 1979, pp. 2–4.
13. McLellan, Robert W., and Pellet, Lane. "Leisure Counseling: The First Step," *Therapeutic Recreation Journal,* Vol. 9, No. 4, 1975, pp. 161–166.
14. Dickason, Jerry. "Approaches and Techniques of Recreation Counseling," *in* Epperson, Arlin, Witt, Peter A., and Hitzhusen, Gerald (eds.), *Leisure Counseling—An Aspect of Leisure Education.* Springfield, Ill.: Charles C Thomas, 1978, pp. 55, 59.
15. O'Morrow, Gerald. "A Study of Recreation Service to Psychiatric Patients in Relation to Pre-Discharge Planning and After Care," Ph.D. Thesis, Columbia University, 1968, p. 17.
16. Wilson, G.T. Mirenda, J.J., and Rutkowski, B.A. "Milwaukee Leisure Counseling Model," *in* Epperson, Arlin, Witt, Peter A., and Hitzhusen, Gerald (eds.), *Leisure Counseling—An Aspect of Leisure Education.* Springfield, Ill.: Charles C Thomas, 1978, pp. 274, 276.
17. McDowell, Chester. "Toward A Healthy Leisure Mode: Leisure Counseling," *Therapeutic Recreation Journal,* Vol. 8, No. 4, 1974, p. 101.
18. Hitzhusen, Gerald. "Recreation and Leisure Counseling for Adult Psychiatric and Alcoholic Patients," *Therapeutic Recreation Journal,* Vol. 7, No. 1, 1973, pp. 16–22.
19. Pieper, Josef. *Leisure—The Basis of Culture.* New York: New American Library, 1952, p. 41.
20. Bly, Robert. *Silence in the Snowy Fields.* Middletown, Conn.: Wesleyan University Press, 1972, p. 38. Copyright by Robert Bly.
21. Bundy, Robert. "Leisure: The Missing Future's Perspective in Educational Policy," *Journal of Education,* May, 1977, pp. 93–104.
22. Kelly, John. "Socialization Toward Leisure: A Developmental Approach," *Journal of Leisure Research,* Vol. 6, No. 3, pp. 181–193.

23. Roberts, Kenneth. *Leisure.* London: Longmans, 1970, pp. 116–119.

24. Godbey, Geoffrey. "Letter to the Editor. Harper's, August, 1972, p. 6; reply by John Holt.

25. Johnstone, John, and Rivera, Ramon. *Volunteers for Learning.* Chicago: Aldine, 1965, p. 79.

26. "Back To School For Millions of Adults," *U.S. News and World Report,* April 2, 1973, pp. 73–74.

27. Godbey, Gordon. "Leisure Service Organizations: Adult Education," *in* Godbey, Geoffrey (ed.), *Recreation, Park and Leisure Services: Foundations, Organization, Administration.* Philadelphia: W. B. Saunders, 1978, pp. 202–217.

28. Bergsten, Urban. *Adult Education in Relation to Work and Leisure.* Stockholm: Almqvist and Wiksell, 1977, p. 000.

# chapter 9

# Everything you ever wanted to know about leisure and sexual behavior

**I**f leisure behavior is thought of as activity which is voluntary and/or pleasurable, then many kinds of sexual and sexually related activity are an increasingly important component of leisure behavior. In spite of this, sexual behavior isn't often studied from the standpoint of leisure behavior. When subjects such as the Sociology of Leisure and Recreation Education were offered in colleges and universities in the 1940s, studying leisure was hardly considered respectable, let alone the study of sexually related uses of leisure. Undertaking research concerning recreational uses of sex was also extremely difficult.

If you think about human sexual behavior for a minute, it's very easy to understand its potential for leisure. First, all sexual behavior, even intercourse, is learned. Human beings are not born knowing how to kiss or have intercourse or with any fixed definitions of what is erotic, although we

**223**

develop sexual needs without being taught. We learn how to express these needs by seeing other people (or other animals), by experimentation, by reading or observing pictures, or by formal instruction. If none of these learning devices are utilized, the individual remains ignorant. Researchers at sex clinics have found that many childless couples who visit the clinic were not able to have children because they didn't know how to have sexual intercourse. They hadn't learned how. "Going to bed" had not been sufficiently explained.

Also, as sociologist Nelson Foote has observed, the stimuli which cause sexual desire among males and females are primarily symbolic rather than physiological.[1] That is, the things that stimulate us sexually are not fixed by our bodies' chemistry as much as they are learned symbols. In some societies, for instance, a woman's breast may be considered sexually arousing, while in another society women may go bare-breasted. Large biceps and chest may make a man more sexually appealing in one era but not another. Consequently, we are not compelled by heredity to respond in fixed ways to certain sexual stimuli (although we may be highly conditioned by our culture). A related circumstance is that the human female, unlike other mammals, will potentially accept intercourse at any time. Therefore, humans develop longings for or aversions to sexual activity quite apart from instinct. Anthropologists have observed that in societies in which children are permitted to observe the sexual intercourse of adults, they may become active participants in full sexual relations several years before puberty. Freud contended that sexual energy (libido) was not a product of puberty, but a basic life force from birth to death.[2] How this energy is expressed is determined more by family relations and social experiences than by biological factors.

## HISTORICAL PERSPECTIVES

Sexual activity has always had the potential to be a form of leisure behavior, and the beliefs of various societies and the difficulty with which they struggled for survival have greatly influenced that potential. The earliest influences upon attitudes toward sexual behavior in the Western World were the Talmud and the Old Testament.[3] Marriage and children were of the greatest importance to the ancient Hebrews and all men, including priests, had to marry. A woman could be divorced for failing to have children.

In Greece's Classical Period, the main function of women was still childbearing. The Greek gods and goddesses were believed to have active sex lives and, perhaps because of this, many prohibitions against sex were absent in Greek society. The double standard was accepted in regard to sexual behavior: it was expected that married men would have sexual relations with women other than their wives, but this freedom did not apply to women. Marriage in Greece, Rome, and other ancient societies typically was not based upon love, especially not upon romantic love. Since love was not part of marriage, men sought amorous activity outside of marriage. Women, other than prostitutes, were prevented from doing so by their home-based existence and second-class status in society. Finally, since homosexuality was more acceptable than in many other societies, it was common for older men to have sexual relations with young boys, and provisions were made for them to meet, both in temples and in private residences. The Greek island of Lesbos, which was inhabited by a number of female homosexuals, gave rise to the term "lesbian."

The emergence of Christianity reinforced women's second-class status. Man was considered superior, and woman was thought to be the cause of his downfall and misfortune since Adam and Eve. Even the institution of marriage was not made one of the seven sacraments until the sixteenth century. The worship of the Virgin Mary in the Middle Ages was responsible for the development of the code of chivalry by the aristocracy. According to this code women were to be idolized for their character and, originally, sexual relations had no place in this concept. It was the beginning of romantic love, full of emotion and longing. Virginity was a virtue and a sign of women's moral superiority. As with many ideals, the reality of sexual relations during this period was far different: rape was common, and adultery flourished among nobility and peasant. While the Church may have had strict prohibitions against many forms of sexual expression, priests themselves often used their religious authority to seduce women. Also, as historian Barbara Tuchman has

FIGURE 9-1 Is romantic courtship today an extension of male-female roles from the Middle Ages? (Courtesy of H. Armstrong Roberts)

observed: "While the cult of courtly love supposedly raised the standing of noble ladies, the fervid adoration of the Virgin (Mary), which developed as a cult . . . left little deposit on the status of women as a whole."[4] Women were commonly considered inferior to men, and this belief was reinforced by the all-male clergy.

During the Reformation, Martin Luther and other religious leaders began to recognize the sexual needs of men and women, declaring that intercourse between man and wife was normally permissible, and that frigidity and impotence were grounds for divorce. As the concept of chivalry spread to the middle classes, love became the basis for many marriages.

The Puritans who arrived in the New World were trying to keep their own way of life, which included the belief that sex was sinful. The Calvinist belief in thrift, salvation through work, and the distrust of all forms of pleasure and idleness became part of the American character. Even in the mid-1800s there was shocked criticism concerning the introduction into society of dances such as the waltz and the polka. Members of the clergy complained of "the abomination of permitting a man who is neither your lover or your husband to encircle you with his arms, and lightly press the contour of your waist."[5] Nevertheless, these dances became popular. Even prejudice toward mixed swimming gave way, although very slowly.

Victorian England maintained a double standard in regard to sex. While a proper lady was expected to be ignorant about sex, acting as if she did not even know of its existence, Brewer has referred to her male counterpart as "the boozing, whoring, one standard for me, another for my wife, typical Victorian male."[6]

Such attitudes are still found in our society, reflected in our beliefs and in the laws concerning what we may do during our leisure time. There are still laws against adultery in some states today, although they are increasingly unenforceable. In the early 1900s such laws brought severe consequences to offenders, as the Chicago Code of Ordinances of 1911 demonstrated:

> If any man and woman live together in an open state of adultery or fornication or adultery and fornication, every such person shall be fined not exceeding $500, or confined in the county jail not exceeding one year. For a second offense, such man and woman shall be severely punished twice as much as the former punishment, and for a third offense, treble, and thus increasing the punishment for each succeeding offense. Provided, however, that it shall be in the power of the party or parties offending, to prevent or suspend the prosecution by their intermarriage, if such marriage can be legally solemnized, and upon the payment of the costs of such prosecution.[7]

The revolution in sexual mores and behavior which has occurred, however, has blunted our distrust of sensual pleasure. Fewer laws exist governing sexual behavior, and those which do exist are often not enforced or are not enforceable.

## The Impact of Changing Women's Roles

As women's roles began to change, and as the drive for women's rights intensified in the United States, a number of changes occurred which influenced sexual behavior and relations. The gap between accepted ways of behaving for men and women began to close in regard to sexual behavior, although such differences are still generally identifiable. Women's rights groups have sought ways of putting an end to women being treated as sex objects; specific concerns have dealt with the right to abortion, rape prevention and more humane ways of dealing with rape victims, dissemination of birth control information, ending sexual harassment on the job, and prohibiting degrading sexual displays and exhibitions involving women. Also, they have dealt with increasing sexual freedom for women and minimizing or eliminating the double standard for men and women in sexual matters.

In seeking to accomplish such aims, the notion of a woman being more "passive" than a man had to be changed. In sexual matters, as in others, males historically have been more likely to be the initiators of behavior while females have been more likely to be in a position of responding. Effecting change in matters of sexual and other behavior, therefore, has involved either seeking to protect the passive behavior of females through legal and other means and/or restructuring social behavior in ways to make the female less passive.

Think about this active-passive or actor-receiver division as it relates to males and females you know. Let's examine this active-passive dichotomy with regard to their sexually related behavior. Keep in mind that, as discussed in Chapter 1, the medieval ideal of chivalry established, as ideals of behavior, a passive, virtuous (and virginal) woman, ignorant of the ways of the world, who was to be worshipped and won over by the heroic deeds and courteous attention of a pursuing male. Such roles, in which women were both idealized (as an extention of the worship of the Virgin Mary) and considered as objects to be won, may still be with us today. Let's find out. In the following exercise, mark the statements true or false as they apply to your social circle or friends.

NAME _____

DATE _____

# Leisure Exercise 9·1

Among your friends, which of the following are true?

**1.** T F  Males are more likely to initiate dates than females.

**2.** T F  Males are more likely to pay for expenses during dates than females.

**3.** T F  Females are expected to be less sexually aggressive than males.

**4.** T F  Females are less likely to read "dirty" books and magazines than males.

**5.** T F  Males are more likely to propose marriage or living together than a female.

**6.** T F  Males are more likely to perform courtesies such as holding doors open for females than females are for males.

**7.** T F  Males are more likely to seek to attract the attention of females by "showing off" than females are likely to show off to attract males.

The higher the number of "true" statements, the more the "actor-receiver" roles are divided between males and females. If the majority of your answers are "true," discuss in the space below whether or not you consider these divisions between males and females to be a problem. If you do think these divisions create problems, what are they? Why?

**229**

# LEISURE AND SEXUAL BEHAVIOR TODAY

Sex today has three important uses in our society, according to Alexander Comfort: (1) sex as parenthood (procreational sex); (2) sex as total intimacy between two people (relational sex); and (3) sex as physical play (recreational sex).[8] While organized religion in our society hasn't traditionally accepted pleasure as a legitimate motive for engaging in sexual activity, it has recently tried to head off the movement toward recreational sex by asserting that worthy sexual activity must be relational.

Recreational sex is, of course, nothing new. In even the strongest kin-based cultures the gap left between relational sex and sex designed to produce offspring has been filled by recreational sex. While some forms of sexuality expressed total involvement between two people, others reflected "an old human pattern in which sexual contacts were permitted between a woman and all her husband's clan brothers or a man and all his wife's titular sisters."[8] Today, many in our society are beginning to believe that procreational, relational, and recreational sex all have a role to play. Let's examine your attitudes toward recreational sex.

# Leisure Exercise 9·2

We have distinguished between procreational, relational, and recreational
sexual activity. On the front and back of this page, describe whether you
believe recreational sex is justified in moral terms. If you believe it is, explain
why and under what conditions. If you believe it is not, explain why not.

## Sex-Related Games and Contests

Many popular songs observe that love is a game or has elements of games. If games are considered to be forms of play which have specific rules and require skills, knowledge, or endurance on the part of the players, then many forms of behavior relating to love and sex can be considered games.

Many such games and contests are related to courtship. Traditionally, adolescent males have engaged in competitive games and contests with each other for the right to court or receive the affection of a female of their choice. From the jousting of knights to high school football games, in which young men butt heads while female cheerleaders watch admiringly, such events are based upon the traditional notion of the aggressive man and the submissive woman.

The early New England custom of bundling represented a kind of courtship contest in which a girl and her suitor were allowed to get into a bed together, keeping their undergarments on, after the girl's parents had retired for the night. Although the practice of bundling came about so that the courting male would not have to walk home through a freezing night, the sexual overtones are obvious. In some cases, parents provided obstacles such as a board fitted into a slot which divided the bed in two, encasing the lower parts of their bodies in tight garments, or even tying the girl's legs together. The degree of freedom parents gave such couples was often related to the desire for their daughter to be married.

Kissing games represent a form of courtship behavior which continued in this country after the more formal elements of courtship had largely been abandoned. A study by Avedon and Sutton-Smith of adolescents in rural Ohio found three distinct groupings of such games: (1) chasing kissing games usually played out of doors by pre-adolescents; (2) mixed kissing games of junior and senior high school students in which couples are not paired off before the game, but pair off momentarily once the game has started; and (3) couple kissing games in which coupling occurs before the game, which permits them to continue to enjoy their interest in each other.[9] Such games provide a kind of bridge in the social development of teenagers by allowing for the expression of given impulses while simultaneously safeguarding the players by placing limits on the expression of such impulses.[9]

The process of searching out members of the opposite sex can figuratively or literally take on the aspects of a game. Proulx has provided an example of each in her examination of sex activities in a "swinging singles" apartment complex.[10] In a figurative sense, the social activities provided at the singles complex constitute a game in which males and females seek to meet, couple off, and go back to one of their apartments for lovemaking. Women seek to determine the socioeconomic status of those they dance with ("What do you do? Does that pay pretty good?"), while men seek the female with the prettiest face and the best build. In Proulx's study, this process was literally turned into a game by a group of men who decided to hold a contest for 1 year to see who could take the most women to bed—the winning score was 79.

Such behavior, with its emphasis on conquering, is part of a mentality which could be called *macho* (Spanish for "male"). To be macho is to be in control, to conquer, to demonstrate virility. For the macho man, male and female are absolute opposites. The games previously discussed, as well as other chances to experiment with sexual behavior, help determine whether macho behavior will prevail in later life. It would be a mistake, of course, to assume that males are the only ones who exhibit macho behavior. Females also seek to control and conquer men, although their means of achieving this are often different

**FIGURE 9-2** Porno films have become a part of our urban culture. (Courtesy of Lessa Massey)

# Pornography

The many forms of pornography constitute a use of leisure time in our society. Most of us have at some time been exposed to reading matter, pictures, movies, or other forms of material that our society, or some members of our society, consider to be obscene, although that which is considered lewd or obscene, of course, is culturally determined: the art that is sacred in one civilization may be considered lewd in another; one society may require women to cover their breasts, while another requires that they cover their faces in public. Not all obscene displays that serve as leisure activity are so considered because of their sexual aspect. Our own society, for instance, bans certain forms of entertainment that were popular in other times or other cultures. Such pursuits as bull- or bear-baiting, in which large dogs were set on a bull or bear with a bloody fight ensuing, are now prohibited because the cruelty and violence to the animals are considered to be obscene. It should be noted, however, that our society does not seek to ban fictionalized violence as it prohibits fictionalized sex. Thus, a child watching television may watch one person murder another but may not watch them have sexual intercourse or even swim in the nude.

Leisure activity that could be considered pornographic may take many forms. *The Report of the Task Force on Pornography and Obscenity* has classified types of pornography in contemporary society as (1) books and manuscripts, (2) film and plays, (3) the spoken word, (4) art, pictures and music, and (5) advertising.[11] The *Yale Law Review* has provided a listing of 68 methods of dissemination that have at one time been banned or prohibited by the courts of some states when they were thought to transmit obscenity.[12] Such methods include dancing, photographs, records, statues, and drawings.

Books and magazines cover a wide range of written material of various quality, style, and intent. Some serious literature, such as James Joyce's *Ulysses*, has sometimes been held to be obscene. Other books are intentionally written without "socially redeeming value," primarily to arouse the sexual interest of the reader. (Sexual arousal is generally not considered a socially redeeming value, although some social scientists feel it has a positive effect upon behavior.) Many such books seek to use the frankest possible language. Some magazines, such as *Playboy*, have enjoyed huge success by combining sexually oriented material with other articles and features not related to sex.

Films and plays may also be classified as "skin flicks," "stag films" and plays which exist primarily in order to exhibit sexual activity, as opposed to those in which such activity is a natural and necessary occurrence in the development of the story line. As movies have become more explicit, the film industry has developed a code to distinguish the degree of sexual frankness or level of maturity for which the film is appropriate. This, of course, has also made it easier for those who want to attend sexually explicit films to do so by looking for the X-rated ones. Television, which is presenting more sexually explicit material, has also begun to inform viewers about the "mature" nature of certain shows. The issue of how far television should go in presenting sexually explicit material is an explosive one, since it is impossible to prevent children from viewing such programs.

Most societies consider certain words to be obscene, and therefore seek to curtail or limit their use. Part of the negative reaction presumably caused by such words is based upon linguistic custom and tradition. A word such as "shit," therefore, has a different value than a word such as "feces," even though they are synonymous. Such linguistic values are constantly changing; it is hard for us to imagine how Clark Gable shocked the nation in *Gone With the Wind* by uttering "Damn!" One form of leisure activity that often uses words considered to be obscene is graffiti, written slogans and risqué or obscene comments in public places. In many ancient cultures there is evidence of graffiti of the same type found today on the walls of public restrooms and covering our urban areas.

In some societies the visual arts may be considered lewd simply by revealing the human body. The recent *Report of the Task Force on Pornography and Obscenity* bemoaned the "disturbing tendency of religious greeting cards to expose areas of cherubim's bodies which are best left private."[11] Erotic art is found in most societies, and attitudes toward it vary; some consider it to be of religious significance, while others imprison those who produce it. Music and advertising are usually considered pornographic only in a subliminal manner. Such music motifs or rhythmic patterns are considered to be sensual or suggestive. Advertising often implies sexual rewards for those who use the product in question, or associates its use with virile, sexually attractive people.

What is pornographic and what is not are often analyzed in our society on the following bases. Is it offensive? Does it incite to lust? Is it repulsive and without redeeming value? In a multicultural society such as our own, the range of opinion concerning what is offensive, repulsive, and without redeeming value is extremely broad. This has made it quite difficult to interpret the test of pornography as stated by Chief Justice Alexander Cockburn in England in 1868, which was used in this country until the late 1950s. The test was "whether the tendency of the matter charged as obscenity is to deprave and corrupt those whose minds are open to such immoral influences, and into whose hands a publication of this kind may fall."[12]

The relationship between exposure to material considered to be obscene and the committing of sex crimes is not yet clearly understood. There is evidence that viewing sexual material does cause an erotic response in some people, but so does daydreaming. The effect of this erotic response, which is more prevalent in males than in females, is subjective to question. Some scholars have argued that pornography acts as a substitute for antisocial sexual behavior; others have contended that it stimulates such behavior.

Today the Supreme Court leaves judgments concerning obscenity as a matter to be interpreted according to local community standards. Two difficulties arise from this approach: (1) There may be great variation of opinion and attitude among those of the local community; and (2) many materials in question are distributed nationally through the mails or produced for a national readership or viewership. Differing local standards make the operation of such undertakings difficult.

Pornography in all its forms is primarily a product of the male imagination. There is little history of pornography designed for females, except that produced for lesbians. The current Women's Liberation Movement, which has sought to make the roles of men and women in our society more equal, may be partially responsible for the beginnings of a pornography industry designed for women. *Playgirl* and other such magazines portray the male in photographic displays in much the same manner that magazines aimed at males have traditionally treated females. Also, the go-go girl has been joined by the male exotic dancer, performing in bars for a female audience.

It is difficult to predict the future of pornography. There is some evidence that after the initial exposure to pornographic films many viewers do not attend others. Pornography is ultimately repetitious, since the number of sex acts and displays is limited. Some observers believe that the widespread availability of pornography is one more indication of the extent to which sex has become shallow or meaningless in our society, with a corresponding loss of the capacity for deep love. Others, however, feel that pornography may help free us from our puritanical inhibitions and disgust with our own bodies, and may actually enhance our capacity to love. In nearly all forms, pornography represents sex as a consumable item.

## Prostitution

Prostitution, which has been called the world's oldest profession, has always been dependent upon men choosing to use their leisure time for sexual activity outside of marriage. In early Greece, where the double standard existed for men and women, two types of prostitution flourished. Since the Greek male believed that sexual intercourse was not only his right but essential to his health, prostitutes were considered necessary and were expected to accompany men in public, where wives were forbidden. Such prostitutes were usually intelligent and well educated. The second form of prostitution began as a means of worship, since money paid to certain prostitutes was used for the upkeep of the temples. Some of these "love goddesses" were slaves in supervised brothels, while others were women who voluntarily sacrificed their virginity to the gods and goddesses. Male prostitution also existed, since homosexuality was accepted.

Prostitution was evident in Christian societies in the Middle Ages. Although Christian emperors tried to abolish it, prostitution was finally accepted as a necessary evil in order to control adultery and rape. Prostitutes were sometimes organized into guilds, and lived in designated houses in special districts. Unlike the Greek courtesans, however, they were often abused by their masters.

In industrialized nations prostitution became a by-product of urbanization. It was reported that there were 80,000 prostitutes in London in 1861, even though the entire male population only numbered 1,300,200. In the United States every large city had its red-light district, where men could gamble, drink, and hire the services of prostitutes.[3]

Increasing sexual permissiveness is thought to have caused some decline in prostitution during the last few decades. Today, however, prostitution is legal in several counties in Nevada, and illegal "free-lance" prostitutes are making a comeback in American towns and cities. Additionally, male homosexuality is flourishing. Pittman described today's male houses of prostitution, which exist in every major city, as ones in which a number of male "models," managed by a male "madam," perform sexual acts for homosexual and bisexual customers. The homosexual market values novelty and youth above all else.[13]

If we consider prostitution to be engaging in sexual behavior to gain some reward other than the experience itself, then prostitution may be extremely common. Engaging in sexual activity to be popular, to obtain a favor, to get or hold a job, to achieve power over an individual, or to become a member of a certain social circle appears to be common. The joys of sex, in other words, are "prostituted" in many ways.

## CONTEMPORARY TRENDS IN LEISURE-RELATED SEXUAL ACTIVITY

A number of trends have dramatically influenced sexual behavior during the last few decades. Many of these trends are similar to those that have influenced other forms of leisure behavior.

There is little doubt that technology has been responsible for the leisure potential of much sexual activity. Effective means of contraception have drastically reduced the incidence of procreation in sexual intercourse. Kinsey has reported that the ratio of sexual intercourse to pregnancy in a sample of over 2,000 women was approximately 1,000 to 1.[14] Other significant findings included (1) increased pre-marital intercourse among females to levels more nearly comparable to those of males, (2) an increasing percentage of marital copulations leading to orgasm decade by decade, (3) a steady approach to equivalence of males and females in pre-marital petting and marital sex play techniques, (4) an increase in extra-marital intercourse, and (5) declining insistence by males on pre-marital female virginity. More recent studies further demonstrate such changes in sexual behavior. Zelnick and Kanter found that 75 per cent of American girls who became pregnant while in their teens were unmarried at the time of conception.[15] Fifty-eight per cent of the girls who got married in their teens said they had engaged in sexual intercourse before they were married. Psychiatrists at some universities report that students who are still virgins feel insecure and hurt because of their lack of sexual experience and because of peer group pressure to become sexually active. Other students embrace a "secondary virginity" in which the individual becomes celibate after a disillusioning period of sexual promiscuity.

A Gallup Poll in 1972 found that only 27 per cent of the public thought it was not wrong at all for a man and woman to have sexual relations before marriage but, by 1977, 37 per cent thought so.[16] Whatever people think, young people are increasingly sexually active. Among America's young women, one in five have engaged in sexual relations by age 16, two-thirds have done so by age 19, and over nine out of ten have had sex prior to marriage. One quarter of American females get pregnant before age 19 but, by using legal abortion, birth rates have been kept low. Because white females are more likely to use legal abortion than black females, the proportion of whites giving birth has declined substantially. In summary, sex before marriage has become a normal way of behaving for American youth, even if such ways of behavior are not fully acceptable to many.

As sexual intercourse has become increasingly separated from childbearing and we, as a society, have become more accepting of a wide range of sexually related behavior, our attitudes toward it have changed. Today we are likely to view many forms of sexual behavior in the same terms as other leisure activity. Sexually related activity has become part of what has been called a "fun morality." That is, we tend to judge it using standards that were previously acceptable only to work.[17] We tend to wonder if we are doing as well as we should. Our behavior shows many of the values of work: our activity is pre-scheduled and planned, goals are established, an attempt is made to improve technique through education; even evaluation and feedback become part of such behavior.

A study of marriage manuals, for instance, found the approach of most of them to be completely work-oriented. One manual cautioned housewives that sex was too important an activity to be given less energy than cooking and doing the laundry. The marriage bed was often referred to as a training ground. Intercourse was divided into progressive stages, each with certain activities to be performed and each with specified time limits.[18]

Such an approach is not limited to marriage manuals. A number of best-selling books have taken a salvation-through-effort approach to sex. In advising women to undertake masturbation exercises, the author of *The Sensuous Woman* said: "In a few months of work you should be able to have several orgasms with him in the time it takes you now to feel the first real glow of arousal."[19] The book also provides ten exercises to help the reader learn how to be sensual, and gives eleven pointers for those who are attending a sex orgy for the first time. Treating sex in such a fashion is symptomatic of materialism, where emphasis is placed upon the act or material good rather than upon its meaning or consequence.

## Recent Sexual Literature

More recent sexual literature has dealt more with understanding sexual meaning, functioning, and problems. Additionally, much recent literature has stressed the ideas that humans must define what is sexually "normal" in individual terms rather than in terms of "average" behavior: What is right for one couple may not be right for another. Sexual advice has become an industry, whether in highly technical books or in "Dear Abby."

## Recognizing Sexual Needs

One of the most far-reaching trends affecting current sexual behavior is the increasing recognition of the sexual needs of many segments of our population for whom it was frequently assumed that sex was inappropriate. These include the elderly, the physically handicapped, prisoners, the mentally retarded, and (even) single adults. Because sexual behavior has traditionally been legitimatized in terms of child rearing, for instance, the elderly were thought of as somehow asexual (think about your grandparents for a minute). It was often assumed that old people's interest in and ability to undertake sexual relations had ceased. A number of studies, however, demonstrate that this simply is not the case. One study at Duke University found that "The median age for stopping intercourse was sixty-eight in men, with a range of forty-nine to ninety, and sixty in women, with a high of eighty-one."[20] Another survey questioned men and women between 60 and 93 years of age. Fifty-four per cent were found to be sexually active.[21] Age does induce some changes in sexual performance, chiefly in males for whom orgasm becomes less frequent and more direct physical stimulation is needed to produce an erection. Barring disease, however, most older people are capable of sex and, as sexual attitudes among the elderly become more liberal, they will increasingly insist on using that ability. This has tremendous implications for many areas of life for the elderly. Old age homes, for example, often segregate their room arrangements by sex and make no provision for elderly males and females to be alone with each other.

Society is increasingly recognizing that the physical or mental condition of a person does not and should not cause the removal of sexual expression. Seeking to suppress sexual expression of such individuals, in fact, is likely to compound problems. The same may be said for many special groups who are institutionalized. Pretending that those who have been removed from society have no sexual needs is quite likely to compound existing problems. This is

**FIGURE 9-3** Growing older does not mean that people lose their sexual interests. (Courtesy of H. Armstrong Roberts)

being realized by some authorities responsible for the management of some prisons, schools for the retarded, hospitals, etc., but not by others. Even in a supposedly sexually liberated society, the recognition of sexual needs is slow.

The treatment of sexual matters in recent fiction and nonfictional writing reflects a number of diverse themes, including sexual politics, sex education, pornography for women, sexual therapy, and the sexual capacity and needs of groups such as the elderly and institutionalized populations. A number of novels (and nonfiction as well) have dealt with the liberation of women from the standpoint of sex. Erica Jong, in the best seller *Fear of Flying*, wrote:

> I thought of all those centuries in which men adored women for their bodies while they despised their minds. Back in my days of worshipping the Woolfs and the Webbs it had seemed inconceivable to me, but now I understood it. Because that was how I so often felt about men. Their minds were hopelessly befuddled, but their bodies were so nice. Their ideas were intolerable, but their penises were silky. I had been a feminist all my life. . . , but the big problem was how to make your feminism jibe with your unappeasable hunger for male bodies.[22]

Similarly, other authors deal with the sexual needs of women, confinement of women's roles to sex objects and child raisers, stereotyping of women's behavior by men, and the role of sex in power relationships between men and women.

Some feminist authors, however, see the sexual freedom issue as a smoke screen. Radical feminist Dana Densmore has argued that the freedom given women in the last decade has largely been freedom to engage in sexual activity but that "spiritual freedom, intellectual freedom, freedom from invasions of privacy and the insults of degrading stereotypes—these are appropriate only to men."[23]

## Marriage and Divorce

Another trend affecting the sexual patterns of Americans is the continuing popularity of marriage, despite its increasingly temporary nature. While much publicity has been given to swinging singles and couples living together out of wedlock, 95 per cent of all Americans are married or will get married at some point in their lives. While marriage continues to be an experience common to the overwhelming majority of Americans, one out of every five married persons in this country has been divorced.[24] The reasons for the increase in the divorce rate are complex, but Toffler has explained it as follows:

> As human relationships grow more transient and modular, the pursuit of love becomes, if anything, more frenzied. But the temporal expectations change. As conventional marriage proves itself less and less capable of delivering on its promise of lifelong love, therefore, we can anticipate open public acceptance of temporary marriages. Instead of wedding "until death us do part," couples will enter into matrimony knowing from the first that the relationship is likely to be short-lived.
>
> They will know, too, that when the paths of husband and wife diverge, then there is too great a discrepancy in developmental stages, they may call it quits— without shock or embarrassment, perhaps even without some of the pain that goes with divorce today. And when the opportunity presents itself, they will marry again . . . and again . . . and again.[25]

Serial marriage, to the extent that it replaces lifelong marriage, will further break down the idea of maintaining one sexual partner throughout adult life. It also will result in more one-parent families and greater exposure of children to parents in dating and courtship situations.

The increasing acceptance of living together before marriage, which is often a trial marriage, and the increasing prevalence of serial marriage means that marriage is less important in our society in its impact on our sexual behavior.

## Time-Deepening and Sexual Behavior

Current sexual activity often shows great emphasis upon time saving behavior. Time deepening, mentioned in Chapter 1, applies to sexual and nonsexual behavior alike. While many do not agree with Linder's notion of a "harried leisure class," much of our contemporary sexual behavior would seem to support it.[26] As mentioned above, many desire to be efficient in sexual activity, not to waste time. Linder has argued that the amount of sexual activity in our society may actually be decreasing, if measured from the standpoint of the amount of time devoted to it. What is often thought of as promiscuity on the part of today's females, Linder suggested, may only be an acceleration aimed at saving time for both male and female. Furthermore, he suggested that conjugal fidelity may be increasing, in fact if not in mind, simply because it takes too much time to establish new contacts.[26] This notion is borne out by the fact that many of today's prostitutes meet their customers in cars in indoor parking garages for "quickies." Certainly, one reason for the success of many discos in the 1970s was their ability to provide an attractive place for males and females where they could quickly make "pickups" for sexual purposes. Humphries, in his study of impersonal sexual behavior in public restrooms, found that many men who did not have a homosexual identity and self-image were nevertheless turning to the impersonal sexual activity in public restrooms offered by the homosexual world. He has referred to such activity as "America's sexual answer to the increasing scarcity of time. . . ."[27]

The increase in pornography may also be considered as evidence of the desire to save time in sexual relations. Pornography may offer a convenient way of providing some of the sensations of other forms of sexual activity in a less time-consuming manner. In addition, it may serve as a kind of compensation for the frustrations produced by a lifestyle in which one's love life is reduced to a series of brief and impersonal encounters.

Many sexual institutions and customs have been almost eliminated from our society owing to time consciousness. Taking a mistress, for instance (the practice of a married man establishing a long-term relationship of an emotional and sexual nature with another woman), requires considerable time, which many of today's males simply do not have. The rigid scheduling and pre-planning of all activity also makes it difficult to obtain the social freedom needed to prepare the groundwork for such a sustained affair. The love affair has often been replaced by the "one-nighter": an impersonal, hurried sexual liaison between near strangers. Although Baudelaire asserted that the natural occupation of the leisured was love, impersonal sex is the occupation of the harried leisure class.

## Blurring Distinctions Between the Sexes

A final trend in leisure-related sexual activity is the blurring of distinctions between sexual roles, resulting in an increase in the range of acceptable behavior of males and females. Since many forms of leisure behavior are directly related to gender, changes in the concepts of masculinity and femininity may alter future leisure patterns radically. A number of factors have changed the images of male and female from polar extremes to a continuum, with very few individuals at either end. Much of this change has resulted from a new societal permissiveness and emphasis upon achieved status rather than ascribed status. Furthermore, today's society is more accepting of deviant sexual patterns. Indeed, with the development of effective means of contraception, movements such as Gay Liberation and Women's Liberation, bisexual social functions, sex change operations, sex therapy, and increased pornography, it has become increasingly difficult to determine what sexual patterns are truly deviant.

As the potential of sex to become leisure activity has increased, its practice has become more diverse. In such a period of change the link between politics and sexual behavior is becoming stronger and stronger. The Gay Liberation Movement, for instance, has concentrated on increasing the protection of the homosexuals' rights under the law and developing a political power base. In cities such as San Francisco, this political power is already a reality.

In issues such as abortion, providing birth control devices and information through the schools, allowing massage parlors or porno bookstores in downtown areas, no-fault divorce, and other issues, change is being effected through the political system; this period of testing seems likely to continue.

# STUDY QUESTIONS

1. Should a book dealing with leisure behavior contain a chapter dealing with sexual behavior? Why or why not?

2. Why do you think there has been little pornography over the ages designed for females?

3. What would be the advantages and disadvantages of legalizing prostitution? Do you favor it?

4. In what ways does human sexuality diminish with age? Do the aged continue to have sexual needs?

5. How has "time deepening" influenced leisure behavior during the last decade?

## REFERENCES

1. Foote, Nelson, "Sex As Play," *Social Problems*, Vol. XV, April, 1954, p. 159.
2. Freud, Sigmund, "Three Contributions to the Theory of Sex," in Brill, A. (ed.), *The Basic Writings of Sigmund Freud.* New York: The Modern Library, 1938, p. 128.
3. Juhasz, A. *Sexual Development and Behavior: Selected Readings.* Homewood, Ill.: Dorsey Press, 1973, pp. 84, 193.
4. Tuchman, Barbara. *A Distant Mirror: The Calamitous Fourteenth Century.* New York: Alfred Knopf, 1978, p. 215.
5. Dulles, Rhea F. *A History of Recreation: America Learns to Play.* New York: Appleton-Century-Crofts, 1965, p. 151.
6. Brewer, L. *The Good News.* London: G. P. Putnam's Sons, 1962, p. 95.
7. Cited by Worthington, G. E., and Topping, R., *in Specialized Courts Dealing With Sex Delinquency.* Montclair, N. J.: Patterson Smith, 1925, p. 11.
8. Comfort, Alexander. "Future Sexual Mores: Sexuality In A Zero Growth Society," *Current,* February, 1973, pp. 29-34.
9. Avedon, E., and Sutton-Smith, B. *The Study of Games.* New York: John Wiley and Sons, 1971, pp. 194-216.
10. Proulx, C. "Sex As Athletics In the Singles Complex," *Saturday Review of the Society,* May, 1973, pp. 61-66.
11. *The Obscenity Report—The Report of the Task Force on Pornography and Obscenity.* New York: Stein and Day, 1970, pp. 27-34, 80.
12. *Yale Law Review,* 1966, pp. 1409-1410.
13. Pittman, D. J. "The Male House of Prostitution," *Transaction,* March-April, 1971, pp. 21-26.
14. Kinsey, A. C., et al., *Sexual Behavior in the Human Female.* Philadelphia: W. B. Saunders, 1953, p. 60.
15. Zelnick, M., and Kanter, J. Cited by Swift, P., in "Teen-Agers and Sex," *Parade,* August 18, 1974, p. 18.
16. McBee Susanna. "Americans Remain the Marrying Kind," *Washington Post,* January 14, 1979, p. 34.

17. Wolfenstein, M. "The Emergence of Fun Morality," *in* Larrabee, E., and Meyersohn, R. (eds.), *Mass Leisure.* Glencoe, Ill.: The Free Press, 1958, p. 93.

18. Lewis, S., and Brissett, D. "Sex As Work," *Social Problems,* Vol. XV, 1967, pp. 9-18.

19. "J." *The Sensuous Woman.* New York: Dell, 1969, p. 41.

20. Comfort, Alex. *A Good Age.* New York: Crown Publishers, 1976, p. 88.

21. *Ibid.*

22. Jong, Erica. *Fear of Flying.* New York: Signet Books, 1973, p. 89.

23. Densmore, Dana. "Independence From the Sexual Revolution," *in* Koedt, A., et al. (eds.), *Radical Feminism.* New York: Quadrangle Books, 1973, p. 119.

24. Zelnik, Melvin, and Kanter, John. "Probabilities of Intercourse and Conception Among U.S. Teenage Women—1971 and 1976," *Family Planning Perspectives,* May/June, 1979, p. 18.

25. Toffler, Alvin. *Future Shock.* New York: Bantam Books, 1970, p. 251.

26. Linder, Staffan. *The Harried Leisure Class.* New York: Columbia University Press, 1970, p. 77-93.

27. Humphries, L. "New Styles in Homosexual Manliness," *Transaction,* March-April, 1974, pp. 38-46, 64, 66.

# Leisure behavior- getting organized

**M**any of the leisure activities in which you participate are sponsored by a formal organization. Lots of you have gone swimming at the "Y," gone camping with the Girl Scouts, joined stamp collecting clubs, become members of theater guilds or choral societies, played in parks administered by municipal recreation and park departments, and gone on guided tours arranged by commercial travel agencies. In short, formal organizations play an important part in shaping our leisure behavior.

## ROLES OF LEISURE SERVICE ORGANIZATIONS

There are many ways to try and identify types of leisure service organizations; one is to identify such organizations by their role. Most leisure service organizations fulfill one or more of the following roles.

### Promoter of Specific Leisure Activities and Facilities

Many leisure service organizations seek to interest people in participating in specific recreation and leisure activities with which they are not presently involved. In some cases, this is done in the belief that the leisure activity being

**249**

promoted is "superior" to other choices of activity which the individual might make during his/her free time. Many outdoor recreation organizations act on the assumption that the activities they promote are more worthwhile than other activities.

Bowling centers, for instance, sponsor advertisements concerning the joy of bowling. Some state or provincial leisure service agencies promote various sports and athletic activities in the hope that, if people become involved in such sports, they will become more physically fit, both for their own betterment and that of society. In some mental hospitals therapeutic recreation workers encourage emotionally disturbed patients to grow plants, whether or not the patient had such an interest previously, in the belief that it is a valuable step in learning to accept responsibility. In all these cases the agency wants the person to modify his/her behavior to include certain forms of leisure activity. The leisure service organization serves as a stimulus to awaken this interest. Since a given leisure activity is often valued only after some form of exposure to it, the organization justifies its approach by saying that the individual may not appreciate the happiness found in sailing, for instance, because he/she has never been exposed to it. A child playing basketball all summer in a ghetto area may not desire to go camping until exposed to a camping program, and may need to be introduced to such a program one step at a time or on a number of occasions before he/she can decide whether or not it is worth doing.

## Culturally Neutral Provider

*Provide whatever leisure activity, facility or services in which its clients express interest*

When acting as a neutral agent the leisure service organization seeks to provide or sponsor whatever leisure activities, facilities, or services in which its clients express interest. In this role it is assumed that the agency has no right to impose its own values upon its clients, and should cater to existing leisure interests rather than attempting to create new ones. The chief task of the agency is to identify accurately and supply those leisure experiences in which people wish to participate. The determination of leisure desires may involve community surveys, citizens' boards or councils, public hearings, or the collection of information concerning participation in a variety of leisure activities. As stated earlier, it is impossible for the agency to avoid having its own values enter into the decision-making process. The agency may, however, consciously seek to minimize the role its own values play in the operation of its program.

## Social Change Agent

*attempts to change people's behavior or social condition through the use of leisure activity.*

Some leisure service agencies attempt to change people's behavior or social condition through the use of leisure activity. Such change goes beyond creating interest in a given activity. In such "social engineering" the leisure activity serves as a means to an end; it is a technique or tool to change and, hopefully, to improve society. Some commercial leisure service organizations use golf or tennis as a means of interesting people in purchasing condominiums. Boys' Clubs sponsor after-school programs for teenage boys in the hope of averting delinquent behavior. Nature programs in county park systems may be initiated to change the attitudes of young children toward the outdoors, and to foster an attitude of "stewardship" toward the land. Employee-based recreation programs are often sponsored to help attract potential employees and to improve the morale of those already employed in order to improve company productivity. For a leisure service organization to act effectively as an agent for change, however, there must be an ideal situation articulated by the agency as a goal. Sometimes these are criticized for being incomplete or even unworthy. Thus, the goal of providing elder citizens with "something to do" may be criticized for seeming to assume that the elderly would have nothing to do unless some activity were "given" to them. Another criticism is that the purpose of an activity is often left unstated, as is the question of its importance.

The recent interest in "leisure counseling" reflects the belief that people can be helped to use their leisure in more satisfying ways. However, leisure service agencies that sponsor such programs often find that counseling leads to the agency's making judgments about which activities are potentially more worthwhile, which may not always be desirable.

## Coordinator of Leisure Opportunities

As a coordinator of leisure opportunities within a community, leisure service organizations seek to maximize the citizen's opportunities to participate in a wide variety of leisure activities. The organization, in this role, takes the initiative in bringing together representatives of commercial, private, and public leisure service agencies in order to share information, avoid duplicating each other's efforts, and plan ways to allow joint cooperative use of each agency's programs and facilities. As a coordinator of leisure opportunities, the leisure service agency tries to make the citizen familiar with the total range of leisure opportunities within his/her community. Often particular attention is given to informing new community residents about such opportunities. The coordinator role assumes that it is desirable for the agency to take a "systems" approach to leisure opportunity rather than to act independently or in conflict with other agencies. In many cases the citizen is primarily interested in a given leisure activity rather than in its sponsor. A swimmer, for instance, will be interested in swimming in a clean, well maintained pool at a nominal cost regardless of the organization maintaining the pool. It is conceivable that many different leisure service organizations could provide this service successfully: commercial neighborhood pools, YMCAs, municipal recreation and park departments, public schools, and so on. Therefore it would appear desirable for all the agencies who could provide this service to consult with each other to avoid duplicating services. This belief, however, is by no means unchallenged. Grodzins, for instance, has argued that an overlapping of functions by leisure service agencies is actually desirable.[1]

## Provider for the Recreationally Dependent

Here, it is assumed that the leisure service agency should direct its major effort toward providing services to those who are highly dependent upon the agency for meaningful leisure experience or who have a minimum of alternatives to the use of these services. Some people are fortunate enough to have a wide variety of leisure opportunities to choose from because of their relatively good health, income, mobility, education, and so forth. While these individuals may depend upon leisure service agencies for some of their leisure experiences, they are not dependent *to the same extent* as those who are in poor physical or mental health or who have less income, less mobility, or less education. The leisure service organization tries to compensate for this inequity of opportunity in regard to play, recreation, open space, and related areas. There are, of course, no absolute guidelines as to those characteristics that constitute a high degree of recreation dependency. Many would argue that it is possible to be poor and still enjoy a rewarding variety of leisure experiences. When dealing with an issue as basic as where children can play, however, it quickly becomes apparent that, in urban poverty areas where apartments are small and overcrowded, children's play opportunities are very limited unless some organized effort is made to provide parks, playgrounds, and leisure activity programs. The physically handicapped may likewise enjoy a variety of leisure activities with the support of interested organizations in their community, but such help is not always forthcoming. The rationale for a public leisure service agency to provide services for the recreationally dependent is that it should be a "provider of last resort," responsible for helping meet the leisure needs and desires of those for whom no one else can or will provide. Much the same argument is presented concerning the responsibility of government to provide employment for those who cannot find work during a recession or depression.

## Enhancement of the Physical Environment

Many leisure service agencies have, as a primary role, the protection and improvement of the environment. Many types of leisure activities are dependent upon certain environmental features or conditions which most people cannot supply individually in urban or suburban areas. In addition, the *quality* of the leisure experience may be highly dependent upon environmental conditions. Boating in a polluted lake is a markedly different experience from boating in a clear, clean one. A number of these leisure activities are often referred to as "land-based" and include boating, camping, backpacking, hunting, and mountaineering. Leisure service agencies maintain a variety of areas and facilities to accommodate such activities.

Some leisure service agencies also perform services that contribute to the "quality of life" of a community, such as planting shade trees, acquiring stream valley parks, preserving historical sites and unique natural areas, and protecting wildlife.

# THE SCOPE OF LEISURE SERVICE ORGANIZATIONS

As it has been shown, leisure service organizations have a wide variety of roles. We may also distinguish these agencies according to how they are financed and administered and, when this is done, such organizations are often divided into public, private, and commercial categories. Such organizations are compared and contrasted in Table 10-1.

## Commercial Leisure Services

{We spend more ~~time~~ of our free time with commercial leisures than without. Often high risk ventures.}

It is difficult to imagine all the ways whereby leisure service organizations shape our leisure behavior, and to imagine their sheer size. The commercial

**TABLE 10-1  COMPARISON AND CONTRAST STUDY OF PUBLIC, PRIVATE (VOLUNTARY AGENCIES), AND COMMERCIAL RECREATION\***

|  | Public | Private | Commercial |
|---|---|---|---|
| Philosophy of Recreation | Enrichment of the life of the total community by providing opportunities for the worthy use of leisure. Nonprofit in nature. | Enrichment of the life of participating members by offering opportunities for worthy use of leisure, frequently with emphasis on the group and the individual. Nonprofit in nature. | Attempt to satisfy public demands in an effort to produce profit. Dollars from, as well as for, recreation. |
| Objectives of Recreation | To provide leisure opportunities that contribute to the social, physical, educational, cultural, and general well-being of the community and its people. | Similar to public, but limited by membership, race, religion, age, and the like. To provide opportunities for close group association with emphasis on citizenship, behavior, and life philosophy values. To provide activities that appeal to members. | To provide activities or programs which will appeal to customers. To meet competition. To net profit. To serve the public. |

(continued)

**TABLE 10-1   COMPARISON AND CONTRAST STUDY OF PUBLIC, PRIVATE (VOLUNTARY AGENCIES), AND COMMERCIAL RECREATION\*** *(continued)*

|  | Public | Private | Commercial |
|---|---|---|---|
| *Administrative Organization* | Governmental agencies (federal, state, county, and local). | Boy Scouts, settlements, Girl Scouts, Camp Fire Girls, "Y" organizations, and others. | Corporations, syndicates, partnerships, private ownerships. Examples: motion picture, television, and radio companies, resorts, bowling centers, skating rinks. |
| *Finance* | Primarily by taxes. Also by gifts, grants, trust funds, small charges, and fees to defray cost. | By gifts, grants, endowments, donations, drives, and membership fees. | By the owner or promoters. By the users; admission and charges. |
| *Program* | Designed to provide a wide variety of activities, year-round, for all groups, regardless of age, sex, race, creed, social, or economic status. | Designed to provide programs of a specialized nature for groups and in keeping with the aims and objectives of the agency. | Program designed to tap spending power in compliance with state and local laws. |
| *Membership* | Unlimited—open to all. | Limited by organizational restrictions such as age, sex, and religion. | Limited by law (local, state, and federal), social conception regarding status and strata in some places, economics—those who have the ability to pay. |
| *Facilities* | Community buildings, parks (national, state, local), athletic fields, playgrounds, playfields, stadiums, camps, beaches, museums, zoos, golf courses, school facilities, etc. | Settlement houses, youth centers, churches, play areas, clubs, camps, and others. | Theaters, clubs, taverns, nightclubs, lodges, racetracks, bowling lanes, stadiums and others. |
| *Leadership* | Professionally prepared to provide extensive recreation programs for large numbers of people. Frequently subject to Civil Service regulations. Volunteers as well as professionals. College training facilities growing. | Professionally prepared to provide programs on a social group-work basis. Employed at discretion of managing agency. Volunteers as well as professionals. | Frequently trained by employing agency. Employed to secure greatest financial returns. Employed and retained at the discretion of the employer. No volunteers. |

\*SOURCE: H. Douglas Sessoms, Harold D. Meyer, and Charles K. Brightbill, *Leisure Services: The Organized Recreation and Park System.* Englewood Cliffs, N.J.: Prentice-Hall, 1975, pp. 13–15.

sector is by far the most pervasive. As a nation, we spend more of our free time with the products and services of the commercial sector than we do without them. Television and other mass media, travel and tourism, theme parks, professional and commercial sport facilities, and many other commercial ventures occupy, in some manner, the majority of our leisure time. The impact of such commercial outlets on our daily lives is enormous. Commercial leisure resources have been developed to a particularly great extent in the United States. More tourists, for example, visit Disney World than visit the United Kingdom.[2]

Commercial leisure services are often high-risk ventures, since it is difficult to determine what people will spend their time and money for. Interest in many leisure activities may rise or fall rapidly. Enthusiasm for such activities as trampoline centers, miniature golf, cross-country skiing, or disco dancing may change rapidly, making it difficult for such organizations to plan future development. Consequently, commercial organizations often try to diversify their activities or products. They also use advertising extensively to try and create a favorable image with the public.

According to Munson,[2] these organizations may be organized as (1) an individually owned enterprise, such as a dude ranch, (2) a local corporation, such as a ski resort, (3) a large nationwide corporation, such as the chain of tennis facilities owned by Tennis Corporation of America, (4) a concession operation, where a campsite or other facility is operated on public property under a contractual agreement, and (5) a manufacturer-operated enterprise, such as a bowling alley which is operated by a manufacturer of bowling equipment.

Let's examine how many forms of commercial leisure services exist in your community.

NAME _____

DATE _____

# Leisure Exercise 10·1

Select one square block of the downtown business district in your town. By walking the block, identify each commercial establishment which provides a leisure service, leisure equipment, or facilities. List the name of these establishments below. What percentage of the businesses on the square block you examined were devoted *primarily* to leisure goods and services? _____%

| Name of Business | Leisure Service Provided | Leisure Equipment or Facilities |
|---|---|---|
| 1. | | |
| 2. | | |
| 3. | | |
| 4. | | |
| 5. | | |
| 6. | | |
| 7. | | |
| 8. | | |
| 9. | | |
| 10. | | |
| 11. | | |
| 12. | | |
| 13. | | |

14.

15.

16.

17.

18.

19.

20.

21.

22.

23.

24.

25.

26.

27.

28.

29.

30.

31.

32.

33.

34.

35.

36.

37.

38.

39.

40.

41.

42.

43.

44.

45.

46.

47.

48.

49.

50.

## Organizations for Special Groups

Some leisure service organizations have emerged in order to meet the leisure needs of a specific subsection of the population. Therapeutic recreation, for instance, refers to both indirect and direct recreation or leisure services provided to special populations such as the mentally retarded, emotionally disturbed, physically handicapped, and other groups whose special needs limit their recreation opportunities. Organizations providing such services include not only residential institutions, such as state schools for the mentally retarded, but also community organizations, such as municipal recreation and park departments and "transitional" organizations such as "halfway houses," sheltered workshops, and others.

Residential institutions serving these groups vary widely in the leisure activities and facilities they provide or allow to be undertaken. Some of the goals of institutionalized leisure services include the following: (1) to aid in adjustment to institutional living; (2) to make the person more receptive to other forms of treatment or therapy; (3) to provide a means for catharsis through wholesome leisure activity and thus lessen antisocial behavior; (4) to provide opportunities for self-expression; (5) to provide activity that is, in itself, therapeutic and contributes to the improvement or adjustment of the individual; (6) to aid in the acquisition of leisure interests and skills that can be used in the outside world; and (7) to facilitate better intergroup relations within the institution.

Community-based organizations providing therapeutic recreation services may concentrate on making recreation areas, facilities, and equipment available or usable by some special population group, teaching leisure skills, and counseling those they serve in terms of leisure behavior and available leisure resources.

Many private nonprofit organizations provide leisure services primarily for youth. Such organizations often sprang up in the early twentieth century out of concern for children of the urban poor. Many have been concerned, in some way, with "character-building." Such organizations, according to Farrell, may be religion-oriented, such as the Catholic Youth Organization or YMCA, or social service-oriented, such as the Police Athletic League.[3] Such organizations typically involve a central national office with a specialized professional staff, regional offices, and local or neighborhood associations made up of volunteers.

Another type of leisure organization concerned with a specialized clientele is the employee recreation organization. These are usually involved in providing recreation and leisure services to employees of a medium- or large-sized company. Such organizations may provide athletic programs, social and educational activities, recreation activities for company employees who have retired, lunchtime or coffee break programs at the workplace, or organized vacations. Many such programs have been initiated by management to improve worker productivity and their image of the company. Employee recreation services are sometimes organized and financed by workers or management, but in most cases employee recreation services represent the combined financial and organizational efforts of both management and labor.

# Government Leisure Service Organizations

During the twentieth century, government has become involved in the provision of leisure services at the municipal, state, and federal levels.

### Municipal Services

At the local level, concern for bringing a bit of nature to the city has resulted in the creation of park departments, while concern for children's play has gradually led to the creation of recreation departments.

Local recreation and park departments have became a common feature of cities and towns in North America and, increasingly, in other industrialized nations. Among the functions they commonly perform are the following.

*Planning, Acquiring, Developing, and Maintaining Park Land and Recreation Areas and Facilities.* Such facilities may include athletic fields, day camps, beaches, nature centers, multipurpose buildings (recreation centers), arenas, theaters, golf courses, marinas, zoos, picnic areas, playgrounds, stadiums, swimming pools, "vest pocket" parks, music shells, cultural centers, and many others. Outdoor recreation areas administered by municipalities are likely to be smaller in size than those owned by the county, state, or federal government, but are more highly programmed and more heavily used.

*Providing Services for Groups or Individuals with Special Leisure Service Needs.* A study by the National Recreation and Park Association found that nearly four-fifths of local recreation and park agencies provide leisure services for senior citizens, and over one-fifth for preschool children.[4] Over half of these organizations provide services for mentally retarded youths, while 13 per cent do so for retarded adults. Physically handicapped youths and adults are provided some services by approximately 15 per cent of these agencies. With the movement toward the integration of the handicapped into the community, municipal leisure service agencies may assume a greater role in the provision of leisure services for them.

*Educating for Specific Leisure Skills.* Most municipal leisure service agencies provide instruction in a number of leisure activities, including sports and athletics, the visual and performing arts, crafts, and a range of nonvocational adult education courses. The bulk of such instruction is at an introductory level, although opportunity is increasingly being provided for more advanced instruction or some progression of learning experiences. Instruction is provided for leisure activities ranging from ice skating and macramé to vegetable gardening for urban youths. In some cases such instruction involves the resources of the public school system or is co-sponsored with special interest groups within the community.

*Sponsoring Special Community Events and Celebrations.* Municipal leisure service agencies often coordinate parades, exhibitions, demonstrations, celebrations marking holidays or days of special community significance, and festivals or pageants that are part of the community's cultural life. Such celebrations range from Black art expositions to Octoberfests and Halloween parades.

*Sponsoring Social, Cultural, and Athletic Programs on a Continuing Basis.* This includes such programs as athletic leagues, teen dances, contests and tournaments, organized playground and recreation center programs, adult bridge clubs, and so forth.

## State Involvement

All state governments and most provinces of Canada perform a number of functions directly related to leisure. Each of the 50 states has an agency whose primary responsibility is outdoor recreation. Additionally, other state agencies dealing with youth, the aged, education, conservation, planning, and other functions usually provide recreational services to their clientele. Each state has developed a network of areas and facilities used for recreation, including parks, forests, game preserves, conservation areas, historic sites and monuments, beaches, and marinas. State governments promote the use of these recreation areas and facilities, as well as other aspects of leisure activity in their state, in order to promote tourism and the spending it generates.

State governments affect the municipal role in recreation and parks in various ways. They formally authorize county and local governments to undertake the provision of recreation and park services through enabling legislation. States also help local governments by providing funds and technical assistance concerning leisure-related undertakings. Most states, for instance, provide funds to municipalities for the acquisition and development of open spaces. They may also provide consultants to help municipalities establish recreation and park departments, undertake master plans for recreation and parks, or provide leisure programs for the aged.

State governments may seek to encourage more skilled professionals in recreation and parks by certifying those who work in such occupations and by providing college and university courses to prepare them. In nearly every state at least one public university has such a program of study.

Since state governments are responsible for the operation of institutions for those who are segregated from society, such as hospitals, prisons, and homes for the aged, the provision of recreation and leisure-related experiences for such groups is also a responsibility of the state. State governments also provide services to private and commercial recreation and leisure-related undertakings, which might include the management of private campgrounds or inner city Boys' Clubs.

### Federal Involvement

The federal government is directly and indirectly involved in many undertakings which influence our recreation and leisure. You may have visited one of the national parks or forests for camping, fishing, sightseeing, or other activities. One reason for the involvement of the federal government in leisure services is land management. As Table 10-2 shows, the federal government serves as the "owner" of about one-third of the land mass of the United States.

Although most federal land management agencies were not originally created with any thought of outdoor recreation, they gradually became involved. The United States Forest Service, for instance, was formed in 1905 to protect and develop forest reserves in the public domain. The increasing use of these areas for camping by the public and resulting forest fires brought about the agency's involvement in outdoor recreation management. In 1960 the Multiple Use-Sustained Yield Act recognized recreation as a legitimate management purpose. Other land management agencies include the following: Bureau of Land Management, which conserves, manages, and develops 470 million acres in the Western states and Alaska; the Bureau of Reclamation, which is involved in the development of water resources; the Fish and Wildlife Service, which is responsible for wild birds, mammals (except certain marine mammals), inland sport fisheries, and fishery research activities; the Army Corps of Engineers, which undertakes civil works such as improvement of rivers, harbors, and waterways for navigation, fish, and wildlife, and shore protection; and the Tennessee Valley Authority, which conducts resource development for economic growth in the Tennessee Valley Region through the development of a system of dams providing outdoor recreation along with flood control and electric power. Even the National Park Service did not originally recognize recreation as such to be a sufficient reason for the establishment of a national park. Today, however, it ad-

**TABLE 10-2 DISTRIBUTION OF UNITED STATES LAND BY OWNERSHIP***

| Private Owners | Federal Government | State and Municipal Government | Indians |
|---|---|---|---|
| 58% | 34% | 6% | 2% |

*SOURCE: Bureau of Land Management, U.S. Department of the Interior, Federal Land Statistics. Washington, D.C.: 1977, p. 1.

ministers 30 million acres of outdoor areas which are of national historic, cultural, natural, or recreational significance.

Many other federal agencies are indirectly concerned with recreation and leisure because of their concern with a myriad of subjects, such as the elderly, the mentally retarded, transportation, commerce, and the arts. The only agency directly concerned with recreation is the Heritage Conservation and Recreation Service in the Department of the Interior, which plays a major role in planning and attempting to coordinate federal, state, and local public involvement in outdoor recreation. Generally, it may be said that the federal government has not developed much comprehensive policy with regard to recreation and leisure. I happen to think that in a diverse society such as our own it is better for the federal government not to have highly developed policies in regard to leisure. What do you think?

## The Question of Government Involvement

Why should government be involved in the provision of leisure services to citizens? Couldn't our leisure or recreational needs and desires be met through special interest clubs and organizations, commercial recreation opportunities, and individual efforts? The traditional justification for government involvement in leisure services has been that such involvement is necessary to provide for the general welfare of the population. As society

**FIGURE 10-1** Should government be involved in the provision of leisure services to its citizens? (Courtesy of the U.S. Bureau of Outdoor Recreation)

becomes more urbanized and people become more interdependent, the argument goes, public leisure services can provide an "enabling" role through the provision of leisure services not possible without such involvement. Furthermore, it is argued, government can provide a "stimulating" role in regard to leisure by providing unique opportunities for new leisure experiences that contribute to the redefinition of existing culture.

To understand some reasons for government involvement in leisure services, it is necessary to determine what would be missed if the government were not involved. One of the greatest contributions made by the government is the provision of recreation facilities that are not economically feasible for commercial organizations to undertake. Large parks in urban areas, for instance, require large expenditures for acquisition and development, as well as for maintenance. Government leisure service agencies also may help mobilize the resources of a community in a way that could not be done without them, because of the sustained effort required. In some instances, for example, government leisure service agencies have had more success in opening public schools for recreational use than have private citizen groups.

Some art forms are partially dependent upon the government for their survival. The government serves as a patron of such art forms as ballet, opera, sculpture, and poetry, providing financial assistance and promotion. The National Endowment for the Arts, for instance, makes financial grants to small publishers to enable them to produce books of poetry which, even though written by talented poets, would not make a profit as commercial undertakings. Additionally, government seeks to preserve areas of historical importance or with unique physical characteristics for the public.

The provision of leisure services to segments of the population with special needs or disabilities, such as the emotionally disturbed, the mentally retarded, the physically handicapped, the aged, and prisoners is also undertaken largely by government, although special purpose organizations also make important contributions. Certainly, it is difficult for government to identify what people want to do during their leisure or what indicates a need for recreation or leisure services.

A second criticism of government involvement in leisure services is that government will attempt to use leisure as a means of social control. Leisure may be used as a means to engender political support for those in office—to shape people's values and behavior in accordance with the wishes of those in power. Many governments, for instance, provide funding for superior athletes and promote excellence in certain sports in the hopes that they will bring glory to the country and, hence, the government in the Olympics. When the East German government spent $100,000 developing a new helmet for its luge (sled) drivers, it was not done for the glory of amateur sport, but for the glory of the state. The provision of health spas for Russian workers by the state, and the practice of husband and wife (both of whom are employed) taking separate vacations, reinforces the model of recreation as reward for work and the role of worker being more important than the role of husband or wife.

In our own country, the urban riots and racial disturbances of the 1960s provide an example of the use of leisure services as a means of social control. Immediately after such riots, in many large urban areas, local recreation and park agencies received large federal grants to provide summer recreation programs which were designed to "cool" the tense social atmosphere. It has also been charged that government may sponsor leisure services rather than attempt to deal with more basic problems of housing, education, and employment.

In many instances government's massive support of outdoor recreation appears to affect the behavior of those who live near such areas. The decision to support outdoor recreation at high funding levels reflects the conviction of many in government that such participation is superior to other recreation alternatives.

All government leisure services, to the extent that they involve some change in behavior, have the potential for social control. Even the decision to allow or not allow drinking in a public park controls or shapes behavior.

In short, government affects and controls leisure behavior both because of what it will not allow and through the encouragement of certain uses of leisure. If leisure is thought of as voluntary and pleasurable or, as I have suggested, internally compelled rather than externally compelled, then government always has the potential to change, even destroy, it.

Certainly it can't be argued that government can or should avoid all attempts at social control; regulation is a necessity in our complex society. If government acts as the owner of forest land, on behalf of the public, some control must be exerted on the public's recreational use of such areas. The alternative has proven to be a continuous round of forest fires. In local parks, government may either provide or not provide picnic tables, tennis courts, or separate sitting areas for older people. These decisions, regardless of what they are, will shape and control behavior. The question here is which areas of behavior should be controlled, and to what degree.

If government seeks to promote the performing arts, some forms and styles of artistic expression are likely to be promoted at the exclusion of others. This, in turn, may begin to shape the direction of artistic endeavor.

In the following exercise you are asked to act as a government recreation and park official and deal with some issues of social control.

## Decision-Making in State Parks

Assume that you are the Director of State Parks for your state. As such, it is your duty to deal with policy-making for the state park system. Many of these policy areas have to do with issues relating to social control. Answer the following questions and then discuss them in small groups with your classmates.

1. *How* would you decide whether or not to allow trail bikes and snowmobiles in the parks? Why? What is your *personal* belief on this issue?

2. How would you decide whether or not to allow alcoholic beverages in the parks? Why? What is your *personal* belief on this issue?

3. How would you decide whether or not to sponsor educational programs of nature interpretation in the parks? Why? What is your *personal* belief on this issue?

4. How would you decide whether or not special interest clubs and organizations should be able to use the park for meetings and rallies? Why? What is your *personal* belief on this issue?

5. How would you decide whether or not to develop cross-country skiing trails? Why? What is your *personal* belief on this issue?

Reynolds has suggested that the following steps would help return control of public leisure services to the participant and minimize social control:

> (1) encourage development of leisure lifestyles which are consistent with the financial means of people and therefore under their control; (2) broaden the educational base of leisure service professionals so they will deal with people's leisure needs as a whole rather than dealing only with compartmentalized activities or with the provision of traditional recreation facilities; (3) recognize that participants themselves are the only relevant judges of how effective leisure services are; and (4) help individuals develop independent leisure skills.[5]

If these changes were effected, government leisure services would take more of an educating, counseling, and facilitating role, with a greater degree of direction from those they serve. It seems probable that greater citizen involvement in the decision-making process of leisure service agencies has the potential to minimize government's use of leisure services.

Certainly government is not alone in its use of leisure as a means of social control. Industries and other companies sponsor recreation, doing so in an attempt to improve the "morale" of their workers and their job performance. Youth-serving organizations and voluntary organizations, such as the YMCA, Boys' Clubs, or Girl Scouts, also seek to change the behavior of those who participate in their programs. Often such agencies will define their ideals in terms of behavior or attitudes, and then will sponsor programs that they believe will meet or help foster these "ideals." Commercial recreation, through the use of advertising, often seeks to control the behavior of people by creating a need for their service in the mind of the individual. Thus, all types of leisure service agencies may seek to use leisure as a means of social control.

A third criticism of government involvement in the provision of leisure services is that government has been reactionary in its provision of such services. That is, it has often not sponsored innovative leisure activities or facilities, preferring to play it safe and avoid experimentation. To a great extent this criticism appears to be valid. Many leisure service agencies have shied away from programs such as bowling, despite obvious public interest, because of the "poolroom" stigma once attached to the sport. Park managers have often failed to recognize changes in people's tastes in camping, or still believe that everyone prefers to "rough it" while in the outdoors. In many instances it may be said that government leisure services wait for an activity to become widely accepted and noncontroversial before becoming involved with it.

## RECREATION AND LEISURE NEED

You have often heard people around you express their opinions about need or demand for recreation and leisure. "The kids around here need a place to play." "This town needs a swimming pool." "Why aren't there more movies for the whole family?" "I'd like to learn to play the guitar." It is difficult to try to measure the actual "need" or "demand" for recreation and leisure. While we can determine certain symptoms of people who need food, air, water, or sleep, leisure needs are more elusive.

Mercer[6] and others have correctly argued that the bases of recreation or leisure need are pluralistic, which is to say that they are capable of being conceptualized and acted upon within more than one value framework. Certainly this is true. It may even be argued that recreation and leisure behavior represent, for many, an ultimate expression of individual values. It does not necessarily follow, however, that public recreation, park, and leisure service agencies can adopt all individuals' values in planning. By necessity, the field of service and values inherent in such service must be limited. Agency staff, areas and facilities, and fiscal resources are all limited, and the only alternative to limiting their operation by identifying and delimiting values is to attempt to please everyone: today fighting stream pollution,

**FIGURE 10-2** Expressed need for leisure activity is demonstrated by what people actually do. (Courtesy of the U.S. Bureau of Reclamation, Department of the Interior)

tomorrow organizing junior competitive sports programs, the next day claiming to be the saviors of the inner city and, finally, claiming to be value-free—just giving the people what they want. While all such activity is potentially worthwhile, and there is great benefit from amalgamating professionals into national organizations with such diverse goals, it is a cop-out to argue that leisure or recreation should be concerned with "the quality of life," since no specific values are enunciated in such a statement. All human activities affect the quality of life. Additionally, the statement assumes that what constitutes superior quality can be readily agreed upon.

In short, some specific concept of public need for recreation must be internalized before recreation or leisure service planners can systematically develop goals and utilize research in that process. Let us examine four concepts of recreation need identified by Mercer[6] and a fifth added by this author in an attempt to determine from what definitions of recreation or leisure and value assumptions they have proceeded, and how research could be utilized to make such conceptualizations operational. Table 10-3 shows these concepts of need, the definitions of recreation they imply, the value assumptions implicit in them, and the type of research which will facilitate their use.

As you can see, the values inherent in these conceptualizations are in conflict. One believes either that each citizen should have an equal amount of public recreation resources or that some subgroup should be given priority. One believes either that government should seek to be culturally neutral, reacting to what the public says about and does during leisure, or that government should promote certain activities and experiences and discourage others. You believe either that experts are in a position to prescribe desirable minimums of certain types of recreation resources, or you do not. These conflicts of values and the inability of recreation and park professionals to take stands on them is probably indicative of the fact that, philosophically, there is no unified social movement in public recreation, parks, or leisure services, if by social movement we mean "an important form of collective behavior in which large numbers of people are organized or alerted to support and bring about or to resist social change."[2]

Thus, in the public sector, there are no agreed-upon assumptions about how to measure leisure needs. How a public agency measures leisure need will have a direct relation to how the agency serves the public. For example, if an agency uses only an "expressed need" model of recreation need, it may assume that those who "need" or "demand" to go camping are doing so. Future provision of campsites, therefore, may be targeted to those who already use them. If the same agency used "felt need" as a basis for providing campsites, it would try to provide campsites for those who said they "wanted" to go camping, whether or not they had actually been camping. It is perhaps natural that public leisure service agencies, in a pluralistic society such as ours,

**TABLE 10-3   RECREATION NEEDS***

| | Conceptualizations of Recreation Need | Definitions of Recreation | Value Assumptions | Information Needs |
|---|---|---|---|---|
| Expressed Need | Individuals need for leisure is determined by individual's current leisure activity patterns. | The expression of individual values through participation in freely chosen activities. | Government should be a culturally neutral provider. There is a relatively just distribution of recreation resources. Individuals have a relatively easy and equal access to recreation resources. Individuals don't have a similar need for publicly sponsored recreation services. Variation in need is expressed through differences in participation rate. | Determining what people do during leisure: activities participated in, duration, frequency, sequencing, and scheduling. |
| Comparative Need | Need for leisure services of government as systematically related to both supply of leisure resources available to an individual and his/her socioeconomic characteristics. | High autonomy in non-work activity which is the prerogative of an elite; a right to pursue happiness which is systematically inequitably distributed. | Government should not be a culturally neutral provider. People do not have similar need for public recreation resources. Those with low socioeconomic statuses have higher need. There may not be a relatively just distribution of recreation resources. Individuals may have relatively difficult and unequal access to public recreation services. | Studies of participation and non-participation and relationship to socioeconomic variables. Studies of relationship of supply of recreation resources to socioeconomic status. Case studies examining reasons for participation among various subcultures. |

| | | | |
|---|---|---|---|
| Created Need | Leisure need is determined by individual choosing to participate in activity after being taught to value it. | Any activity in which, after sufficient introduction, an individual will freely and pleasurably participate. | Government should not be a culturally neutral provider. Individuals often don't know what they want to do during leisure and are happier if given guidance. Leisure activities are substitutable since the individual seeks certain environmental conditions, not specific activities. It is legitimate to use recreation to promote the desired goals of the state. | Pre- and post-testing of behavior and attitudes as a result of participation in public recreation services. |
| Normative Need | Experts can establish precise, objective standards to establish desirable minimum supply in quantitative terms. Implies physiological need for leisure. | A set of physiologically necessary yet pleasurable activities undertaken during non-work time which restore and refresh the individual and prepare him/her for work again and otherwise contribute to his/her well-being. | Government should not be a culturally neutral provider. Individuals have similar need for public recreation. Certain well established kinds of recreation resources are inherently in the public interest. Recreation resources should be equally distributed through space. | Testing of assumptions of standards; e.g., accuracy of service radii. Testing relationship between perceived satisfaction and social quality indicators; e.g., crime rate, and having met standards. |
| Felt Need | Individuals need for leisure activity as a function of individual belief, perception, and attitude. | What an individual would choose to do given a minimum of constraints or high autonomy. It is a set of personally ideal activities in the mind of the individual which, | Government should be a culturally neutral provider. Many individuals desire to participate in activities which they currently do not. | Attitudinal research concerning people's desire for recreation experiences and environments and intensity of desire. |

(continued)

**TABLE 10-3  RECREATION NEEDS*** (continued)

| Conceptualizations of Recreation Need | Definitions of Recreation | Value Assumptions | Information Needs |
|---|---|---|---|
| | given the opportunity, he/she will undertake. | There may not be a relatively just distribution of recreation resources. Individuals often have legitimate reasons for not using public recreation resources. Individuals may not have relatively easy or equal access to public recreation resources. Individuals will be happier participating in what they "perceive" they want to do than in what they are currently doing. | |

*SOURCE: David Mercer, "The Concept of Recreation Need," *Journal of Leisure Research,* Winter, 1973, p. 39; and Geoffrey Godbey.

increasingly recognize that there is more than one way of determining need for recreation or leisure.

In private, nonprofit, and commercial leisure service organizations, determining recreation or leisure need assumes different dimensions. Private nonprofit organizations may make assumptions about what changes should be made in society and use leisure activity as a means of bringing about such change. Thus, the organization's concern will not be with leisure needs but with other kinds of need. The YMCA, for instance, may be interested in promoting Christian living. Commercial leisure service organizations often seek to create a need through advertising or by teaching people how to participate in or enjoy their services. They also try to measure felt and expressed need accurately to determine more exactly who uses the type of service or products they provide and who would like to.

Leisure service organizations can never determine "need" for leisure in a completely scientific or objective way. As recreation educator Harlan G. Metcalf stated in his class many years ago, recreation (and leisure) are as broad as the interests of mankind and as deep as his imagination.

## STUDY QUESTIONS

1. Identify some important differences between public, private, and commercial leisure service organizations.

2. What are some major criticisms of government involvement in the provision of leisure services?

3. What does it mean that the bases of recreation need are "pluralistic?"

4. Discuss some leisure services typically provided by local government.

5. What is "therapeutic recreation?"

### REFERENCES

1. Grodzins,
2. Munson, Karl. "Commercial and Member-Owned Recreation Forms," in Godbey, Geoffrey, *Recreation, Park and Leisure Services.* Philadelphia: W. B. Saunders, 1978, p. 133-175.
3. Farrell, Pat. "Recreation Youth-Serving Agencies," in Godbey, Geoffrey, *Recreation, Park and Leisure Services: Foundations, Organization, Administration.* Philadelphia: W. B. Saunders, 1978, p. 187-201.

4. National Recreation and Park Association, "Local Parks and Recreation," *Parks and Recreation,* Vol. 8, No. 6, August 1971, p. 19.

5. Reynolds, Ronald P. "Leisure Services and Social Control," in Goodale, Thomas, and Witt, Peter (eds.), *Recreation and Leisure: Issues In An Era of Change.* State College, Pa.: Venture Publishing, 1980, p. 246–260.

6. Mercer, David. "The Concept of Recreation Need," *Journal of Leisure Research,* Winter, 1973, p. 39.

# Some leisure ideals

**T**he next consideration of this book is perhaps the most important one: leisure ideals. What part does leisure, ideally, play in our lives? In previous chapters we examined how you spend your time and money, work-leisure relations, changes in leisure behavior throughout the life cycle, and other topics which, hopefully, have expanded your consciousness about leisure in your own life. In this chapter we will examine the reasons for desiring leisure, consider some successful as well as unsuccessful ways of using leisure, and attempt to provide some goals for the use of leisure time. All of these can be applied to each of us at a personal level.

## THE DESIRE FOR LEISURE

Perhaps the first consideration should be whether or not you want leisure. Many in our society demonstrate that they are uncomfortable with leisure and do not really want it, choosing to avoid situations that would allow them leisure time. Many factory workers, for instance, when given a 6-month vacation or sabbatical, soon find that what they do during this time is not satisfying and therefore try to return to work or else take on an additional job. As noted earlier, the final test of a civilization may be the ability to use leisure intelligently.

In our own civilization, there is much evidence that we are not ready for such a final test. Many of us would trade more leisure for more money, are uneasy or bored with leisure, or use it in ways which are personally

**279**

destructive. You may not want leisure—there is great comfort in letting other people shape your life for you. Many people find salvation in blind obedience and acceptance of work, and many seek to purify through suffering. Work, said de Grazia, may make us rich or noble, but it cannot perfect us; only leisure can do that.[1]

Let us assume that you want some leisure time in your life, for various reasons. You might want leisure because of the pleasure involved in the activities you could undertake. Conversely, leisure might merely be an escape from unpleasant work or other obligations. Or, your leisure activity might be an attempt to define who you are by achieving or accomplishing certain things, or it could be merely a way of "passing" time instead of "using" time.

## SUCCESSFUL AND UNSUCCESSFUL USES OF LEISURE

What constitutes the successful use of leisure? Obviously, people with different values judge success in leisure activity quite differently. The model of leisure activity and the lifestyle advocated in *Playboy*, for instance, with its emphasis upon pleasure, sexual freedom, travel, and stylish consumerism, might constitute the successful use of leisure for some, but not for others. Some people believe that camping and outdoor recreation activities have qualities that make them more important or "better" leisure activities than other alternatives. Those in citizen action groups, however, may feel that the successful use of leisure involves spending time in worthwhile community improvement projects. Part of the concern expressed by social critics of mass leisure is that the quality of individual leisure activity would be diminished if some "common denominator" were sought in providing leisure activities to the masses.

All of us have somewhat different models of what constitutes successful leisure experience presented to us every day. Television advertising frequently shows models of leisure behavior in connection with a particular product. Often such advertising promotes a leisure image of young, sexually attractive people having "fun" in high status activities such as skiing or sailing; these people appear to compete successfully with great ease and style. Successful use of leisure, in fact, may seem to imply a competitive approach to leisure in which one uses time efficiently in order to perform various activities better than other people. To some extent we all are urged to assume a competitive posture during our leisure, to "spend" our time wisely and have a recognizable result to show for our effort. This represents the carry-over of our work ethic into our leisure. We are urged to plan our leisure activity carefully, set goals, and learn techniques that will allow mastery over certain activities. While it is impossible to substantiate, it would appear that those who are highly competitive and compete with other people in their work roles also do this in their leisure roles. Whether this competitive ability constitutes the successful use of leisure, however, is open to question. Perhaps we should ask how the competition affects the individual.

Some may say that the successful use of leisure does not waste time. Others find leisure as an opportunity to escape the pressures of time. It may be, however, that many who have "dropped out" of society have done so in order to use their leisure time successfully in ways that the established system has denied them: time to really look into a face, time to meditate, sleep, read, loaf, or drift in the direction time takes them. They try to simplify, to let go, to dream. To succeed in using leisure in this sense may mean failing to use leisure successfully in the opinion of those who employ it for more competitive pursuits.

Success in the use of leisure may also be related to social role performance. Havighurst and Feigenbaum have suggested that unsuccessful users of leisure either invest most of their energies in work and other commitments, or else demand too much from leisure to compensate for their shortcomings in other areas of endeavor.[2] This assessment, however, seems to advocate an individual's being "well rounded" in regard to leisure and work. Many have developed skills which we admire, solely by concentrating on that particular skill. Some Olympic athletes, for instance, may accept a job merely because it enables them to partake of the sport of their choice. Many important artists have had a singular devotion to their art form, which served as their only important means of self-identification. Dylan Thomas was not well rounded, nor was van Gogh. Both, however, were successful in terms of their contribution to important forms of human expression. For such individuals it may not make sense to regard the central form of expression around which their lives revolved as "leisure." Nor, in many senses of the word, would it be "work." The fact remains, however, that we as a society benefit from those who are not "well rounded" in terms of the activities they choose to pursue, just as we benefit from those who are.

## A Hierarchy of Leisure Values

Jay B. Nash has provided a model showing a hierarchy of leisure values.[3] As may be noticed, creative activity is the highest use of leisure, while criminal activity is the lowest. This model provides a useful critique of the levels and kinds of involvement in leisure activity although, in theory, criminal activity as leisure could also be seen as creative participation or an antidote to boredom (Table 11-1).

Perhaps the first four levels of this model are the most useful, since they specify a continuum for the use of leisure from a standpoint of the degree of self-investment in activity undertaken during leisure. The zero level, however, begins to sound like Havighurst and Feigenbaum's implication that a person be well rounded in work and leisure. There may be instances when

**TABLE 11-1   MAN'S USE OF LEISURE TIME PARTICIPATION BROADLY INTERPRETED\***

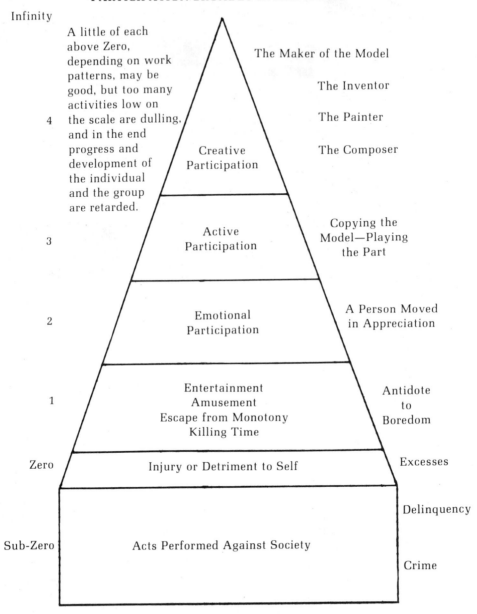

Infinity

A little of each above Zero, depending on work patterns, may be good, but too many activities low on the scale are dulling, and in the end progress and development of the individual and the group are retarded.

4

The Maker of the Model

The Inventor

The Painter

The Composer

Creative Participation

3

Active Participation

Copying the Model—Playing the Part

2

Emotional Participation

A Person Moved in Appreciation

1

Entertainment Amusement Escape from Monotony Killing Time

Antidote to Boredom

Zero

Injury or Detriment to Self

Excesses

Sub-Zero

Acts Performed Against Society

Delinquency

Crime

How Do You Rate?

*J. B. Nash, *Philosophy of Recreation and Leisure*, Dubuque, Iowa: William C. Brown Company, 1953, p. 89. Reprinted with permission.

**FIGURE 11-1** According to Nash, emotional participation or entertainment is a less desirable use of leisure time than active or creative participation. (Courtesy of AAHPERD)

"excesses" are necessary to produce great music, Olympic athletes, or a new chess strategy.

## Pleasure-Seeking

A seemingly related but actually quite different conceptualization of leisure has been propounded by Smith.[4] Smith argued that pleasure-seeking may be divided into three types: sensory, expressive-cortical, and intellectual-cortical. The basis of difference among these three types is the importance of the cortex area of the brain in generating feelings of pleasure.

Sensory recreation, which includes activities such as eating, children's play, rock music, vandalism, hunting, sports, snowmobiling, flirting, and rape, all involve the pleasurable use of muscles which are sensed by the proprioceptors (nerves sensing muscular movement). Some of these activities involve physiologically pleasurable fear. Smith described some sexual activity as follows:

> A lot of so-called sexual activity pleasure also stems from [a] "playground mentality." Caressing, kissing and intercourse provide many pleasurable stim-

uli, but not all apparently sexual activity is truly sexual. The first adolescent contacts between boys and girls generate great feelings of excitement and pleasure, but these are largely autonomic, arising from the pleasurable sensations in changes in the heart rate, respiration rate and movement of the stomach and intestines. Because these early pleasures are primarily autonomic, they inevitably decline as the two people become more familiar with each other. The mystery and intrigue are gone; sex becomes routine; the flame has gone out of their romance. Some change is necessary to rekindle the feelings: having sex in more exotic or naughty ways, in semi-public places or with new partners. Truly sexual feelings intensify with familiarity as the couple begins to draw together emotionally and become more skilled in their caresses. In brief, much so-called sexual attraction is basically pleasurable fear—like a roller coaster ride. In fact a roller coaster is a not unknown analogy in describing many love affairs.[4]

Expressive-cortical recreation is activities which are based upon a mingling of man's sensory and intellectual characteristics. The activities which use creative thought to produce something which gives sensual pleasure or adds a major intellectual dimension to a sensory experience might include wine tasting, painting, film making, or sex based upon emotional closeness.

Intellectual-cortical recreation involves activities where pleasure is obtained from intellectual activities which don't involve sensory stimulation. "Participants in such activities form an elite in any society which is regularly singled out for admiration or, as is much more common because of common social values, ridicule. These are the philosophers, theologians, linguists, mathematicians, logicians, certain historians, theoretical physicists, mystics and, at times, politicians."[4]

Smith advocated a minimum of support for sensory recreation activities, which he termed "sub-human."[4] The human being is unique from other animals, Smith argued, and his recreation should stress this uniqueness. Thus, Steve Smith has delineated a major question concerning leisure ideals. Do we seek sensory pleasure or pleasure which transcends the senses? Do we take our place with the other animals or seek our uniqueness, which is surely our more highly developed intellect, during our leisure? Should we seek to live, as Keynes advocated, increasingly in the mind? I find it hard to react to this proposition with any but mixed feelings. Surely we must admire leisure activity which transcends the body, which rises above the unconscious, automatic responses of our physical selves. Rising above the physical is, in many ways, rising above one more form of enslavement to the freely chosen, the God-like realm of the mind and spirit. Still—we are animals. We belong here no less than they and we would be deceiving ourselves to ignore our bodies, our physical desires, the pleasures of food, of touch. Also, how alone from the rest of the world we would be. Smith's typology and his view toward it appear to be one more schema for our perfection. It is distressing to think that, as a species, we may have to come much closer to perfecting ourselves, and our use of freedom, to survive. The lessons of history seem to

**FIGURE 11-2** Smith advocates minimum support for "sensory" recreation such as lacrosse. (Courtesy of Laurie Usher)

tell us this, though, particularly when technology has begun to give us greater power for harming ourselves. How can we act and enjoy with the other animals when we have tools, weapons, a self-consciousness, an awareness of death which they don't have? Yet, how can we act differently without becoming lonely little gods?

Paul Goodman has challenged the model for the successful use of leisure as presented by many recreation-oriented organizations.[5] Suppose that the goals of the National Recreation Association (now the National Recreation and Park Association) were achieved, he wrote:

> There would be a hundred million adults who have cultured hobbies to occupy their spare time—some expert on the flute, some with do-it-yourself kits, some good at chess and go, some square dancing, some camping out and enjoying nature, and all playing athletic games. . . . Now even if people were indeed getting deep personal satisfaction from these activities, this is a dismaying

picture. It doesn't add up to anything. It isn't important. There is no ethical necessity to it, no standard. One cannot waste a hundred million people that way.[5]

Goodman believed that the NRA's mistake was to consider recreation as "any activity participated in . . . merely for the enjoyment it affords."[5] Enjoyment, he said, is not a goal; it is a feeling that accompanies important ongoing activity. Pleasure depends upon function. No new culture can emerge from such activity unless it has some communal necessity. In defense of such organizations, however, it should be noted that their sense of what is communally necessary is starting to be renewed through emphasis upon the problems of the inner city, the aged and handicapped, open space preservation, community beautification, and minority group culture and art. Many such organizations, as noted previously, initially grew out of a concern for children's recreational needs, open space preservation, and similar interests of great communal necessity.

Perhaps such organizations should promote a mixture of leisure-related activities, the more important being those serving as means to culturally necessary ends, and the less important those that are done merely for the enjoyment they afford. Ultimately, this means that government leisure service agencies will play a more direct role in defining and shaping our culture and, thus, further increasing the need for effective citizen representation in the decision-making of such agencies.

## AN INTERNATIONAL CHARTER FOR LEISURE

The *Charter for Leisure*, developed by the World Leisure and Recreation Association (formerly the International Recreation Association) in conjunction with other international agencies operating in the field of play, constitutes a vision of the successful use of leisure and the role of leisure service organizations.[6]

## CHARTER FOR LEISURE

### Preface

Leisure time is that period of time at the complete disposal of an individual, after he has completed his work and fulfilled his other obligations. The uses of this time are of vital importance.

Leisure and recreation create a basis for compensating for many of the demands placed upon man by today's way of life. More important, they present a possibility of enriching life through participation in physical relaxation and sports, through an enjoyment of art, science, and nature. Leisure is important in all spheres of life, both urban and rural. Leisure pursuits offer man the chance of activating his essential gifts (a free development of the will, intelligence, sense of responsibility and creative faculty). Leisure hours are a period of freedom, when man is able to enhance his value as a human being and as a productive member of his society. Recreation and leisure activities play an important part in establishing good relations between peoples and nations of the world.

## Article 1

Every man has a right to leisure time. This right comprises reasonable working hours, regular paid holidays, favorable traveling conditions and suitable social planning, including reasonable access to leisure facilities, areas and equipment in order to enhance the advantages of leisure time.

## Article 2

The right to enjoy leisure time with complete freedom is absolute. The prerequisites for undertaking individual leisure pursuits should be safeguarded to the same extent as those for collective enjoyment of leisure time.

## Article 3

Every man has a right to easy access to recreational facilities open to the public, and to nature reserves by lakes, seas, wooded areas, in the mountains and to open spaces in general. These areas, their fauna and flora, must be protected and conserved.

## Article 4

Every man has a right to participate in and be introduced to all types of recreation during leisure time, such as sports and games, open-air living, travel, theatre, dancing, pictorial art, music, science and handicrafts, irrespective of age, sex or level of education. *Ethnic, Religion, Ability*

## Article 5

Leisure time should be unorganized in the sense that official authorities, urban planners, architects and private groups of individuals do not decide how others are to use their leisure time. The above-mentioned should create or assist in the planning of the leisure opportunities, aesthetic environments and recreation facilities required to enable man to exercise individual choice in the use of his leisure according to his personal tastes and under his own responsibility.

## Article 6

Every man has a right to the opportunity for learning how to enjoy his leisure time. Family, school, and community should instruct him in the art of exploiting his leisure time in the most sensible fashion. In schools, classes, and courses of instruction, children, adolescents, and adults must be given the opportunity to develop the skills, attitudes and understandings essential for leisure literacy.

## Article 7

The responsibility for education for leisure is still divided among a large number of disciplines and institutions. In the interests of everyone and in order to utilize purposefully all the funds and assistance available in the various administrative levels, this responsibility should be fully coordinated among all public and private bodies concerned with leisure. The goal should be for a community of leisure. In countries, where feasible, special schools for recreational studies should be established. These schools would train leaders to help promote recreational programs and assist individuals and groups during their leisure hours, insofar as they can, without restricting freedom of choice. Such service is worthy of the finest creative efforts of man.

This is a fairly comprehensive statement, but it has not been reproduced simply to invite your agreement with what it presents. Rather, I urge you to use it—and any other such statements that you may come across—as a basis for working out your own approach to leisure. The preface to the *Charter* refers to leisure *time* at the *complete* disposal of an individual; however, as we saw at the beginning of this book, leisure refers not just to the amount of time but also to the quality of activity. Furthermore, since we live in a society in which we have to consider the needs of other people as well as ourselves, can any time be completely at our disposal?

Leisure and recreation, according to the *Charter*, compensate for the many demands upon us today. Does this mean that we can be adequately compensated in leisure for what society may do to us in work and other spheres? If you are tempted to agree, then reflect upon what was said in Chapter 3 about the difficulty of isolating leisure from the rest of life. Furthermore, the *Charter* offers a goal of perfection and sometimes advocates incompatible objectives. Fundamental assumptions are made about the government's responsibility for leisure. Leisure is regarded as a "right" which is easily accessible through a number of public recreational facilities and by introduction to and participation in all types of leisure activities. This would seem to imply substantial government involvement in the provision of leisure facilities and programs. At the same time, however, the document asserts that "The right to enjoy leisure time with complete freedom is absolute." This ideal contradicts the notion of substantial governmental involvement in education for leisure and governmental provision of substantial leisure services. It should be remembered that there are different kinds of freedom—freedom of access or freedom of lifestyle. The freedom of easy access to leisure services may well limit some other freedom, and vice versa.

# LEISURE GOALS AND IDEALS

Ultimately you must determine your own leisure goals and ideals; no one else can do it for you. This is not the same, however, as saying that all leisure values and ideals are of equal worth. Often college students argue that all leisure activity is of equal worth as long as the individual in question likes it and doesn't hurt others by doing it. While this position can certainly be defended, it may indicate that the proponent of this viewpoint has not yet developed a personal philosophy of leisure. That is, he or she has not yet developed "a point of view from which to take in the world" in regard to freely chosen activity. Individuals, of course, should be free to use their leisure as they choose provided it doesn't hurt others. As a philosophical position, however, this is a necessary but not sufficient viewpoint. Freedom is opportunity and opportunity is important only when it is responded to, and how we respond, what we do, and how we do it is important. As we develop as unique human beings we begin to develop unique views of what is worthwhile, important, and good. To believe that all leisure behavior is the same is to believe that what the individual does is of little consequence, that human uniqueness is not important. This is not to say that we should penalize those whose leisure ideals are different from our own, or that we should spend all our energies seeking to convert the world to our leisure values, but only that we should develop some leisure ideals as a necessary step in becoming who we will be.

## Leisure Values

Allow me to present some leisure values for your consideration. In doing so, I must start by suggesting that any leisure goals should be situationally determined. For instance, most of us speak of puritanism in negative terms because of the puritanical prohibitions against pleasure. Given the situation of the early Puritans, however, who were seeking to survive in a strange land where winters were cold and life was hard, the puritan ethic was quite functional. In a society that meets material needs more easily, however, a strong distrust of pleasure is not as functional. The following leisure ideals, therefore, are suggested in light of our own culture, although I do not mean to suggest that this is the best of all possible cultures.

In choosing leisure activity, I believe that the first question is not "What is pleasurable?" but rather "What is worth doing?" Leisure is ultimately freedom, and freedom must be used for activity that the individual believes is worthwhile. Some worthwhile activities are also pleasurable at the time they are done, but some are not; some pleasurable activities are not worthwhile, while others are. This does not negate the importance of pleasure—it simply points out that the issue of pleasure is not primary. Additionally, many activities which the individual believes are worthwhile produce pleasure via a by-product even though the actual performance of the activity is not pleasurable. For instance, learning to ski may not be fun, campaigning against a government policy can be painful, weeding a tomato patch or flower bed can be drudgery, and a first attempt at skydiving may be a nightmare. If these activities have meaning and worth to the individual, however, the question of direct or immediate pleasure becomes less important.

Given the rate of change in present Western society it would appear logical for us to retain the Romantic ideal, which valued new experience for its own sake. Our relationships with people and things are becoming increasingly shorter and, as Toffler has observed, experience is the only thing that cannot be taken from us.[7] Seeking new leisure experiences may serve both as an educational experience for the individual and as an affirmation and acceptance of what life has to offer. This does not imply that one should forsake old activities which are valued all through a lifetime, but only that it seems important to maintain an openness and receptiveness to new experience. This indicates a continued willingness to explore, to learn, to change, and to grow.

Learning may actually have the greatest leisure potential of all, not only learning as formal education, but also in terms of other activities from which we gain new discoveries, understandings, and changes in our behavior. It is difficult for us to value learning as a means to an end. Many of you, for instance, may be reading this book in hope of getting a good grade in a course, thus giving you the credentials to get a job in the vocational area of your choice. Learning as a desired leisure experience throughout a lifetime may appear to be an unrealistic ideal. Learning, however, is an activity with infinite potential, of the greatest importance for those who seek to be free. Learning, therefore, can be a way of becoming free.

Another leisure ideal is to maintain the spirit of playfulness in leisure activity, a spirit which our society has largely lost. Overseriousness pervades many of our leisure activities; we approach them industriously, even scientifically. The late Vince Lombardi, formerly coach of the Green Bay Packers, is alleged to have said that winning football games is not the important thing—it's the *only* thing. Such an attitude insured that his team would not "play" football, it would "work" football. The spontaneity and ritual of sport is lost when calculation and machine-like performance become everything.

Leisure activity ultimately finds its meaning in a sense of celebration, activity that affirms the universe and our place in it. I would agree with Josef Pieper who said "What is true of celebration is true of leisure: its possibility, its ultimate justification derive from its roots in divine worship."[8] Such a celebration must stem from a sense of wonder, a holy curiosity, a letting go based upon some universal belief or trust. As the Chippewa Indian poem stated:

Sometimes I go about pitying myself,
and all the time I am being carried
on great winds across the sky.[9]

The worship of work, so predominant in our society, kills the opportunity for leisure as celebration. As Pieper remarked, "the ultimate root of leisure is not susceptible to the human will."[8] We cannot, in other words, become celebrants of life by working at it. Sometimes it is worthwhile to let things happen to us, to be still, to go inside ourselves and grope with what is there.

To celebrate life requires that its mysteries be celebrated, as well as its certainties. To be content with the unknown and to take joy from it is necessary if leisure activity is to provide some basis for holiness, for going beyond the purely rational. We cannot, for instance, explain why a particular painting pleases us. Part of man's ancient fascination with art is that most art forms produce something which cannot be translated or substituted. The mystery is partially one of uniqueness. Likewise, in our leisure activity, we must seek our own sense of uniqueness.

In doing this, we are dealing with man's highest need: self-actualization. Leisure activity in its highest form provides self-actualization or self-definition, as does "work" in its highest form. Seeking self-definition in leisure activity, however, should not merely be a matter of what one does, but also an expression of what one is. Too often our society uses only proficiency as the medium for identifying and judging other people in both their leisure activity and their work. Bertrand Russell once suggested that society should reward its members according to their morality rather than according to their productivity. Self-defining leisure activity is not at all synonymous with a level of achievement or the number of achievements. *How* the individual does something may be far more important in terms of self-definition than the *amount* of productivity or accomplishments.

Another leisure ideal, which somewhat overlaps several of the others we have mentioned, is that of leisure as a transcendental or authenticating experience. Existential man, according to William Barrett, is coming more and more to believe that "an authentic life is not handed to us on a platter but involves our own act of self-determination (self-finitization) within our time and place."[10] Man breaks through to the authentic, or transcends his condition, when he loses himself totally to activity so as to make a place for himself in the universe. In such activity there is a loss of self-consciousness because of the total immersion in the activity. But, because our society is extremely self-conscious, this may rarely happen and, because our society is extremely rational (but not always reasonable), there is a tendency for us to be self-analytic even during leisure activity. We may, for instance, go to a party and mentally analyze the situation: Am I with my friends? Are the refreshments good? Do I like the music? Then we decide if we are having a good time. If the party were to serve as a transcendental leisure experience, however, the individual would make no conscious analysis while at the party and, only later, on the way home, would say to himself "Hey, I had a good time!" In such an authenticating leisure experience the individual also loses his sense of time, momentarily stepping outside of time. As W.H. Auden said:

> Time will say nothing but I told you so
> Time only knows the price we have to pay[11]

The desire to conquer time is ultimately futile, because in becoming "efficient" our awareness of time increases. It is only through transcendental activity that man defeats time, because in such activity he separates himself from it. The substance of such activity may be almost anything: sports, arts, hobbies, reading. It may be called either leisure or work. The important thing is to give oneself to the activity.

In doing this, one moves beyond the realm of seriousness to what Huizinga has called "that more primitive and original level where the child, the animal, the savage and the seer belong, in the region of dream, enchantment, ecstasy, laughter."[12] It is in this realm, and only in this realm, that man can truly be free and become whole again.

## STUDY QUESTIONS

1. Do you agree with the hierarchy of leisure time usage as described by Nash?

2. Smith believes that "sensory recreation" should be minimized in our society? Do you agree? Why?

3. Review the *Charter for Leisure*. Do you believe it is a meaningful document? What contradictions, if any, do you find in it?

4. Is seeking pleasure in and of itself a worthy use of leisure? Why or why not?

5. What is the existential view of leisure? Do you share this view?

### REFERENCES

1. de Grazia, Sebastian. *Of Time, Work and Leisure.* New York: Twentieth Century Fund, 1962, pp. 1-365.
2. Havighurst, R., and Feigenbaum, L. "Leisure and Life Style," *American Journal of Sociology,* Vol. LXVIII, January, 1969, pp. 295-307.

3. Nash, Jay B. *Philosophy of Recreation and Leisure.* Dubuque, Iowa: William C. Brown, 1953, p. 89.

4. Smith, Stephen L.J. "On the Basis of Pleasure: Some Implications for Leisure Policy," *in* Goodale, Thomas, and Witt, Peter (eds.), *Recreation and Leisure: Issues In An Era of Change.* State College, Pa.: Venture Publishing, 1980, p. 57.

5. Goodman, Paul. *Growing Up Absurd.* New York: Vintage Books, 1956, pp. 234-235.

6. *Charter For Leisure.* World Leisure and Recreation Association, 1974.

7. Toffler, Alvin. *Future Shock.* New York: Bantam Books, 1970, p. 87.

8. Pieper, Josef. *Leisure: The Basis of Culture.* New York: New American Library, 1952, pp. 57, 62.

9. American Indian Anonymous. *In* Bly, R. (ed.), *The Sea and the Honeycomb.* Boston: Beacon Press, 1972, p. 15.

10. Barrett, William. *Existential Man—A Study In Existential Philosophy.* New York: Doubleday, 1962, p. 271.

11. Auden, W. H. *Selected Poetry of W.H. Auden.* New York: Random House, 1933, p. 69.

12. Huizinga, Johan. *Homo Ludens.* London: Paladin Books, 1970, p. 141.

# The future of leisure

**I**n a society as complex as ours, the forces which have an impact upon our leisure are too numerous even to identify. Nevertheless, several trends can be noted which are likely to shape our leisure behavior in the decade of the 1980s and beyond. Examining these trends will be our last concern and the one about which we can be least certain.

## A MORE CENTRAL ROLE FOR LEISURE

It seems likely that during the next decade our uses of leisure will be less a matter of division or refreshment after work and more a matter of pursuing interests which are central to the lives of participants. Accompanying this trend will be an increasing inability to determine whether or not a person is at work or at leisure merely by knowing the activity in which he or she is participating. Leisure will be different from work because of the individual's attitude toward the activity, the activity's personal meaning to the individual. Sociologists Cheek and Burch have argued that already the difference between work and leisure is not a conceptual one. They stated that:

> All persons clearly know when they are working and when they are off duty. Unlike social life with intimates—kin, friends, peers—or the large social spheres concerned with sustaining myth—such as religion, sports, and politics—work exhibits a fundamentally different pattern of organization. In work, participation is coerced by necessity, only a narrow segment of one's person is required,

the selection of co-workers is made by necessity rather than choice, and the timing and sequence of action is usually external to the worker; that is, set by seasons, tools, machines, materials, or work organization—and finally, there is usually a tangible outcome. In short, the significant difference between work and non-work is not a conceptual one or one that inheres in a specific activity or specific person, rather the significant difference is in the kinds of social organization that are involved.[1]

Thus, we cannot determine whether Activity A is work or leisure without understanding something about its social organization. While many have speculated that the line between work and leisure is likely to disappear in the near future, it seems probable that leisure will still be distinguishable from work according to how it is organized and with whom it is undertaken. While we will continue to distinguish between work and leisure, the primacy of work may be balanced.

## A Balancing of Work Centrality

As we move into the final quarter of the twentieth century the central role of work for many is likely to be altered. While many social scientists such as Golding have believed that "work experience is a central determinant of the amount and type of leisure demands an individual will make,"[2] this presently seems to be true to a lesser and lesser extent. Leisure, as Roberts and others have pointed out, is increasingly not dependent upon work role and exists as a category of behavior which is more and more independent of work role.[3] This independence appears to be increasing, both in the content of leisure and in its meaning. It seems difficult to connect occupation to employment systematically in a society where a higher percentage of those who are unemployed go horseback riding than professional workers, where almost one out of ten housewives goes hunting, where seven per cent of all farmers play golf, or where a higher percentage of students play tennis than those in the highest status occupations.[4] Similarly, it is difficult to connect occupation to leisure when professionals, farmers, and housewives are almost equally likely to identify lack of money as the reason preventing their use of outdoor recreation areas. While occupational status—student, unemployed, employed part-time, employed full-time, housewife, retired—does influence the content and meaning of our leisure, even these relations are becoming less pronounced.

In short, leisure is becoming more independent of work. As Roberts stated, the growth of leisure has come about through the containment of work rather than its decline: "Leisure has developed alongside work, and functions alongside it in identity formation and maintenance."[3] One piece of evidence of the increased importance of leisure and its independence from work is flexible work hours. In the future it is likely that rigid scheduling of work, which began during the industrial revolution, will give way to more flexible and less uniform patterns of work and work-related activity.

# A Decline of Standardization and Centralization

As the industrialization of America occurred many aspects of our life, from clothing to formal education to food to entertainment, became more standardized. Mass production and consumption, mass media, mass leisure, and mass education arose from the standardization that accompanied industrial applications of technology. When work became standardized a process was begun which resulted in the standardization of many other areas of our lives. In similar fashion, the centralization of work led to centralization in other spheres of life. The giant bowling center, the package tour of Europe, the "made for television" film, and many other forms of leisure activity reflect this centralization and standardization.

Today we are beginning what Alvin Toffler has called "The Third Wave."[5] In first wave civilizations, which were basically agricultural, work was not highly interdependent. In second wave cultures the synchronization of man's machine led to standardization and centralization. Today, in the emerging third wave civilization, there is a marked movement toward decentralization and individualization, evident in many spheres of life.

In regard to government, the desire for neighborhood control and revolts against centralized federal taxation, control, and centralized social schemes are occurring across the nation. Organizations, which were formerly often centralized bureaucracies, are increasingly "ad-hocracies" in which different groups and individuals are in charge in different circumstances.[5] The desire to be self-sufficient and self-reliant has led to growing small plots of vegetables, relearning handyman skills, and experimenting with energy sources which can be used independently of large public utilities.

All these attempts to decentralize and avoid standardization are manifestations of what Toffler has called "the post-standardized mind."[5] Consumption of goods is affected by this because the lifestyle of the consumer will become an increasingly important consideration in the decision to buy or not buy a given item. Products must "fit in" with the configuration of other products and services used by the consumer; this has led to more specialized retail stores and boutiques.

The post-standardized mind will certainly be getting more and more of its information from decentralized sources. The "mass media" are breaking up quickly; the use of specialized newsletters and magazines, photostated written communication, home computers, miniature tape recorders, video cassettes, Home Box Office and other cable television, and other new forms of communication are decentralizing our communication and individualizing our leisure behavior.

Decentralization and less standardization will certainly shape our leisure behavior in a number of ways. While predicting this impact is risky, perhaps some of the following will occur:

1. A breakup of a common rhythm of work and leisure will mean that

leisure will occur at different periods of time for different people. The organizations and institutions which sponsor leisure activity will have to be increasingly flexible as to when and for what lengths of time they will offer their services.

2. We will be less and less likely to share a common popular culture. What we see on television, or how or even if we use it, will vary greatly. Where and how we are entertained, the popular art forms which emerge, what we read for pleasure, and even our games will be increasingly different.

3. Determining what recreation or leisure activity should be provided by government will be increasingly difficult and will require more of a grass roots approach. Our definitions of what a park, playground, or swimming pool is will fluctuate in different regions of the country or neighborhoods within a region.

4. The "franchise" approach to offering recreation by the commercial sector will have to be modified so that each "unit" will match local interests and lifestyles more closely. Merely providing the "standard" model racquetball center in town X will not be likely to work. In the field of travel and tourism, futurist Herman Kahn has predicted an increasing role for travel advisors who are more than merely sellers of transportation.[6] Such advisors will individualize travel packages and experiences to suit customers.

In these and other ways, decentralization and decreased standardization will shape our leisure. As this occurs, our basic notions of what leisure is and what is worthwhile during leisure will have less in common. Leisure expression will reflect more our personality and the values and lifestyles of those in our own social circles.

## GREATER USE OF LEISURE FOR EDUCATIONAL AND RELIGIOUS PURPOSES

Will human beings still be on this planet in the twenty-first century? Many of our greatest thinkers are not at all sure. Buckminster Fuller stated that whether or not we will survive will depend upon whether muscle and power continue to have complete dominance over world affairs:

> Humans will be alive aboard our planet Earth in the twenty-first century only if the struggle for existence has been completely disposed of by providing abundant life support and accommodation for all humans. Only under these conditions can all humans function as competent local Universe problem solvers. That is what humans were invented for. Only if Abraham Lincoln's "right" has come into complete ascendancy over "might" will humanity remain alive on board our planet in the twenty-first century. . . .[7]

As the nations of the world become more and more interdependent, it will be more and more difficult for anyone to exist independently of others. Your life, in other words, will increasingly be interrelated to the lives of others living in Brazil, China, or France; what happens in Pakistan or Haiti will affect your life in increasingly direct terms. As we become more interdependent, it will be more important that no segment of the world's population remain ignorant. As our power to do harm to each other increases, the power of those with the lowest education levels to do harm to those with higher levels will increase. As much of American literature since Melville and Hawthorne has warned us, as our knowledge increases, our mortality must increase correspondingly if we are to survive. In the Western World, and increasingly the Eastern, we have come to believe that the best chance of improving our mortality is more education.

If the previous assumptions are true, leisure may be affected in two ways. First, our use of leisure for educational purposes will become more important. "Continuing education" using both formal and informal methods will become a more important use of our non-work time. Such education is likely to occur through various media, including television, print, travel and living in other countries, formal instruction, lectures, exhibits, and small group discussions. Colleges and universities, whose enrollment of full-time students in the 18 to 25 age range will decline slightly during the 1980s, are likely to make far greater efforts to meet the continuing education needs of older adults. Leisure, defined as free time, may increasingly be used for learning which serves as a means to an end: our survival.

Leisure may also be restricted due to our increased power over each other. The major unanswered question of the Western World is whether our collective survival is imperiled if individuals are allowed to be free to pursue their own interests during leisure. It appears that the liberal democratic idea of individual rights being more important than group rights can only be maintained if individuals exhibit more concern for others. When we act, as Jean Paul Sartre said, we must act for all mankind. Our leisure activity will increasingly have to show our ecological understanding. It will, for instance, be less and less feasible to destroy the desert habitat by riding motorcycles and dune buggies over it for the sake of freedom and pleasure. It will be less and less defensible to consume vast quantities of the world's non-renewable resources during leisure, and education must help show us why.

The use of leisure may also increasingly become a search for spiritual meaning. Much of the pleasure-seeking behavior of the so-called "me" generation of the 1970s was characterized by a spiritual emptiness. Sara Davidson described life among the pleasure seekers of Venice, California, thusly:

> Rolling, Rolling. The wind is blowing, the palms are blowing, and people are blowing every which way. I cannot walk on the boardwalk these days without feeling it in my stomach. Something is wrong. There are too many people on

wheels. The skaters will fall, the bikers will crash, they will fly out of control, and there is nothing to hold on to.

I retreat to my house and remain indoors all weekend. Venice is odd, unique, and yet I see among the crowds on the boardwalk an exaggeration of common symptoms: the worship of wealth; the insatiable partying; the loss of commitment and ideals; the cult of the body; the wandering of children in a sexual wilderness.

What does it mean, I ask myself, to be dressed as a striptease artist on skates?

What does it mean to pay half a million dollars for a tacky two-bedroom condo on the sand?

What does it mean that everyone I know is looking to make some kind of "killing"?

It means, I think, that we are in far deeper than we know.[8]

It seems likely that the search for spiritual satisfaction will grow more intense during the next few decades, even though those in the upper middle class have been described by Kahn as being increasingly atheistic, especially those who earn their living by analytic, literary, and aesthetic skills.[9]

## CHANGES IN LEISURE LIFESTYLE OF AN AGING POPULATION

Our population is growing older. In terms of those 65 and older, in 1900 they constituted only 3 per cent of the population, 8 per cent in 1950, 11 per cent in 1980, and are expected to constitute 17 per cent by the year 2030, which is less than 50 years away.[10] Our rapidly aging population can be traced to the "baby boom" of 1947 to 1957, when 43 million children were born who now comprise one-fifth of our total population—and they will be middle-aged in the 1980s and 1990s.

It is difficult to delineate what the impact of an aging society will be on leisure behavior, since those who are growing old now are likely to be different from those who are already old. The life experiences of those old now are different from those who will be old in coming decades. Since these generational effects mean that old people are not the same now as those in the future, caution must be exercised in trying to estimate how an older population will change recreation and leisure. Today's young adults, for instance, have been socialized into a number of sports which the older generation have not, they have also not lived through the Depression, they are less likely than their predecessors to think that pleasure-seeking is sinful, and they are better educated and in better health.

While we can't assume that tomorrow's older citizens will be the same as today's, perhaps the biggest predictable impact will be the need to "retro-fit" our recreation and leisure resources for an aging population. The disco which is of interest to many younger people may not be a suitable place for older people to dance because older people often have different styles of dancing, different motivations for going dancing, and can do very nicely without a lot of loud noise and flashing lights, thank you. Public recreation and park agencies cater disproportionately to the adolescent; many parks have specialized play equipment for the young but not for the old. In many often unnoticed ways our recreation and leisure resources are geared to the young. As our population grows older, it is likely that many leisure activities will increasingly be undertaken for social rather than achievement reasons, for expressive rather than instrumental reasons.

## SMALLER LIVING UNITS

As America moves into the last fifth of the twentieth century, the number of households will increase by over twice the percentage as the population. Married couples, who made up 70 per cent of the households in 1970, will comprise only 55 per cent in 1999. One out of three people will live alone or with a non-relative, as compared to one in five in 1970.[11]

A number of changes are likely to result from the increase in smaller living units. Many forms of "family-oriented" recreation are likely to decrease. As more and more people live alone, leisure activity which emphasizes "socializing" and establishing meaningful interpersonal relations will become more important. Leisure behavior will increasingly become the vehicle for bringing individuals together into social groups.

## FURTHER MIGRATION TO THE SUN BELT
## AND TO SMALLER COMMUNITIES

During the 1980s, the migration of population to southern states will continue, while northeastern states such as Pennsylvania and New York will experience practically no population growth. Migration is also expected to continue to non-metropolitan areas from larger urban centers. During the 1970s, such non-metropolitan areas grew in population by 14.3 per cent while the population of metropolitan areas increased by only 5.7 per cent.[12] Such migration appears to be motivated not only to escape the crime, pollution, and complexity of urban life, but also to return to closer relations with neighbors and to have a more active role in an environment whose dimensions are known. Futurist Herman Kahn has stated that the number one social concern of the 1980s will continue to be "Do I live in a good place to raise my children? Can I afford it?"[9] The migration to smaller communities reflects this concern.

These two migration trends, coupled with the limits of growth in government spending, would seem to indicate that people will have to be more involved in planning and organizing their own recreation and leisure activity. In smaller communities, with reduced government spending, people will increasingly have to serve as volunteers if libraries, parks, and senior citizen centers are to remain open. Leisure may take on more of the qualities associated with *Gemeinschaft* (rural community)—group-centered, outdoor, spontaneous, classless, conservative.

Migration to warmer states will also increase participation in many forms of outdoor recreation and sports activities, as well as perhaps bring about a more "leisurely" lifestyle often associated with subtropical climates.

## ENERGY AVAILABILITY

The availability of energy and its costs will shape our leisure in many ways, both direct and indirect. It is not possible even to identify all the indirect ways in which energy affects our leisure. Who works, how they work, and how close they live to work are all influenced by the availability of energy. So, too, is the level of goods and services which we enjoy. Because of this, energy availability will determine, to a certain extent, the style of our leisure behavior.

In addition to these effects, participation in many forms of leisure experience will be shaped by energy requirements if energy is in short supply or is very expensive. Many leisure activities, such as motorboating, consume significant amounts of energy, both in travel to and from the activity and in participation in the actual activity itself. It seems likely that in a situation of scarce energy, home-based recreation will become more prevalent. As Table 12-1 shows, many forms of outdoor recreation take place at a considerable distance from one's home.[4] These activities may be partially replaced by activities done around and in the home. Those who wish to camp in developed areas may not be able to afford to travel for over 1 hour to do so. Travel and tourism will also be negatively affected by restricted energy availability. Fewer people will travel or will travel for shorter distances (and in more fuel-efficient ways) than currently.

Such changes, of course, will only occur if energy supply is low throughout the world. Many, including Herman Kahn, have not made that assumption:

> I do not foresee a long-term energy crisis. Many scenarios can be developed for a short-term crisis (5 or 10 years or, in the case of gross incompetence, perhaps 15 years) but none are plausible for the long term, certainly nothing catastrophic. There is just too much energy around.

> Should Saudi Arabia or Iran go out of production for a long term or permanently, the world might take 5 to 10 years to adjust, but the adjustment would be made and substitute energy sources brought on line.[6]

**FIGURE 12-1** Future leisure patterns will depend upon new forms of transportation such as this electric car, scheduled for production in the mid-1980s. (Courtesy of the General Motors Corporation)

**TABLE 12-1 PERCENTAGE OF THE POPULATION PARTICIPATING IN OUTDOOR RECREATION BY DISTANCE FROM RESIDENCE***

|  | At Your Residence | Within 15 Minutes' Walk of Residence | Within 1 Hour's Travel From Residence | More Than 1 Hour's Travel From Residence |
|---|---|---|---|---|
| Camping in developed area | 0 | 1 | 18 | 21 |
| Fishing | 1 | 7 | 38 | 28 |
| Outdoor pool swimming and sunbathing | 3 | 8 | 40 | 20 |
| Bicycling | 3 | 23 | 28 | 9 |
| Golf | 2 | 3 | 11 | 5 |
| Tennis | 4 | 15 | 21 | 6 |
| Downhill skiing | 0 | 0 | 3 | 5 |
| Snowmobiling | 1 | 2 | 4 | 3 |
| Hunting | 1 | 2 | 3 | 10 |

*SOURCE: Heritage Conservation and Recreation Service, *National Outdoor Recreation Survey.* Washington, D.C.: U.S. Department of the Interior, 1978, p. 36.

Hydrogen and alcohol are easily produced substitutes, and electricity will be used extensively for ground transportation. Barring unforeseen developments, the price of fuel will decline. According to Kahn, business travel will not increase faster than the overall rate of economic growth, but leisure travel will rise from 1.5 to 2.0 times faster than this rate. Abundant energy, in other words, will mean that traveling for pleasure will become increasingly popular.

## BEYOND THE "NEAR" FUTURE

Our discussion so far has dealt with the near future, perhaps the next 20 to 50 years. If we think about the more distant future, our ability to speculate correctly becomes even more limited than in forecasting the near future. It may be best, therefore, if we develop two different "scenarios," or likely futures. But first let's recall the stages of historical development with regard to work and leisure. In making these generalizations, of course, we are dealing with central themes or tendencies. Perhaps the following can be used to make sense historically out of the evolution of leisure.

### Pre-Industrial Societies

**Phase One.**   Tribal, hunter-gatherer, agricultural—work and leisure usually not concepts used to divide human activities. Cyclic concept of time taken from natural environment.

**Phase Two.**   Agricultural, trade, crafts—work shows more specialization and division of labor. Cyclic and mechanical concepts of time coexist. Beginnings of separation between work and non-work activity (recreation).

### Industrial Society

**Phase One.**   Manufacturing combines people, machines, and technology. Work scheduled first and central in lives of workers. Leisure limited to an elite. Non-work time for most spent in rest and recovery. Mechanical time dominates.

**Phase Two.**   Manufacturing becomes somewhat more humanized. Common rhythm of work and leisure. Opportunities for recreation available to many workers. Content and scheduling of leisure still highly shaped by work. Mechanical time continues to dominate.

**Phase Three.**   Service industries join manufacturing. Division between work and leisure minimized for some. Content, scheduling, and style of leisure vary greatly. Both mechanical time and psychological time become important.

Let us assume that during the next 100 years one of the following two scenarios will follow Phase Three of industrial society.

# The Integrated Future

Although energy shortages exist throughout the 1980s, a combination of conservation, synthetic fuels, alcohol, wood, wind, and biomass avert an economic catastrophy. Public education shifts toward a lifelong learning model in which citizens maintain some contact with schools for most of their lives. Learning, even in colleges, is no longer geared to careers, which may become obsolete in a decade, but toward broad themes centering around what the student gradually identifies as desired major life experiences and contributions. Such freely chosen experiences may be done for pay in the private or public sector or may not earn money at all. Government will provide a subsistence wage for those whose desired major life experiences will earn no money. The line between work and leisure will almost disappear, although some diversionary recreation activity, similar to that found in the second phase of industrialism, will appear. Less time will be spent with the mass media, and more time in travel. Entertainment will be limited. Social barriers to undertaking desired major life experiences, such as race, sex, religious affiliation, origin, physical handicaps, addictions, physical appearance, and sexual preference will be minimized. People will increasingly be judged according to their virtue and their intelligence. The common rhythm of daily life will be completely broken. Urban centers will bustle with activity around the clock. Devoting one's life to seeking individual sensual pleasure will be allowed but considered unworthy. Facilitating individual major life experiences will involve more participatory democracy and less emphasis on efficiency and other industrial goals. It will subsequently cost more to build a house, buy a loaf of bread, or purchase life insurance. Ownership of things will be much more limited than today, although material goods purchased will be of better quality and selected more carefully. People's interaction with others will be comparatively more important than their interaction with things.

Those in the less educated lower classes will increasingly do the undesirable work of society, but will be paid in accord with how disagreeable the work is considered by society; the most disagreeable tasks will be the highest paid. Third world nations will increasingly supply the workers to perform these tasks and will receive government-guaranteed educational programs as part of their work visa agreements.

In regard to specific forms of behavior which we now call leisure, the following will occur. Sport will increasingly become religious ritual. Interest in travel and tourism will become heightened, with emphasis upon experiencing everyday life in other cultures. Moon visitation will be popular, but available to only a few as selected by lottery. Television will serve many functions, including instruction, counseling, personal communication, historic preservation, organizational meetings, intercultural exchange and, to a very small extent, entertainment.

Outdoor recreation forms will show increased concern for the protection of the natural environment. Hunting will largely disappear. Any and all forms of sexual behavior between those capable of informed consent (based upon their knowledge, not age) will be permitted and considered not to be the business of the state. Non-chemical forms of altering the senses will be found, which will be considered enlightened alternatives to alcohol and marijuana, although a number of carefully licensed drugs will be used for pleasurable purposes. The term "volunteer" work will lose much of its meaning, since it will be assumed that one's central life work is voluntary.

People will be more consistent in terms of how they treat other people, and will be forced to be more tolerant of individual variation. This will be a major source of stress and will require training and practice. The industrial revolution will, in many respects, have come full cycle.

## The Segregated Future

Energy shortages of the 1980s will be made worse by increasing instability of several Middle East governments. The Moslem nations, although in political disarray, decide to supply less and less oil to the world. Other international cartels form, raising the price of wheat, aluminum, coal, and other raw materials. Travel within North America becomes severely restricted, causing a movement back to cities and small towns and out of suburbs and rural areas. Many service occupations, particularly in the professions, begin to decline. Manual labor becomes a more important source of energy. Craftsmanship is increasingly important since the operation of machines will become more costly. Formal education moves away from liberal education and toward vocational training to an even greater extent than in the 1970s. Government will seek to reinforce the work ethic in a number of ways. Social welfare benefits are reduced. New machines and technologies are carefully examined by government and are banned if it is believed they will throw people out of work. Additionally, government will take renewed efforts to see that employment is not denied based upon race, gender, age, physical handicaps, or other bases of discrimination.

Private cooperatives will be formed among groups of people who live close to each other in order to pool material resources and provide other kinds of mutual assistance. Millions of people will attempt to start small businesses and "cottage industries."

Leisure, for many, will take on a recreational and diversionary quality. The line between work and leisure will become a rigid one. Use of community recreation resources, such as parks and libraries, will expand tremendously. People will become more self-reliant during their non-working hours, although they will continue to depend upon the mass media, particularly television, for entertainment. Government will ban or discourage many forms of recreation and leisure which consume great amounts of energy. Most forms of motorized recreation vehicles will disappear, including motorized vacation homes. Non-business use of airlines will be taxed. Commercial leisure services will increasingly coordinate their services with mass transportation or supply their own mass transit. Indoor tennis will largely disappear due to high energy costs. Golf will be limited to the rich. People will camp close to home, garden, and spend more time in do-it-yourself activities. Additionally, they will become more conservative in their attitudes toward sexual behavior, use of drugs, and pornography. Deviant leisure behavior will go underground.

In this scenario a work-leisure cycle will emerge even more strongly than today. Work will not be expected to provide individual fulfillment. Money and security will be sought from work. People's lives will be segmented into spheres of work and leisure.

Regardless of whether or not one of these scenarios unfolds, leisure will continue to be the ideal about which we dream. And, in any future, we shall continue to dream.

*Leisure*

A few miles from here a rhinoceros sleeps;
a man born in a boulder.
every night his dream is the same:

the armor is pierced.

He glides among the murderous streets
and makes, at last, rhinoceros music,
a Christly cello, centuries ripe.

The morning world is cageless
and naked and near
and whole.[13]

## STUDY QUESTIONS

1. What does it mean that the difference between work and leisure is that they involve different kinds of social organization?

2. Do you agree that what we do during leisure has increasingly less connection with our work? Why or why not?

3. In your future, will any of your personal leisure be devoted to continuing education? Please discuss.

4. Do you believe our future society will be better off if the line between work and leisure disappears? Why or why not?

**5.** Summarize how your ideas about leisure have changed as a result of reading this book.

## REFERENCES

1. Cheek, Neil, and Burch, William. *The Social Organization of Leisure in Human Society.* New York: Harper and Row, 1976, p. 41.
2. Golding, P. *The Mass Media.* London: Longmans, 1974, p. 3.
3. Roberts, Kenneth. *Contemporary Society and the Growth of Leisure.* New York: Longmans, 1978, p. 144.
4. Heritage Conservation and Recreation Service. *Nationwide Outdoor Recreation Survey.* Washington, D.C.: U.S. Department of the Interior, 1978, pp. 1–87.
5. Toffler, Alvin. "The Third Wave," *Playboy,* January, 1980, pp. 146, 152, 180, 268–274.
6. Kahn, Herman. "Leading Futurist Traces Next Half Century in Travel," *Travel Trade News Edition,* January 31, 1979, p. 6.
7. Fuller, Buckminster. *On Education.* Amherst: University of Massachusetts Press, 1979, p. 156.
8. Davidson, Sara. "Rolling Into the Eighties," *Esquire.* Vol. 93, No. 2, 1980, pp. 18–25.
9. Kahn, Herman. "Next Decade Will Be the Sobering '80's," *U.S. News and World Report,* August 20, 1979, p. 53.
10. McBee, Susanna. "Census Sees More Elderly By Next Century Than Anticipated," *Washington Post,* June 11, 1978, p. A7.
11. "A Peek at a Changing America," *U.S. News and World Report.* December 10, 1979, p. 8.
12. "What Lures Americans Back To The Land?" *U.S. News and World Report.* November 26, 1979, p. 85.
13. Godbey, Geoffrey. *Leisure.* This poem originally appeared in *The Little Magazine.* New York, New York, Winter, 1970, and is reproduced by permission.

# Some suggested further readings

## LEISURE STUDIES

Bryan, H. *Conflict in the Great Outdoors.* University, Ala.: University of Alabama, Bureau of Administration, 1979.

Burton, T.L. *Experiments in Outdoor Recreation.* Totawa, N.J.: Rowman and Littlefield, 1971.

Cheek, N.H., Jr., Field, D.R., and Burdge, R.J. *Leisure and Recreation Places.* Ann Arbor: Ann Arbor Science Publishers, 1976.

Csikszentmihalyi, M. *Beyond Boredom and Anxiety.* Washington, D.C.: Jossey-Bass, 1975.

de Grazia, S. *Of Time, Work, and Leisure.* Garden City, N.Y.: Doubleday and Company (Anchor Book Edition), 1964.

Dulles, F.R. *A History of Recreation: America Learns to Play.* New York: Meredith Publishing, 1965.

Ellis, M.G. *Why People Play.* Englewood Cliffs, N.J.: Prentice-Hall, 1973.

Godbey, G., and Parker, S., *Leisure Studies and Services: An Overview.* Philadelphia: W.B. Saunders, 1976.

Goodale, T., and Witt, P. *Recreation and Leisure: Issues in an Era of Change.* State College, Pa.: Venture Publishing, 1980.

Huizinga, J. *Homo Ludens: A Study of the Play-Element in Culture.* Boston: The Beacon Press, 1962.

Kraus, R. *Recreation and Leisure in Modern Society.* New York: Appleton-Century-Crofts, 1971.

Murphy, J.F. *Concepts of Leisure.* Englewood Cliffs, N.J.: Prentice-Hall, 1974.

Nash, J.B. *Philosophy of Recreation and Leisure.* Dubuque, Iowa: William C. Brown, 1960.

Neulinger, J. *Psychology of Leisure.* Springfield, Ill.: Charles C Thomas, 1974.

Pieper, J. *Leisure—The Basis of Culture.* New York: New American Library, 1952.

Rapaport, R., and Rapaport, R. *Leisure and the Family Life Cycle.* Boston: Routledge and Kegan Paul, 1975.

Roberts, K. *Contemporary Society and the Growth of Leisure.* London: Longmans, 1978.

## DELIVERY OF LEISURE SERVICES

Avedon, E. M. *Therapeutic Recreation Services: An Applied Behavioral Science Approach.* Englewood Cliffs, N.J.: Prentice-Hall, 1974.

Avedon, E. M., and Sutton-Smith, B. *The Study of Games.* New York: John Wiley and Sons, 1971.

Bannon, J. J. *Problem Solving in Recreation and Parks.* Englewood Cliffs, N.J.: Prentice-Hall, 1972.

Bannon, J. J. *Leisure Resources: Its Comprehensive Planning.* Englewood Cliffs, N.J.: Prentice-Hall, 1976.

**308**

Brockman, C. F., Merriam, L. C., Jr., Catton, W. R., Jr., and Dowdle, B. *Recreational Use of Wild Lands*, 2nd ed. New York: McGraw-Hill, 1973.

Christiansen, M. L. *Park Planning Handbook: Fundamentals of Physical Planning for Parks and Recreation Areas*. New York: John Wiley and Sons, 1977.

Dimock, H. S. (ed.). *Administration of the Modern Camp*. New York: Association Press, 1967.

Driver, B. L. (ed.). *Elements of Outdoor Recreation Planning*. Ann Arbor: University of Michigan Press, 1970.

Edginton, C., and Williams, J. *Productive Management of Leisure Service Organizations*. New York: John Wiley and Sons, 1978.

Epperson, A. F. *Private and Commercial Recreation*. New York: John Wiley and Sons, 1977.

Farrell, P., and Lundegren, H. M. *The Process of Recreation Programming*. New York: John Wiley and Sons, 1978.

Fischer, D. W., Lewis, J. E., and Priddle, G. B. (eds.). *Land and Leisure: Concepts and Methods in Outdoor Recreation*. Chicago: Maaroufa Press, 1974.

Frye, V., and Peters, M. *Therapeutic Recreation: Its Theory, Philosophy, and Practice*. Harrisburg: Stackpole Books, 1972.

Godbey, G. *Recreation, Park and Leisure Services: Foundations, Organization, Administration*. Philadelphia: W. B. Saunders, 1978.

Gold, S. M. *Urban Recreation Planning*. Philadelphia: Lea and Febiger, 1973.

Gunn, S. L., and Peterson, C. A. *Therapeutic Recreation Program Design: Principles and Procedures*. Englewood Cliffs, N.J.: Prentice-Hall, 1978.

Hammerman, D. R., and Hammerman, W. M. *Teaching in the Outdoors*, 2nd ed. Minneapolis: Burgess Publishing, 1973.

Howard, D., and Crompton, J. *Financing, Managing and Marketing Recreation and Park Resources*. Dubuque: William C. Brown, 1980.

Kaplan, M. *Leisure: Lifespan and Lifestyle*. Philadelphia: W. B. Saunders, 1979.

McCall, J. R., and McCall, V. N. *Outdoor Recreation: Forest, Park, and Wilderness*. Beverly Hills: Bruce, 1977.

Mitchell, A. V., Robberson, J. D., and Obley, J. W. *Camp Counseling*, 5th ed. Philadelphia: W. B. Saunders, 1977.

Sessoms, H., Meyer, H. D., and Brightbill, C. K. *Leisure Services: The Organized Recreation and Park System*, 5th ed. Englewood Cliffs, N.J.: Prentice-Hall, 1975.

Sharpe, G. W. *Interpreting the Environment*. New York: John Wiley and Sons, 1976.

Theobald, W. F. *Evaluation of Recreation and Park Programs*. New York: John Wiley and Sons, 1979.

van Matre, S. *Acclimatization: A Sensory and Conceptual Approach to Ecological Involvement*. Martinsville, Ind.: American Camping Association, 1972.

van Matre, S. *Acclimatizing: A Personal and Reflective Approach to a Natural Relationship*. Martinsville, Ind.: American Camping Association, 1972.

# Index

Page numbers followed by an italic *t* refer to tables.

**Second Edition**

# A Course for Teaching English Learners

**Lynne T. Díaz-Rico**

*California State University, San Bernardino*

PEARSON

Boston   Columbus   Indianapolis   New York   San Francisco   Upper Saddle River
Amsterdam   Cape Town   Dubai   London   Madrid   Milan   Munich   Paris   Montreal   Toronto
Delhi   Mexico City   Sao Paulo   Sydney   Hong Kong   Seoul   Singapore   Taipei   Tokyo

Vice President, Editor-in-Chief: Aurora Martínez Ramos
Series Editor: Erin K. L. Grelak
Editorial Assistant: Meagan French
Executive Marketing Manager: Krista Clark
Editorial Production Service: Omegatype Typography, Inc.
Manufacturing Buyer: Megan Cochran
Electronic Composition: Omegatype Typography, Inc.
Interior Design: Omegatype Typography, Inc.
Photo Researcher: Annie Pickert
Cover Designer: Elena Sidorova

Library of Congress Cataloging-in-Publication Data

Díaz-Rico, Lynne T.
    A course for teaching English learners / Lynne T. Díaz-Rico.—2nd ed.
        p.   cm.
    Includes bibliographical references and index.
    ISBN-13: 978-0-13-249035-1 (pbk.)
    ISBN-10: 0-13-249035-8 (pbk.)
    1. English language—Study and teaching—Foreign speakers.   2. English language—Study and teaching—United States.   3. English language—Study and teaching—Handbooks, manuals, etc.   I. Title.
    PE1128.A2D448   2012
    428.2'4—dc22

                                                                        2010041646

Printed in the United States of America
10  9  8  7  6  5  4  3  2  1   RRD-VA   14  13  12  11  10

www.pearsonhighered.com

ISBN-10:  0-13-249035-8
ISBN-13:  978-0-13-249035-1

# ABOUT THE AUTHOR

*Lynne T. Díaz-Rico* is professor of education at California State University, San Bernardino. She has worked with public and private teacher education institutions and agencies around the world to prepare teachers for classrooms with diverse students and English-language pedagogy. Her books *Crosscultural, Language, and Academic Development Handbook* and *Strategies for Teaching English Learners* are widely used to educate English-language development teachers. Her research interests are in pedagogies for multilingual classrooms; creative, innovative English teaching strategies; critical discourse analysis; and visual literacy.

# CONTENTS

## CHAPTER TWO

## First- and Second-Language Development and Their Relationship to Academic Achievement   47

## PART TWO   Assessment and Instruction

## CHAPTER THREE

## Assessment of English Learners   87

# CHAPTER FOUR
## Programs for English Learners 115

# CHAPTER FIVE
## English-Language Literacy Development, Lesson Planning, and Specially Designed Content Instruction in English 149

## CHAPTER SIX
## English-Language Oracy Development   211

## CHAPTER SEVEN
## English-Language Literacy Development   235

## PART THREE    Culture and Inclusion

### CHAPTER EIGHT
### Culture and Cultural Diversity and Their Relationship to Academic Achievement    279

### CHAPTER NINE
### Culturally Inclusive Instruction    325

# PREFACE

To educate English learners, teachers need not only basic principles but also specific practices and methods. This book is designed to help teachers become more effective in expanding English learners' access to the core curriculum, instructing all students with a rich and demanding curriculum, and making crosscultural connections by means of teaching practices and curricular content. Coverage includes a broad foundation in second-language acquisition issues and techniques, the influence of culture on schooling, cultural practices of schooling, and the sociopolitical context of education, as well as strategies for teaching content subjects such as mathematics, sciences, and social studies.

*A Course for Teaching English Learners* offers an opportunity for educators to access in a single volume the information necessary to educate practicing and prospective teachers in principles for working with students who are English learners. Not only teachers, but also program coordinators, curriculum developers, administrators, and materials designers can use up-to-date research and methods to work successfully with this group.

This work contains the most recent teaching techniques, cultural knowledge, and language proficiency assessment strategies now available, and offers activities to help teachers better understand their English learners and their families, communities, languages, and cultures. Readers of this book not only learn about theories of language acquisition but also how the theories are applied in the classroom, highlighting successful features of English-language development programs and drawing examples from the classrooms of practicing teachers.

After a brief Introduction that surveys the demographics of English learners across the United States as well as the extent of the need for qualified teachers, Chapter 1 offers fundamentals in the nature of language, including its structure, function, and variation. Chapter 2 introduces language learning, comparing first- and second-language acquisition processes. Essentials of assessment follow in Chapter 3, which addresses issues of standardized testing under federal mandates and weighs the pros and cons of testing English learners for purposes of placement and evaluation.

Chapter 4 compares program models for educating English learners and includes a discussion of controversies about current legal requirements, best practices, and school reform efforts in the area of bilingual education. Chapter 5, on English-language development and specially designed academic instruction in English (SDAIE), offers frameworks within which teachers can plan, implement, and assess their lessons. Chapters 6 and 7 address oracy and literacy development. Chapters 8 and 9, on cultural diversity and culturally inclusive instruction, bring to the fore best practices in motivating English learners toward high academic achievement in line with the values and practices of home and community.

Teachers who can plan and carry out effective instruction that incorporates knowledge of intercultural communication can be expected to build a base of personal knowledge about the ways in which language, content knowledge, culture, and schooling are connected. This book is designed to offer a solid foundation in core techniques, in a manner that balances a growth in theoretical understanding with exposure to effective practice. One goal of this course is to increase teachers' confidence in their teaching ability. Simultaneously, a focus on issues of social justice and a moral commitment to democracy within the context of cultural values and individual rights and responsibilities brings to this book the themes that have sustained and inspired me throughout my professional life. I offer my thanks and tribute to colleagues in the profession of teaching English learners who have shared with me their like-minded dedication.

The methods and strategies included in this course reflect current practice in the field of teaching English learners. A carefully structured tool kit of strategies, with a clear process for use, permits educators to act clearly and consistently as professionals. The complex texture of native and target cultures, diverse languages, social and political forces, socioeconomic status, and individual differences in learners that one faces when teaching English learners demands continuous innovation and experimentation with teaching and learning strategies.

This book features specific, anecdotal documentation of the use and success of actual strategies in the context of the classroom. Examples in the book are drawn from classrooms spanning kindergarten through high school levels and across a variety of contexts. I hope that the reader as practitioner can apply these strategies with both immediate and long-term success.

Due to constraints of time and space this book does not include an in-depth coverage of second-language acquisition theory, the complexity of which remains a fascinating subject of intensive empirical and theoretical study. I hope instead that the reader will become curious about the issues and research in this field and seek further education in this area.

# MyEducationLab

In *Preparing Teachers for a Changing World*, Linda Darling-Hammond and her colleagues point out that grounding teacher education in real classrooms—among real teachers and students and among actual examples of students' and teachers' work—is an important, and perhaps even an essential, part of training teachers for the complexities of teaching in today's classrooms. MyEducationLab is an online learning solution that provides contextualized interactive exercises, simulations, and other resources designed to help develop the knowledge and skills teachers need. All of the activities and exercises in MyEducationLab are built around essential learning outcomes for teachers and are mapped to professional teaching standards. Utilizing classroom video, authentic student and teacher artifacts, case studies, and other resources and assessments, the scaffolded learning experiences in MyEducationLab offer pre-service teachers and those who teach them a unique and valuable education tool.

PEARSON
**myeducationlab**
The Power of Classroom Practice
www.myeducationlab.com

For each topic covered in the course you will find most or all of the following features and resources.

## Connection to National Standards

Now it is easier than ever to see how coursework is connected to national standards. Each topic on MyEducationLab lists intended learning outcomes connected to the appropriate national standards. All of the activities and exercises in MyEducationLab are mapped to the appropriate national standards and learning outcomes as well.

## Assignments and Activities

Designed to enhance student understanding of concepts covered in class and save instructors preparation and grading time, these assignable exercises show concepts in action (through video, cases, and/or student and teacher artifacts). They help students deepen content knowledge and synthesize and apply concepts and strategies they read about in the book. (Correct answers for these assignments are available to only the instructor under the Instructor Resource tab.)

## Building Teaching Skills and Dispositions

These learning units help students practice and strengthen skills that are essential to quality teaching. After presenting the steps involved in a core teaching process, students are given an opportunity to practice applying this skill via videos, student and teacher artifacts, and/or case studies of authentic classrooms. Providing multiple opportunities to practice a single teaching concept, each activity encourages a deeper understanding and application of concepts, as well as the use of critical thinking skills.

**As part of your access to MyEducationLab.**

A+RISE®, developed by three-time Teacher of the Year and administrator, Evelyn Arroyo, gives new teachers in grades K–12 quick, research-based strategies that get to the "how" of targeting their instruction and making content accessible for all students, including English language learners.

A+RISE® Standards2Strategy™ is an innovative and interactive online resource that offers new teachers in grades K–12 just-in-time, research-based instructional strategies that:

- Meet the linguistic needs of ELLs as they learn content
- Differentiate instruction for all grades and abilities
- Offer reading and writing techniques, cooperative learning, use of linguistic and nonlinguistic representations, scaffolding, teacher modeling, higher order thinking, and alternative classroom ELL assessment
- Provide support to help teachers be effective through the integration of listening, speaking, reading, and writing along with the content curriculum
- Improve student achievement
- Are aligned to Common Core Elementary Language Arts standards (for the literacy strategies) and to English language proficiency standards in WIDA, Texas, California, and Florida.

## IRIS Center Resources

The IRIS Center at Vanderbilt University (http://iris.peabody.vanderbilt.edu)—funded by the U.S. Department of Education's Office of Special Education Programs (OSEP)—develops training enhancement materials for pre-service and in-service teachers. The Center works with experts from across the country to create challenge-based interactive modules, case study units, and podcasts that provide research-validated information about working with students in inclusive settings. In your MyEducationLab course we have integrated this content where appropriate.

## Study Plan Specific to A Course for Teaching English Learners, 2nd Edition

A MyEducationLab Study Plan is a multiple choice assessment tied to chapter objectives, supported by study material. A well-designed Study Plan offers multiple opportunities to fully master required course content as identified by the objectives in each chapter:

- *Chapter Objectives* identify the learning outcomes for the chapter and give students targets to shoot for as they read and study.
- *Multiple Choice Assessments* assess mastery of the content. These assessments are mapped to chapter objectives, and students can take the multiple choice quiz as many times as they want. Not only do these quizzes provide overall scores for each objective, but they also explain why responses to particular items are correct or incorrect.
- *Study Material: Review, Practice, and Enrichment* give students a deeper understanding of what they do and do not know related to chapter content. This material includes text excerpts, activities that include hints and feedback, and interactive multimedia exercises built around videos, simulations, cases, or classroom artifacts.

## Course Resources

The Course Resources section on MyEducationLab is designed to help students put together an effective lesson plan, prepare for and begin their career, navigate their first year of teaching, and understand key educational standards, policies, and laws. The Course Resources tab includes the following:

- The **Lesson Plan Builder** is an effective and easy-to-use tool that students can use to create, update, and share quality lesson plans. The software also makes it easy to integrate state content standards into any lesson plan.
- The **Preparing a Portfolio** module provides guidelines for creating a high-quality teaching portfolio.
- **Beginning Your Career** offers tips, advice, and other valuable information on:
  - *Resume Writing and Interviewing:* Includes expert advice on how to write impressive resumes and prepare for job interviews.
  - *Your First Year of Teaching:* Provides practical tips to set up a first classroom, manage student behavior, and more easily organize for instruction and assessment.
  - *Law and Public Policies:* Details specific directives and requirements teachers need to understand under the No Child Left Behind Act and the Individuals with Disabilities Education Improvement Act of 2004.
- **Longman Dictionary of Contemporary English Online:** Make use of this online version of the CD-ROM of the Longman Dictionary of Contemporary English—the quickest and easiest way to look up any word while you are working on MyEducationLab.

## Certification and Licensure

The Certification and Licensure section is designed to help students pass their licensure exam by giving them access to state test requirements, overviews of what tests cover, and sample test items.

The Certification and Licensure tab includes the following:

- **State Certification Test Requirements:** Here students can click on a state and be taken to a list of state certification tests.
- Students can click on the **Licensure Exams** they need to take to find:
  - Basic information about each test
  - Descriptions of what is covered on each test
  - Sample test questions with explanations of correct answers
- **National Evaluation Series™** by Pearson: Here students can see the tests in the NES, learn what is covered on each exam, and access sample test items with descriptions and rationales of correct answers. They can also purchase interactive online tutorials developed by Pearson Evaluation Systems and the Pearson Teacher Education and Development group.
- **ETS Online Praxis Tutorials:** Here students can purchase interactive online tutorials developed by ETS and by the Pearson Teacher Education and Development group. Tutorials are available for the Praxis I exams and for select Praxis II exams.

Visit **www.myeducationlab.com** for a demonstration of this exciting new online teaching resource.

# Acknowledgments

This book was made possible through the help of many people. I credit my editor Aurora Martínez Ramos with the vision to foresee the publications needed by teachers of English learners. I wish to thank my colleagues in the field of teaching English to speakers of other languages and applied linguistics for their encouragement, including Larry Selinker, Gertrude Tinker-Sachs, Suchada Nimmannit, Shelley Wong, Connie Williams, Su Motha, Theresa Austin, Ryuko Kubota, Natalie Hess, Lia Kamhi-Stein, Suzanne Medina, Stephen Stoynoff, Charles S. Amorosino, Jr., Jun Liu, Sandy Briggs, Mabel Gallo, Liz England, Christine Coombe, and so many others. I acknowledge the support of my students, who gave me feedback on early drafts. Thanks to my colleagues at California State University, San Bernardino, for their collegial support, including María Balderrama, Barbara Flores, Nena Torrez, Mónika Niehus, Julie Ciancio, Peggy Marcy, and Starley Dullien.

My sincere thanks goes to the editorial staff at Pearson Teacher Education and to Diana Neatrour and the team at Omegatype Typography. Also my deep thanks to the reviewers, Cheryl Caldera, CSU Fresno; Zaida McCall-Perez, Holy Names University; Terri Mossgrove, St. Petersburg College; Deborah L. Norland, Luther College; and Pal Chamness Reece-Miller, Texas Tech University, for their dedication and diligence.

# INTRODUCTION

## Teaching English Learners

Teachers in elementary and secondary schools in the United States face an unprecedented challenge—educating the growing number of students whose families speak a language other than English or whose backgrounds are culturally diverse. In addition to accommodating recently arrived immigrants with limited English proficiency, schools need to offer a high-quality, college-bound curriculum to English-speaking students whose heritage is Native American or who are second-generation immigrants.

In the face of this diverse linguistic and cultural terrain, the responsibilities of the U.S. educator have become increasingly complex. Teachers must now modify instruction to meet the specific needs of culturally and linguistically diverse (CLD) students, especially English learners, using English-language development (ELD) techniques and other instructional adaptations to ensure that all students have access to an excellent education. In turn, educators are finding that these diverse cultures and languages add richness and depth to their teaching experience. Because the core of the teaching profession in the United States remains monolingual, teachers can benefit from teacher education that includes specialized methods and strategies for the effective education of CLD students.

Language learning is a complex process that forms the foundation for academic achievement. Competence in more than one language is a valuable skill. Students who come to school already speaking a home language other than English have the potential to become bilingual if schooling can preserve and augment their native-language proficiency. One exciting trend is the spread of two-way immersion (TWI) programs, which enable monolingual English-speaking students to learn a second language in the company of English learners.

This book uses the term *English learner* to mean "students whose first (primary, native) language is not English and who are learning English at school." This chapter offers an overview of the demographics of English learners.

# English Learners in U.S. Schools

## Demographics of English Learners in the United States

The National Clearinghouse for English Language Acquisition and Language Instruction Educational Programs (NCELA, 2008) put the number of English learners (K–12) in the United States at 5 million for 2004–2005. Nearly half of the nation's children under age five (45 percent) are racial or ethnic minorities (Cohn & Bahrampour, 2006), and the percentage is increasing mainly because the Hispanic population is growing so rapidly. This accounted for 49 percent of the country's growth from 2004 to 2005, driving 70 percent of the growth in children younger than five. Of the population under age five, 22 percent is Hispanic.

California has more residents—and students—than any other state, with 6,259,972 students in 2008, nearly 2 million more students than Texas, the next largest state (4,317,427). With a school enrollment of approximately 1.6 million English learners, in 2007–2008 California led the states in the need for English-as-a-second-language (ESL) services at the K–12 level teaching speakers of over 100 languages (California Department of Education [CDE], 2008). Primary languages included Khmu, Albanian, Marshallese, and Chamorro, with the largest number of students speaking Spanish (85.3 percent) and Vietnamese (2.2 percent). One in four pupils in K–12 schools is an English learner, comprising one-third of the English learners in the United States (CDE, 2010).

*English learners comprise a growing proportion of school children in the United States.*

Whereas 25.1 percent of California students are English learners, Texas, Florida, and New York have 16.8, 8.4, and 7.3 percent, respectively. Texas and Florida are expected to have continuous and rapid enrollment growth. Although enrollment in California will increase by about 14 percent between 1998 and 2016, Texas and Florida will see increases of about 41 and 39 percent, respectively, over the same time period. Enrollment in New York is projected to decline (EdData, 2008).

## Spanish-Speaking English Learners

The majority of households in the United States in which English is not spoken are Spanish-speaking (28.1 million), a number that increased 62 percent over the decade 1990 to 2000. Latinos are the fastest-growing segment of the population, with a 24.3 percent growth rate (U.S. Census Bureau, 2006), fueled largely by births rather than immigration (Gaouette, 2006). In 2008, 46.9 million Latinos resided in the United States, constituting 15.4 percent of the total U.S. population (the terms *Hispanic* and *Latino* are used interchangeably in the census reports). Of the Spanish-speaking households, 66.1 percent are from Mexico or of Mexican-American origin; 14.5 percent

Mary Kate Denny/PhotoEdit

from Central or South America; 9 percent from Puerto Rico or of Puerto Rican origin; 4 percent from Cuba or of Cuban-American origin; and 6.4 percent from other Hispanic/Latino origin. Latinos make up more than 30 percent of the population of New York City (Wallraff, 2000) and at 13 million comprise 35 percent of the population of California.

Nearly half of all Latinos live in a central city within a metropolitan area (46.4 percent); more than 45 percent live in the West. However, Arkansas leads the United States in growth rate at 60.9 percent from 2000 to 2006 (U.S. Census Bureau, 2006). Many Spanish speakers are poor—in 1999, 22.8 percent of all Latinos were living in poverty (compared to 7.7 percent of non-Latino Whites). In addition, Latino children under age eighteen were more likely than non-Latino White children to be living in poverty (30.3 percent versus 9.4 percent) (U.S. Census Bureau, 2000).

## Asian/Pacific English Learners

The second largest non-English-speaking population comprises Asians and Pacific Islanders. In 2008, the Asian and Pacific Islander population in the United States numbered about 15 million, constituting 5 percent of the population (Asian Nation, 2010). *Asian* refers to those having origins in any of the original peoples of the Far East, Southeast Asia, or the Indian subcontinent, including Cambodia, China, India, Japan, Korea, Malaysia, Pakistan, the Philippine Islands, Thailand, and Vietnam. *Pacific Islander* refers to those having origins in any of the original peoples of Hawai'i, Guam, Samoa, or other Pacific islands.

Like Spanish speakers, the Asian and Pacific Islander population (5 percent of the United States) lives in metropolitan areas (nearly 96 percent), with 45 percent living in central cities, double the proportion for non-Hispanic Whites (22 percent) (U.S. Census Bureau, 2001a). Approximately 2.4 percent of these Asians are Chinese speakers, about two million speakers of Chinese (Mandarin). Four out of five of these report that they prefer to speak Chinese at home (Wallraff, 2000).

By and large, then, in the United States, those who educate English learners are more likely to find employment in California, New Mexico, New York, or Texas, in central city schools, serving Hispanics or Asian/Pacific Islanders. Aside from this employment likelihood, however, demographics indicate that services for English learners are needed in every state and large city.

To educate these students, resources are badly needed. However, inner-city schools are faced with large numbers of poor children, fewer books and supplies, and teachers with less training and experience. Thus, excellence in education for English learners is frequently compromised by the fact that such students may be poor and attending underfunded and poorly equipped schools.

## Putting Faces to Demographics

English learners in the United States present a kaleidoscope of faces, languages, and cultures:

Hayat, eleventh grade, refugee from Afghanistan, living in Oakland, California . . .

Rodica, eighth grade, adoptee from Romania, living in Kansas City, Missouri . . .

Viviana, third grade, second-generation Mexican American living in Prescott, Arizona, whose parents speak no English . . .

Muhubo, sixth grade, immigrant from Somalia, living in Lewiston, Maine . . .

Hae Lim, second grade, visitor from Pusan, Korea, "temporarily" living with an aunt in Torrance, California . . .

Lei Li, kindergartner, attending a neighborhood school in Amherst, Massachusetts, while her mother is an international student at a nearby university . . .

Tram, tenth grade, living in inner-city San José, whose parents speak Vietnamese but who has lived in the United States since he was two years old . . .

Augustín, fourth grade, a Trique Indian from San Juan Copala in the Oaxaca state in Mexico, who speaks Spanish as a second language and is learning English as a third language . . .

Juan Ramon, second grade, whose mother recently moved from San Juan, Puerto Rico, to live with relatives in Teaneck, New Jersey . . . .

Some of these students may be offered primary-language instruction as a part of the school curriculum, but those students whose language is represented by few other students in the school district face structured English immersion, with little support in their native language.

## English Learners with Learning Challenges

Some English learners face academic learning challenges in addition to the need to acquire a second language. They may be diagnosed with learning disabilities and referred to special education services; they may suffer culture shock during the process of acculturation; or they may experience other difficulties that require counseling services or situations in which their families are not able to meet their social, emotional, or health needs.

Like their counterparts who are native English speakers, English learners may require special services, including referral to gifted-and-talented programs, resource specialists, reading-resource programs, counseling, and/or tutoring.

# English Learners around the World

Teaching English is one of the fastest-growing global professions. In countries such as Canada, England, and Australia, immigrants study English as a second language, just as they do in the United States, making ESL a well-established curriculum in English-dominant countries. The term *English learners* also includes those studying English as a foreign language (EFL), usually as an academic subject in elementary, middle, or high schools—but also in private, proprietary institutes that cater to those who must learn English for business, scientific, or other career-related purposes. This division is not clean-cut, because English is widely used for international communication, especially with the Internet. English for speakers of other languages (ESOL) is also a widely used term; hence, Teaching English to Speakers of Other Languages (TESOL) is the term for the profession.

Teaching English learners is a broad and flexible profession. ESOL educators can be found in Mandarin–English dual-language immersion kindergartens in Seattle, college classrooms in Tokyo, adult education classes in Florida, "cram" schools in Seoul, precollegiate preparation courses in Texas, middle school social studies classes in California, five-year vocational colleges in Taiwan, private schools in the United Arab Emirates, or in summer intensive programs in Uzbekistan—at a myriad of levels from preschool to postgraduate in a host of countries around the world.

# Teaching with Integrity

This book takes a critical perspective on the education of English learners—one that looks at dual-language proficiency and language policy in the context of broader issues of social equity and social justice. Teachers who develop a deeper understanding of the effects of culture and language on the success—or disenfranchisement—of CLD students through school culture, curricula, and instructional methods are better prepared to promote social change. Teachers with a critical perspective look within, around, and beyond educational issues; ask probing questions about the role of educators in the struggle to attain fairness, justice, equity, and equal opportunity in the world; and work toward social equity and justice as a part of their role as language educators.

One of the major challenges for those who teach English learners is to motivate them to reach the highest possible level of school achievement. In this process, teachers work to create a classroom environment characterized by equal opportunity and a democratic process so that English learning represents a positive experience. A second challenge is to respect native languages and the rights of their speakers. Teachers who make sincere attempts to learn the languages of their students and build English on students' prior language expertise serve as intercultural and interlingual educators. Only in the context of full support for the bilingual, bicultural learner does the teaching of English respect the learner's linguistic and cultural heritage.

Critical educators are those who teach with integrity (Balderrama & Díaz-Rico, 2006). Their passion for teaching and learning fosters within their students the capacity for joyful lifelong learning, a feeling of respect for and pride in their own culture, and a sense of curiosity regarding human diversity. Colleagues can undertake together the task of achieving social justice: equal access to, and opportunity for, quality education for all students. Critical educators advocate an inclusive society in which language, literacy, and culture are integrated with respect and not compromised in any way.

Teachers are intellectual workers, knowledge professionals with cultural expertise. As such, the role of teachers is to help students attain the wisdom and skills the whole community needs in order to prosper. Teachers of English learners provide academic content and English-language development while upholding high professional standards within an intellectually challenging context grounded in academic knowledge that is humane and ethical, upholding intercultural relationships and promoting educational equity. Teaching with integrity includes six elements.

## The Willingness to Be Fully Human

First, teachers must be willing to be human and to treat others with humanity. This is partially fulfilled when the teacher deeply believes—and communicates the belief—that teachers and students have equal civil rights in the classroom as well as parity as fellow human beings. One way of looking at the humanity of teaching is to examine the ways in which teachers and students mutually socialize one another in classroom interaction. Cole (2003) has called this *intersubjectivity*—the co-creation of joint activity. Intersubjectivity in the classroom features nonthreatening interaction that communicates a sense of mutual respect with nonverbal immediacy, in a shared atmosphere of pacing and activity and enjoyment of shared cultural commonplaces.

This does not mean teachers act as "buddies" to students, but rather as fully actualized human beings who are able to apologize when wrong, seek peer help when unsure, and grow and learn alongside students. Teachers with integrity have compassion at their core because they are conscious of others' misfortunes and distress and have an active desire to alleviate such hardships.

## High Expectations for Students

A second facet of teaching with integrity is having high academic expectations for students, a deep commitment to the idea that all students can achieve academic success. Teacher expectations operate as a cycle of teacher–student mutual perceptions: Teachers and students each form ideas about the other, which they communicate in their interactions, causing both to respond in positive or negative ways (Jussim, 1986).

Recognizing, addressing, and understanding these expectations and how they operate are therefore essential parts of examining the role of a teacher's integrity with English learners. Teachers must learn to avoid prejudgments and stereotypes so that such negativity does not produce a self-fulfilling prophecy of low achievement. Even if students have internalized low expectations for themselves, teachers who strive to change students' low academic performance can sow seeds of improved self-esteem. The strongest teachers are those who believe in students' success more than students believe in their own failure. Teachers with flexible expectations readily revise their impressions when direct information about student achievement is available.

## Being "Fully Qualified"

A third aspect of teaching with integrity is expertise in content. The No Child Left Behind federal education legislation (2001) specifically requires schools to employ teachers who are fully qualified in the areas they will instruct. Two areas of content expertise related specifically to English learners that are not often required—but should be—are the following: (1) theories and pedagogy relevant to teaching English learners academic literacy and (2) some degree of proficiency in the primary language of their students.

Given the existing linguistic diversity prevalent in U.S. classrooms, these two areas of expertise are central to the implementation of content knowledge. The widely accepted mythology in the United States that a person can be well educated and remain monolingual is questionable with regard to being "fully qualified" as an educator. The Latino population has become the largest minority in the United States, and educators who are able to augment their teaching using both second-language acquisition principles and Spanish-language skills are increasingly needed.

## Maintaining Professional Ethics

Another element of teaching with integrity is ethical teaching. Upholding the morals of the profession of teaching includes believing in the worth and dignity of each human being and recognizing the supreme importance of democratic principles (National Education Association, *Code of Ethics of the Education Profession,* 1975). Ethical teachers understand the importance of professional conduct and are willing to accept a role in protecting the freedom to teach and learn; they work toward providing equal educational opportunity for all.

The NEA's code of ethics frames the teacher's commitment to the student. For example, teachers shall not knowingly distort subject matter relevant to the student's progress; grant advantage or deny benefit on the grounds of race, color, creed, sex, national origin, marital status, political or religious beliefs, family, social or cultural background, or sexual orientations; or use professional relationships with students for private advantage (such as receiving money for privately tutoring after school the same students they teach during the day—which represents a conflict of interest).

Other aspects of ethical behavior address an educator's commitment to the profession, forbidding, for example, misrepresenting one's qualifications, disclosing information about colleagues obtained during the course of professional service, or receiving gifts or favors that might compromise one's professional decisions. *Ethical Issues for ESL Faculty* (Hafernik, Messerschmitt, & Vandrick, 2002) touches on problematic issues that may arise when students come from countries with social norms that are quite different from those in the United States.

## Being an Intercultural Educator

A teacher with integrity has an intercultural repertoire. The ability to communicate effectively with people from other cultures is the hallmark of the intercultural educator. According to Smith, Paige, and Steglitz (1998), a person with an intercultural perspective has incorporated a set of core elements into a repertoire that facilitates, and forms the foundation for, intercultural communication. These core elements are complex and subtle, yet represent a clear and useful body of knowledge, skills, and dispositions that educators need to function professionally in a diverse society.

These elements include engagement in face-to-face interactive communication that shows sensitivity to the different ways in which individuals construct their social reality, compassionate involvement as a whole person, and commitment to the social context of communication. Intercultural educators recognize that they must work on themselves in order to progress from ethnocentric to ethnorelative views. An individual's culture provides tools to interpret reality only one way; intercultural educators must move beyond this limitation, as is discussed further in Chapter 9.

## Clarity of Vision

The sixth and last facet of integrity is clarity of vision: being able to see clearly the social and political realities surrounding teaching. Teachers of English learners must consider several fundamental questions. Why do some individual students achieve, whereas others fail academically? Why is there disproportionate academic failure among certain groups of students, particularly regarding differences between majority Whites and African Americans, Latinos, English learners, or low-income students, for example? Why do European-American, White, monolingual, English-speaking students, including those who come from high-income groups, succeed disproportionately? Thinking teachers interrogate those processes that affect their teaching and professional performance; in turn, they sustain political and ideological insight about the process of schooling and their role as teachers.

This political clarity is important if teachers are to act effectively and facilitate student empowerment. First and foremost, teachers can function as more conscientious professionals when they understand the larger social and political forces that affect their professional lives. With this understanding, teachers can confront these forces with the tools to change those aspects of society that undermine educational success, particularly for low-status student groups such as English learners.

As suggested in the definition of political clarity, teachers must be cognizant that they do not teach in a vacuum, but that instead their work is interconnected with broader social processes that affect their teaching. Commonly accepted belief systems justify and rationalize the existing social order. How do teachers explain the fact that multilingualism is facilitated for the privileged but not encouraged for those students who come from lower socioeconomic backgrounds? The ideology of unexamined beliefs affects teaching and schooling practices at the level of microinteractions in daily classroom life.

Social institutions such as schools play major roles in maintaining and perpetuating processes important to society. Certain groups manage to dominate others and determine how people in positions of privilege maintain those positions with the support and approval of the disempowered—a process Leistyna, Woodrum, and Sherblom (1996) define as *hegemony*, the unexamined acceptance of the social order—even when the social classes in power make decisions that disempower others.

Beliefs about language are powerful hegemonic devices, intimately connected to social position. For example, beliefs about second-language acquisition in the United States privileges French above Spanish as a preferred foreign language of study and stigmatizes non-native speakers of English through roles of English teachers that privilege native speakers. However, at every opportunity, teachers with integrity oppose attitudes based on hegemonic ideas or folk beliefs, upholding professional practices that are substantiated by research or infused with clarity of vision about the all-too-hidden processes that perpetuate unequal power relations and inequality.

Teaching with integrity means wholeness in all that teachers do. This implies a genuine vision of social justice in the classroom. Teachers with integrity are able to sustain their humanity in the face of potentially dehumanizing forces that would reduce teaching and learning to mechanical enterprises devoid of intrinsic interest and personal investment (Bartolomé, 1994; Freire, 1970; Giroux, 1988). As suggested earlier, teaching English learners is a challenging and complex task requiring both integrity in teaching and pedagogical skills and knowledge along various dimensions of instruction. Teaching with integrity provides a model for a professional approach that is humane, student-centered, and equitable.

## The Professional Preparation of Teachers to Educate English Learners

School districts seeking highly qualified teachers for English-language development programs employ teachers with bilingual certification who can deliver primary-language education, in recognition of the fact that these teachers have additional preparation and expertise relevant to the position. These teachers are expected to deliver ELD instruction along with primary-language instruction for literacy as well as content. In states where structured English immersion (content delivery in English without support for primary-language literacy) is the specified model for English learners, teachers use specially designed academic instruction in English (SDAIE) strategies in addition to ELD.

The availability of employment for ELD teachers in the United States depends on local population demographics, the role of ELD teaching in relation to bilingual education, and the local need for teachers qualified for ELD. One fact, however, remains a constant: the current shortage of teachers in U.S. classrooms. The United States is expected to need from two to four million teachers by 2013, as one-third of the 3.2 million teachers are expected to retire (Dillon, 2009). The teacher shortage is particularly acute in urban areas, where 40 to 50 percent of English learners are found. Almost half of new teachers leave the profession within five years, and the rate is even higher in low-income communities (National Commission on Teaching and America's Future, 2002). Districts are setting aside funds for training new teachers, raising starting salaries, and recruiting teachers for bilingual education. The employability outlook has never been better for teachers who specialize in teaching English learners.

## Career Preparation for Teachers

To prepare for teaching English learners, an individual can pursue various levels of precareer training, from BA programs with a special emphasis, to post-BA teacher credential programs, to MA programs that include teacher certification. TESOL's website (www.tesol.org) has a link (www.tesol.org/careers/seekers-faq1.html#2) that may help to clarify these terms and the important differences that distinguish preparation programs and levels of career training. Regardless of the widely varying career ladders available to educators, the demand for English-language teaching professionals has steadily grown, not only in the United States but also throughout the world.

Because each state has the authority to set its own certification requirements, professional qualifications for teachers of English learners can vary. The NCELA website (www.ncela .gwu.edu/policy/states/index.htm) offers a complete listing of requirements for teaching English learners by state.

The field of teaching English learners is equally open to native English speakers and non-native speakers alike. A speaker of another language who has learned English and has achieved some measure of bilingual competence is uniquely qualified to understand the needs of English learners (see Brutt-Griffler & Samimy, 1999). The Nonnative English Speakers in TESOL (NNEST) Interest Section can provide more information about this topic.

The Internet can help to provide a broad picture of the possibilities available to those who specialize in teaching English learners. The Center for Research on Education, Diversity, and Excellence at the University of California, Berkeley, offers a range of resources, including research articles and teaching guides (http://crede.berkeley.edu). Another site hosted by the Center for Multilingual Multicultural Research at the University of Southern California contains links to scholarships and teacher training programs (www.usc.edu/dept/education/ CMMR).

## Professional Organizations for Teachers

Teachers of English learners can choose as their major professional affiliation such organizations as the National Association for Bilingual Education (NABE, online at www.nabe.org), Teachers of English to Speakers of Other Languages (TESOL, Inc., online at www.tesol.org), National Council of Teachers of English (NCTE, online at www.ncte.org), the International Reading Association (IRA, online at www.ira.org), or state, regional, or local affiliates of these organizations. These groups increasingly include a focus on English learners in their publications and conference sessions. However, NABE and TESOL are the only U.S.-based professional organizations with the teaching of English learners as their central mission.

## Information about Teaching English Learners

The professional information available from the National Clearinghouse for English Language Acquisition (www.ncela.gwu.edu) includes an archive of newsletters, a conference calendar, links to scholarly journals, statistics about English learners, and resources on heritage languages, such as Tagalog, for example. NCELA's website offers links to Tagalog (Filipino) curriculum materials, multilingual books in Tagalog, and lists of language and cultural resources, Web resources and organizations, and colleges and universities in North America that teach Tagalog. Resources for many other languages are equally available.

*It is not necessary to be a native English speaker to teach English learners.*

Karen A. Heath

For ELD teaching, Dave's ESL Cafe (www.eslcafe.com) is a popular site for English learning, featuring chatrooms, an online bookstore, job listings, and sections on slang, idioms, and other language-teaching tips. The site also includes thousands of links to other topics (flash cards, multicultural issues, lesson plans, online help, newsgroups, and tongue twisters, to name a few categories).

Those who teach English learners work within a variety of cultural, linguistic, and socioeconomic contexts. They honor the diversity in culture, language, social class, and talents that makes their students unique. The intellectual and pedagogical challenges of teaching in a language-acquisition classroom offer rich opportunities for personal and professional growth. Those who offer cultural understanding receive it; those who offer language exchange expand their language skills; those who offer empathy grow as human beings. No other teaching profession provides such possibilities for intercultural communication, literacy development, creative instruction, and reflective social praxis. Using this text, prospective teachers of English learners can prepare for a successful career and current teachers can update their expertise in teaching English learners.

# Language Structure and Use

## Ah, Language!

Verbal language is unique to human beings. It allows us to express our deepest feelings, our broadest concepts, our highest ideals. It takes us beyond the here and now, and even beyond the possible—by means of language, we might join the attackers at the siege of Troy or journey through the looking glass with Alice. Language can connect humans as children listen to stories before the fireplace on a cold winter night; or it can, together with culture, divide two peoples into bitter sectarian warfare. Language communicates the heights of joy and the depths of despair.

Language equalizes—preschoolers as well as professors can be considered native speakers of their first language. Alternatively, language reflects inequality—dialect distinctions often demarcate social class. Almost all aspects of a person's life are touched by language. Although language is universal, each language has evolved to meet the experiences, needs, and desires of a particular community.

Understanding language structure and use provides teachers with essential tools to help students learn. All languages share universal features, such as the ability to label objects and to describe actions and events. All languages are divided into various subsystems (phonology, morphology, syntax, semantics, and pragmatics). What is most amazing is that language users learn all these subsystems of their first language without realizing it—native speakers are not necessarily able to explain a sound pattern, a grammatical point, or the use of idiomatic expression. To them, that is "just the way it is." Language, then, is a system that works even without conscious awareness, an inborn competence that unfolds and matures when given adequate stimulation from others.

This chapter explores the various aspects of language and provides suggestions to help English-language development (ELD) teachers identify student needs and provide appropriate instruction. Knowledge about language structure and use also helps teachers recognize the richness and variety of students' skills in both first and second languages. Linguistic knowledge—not only about English but also

13

about the possibilities inherent in other languages—helps teachers view the language world of the English learner with insight and empathy.

## Language Universals

At last count, 6,912 languages are spoken in today's world (SIL International, 2000). Although not all of these have been intensely studied, linguists have carried out enough investigations over the centuries to posit some universal facts about language.

### All Languages Have Structure

All human languages use a finite set of sounds (or gestures) that are combined to form meaningful elements or words, which themselves form an infinite set of possible sentences. Every spoken language also divides these discrete sound segments—phonemes—such as /t/, /m/, or /e/ into a class of vowels and a class of consonants.

All grammars contain rules for the formation of words, and sentences of definite types, kind, and similar grammatical categories (for example, nouns and verbs) are found in all languages. Every language has a way of referring to past time; the ability to negate; and ways to form questions, issue commands, and so on.

Although human languages are specific to their places of use and origin (for example, languages of seafaring cultures have more specific words for oceanic phenomena than do languages of desert tribes), semantic universals, such as "male" or "female," are found in every language in the world. No matter how exotic a language may appear to a native English speaker, all human languages in fact share the same features, most of which are lacking in the language of apes, dolphins, or birds.

### Language Is Dynamic

Languages change over time. Pronunciation (phonology) changes—across 400 years, for example, Shakespeare's plays often feature scene-ending couplets whose words may have rhymed in his day but do not in modern translations. We recognize that pronunciation in English has altered over time, because the spelling of some words is archaic: We no longer pronounce the /k/ in *knight* or the /w/ in *write*. Semantics change over time, and words disappear, such as the archaic English words *bilbo, costermonger, fluey,* and *shew.* Words expand their meanings, as with *geek* and *mouse.* New words appear, such as *nannycam* and *freeware.* Some languages change more than others: Written Icelandic has changed relatively little since the thirteenth century, whereas writers for *Wired,* a New York–based technology magazine, coin an average of thirty new words in English with each month's edition.

Teachers who respect the dynamic nature of language can take delight in learners' approximations of English. When Chinese speakers fail to produce past-tense markers (*Yesterday I download a file),[1] they may be speaking the English of the future, when the past-

---

[1]An asterisk (*) before a word or a sentence indicates that it is phonetically or grammatically incorrect.

tense morpheme (-*d, -ed, -t*) may be dropped, just as the second-person inflection (-*est,* as in "thou goest") has disappeared.

## Language Is Complex

Without question, using language is one of the most complex of human activities, providing the human race with a psychological tool unmatched in power and flexibility. It is normal for humans no matter their native language to be able to communicate a wide range of concepts, both concrete and abstract. All languages are equally complex, capable of expressing a wide range of ideas and expandable to include new words for new concepts. Motu, one of 715 indigenous languages in Papua New Guinea, has a complex vocabulary for indigenous plants, whereas Icelandic has an elaborate system of kinship names that allows people to trace their ancestry for hundreds of years.

Language is arbitrary, meaning that we cannot guess the meaning of a word from its sound (except for a few words such as *buzz*)—there is no inherent reason to link the sound and meaning of a word. Because the meaning–symbol connection is arbitrary, language gains an abstracting power removed from direct ties to the here and now of objects or events. Moreover, language is open-ended—an infinite set of sentences can be produced in any language.

Even though language is complicated, every healthy child—regardless of racial, geographical, social, or economic heritage—is capable of learning any language to which he or she is exposed. By the age of five, most children have learned how to make well-formed sentences in their native language and are thus considered native speakers. Although some students may be shy or their language skills delayed in development, it is incorrect to say that a young child "doesn't have language."

─────────────── **DID YOU KNOW?** ───────────────

**THE KOREAN LANGUAGE**

Korean is the only language to have a true alphabet completely native to East Asia, with each character corresponding to a phoneme (10 vowels, 19 consonants, and vowel-like consonants called *glides*). Korean has no articles, word gender, or declensions. There are no adjectives; instead, verbs can be used as adjectives. There are also extensive variations of verb forms used to indicate tenses and honorifics.

Adapted from Herrera, Pérez, & Escamilla, 2010, pp. 94–95.

# Phonology: The Sound Patterns of Language

Phonology is the study of the sound system of a language. Phonetics is the science of the production, reception, analysis, transcription, and classification of speech sounds, and also, "the relation of speech sounds to the total language process" (Heilman, 2002, p. 4).

―――――――――――――――――――― **DID YOU KNOW** ――――――――――――――――――――

**IS IT ENGLISH?**

These activities illustrate the characteristics of the English sound system:

■ Which of the following are possible English words and which would be impossible because they do not fit the English sound system? *stgmonic, chetelogo, ndele, tassitic*

(Answer: not *stgmonic* and *ndele*—they contain non-English-like consonant clusters)

■ Products are often brought to the market with names that use phonemic enhancement: The gasoline company and product Esso was renamed Exxon in 1973 in part because test marketing showed that people responded more strongly to the look and sound of the double *X* than the double *S*.

## Phonemes

Phonemes are the individual sounds in a language, the distinctive units that "make a difference" when sounds distinguish words. For example, in English the initial consonant sounds /p/ and /b/ are the only difference between the words *park* and *bark* and thus are phonemes. The number of phonemes in a language ranges between twenty and fifty; English has a high average count, from thirty-four to forty-five, depending on the dialect. Hawai'ian, in contrast, has one of the lowest phoneme counts, with eight consonants and ten vowels. Table 1.1 lists the phonemes in English (using the International Phonetic Alphabet) with example words.

If phonemic variations do not distinguish words, they are considered variations of one phoneme rather than completely different phonemes. For example, in English—at least in the Pittsburgh dialect—the name "Lynne" is pronounced with the tongue to the back of the roof of the mouth, whereas when pronouncing the name "Linda" the tongue is tipped farther forward. However, both are acceptable versions of the /l/ phoneme because this difference alone does not distinguish two word meanings, as does the difference between *pan* and *ban*.

―――――――――――**DID YOU KNOW?**―――――――――――

**ENGLISH PHONEMES NOT FOUND IN OTHER LANGUAGES**

Some phonemes in English do not exist in certain other languages. English learners from these backgrounds might experience difficulty in hearing and producing these sounds.

Not in Japanese: /dg/ /f/ /i/ /th/ /oo/ /v/ /schwa/

Not in Spanish: /dg/ /j/ /sh/ /th/ /z/

English learners' aural comprehension and pronunciation may be affected when English words contain phonemes that are unfamiliar to them. The schwa (the sound of the "e" in the phrase "the hat") is often difficult for Spanish speakers because Spanish vowels rarely alter their sound quality in unaccented syllables. A digraph—a pair of letters used to write one sound or a combination of sounds that does not correspond to the written letters combined—may confuse the English learner who attempts to separate the digraph into two separate phonemes. The concept of diphthong (defined as a vowel blend with two adjacent vowels, each of which is sounded) may transfer in principle from another

**TABLE 1.1** Phonemes in English: Vowels and Consonants

| Vowels | Examples | Consonants | Examples |
|--------|----------|------------|----------|
| /A/ | wake, pain, tray | /b/ | bet, habit, rub |
| /a/ | pat | /k/ | cake, naked, lack |
| /E/ | be, beat, flee | /d/ | do, sadder, wed |
| /e/ | set | /f/ | far, offer, half, phony |
| /I/ | I, tie, by | /g/ | gone, digger, beg |
| /i/ | if, tin | /h/ | head, behold |
| /O/ | no, moat, stone | /j/ | jam, tragic, stage, ledge |
| /o/ | pot | /l/ | light, willow, well |
| /U/ | futile, Tuesday | /m/ | mine, dim |
| /u/ | cup, dumb | /n/ | none, fun, Lynne |
| /OO/ | to, rue, chew, boot | /p/ | push, topple, step |
| /oo/ | soot, put | /kw/ | quiet |
| /oi/ | toil, boy | /r/ | rope, Larry, bar |
| /ou/ | pout, how, mouse | /s/ | sip, hustle, miss |
| /aw/ | saw, call, caught | /t/ | tip, after, bat |
| /ar/ | far | /v/ | vet, hover, gave |
| | | /w/ | wag, away |
| | | /ks/ or /gz/ | sox, exit |
| | | /y/ | your, yet |
| | | /z/ | zip, noisy, buzz |
| | | /sh/ | shout, lotion, wash |
| | | /hw/ | what |
| | | /ch/ | chop, pitch |
| | | /th/ | thing, southside, north |
| | | /th/ or $\partial$ | that, mother, soothe |
| | | /ng/ | wing, running |
| | | /zh/ | genre, collision, pleasure |

language, although the diphthongs may differ from language to language. Mandarin has diphthongs (*shyueh*), as does Spanish (*hay*).

*Phonemic sequences* are the permissible ways in which phonemes can be combined in a language. Languages also have permissible places for these sequences: initial (at the beginning of a word), medial (between initial and final position), and final (at the end of a word), or in a combination of these positions. In English, /spr/ as in *spring*, /nd/ as in *handle*, and /kt/ as in *talked* are permissible phonemic sequences, but neither /nd/ nor /kt/ can be used initially (*ndaft* is not permissible). English allows /sp/ in all three positions—*speak, respect, grasp*—but restricts /pt/ to only one—*apt* (the word *optic* splits the phonemes into two syllables; the word *pterodactyl* has a silent *p*).

Phonemes can be described in terms of their characteristic point of articulation (tip, front, or back of the tongue), the manner of articulation (the way the airstream is obstructed), and whether the vocal cords vibrate or not (voiced versus voiceless sounds). Not all languages distinguish between voiced and voiceless sounds. Arabic speakers may say "barking lot" instead of "parking lot" because to them /p/ and /b/ are not distinguishable.

## Phonemic Awareness

As children learn language, they acquire phonological awareness in the process of separating the oral sound stream they encounter into syllables and words. Literacy development builds on this ability, helping young readers connect sounds to written symbols (Burns, Griffin, & Snow, 1999). *Phonemic awareness* is the ability to use the sound–symbol connection to separate sentences into words and words into syllables in order to hear, identify, and manipulate the individual phonemes within spoken words (Block & Israel, 2005). This is not an easy task, with ten to twenty phonemes articulated per second in normal speech. Phonemic awareness tasks help students hear and isolate individual phonemes. This is the basis of phonics instruction (see Chapter 7).

## Stress

Besides phonemes, characteristics of language sounds include stress, pitch/tone, and intonation. Stress, the amount of volume a speaker gives to a particular sound, operates at two levels: word and sentence. Stress is a property of syllables—stressed syllables are longer and louder than unstressed syllables. Within words, specific syllables are stressed. In some languages, stress is predictable; in Czech, stress is usually on the first syllable of a word; in French, on the last syllable of a phrase. Stress is difficult to learn in English because there are "no consistent rules" (Dale & Poms, 2005, p. 84). Incorrect stress can alter the meanings of words. In the following examples, the stressed syllable is indicated by the accent mark ´:

> désert   noun, "dry region"
>
> dessért   noun, "sweet foods after the main meal"
>
> ínvalid   noun, as in "person with long-term, debilitating illness"
>
> inválid   adjective, as in "null, void" (Dale & Poms, 2005, p. 84)

Stress can further be used at the sentence level to vary emphasis. For example, the following sentences all carry different emphases:

> *Kimberly* walked home. (It was Kimberly who walked home.)
>
> Kimberly *walked* home. (She walked; she did not ride.)
>
> She walked *home.* (She walked home, not to Grandma's house.)

In some cases, the wrong stress on a word completely undermines comprehension.

Students who learn a second language sometimes have difficulty altering the sounds of words in the context of whole sentences. Thus, teachers are better served by teaching words in context rather than in lists.

**Classroom Glimpse**

### A MISPLACED WORD STRESS

Rashid sat down, shoulders slumped. "I'm beginning to get discouraged. People don't understand my speaking."

"Give me an example," I suggested.

Rashid continued, "At lunch my friend was eating something mashed. I said 'That looks like potty toe.' She gave me a strange look."

"Potty toe?" I asked. "What in the world do you mean? You'd better write down the word." (He wrote the word.)

"Oh!" I exclaimed, looking at the paper. "Potato!"

## Pitch and Rhythm

Another sound quality is important in oral speech. Pitch at the word or sentence level is a phonological component of language that plays a key role in determining meaning. "Eva is going," as a statement, is said with a rise on the syllable "go," followed by "-ing" with a falling pitch; but said as a question, the pitch rises at the end. *Tone languages* use the pitch of individual syllables to contrast meanings (examples are Thai, Mandarin, Vietnamese, Zulu, Apache, Navajo, and Kiowa).

Pitch interacts with word stress to produce prosody, the underlying rhythm of the language. The way an individual word fits into a sentence may change the stress. For example, in the sentence "He's my uncle—Uncle Bob," the first use of "uncle" is heavily stressed on the first syllable because the syllable is placed in the first clause at the climax of the prosodic contour, just before the final pitch drop. During the second "uncle," neither syllable is stressed, because the name "Bob" carries the emphasis, hence the stress.

Because English words are pronounced with different stress depending on their locations in sentences, in contrast to Spanish, in which the vowels are more apt to maintain their sound values irrespective of placement, Spanish speakers may have difficulty achieving the prosody of the native speaker of English.

Typical problems in oral speech include the tendency to pronounce all words with equal emphasis, avoiding contractions (thus sounding stilted), and pausing incorrectly between words. To achieve proper prosody, words in phrases are blended together and functional words are reduced in emphasis ("How are you" sounds like "Howaru?"), and sounds are linked across words, so that "We've eaten" sounds like "We veaten." Smooth prosody is a combination of phrasing and pausing: "Please//do your chores//before you go out."

## Intonation Patterns

The use of pitch to modify sentence meaning is called *intonation*. Each language has a distinctive sound flow across the sentence. The English pattern is characterized by accented and unaccented syllables, the same patterns found in English poetry. The *iamb* is a beat with one unaccented syllable followed by an accented one, as in the phrase "too late to go." An *anapest* is a beat with two unaccented syllables followed by an accented one: "in the heat of the night." Most sentences in English combine accented and unaccented syllables in an undulating rhythm until just before the end of the sentence, at which time the pitch rises and then drops briefly.

In contrast, Cantonese, as a tonal language, has intonation variation that distinguishes words by tone, but an entire sentence does not have a rise-and-fall curve. Because English, for example, makes use of a questioning intonation to soften the demanding nature of a request ("Could you sit down over there?"), a Cantonese speaker may sound impolite to English ears ("Could! You! Go! Sit! Down! Over! There!"). Intonation matters a great deal when language fulfills social functions.

*Contrastive analysis*—paying careful attention to phonemic differences between languages and then spending more time teaching those phonemes that differ—has been found to be relatively nonproductive as a teaching methodology. There is little evidence that learners will find general phonemic differences between languages to be difficult. *Error analysis,* however, can guide teachers; making careful note of a learner's difficulties can provide evidence about the need for specific interventions. Empirical teaching—teaching guided by data—helps to focus phonological training directly on the learner's difficulties. Guidelines for teaching pronunciation are featured in Chapter 6.

## Morphology: The Words of Language

Morphology is the study of the meaning units in a language. In some cases in English, individual words constitute these basic meaning units (e.g., *chase*). However, many words can be broken down into smaller segments—morphemes—that still retain meaning.

### Morphemes

Morphemes, small units that cannot be further subdivided, are the basic building blocks of meaning. *Fundamentalists* is an English word composed of five morphemes: *funda + ment + al + ist + s* (root + noun-forming suffix + adjective-forming suffix + noun-forming suffix + plural marker). Morphemes can be represented by a single sound, such as /a/ (a morpheme with two meanings—a stand-alone, or free, morpheme meaning an indefinite article ["a girl"] or a bound morpheme meaning "without," as in *amoral* or *asexual*). Morphemes can be a single syllable, such as the noun-forming suffix -*ment* in *amendment,* or two or more syllables, such as in *lion* or *parsley*. Two different morphemes may have the same sound, such as the -*er* in danc*er* ("one who dances") and the -*er* in fanci*er* (the comparative form of *fancy*). A morpheme may also have alternate phonetic forms: The regular plural -*s* can be pronounced either /z/ (*bags*), /s/ (*cats*), or /iz/ (*bushes*).

Morphemes are of different types and serve different purposes. Free morphemes can stand alone (*envelope, the, through*), whereas bound morphemes occur only in conjunction with others (-*ing, dis-, -ceive),* either as *affixes* or as *bound roots*. Affixes at the beginnings of words are *prefixes* (*un-* in the word *unafraid*); those added at the ends are *suffixes* (-*able* in the word *believable*); and *infixes* are morphemes inserted between other morphemes (-*s-* in *mothers-in-law*).

Part of the power and flexibility of English is the ease with which longer English words are formed by adding prefixes and suffixes to root words (*cycle, cyclist; fix, fixation*). The predictability of meaning carried by standard affixes can make it easier for students to learn to infer words from context rather than relying on rote memorization.

---

**Best Practice**    MORPHEMES

To generate interest in science concepts, at the beginning of each general science unit Mrs. Silvestri selected several roots from a general list (*astro, bio, geo, hydr, luna, photo, phys, terr*). She then asked students to work in pairs to search their texts for words with those roots from the relevant chapter in the science text. Next she handed out a list of prefixes and affixes and asked each pair to generate five to ten new words, including definitions. Students wrote each new word and its definition on two index cards and played a memory matching game with their card decks.

---

## Word-Formation Processes

English has historically been a language that has borrowed extensively from other languages or coined new words from extant terms. Studying how new words are formed—largely from existing morphemes—helps English learners understand morphemes. Table 1.2 displays new words that have been published in *Wired* magazine in recent years. Each is derived in part from an existing word in English.

**TABLE 1.2**    Neologisms (New Words and Phrases) from *Wired* Magazine (April 2006)

| New Word or Phrase | Derivation | Meaning |
|---|---|---|
| @homer | @ = at + home + er | one who stays at home |
| funkatizing | funk + atize + ing | making something funky |
| geekonomics | geek + economics | finance for computer aficionados |
| geek-year | geek + year | like "dog year"; different timescale for nerds |
| middleware | middle + ware as in hardware ↔ software | hybrid form of hardware-software |
| office-chairy | office chair + like | adj. form of office chair |
| paraspam | para = almost + spam | something like spam |
| transgenic | trans = across + genic = life | hybrid species |
| trigger species | trigger = early tip-off | the first species to be affected, as by global warming |
| übergroovy | über = over the top + groovy | supercool |
| viral video | viral = contagious + video | video that is rapidly disseminated via the Internet |

**Clipping**    Clipping is a process of shortening words, such as *prof* for *professor* or the slangy *teach* for *teacher*. If students learn both the original and the clipped versions, they gain the sense that they are mastering both colloquial and academic speech.

**Acronyms**    In English, acronyms are plentiful, and many are already familiar to students—USA, CNN, and NASA, for example. A list of acronyms helps students increase their vocabulary of both the words forming the acronyms and the acronyms themselves. Who can resist knowing that *laser* is light amplification by stimulated emission of radiation?

**Blends**    Words formed from parts of two words are called blends—for example, *chortle* from *chuckle* + *snort* and *travelogue* from *travel* + *monologue*. Students can become word detectives and discover new blends (*Spanglish, jazzercise, rockumentary*) or create their own blends (a hot dog in a hamburger bun can be a *hotburger*).

## Using Morphemes in Teaching

Students can add to their enjoyment of learning English by finding new words and creating their own. Those who play video games can make up new names for characters using morphemes that evoke pieces of meaning. Advertising copywriters and magazine writers do this on a daily basis; the word *blog* is a combination of the free morphemes *web* and *log;* then came *vlog* (*video* added to *blog*). The prefixes *e-* and *i-* have combined to form many new words and concepts over recent decades (e.g., *e-pets* and *iTunes*). The study of morphology is fun and increases word power.

Depending on the student's first language, some morphemes are easier to acquire than others. For example, the prefix *en-*, meaning "to bring about, to make, or to put into," is more often used to make verbs from nouns or adjectives that derive from the Anglo-Saxon side of English—that is, words not directly related to cognates in Romance languages. For example, one can say "enjoy" but not "\*enmuse." In contrast, words ending in the noun suffix *-ion* are relatively easy for Spanish speakers because they are usually words that have cognates in Spanish. Therefore, students may not as easily acquire the words in Table 1.3 as they might those in Table 1.4.

Attention to morphemes in the classroom can accelerate language acquisition if students are exposed to families of words across parts of speech—that is, if *courage* is taught alongside *courageous, discourage,* and *encourage* or *ice* is taught with *icy, ice cream, icicle, ice age,* and *iceberg*. Instead of defining new words, students

**TABLE 1.3**   Words with Morpheme *en-* as Prefix

| | | |
|---|---|---|
| enjoy | enact | enliven |
| enlarge | enclose | ensure |
| enrich | encourage | entrust |
| entrap | entangle | enroll |
| enable | encrust | enforce |

**TABLE 1.4**   Words with Morpheme *-ion* as Suffix

| | | |
|---|---|---|
| transportation | division | translation |
| action | succession | comparison |
| examination | combination | validation |
| preparation | signification | respiration |
| certification | termination | separation |

may enjoy separating new words into morphemes and finding other words that match these morphemes. This activity is consonant with a key principle of brain-based learning (see Chapter 2): The brain learns faster when engaged in pattern-matching or pattern-finding activities.

**Best Practice** WORKING WITH MORPHEMES

The teacher can encourage awareness of comparatives and superlatives using the following game, called Speed Search.

Students circulate around the room to see how many people they can find who fit the description on the slip of paper they have drawn from a box. After two minutes, they draw another slip for a second round of play. Students win if they have the <u>most</u> points after a designated number of rounds. Sample descriptions: Find a person who believes that dogs are <u>less</u> intelligent than cats. Find a person who has <u>more</u> than two brothers. Find a person who is the old<u>est</u> child in the family. (Kealey & Inness, 1997, pp. 24–25)

# Syntax: The Sentence Patterns of Language

Syntax refers to the rules that govern the formation of phrases and sentences. The words in a language have semantic properties that entail their use in sentences in some ways and not in others. A well-formed sentence is more than the sum of the meanings of the words; in English the position of the word in a sentence is an important part of the overall meaning. Sentence A, "The teacher asked the students to sit down," has the same words as sentence B, "The students asked the teacher to sit down," but not the same meaning. Not every sequence of words is a sentence: Sentence C, "*Asked the the teacher to down students sit," violates syntactic rules in English and thus has no meaning.

Native speakers of a language have syntactic proficiency—they can distinguish syntactically correct from incorrect combinations of words, even though they may not be able to explain what syntactic rules have been violated. Even very young English-speaking children know that sentences A and B are meaningful but sentence C is not. Moreover, the mind is a strong organizing force, constantly striving to gain meaning, so speakers of a language can comprehend even imperfectly formed sentences.

Whereas syntax refers to the internally constructed rules that make sentences, grammar looks at whether a sentence conforms to some standard. An important distinction, therefore, is the one between standard and colloquial use. Many colloquial usages feature acceptable sentence patterns in English, even though their usage is not standard—for example, "I ain't got a pen" is acceptable English syntax but not standard usage. Teachers who are promoting the standard dialect need to be aware that students' developing competence will not always conform to that standard.

Besides grammaticality and word order, speakers' syntactic knowledge helps them understand three other sentence features. Double meaning, or *ambiguity*, occurs in sentences such as "She is a Korean karate expert" or the frequently seen "Please wait for the hostess to be seated." On the other hand, sentences can have different structures but mean the same thing:

"He is hard to please," "Pleasing him is hard," "It is hard to please him." Finally, speakers can understand and produce novel utterances, the creative aspect of language.

## Explicit Teaching of Syntax

In the late twentieth century, it was widely believed that students could acquire a second language without explicit teaching of syntactic structures. However, because the mind seeks to acquire patterns, and syntax is a pattern, it is now thought that creative and systematic teaching of syntax can accelerate language learning. Grammar books that teach students to label the parts of speech and build up sentence structures from simple to complex are useful. Balancing this systematic instruction with grammar games and creative language engagement such as poetry—or even Mad Libs, the game that has students blindly providing nouns, adjectives, and verbs without knowing the story plot—helps students to learn the parts of speech.

Figure 1.1 presents a simple card for teaching sentence syntax. A pocket chart in a learning center can be used to teach sentence structure. Students can work in pairs to assemble meaningful sentences using packs of sentence components. Words in the same sentence should be on the same color of index card so that multiple sentences can be kept separated as students work.

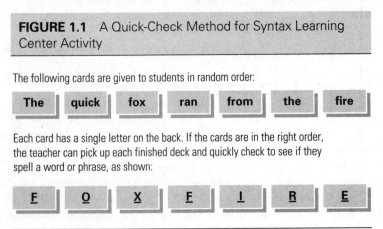

**FIGURE 1.1**  A Quick-Check Method for Syntax Learning Center Activity

The following cards are given to students in random order:

| The | quick | fox | ran | from | the | fire |

Each card has a single letter on the back. If the cards are in the right order, the teacher can pick up each finished deck and quickly check to see if they spell a word or phrase, as shown:

| F | O | X | F | I | R | E |

A trick to checking students' work quickly is for each set of cards to spell out a word on the back of the cards if the cards are in the correct order.

Some students have more *metalinguistic knowledge* than others—that is, they have the vocabulary to talk about grammar because they learned the grammar of their native language. As with other kinds of learning, the wise teacher assesses students' prior knowledge to learn where to begin instruction.

Describing the characteristic differences between languages—contrastive analysis—is useful to some degree in predicting what kinds of syntax errors students make (see Box 1.1 for Mandarin and Box 1.2 for Spanish). However, direct instruction must also be balanced with rich, authentic exposure to English sentences, both spoken and written, and the learner must be allowed time for syntactic structures to be absorbed, consolidated, and deployed in many situations before a given structure can be said to be a stable feature of the learner's repertoire.

## Semantics: The Meanings of Language

Semantics is the study of the meanings of individual words and of larger units such as phrases and sentences. Speakers of a language learn the "agreed-on" meanings of words and phrases in their language; these meanings must be shared, or communication becomes impossible.

**Box 1.1**   English Syntax Contrasted with Chinese (Mandarin)

English learners with Chinese as a mother tongue may need additional teacher assistance with the following aspects of English:

- Verb tense: *I see him yesterday.* In Chinese, the verb form is not changed to mark the time during which the action occurred—the adverb, not the verb, signals the time. Conjugating the verb form in English may prove to be difficult for the learner.
- Subject–verb agreement: *He see me.* In Chinese, verbs do not change form to create subject–verb agreement.
- Word order: *I at home ate.* In Chinese, prepositional phrases usually come before the verb—the rules governing adverb placement in English are difficult for many learners.
- Plurals: *They give me 3 dollar.* In Chinese, like English, the marker indicates number, but the noun form does not change to indicate plural; in English the noun form changes.
- Articles: *No one knows correct time.* Chinese uses demonstrative pronouns [*this one, that one*] but not definite or indefinite articles [*a, the*]. The rules for such use in English are complex.

However, English is a flexible language that is responsive to the needs of a dynamic culture, and new concepts emerge daily that require new words; English learners must acquire vocabulary continuously in order to keep up with semantic demands.

Some words carry a high degree of stability and conformity in the ways they are used (*slap* as a verb, for example, must involve the hand or some other flat object—"He slapped me with his ball" is not semantically meaningful). Other words carry multiple meanings (e.g.,

**Box 1.2**   English Syntax Contrasted with Spanish

English learners with Spanish as a mother tongue may need additional teacher assistance with the following aspects of English:

- Verb conjugation: Spanish has three groups of regular verbs, in contrast to one group in English (those that add *-ed* or *-d*), but English has more classes of irregular verbs (wildly irregular *go/went/gone* versus mildly irregular like *send/sent, break/broke,* etc.).
- Subject–verb agreement: In Spanish, first-, second-, and third-person forms must be changed from the base form to create subject–verb agreement. It is sometimes hard to remember that in English only the third-person form is changed.
- Noun/adjective order: In Spanish, adjectives come sometimes before and sometimes after the noun (*un buen día, un día linda*). These alterations, however, obey regular rules.
- Articles: Spanish, like English, uses both definite and indefinite articles, but with different rules (for example, languages need the definite article, *el ingles*). Both definite and indefinite articles must match the noun to which they refer (*unos muchachos, las mujeres*).

*Source:* Spinelli (1994).

**TABLE 1.5** Examples of English–Spanish Cognates

(Same meaning, same spelling; may be pronounced differently)

| | |
|---|---|
| club | plural |
| director | radio |
| hotel | rural |
| hospital | salmon (Spanish salmón) |
| mineral | sofa (Spanish sofá) |
| postal | tenor |
| perfume | violin (Spanish violín) |

*scrap*), ambiguous meanings (*bank,* as in "They're at the bank"), or debatable meanings (*marriage,* for example, for many people can refer only to heterosexual alliances, whereas others might apply it to nonheterosexual contexts).

## Semantic Challenges

In second-language acquisition, there are three basic semantic challenges. First is the process of translating—finding words (lexical items) in the second language that correspond to those already known in the first. The second challenge is learning words for ideas and concepts that are new in the second language for which there is no first-language counterpart (for example, the Polish term *fúcha*—"to use company time and resources to one's private ends"—has no equivalent in English) (de Boinod, 2006). The third challenge involves similar words that are in both languages whose meanings differ in small or large ways. Table 1.5 lists words that are cognates in English and Spanish—their meaning is identical. Table 1.6 lists near cognates, and Table 1.7 lists false cognates—those in which the similar appearance is misleading.

Another challenge in English is the extraordinary wealth of synonyms. One estimate of English vocabulary places the number at over 3 million words; the *Oxford English Dictionary* contains some 290,000 entries with some 616,500 word forms. Fortunately, only about 200,000 words are in common use, and an educated person draws from a stock of about 20,000 to use about 2,000 in a week (Wilton, 2003). The challenge when learning this vast vocabulary is to distinguish denotations, connotations, and other shades of meaning.

**Best Practice** NUANCES OF MEANING

- For adolescent learners, the teacher provides a list of a dozen common emotions (love, anger, fear, and fright are the big four; a few others are thankfulness, doubt, guilt, surprise, contempt, delight, hunger, nervousness).
- Students, working in pairs, make up situations that would engender the emotion.
- Rich discussion about nuances of meaning might result!

## Acquiring Vocabulary

What does it mean to "know" a word? Recognizing a word involves matching stored meaning with meaning derived from context. In addition, knowing a word includes the ability to pronounce the word correctly, to use it grammatically in a sentence, and to know with which morphemes it is appropriately connected. This knowledge is acquired as the brain absorbs and

**TABLE 1.6**  Examples of English–Spanish Near Cognates

(Same meaning, slightly different spelling; may be pronounced differently)

| English | Spanish | English | Spanish |
|---------|---------|---------|---------|
| February | febrero | tranquil | tranquilo |
| March | marzo | salt | sal |
| April | abril | violet | violeta |
| May | mayo | second | segundo |
| June | junio | intelligent | inteligente |
| July | julio | problem | problema |
| August | agosto | cream | crema |
| button | botón | check (bank) | cheque |
| much | mucho | deodorant | desodorante |
| office | oficina | garden | jardin |
| courtesy | cortesía | map | mapa |
| lamp | lámpara | paper | papel |
| medal | medalla | use | uso |

interacts with the meaning in context, possibly due to the important role that context plays in forming episodic memory—memory that is tied to emotionally rich experience.

Nation (1990) lists the following as the types of word knowledge necessary for complete comprehension of a given word: its spoken form, written form, grammatical behavior,

**TABLE 1.7**  Examples of English–Spanish False Cognates

(Close in sound; slightly different spelling; different meaning)

| Spanish | Meaning in Spanish | English False Cognate | Meaning in English |
|---------|--------------------|-----------------------|--------------------|
| blando | soft | bland | soothing; not stimulating or irritating |
| blanco | white | blank | colorless; free of writing |
| campo | country | camp | place for tents or temporary shelter |
| codo | elbow | code | a system of signals |
| despertador | alarm clock | desperate | almost beyond hope |
| dirección | address | direction | the way to go; authoritative instruction |
| cola | tail | cola | drink |
| plata | silver | plate | sheet of metal, food dish |

collocational behavior (what words are frequently found next to the word), frequency, stylistic register constraints (such as formal/informal contexts), conceptual meaning, and word associations (such as connotations).

Vocabulary knowledge can be *passive, controlled active,* or *free active* (Laufer & Paribakht, 1998). Passive knowledge involves understanding the most frequent meaning of a word (e.g., *break*—He breaks a pencil). Controlled active knowledge can be described as cued recall (e.g., The railway con_____ the city with its suburbs), and free active knowledge describes the ability to spontaneously use words. Each type of knowledge develops at a different rate, with passive understanding growing faster than active word use. Passive vocabulary is always larger than active vocabulary.

## Academic Vocabulary

Acquiring the vocabulary used to educate is essential to school success; it is a large part of what Cummins (1979, 1980) called cognitive academic language proficiency. This vocabulary has been compiled by various researchers (c.f., Bromberg, Liebb, & Traiger, 2005; Huntley, 2006). Although no exhaustive list exists of academic terms by grade level, Table 1.8 presents academic terms by approximate grade level. Table 1.9 displays examples of academic vocabulary.

## Vocabulary Teaching and Concept Development

Many methods have been used to teach vocabulary during second-language acquisition; rote memorization of lists or flash cards with words and meanings is probably the least effective, even when picture cues are provided. Rich experience of new words in the context of their use is the way words are usually acquired in the first language. Games such as Pictionary and Total Physical Response are useful when objects and actions are simple. More nuanced or complex knowledge requires careful work at all the levels described earlier by Nation (1990).

**TABLE 1.8** Examples of Cognitive Academic Words by Approximate Grade Level

| Grade 1 | Grade 2 | Grade 3 | Grade 4 | Grade 5 | Grade 6 |
|---|---|---|---|---|---|
| connect | measure | indent | define | summarize | minimum |
| check | width | proofread | method | evidence | initial |
| ruler | margin | paragraph | highlight | energy | estimate |
| period | dictionary | hyphen | environment | positive | factor |
| capital letter | schedule | topic | exhibit | gender | percent |
| grade | label | graph | layer | nuclear | simulate |
| mistake | draft | edit | region | source | transfer |
| chalk | chart | ignore | research | substitute | variable |
| file | margin | select | style | theme | volume |

**TABLE 1.9**   Examples of Academic Vocabulary

| | | | | |
|---|---|---|---|---|
| access | available | component | element | sufficient |
| adjust | capacity | confirm | emphasis | supplement |
| alter | clarify | consistent | instance | survey |
| approach | comment | contrast | random | undergo |
| aspect | complex | core | specific | visible |

*Source:* From Huntley (2006).

**Best Practice**   **KEY PRINCIPLES FOR TEACHING VOCABULARY**

- Vocabulary taught with collocations—words that co-appear commonly (for example, the verb *lose* is presented as "lose your way," "lose your temper," "lose your keys," etc.)
- Vocabulary taught within its grammatical environment (for example, verbs are always introduced with *to*—"to apply," "to return")
- Emphasis on register (teach where, when, with whom a word is used; in a formal or informal setting?)
- Emphasis on word form (does it include a prefix or suffix as a clue toward meaning?)
- Emphasis on connotation (nuances of meaning differentiating one word from another) (Daloğlu, 2005)

## Semantic Shifts

Language users must become aware of the semantic requirements when writing. It may be understandable when a speaker overuses the colloquial "you know" when telling a story, but in written English, one must shift toward more formal expression. Learning to make this shift is an important part of cognitive academic language. Only in certain types of writing—such as literature when a colloquial dialect is expressed, or in gonzo journalism, a flamboyant, first-person genre—is the colloquial form acceptable.

Teachers can emphasize this semantic shift by, for example, using a chart that compares "talk written down" with "more thoughtful writing." Table 1.10 contrasts these two writing styles as semantic shifts.

Semantics is a domain in which growth must be sustained at every level of schooling and in every content domain. Teacher education, for example, has its own lexicon; prospective teachers are asked to master such terms as *assertive discipline, wait-time, manipulatives, mind mapping, retelling, writing genre, mini-lesson,* and so forth. Demonstrating proficiency in these and similar terms is a measure of professionalism.

| **TABLE 1.10** Semantic Shifts When Writing | |
| --- | --- |
| **Informal Register** | **Formal Register** |
| you know | it is evident |
| a lot of, a whole bunch of | multiple |
| getting (dark, warm) | becoming |
| a piece of | a component of |
| to take a chance | to attempt |
| to make an offer | to offer |
| to keep on doing | to continue |

# Language Functions

Language proficiency is not an end in itself; language is used for various purposes—to solve problems, communicate feelings, or keep records as people go about their daily routines. Halliday (1978) has distinguished seven different functions for language: *instrumental* (getting needs met), *regulatory* (controlling others' behavior), *informative* (communicating information), *interactional* (establishing social relationships), *personal* (expressing individuality), *heuristic* (investigating and acquiring knowledge), and *imaginative* (expressing fantasy or possibility).

A curriculum might encourage students to perform a wide variety of functions such as reporting, evaluating, questioning, and critiquing. Many other functions are not necessarily encouraged by schools but take place nonetheless: interrupting, shifting the blame, threatening, accusing, arguing, demanding, and making excuses. Learners must begin to understand how language functions to acquire written as well as spoken competence in the effort to match forms with functions.

## Academic Language Functions

Academic language functions include explaining, informing, justifying, comparing, describing, proving, debating, and so forth. There is some overlap in the terminology of academic functions and of thinking skills. Academic English—also called cognitive academic language proficiency (CALP)—is designed for abstract, decontextualized performance across a variety of content domains, which requires a long period of successful schooling; exposure to academic language, feedback, and support in its use by students; and explicit instruction in vocabulary, morphology, syntax, and cognitive strategies (see Chapter 5). Table 1.11 aligns academic language functions with typical phrases that are used during that function.

Providing English learners with opportunities to engage in the various functions of language is critical for enabling them to develop a full range of proficiency in English. In school, however, rarely do teachers allow students to practice "out of school" social functions; the emphasis is usually on language functions necessary for the work of learning.

## Functions and Classroom Routines

In every situation, participants are expected to use language to carry out specific routines. One of the important tasks of kindergarten and first-grade teachers is to teach children how to respond appropriately in the school setting. Confusion and a sense of alienation can arise for English learners who are used to the school routines in their own countries and face the unexpected in U.S. schools. A knowledgeable teacher recognizes that these students are acting according to the routines with which they are familiar. It may take time—and explicit language coaching—for students to learn the language functions appropriate for a U.S. school context.

**TABLE 1.11** Phrases Associated with Academic Functions of Language

| Function of Language | Sample Phrase(s) |
|---|---|
| Indicating cause and effect | Therefore, as a result, gradually |
| Providing example | For instance, that is, one sample, such as, in fact |
| Comparing | Like, likewise, similarly, in much the same way, equally |
| Emphasizing | Moreover, chiefly, above all |
| Indicating sequence | In the first place, starting with, consequently, finally |
| Summarizing | To conclude, in other words, thus |

---

**Best Practice** ACQUIRING LANGUAGE FUNCTIONS

- *Instrumental:* Students practice a list of ways to request actions of others, including "Could you . . ." "Would you mind . . . ."
- *Regulatory:* Students take turns acting as timekeeper and taskmaster in cooperative groups.
- *Informative:* Students keep records of classroom pets, weather patterns, or commonly misspelled words on a bulletin board.
- *Interactional:* Students work together to plan field trips, social events, and classroom and school projects.
- *Personal:* Students use personal language in a journal and then share their thoughts and opinions on a voluntary basis.
- *Heuristic:* During projects, students brainstorm questions about which no one knows the answer.
- *Imaginative:* Students "play" with language—the sounds of words and the images they convey.

*Source:* Adapted from Pinnell (1985).

# Discourse

Discourse is classified using various dimensions, such as *written versus spoken.* Other dimensions include *register* (formal versus informal) and *genre* (a combination of communicative purpose, audience, and format) as well as considerations of number—*monologic, dialogic,* or *multiparty* (how many are involved) (Celce-Murcia & Olshtain, 2001). Many kinds of analysis have been used in examining discourse: studies of information structure, coherence, cohesion, turn-taking, and critical discourse analysis.

Discourse analysis can be defined as the study of language "beyond the sentence" (Tannen, 2001). Discourse might be characterized as "language associated with a particular activity, a particular kind of knowledge, a particular group of people or a particular institution"

(Peim, 1993). The study of discourse looks at language in its larger units, such as oral text (classroom talk, speeches, casual conversation) and written text (magazine articles, school assignments, signs, and posters). Discourse specialists have looked at such behavior as how people take turns, how speakers use contextual cues as they interact, and how people show others they are listening. These features are heavily influenced by culture.

In school, language is used differently than in the experiences of everyday life. As students acquire a second language—English—they are exposed to a distinct set of language functions that are specially adapted for school. This can work to the benefit of English learners if educators can affirm the voices that students bring to school and encourage them to build the second language on the knowledge they have gained in their first language, thus increasing their academic potential.

## Academic Discourse

What does it mean to use language for academic purposes? An educated person lives in a world in which discourse is used for a wide range of purposes. For many, literacy at work has become highly computer dependent, with word processing, databases, telephone number files, e-mail, and Web-based activities, as well as paper dependent, with piles of various folders containing information, along with books, journals, and newsletters. At home, personal literacy may include cookbooks, hobby materials, newsmagazines, correspondence, and bill-paying. All these reading materials have their own place, time, and task orientation.

*Classroom discourse patterns involve students as active language users.*

Bob Daemmrich Photography

Literacy practices are activities that form discourses within the culture or society at large. By the time a student enters undergraduate education, the discourse demands are intense: reading course syllabi, textbooks, study guides, handouts, laboratory manuals, tests, online materials, and reference materials; listening to lectures and peer discussions; writing tests, research papers, and other notes; making formal oral presentations; and informally contributing orally in class or in group working sessions. English learners must prepare for these discourse registers and activities in elementary and secondary school programs.

**Academic Competence: Psychological Factors**   The demands of producing and understanding academic discourse depend not only on acquiring cognitive academic language proficiency, but also on developing qualities such as persistence, rapport with one's teachers, and attunement to the demands of the task, as well as the ability to seek, obtain, and benefit from help. These personality features help an individual accommodate the demands of a situation.

**Academic Competence: Sociocultural Factors**   Success in previous schooling makes present and future accommodations easier. The peer culture must sustain patterns of academic activity; the parental/cultural standards of achievement must also be appropriately demanding and supportive; and the school must enforce high educational standards, with expert management, well-certified staff, and adequate resources. In this way, the individual is situated within a social and cultural context that sustains academic activity.

## Oral Discourse in the Classroom

Classroom discourse is a special type of conversation. Intonation, pausing, and phrasing determine when one person's turn to speak is over and the next person's turn begins. Markers signal the circulation of power. As Foucault (1979) noted, discursive practices in the modern world prepare the individual for power. Schooling can shape an average person into a "good" student using discourse.

Good language learners are able to gain access to a variety of conversations in their communities. The communities of practice (Lave & Wenger, 1991) in which they participate—even peripherally—provide access to the utterances of others and the cultural practices they need to become engaged in community life. This means that the community of practice in a classroom does as much to create a good learner as the individual's cognition and striving.

Linguistic features are useful ways to examine classroom discourse. Turn markers governing who takes the floor signal speaking and listening. Some listeners nod frequently, and others offer eye contact or feedback such as "hmm," "uh huh," and "yeah." If a teacher is speaking, the type of listening that a learner signals is an important part of that learner's image in the mind of the teacher. If someone seems uninterested or uncomprehending (whether or not they truly are), the speaker tends to slow down, repeat, or overexplain, giving the impression of "talking down."

**The Recitation Pattern: A Typical Learning Encounter**   Classrooms in the United States often follow a model of instruction based on recitation (Mehan, 1979). Typically, the pattern has three parts, called the IRE sequence. First, the teacher initiates (I) an interaction by asking a question. A student responds (R), and the teacher follows up with evaluation (E). Alternatively, this may be called the IRF pattern, replacing the term *evaluation* with *feedback*, which consists not only of praise or disguised evaluation but also of reformulation, repetition of the student's answer, and summarizing or delivering information.

The IRF pattern shares characteristics of other kinds of teacher talk. The teacher not only produces the most language but also takes the most turns. Questions asked in this way usually call for simple information recall, and the responses are limited to this type of thinking. The teacher tends to ask "known-answer" questions in which students' responses can be easily evaluated (Pridham, 2001). The IRF pattern is easy to identify, partially because of its prevalence.

*I*nvitation to respond:
> **Teacher:** Who knows why names are capitalized? (Some students are wildly waving their hands, begging to be chosen to respond; others are averting their eyes, hoping *not* to be called on) Alma?

*R*esponse:
> **Alma:** It's somebody's name.

*E*valuation or *F*eedback:
> **Teacher:** That's true. Good, Alma.

*I*nvitation to respond: (pattern repeats) . . .
> **Teacher:** But who can tell me what the term for that is?

The IRF is not the only discourse pattern in which the teacher dominates, but it is the most frequent. In *teacher-fronted* classrooms in general (Harel, 1992), the teacher takes the central role in controlling the flow of information, and students compete for attention and permission to speak. English learners are dependent on their ability to understand the teacher's explanations and directions.

Clearly the IRF pattern has positive instructional features—to activate students' prior knowledge about a topic, review material already covered, present new information, calm a noisy room, check on the general state of group knowledge on a topic, or evaluate the discipline and cooperation of individual students. This evaluation of the student seems to shape a teacher's academic expectations for that student. Many features of the recitation pattern work for the benefit of instruction, although the same features that benefit some students may create difficulties for English learners (see Table 1.12).

**Recitation Pattern: Questioning Strategies**   Through skilled questioning, teachers lead discussions and ascertain students' understanding. Questions should be framed to match students' proficiency levels and to evoke the level of critical or creative thinking sought in the response. Teachers who are sensitive to varying cultural styles are aware that in some cultures students are reluctant to display knowledge before a large group. The teacher must organize other means for students to demonstrate language and content knowledge, such as small-group discussions.

A hierarchy of question types can be matched to students' proficiency levels. Beginning English learners in the "silent period" may be asked a question requiring a nonverbal response—a head movement, pointing, or manipulating materials. Once students begin to speak, either/or questions allow them merely to choose the correct word or phrase to demonstrate understanding: "Is the water evaporating or condensing?"; "Did explorers come to the Americas from Europe or Asia?" Once students can produce language, *wh-* questions are

**TABLE 1.12**   Positive and Negative Features of the IRF for English Learners

| Positive Features | Possible Negative Features for English Learners |
|---|---|
| *Invitation to Bid* | |
| Teacher waits for silence and imposes order on student behavior. | English learners may not appear as attentive as English speakers because they might have difficulty comprehending instruction. |
| Teacher controls the scope of the lesson by asking selected questions. | English learners may need more time than English speakers to understand questions and frame responses. |
| Teacher determines order and importance of information by posing questions. | Students with creative and individualistic thinking may wish to contribute related ideas outside the scope of the immediate topic. |
| Teacher controls the level of language displayed in class by choice of lexicon and complexity of sentence structure. | Instructional language, including vocabulary, may be too complex for English learners. |
| Teacher controls pace and rhythm of discourse. | Pace and rhythm of discourse may be different in students' native language, causing discomfort. |
| *Response* | |
| Teacher evaluates behavior of individuals by looking to see who is willing and ready to participate. | English learners may be reluctant to bring attention to themselves because they are insecure about their oral language, see such an action as incompatible with group cohesiveness and cultural norms, or are reluctant to display knowledge in front of others. |
| Teacher controls potential for reward by choosing respondent. | |
| By acting eager to answer, students can demonstrate responsivity to instruction, attention, and cooperation even if they do not really know the answer the teacher expects to hear. | Students may lack experience in particular topics under discussion, although their background may be rich in topics that are not curriculum related. |
| Teacher controls behavior by calling on students who may not be attentive. | Students from cultures in which children do not make direct eye contact with adults may not appear attentive during instruction. |
| Students can practice risk-taking by volunteering to answer. | English learners may be reluctant to volunteer to answer if they are not 100 percent sure their idea is correct and their culture does not reward ambiguity. |
| Students can show knowledge whether from prior instruction or experience. | |
| *Evaluation (Feedback)* | |
| Teacher is able to evaluate students' level of oral participation. | Students may need prior language development in oral participation, including turn-taking, listening, and speaking. |
| Teacher is able to use teacher approval as a reinforcer. | |
| Teacher is able to establish public recognition for those who answer correctly. | Students from certain cultures may not depend on teacher for approval. |
| Teacher may use the evaluation turn to correct sentence grammar. | Individual public recognition may be taboo in some cultures. |

*(continued)*

**TABLE 1.12** Continued

| Positive Features | Possible Negative Features for English Learners |
|---|---|
| *Evaluation (Feedback)* *(Continued)* | |
| Teacher can withhold negative evaluation by partially accepting an incomplete answer. | Research shows that second-language grammar is not improved by public correction of grammar, but by gradual acquisition of forms during language input and output. |
| Teacher can avoid direct negative evaluation by asking one student to "help" another to improve an answer. | |
| Teacher may evaluate students' success in the recitation pattern as an indicator of facility with "display knowledge" cultural pattern. | Indirect negative evaluation may be confusing for some students, leaving them with unclear concept formation. |
| | Students who are unfamiliar with "display knowledge" cultural pattern may appear uncooperative. |
| Teacher can elaborate on answer and expand a concept by delivering direct instruction at this point. | Students who are not rewarded by encouragement of more complex questions and responses gradually receive fewer hours of attention and instruction. |
| Teacher can improve a poor answer by substituting more correct terminology or restating a sentence in more correct grammar. | |
| As teacher evaluates students' responses, he or she determines what question comes next. | |

appropriate: "What is happening to the water?"; "Which countries sent explorers to the Americas?"; "What was the purpose of their exploration?"

If a teacher is seeking evaluative responses requiring critical thinking by means of questioning strategies, more wait-time is necessary for students to understand the question and frame a thoughtful response. Bias is avoided if all respondents are given equal feedback and support in increasing the cognitive complexity of the answer.

Teachers of English learners cannot avoid using teacher-fronted discourse patterns to some extent, because of the legacy of traditional teaching discourse. However, awareness of its strengths (in summary, ease of use, effectiveness for controlling attention and behavior, and diagnosis of a learner's responsiveness) and weaknesses (for example, lack of emphasis on learner oral production, limited peer interaction, and inequity of reinforcement) may encourage teachers to better focus the use of teacher-fronted discourse for English learners.

**Cooperative Learning as a Discourse Alternative**   The organization of discourse is important for second-language acquisition in content classes. Classrooms that feature flexible grouping patterns and cooperative learning permit students greater access to the flow of information as they talk and listen to peers, interact with the teacher or another adult in small groups, and use their home language for clarification purposes (Wells, 1981).

In cooperative-learning classrooms, the style of teacher talk often changes: Teachers assist students with the learning tasks, give fewer commands, and impose less disciplinary control (Harel, 1992). The teacher plans tasks so that students use language in academic ways. Students are placed in different groups for different activities. Teachers work with small groups to achieve specific instructional objectives (e.g., in literature response groups or instructional conversations, as discussed next).

**The Instructional Conversation as a Discourse Alternative** An instructional discourse format called the *instructional conversation* is one alternative to a teacher-fronted classroom. With a group of six to eight students, the teacher acts as a discussion leader, following up a literature, social studies, or math lesson with a directed conversation that invites a deeper understanding of the issues raised (Tharp & Gallimore, 1991). The focus is on assisted understanding of complex ideas, concepts, and texts, permitting a more satisfying intellectual relationship between teacher and students.

Learning to manage and appreciate the instructional conversation takes time, but many teachers find that the increased attention paid to students' assisted thinking reaps great benefits in increased understanding of students' thought processes as well as in students' sense of instructional co-ownership. It is difficult for most teachers to keep silent and let students think and volunteer their thoughts in good time, to move the conversation forward by building on students' ideas rather than the teacher's, to select topics that students find genuinely interesting and comprehensible, and to have patience with English learners' struggle to find the words for their thoughts. However, the rewards are great—a satisfying instructional conversation is the event for which, at heart, every good teacher yearns.

## Discourse That Affirms Students' Voices

Throughout this book, the emphasis is on the co-participation of the learner in learning. It is imperative that teachers encourage the language that is needed and desired by the student, and if that desire does not exist, to evoke those emotions and motivations as an integral part of instruction. Instruction—particularly in a second language—that is not meaningful and motivating to the learner becomes empty.

What kind of participation enhances motivation and promotes acquisition? *Co-construction of meaning* permits the learner to plan, choose, and evaluate knowledge in relation to personal needs and goals. *Participatory genres* help the student to bridge the home–school divide. For example, the "talk-story" of Hawai'ian culture, when brought into the classroom, can open up the discourse around reading (Jordan, Tharp, & Baird-Vogt, 1992). By working in acknowledgment of, rather than at cross-purposes to, these community patterns of discourse, teachers can choose modifications to teacher-fronted discourse that will be successful for a particular group of learners.

In summary, using the tools of ethnography and community participation, teachers can learn how to help the learner participate in meaningful English-language instruction. Studying how the community uses discourse can help teachers pattern their classroom activities in ways that increase the likelihood that students' English proficiency will grow.

# Pragmatics: The Influence of Context

Pragmatics is the study of communication in context. It includes three major communication skills. The first is the ability to use language for different functions—greeting, informing, demanding, promising, requesting, and so on. The second involves appropriately adapting or changing language according to the listener or situation—talking differently to a friend than to a principal or speaking differently in a classroom than on a playground. The third skill is the ability to follow rules for conversations and narrative, knowing how to tell a story, give a book report, or recount events of the day.

Linguists who study pragmatics examine the ways that people take turns in conversation, introduce topics and stay on topic, and rephrase their words when they are misunderstood, as well as how people use nonverbal signals in conversation: body language, gestures, facial expressions, eye contact, and distance between speaker and listener. Because these pragmatic ways of using speech vary depending on language and culture (Maciejewski, 2003), teachers who understand these differences can help learners adjust their pragmatics to those that "work" when speaking English.

## Appropriate Language

To speak appropriately, the speaker must take into account the gender, status, age, and cultural background of the listener. For example, a teacher's assistant in a classroom may be an older woman who shares the language and culture of the children and addresses students in a manner similar to the way she interacts with her own children, whereas the teacher might use more formal language. Similarly, a former second-grade teacher who takes a job at the sixth-grade level must learn to make adjustments in tone of voice to an appropriate level for older students.

**Language Contexts and Register Shifts** Various *language registers* match language to contexts—whether the classroom, a social event, a store, or different types of written correspondence—using a formal or informal tone, specific vocabulary and sentence structures, or even vocal pitch changes to suit different situations. Language registers are in turn enveloped by other verbal and nonverbal clues. In written genres, for example, the paper and ink quality varies according to the purpose and content of the written message; for oral genres, variation can be found in the distance between speakers, the roles of men versus women, and the tone and pitch of the voice.

There is a great contrast, for example, in the pitch of a kindergarten teacher's voice when reading a story aloud versus a high school football coach's instruction on the gridiron. These differences are adapted to the verbal and nonverbal—sometimes physical—features of the context. Factors that affect a speaker's or writer's choice of pragmatic features include cultural and social norms, the social and physical setting, goals and purpose of the language used, the identities of the participants, the subject matter involved, and the role of the speaker or writer vis-á-vis the audience.

 **Classroom Glimpse**

### LEARNING TO BE APPROPRIATE

In preparation for a drama unit, Mrs. Morley has her students develop short conversations that might occur with different people in different situations, such as selling ice cream to a child, a teenager, a working adult, and a retiree. Pairs of students perform their conversations and the class critiques the appropriateness of the language. Students develop a feel for appropriate expressions, tones, and stances before working on plays and skits.

**Teaching Oral Register Shifts**   Registers may involve conventions of intonation, vocabulary, or topic that meet the needs of the people and the tasks to be performed in that situation. For example, car advertising commercials filmed locally often use "car commercial register," a kind of frenzied tone performed by a man speaking loudly and quickly, whereas airline pilots who use the public address system of the airplane adopt a folksy tone, a "captain register" that is reassuring and paternal. Kindergarten teachers who read fairy tales aloud use storytelling register, featuring a tone of wonder and suppressed excitement. Understanding *register shifts* enables a language user to adapt to these rules.

Formal oral presentations, for example, may resemble written language, with scholarly sounding words, passive voice, or use of the subjunctive, because many speakers write out a presentation in advance. Informal, casual speech often features contractions, slang, and incomplete sentences (Cipollone, Keiser, & Vasishth, 1998). Table 1.13 displays a variety of registers that students might master for use in a classroom.

---

**Best Practice**   TRAINING STUDENTS IN ORAL REGISTER SHIFTS

- Set up opportunities for situated practice, require oral presentations, stage dramatic events, and engage older students in storytelling to children.
- Offer repeated trials with feedback to help students improve the ability to shift registers.
- Let students take the initiative in creating settings and events for a variety of register usages that require leadership and talent in language use.
- Apply strategies for identifying and addressing difficulties English learners may encounter in comprehending regional dialects or other varieties of English.
- Create an instructional environment that respects English learners' home language and variety of English.

---

**TABLE 1.13**   Typical Oral Registers in the Classroom

| Register | Description or Example |
|---|---|
| Student response register | A firm tone, spoken confidently, that reaches all other students in the room |
| Leadership register | The voice of roll call, the call to line up for lunch, or the call to be quiet and listen |
| Classroom presentation register | Involves eye contact with an audience, confident bearing, pleasing and varied tone of voice, and an inviting sense of two-way communication with listeners |
| Dramatic register | Spoken dialogue in a play, in the role of narrator or announcer; it is "larger than life," with exaggerated emotion and voice |
| Storytelling to children | Features simplification and a sense of warmth and intimacy, no matter what the size of the crowd |
| Cooperative work register | The "ten-inch voice"; able to be heard within one's group but not by the next group |

**Turn-Taking**    A key aspect of learning to be appropriate is understanding how to take turns. Native speakers of a language have internalized guidelines for when to speak, when to remain silent, how long to speak, how long to remain silent, how to give up "the floor," how to enter into a conversation, and so on, including how to show respect when doing so. Linguistic devices such as intonation, pausing, and phrasing are used to signal an exchange of turns. In some cultures, people wait for a clear pause before beginning their turn to speak, whereas others start while the speaker is winding down.

In some cultures, overlapping a turn with the speaker is acceptable; in other cultures, this is considered rude and causes feelings of unease or hostility. Some children can interrupt instruction without receiving negative sanction, whereas others are chided for frequent interruption. Punishing some students while letting others take unwarranted turns is tantamount to linguistic discrimination. To avoid this, a skilled teacher instructs second-language students about how to get turns and monitors instruction to ensure fairness. (It is difficult to see one's own behavior in this; it is best for the teacher to ask a peer to observe.)

## Nonverbal Communication

An important part of the pragmatic dimension of language is the complex nonverbal system that accompanies, complements, or takes the place of the verbal: "An elaborate and secret code that is written nowhere, known by none, and understood by all" (Sapir, quoted in Miller, 1985). This nonverbal system, estimated to account for up to 93 percent of communication (Mehrabian, 1969), involves sending and receiving messages through eye contact, facial expression, gesture, posture, and tone of voice.

Everyone is adept at sending and receiving these nonverbal messages, but, as in oral language, people are often unconscious of the information they are receiving. Because this nonverbal system accounts for a large part of the emotional message given and received, awareness of its various aspects helps teachers to recognize when students' nonverbal messages may not fit with expected school norms.

**Body Language**    The way one holds and positions oneself—one's body language—is a means of communication. Body language can convey power and confidence, or submission and timidity, merely by the tilt of the head, the position of the shoulders, or the grip of a handshake.

Gestures—expressive motions or actions made with hands, arms, head, or even the whole body—are ways to add meaning to verbal language or to substitute for words. Through the use of eyebrows, eyes, cheeks, nose, lips, tongue, and chin, people nonverbally signal any number of emotions, opinions, and moods.

Eye contact is another communication device that is highly variable. Many folk sayings express the idea that "the eyes are the windows of the soul," and it is important for some that the gaze be direct but not too bold. Eyes can reveal or hide emotions; not only the gaze but also the shape of the eye and even the size of the pupil convey emotions.

**Conceptions of Space and Time**    Physical distance between people, the invisible "bubble" that defines individual personal space, varies according to relationships. People usually stand closest to relatives, close to friends, and farther from strangers. Coming too close can be interpreted as aggressive behavior; conversely, staying too far away may be perceived as cold. Teachers with students of many cultures in their classes may have the opportunity to observe many spatial facets of communication.

Use of time, even daily rhythms, varies across cultures. Hall (1959) pointed out that for speakers of English, time is treated as a material object—a commodity—rather than an objective experience. English expressions include "saving time," "spending time," and "wasting time." Teachers often reprove students for idling and admonish students to "get busy." Standardized tests record higher scores for students who work quickly. In fact, teachers correlate rapid learning with intelligence.

With an awareness of mainstream U.S. conceptions of time, teachers become more understanding of students and families whose time values differ from their own. Some students may need more time to express themselves orally because the timing of oral discourse is slower in their culture. Parents who were raised in cultures with radically different concepts of time may not be punctual for parent conferences. One group of teachers allowed for this by designating blocks of three hours when they would be available for conferences, letting parents arrive when they could without fixed appointment times. Thus, teachers' accommodation to the intercultural pragmatics of the situation was key to an improved school climate.

## Evaluating the Pragmatic Features of School Programs

Intercultural pragmatics often involves concepts, feelings, and attitudes that are difficult for teachers and school administrators to discuss. Some teachers, lacking a more nuanced vocabulary, focus on teaching students *manners*, a term that carries a variety of meanings, from interpersonal respect to reliance on traditional, hierarchical adult–child rituals. Seeing others' beliefs, values, and behaviors through the lens of one's own culture often means that others' culturally based behavior—that of students and their families—is viewed as wrong, maladapted, or rude. Teachers who avoid the trap of "right" versus "wrong" can set an open and accepting tone.

Making the pragmatic features of the school and other settings explicit for English learners helps students engage in oral and written discourse that is appropriate for a given context, purpose, and audience. One teacher wrote a Welcome Book for newcomers to the classroom that explained routines, procedures, expected behaviors, and shared values. A student's "buddy" would have the chance every day to go over sections of the manual with the newcomer, and a copy was sent home. This helped students and their families know what to expect.

# Dialects and Language Variation

The language used in a certain context varies not only according to pragmatic factors of register shift (cultural and social norms, social and physical setting, goals, purpose, participants, audience, and subject matter) but also in long-term variations that influence the way people produce language. An oral dialect is evinced when people talk a certain way in order to feel appropriate within a given context. Teachers who take such variation into consideration communicate respect and understanding of contextual influences on English-language use.

Within the first few seconds of listening to the voice of a stranger, native speakers can usually identify not only whether the speaker's voice is familiar but also a host of other information about that person. As Wolfram (1991) noted, "It is surprising how little conversation it takes to draw conclusions about a speaker's 'background'—a sentence, a phrase, or even a word is adequate to trigger a regional, social, or ethnic classification" (p. 1). *Dialect* refers to "any variety of language which is shared by a group of speakers" (p. 2). Dialect varies with region, social class, and ethnic origin.

## Dialects and the Education of English Learners

Language educators cannot help being influenced by dialect considerations. Wolfram (1995) emphasized the importance of dialect issues for educators of English learners:

> The standard version of English provided in most ESL curricula aims unrealistically at a dialect-neutral variety of English. At the same time, the majority of ESL learners are surrounded by an array of dialects, including some well-established vernacular dialects for those who live in economically impoverished conditions. The socialization of many ESL learners into US culture may lead them to adopt the same uncharitable, biased opinion of vernaculars that is often found among native speakers of English. . . . It thus seems appropriate to incorporate dimensions of language variation into the ESL curriculum. (p. 1)

A student's dialect may affect teacher expectations. The ESL teacher may be tempted to oversimplify classroom language to match students' acquisition level. Finding the appropriate balance of language knowledge, pedagogical skill, dialect accommodation, and standard-language modeling is a challenge for teachers of English learners.

One important question is whether ESL teachers should model Standard English. In many urban schools, bilingual (Spanish–English) teachers are in demand in elementary schools, and personnel administrators do not seem to see Spanish-accented English as a negative in this context. However, some personnel administrators still seem to prefer to hire high school English teachers who are native speakers, or who speak English without a "foreign" accent.

A central issue, that of honoring the dialect of the learner, means finding the appropriate balance between respecting the home dialect of the student and modeling and teaching Standard English. Prejudice may be an issue in ESL contexts. Speakers of a regional dialect (for example, a Mexican-American dialect in Fresno) may not be accorded the same respect as speakers of Standard English. Yet within a specific community, a dialect may be the norm. Should English teachers enforce Standard English even if it is not the norm in the students' community? Thus, dialect issues are also issues of social power and status in society.

Students who speak nonstandard dialects are very aware when they have difficulty acquiring standard forms for academic writing and avoiding stereotyping and discrimination (Nero, 1997). But they are also aware that their very identity and deepest values are linked to their language, leading to potential conflicts in self-evaluation and acculturation—but also to possible positive biculturality (Bosher, 1997; LePage & Tabouret-Keller, 1985). The role of dialect is complex. This section examines dialect from a linguist's point of view: common features of dialects, how dialects reflect social and ethnic differences, what types of attitudes people have toward dialects, and how dialects affect style.

## Common Features That Constitute Dialects

Why do languages have dialects? Language differences go hand-in-hand with social differentiation. People speak differently because they are physically separated (regional dialects) or because they are socially separated (by means of economic ecology and social stratification). A third explanation is based on linguistic differences between the dialects themselves.

**Regional Dialects**    Sometimes physical terrain keeps dialects isolated and intact. In the United States, the geographic isolation of some Southern communities has given rise to so-called Appalachian English (Wolfram, 1991). The overall dialect terrain of the United States is an example of regional dialects. The four distinct dialects that most Americans find recognizable in the United States today can be roughly characterized as (1) New York City, (2) New England, (3) the South, and (4) everyone else. The use of these dialects often has cultural implications.

**Social-Stratification Dialects**    Within social groups, language establishes and maintains social distinctions. If people want to be considered a part of a particular social group, they consciously or unconsciously adopt the vocabulary items, pronunciation, and grammatical patterns of that group. This is easy to see in the case of teenage slang. Even when people's language receives negative social evaluation from mainstream English speakers, they continue to use the language of their in-group. Features of the dialect may be associated with ethnic solidarity, whereas speaking in the mainstream style may cause loss of friends or weakening of family ties. It is not uncommon for speakers to try to live in two or more worlds.

**Deeper Syntactic Causes for Dialects**    The third explanation for the origin and persistence of dialects is based on linguistic analysis. Double negation within a sentence, as in the Southern U.S. dialect construction "The dog didn't like nobody," is also found in European languages. Deletion of the copula ("They late") is a feature of African-American Vernacular English (AAVE) but also of Chinese and other languages. Lack of the *'s* in the possessive structure ("that man hat") in AAVE is true for other possessive structures in English ("her hat"); similarly, the lack of the noun plural ending ("four girl") in AAVE is common in many languages. Thus, dialects persist based on the ways in which languages are constructed.

## How Dialects Exhibit Social and Ethnic Differences

Whether dialects have a regional, social, or linguistic explanation, speakers acquire a dialect of English based on the language used by others of their region, social class, and native language. The most obvious form of dialect usage is in the sound of the language—the *accent*. People use accent to make judgments on a range of personal qualities and capabilities, such as innate intelligence, morality, and employability (Wolfram, 1991). Just because someone speaks with an accent does not mean he or she is less competent in the language. In fact, as Lippi-Green asserts,

> [D]egree of accentedness, whether from L1 interference, or a socially or geographically marked language variety, cannot predict the level of an individual's competency in the target language. In fact . . . high degrees of competence are often attained by persons with especially strong L2 accents. (1997, p. 70)

Standard pronunciation (an accent known as General American or Midwestern) has become associated with high-status occupations, such as doctors, lawyers, professionals, and executives of large companies. Thus, language variation is associated with a person's economic activity. Economic discrimination based on language is enforced by means of informal, often invisible, social networks that intersect with social-class stratification.

Many people live in communities in which people are multidialectic, code-switching back and forth easily between multiple languages, each with its own repertoire of styles. To overcome the negative effects of social stratification, many people who are non-native speakers of English seek to lose the accent that they feel hinders them from assimilating into the mainstream. On the other hand, in many cultures the dialect they speak *is* the mainstream, and to acquire any other accent risks social stigma. In some cultures, being bilingual is acceptable only to a limited degree.

## Attitudes toward Dialects

People who are forbidden by law from discriminating against others on the basis of race or ethnicity may use accent as a means of social stigmatization or exclusion (Lippi-Green, 1997). Teachers may unwittingly communicate a negative social evaluation to a non-native-English-speaking student by speaking louder, using shorter sentences, slowing speech, restricting vocabulary and range of topics, or signaling a patronizing attitude (curiously enough, this is also done to the elderly). This puts the non-native speaker in a position of lower status.

Americans, consciously or unconsciously, view certain "foreign" languages as less prestigious than others. Because of racism, the French spoken by Haitians may not be evaluated as positively as French spoken by a Canadian. Status issues are prevalent in dialect differences among native speakers of English. In many parts of the world, the prestige form of British English is considered a preferable dialect to any form of American English.

Language is central to the identification of self and group. Teachers can damage the teacher–student relationship through prejudice or impair students' academic success through lower academic expectations. Student who are made to feel inferior for reasons of accent may internalize the shame associated with discrimination or maintain a negative attitude toward learning English. As Lippi-Green (1997) states, "When an individual cannot find any social acceptance for her language outside her own speech communities, she may come to denigrate her own language, even when she continues to use it."

## Dialects and Style

A speaker's or writer's choice of language variation for a given discourse may be influenced by the context or setting of the discourse and by the speaker's age, gender, culture, level of education, social class, or vocation. Formal settings call for formal language; a student skilled in making this distinction may be chosen for public speaking at school assemblies.

Male–female differences have been shown in women's greater pitch changes to show emotion, higher overall pitch, and greater use of expressive adjectives and intensifiers (Brend, 1975). Characteristics of female speech are related more to powerlessness than gender, suggesting that women have learned to use these linguistic forms because they have traditionally been relegated to relatively powerless social positions (O'Barr & Atkins, 1980). English educators may find that male and female learners acquire different dialects of English, transferring to English the different roles and speech patterns in the native language. For example, female students may be more reticent to speak than male students, or vice versa. In these cases, a teacher might openly discuss the differences and find ways to equalize speaking opportunities.

## Vernacular Dialects and Language Teaching

Because accent and intonation patterns are important in second-language acquisition, students need to understand four basic truths about dialect usage in English: (1) One's dialect, if widely used by the surrounding racial, ethnic, or cultural community, is equally valid as a subset of English as any other dialect; (2) dialects are often used as a basis for discrimination, combining with underlying issues of power and race relations; (3) it is common for individuals all over the world to learn more than one dialect of English and to switch from one dialect to another depending on the context; and (4) such features of dialect as accent can be altered, if so desired, by specific, albeit time-intensive, drill.

**Teaching Standard English: Whose Standard?**   In a language as varied as English, there are naturally some who feel that it is important to establish a standard, or norm, against which usage is measured. Experts who publish grammar and usage books usually prescribe correct or standard language forms, but in English, no such standard in fact exists. Generally speaking, Standard American English is a composite of several subdialects spoken by the educated professional middle class. People seeking success in school and in the job market tend to adopt the language used by people in positions of power.

Many educators feel it is their right and privilege to enforce Standard English on their students. Teachers may subordinate the language of their students using a variety of messages, both overt and covert. Some teachers believe it is their right to correct students in public, to reprimand them for incorrect usage, or to refuse to communicate until a standard is reached ("You must answer in a complete sentence," "I can't understand you—say it again") (Lippi-Green, 1997).

Varieties of language are a result of normal social processes rather than inadequacies of individual speakers. The unique voice of the student is lost if educators insist on the use of Standard English exclusively in the classroom. Just as the worldview of the Native American is

*Students speaking a nonstandard dialect of English are a rich source of language input to English learners in urban schools.*

lost if the indigenous language dies away, so is the interlanguage of the student lost if no one listens. By balancing the need to teach Standard English with the zest and delight in each individual's vernacular, education can become a reservoir of English-language diversity.

In summary, language affords rich and dynamic expression. Familiarity with the structures and functions of language helps teachers to promote English-language development while supporting students' self-expression in their primary languages. Teachers with knowledge about the various subsystems of language can recognize the effort involved in developing English ability and incorporate students' language-development objectives into all facets of the daily program.

Language is accompanied by a nonverbal system that surrounds and supports grammatical competence. Knowledge about and skill in nonverbal communication enhances teachers' rapport with students. Understanding the basics of language helps to make language learning a meaningful, purposeful, and shared endeavor.

---

**PEARSON**
**myeducationlab**
The Power of Classroom Practice
www.myeducationlab.com

Go to the Topic Vocabulary Development in the MyEducationLab (www.myeducationlab.com) for your course, where you can:

- Find learning outcomes for Vocabulary Development along with the national standards that connect to these outcomes.
- Complete Assignments and Activities that can help you more deeply understand the chapter content.
- Apply and practice your understanding of the core teaching skills identified in the chapter with the Building Teaching Skills and Dispositions learning units.
- Examine challenging situations and cases presented in the IRIS Center Resources.
- Check your comprehension on the content covered in the chapter by going to the Study Plan in the Book Resources for your text. Here you will be able to take a chapter quiz, receive feedback on your answers, and then access Review, Practice, and Enrichment activities to enhance your understanding of chapter content.

Go to the Topic A+RISE in the MyEducationLab (www.myeducationlab.com) for your course. A+RISE® Standards2Strategy™ is an innovative and interactive online resource that offers new teachers in grades K–12 just-in-time, research-based instructional strategies that:

- Meet the linguistic needs of ELLs as they learn content
- Differentiate instruction for all grades and abilities
- Offer reading and writing techniques, cooperative learning, use of linguistic and nonlinguistic representations, scaffolding, teacher modeling, higher order thinking, and alternative classroom ELL assessment
- Provide support to help teachers be effective through the integration of listening, speaking, reading, and writing along with the content curriculum
- Improve student achievement
- Are aligned to Common Core Elementary Language Arts standards (for the literacy strategies) and to English language proficiency standards in WIDA, Texas, California, and Florida.

# 2

# First- and Second-Language Development and Their Relationship to Academic Achievement

Attending school in a second language is a challenge. English learners' futures—their dreams, identities, and expectations of success—are enhanced if they have a successful school experience. By knowing about how language is acquired, teachers can recognize and use communication strategies that help students succeed. As an introduction to the study of language acquisition and learning, this chapter presents an overview of historical and contemporary theories that provide an orientation to English-language development.

## Processes and Stages of Language Acquisition

Learning a language—the first or the second (second-language acquisition means learning any language after the first, whether it is the second, third, etc.)—is only partially a conscious activity. Most people retain very little awareness of having actually learned the first language. In contrast, people tend to remember learning the second language, especially if it is learned in school. Often learners are self-conscious about second-language acquisition. Even so, some of the same unconscious processes that helped us acquire the first language continue to underlie acquisition of the second.

Learning a language, even for children, requires a fully functioning mind. The mind processes a vast amount of verbal and nonverbal input and extracts meaning. Perceptual processes (listening and looking at the world and listening to ourselves) operate together with automatic language centers (involving phonemic awareness, linear-syntactic assembly, emotional circuits, and speech production), which in turn are synthesized with higher-order thinking (cognitive processes such as memorization, categorization, generalization and overgeneralization, and metacognition) to produce and understand language.

## First-Language Acquisition

By the age of five, a normal child can operate in the world with a full range of phonemic, syntactic, semantic, and pragmatic skills. The pronunciation resembles that of other speakers of the first language; the sentence structure is adequate; vocabulary amounts to several thousand words; and discourse skills include command of basic conversational skills, such as talking about a variety of topics with different audiences. Although parental input is useful for developing a large vocabulary, children learn language from other speakers, whether other children, neighbors, or television.

**The Innateness Hypothesis**   A child not only imitates the language in the environment but also seeks out patterns and tests rules by creating novel sentences. Lenneberg (1967) claimed that language is a biologically controlled behavior that develops from within, triggered by age and environment. Direct teaching and intensive practice have little effect on this "unfolding," but there are characteristic stages associated with language development. From birth to age two is a critical period for language emergence, during which crucial brain structures must develop. A second critical period, from the ages of ten to sixteen, allows the individual to learn language easily but not with native-speaker competence (Cipollone, Keiser, & Vasishth, 1998).

**Stages of First-Language Acquisition**   After only a few weeks of crying, infants begin to coo in vowel-like sounds such as "oooooh" or "aaaaah" in addition to crying. At around three or four months, infants start to add consonant sounds to their cooing, and they begin to babble at between four and six months of age using consonant and vowel sounds together. By the end of the first year, infants develop a sense of the role of language in communication (Lu, 2000).

When children first speak, they seem to utter single words to represent the whole meaning of an entire sentence, the so-called holophrastic utterance (Shaffer, 1999); for example, "ball" can mean "Throw me the ball" or "Where did the ball go?" Children's first words are contextual and identify people or things or express needs. In their second year, children begin to produce two-word phrases; later, this expands to three or more words, generating simple sentences in "telegraphic speech" that contain mainly the essential content words, such as verbs and nouns, but omit the function words, such as articles, auxiliary verbs, prepositions, and pronouns. Although these first sentences seem to be ungrammatical in terms of adult standards, they have a structure of their own.

As children's use of simple sentences increases, their sentences become increasingly elaborate and sophisticated. Language development, especially vocabulary growth and conversational skills, continues at a rapid pace throughout the preschool years. The development of conversational skills requires children to interact actively with other people. Through interacting with other, more experienced language users, children modify and elaborate their sentences in response to requests for more information, learn to take turns in speaking, and adjust their messages to their listeners' level of understanding.

**The Role of the First Language in Schooling**   Research has shown that proficiency in the first language helps students to achieve in school. To learn about a student's strengths in the first language, a teacher, primary-language-speaking aide, or parent who is fluent in the language of the student might observe a student working or playing in the primary language and take notes on the child's language behavior. Some schools may test students' first-language (L1) proficiency using such measures as the Bilingual Syntax Measure (BSM), which measures oral proficiency in English and/or Spanish grammatical structures. Knowledge about the student's linguistic and academic abilities may assist the teacher in second-language (L2) academic content instruction.

## Second-Language Acquisition

How many people can say they are truly fluent in more than one language? In many parts of the world, people undergo schooling in multiple foreign languages as a widely accepted component of being well educated. In Canada and elsewhere, the ability to communicate, read, and write in two languages is encouraged. Millions of people around the world are *multicompetent language users* (Cook, 1999), meaning their bilingualism or trilingualism acts as an asset to them or to their society.

The United States is one of the few countries in which a young person can graduate from secondary school without ever studying a second language. Yet many young people enter schooling fluent in a primary language other than English, a proficiency that can function as a resource. Ideally, schools can help students whose families speak a language other than English to sustain fluency and develop academic competence in their heritage language while acquiring fluency and literacy in English.

**Types of Bilingualism**   Cummins (1979) analyzed the language characteristics of the children he studied and suggested that the level of bilingualism attained is an important factor in educational development. *Limited bilingualism*, or subtractive bilingualism, can occur when children's first language is gradually replaced by a more dominant and prestigious language. In this case, children may develop relatively low levels of academic proficiency in both languages. *Partial bilingualism*, in which students achieve a nativelike level in one of their languages, has neither positive nor negative cognitive effects. The most positive cognitive effects are experienced in *proficient (additive) bilingualism*, when students attain high levels of proficiency in both languages.

---
──────────────────────── DID YOU KNOW? ────────────────────────

**THE COGNITIVE BENEFITS OF BILINGUALISM**

After the first three or four years of second-language instruction, students outperform their monolingual peers in many ways:

- Enhanced pattern recognition, problem solving, divergent thinking, and creativity
- Better metalinguistic and critical thinking
- Improved performance on standardized tests—not only verbal, but also mathematical
- Sharper task focus
- Increased understanding of the contextual use of language

(Porter, 2010)

**Simultaneous Dual-Language Acquisition**    Preschool bilingual programs are pushing the age ever lower for children to acquire a second language: almost at the same time as the first language. Parents and teachers sometimes express concern about children's ability to become proficient simultaneously in two languages. What does research indicate about such a process? Does this negatively affect first-language acquisition?

Before the age of three, children have acquired the basic elements of grammar: how words go together to make meaning. Bilingual children may sometimes mix the grammar and vocabulary of their two languages, but such errors are temporary; however, they rarely use phonemes of one language in the other unless their pronunciation models have an accent. For example, if young speakers of Spanish are exposed to English with a standard (U.S. Midwest) accent, they will acquire that accent; if they learn English from speakers whose English has a Spanish accent, they will learn English with that accent.

Some phonemes in both languages develop later even for native speakers (the /th/ in *thin*, for example, for native English speakers, and the trilled /r/ in *arroz* for Spanish speakers), so it is to be expected that some second-language speakers will show the same kind of development. Most important, by the age of five or six, bilingual speakers show great progress in two languages: They can use and repeat complex sentences; they have mastered 90 percent of the sound systems; and they can apply prepositions correctly, use slang and make jokes, modify their speech if necessary to talk to younger children, and take conversational turns without being seen as interruptive or rude. These are impressive advances in language and well worth any temporary confusion along the way.

**Proficiency Levels of Second-Language Acquisition as Identified in the CELDT**    The main purpose of the California English Language Development Test (CELDT) is to assess English learners at the K–12 level to determine their levels of English proficiency, while also annually assessing their progress toward becoming fluently English proficient. The CELDT covers four skill areas: listening, speaking, reading, and writing. Students in kindergarten and grade 1 are assessed only in listening and speaking. Students in grades 2 through 12 are assessed in all four areas.

The CELDT contains five proficiency levels: beginning, early intermediate, intermediate, early advanced, and advanced, along the four dimensions of language (listening, speaking, reading, and writing). Table 2.1 describes in general the five levels of the CELDT and the language proficiency associated with each level.

Because the CELDT is aligned with California's English Language Development standards (California Department of Education, 1999) and closely tied to the state's language arts standards, a teacher can use an English learner's CELDT levels as a guide to match specific language objectives in the lesson plan with the linguistic needs of the student.

## First- and Second-Language Acquisition: Commonalities

Language acquisition is furthered when the learner is immersed in a stimulating environment. Language knowledge builds on prior knowledge of concepts and is vocabulary intensive. The brain operates as a pattern-seeking processor with a high motivation to understand communication it deems important. Accompanying verbal language is a rich and informative system of nonverbal communication, supplying and interpreting the underlying emotions and gestural

**TABLE 2.1** CELDT Levels and Associated Proficiency Descriptor

| Level | | Proficiency Descriptors |
|---|---|---|
| Beginning | Listening/Speaking | May be able to recognize and speak a few isolated words and phrases |
| | Reading | May be able to recognize a few isolated words |
| | Writing | May be able to write a few isolated words |
| Early Intermediate | Listening/Speaking | Can produce words or phrases; can separate spoken sounds into words and respond to questions using simple vocabulary |
| | Reading | Can recognize words and phrases in print and match words to pictures |
| | Writing | Can respond to a writing prompt with a simple sentence |
| Intermediate | Listening/Speaking | Can produce relevant sentences using increasingly complex vocabulary |
| | Reading | Can read text with basic comprehension |
| | Writing | Can respond to a writing prompt with sentences or write a story with a sequence of events |
| Early Advanced | Listening/Speaking | Can understand instructional delivery and respond relevantly |
| | Reading | Can read text using skills of inferencing, drawing conclusions, and making predictions |
| | Writing | Can write with well-formed sentences and paragraphs, communicating ideas with organization |
| Advanced | Listening/Speaking | Can understand and respond to instructional delivery on increasingly complex topics |
| | Reading | Can read narrative and expository texts with comprehension requiring a range of thinking skills |
| | Writing | Writing is fluent and accurate, communicating ideas with organization, few grammatical errors, and specific vocabulary |

components. All language learning is time consuming, with an accumulation of skill that cannot be rushed.

A second language is built on the foundation of the first language; this is the only way the learner can make sense of the world. This development is cultural as well as linguistic. Therefore, supporting the learner's meaning-making efforts furthers English acquisition. Providing linguistic and cultural support for the learner is a major theme of this book.

**Separate or Common Underlying Proficiency** Some critics of bilingual education claim that educating children in the primary language reduces their opportunity to acquire English. This argument assumes that proficiency in English is separate from proficiency in a primary language and that content and skills learned through the primary language do not transfer to English—a notion that Cummins (1981b) has termed *separate underlying proficiency* (SUP). In contrast, Cummins asserted that cognition and language, once developed in the primary language, form a basis for subsequent learning in any language. This position assumes a *common underlying proficiency* (CUP), the belief that a second language and the primary language have a shared foundation and that competence in the primary language provides the basis for competence in the second language.

For example, children learning to read and write in Korean develop concepts about print and the role of literacy that make learning to read and think in English easier, despite the fact that these languages do not share a similar writing system. The surface differences in the languages are less important than the deeper understandings about the function of reading and its relationship to thought and learning. According to Cummins (1981b), students do not have to relearn in a second language the essentials of schooling: how to communicate, how to think critically, and how to read and write.

# Theories and Models of Second-Language Acquisition

Various theories and methods of second-language teaching have been used throughout recorded history, each based on an underlying rationale or set of beliefs about how language is best learned. These range in type from traditional to innovative. This chapter provides a historical context, with a focus on contemporary theories and models that underlie current instructional models.

## Former Theories That Still Influence Current Practice

Latin was the model for grammar throughout the Middle Ages, even though it was not an appropriate model for most European languages. Some current grammar-centered teaching practices sustain this model. Similarly, outdated practices of language teaching carry the legacy of now-discredited theories. Table 2.2 presents an overview of historical methods of language acquisition, the underlying theoretical premises of these methods, and their legacy of beliefs and justification for current teaching practices.

**Grammar Translation**    When Latin was the focus of second-language schooling, teachers translated and drilled on vocabulary, verb tenses, and parts of speech. The grammar-translation method of instruction is still widely used in settings in which the main goal is reading and grammar knowledge. Students learn in a carefully controlled curriculum and are rewarded for memorization. However, students have little choice in what they learn, little contact with actual speakers of the language they are acquiring, almost no actual use of the language in a social context, and little stimulation of curiosity, playfulness, and exploration—aspects of learning that are intrinsic to the nature of the mind. In contrast, current second-language teaching, especially in the elementary school, features extensive social interaction and active language use (Takahashi, Austin, & Morimoto, 2000).

**TABLE 2.2** Historical Methods of Second-Language Acquisition, Underlying Theoretical Premise, and Contribution to Second-Language Teaching

| Method of Instruction | Underlying Theory | Legacy in Current Beliefs about Second-Language Teaching |
|---|---|---|
| Grammatical analysis | Learning a language is equivalent to knowing about the structure of the language. | Emphasis on following rules of grammar |
| Grammar translation | Second language is learned by translating second-language structures into first language, emphasizing grammar and vocabulary. | Focus on vocabulary memorization |
| Structural linguistics and contrastive analysis | Second language is learned by classifying similar languages into groups and comparing the structures of two languages with each other to note similarities and differences. | Language comparison as a teaching methodology |
| Behaviorism as audiolingualism | Second language is learned by habit formation, especially by training in correct pronunciation. | Used to justify repetitious, structured practice in which learners are drilled on correct pronunciation |
| Behaviorism as direct teaching and mastery learning | Second language is learned by dividing what is to be learned into small units and using rote repetition, with much drill and practice. | Used to justify scripted lessons with controlled vocabulary and extensive testing |

**Focus on Structure**   The descriptive and structural linguistics of the nineteenth century led to the comparison of languages for the purpose of teaching. *Contrastive analysis* is the theory that comparing the first and second languages can predict what might be easy or difficult for the learner. However, its central premise—that the more similar two languages are, the more easily a speaker of the first will learn the second—was impossible to prove (Gass & Selinker, 2008), and contrastive linguistics has been largely an ineffectual way to teach a second language except in small areas such as cognates.

**Behaviorism**   When behaviorism dominated learning theory, it greatly influenced second-language teaching. Principles of repetition and reward led to classroom methodologies of drill and practice. Three aspects of behaviorism are still used in contemporary language teaching: audiolingualism, direct teaching/mastery learning, and total physical response (TPR).

The audiolingual method of language learning is behavioral, emphasizing oral practice such as pattern drills of specific grammatical forms ("It's cold today, *isn't it?*"). The goal for the learner is to learn new habits of speech, including correct pronunciation, in the second language through repetitious training directed and controlled by the teacher. Errors are corrected immediately to discourage "bad" habit formation. Reading and writing are often delayed until the student has an adequate oral base. The strength of the audiolingual method is its repetitious drill to achieve correct pronunciation; drawbacks include limited exposure to the target culture and failure to emphasize self-motivated language acquisition.

Direct teaching and mastery learning are also forms of behaviorist instruction, and their widespread use in classrooms of English learners through reading programs such as Open Court and Direct Instruction demonstrates that behaviorism is still widely practiced. Direct teaching incorporates explicit instructional objectives for students and promotes the learning of facts, sequenced steps, or rules. The instructor uses carefully scripted lessons divided into small units with specific objectives that move at a lockstep pace. Students are regularly tested over the material that is covered and receive immediate remediation if performance lags.

An advantage of direct teaching and mastery learning is the focus on the subskills of language, including word recognition and low-level comprehension skills. The weakest part of direct teaching is that students are seldom asked to set their own goals in learning or pursue their own interests, and they have little time to explore language creatively. Balancing the strengths and weaknesses of behavioral-based pedagogy, one might conclude that these teaching approaches have a distinct, yet limited, role in instruction.

**Total Physical Response (TPR)**   In TPR, students respond to an oral command that is simultaneously being modeled. For example, the teacher says "Stand" while standing up and "Sit" while sitting down, and students follow along (Asher, 1982). The instructor repeats the commands followed by the appropriate action until students perform without hesitation. The instructor then begins to delay his or her own action to allow students the opportunity to respond and thus demonstrate understanding. Eventually, the students, first as a whole group and then as individuals, act on the instructor's voice command alone. The number of commands is gradually increased. Students continue to respond in a nonverbal manner until they feel comfortable issuing their own commands.

Reading and writing can also be introduced through commands. The instructor may write on the board "Stand" and gesture to the students to perform the action. After practice with the written form in class, students can be given lists of familiar commands that they can then manipulate in their own fashion. The concrete, hands-on methodology recommended by Asher (1982) is associated with early stages of second-language learning and is recommended by Krashen and Terrell (1983) for promoting comprehension in a low-anxiety environment.

## Current Theories of Language Development

Starting in the mid-twentieth century, several important theories have shaped current understanding of language acquisition and development. In 1959, Chomsky criticized the prevailing belief that language is learned through constant verbal input shaped by reinforcement. He claimed that language is not learned solely through a process of memorizing and repeating, but that the mind contains an active language processor, the language acquisition device (LAD), that generates rules through the unconscious acquisition of grammar. This led to a cognitive emphasis, focusing on the role of the mind.

The idea of communicative competence—that the social setting of language is important in language performance—directed attention away from the structural analysis of language toward a more anthropological or cultural approach. Halliday (1975) emphasized the role of social relations in language. Vygotsky was a prime mover in social interactionist theories of learning. Current conceptions of language have thus moved away from the merely linguistic components of a language to the more inclusive realm of language in use, which includes its psychological, social, and political domains.

**Transformational Grammar**   Chomsky envisioned language as a set of rules that human beings unconsciously know and use. He postulated that human beings, once exposed to the language(s) of their environment, use their innate ability to understand and produce sentences they have never before heard, because the mind has the capacity to internalize and construct language rules. The rules help native speakers distinguish whether a group of words forms a sentence in their language. Chomsky upheld the idea that children do not need to be taught language.

> Children hear people speaking as they do naturally, in bits of sentences, with hesitations, breaks, and repetitions . . . [yet] by and large they grow up competent speakers of the language(s) they hear . . . they (unconsciously) apply certain rules and representations in order to become users of a specific language. (Gillen, 2003, p. 83)

The goal of transformational grammar is to understand and describe these internalized rules. Much of Krashen's monitor model can be traced to Chomsky's influence.

**Communicative Competence**   Hymes (1972) introduced the term *communicative competence,* meaning the knowledge that enables language users to "convey and interpret messages and to negotiate meanings interpersonally within specific contexts" (Brown, 1987). Rather than merely knowing grammatical forms, the competent speaker is one who knows when, where, and how to use language appropriately, including producing and understanding in different social contexts. As Taylor (1987) noted,

> Real communication is a shared activity which requires the active involvement of its participants. . . . We have a responsibility to create an atmosphere in which communication is possible, one in which students can feel free to take communicating initiative and are motivated to do so. Making classes "student-centered" can contribute to creating such an atmosphere. (p. 49)

Communicative language teaching involves social functions of language, such as requesting, agreeing, refusing, telling a story, expressing disappointment, and so forth. Even at the beginning level of English, students learn how to meet their needs through communication. At the early intermediate CELDT level, students might listen to and repeat conversations; role-play situations involving complaints ("Sorry to bother you, but . . .") or apologies ("I'm sorry that . . ."); or work to expand their repertoire of common phrases, such as "How's it going?"; "I hope so"; "I doubt it"; and a hundred other useful expressions (see Spears, 1992).

Task-based learning (TBL) is part of communicative language teaching. Students use real-life language as they perform authentic activities that accomplish the language objectives or content objectives of a lesson; the focus is on meaning, rather than form. Often these activities are in a sequence, called a task chain. For example, students might have as their objective "to use the format of a personal letter." The task chain is a set of tasks that involve comprehending, manipulating, producing, or interacting in the target language—for example, reading letters, discussing the various parts of the letter, and then producing a letter, perhaps to thank a recent classroom visitor.

Communicative language teaching has also led to greater use of games and communicative activities that lighten the spirit of learning, reduce anxiety, add excitement to a lesson, and make review and practice more fun. Box 2.1 offers a variety of resources for communicative games.

**Box 2.1**    Resources for Communicative Games

Blair, R. W. (Ed.). (1982). *Innovative approaches to language teaching.* Boston: Heinle and Heinle.

Danesi, M. (1985). *A guide to puzzles and games in second language pedagogy.* Toronto: Ontario Institute for Studies in Education.

Lewis, G., & Bedson, G. (1999). *Games for children.* Oxford: Oxford University Press.

Lewis, M. (1997). *New ways in teaching adults.* Alexandria, VA: Teachers of English to Speakers of Other Languages.

Maculaitis, J. (1988). *The complete ESL/EFL resource book: Strategies, activities, and units for the classroom.* Lincolnwood, IL: National Textbook Company.

Nation, P. (1994). *New ways in teaching vocabulary.* Alexandria, VA: Teachers of English to Speakers of Other Languages.

Omaggio, A. (1978). *Games and simulations in the foreign language classroom.* Washington, DC: Center for Applied Linguistics.

---

**Best Practice**    ENHANCING COMMUNICATIVE COMPETENCE

In a high school ESL class, Mr. Thurmond demonstrates grammatical, sociolinguistic, strategic, and discourse competence to students by having them role-play a job interview. As students conduct and analyze the interview situation, they identify such aspects as the need for forms of politeness and the inappropriate use of slang. In one such activity, the final winner was the applicant who, having at first been turned down, used strategic competence—she asked to be put on a waiting list and then got the job when the first-choice candidate accepted "a better offer"!

---

Chesterfield and Chesterfield (1985) found that students used communicative strategies to enhance their second-language competence. Table 2.3 presents these in order of their development.

These communication strategies are employed for transmitting an idea when the learner cannot produce precise linguistic forms. Brown (2000) groups communication strategies into five main categories: avoidance (evading sounds, structures, or topics that are beyond current proficiency); prefabricated patterns (memorizing stock phrases to rely on when all else fails); cognitive and personality styles to compensate for unknown language structures; appeals for help; and language switch (falling back on the primary language for help in communication).

This last strategy, often called *code-switching,* has been studied extensively because it permeates a learner's progression in a second language. Code-switching—the alternating use of two languages on the word, phrase, clause, or sentence level—is used by many bilingual speakers for a variety of purposes, not just as a strategy to help when expressions in the second language are lacking.

Baker (1993) lists ten purposes for code-switching: (1) to emphasize a point, (2) because a word is unknown in one of the languages, (3) for ease and efficiency of expression, (4) as a repetition to clarify, (5) to express group identity and status or to be accepted by a group, (6) to quote someone, (7) to interject in a conversation, (8) to exclude someone, (9) to cross social or

**TABLE 2.3**    Second-Language Communication Strategies

| Strategy | Description |
| --- | --- |
| Repetition in short-term memory | Imitating a word or structure used by another |
| Use of formulaic expressions | Using words or phrases that function as units, such as greetings ("Hi! How are you?") |
| Use of verbal attention-getters | Initiating interaction with language ("Hey!" "I think") |
| Answering in unison | Responding with others |
| Talking to self | Engaging in subvocal or internal monologue |
| Elaboration | Providing information beyond that which is necessary |
| Anticipatory answers | Answering an anticipated question or completing another's phrase or statement |
| Monitoring | Correcting one's own errors in vocabulary, style, and grammar |
| Appeal for assistance | Seeking help from another |
| Request for clarification | Asking the speaker to explain or repeat |

*Source:* Chesterfield & Chesterfield (1985).

ethnic boundaries, and (10) to ease tension in a conversation. Code-switching thus plays a key role in bilingual communicative competence.

 **Classroom Glimpse**

**MATILDE'S CODE-SWITCHING**

Matilde's use of two languages makes a fascinating study in code-switching. She grew up in a Puerto Rican family in New York and has always lived in communities in which both English and Spanish are used, separately and together. Because all her schooling was in English, Matilde considers that to be her stronger language, but her Spanish is totally fluent, if not always correct according to "standard" Spanish. Her code switches are fluent, grammatical, and usually motivated by something in the situational or linguistic context. It may be the person she is talking to, the language used by that person, the thing she is talking about, the desire to ensure that everybody understands, or a borrowed word that triggers a switch. For example, a change from talking to the entire class to talking to a single student can cause a switch.

(Irujo, 1998, p. 47)

Although language purists look down on language mixing, a more fruitful approach is letting children learn in whatever manner they feel most comfortable so that anxiety about language will not interfere with concept acquisition. In fact, a teacher who learns and uses words and expressions in the students' home language is able to express solidarity and share personal feelings when appropriate.

**Sociocultural Models of Second-Language Acquisition**   Schools, as institutions of learning and socialization, represent the larger culture. Culture, though largely invisible, influences instruction, policy, and learning in schools (Trueba, 1989). Knowledge of the deeper elements of culture—beyond superficial aspects such as food, clothing, holidays, and celebrations—can give teachers a crosscultural perspective that allows them to educate students to the greatest extent possible.

Anthropologists have joined with educators to view closely the culture of schooling and the language learning that takes place therein. Intensive studies of Hawai'ian and Native-American cultural practices of learning helped Mehan (1981), Tharp (1989), and other educational researchers (Philips, 1972; Phillips, 1978) recommend ways in which schools could institute culturally compatible practices (see Chapter 9).

Learning is not a separate and independent activity of individuals but an integral part of participation in a community (Lave & Wenger, 1991). Children return to dynamic and interactive communities after a day at school. Teachers must come to know and respect what the community offers students and encourage knowledge to travel a two-way path as it circulates from school to home and back to school. Thus, learning is both an individual and communal activity.

**The Interactionist Model**   Extending the notion of communicative competence, Long (1980) developed the interactionist model. Using peer conversation as a means of enriching a student's exposure to language maximizes the opportunity for a student to hear and enjoy English; teachers need to provide many opportunities for English learners to engage in discourse with native speakers of English, in a variety of situations. ELD programs that restrict English learners to certain tracks or special classrooms, without incorporating specific opportunities for interaction between native and non-native speakers, do a disservice to English learners.

Interaction theorists have analyzed conversation to understand how meaning is negotiated. According to them, face-to-face interaction is a key to second-language acquisition. By holding conversations, non-native speakers acquire commonly occurring formulas and grammar as they attend to the various features in the input they obtain. Through their own speech output, they affect both the quantity and the quality of the language they receive. The more learners talk, the more other people will talk to them. The more they converse, the more opportunity they have to initiate and expand topics, signal comprehension breakdowns, and try out new formulas and expressions.

**Best Practice**   ENCOURAGING INTERACTION BETWEEN NATIVE AND NON-NATIVE SPEAKERS

- Students can interview others briefly on topics such as "My favorite sport" or "My favorite tool." The responses from the interviews can be tallied and form the basis for subsequent class discussion.
- English learners can interact with native English speakers during school hours through cross-age or peer interactions.

**Constructivist Views of Learning**   Constructivism is an offshoot of the cognitivist tradition in which complex, challenging learning environments help students take responsibility for constructing their own knowledge. As students deal with complex situations, the teacher provides support. Thus, students and teachers share responsibility for the knowledge construction process, collaborating on the goals of instruction and the planning needed for learning to take place (Fosnot, 1989; Wells & Chang-Wells, 1992).

Key elements of constructivist learning are the encouragement of student autonomy and initiative, the expectation that student responses will drive lesson content and instructional strategies, learning experiences that provoke discussion, a focus on students' concept understanding rather than teachers' concept explanation, and an emphasis on critical thinking and student dialogue. Constructivist methods make minimal use of rote memorization and instead focus on problem solving. Students discuss, ask questions, give explanations to one another, present ideas, and solve problems together.

Constructivist learning in the elementary years helps students maintain their curiosity and zest for learning. Typical constructivist environments are found in children's museums, rich worlds in which children can be exposed to many different stimuli. At the middle and high school levels, students use research resources featuring various types of information representation. Conducting research need not be a solitary occupation; project-based learning, for example, is a constructivist technique in which teams of students pool resources and expertise in the service of large undertakings.

---

**Best Practice**   PROMOTING STUDENTS' KNOWLEDGE CONSTRUCTION

- Instructional objectives are compelling and comprehensible.
- Complex problems require teachers to become learners as well as students.
- Students are exposed to a variety of representational formats for knowledge (text, visual, oral, figurative, etc.).
- Working in teams, students learn conflict resolution skills as well as receptive and productive language skills.

---

**Social Constructionist Views of Language Learning**   The Russian psychologist Lev Vygotsky emphasized the role of social interaction in the development of language and thought, in which language joins with thought to create meaning (Wink, 2000). Interaction occurs in a cultural, historical, and institutional context that shapes the availability and quality of the tools and signs that mediate higher mental functions. Vygotsky recognized that all teaching and learning takes place within the context of the memories, experiences, and cultural habits found within families.

A social-constructivist view of language acquisition takes into account the role that language plays in social interaction. As Gillen stated,

> Children make sense of symbolic practices . . . through their presence in communities. People create and interpret meanings together. . . . Children learn how to dance or how to draw, partly

through watching others, partly through responses that others make to their own efforts, and partly through the special individually motivated capabilities they bring to the activity in question. (2003, p. 13)

According to Vygotsky (1981), teaching must take into consideration the student's *zone of proximal development,* defined as "the distance between the actual developmental level as determined by independent problem solving and the level of potential development . . . under adult guidance or in collaboration with more capable peers" (p. 86). Social interaction between adults and students operates within this zone. Mediation of learning—assisting students' performance—requires teachers to adapt to the level of the student, provide guidance when needed, and help students to work with one another and the teacher to co-construct meaning.

---

**Best Practice**    **USING SOCIAL INTERACTION TO LEARN ENGLISH**

The social uses of language are advanced when students engage in communicative pair or group tasks. Students benefit from communication with one another, members of the school community, and the community at large, as in the following examples:

- Practice reader's theater with other students
- Develop interview questions for a community survey
- Plan an exhibition of art or written work to which the public will be invited

---

**Interlanguage Theory**    In second-language learning, learners use four kinds of knowledge: (1) knowledge about the second language, (2) competence in the native language, (3) ability to use the functions of language, and (4) general world knowledge. The language they produce is an *interlanguage,* an intermediate system they create as they attempt to achieve nativelike competence.

Selinker's interlanguage hypothesis (1972, 1991) asserted that the learner's language should be viewed as creative, with rules unique to itself, and not just a borrowed or incomplete form of the target language. Although imperfect compared to target-language proficiency, it represents a learner variety of the target language. The view that learners have intermediary language modes that are natural and normal ways of learning offers a refreshing opportunity for teachers to view second-language learning as a productive pathway whose features have unique interest.

According to interlanguage theory, second-language learners draw from three sources of information: the rules of their own language (such as the way phonemes sound, the way sentences are formed, and so forth), a general knowledge about the way languages work, and the rules of the new language that they acquire gradually. Therefore it is common that they produce an imperfect approximation as they learn. Instead of seeing their errors as failures, they are in fact clues to the learners' beliefs about the way the language works. The teacher can use these errors to gain insight into the instruction that must follow. Thus, interlanguage theory is compatible with error analysis and data-driven teaching: using assessment to shape subsequent instruction.

**Krashen's Monitor Model**    Five distinct hypotheses make up Krashen's (1981, 1982) monitor model, which claims that languages are acquired best when language acquirers comprehend messages and lower the mental and emotional blocks that can prevent them from fully comprehending input.

In the *acquisition-learning hypothesis,* Krashen (1985) distinguishes second-language *acquisition* from *learning*. Learning is "knowing about" a language (formal knowledge). Grammar teaching promotes learning by providing the learner with explicit knowledge about the rules of a language. Acquisition, on the other hand, is an unconscious process that occurs when language is used for real communication. Most teachers acknowledge the fact that students produce some language structures unselfconsciously and need rules and help for others. Krashen considered acquisition more important than learning.

Krashen's *natural order hypothesis* states that there appears to be a predictable order of acquisition of English morphemes. The order is slightly different for second-language learners from the first-language order, but there are similarities. For example, children learn how to express a negative structure in the first and second languages in a similar way, first putting the negative marker outside the sentence (L1, "No Mom sharpen it"; L2, "Not like it now"); then putting the negative marker between the subject and the verb (L1, "I no like this one"; L2, "This no have calendar"); and finally, putting the negative marker in the correct position (L1, L2, "I don't like this one"). This example illustrates the idea that children acquire correct usage of grammatical structures in their second language gradually.

The *monitor hypothesis* postulates an error-detecting mechanism, the monitor, which scans an utterance for accuracy and edits—that is, confirms or repairs—the utterance either before or after attempted communication. However, the monitor cannot always be used. In a situation involving rapid verbal exchange, an individual may have little time to be concerned with correctness.

The *input hypothesis* claims that language is acquired in an "amazingly simple way—when we understand messages" (Krashen, 1985, p. vii). Contrary to popular belief, simply immersing a learner in a second language is not sufficient. Language must contain what Krashen calls "comprehensible" input. Critics have pointed out that it is impossible to tell what "comprehensible input" really means, and, as Marton (1994) pointed out, Krashen's emphasis on comprehensible input ignores the active role of the learner in communicating and negotiating useful and understandable language. Nonetheless, when working with English learners, teachers need to use a variety of techniques and modalities, including visual and kinesthetic, to ensure that their speech is comprehensible.

The *affective filter hypothesis* addresses emotional variables, including anxiety, motivation, and self-confidence, which are crucial because they can block input from reaching the language acquisition device. If the affective filter blocks some of the comprehensible input, less information enters the learner's LAD and thus less language is acquired. On the other hand, a positive affective context increases input. Most teachers understand that a nonthreatening and encouraging environment promotes learning and that it is important to increase the enjoyment of learning, raise self-esteem, and blend self-awareness with an increase in proficiency as students learn English.

### Cummins's Theories of Bilingualism and Cognition

Jim Cummins's work (1981b) falls within the cognitive approach to language, with its emphasis on the strengths the learner brings to the task of learning a second language. The cognitive approach to learning is based on the premise that learners already have considerable knowledge of the world. Cummins's research has furthered the belief that being bilingual is a cognitive advantage and that knowledge of

*Language is acquired best when students are actively engaged in interesting, comprehensible activities.*

the first language provides a firm foundation for second-language acquisition. Moreover, Cummins's concept of cognitive academic language proficiency helps teachers identify and teach the type of language that students need to acquire for academic success.

Cummins is also a vocal advocate of "critical literacy" as an essential component of educational reform to promote achievement for Latino/Latina students. According to Cummins, students who achieve only "functional literacy" often fail to develop a sense of empowerment through acquisition of cultural and critical literacy, and cannot successfully challenge the "status quo" in which their culture and language is relegated to a second-class status. Cummins (2010) also distinguishes between coercive and collaborative relations of power. "Coercive relations of power refer to the exercise of power by a dominant group (or individual) to the detriment of a subordinated group (or individual)" (2010, n.p.).

Cummins (2010) goes on to state,

> Collaborative relations of power, on the other hand, operate on the assumption that power is not a fixed pre-determined quantity but rather can be *generated* in interpersonal and intergroup relations, thereby becoming "additive" rather than "subtractive." In other words, participants in the relationship are *empowered* through their collaboration such that each is more affirmed in her or his identity and has a greater sense of efficacy to effect change in her or his life or social situation. Thus, power is created in the relationship and shared among participants. Collaborative relations of power create *empowerment; transformative pedagogy* refers to interactions between educators and students that foster the collaborative relations. (n.p.)

**Meaning-Centered Approaches**    Researchers (Goodman, 1986; Smith, 1983) looking at children learning to read in naturalistic settings noticed that they actively seek meaning. They work to make sense of text, combining text clues with their own prior knowledge to construct meanings. The theory called *whole language* arose from the idea that meaning plays a central role in learning and that language modes (speaking, listening, reading, writing) interact and are interdependent. Whole language, a philosophy of reading instruction, complemented many findings of studies in first- and second-language acquisition.

Meaning-centered systems of language acquisition (also called *top-down* systems—see Weaver [1988]) support the view of language espoused by Halliday (1978)—that language is a complex system for creating meanings through socially shared conventions. The notion of *meaning-making* implies that learners are generating hypotheses from and actively constructing interpretations about the input they receive, be it oral or written. Language is social in that it occurs within a community of users who attach agreed-on meaning to their experiences.

**Semiotics**    Not all second-language acquisition depends on verbal language. Semiotics is a discipline that studies the ways in which humans use signs, symbols, icons, and indexes to create meaning. Signs—and the meanings they carry—vary across cultures and languages, adding richness to the study of second language that words alone seldom express fully.

Semiotics provides a perspective for examining human development through the interplay of multiple meaning systems. Semiotics has become increasingly important within the last decade, as sophisticated computer art, animation, and graphics programs available through the Internet have opened up a language of two-dimensional shape and color that supplements, if not replaces, text as a source of information and experience for many young people. For those interested in knowing more about this field, see Chandler (2005), Kress and Van Leeuwen (1995), and Scollon and Scollon (2003).

---

**Best Practice**    USING SEMIOTICS TO ACQUIRE A SECOND LANGUAGE

- Students can view themselves, other students, teachers, the community, and culturally authentic materials (phone books, voicemail messages, advertising brochures, music videos, etc.) to examine ways that meaning is communicated using both verbal and nonverbal messages.
- Students can engage in a variety of purposeful cross-media activities—produce music, create collages, and write poems, journal entries, or advertising slogans—to display their identities, values, or ideas.
- Students can "people-watch" using semiotics to read nonverbal messages sent by dress styles, posture, demeanor, and so forth as a way to increase their interactions with one another at all levels of language proficiency. (Díaz-Rico & Dullien, 2004)

---

**Contributions of Research about the Brain**    A basic question concerning second-language acquisition is "What is the role of the brain in learning language?" Neurolinguists attempt to explain the connection between language function and neuroanatomy and to identify, if possible, the areas of the brain responsible for language functioning. Recent studies have looked at the role of emotions and visual and gestural processing in second-language acquisition, tracing the brain processing of not only verbal language but also nonverbal input such as gestures, facial expressions, and intonation (Schumann, 1994).

Several contemporary educators have developed learning methods that take into consideration brain processing. According to their research, learning is the brain's primary function. Many parts of the brain process reality simultaneously, facilitating language acquisition (see Table 2.4). For further information about brain-based learning, see *Brain/Mind Learning Principles in Action: The Fieldbook for Making Connections, Teaching, and the Human Brain* by Caine, Caine, McClintic, and Klimek (2004); Haley's *Brain-Compatible Differentiated Instruction for English Language Learners* (2010); Jensen's *Teaching with the Brain in Mind* (1998); Lyons and Clay's *Teaching Struggling Readers: How to Use Brain-Based Research to Maximize Learning* (2003); Smilkstein's *We're Born to Learn* (2002); and Sousa's *How the Brain Learns to Read* (2005).

---

**Best Practice**   USING PRINCIPLES OF BRAIN-BASED LEARNING
IN ORAL PRESENTATIONS

**Before a Presentation**

- Students can lower anxiety by taking a few deep breaths, visualizing success, and repeating positive self-talk phrases (brain-based principle 2: Learning engages the entire physiology).
- Students can review the structure of the information, especially how the parts of the presentation fit together (brain-based principle 6: The brain processes parts and wholes simultaneously).

**During the Presentation**

- The speaker concentrates on the task while staying tuned to the needs of the audience (brain-based principle 7: Learning involves both focused attention and peripheral perception).
- Tenseness that is redefined as "eustress" ("good stress") supplies energy for learning rather than inhibits performance (brain-based principle 11: Learning is enhanced by challenge and inhibited by threat).

**After the Presentation**

- Students can evaluate their accomplishments, ask for feedback and tune in to the reactions of others, identify problem areas, and make a plan for improvement (brain-based principle 10: Learning occurs best when facts and skills are embedded in natural, spatial memory—including the memory of positive performance).

---

# Factors That Influence Second-Language Acquisition

Learners do not acquire language in a vacuum; rather, they learn it by interacting with others. Psychological and sociocultural factors play important roles in a learner's acquisition and use of a second language (see Figure 2.1). Simultaneously an individual and a member of a group,

**TABLE 2.4**   Principles and Implications for Brain-Based Instruction

| Principle | Implications for Instruction |
|---|---|
| 1. The brain can perform multiple processes simultaneously. | Learning experiences can be multimodal. As students perform experiments, develop a play from the text of a story, or take on complex projects, many facets of the brain are involved. |
| 2. Learning engages the entire physiology. | Stress management, nutrition, exercise, relaxation, and natural rhythms and timing should be taken into consideration during teaching and learning. |
| 3. The search for meaning is innate. | Language-learning activities should involve a focus on meaning; language used in the context of interesting activities provides a situated, meaningful experience. |
| 4. The brain is designed to perceive and generate patterns. | Information is presented in a way that allows brains to extract patterns and create meaning rather than react passively. |
| 5. Emotions are crucial to memory. | Instruction should support the students' backgrounds and languages. Interaction should be marked by mutual respect and acceptance. |
| 6. The brain processes parts and wholes simultaneously. | Language skills, such as vocabulary and grammar, are best learned in authentic language environments (solving a problem, debating an issue, exploring) in which *parts* (specific language skills) are learned together with *wholes* (problems to be solved). |
| 7. Learning involves both focused attention and peripheral perception. | Music, art, and other rich environmental stimuli can enhance and influence the natural acquisition of language. Subtle signals from the teacher (processed peripherally by students) communicate enthusiasm and interest. |
| 8. Learning always involves conscious and unconscious processes. | Students need opportunities to review what they learn consciously so they can reflect on, take charge of, and develop personal meaning. |
| 9. There are at least two types of memory: spatial memory and rote learning systems. | Teaching techniques that focus on the memorization of language bits—words and grammar points—use the rote learning system. Teaching that actively involves the learner in novel experiences taps into the spatial system. |
| 10. Learning occurs best when facts and skills are embedded in natural, spatial memory. | Discrete language skills can be learned when they are embedded in real-life activities (demonstrations, field trips, performances, stories, drama, visual imagery). |
| 11. Learning is enhanced by challenge and inhibited by threat. | Teachers need to create an atmosphere of acceptance. Learners are taken from the point they are at present to the next level of competence through a balance of support and challenge. |
| 12. Each brain is unique. | Teaching should be multifaceted. English learners can express developing understanding through visual, tactile, emotional, and auditory means. |

*Source:* Caine, Caine, McClintic, & Klimek (2004).

---

**FIGURE 2.1** English Learner Profile

**Psychological Factors: Learner's Background**

Learner's name _____ Age _____ Gender ( M / F )

Grade _____ L1 proficiency _____

Type of bilingualism _____

Previous L2 experience _____

Assessed L2 level: Reading ____ Writing ____ Listening ____ Speaking ____

Academic success _____

Likes/dislikes _____

**Social–Emotional Psychological Factors**

Self-esteem _____

Motivation _____

Anxiety level _____

Attitudes toward L1/L2 _____

Attitudes toward the teacher and the class _____

**Cognitive Psychological Factors**

Stage of L2 acquisition _____

Cognitive style/learning style _____

Learning strategies _____

**Sociocultural Factors**

Family acculturation and use of L1 and L2 _____

Family values _____

Institutional support for L1 _____

Sociocultural support for L1 in the classroom environment _____

---

each learner's character traits enable specific types of functioning, while group membership leads a person—largely unconsciously—to adopt rules for interaction and take on roles appropriate for effective functioning in that group. Teachers who are aware of these individual (psychological) and group (sociocultural) factors are able to adapt instruction to meet individual needs so that each learner can achieve academic success. Figure 2.1 offers an outline that can help teachers organize what they know about a given learner.

Psychological factors are traits specific to individuals that enable them to acquire a second language (L2). Learners use their personalities to process the language they hear and to create meaningful responses. Psychological factors can be divided into three categories: *background, social–emotional* aspects, and *cognitive* skills. A learner's age, prior language experience, and prior schooling affect current school performance. Learning creates a sense of mastery of the language, producing an affective–emotional response: enjoyment, pride, and competence. The work of mastering a second language can be considered cognitive. Teachers can help students be aware of those psychological factors that further their language learning and can work with students to ensure that these factors promote rather than impede their learning.

## Psychological Factors: The Learner's Background

**Naming Practices and Forms of Address**    A learner's name represents the individual as well as a family connection. People feel validated if their names are treated with respect. Teachers who care make an effort to pronounce students' names accurately. Taking extra time to talk privately with a student is preferable to practicing an unfamiliar name in public, which may be embarrassing for the student.

Naming practices differ across cultures. In the United States, people use a first (or given), middle, and last (or family) name. Around the world, naming order can vary. In Taiwan, for example, the family name goes first, followed by given names. In Vietnam, names are also ordered as family name, middle name, and given name. Puerto Ricans, as well as other Hispanics, generally use three names: a given name, followed by the father's surname and then the mother's surname. If one last name must be used, it is generally the father's. Thus, Esther Reyes Mimosa can be addressed as Esther Reyes. If the first name is composed of two given names (Hector Luis), both are used.

In many cultures, adults are referred to by function rather than name. In Hmong, *xib fwb* means "teacher," and Hmong children may use the English term *teacher* in the classroom rather than a title plus surname, as in "Mrs. Jasko." Middle-class European-American teachers may consider this to be rude rather than understanding it as a culturally based practice.

---

**Best Practice**    STUDENTS' NAMES

- Understand the use and order of names but also pronounce them correctly.
- Work with the student privately to practice his or her name.
- Don't change a student's name, apply a nickname, or use an "English" version of a student's name (even at the student's request) without first checking with a member of the student's family.

---

**Age**    Second-language acquisition (SLA) is a complex process that occurs over a long period of time, and the optimum age for its inception has been widely debated. Many people believe that children acquire a second language more rapidly than adults, but recent research counters this notion. Although it is true that the kind of instruction varies greatly according to the age of the learner—how formal the treatment of grammar and rules can be and what kind of communicative activities are appropriate—there is little evidence to indicate that biology closes

**Box 2.2**   What Is the Best Age for Second-Language Acquisition?

For adults, learning a second language can be a frustrating and difficult experience. In contrast, it seems so easy for children. Is there a best age for learning a second language?

### *Point:* Children Learn Second Languages Easily

Those who argue the *critical period hypothesis* believe that a child can learn a second language more rapidly than an adult because the brain has a language-acquisition processor that functions best before puberty (Lenneberg, 1967)—despite the fact that the critical period hypothesis has not been proved.

Evidence from child second-language studies indicates that the language children speak is relatively simple compared to that of adults, with shorter constructions and fewer vocabulary words, and therefore appears more fluent. Moreover, adults are often unaware that a child's silence indicates lack of understanding or shyness, and they underestimate the limitations of a child's second-language acquisition skills. One area that seems to be a clear advantage for children is phonology: The earlier a person begins to learn a second language, the closer the accent may approach that of a native speaker (Oyama, 1976).

### *Counterpoint:* Adults Learn Languages More Skillfully Than Children

Research comparing adults to children has consistently demonstrated that adolescents and adults outperform children in controlled language-learning studies (e.g., Snow & Hoefnagel-Hoehle, 1978). Adults have access to more memory strategies; are, as a rule, more socially comfortable; and have greater experience with language in general. The self-discipline, strategy use, prior knowledge, and metalinguistic ability of the older learner create a distinct advantage for the adult over the child in language acquisition.

Marinova-Todd, Marshall, and Snow (2000) analyzed misconceptions about age and second-language learning and reached the following conclusions: "Older learners have the potential to learn second languages to a very high level and introducing foreign languages to very young learners cannot be justified on grounds of biological readiness to learn languages" (p. 10). "Age does influence language learning, but primarily because it is associated with social, psychological, educational, and other factors that can affect L2 proficiency, not because of any critical period that limits the possibility of language learning by adults" (p. 28).

### Implications for Teaching

Teachers need to be aware that learning a second language is difficult for children as well as for adults. Helping children to feel socially comfortable reduces their anxiety and assists acquisition.

the door to learning a second language at certain ages (see Singleton and Ryan [2004] and Han [2004] for further discussion of age-related issues in SLA, as well as Box 2.2).

**First-Language Proficiency**   Research has shown that proficiency in the first language helps students to achieve in school. To learn about a student's first-language strengths, a teacher, primary-language-speaking aide, or parent might observe a student working or playing and take notes on the child's primary-language behavior. Knowledge about the student's linguistic and academic abilities may assist the teacher in first- or second-language academic content instruction.

Acceptance of the first language and allowing its use to support instruction promote a low-anxiety environment for students. A lower anxiety level in turn promotes increased learning.

**Previous L2 Experience**   English learners in the same grade may have had vastly different prior exposure to English, ranging from none to previous submersion in English—including students with no prior schooling at all. Moreover, no two students have been exposed to exactly the same input of English outside of class. Therefore, students' prior exposure to English and achievement of proficiency are often highly varied. Teachers may need to ascertain what degree of L2 instruction students have previously attained in order to design English-language instruction at the appropriate level.

Students who have not had a positive experience when first learning English may have "shut down" and become unwilling to speak. It may take time for a more positive approach to L2 instruction combined with a supportive attitude toward L1 maintenance to produce results.

**Best Practice**   **EQUALIZING PRIOR L2 EXPERIENCE**

- If students in the same class have drastically different prior experience in L2, it may be necessary to group students who are at about the same level of English skills (homogeneous grouping) for targeted ELD instruction.
- Heterogeneous groups—each group containing students who are at different levels of English proficiency—can be used for cross-level language stimulation.
- For students who seem unwilling to speak English, small-group language games within homogeneous groups may lower anxiety and increase fluency.

**Assessed L2 Level**   An important part of knowledge about learners that teachers amass as a foundation for instruction is each student's assessed level of proficiency in listening, speaking, reading, and writing in English. This can be obtained during the process of assessment for placement. In California, the California English Language Development Test (online at www.cde.ca.gov/ta/tg/el) is the designated placement instrument. Other states have other ways to assess proficiency (see each state's department of education website). No matter the source of information, the student's L2 level is the beginning point of instruction in English.

**Best Practice**   **ASSESSING L2 PROFICIENCY LEVELS**

- Be aware that a student's listening and speaking proficiency may surpass that for reading and writing, or vice versa.
- Assess each language skill independently.
- Use a measure such as the Student Oral Language Observation Matrix (SOLOM) to assess students' oral proficiency.
- Use *The English–Español Reading Inventory for the Classroom* (Flynt & Cooter, 1999) to provide a quick assessment of reading levels in the two languages.

**Stages of Second-Language Acquisition**    Despite the great variance in levels of second-language acquisition, there are generally accepted stages of development through which all learners progress. These stages include *preproduction, early production, speech emergence,* and *intermediate fluency.* In preproduction—also called the silent period—the learner is absorbing the sounds and rhythms of the new language, becoming attuned to the flow of the speech stream, and beginning to isolate specific words. In this stage, the learner relies on contextual clues to understand key words and generally communicates nonverbally. For the most part, learners in the silent period feel anxious when expected to produce speech. This stage corresponds to the beginner level of the California English-language development framework.

Once a learner feels more confident, words and phrases are attempted—the early production stage (California's early intermediate stage). Responses can consist of single words ("yes," "no," "OK," "come") or two or three word combinations ("where book," "don't go," "teacher help"). Students can sometimes recite simple poems and sing songs at this point. In the third stage, speech emergence (California's intermediate stage), learners respond more freely. Utterances become longer and more complex, but as utterances begin to resemble sentences, syntax errors are more noticeable than in the earlier stage ("Where you going?" "The boy running"). After further progress, learners reach intermediate fluency (California's early advanced or advanced level) and begin to initiate and sustain conversations while often being able to recognize and correct their own errors. ("Advanced" proficiency for English learners simply means that the student has achieved a set of beginning stages. This does not correspond to the label of "Advanced" on the proficiency guidelines of the American Council for the Teaching of Foreign Languages, indicating a near nativelike fluency and depth of knowledge.)

Regardless of the way one labels the stages of second-language acquisition, it is now recognized that, in natural situations, learners progress through predictable stages, and learners advance through them at their own pace. Undue pressure to move through the stages rapidly only frustrates learners and retards language learning.

---

**Best Practice**    MATCHING INSTRUCTION TO STUDENTS' L2 LEVELS

Ideally, classroom activities match the students' second-language acquisition levels.

**Beginning Level**
- Provide concrete activities featuring input that is augmented by pictures, real objects, carefully modified teacher speech, and frequent repetition of new vocabulary.

**Early Intermediate and Intermediate Levels**
- Ask questions that produce single words and brief phrases.
- Provide opportunities for students to use their primary language as they acquire the second language.

**Early Advanced Level**
- Engage students in opportunities to speak with greater complexity, read several pages of text even though they have limited comprehension, and write paragraphs.
- Offer a curriculum that supports and explicitly teaches learning strategies.

**Academic Success**   A valid predictor of school success is prior academic success. By reading cumulative academic records, a teacher should get a sense of students' strengths and weaknesses. This can be augmented by observations of students during academic activities, as well as interviews with family members and former teachers. It is important for the current teacher to assemble as complete a record of students' prior schooling as possible to best inform instructional decisions.

**Likes/Dislikes**   Inquiring about students' favorite academic subjects, television shows, and extracurricular activities is one way of bridging adult–child, teacher–student, or intercultural gaps. Getting-to-know-you activities can be based on the following questions: Who/what is your favorite [native-language/culture] singer? Actor? Video game? Outdoor game? Storybook? Holiday? What do you like about it? Students can write about favorite subjects, and teachers can then use these culturally familiar ideas in classroom math story problems and other content. This conversation may need to occur using the home language.

## Psychological Factors: Social–Emotional

The affective domain, the emotional side of human behavior, is the means through which individuals respond to their environment with feeling. Some affective factors pertain specifically to individuals' feelings about themselves, whereas other factors pertain to their ability to interact with others. This emotional dimension, through such affective factors as self-esteem, motivation, anxiety, and learner attitudes, helps determine how language acquisition and communication take place.

**Self-Esteem**   Many teachers intuitively recognize that self-esteem issues play important roles in their classrooms, and they encourage students to feel proud of their successes and abilities. Efforts to empower students with positive images of self, family, and culture may facilitate language learning. Teachers should also strive to ensure that learners feel good about specific aspects of their language learning (e.g., speaking, writing) or about their success with particular tasks.

Self-esteem is particularly at risk when an individual is learning a second language, because so much identity and pride are associated with language competence. Schools that honor the primary languages and cultures of students and help students to develop additive bilingualism foster strong identities, whereas schools in which students face disrespect and discrimination hinder healthy social and emotional development (Cummins, 1996).

 **Classroom Glimpse**

### BUILDING SELF-ESTEEM

Anita Álvarez was a Spanish-speaking first-grade student at the beginning stages of English-language acquisition. She was shy and retiring, and Mrs. Figueroa noticed that she seldom took advantage of opportunities to chat with her peers. Anita seemed to have good sensorimotor abilities and to be particularly adept at building three-dimensional models following printed diagrams. When Mrs. Figueroa observed that Mary, another student in the class, had a lot of difficulty in constructing objects, she teamed the students, and, with Anita's help, Mary completed her project successfully.

Noting this success, Mrs. Figueroa "assigned competence" to Anita by publicly praising her to the class and referring students to her for help. This boosted Anita's feelings of worth—her "task" self-esteem—and the effects transferred to academic areas. Mrs. Figueroa was pleased to see that, subsequently, Anita talked more with other students and seemed to acquire English at a faster rate.

Many classroom activities can be used to enhance students' self-esteem, such as Press Release, which asks students to write a news story about an incident in which they achieved a victory or reached a goal. A second activity, Age Power, asks students to think positively about their age and answer the question, "What do you like about being your present age?" (Moskowitz, 1978).

In the Name Game, students introduce themselves by first name, adding a word that describes how they are feeling that day, a word that begins with the same letter as the first name (the teacher may provide English learners with an alphabetized list of adjectives). Each subsequent person repeats what the others have said in sequence. Another activity, Name Interviews, lets students work in pairs on a teacher-provided questionnaire with questions such as "What do you like about your name? Who named you? Were you named for someone? Are there members of your family who have the same name?" and more (Siccone, 1995).

## Best Practice    FOSTERING SELF-ESTEEM IN THE CLASSROOM

If classroom teachers can foster students' self-esteem, students will . . .

- Feel free to express their minds, with respect, and without any attack in response
- Expect the best from others, but also accept imperfections
- Contribute freely to ideas and feel valued in small teams and in class
- Show positive attitudes to others' different ideas, even when they disagree
- Apologize whenever offense is taken by any member of the group
- Laugh at themselves and shake off personal offense if they [feel insulted]. (Adapted from Weber, 2005, p. 16)

A concept related to self-esteem is *inhibition,* a term that suggests defensiveness against new experiences and feelings. Emphasizing fluency over accuracy in the first stages of language learning may help students feel less inhibited.

The ability to take risks, to "gamble," may facilitate second-language acquisition. Educators believe that those who are willing to guess at meaning when it is not clear and to be relatively unconcerned about making errors will progress in language skills more rapidly than their more inhibited colleagues. As Brown (2000) pointed out, however, students who make random guesses and blurt out meaningless phrases have not been as successful. It appears that moderate risk-takers stand the best chance at language development.

**Motivation**  "The impulse, emotion, or desire that causes one to act in a certain way" is one way to define motivation, which can be affected by various individual, sociocultural, and instructional factors. Gardner and Lambert (1972) postulated two types of motivation in learning a second language: *instrumental,* the need to acquire a language for a specific purpose such as reading technical material or getting a job, and *integrative,* the desire to become a member of the culture of the second-language group. Most situations involve a mixture of both types.

---

### Best Practice    MOTIVATING STUDENTS

- Give pep talks to remind students that anything worth doing may seem difficult at first.
- Provide students with a list of encouraging phrases to repeat to themselves as self-talk.
- Make sure a student's peer group consists of academic achievers.

---

**Anxiety Level**  Anxiety when learning a second language can be seen as similar to general feelings of tension that students experience in the classroom. Almost everyone feels some anxiety when learning a new language—that is, feelings of self-consciousness, desire to be perfect when speaking, and fear of making mistakes. Using a foreign language can threaten a person's sense of self because speakers know they cannot represent themselves fully in a new language or understand others readily (Horwitz, Horwitz, & Cope, 1991).

Because anxiety can cause learners to feel defensive and block effective learning, language educators strive to make the classroom a place of warmth and friendliness, where risk-taking is rewarded and encouraged and where peer work, small-group activity, games, and simulations are featured. In such contexts, student-to-student communication is increased. Classroom techniques can teach students to confront anxiety directly.

 **Classroom Glimpse**

### DISCUSSING ANXIETY

In a series of lessons, Mr. Green has students write a letter to an imaginary advice columnist, relating a particular difficulty they have in language learning and asking for advice. Working in groups, the students read and discuss the letters, offer advice, and return the letters to their originators for follow-up discussion.

In a second exercise, students collect mistakes over a number of class periods and, in groups, assess the errors. They then rate the errors on a scale of 1 to 3 for such qualities as amusement, originality, and intelligibility, and they tally points to reward the "winning" mistake. Again, class discussion follows. By working together and performing interviews in pairs, students begin to feel more comfortable because they have the opportunity to get to know a classmate and to work with others.

**Best Practice** REDUCING EXCESSIVE STUDENT ANXIETY

- Monitor activities to ensure that students are receiving no undue pressure.
- Use competitive tasks in which students have a reasonable chance to succeed.
- Avoid having anxious students perform in front of large groups.
- When using a novel format or starting a new type of task, provide students with examples or models of how the task is done.
- Occasionally make available take-home tests to lower unnecessary time pressures for performance.
- Teach test-taking skills explicitly and provide study guides to help students who may need extra academic preparation.
- To increase energy levels in class, give students a brief chance to be physically active by introducing stimuli that whet their curiosity or that surprise them. (Adapted from Woolfolk, 2003, p. 367)

**Attitudes of the Learner**   Attitudes play a critical role in learning English. Attitudes toward self, toward language (one's own and English), toward English-speaking people (particularly peers), and toward the teacher and the classroom environment affect students (Richard-Amato, 2003). One's attitude toward the self involves cognition about one's ability in general, the ability to learn language, and self-esteem and its related emotions. These cognitions and feelings are seldom explicit and may be slow to change.

Attitudes toward language and those who speak it are largely a product of experience and the influence of people in the immediate environment, such as peers and parents. Negative reactions are often the result of unfavorable stereotypes or the experience of discrimination or racism. If English learners are made to feel inferior because of accent or language status, they may have a defensive reaction against English and English speakers. Students may also experience ambivalent feelings about their primary language. This can cause problems within the family and create a backlash against English or English speakers.

Attitudes toward the teacher and the classroom environment play an important role in school success in general and English acquisition in particular. Families may promote positive attitudes toward school, thus influencing their children's success. In contrast, parents who have experienced discrimination and had negative experiences at school may subconsciously mirror these same attitudes, adding to their children's ambivalent attitudes toward education. Some theorists have postulated that students' refusal to learn what schools teach can be seen as a form of political resistance, which can include misbehavior, vandalism, and poor relationships with teachers (Nieto, 2007).

Teachers can do much to model positive attitudes toward the students' primary language. However, a teacher–family conference may be advisable if a student continues to show poor attitudes toward the first or second language or the school. Chapter 9 offers strategies for involving the family in schooling.

## Psychological Factors: Cognitive

The cognitive perspective helps educators understand language learners as people who are active processors of information. Language is used in school to create meaning from print, to encode ideas into print, to analyze and compare information, and to respond to classroom discussion. All of these activities involve cognitive factors. Students learn in many different ways using a variety of strategies and styles.

**Learning Styles**    Many researchers have documented differences in the manner in which learners approach the learning task: "Learning styles are the preferences students have for thinking, relating to others, and for particular types of classroom environments and experiences" (Grasha, 1990, p. 23). These preferences serve as models for instructors in their efforts to anticipate the different needs and perspectives of students. Knowing these preferences can assist instructors in helping students to understand themselves as learners and help instructors use the information to both plan and modify certain aspects of courses and assignments.

Keefe (1987) divided learning style variables into four categories: physiological, affective, incentive, and cognitive. *Physiological* variables influence personal nutrition, health, time-of-day preferences, sleeping and waking habits, need for mobility, and requirements for and response to varying levels of light, sound, and temperature. *Affective* variables include how much structure or supervision students need, the degree of anxiety and curiosity they display, and what degree of persistence they use to pursue a task in the face of frustration. *Incentive* variables cover students' personal interests; levels of achievement motivation; enjoyment of competition versus cooperation; risk-taking versus caution; reaction to rewards and punishment; social motivation arising from family, school, and ethnic background; and locus of control (internal, seeing oneself as responsible for one's own behavior, or external, attributing circumstances to luck, chance, or other people).

*Cognitive* learning style variables, for Keefe (1987), include field independent versus field dependent; conceptual/analytical versus perceptual/concrete; broad versus focused attention; easily distracted versus capable of controlled concentration; leveling (tendency to lump new experiences with previous ones) versus sharpening (the ability to distinguish small differences); and high cognitive complexity (accepting of diverse, perhaps conflicting input) versus low cognitive complexity (tendency to reduce conflicting information to a minimum). Table 2.5 sums up the learning style typologies according to Keefe (1987).

Sonbuchner (1991) referred to learning styles as *information-processing styles* (preferences for reading, writing, listening, speaking, visualizing, or manipulating) and *work environment preferences* (differences in motivation, concentration, length of study sessions, involvement with others, level of organization, prime times for study, amount of noise, amount of light, amount of heat, and need for food or drink).

Gardner's theory of multiple intelligences (1983) has made a huge impact on current thinking about differentiating instruction. Assuming that students show a strong predilection for verbal, spatial, logical, interpersonal, intrapersonal, musical, kinesthetic, or nature-based thinking gives the teacher eight ways to think about diversifying teaching and learning. Silver,

**TABLE 2.5** Variables That Constitute Learning Style Differences

| Cognitive | Affective | Incentive | Physiological |
|---|---|---|---|
| ■ Field independent v. field dependent<br>■ Scanning (broad attention) v. focusing (narrow)<br>■ Conceptual/analytical v. perceptual/concrete<br>■ Task constricted (easily distracted) v. task flexible (capable of controlled concentration)<br>■ Reflective v. impulsive<br>■ Leveling (tendency to lump new experiences with previous ones) v. sharpening (ability to distinguish small differences)<br>■ High cognitive complexity (multidimensional discrimination, accepting of diversity and conflict) v. low cognitive complexity (tendency to reduce conflicting information to a minimum) | ■ Need for structure<br>■ Curiosity<br>■ Persistence<br>■ Level of anxiety<br>■ Frustration tolerance | ■ Locus of control (internal: seeing oneself as responsible for own behavior; or external: attributing circumstances to luck, chance, or other people)<br>■ Risk-taking v. caution<br>■ Competition v. cooperation<br>■ Level of achievement motivation (high or low)<br>■ Reaction to external reinforcement (student needs rewards and punishment v. not needing them) | ■ Gender-related differences (typically, males are more visual–spatial and aggressive, females more verbal and tuned to fine-motor control)<br>■ Personal nutrition (healthy v. poor eating habits)<br>■ Health<br>■ Time-of-day preferences (morning, afternoon, evening, night)<br>■ Sleeping and waking habits<br>■ Need for mobility<br>■ Needs for and response to varying levels of light, sound, and temperature<br>■ Social motivation arising from family, school, and ethnic background (high or low)<br>■ Personal interests (hobbies, academic preferences) |

*Source:* Keefe (1987).

Strong, and Perini (2000) offer a valuable summary of methods to integrate learning styles and multiple-intelligence theories, including a distinction between *content* of learning (multiple intelligences) and *process* of learning (learning styles) and a four-part learning style process for looking at content areas (using mastery, interpersonal, understanding, and self-expression as four delivery modalities for each content type).

Neuro-linguistic programming (NLP) provides another framework teachers can use to address students in their dominant modality. For example, visual learners can be presented information through visual channels, whereas auditory learners can receive enhanced listening opportunities, and so forth. Spohrer (2009) offers techniques to apply NLP while teaching.

Table 2.6 provides a list of websites that feature learning style information, diagnostic checklists, and ideas for adapted instruction. Although lessons throughout the school day cannot be adapted for all learning styles, the teacher who builds variety into instruction and helps learners to understand their own styles can enhance students' achievement.

---

**Best Practice**   **TEACHING TO DIVERSE LEARNING STYLES**

Although in the typical classroom it is not possible to tailor instruction precisely to meet each individual's needs, some modifications can be made that take learning styles into account.

- Students who are dependent may benefit from encouragement to become more independent learners. The teacher might offer a choice between two learning activities, for example, or reduce the number of times a student can ask the teacher for help. In contrast, students who are highly independent might be provided activities and assignments that encourage collaboration and teamwork.
- Students who show little tolerance for frustration can be given a range of tasks on the same skill or concept. If the student can complete the first task with no errors, subsequent tasks can slowly increase in complexity, with the student gradually gaining skill and confidence but accepting the fact that he or she may not always be correct.

---

**Learning Strategies**   Aside from general language-acquisition processes that all learners use, learners adopt individual strategies to help them in the acquisition process. Learning strategies include the techniques a person uses to think and to act in order to complete a task. Chamot (2009) has incorporated specific instruction in learning strategies in the Cognitive Academic Language

**TABLE 2.6**   Websites That Feature Learning Style Information, Diagnostic Inventories, and Ideas for Adapted Instruction

| Website | Source | Content |
| --- | --- | --- |
| www.chaminade.org/ inspire/learnstl.htm | Adapted from Colin Rose's *Accelerated Learning* (1987) | Users can take an inventory to determine whether they are visual, auditory, or kinesthetic and tactile learners. |
| www.engr.ncsu.edu/ learningstyles/ilsweb.html | North Carolina State University | Users can take a learning styles questionnaire with 44 items to self-assess. |
| www.aboutlearning.com | About Learning | Explains how to use McCarthy's 4-MAT system. |
| www.usd.edu/trio/tut/ts/ style.html | University of San Diego | Learn about learning styles (auditory, visual, and kinesthetic); identify your own learning style. |
| www.indstate.edu/cirt/id/ pedagogies/styles/learning .html | Indiana State University | Types of learning styles, using learning styles to teach, and applying learning styles to complex projects; links to online learning styles inventories. |

Learning Approach (CALLA). In CALLA, learning strategies are organized into three major types: metacognitive, cognitive, and social-affective. (See Chapter 5 for further discussion.)

## Sociocultural and Political Factors That Influence Instruction

Language learning occurs within social and cultural contexts. Proficiency in a second language also means becoming a member of the community that uses this language to interact, learn, conduct business, and love and hate, among other social activities. Acting appropriately and understanding cultural norms is an important part of the sense of mastery and enjoyment of a language. Learners adapt patterns of behavior in a new language and culture from their home culture as they learn a new language. These patterns of behavior can be helpful but also limiting.

Culture includes the ideas, customs, skills, arts, and tools that characterize a given group of people in a given period of time (Brown, 2000). (See Chapters 8 and 9 for further discussion on culture.) An individual's original culture operates as a lens that allows some information to make sense and other information to remain unperceived. When two cultures come into contact, misunderstandings can result because members of these cultures have different perceptions, behaviors, customs, and ideas. Thus, sociocultural factors—how people interact with one another on a daily basis—play a large role in second-language acquisition.

If, as many believe, English can be learned solely through prolonged exposure, why do so many students fail to master cognitive academic language? Some clues to this perplexity can be found beyond the language itself, in the sociocultural context. Do the students feel that their languages and cultures are validated by the school? Do the patterns of schooling mirror the students' modes of cognition? A well-meaning teacher, even with the most up-to-date pedagogy, may still fail to foster achievement if students are socially and culturally uncomfortable and alienated. Sociocultural issues are explored here with a view toward helping teachers bridge culture and language gaps between home and school.

**Family Acculturation and Use of the First and Second Languages**   Acculturation is the process of adapting to a new culture. Acculturation depends on factors beyond language itself and beyond the individual learner's motivation, capabilities, and learning style; it usually is a familywide phenomenon. Moreover, acculturation may not be a desirable goal for all groups.

Why do some students from certain minority backgrounds do better in school than others? Ogbu (1978) drew a distinction between various types of immigrant groups. *Castelike minorities* are those minority groups that were originally incorporated into society against their will and have been systematically exploited and depreciated over generations through slavery or colonization. Because of discrimination, castelike minorities traditionally work at the lowest paying and least desirable jobs, from which they cannot rise regardless of talent, motivation, or achievement. Therefore, academic success is not always seen as helpful for members of these groups.

On the other hand, immigrant minorities who are relatively free of a history of depreciation, such as immigrants to the United States from El Salvador, Guatemala, and Nicaragua, may view the United States as a land of opportunity. These immigrants do not view education as irrelevant or exploitative but rather as an important investment. Therefore, the internalized attitudes about the value of school success for family members may influence the individual student.

In support of his acculturation model, Schumann (1978) asserted, "the degree to which a learner acculturates to the target language group will control the degree to which he acquires the second language" (p. 34). He concluded that if the following factors are in place, accultura-tion will take place:

- Members of the primary-language and English-language groups view each other with positive attitudes, are of equal status, and expect to share social facilities.
- The primary-language and the English-language groups have congruent cultural pat-terns, and the English-language group desires that the primary-language group assimi-late.
- The primary-language group is small and not very cohesive, and members expect to stay in the area for an extended period.

Schumann's model demonstrates that the factors influencing a student's L1 and L2 use are complicated by sociocultural variables stemming from society at large.

---

**Best Practice**    **LEARNING ABOUT FAMILY ACCULTURATION**

- If possible, visit the student's home.
- Observe the family's degree of acculturation.
- Note the family's media consumption: What television shows does the family watch, in which language? Do family members read books, magazines, or newspapers? In which languages?

---

A family's use of L1 and L2 is also influenced by the relative status of the primary lan-guage in the eyes of the dominant culture. In modern U.S. culture, the social value and prestige of speaking a second language vary with socioeconomic position; they also vary depending on which second language is spoken.

Many middle-class parents believe that having their children learn a second language benefits their children personally and socially and will later benefit them professionally. In fact, it is characteristic of the elite group in the United States who are involved in scholarly work, diplomacy, foreign trade, or travel to desire to be fully competent in two languages. However, the languages that parents wish their children to study are often not those spoken by recently arrived immigrants (Dicker, 1992). This suggests that a certain bias exists in being bilingual—that being competent in a "foreign" language is valuable, whereas proficiency in an immigrant language is a burden to be overcome.

---

**Best Practice**    **RECOGNIZING BIASES**

- Recognize areas in which there may be differences in language use and in which those differences might create friction because the minority group's use may be deemed "inferior" by the majority.
- Be honest about your own biases, recognizing that you communicate these biases whether or not you are aware of them.

- Model correct usage without overt correction and the student in time will self-correct—*if* the student chooses Standard English as the appropriate sociolinguistic choice for that context.

**Family Values and School Values**    As student populations in U.S. schools become increasingly diversified both linguistically and culturally, teachers and students have come to recognize the important role that attitudes and values play in school success. At times the values of the school may differ from those of the home. Not only the individual's attitudes but also the family's values and attitudes toward schooling influence a child's school success.

## Classroom Glimpse

### FAMILY VALUES

Amol is a third-grade student whose parents were born in India. As the only son in a male-dominant culture, he has internalized a strong sense of commitment to becoming a heart surgeon. His approach to classwork is painstaking, slow, and careful, and often he is the last one to finish an assignment during class. His teacher's main frustration with Amol is that he cannot quickly complete his work. However, when talking with Amol's family, the teacher notes that his parents seem pleased with his perfectionism and not at all concerned with his speed at tasks. In this respect, home and school values differ.

In this example, the teacher epitomizes a mainstream U.S. value: speed and efficiency in learning. This value is exemplified in the use of timed standardized testing in the United States. Teachers often describe students of other cultures as being lackadaisical and uncaring about learning, when in fact these students may be operating within a different time frame and value system.

Other values held by teachers and embodied in classroom procedures have to do with task orientation. The typical U.S. classroom is a place of work in which students are expected to conform to a schedule, keep busy, maintain order, avoid wasting time, conform to authority, and achieve academically in order to attain personal worth (LeCompte, 1981). Working alone is also valued, and children often spend a great deal of time in activities that do not allow them to interact verbally with other people or to move physically around the room.

Children need to find within the structure and content of their schooling those behaviors and perspectives that permit them to switch between home and school cultural behaviors and values without inner conflict or crises of identity (Pérez & Torres-Guzmán, 2002). Teachers who examine their feelings about such values as cooperation versus competition, aggression versus compliance, anonymity versus self-assertion, sharing time versus wasting time, and disorder versus order can use this examination to develop a more flexible cultural repertoire.

The danger of excluding the students' cultures from the classroom is that students may become oppositional. Ogbu and Matute-Bianchi (1986) attributed achievement difficulties on the part of some Mexican-American children to a distrust of academic effort, a reflection of the destructive patterns of subordination and social and economic deprivation of the minority group. Segregated schools that offered inferior education resulted in a general mistrust of schooling, and students had difficulty in accepting, internalizing, and following school rules, leading to a lack of achievement. This element of resistance or opposition often takes the form of mental withdrawal, high absenteeism, or reluctance to do classwork.

Schools with high concentrations of English learners may deprive children of the use of their cultural knowledge and experience. If teachers consistently offer examples drawn from the dominant culture and not the students', present literature that displays pictures and photographs of one culture only, and set up classroom procedures that allow some students to feel less comfortable than others, English learners become alienated from their home, family, and culture. This is unfair and damaging. The implementation of a rich and flexible cultural repertoire can encourage students to draw on their culture to promote achievement.

**Institutional Support for the Primary Language and Those Who Speak It**   Educators may view a student's ability to speak a home language other than English as an advantage or as a liability toward school success. Those who blame bilingual students for failing in school often mistakenly believe that they and their parents are uninterested in education and unwilling to comply with teacher-assigned tasks, perhaps from not acquiring sufficient English or from "cultural mismatch" between the ways children learn at home or among their peers and the ways they are expected to learn at school.

In fact, schools often operate in ways that advantage certain children and disadvantage others, causing distinct outcomes that align with social and political forces in the larger cultural context. Institutional support for the primary language and students who speak it is a prime factor in school success for these students. This avoids the outcome of maintaining the poor in a permanent underclass and of legitimizing inequality (Giroux, 1983), with schooling used to reaffirm existing class boundaries.

 **Classroom Glimpse**

### THE WAY SCHOOLS USE LANGUAGE TO PERPETUATE SOCIAL-CLASS INEQUALITY

The fourth-grade class was electing student council representatives. Mrs. Lark called for nominations. Mary, a monolingual-English-speaking European-American student, nominated herself. Mrs. Lark accepted Mary's self-nomination and wrote her name on the board. Rogelio, a Spanish-speaking Mexican-American child with limited English proficiency, nominated Pedro. Mrs. Lark reminded the class that the representative must be "outspoken." Rogelio again said "Pedro." Mrs. Lark announced to the class again that the representative must be "a good outspoken citizen." Pedro turned red and stared at the floor. Rogelio did not pursue Pedro's nomination. No other Mexican-American child was nominated, and Mary won the election. Pedro and Rogelio were unusually quiet for the rest of the school day and avoided making eye contact with the teacher. (Adapted from Erickson, 1977, p. 59)

Incidents like the one in Mrs. Lark's classroom are generally unintentional on the teacher's part. Teachers have specific ideas and guidelines about appropriate conduct, deportment, and language abilities that stem from their own cultural patterns. A beginning step in helping all students feel fully integrated into the class and the learning environment is for teachers to become sensitive to their own cultural and linguistic predispositions.

Nieto (2007) identified numerous structures within schools that affect student learning: tracking, testing, the curriculum, pedagogy, the school's physical structure and disciplinary policies, limitations of both students and teachers, and barriers to parent and community involvement.

*Tracking,* the practice of placing students in groups of matched abilities, despite its superficial advantages, in reality often labels and groups children for years and allows them little or no opportunity to change groups. Secondary school personnel who place English learners in low tracks or in nonacademic ESL classes preclude those students from any opportunity for higher-track, precollege work. In contrast, a supportive school environment offers equal education opportunity to all students, regardless of their language background.

*Testing* results determine the kinds of curricula taught to various groups. Students who respond poorly on standardized tests are often given "basic skills" in a remedial curriculum that is essentially the same as the one in which they were not experiencing success. A supportive school is one that offers testing adaptations for English learners as permitted by law—for example, academic testing in the primary language, extended time for test taking, and fully trained testing administrators.

*Curriculum design* is often at odds with the needs of learners. Only a small fraction of knowledge is codified into textbooks and teacher's guides, and this is rarely the knowledge that English learners bring from their communities. Moreover, the curriculum may be systematically watered down for the "benefit" of children in language-minority communities through the mistaken belief that such students cannot absorb the core curriculum. As a result, students' own experiences are excluded from the classroom, and little of the dominant culture curriculum is provided in any depth. A supportive environment is one that maintains high standards while offering a curriculum that is challenging and meaningful.

*Pedagogy,* the way students are taught, is often tedious and uninteresting, particularly for students who have been given a basic skills curriculum in a lower-track classroom. The pressure to "cover" a curriculum may exclude learning in depth and frustrate teachers and students alike. Pedagogy that is supportive fully involves students—teachers make every effort to present understandable instruction that engages students at high levels of cognitive stimulation.

*The physical structure of the school* also affects the educational environment. Many inner-city schools are built like fortresses to forestall vandalism and theft. Rich suburban school districts, by contrast, may provide more space, more supplies, and campuslike schools for their educationally advantaged students. Supportive schooling is observable: Facilities are humane, well cared for, and materially advantaged.

*Disciplinary policies* may result in certain students being punished more often than others, particularly those who wear high-profile clothing, have high physical activity levels, or tend to hold an attitude of resistance toward schooling. Rather than defining students as deviant or disruptive, teachers can design cooperative groups that allow children to express themselves and learn at the same time, thus supporting rich cultural and linguistic expression.

*The limited role of students* may exclude them from taking an active part in their own schooling, and alienation and passive frustration may result. However, in addition to language barriers, cultural differences may preclude some students from participating in ways that the mainstream culture rewards. The following Classroom Glimpse illustrates the ways in which students' culturally preferred participation styles can differ from the teacher's.

 **Classroom Glimpse**

## CULTURALLY PREFERRED PARTICIPATION STYLES

In classrooms on the Warm Springs (Oregon) Reservation, teacher-controlled activity dominated. All the social and spatial arrangements were created by the teacher: where and when movement took place; where desks were placed and even what furniture was present in the room; and who talked, when, and with whom. For the Warm Springs students, this socialization was difficult. They preferred to wander to various parts of the room, away from the lesson; to talk to other students while the teacher was talking; and to "bid" for one another's attention rather than that of the teacher.

For the Native-American children, the small-reading-group structure in which participation was mandatory, individual, and oral was particularly ill fitting. They frequently refused to read aloud, did not utter a word when called on, or spoke too softly to be audible. On the other hand, when students controlled and directed interaction in small-group projects, they were much more fully involved. They concentrated fully on their work until it was completed and talked a great deal to one another in the group. Very little time was spent disagreeing or arguing about how to go about a task. There was, however, explicit competition with other groups.

A look at the daily life of the Warm Springs children revealed several factors that would account for their willingness to work together and their resistance to teacher-directed activity. First, they spent much time in the company of peers with little disciplinary control from older relatives. Community life encouraged accessible and open community-wide celebrations. No single individual directed and controlled all activity, and there was no sharp distinction between audience and performer. Individuals were permitted to choose for themselves the degree of participation in an activity. Schooling became more successful for these students when they were able to take a more active part. (Adapted from Philips, 1972, pp. 370–394)

*The limited role of teachers* may exclude them from decision making just as students are disenfranchised. This may lead teachers to have negative feelings toward their students. A supportive environment for English learners should be supportive of their teachers as well.

*Barriers to family and community involvement* may exclude families from participation in their children's schooling. Parents may find it difficult to attend meetings, may be only symbolically involved in the governance of the school, or may feel a sense of mismatch with the culture of the school just as their children do. In circumstances like these, it is simplistic to characterize parents as being unconcerned about their children's education. School personnel, in consultation with community and parent representatives, can begin to ameliorate such perceptions by talking with one another and developing means of communication and interaction appropriate for parent and school communities.

### BUILDING HOME–SCHOOL PARTNERSHIPS

When students began skipping classes in high school, several teachers and staff became concerned. The district's ESL and bilingual staff and several school principals met individually with students and parents to search for the reasons why students were missing classes. Community meetings were held with parents, teachers, school principals, central office administrators, and the school superintendent to strengthen the home–school partnership. The community meetings rotated among the elementary, middle, and high schools and included informal potluck suppers and teacher- and parent-facilitated roundtable discussions. Numerous suggestions and positive actions came from these meetings—including the powerful links that were made between the district and the families. (Zacarian, 2004)

A supportive classroom environment for CLD students is less effective if the environment or practices of the school are discriminatory. Teachers can exercise influence within the school and society at large to support the right of CLD students to receive an effective education.

**Sociocultural Support for L1 in the Classroom Environment**    Various sociocultural factors influence the support that is offered for the primary language and its speakers in the classroom. If students are seated in rows, with the teacher instructing the whole group, many students may not be productive. They may benefit more from the opportunity to interact with peers as they learn, speaking their primary language if necessary to exchange information.

Cooperative learning has had positive results in the education of CLD students (Johnson & Johnson, 1995). Positive race relations among students and socialization toward pro-social values and behaviors are potential outcomes of a cooperative learning environment. Students may gain psychological support from one another as they acquire English, and this support can help the students work with the teacher to achieve a workable sociocultural compromise between the use of L1 and L2 in the classroom.

**Best Practice**    SUPPORTING THE PRIMARY LANGUAGE

- Feature the primary language(s) of students on bulletin boards throughout the school and within the classroom.
- Showcase primary-language skills in written and oral reports.
- Involve primary-language speakers as guests, volunteers, and instructional assistants.

**Political Factors**    Why is there disproportionate academic failure among groups of students, particularly comparing majority White with African Americans, Latinos, English learners, or low-income students, for example? Why do those of European-American origin, or those who are White, monolingual-English-speaking students, including those who come from high-income groups, succeed disproportionately? Teachers who are critical thinkers interrogate those processes that affect their teaching and professional performance and, in turn, gain political and ideological insight about the process of schooling and their role as teachers.

All societies in the world have a system of social stratification, meaning that the social system is hierarchically arranged and that some groups have different access to power, resources, and even perceived social worth. The United States, as a complex society, is also stratified, and its social stratification processes are influenced by class, race, occupation, income, and level of education, along with race, gender, age, region of residence, and, in some cases, national origin and levels of English-language proficiency.

Teachers are themselves members of a social class, race, or gender whose perceptions of specific groups, such as English learners, are influenced by their worldviews and preconceptions. Teachers who are clear about the ways in which social-class affiliations influence students' behavior, sense of identity, and academic performance can gain insight, for example, into why low-status students may initially resist the authority of a middle-class teacher.

 **Classroom Glimpse**

### BLAMING THE STUDENTS

One beginning teacher admitted that 70 percent of the students in her sixth-period high school English class were failing. Notice that she could not say, "I have failed 70 percent of my students," or "due to academic tracking, 70 percent of students who cannot meet current standards of performance in English were placed in one class." Admitting that grading and tracking practices are partly to blame for students' failures prevents teachers and administrators from solely blaming the students.

*Institutional racism* is a set of practices and policies condoned by the school that privileges some students and discriminates against others (see also Chapter 8). To counteract institutional racism teachers of English learners can act informally to recruit teachers from underrepresented minorities as colleagues, monitor the academic quality of life available to English learners, volunteer to organize clubs that can effectively recruit English learners, and involve parents and the community in cooperative endeavors.

*Linguistic racism,* discrimination based on language, is taking the place of discrimination once based exclusively on race. For instance, each day millions of Americans are denied their right to speak in their own words. Santa Ana (2004) suggested that this linguistic racism is most evident in schools where the largest silenced group is the millions of American schoolchildren who do not speak English. He stated that although racism based on skin color has been publicly discredited, linguistic discrimination remains largely unexamined by most people in the United States. Teachers with integrity oppose any act that systematically silences students or punishes those who speak their native or home language.

Political clarity can help teachers act together as professionals to question and interrupt unfair and unjust practices in their individual classrooms as well as their schools. Unfortunately, teachers are often isolated in the job, working alone, with few opportunities to interact collegially to address common concerns. However, when teachers remove barriers of isolation, they can compare notes about their collective experiences. They may begin to see that individual concerns are not chance occurrences but are instead related to wider social issues. Teaching with integrity means working collectively with other colleagues and community members to name and oppose institutionalized practices that dehumanize and disempower people based on their racial or linguistic backgrounds.

Theories of second-language acquisition provide the rationale and framework for the daily activities of instruction. Teachers who are aware of the basic principles of contemporary language acquisition and learning are better equipped to plan instruction and explain their practices to peers, parents, students, and administrators.

Although the teacher's role is valuable as students learn a second language, actually learning the language is the responsibility of the learner. Research on cognitive processes shows that learners construct and internalize language-using rules during problem solving or authentic communication. The shift from *what the teacher does* to *what the learner does* is a characteristic of contemporary thinking about learning in general and language acquisition specifically and has wide implications for teaching English learners.

---

**PEARSON**
**myeducationlab**
**The Power of Classroom Practice**
www.myeducationlab.com

Go to the Topic Comprehensible Input in the MyEducationLab (www.myeducationlab.com) for your course, where you can:

- Find learning outcomes for Comprehensible Input along with the national standards that connect to these outcomes.
- Complete Assignments and Activities that can help you more deeply understand the chapter content.
- Apply and practice your understanding of the core teaching skills identified in the chapter with the Building Teaching Skills and Dispositions learning units.
- Examine challenging situations and cases presented in the IRIS Center Resources.
- Check your comprehension on the content covered in the chapter by going to the Study Plan in the Book Resources for your text. Here you will be able to take a chapter quiz, receive feedback on your answers, and then access Review, Practice, and Enrichment activities to enhance your understanding of chapter content.

Go to the Topic A+RISE in the MyEducationLab (www.myeducationlab.com) for your course. A+RISE® Standards2Strategy™ is an innovative and interactive online resource that offers new teachers in grades K–12 just-in-time, research-based instructional strategies that:

- Meet the linguistic needs of ELLs as they learn content
- Differentiate instruction for all grades and abilities
- Offer reading and writing techniques, cooperative learning, use of linguistic and nonlinguistic representations, scaffolding, teacher modeling, higher order thinking, and alternative classroom ELL assessment
- Provide support to help teachers be effective through the integration of listening, speaking, reading, and writing along with the content curriculum
- Improve student achievement
- Are aligned to Common Core Elementary Language Arts standards (for the literacy strategies) and to English language proficiency standards in WIDA, Texas, California, and Florida.

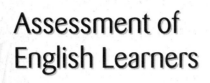

# 3

# Assessment of English Learners

Human beings have been learning for millennia. The traditional proof that learning had taken place was in the product—people could clearly see that a field was plowed productively or a house was built in a sturdy manner. Classroom learning differs because the outcomes are often more abstract and difficult to measure. Assessment is a way of ensuring that students are making progress and that instructional activities are designed wisely. The use of standards helps educators to agree on the expectations and content of English-language instruction and be certain that the school successes of ELD learners are clearly documented. Using these standards, assessment becomes the measure of whether students have acquired the desired skills and knowledge.

Some assessments are informal means of checking to see whether students understand instruction, whereas the purpose of others is to report to the government whether students have met predetermined standards. The emphasis on standards dovetails with outcome-based learning, a philosophy of education that relies on an explicit connection between specific goals and actual outcomes. To receive funds under the federal No Child Left Behind Act of 2001, states must measure student progress on statewide achievement tests. The role of teachers is to describe in detail what students are expected to accomplish in terms of these standards, and then to design learning activities that will enable students to meet the standards.

This chapter addresses the various kinds of assessments, the different educational contexts in which assessments take place, and ways that these assessments can be used to evaluate student learning. Included in this chapter are implications of assessment for English learners and a description of the role of teachers in the assessment process.

# Principles of Standards-Based Assessment and Instruction

## Standards-Based Education: Federal Government Mandates

At the 1989 Education Summit in Charlottesville, Virginia, President George H. Bush and the nation's governors proposed a long-term national education strategy (often referred to as Goals 2000). The call went out for national professional organizations to articulate clear, high standards for what students should know (content standards) and how well they should know it (performance standards). Then the states were supposed to establish delivery standards, a description of what all schools must provide for students to achieve these standards. All students were to be measured at intervals (say, fourth, eighth, and tenth or twelfth grade). These standards and assessments together constituted a voluntary accountability system.

Standards-based reform promoted by the Goals 2000: Educate America Act and the 1994 reauthorization of the Elementary and Secondary Education Act (Improving America's Schools Act) required that each state desiring to receive federal funds for education had to apply standards and assessments to English learners by the 2000–2001 school year, showing that English learners were making adequate yearly progress (AYP). However, rather than develop separate tests designed to accurately measure the progress that English learners make when they are taught and tested in a foreign language (English), most states opted to include English learners in assessments designed and used for mainstream populations, offering English learners testing modification and accommodation (Menken, 2000).

The No Child Left Behind Act (NCLB) incorporated this accountability system into law in 2001, requiring that all students be "proficient" in reading and mathematics by the 2013–2014 school year. Beginning in 2005–2006, all public school students in grades 3 through 8 had to be tested annually, using state achievement tests. This group included English learners, who were to be assessed in a valid and reasonable manner that included fair accommodations and, to the extent practicable, testing in the primary language. Those students who had completed thirty months of schooling, however, had to be tested in English reading (with special exemptions available on a case-by-case basis and students living in Puerto Rico automatically exempted). States also were to establish baseline proficiency goals to which yearly progress would be compared.

In the current climate of standards-driven instruction, the results of student assessment are often used to assess the effectiveness of the teacher's instruction. Often, funds are augmented for schools that show increased test scores or, conversely, withheld from schools in which test scores have not risen over a given period. Under NCLB, schools that fail to make acceptable yearly progress (AYP) for two years in a row are subject to corrective action. This is "high-stakes" assessment—the reputation and resources of schools and teachers rest on students' test performance.

Although NCLB mandated that states desiring federal funds produce adequate yearly progress reporting for students with limited English proficiency (LEP), deep-seated structural flaws undermine the validity and reliability of the data that has been collected to date (Abedi, 2004). For example, the category of "English learner" is not defined in similar ways across states, and in many states, the sparse population of English learners makes comparisons with mainstream populations statistically unreliable. The largest problem, however, is inherent in the logic of the category itself. When an English learner is redesignated, he or she is no longer a member of the subgroup, preventing it from including its most successful members.

Another obstacle comes from testing students whose primary language is not Spanish—6 percent (about 250,000 students) of the English learners in the United States—for whom primary-language tests are often not available. For example, under NCLB, Texas requires English learners to take the state's high-stakes test—the Texas Assessment of Knowledge and Skills (TAKS), even though Valenzuela (2004) and others have argued that this constitutes a profound disservice to this subset of English learners because the TAKS test is only offered in English and Spanish. Non-Spanish-speaking English language learners (ELLs) have no choice but to take the TAKS in English. Although NCLB permits newly arrived English learners to be excluded from the language arts portion of the test during their first year of enrollment, all students must take the math portion of the TAKS, regardless of how long they have been in the United States. Wright and Li (2006) showed that Cambodian students in Texas faced severe linguistic hardship when tested on math concepts in English. The researchers concluded that "linguistically accommodated testing" rarely occurs, causing hardship to students who cannot be tested in their native languages. The unrealistic expectations for student achievement under these conditions undermines the success of accountability; the researchers comment, "Unless policies and programs are made more reasonable for newly arrived ELLS, many of them will likely be left behind" (2006, p. 19).

Teachers also decry the instructional time—and language-learning opportunities—that are lost to preparing English learners for standardized tests. Phipps (2010) commented, "Learning a language takes time and preparing for a test is definitely not learning a language" (p. 19). However, the chief criticism of NCLB in regard to CLD students is the pressure it places on schools with high numbers of English learners: lower baseline achievement scores require greater gains. And when schools who cannot achieve great gains undergo "high-stakes" consequences—with threats to close the schools suffering from low test scores—too often blame falls on the presence of English learners and resentment soon follows.

## Standards for English-Language Development

The aim of standardized measures is to ensure that all students are held to the same level of performance. Yet the net result is often to penalize schools whose English learners do not score well on tests designed for native-English speakers. This poses a dilemma: On the one hand, high standards across schools do not permit school districts to lower academic standards for schools with high percentages of English learners. On the other hand, forcing students to undergo frustrating experiences of repeated testing in English when they are not ready can discourage them. Alternatively, testing students in their primary language is not effective if schools do not offer primary-language instruction.

Many states besides California have adopted standards to guide the process of teaching English to second-language learners. Texas adopted English Language Proficiency Standards (ELPS) in 2007 to replace English as a Second Language Texas Essential Knowledge and Skills (ESL TEKS) beginning in the 2008–2009 school year. The standards are online at www.tea .state.tx.us/curriculum/biling/elps.html. In Florida the Reading/Language Arts Standards with English Language Proficiency Standards in 2007 became part of the Sunshine State Standards. In New York, the Teaching of Language Arts to Limited English Proficient/English Language

Learners: Learning Standards for English as a Second Language document (www.emsc.nysed .gov/biling/resource/ESL/standards.html) serves as the foundation for ESL curriculum, instruction, and assessment in grades Pre-K through 12 as well as being the framework for the New York State ESL Achievement Test (NYSESLAT), which is administered annually to all English learners in New York.

English-language development standards provide teachers with consistent measures of English learners' progress and ensure that English learners can eventually, like English-speaking students, meet and exceed standards for English language arts content. Access to high-quality instruction is accomplished by aligning assessment with instruction so that each student can be taught at the appropriate level. Teachers assess, plan, teach appropriately, and reassess to keep students moving forward. Thus, assessment takes into consideration both ELD skills and content area knowledge.

*Standardized tests are increasingly used to measure educational outcomes.*

Tony Freeman/PhotoEdit

English-language development takes place in stages. Rather than using the four stages introduced in the Natural Approach (preproduction, early production, speech emergence, and intermediate fluency), the California English Language Development Standards (California Department of Education [CDE], 1999) are divided into five levels: beginning, early intermediate, intermediate, early advanced, and advanced. The ELD standards describe expected proficiency on the part of the English learner in each of six key domains of language (listening and speaking, reading/ word analysis, reading fluency and systematic vocabulary development, reading comprehension, reading literary response and analysis, and writing strategies and application).

For example, in the domain of listening and speaking, expected language proficiency increases gradually from beginning to advanced levels. Table 3.1 depicts the expectations for each of the five levels.

### Advantages of Standards-Based Instruction for English Learners

An advantage of establishing content and performance standards for English learners is that teachers can use these standards to focus on what students need to know. Rather than following the traditional ELD emphasis on sentence structure, grammar, and the learning of discrete vocabulary terms, teachers can pursue an articulated sequence of instruction, integrating the

**TABLE 3.1**   Listening and Speaking Expectations in the California English Language Development Standards for English Learners at Five Levels

| ELD Level | Expectations |
|---|---|
| Beginning (K–2) | Begins to speak with a few words or sentences, employing some English phonemes and rudimentary English grammatical phrases. |
| | Answers simple questions with one- or two-word responses. |
| | Responds to simple directions and questions with physical actions and other means of nonverbal communication. |
| | Independently uses common social greetings and simple repetitive phrases. |
| Early Intermediate | Begins to be understood when speaking, but may have some inconsistent use of Standard English grammatical forms and sounds. |
| | Asks/answers questions with phrases or simple sentences. |
| | Retells familiar stories and short conversations by using appropriate gestures, expressions, and illustrative objects. |
| | Orally communicates basic needs. |
| | Recites familiar rhymes, songs, and simple stories. |
| Intermediate | Asks/answers instructional questions with simple sentences. |
| | Listens attentively to stories/information and identifies key details and concepts using both verbal and nonverbal responses. |
| | Can be understood when speaking, employing consistent Standard English forms and sounds; however, some rules may not be in evidence. |
| | Actively participates in social conversations with peers and adults on familiar topics by asking and answering questions and soliciting information. |
| | Retells stories and talks about school-related activities using expanded vocabulary, descriptive words, and paraphrasing. |
| Early Advanced | Listens attentively to stories/information and orally identifies key details and concepts. |
| | Retells stories in greater detail, including characters, setting, and plot. |
| | Is understood when speaking, using consistent Standard English forms, sounds, intonation, pitch, and modulation, but may have random errors. |
| | Actively participates and initiates more extended social conversations with peers and adults on unfamiliar topics by asking and answering questions, restating, and soliciting information. |
| | Recognizes appropriate ways of speaking that vary based on purpose, audience, and subject matter. |
| | Asks and answers instructional questions with more extensive supporting elements. |
| Advanced | Listens attentively to stories/information on new topics and identifies both orally and in writing key details and concepts. |
| | Demonstrates understanding of idiomatic expressions by responding to and using them appropriately. |
| | Negotiates/initiates social conversations by questioning, restating, soliciting information, and paraphrasing. |
| | Consistently employs appropriate ways of speaking and writing that vary based on purpose, audience, and subject matter. |
| | Narrates and paraphrases events in greater detail, using more extended vocabulary. |

*Source:* Adapted from the California English Language Development Standards, online at www.cde.ca.gov/re/pn/fd/englangart-stnd-pdf.asp.

teaching of English into increasingly sophisticated levels of language and meaningful discourse, fluent communication skills, and cognitive academic language proficiency.

The application of standards avoids what has been too-frequent practice in the past: the use in ELD of materials and practices designed for younger students or for special education students (Walqui, 1999). Gándara (1997) reported vast discrepancies between the curricula offered to English speakers and to English learners. The requirements of standards can alter this practice. A standard becomes useful to teachers when they can identify if the standard has been met or progress is being made toward meeting it (Jametz, 1994). Moreover, students can use these standards to evaluate their own performances.

**Disadvantages of Standards-Based Instruction for English Learners**   Although the overall goal of standards-based education is noble—devising a set of very broad standards for all students and measuring success according to a common set of criteria—the ongoing needs of English learners require that school districts remain flexible about the specific means for addressing standards and determining student achievement (Nelson-Barber, 1999). The heavy emphasis on high-stakes testing—and the attendant punitive consequences for schools with low test scores—places English learners at risk of failure.

In fact, schools across the United States report low test scores for students who are linguistically "nonmainstream." The emphasis on testing leaves little time for teachers to focus on teaching the academic subjects and the language that English learners need to acquire to perform well on high-stakes tests.

The answer to this dilemma is for school districts to invest in high-level, late-exit primary-language instruction and to allow students to be tested in their primary language. The catch is the NCLB requirement that students be tested in English reading after three years of schooling. This regulation pressures schools to begin English reading early. English learners, then, are assumed to attain grade-level expectations in English reading that are set for native English speakers, resulting in pressure toward submersion—or, at best, early-exit transition bilingual education programs—as a preferred model.

If testing has become an index used to compare schools competitively, wisdom suggests that high-quality education requires more than high standards. It also requires a high level of resources to accomplish such mandates. In a sense, the whole community must invest in the learning that takes place in a classroom, for the whole community suffers if the learning impetus of the young is misdirected, quashed, or squandered.

# Role, Purposes, and Types of Assessment

What are the components of the assessment picture for English learners? Some assessments used with English learners are required by government programs and legal mandates, and others are a part of standard classroom practice. Ideally, assessment provides information about students' abilities that teachers can use to advance their academic and personal development.

## Assessment-Based Instruction

Assessment is the beginning of instruction. With a valid evaluation of the current level of a learner's knowledge, a teacher knows where to start. Assessment also takes place at intervals in order to modify or improve the learner's performance. Assessment informs educators about the strengths and needs of language learners so that students are properly placed and appropriately instructed while also notifying school authorities, parents, or other concerned parties of the student's progress. A final use of assessment is to compare student achievement against national goals and standards, a significant problem for English learners.

Assessment should not be used merely to place students and design remediation. The best use of assessment is to advance students' understanding and abilities as an integral part of education.

## Identification, Placement, Instruction, Progress Tracking, and Redesignation/Reclassification of English Learners

English learners move through standards-based education in a systematic way. First, procedures are in place in each school district for identifying English learners as they enroll in school. Placement assessment determines the appropriate level of instruction, and, using this placement level as a guideline, teachers design instructional activities and monitor students' progress until they can be reclassified—considered ready to participate in mainstream instruction.

**Universal Access to the Language Arts Curriculum**   California, for example, has its own set of education standards. In the area of English language arts, the draft *Reading/Language Arts Framework* was adopted by the state Board of Education in April 2006 with the intent that it would apply to all reading/language arts instruction. This framework is aligned with the English language arts (ELA) standards. The ELD standards support the ELA standards in two ways: They are aligned with the ELA standards by using similar terminology and categories, and they prepare English learners to advance to a level at which the ELA standards can be used to guide their learning.

Chapter 7 of the *Reading/Language Arts Framework*, "Universal Access to the Language Arts Curriculum," describes the procedures that must be in place in the classroom to ensure that English learners can make adequate yearly progress to meet the standards outlined for mainstream English language arts. These procedures include the following:

- The use of assessment for placement, planning, and monitoring instruction
- Modification of curricula to meet the needs of English learners
- Deployment of a variety of resources and teaching methods adapted to the individual needs of English learners
- Differentiation of instruction in such areas as depth, complexity, and emphasis to ensure students' mastery of key concepts
- Providing flexible grouping strategies according to students' needs
- Marshaling of help from school personnel when appropriate

**Identifying the English Learner**   Various methods are used to identify English learners needing services. *Registration* and *enrollment* information collected from incoming students can help identify those with a home language other than English. A teacher or tutor who has informally observed a student using a language other than English often does identification through observation. Interviews may also provide opportunities to identify students, as may *referrals* made by teachers, counselors, parents, administrators, or community members.

The *home language survey,* a short form administered by school districts to determine the language spoken at home, is a common method of identifying students whose primary language is not English. One difficulty with the home language survey is its dependence on self-report. Some parents simply indicate that the home language is English, a misdirection that usually stems from the desire that the student receive English-only instruction. The resulting submersion in English-only instruction is difficult for both the learner and the teacher, but placement is the parents' decision.

**Assessment for Placement**    Once students are identified, their level of English proficiency needs to be determined. School districts are required by state and federal mandates to administer a placement test before assigning a new student to an instructional program if a home language survey indicates that the student's primary language is not English. The assessment should be done by staff members with the language skills to communicate in the family's native language. Parents and students should be provided with orientation about the assessment and placement process and the expectations and services of the school system. Most important, the school staff needs to be trained in, aware of, and sensitive to the cultural backgrounds and linguistic needs of the student population.

Various states in the United States use a mixture of measures to evaluate students for ELD services, including the following: oral proficiency tests, teacher judgment, parent request, literacy tests in English, prior instructional services, writing samples in English, achievement tests in English, teacher ratings of English proficiency, oral proficiency tests in the native language, and achievement tests in the native language (Hopstock & Stephenson, 2003).

Table 3.2 lists a variety of tests that are used for identification and placement of English learners in various states.

---

**Best Practice**    **LEARNING ABOUT STUDENTS' LANGUAGE ABILITIES**

- Observe students in multiple settings, such as classroom, home, and playground.
- With the help of a trained interpreter if necessary, obtain histories (medical, family, previous education, immigration experience, home languages).
- Interview current or previous classroom teachers for information about a student's learning style and classroom behavior.
- Seek information from other school personnel (e.g., counselor, nurse), especially if they are capable of assessing the home language.
- Ask the student's parents to characterize the student's language and performance skills in the home and the community. (Cheng, 1987)

---

Educators who draw from a variety of information sources can see the students' needs in a broader context and thus design a language program to meet these needs. Teacher-devised checklists and observational data gathered as students participate in learning activities can be used to confirm or adjust student placement (Lucas & Wagner, 1999).

**The California English Language Development Test**    Matched to the California English Language Development Standards, the California English Language Development Test is used to

**TABLE 3.2** Tests Used for Identification and Placement of Language-Minority Students

| | |
|---|---|
| BINL | Basic Inventory of Natural Language |
| BOLT | Bilingual Oral Language Tests |
| Brigance-C | Brigance Comprehensive Inventory of Basic Skills—English and Spanish |
| Brigance-D | Brigance Diagnostic Assessment of Basic Skills—Spanish |
| CAT | California Achievement Test |
| CELT | Comprehensive English Language Test |
| CTBS | Comprehensive Test of Basic Skills |
| FLA | Functional Language Assessment |
| IPT | IDEA (Oral Language) Proficiency Test |
| ITBS | Iowa Test of Basic Skills |
| LAB | Language Assessment Battery |
| LAS | Language Assessment Survey |
| MAP | Maculatis Assessment Program |
| MAT | Metropolitan Achievement Test |
| MRT | Metropolitan Readiness Test |
| PIAT | Peabody Individual Achievement Test |
| PPVT | Peabody Picture Vocabulary Test |
| QSE | Quick Start in English |
| SAT | Stanford Achievement Test |
| SRA | Science Research Associates, Inc. |
| TAP | Total Academic Proficiency |
| WRAT | Wide Range Achievement Test |
| WMLS-R | Woodcock Muñoz Language Survey-Revised |

*Source:* Adapted from DeGeorge (1987–1988).

identify new students who are English learners in grades K–12, determine their proficiency, and annually assess their progress in English skills. It is required to be given within thirty days of enrollment, and is also administered yearly by school-site specialists, either the ELD teacher, an aide, or a program coordinator. The CELDT meets the federal mandate that a state receiving funds under Title III of NCLB define annual measurable achievement objectives (AMAOs) for monitoring the progress of English learners toward attaining proficiency in English. Each school district is responsible for submitting annual assessment reports based on CELDT scores. Other states have similar tests on which to base their progress reports.

Students earn a raw score for proficiency in listening/speaking, reading, and writing (grades kindergarten and 1 are tested in listening/speaking only). These raw scores are converted into scaled scores, which can be used to compare proficiency across repeated administrations of the test. Charts are used to convert scores into the five proficiency levels from beginning to advanced for each grade level.

**Assessment-Based Instruction** Teaching methods that ensure differentiated standards-based instruction for English learners should take into account the range of English proficiency levels represented in the classroom, using multiple means to measure and document the progress of learners.

English learners' achievement in English is made possible by a linkage between standards, placement testing, instruction, and careful record keeping. Placement tests that are directly linked to standards-based classroom instruction for English learners permit teachers to begin using targeted instructional practices as soon as students enter the classroom and provide a seamless system that helps teachers track students' continuous progress toward mainstream instruction. Each linkage—from standards to assessment to instruction and back to assessment—is explained in the following sections.

Ideally, each content lesson in which the student participates has not only a content objective, derived from the relevant content standard, but also a language objective designed to meet one of the ELD standards still to be achieved. The ELD standard is based on the students' assessed level(s); that is, if a group of students has placed in the early intermediate level on a placement proficiency test in reading, the reading objective(s) is drawn from the intermediate level, the level still to be attained. In addition, to promote cognitive academic language proficiency, each lesson should have a learning-strategy objective (further described in Chapter 5).

One might think that moving from assessment to objective is reverse thinking—indeed, Wiggins and McTighe (1998) call it "backwards" lesson planning—but if the goal is to demonstrate progress in English acquisition, one must first determine what ELD standard a student needs to meet and pair that standard with some assessment that would provide the required evidence that the student has met the standard. Thus, assessment is the flip side of setting objectives—one cannot exist without the other. According to curriculum experts (Contra Costa County Office of Education, 2006), the process of instruction consists of the following:

- Aligning curriculum (both teacher-created and textbook assignments) with grade-level standards and students' assessed level(s) (also called *curriculum calibration*)
- Using grade-level formative (in-process) and summative (final) assessments to improve student achievement
- Applying effective instructional strategies to ensure student mastery of the standards taught

---

**Best Practice** "BACKWARDS" PLANNING

Sheni Chen plans a lesson for sixth-grade students at the intermediate and advanced ELD levels. She plans to address two literacy response and analysis (reading) standards from the California ELD standards: (Intermediate) "Read text and use detailed sentences to respond orally to factual questions about brief prose" and (Advanced) "Read a literary selection and orally explain the literary elements of plot, setting, and characters by using detailed sentences." Three objectives result:

1. (Intermediate) Students will work in groups to use complete sentences to make a sequence chain of ten events in the story "Something to Declare" by Julia Alvarez (see Schifini, Short, & Tinajero, 2002, pp. 120–125).

**2.** (Advanced) Students will work in groups, using complete sentences to fill out a plot/setting/character matrix chart about the story "Something to Declare."

**3.** (Intermediate and Advanced) Students will use their charts to play a quiz game with other groups at their level.

Formative Assessment: The teacher will circulate to help the groups plan and complete their charts.

Summative Assessment: Students will receive one point for each of ten questions their group can answer based on their chart.

In subsequent chapters, lesson plans and teaching strategies are presented that differentiate between English learners at various levels of proficiency. Because classrooms invariably include students from more than one level, each lesson plan must include participation for students whose scores represent more than one ELD level. This is the challenge of differentiated instruction.

**Differentiating Instruction to Meet Standards** In designing universal access to the language arts curriculum, Kame'enui and Simmons (2000) proposed that teachers treat students as members of one of three distinct groups: a benchmark group, a strategic group, or an intensive group. Interventions are tailored to the needs of these groups (see Table 3.3).

When interpreting this grouping, it is important to note that the process of acquiring English should not be considered a disability. Just because a student is at the early stage of learning English does not mean that student is in need of intensive intervention. Learning

**TABLE 3.3** Interventions Tailored to Three Need-Based Groups

| Group | Characteristics | Interventions |
|---|---|---|
| Benchmark | May be experiencing minor difficulties. | Reteach concepts. |
| | | Provide additional learning time. |
| | | Offer support, such as a reading tutor. |
| | | Use SDAIE techniques. |
| Strategic | Test results show 1–2 standard deviations below the mean. | Provide specific additional assignments to be done with supervision. |
| | | Schedule extended language arts time. |
| | | Use SDAIE techniques; modify curriculum. |
| | | May be referred to school Student Success Team for intervention strategies; may require a 504 plan for targeted interventions. |
| Intensive | Extremely and chronically low performance in one or more measures. | Refer to Student Success Team for evaluation. Special education placement may entail additional resources or instructional support. |
| | | Student, if placed in special education, will be given an individualized education program (IEP). |

*Source:* California Department of Education, *Reading/Language Arts Framework* (2007), pp. 264–265.

a second language is a social and cognitive achievement that requires time. However, if a student has made no significant progress over a period of four or five months, a referral for a speech/language evaluation may be in order. In bilingual populations, the incidence of special education needs is normally distributed in the same proportion as in the mainstream population.

Gregory (2003) offered strategies for differentiating instruction, particularly in response to standards mandates. Strategies address a range of aspects from learning styles to classroom management.

**Progress Tracking**   In many school districts, each English learner has a progress file in which the yearly proficiency score is recorded. The speaking/listening, reading, and writing standards are listed in the folder, with boxes to check when the student meets each standard. This file also contains writing samples as evidence that the writing standards have been met. This folder travels with the student class by class, providing evidence about which standards are yet to be met and serving as the step-by-step proof that the English learner is making progress toward transition to the reading/language arts standards for the mainstream learner.

**Redesignation/Reclassification/Exit**   When English learners score a certain level on the proficiency test, among other criteria, they are considered ready to participate with English-speaking students in the mainstream classroom. The process for redesignation varies across districts and states. Some districts organize bilingual education advisory committees to ensure parent representation and participation in implementing redesignation criteria that are reliable, valid, and useful. Some states set score targets on language and achievement tests that are used as criteria for proficiency, but in other states the individual districts set their own reclassification criteria. The reclassification process in California uses four criteria:

- CELDT score
- Teacher evaluation of a student's academic performance, based on report card grades, grade point average, or another measure used by the school district
- Consultation with parent or guardian
- Performance in basic skills, as measured by the student's California English Language Arts Standards Test

**Best Practice**   CRITERIA FOR REDESIGNATING ENGLISH LEARNERS

Verdugo Hills High School (Tujunga, California) has various criteria for redesignating students. The school first asserts that "[r]edesignated students speak at least two languages. They learned English as a Second Language and proved their command of English by passing a redesignation test." The students must pass the following:

- CELDT (California English Language Development Test)
- The ELA (English Language Arts) section of the CST (California Standards Test) with a score of basic or higher
- Math and English or ESL 3/4 classes with a C or higher
  (Verdugo Hills High School, 2010)

## Issues of Fairness in Testing English Learners

Tests play a significant role in placing and reclassifying English learners. However, standardized tests are not necessarily well suited as measures of language ability or achievement for English learners. In fact, some have argued that the very use of tests is unfair because they are used to deprive people of color of their place in society. The goal of tests notwithstanding, both the testing situation and the test content may be rife with difficulties for and bias against English learners.

One might ask just how fair it is to test an English learner whose proficiency is at the earliest levels using assessments that are designed for native English speakers.

Zacarian (2006) relayed the following anecdote about a student who was tested in the Massachusetts Comprehensive Assessment System (MCAS). Clearly, this test failed to connect in a positive way to classroom instruction.

> One year ago, An moved from Vietnam to the United States. She could not speak English and required a translator to meaningfully understand all her instructional program. Her motivation to learn and do well in school was quite strong.
>
> A year after An arrived, she was required to take the MCAS. Her translator was not allowed to assist her.
>
> Faced with the MCAS test, An broke down in tears. She fled the exam site and sought out her tutor. Speaking Vietnamese, she sobbed uncontrollably about how bad she felt about not being able to take the test. During the ensuing week, her attitude toward learning dramatically shifted from one of open-minded risk-taker to that of timid, tentative learner. (p. 11)

Factors within the context of testing such as anxiety, lack of experience with testing materials, time limitations, and rapport with the test administrator may also cause difficulties.

**Test Anxiety**  All students experience test anxiety, but this anxiety can be compounded if the test is alien to the students' cultural background and experiences. Certain test formats such as multiple-choice and think-aloud tasks may provoke higher levels of anxiety because students may fear that these assessments inaccurately reflect their true proficiency in English (Scarcella, 1990).

**Time Limitations**  Students may need more time to answer individual questions because of the time needed for mental translation and response formulation. Students from other cultures do not necessarily operate under the same conception of time as do European Americans. Some students may need a time extension or should be given untimed tests.

**Problematic Test Content**  For the most part, language placement tests are well suited for assessing language. Other tests, however, particularly achievement tests, may contain translation problems or bias that affects the performance of English learners. Translating an English-language achievement test into another language, or vice versa, to create equivalent vocabulary items may cause some lack of correspondence in the frequency of the items.

*Geographic bias* might occur when test items feature terms used in particular geographic regions that are not universally shared. *Dialectical bias* occurs when a student is tested using expressions relevant to certain dialect speakers that are not known to others. *Language-specific bias* is created when a test developed for one language is used with another language. *Cultural bias* may occur if the test represents content from the dominant culture that may be understood differently or not at all by English learners. Common European-American food items such as bacon, musical instruments such as a banjo, even nursery rhymes and children's stories may be unfamiliar. Test content may represent a *class bias;* for example, the term *shallots* appeared on a nationally administered standardized achievement test, but only students whose families consume gourmet foods were likely to be familiar with the term.

**Validity**　A test is *valid* if it measures what it claims to be measuring. A test has *content validity* if it samples the content that it claims to test in some representative way. For example, if a reading curriculum includes training in reading for the main idea, then a test of that curriculum would include a test item about reading for the main idea. *Empirical validity* is a measure of how effectively a test relates to some other known measure, such as subsequent success or performance, or with another measure used at the same time.

**Reliability**　A test is *reliable* if it yields predictably similar scores when it is taken again. Although many variables can affect a student's test score—such as error introduced by fatigue, hunger, or poor lighting—test results should be consistent regardless of the examiner, time, place, or other variables related to test administration.

**Practicality**　A test may be valid and reliable but cost too much to administer either in time or money. A highly usable test should be relatively straightforward to administer and score. For example, if a portfolio is kept to document student progress, issues of practicality would require that the portfolio be simple to maintain, accessible to students, and easily scored with a rubric agreed on by teachers and students.

**Best Practice**　**IN TESTING**

The following checklist can be used to monitor testing practices for English learners:

- Does the assessment of what has been learned closely match what has been taught? The test content should reflect the curriculum, with the same type of material being tested as was presented during instruction, with the same language and student interaction.
- Do the conditions for assessment resemble that of instruction? The use of similar conditions helps students access and remember what they have learned.
- Does the assessment build on the experiences of students? Is it relevant to their lives, and can it be matched to their developmental level?
- Is the atmosphere positive, avoiding distractions?

## Types of Classroom Assessments for English Learners

Assessment instruments can be used for a number of purposes: to make determinations about student placement, to make day-to-day instructional adjustments such as when to provide a student with additional mediation, to make resource decisions such as allocation of instructional time or materials, and to measure student achievement against standards. Teachers who apply assessment skillfully can choose which methods of assessment are most useful for classroom decision making; develop effective grading procedures; communicate assessment results to students, parents, and other educators; and recognize unethical, illegal, and otherwise inappropriate assessment methods and uses of assessment information (Ward & Murray-Ward, 1999).

*Formative* and *summative assessments* serve different purposes. Assessment that takes place during instruction is formative; it helps teachers to determine "what and how students are learning, so instruction can be modified while it is still in progress" (Herrera, Murry, & Cabral, 2007, p. 174). This assessment ranges from informal verbal feedback, such as questioning students about their progress or using an informal observation instrument, to more formal instruments such as preliminary scoring with a rubric that will be used again to assess a final score. In contrast, summative assessment occurs at the end point and provides a basis for a letter grade.

*Self-assessment* and *peer assessment* allow students to rate themselves and one another formatively, preferably using rubrics, providing them additional opportunities to apply grading criteria to their work and discuss it with others, while using their metacognitive skills to plan, monitor, and evaluate their efforts. Herrera, Murry, and Cabral (2007, p. 33) offered an "Effort and Achievement Comparison Rubric" that students can use to rate themselves with a five-point scale on how effectively they confront the learning challenges they face. This is an excellent tool to teach time and task management.

**Test Types**    Various types of tests are used for different purposes. Each has its objectives, features, and limitations.

*Textbook tests* are provided by the textbook publisher and designed to correlate with text content. On the plus side, such tests provide a direct measure of what was presented in the text. Another positive feature is the fact that such a text is probably state adopted because of its match with state standards (Linn, 2000). This makes it easier to compare one class with another. One limitation may be the lack of relevance of this content to the student or the culture of the community.

*Performance-based tests* involve "the actual doing of a task" (Linn & Miller, 2005, p. 7), using a product or a performance as an outcome measure. By communicating performance standards to students, schools provide expectations for their work. Outcome-based performance assessment is designed to offer information about students' proficiency (Marzano, 1994), including the ability to analyze and apply, rather than simply recognize or recall information. Performance-based testing procedures can be based on tasks that students are asked to do, including essays, demonstrations, computer simulations, performance events, and open-ended problem solving.

**Best Practice**    PERFORMANCE ASSESSMENT

An ideal performance test for reading would meet the following criteria:

- Contain materials similar to that found in real books rather than reproduced paragraphs written with a controlled vocabulary

- Be administered by a concerned adult who is usually present to help (the teacher or classroom parent volunteer)
- Be observational and interactional, but also valid and reliable, and available for comparison and reporting purposes
- Offer a picture of the student's reading strengths and weaknesses
- Be motivating and fun, so that students, by taking it, would be encouraged to read more (based on Bembridge, 1992)

A positive aspect of performance-based assessment is the targeted feedback that encourages students to compare their work to specific standards. In this way, assessment can provide information about which aspects of instruction need to be redesigned so that both student and teacher performance improves.

*Curriculum tasks* measure the success of activities performed in class. An advantage is that an add-on assessment is not necessary; the class activities themselves can be scored and graded. A limitation is that when students have been given extensive help to complete tasks using formative assessment, it is difficult to assess the skill level they have attained independently of help.

*Authentic tests* measure proficiency on a task commonly found outside the classroom. Examples of authentic assessment include the use of portfolios, projects, experiments, current event debates, and community-based inquiries. Assessments are considered authentic if they stem directly from classroom activities, allow students to share in the process of evaluating their progress, and are valid and reliable in that they truly assess a student's classroom performance in a stable manner (Hancock, 1994; O'Malley & Pierce, 1996).

The advantage of authentic assessment is its direct relation to classroom performance, permitting teachers to design and offer the extra mediation students may need as determined by the assessment. Such real-world relevance is useful to students in the long run, so young people can feel their education is beneficial to themselves and their community.

 **Classroom Glimpse**

### AUTHENTIC ASSESSMENT

At International High School in Queens, New York, authentic assessment is deeply embedded in all activities. In the Global Studies and Art interdisciplinary cluster, students researched a world religion that was unfamiliar to them. Their assignment was to create or re-create a religious artifact typical of the religion.

To begin the project, the film *Little Buddha* was shown, and students brainstormed possible research questions. Other project activities included visiting a museum that exhibits religious artifacts, researching in dyads, and communicating their research in progress to peers.

On the day of the final performance, students sat at tables of six, shared their findings, asked questions, and clarified what they had learned. The culminating activity was an informal conversation in yet another grouping so that students could expand their perspectives.

Although students had their written reports at hand, they could not rely on them for their initial presentations or during the discussion. (Walqui, 1999, p. 74)

*Teacher-made tests* are often used to determine report card grades. They may contain features of performance-based or other kinds of testing, the distinction being that they are teacher-created. Teacher-made language tests can assess skills in reading comprehension, oral fluency, grammatical accuracy, writing proficiency, and listening. Teacher-constructed tests may not be as reliable and valid as tests that have been standardized, but the ease of construction and administration and the relevance to classroom learning make them popular.

**Assessments That Supplement Tests**   *Portfolio assessments* can be used to maintain a long-term record of students' progress, to provide a clear and understandable measure of student productivity instead of a single number, to offer opportunities for improved student self-image as a result of showing progress and accomplishment, to recognize different learning styles, and to allow an active role for students in self-assessment (Gottlieb, 1995). Portfolios can include writing samples (compositions, letters, reports); student self-assessments; audio recordings (retellings, oral think-alouds); photographs and video recordings; semantic webs and concept maps; and teacher notes about students (Glaser & Brown, 1993).

 **Classroom Glimpse**

### USING PORTFOLIO ASSESSMENT

Mr. Zepeda uses a running record to assess each student's reading level as he listens to them read individually. In addition, he schedules individual conferences to learn about students' interests. He sets up a schedule so that he can collect material for student portfolios on a regular basis, and he encourages the students to be involved actively in selecting work for their portfolios.

By the time of parent conferences, student portfolios contain writing samples; anecdotal records; photos; periodic running records; periodic math assessments; records of books the student has read; a complete writing project including prewriting, drafts, and final published copy; a summary of the student's progress; and a list of goals set and accomplished. In preparation for the conference, Mr. Zepeda tells the students, "I want you to select the one piece of work that you feel best about. Write a one-page note to your parents explaining why you are proud of that piece of work and what you learned from doing it." (Herrell, 2000, p. 160)

*Observation-based assessment* is used by a teacher to makes notes of students' learning behavior as they interact and communicate using language. Observations can be formal (e.g., miscue analyses) or informal (such as anecdotal reports to record students' telling a story, giving a report, or using oral language in other ways). Observations should extend across all areas of the curriculum and in all types of interactional situations to show students' progress. An observation checklist allows the teacher to circulate among students while they are working and monitor specific skills, such as emergent literacy skills, word identification skills, and oral reading (Miller, 1995).

---

**Best Practice** ANECDOTAL OBSERVATIONS

Mrs. Feingold keeps a pad of $3'' \times 3''$ sticky notes in the pocket of her jacket. When she observes a student's particular use of language, application of a particular learning style, or other noteworthy behavior, she jots the information on a note, including the student's name, date, and time of day. She then transfers this note to a small notebook for safekeeping. Periodically, she files the notes by transferring them to a sheet of paper in each student's file. Just before parent conferences, she duplicates this page—which contains as many as twelve notes side by side—as a permanent observational record of the student's language behaviors.

---

*Questionnaires and surveys* can help teachers learn about many students' skills and interests at once. These can be given at intervals throughout the year and stored in a student's portfolio.

*Scoring rubrics* created by teachers or obtained commercially can be determined in advance of an assignment, assisting both teacher and student by communicating in advance the basis for scoring. A rubric that provides clear criteria for scoring student work increases the consistency of assessment. It clarifies the expectations for the assignment so that students can focus on what is important; a family member who helps on an assignment can also see clearly what is expected. Using the rubric, students can monitor and critique their own work, adding to a sense of ownership of the knowledge they gain (Airasian, 2005). Rubistar is a free online resource that teachers can use to create rubrics (www.rubistar.com).

---

**Best Practice** DEVELOPING A SCORING RUBRIC

Rubrics are straightforward to develop.

1. First, the teacher identifies desired results. What should students *know* and *be able to do* at the end of the lesson/unit?
2. Then the teacher determines what is considered to be acceptable evidence: What performance (task) will the students do?
3. Finally, the connection to grading is set. What are the criteria for judging—the point values connected to each aspect of the work?
4. If time permits, examples of excellent, acceptable, and poor work help students visualize the grading criteria.
5. The use of a rubric encourages students to check their work against the criteria in a formative way before final grading. This enables "transparent" assessment, which keeps students informed of their progress.

---

**Checking for Comprehension** How does the teacher assess who understands instruction? One part of formative, or in-process, assessment is the use of teacher questions to check an

English learner's comprehension. Depending on the listening skills of the learner, the teacher must ask questions differently for differentiated levels of English proficiency.

At the beginning level, a learner can be asked questions that require a nonverbal answer, or a simple yes/no response: "Is this the Atlantic Ocean?" (pointing to a map). At the early intermediate level, a student can be asked a question requiring a one- or two-word response, or a simple phrase: "Is this the Atlantic or the Pacific Ocean?" At the intermediate level, students can answer in a sentence. "What happened when Columbus first landed?" At the early advanced and advanced levels, the teacher can follow up a single question with another to clarify the students' response or to ask for additional information. Thus, questions are tailored to the student's listening and speaking skills.

## Selecting and Using Appropriate Classroom Assessments

How does a teacher know what, when, and how to test English learners? Tests must be aligned with district curriculum requirements so that test results measure student progress on preselected benchmarks.

Empirical teaching is the foundation for providing additional mediation when necessary to promote the achievement of English learners. Using a variety of assessments the teacher ascertains the factors that contribute to a student's success or difficulties and then designs teaching methods linked to students' needs.

## Assigning Grades to English Learners

Grading and assessment issues concern teachers of all students, but teachers of English learners face additional challenges. English learners' limited English affects their ability to communicate their content knowledge. Should there be two standards of achievement, one for English learners and one for native speakers? Teachers and English learners may have different expectations and interpretations of the grade (Grognet, Jameson, Franco, & Derrick-Mescua, 2000). Answers to these issues are not easy. But by working collaboratively with other teachers in the school, an overall schoolwide plan can be developed.

A variety of approaches have been used to assign grades to English learners. Some schools that assign a *traditional A–F grade scale* in accordance with grade-level expectations do not lower performance standards for English learners in sheltered classes, although assignments are adjusted to meet the students' language levels. A *modified A–F grade scale* is used to assess students' work with an A–F grade based on achievement, effort, and behavior, and with report card grades modified by a qualifier signifying work performed above, at, or below grade level. A third type of grading system is the *pass/fail grade scale* used by schools whose English learners are integrated into the regular classroom. This scale avoids comparing the English learners with English-proficient classmates (From the Classroom, 1991).

Some schools have begun to assign a numerical grade according to a student's knowledge of state standards. For example, in second grade, if a child is required to "read fluently and accurately and with appropriate intonation and expression," the number grade reflects the mastery of this standard. Such ancillary factors as attendance and class participation do not influence this grade.

**Best Practice**    A GRADING AND ASSESSMENT PLAN

- Ensure that the school or school district has a fair policy for grading English learners that everyone follows.
- Grade a combination of *process* and *product* for all students.
- Early in the class, explain to students what and how you grade. Show examples of good, intermediate, and poor work.
- Use rubrics.
- Involve students in developing criteria for evaluating assignments and help them use these criteria to evaluate their own work.
- Use a variety of products to assess (some less dependent on fluent language skills, such as art projects, dramatizations, portfolios, and graphic organizers).
- Adapt tests and test administration (allow more time for English learners; read the test aloud).
- Teach test-taking skills and strategies.
- Grade beginning English learners as satisfactory/unsatisfactory or at/above/below expectations until the end of the year. Then assign a letter grade for the year.
- Put a note on the report card or transcript to identify the student as an English learner. Write comments to clarify how the student was graded. (Adapted from Grognet et al., 2000)

## Reporting Assessment Results to Parents

Teachers are expected to communicate the results of assessment to parents, whether with grades on a report card, through informal conferences (see Chapter 9), or by interpreting the results of standardized tests. Airasian (2005) advised teachers to start with general information about the test and its purpose when explaining standardized test scores. Describe the student's overall performance, with strengths and weaknesses; pick one or two areas (math and reading, for instance) and describe the percentile rank. To help the parent more fully understand the level of achievement, give the context of the student's general classroom performance. One does not need to explain everything on the test report; be brief, but accurate.

## Test Accommodation

Under certain conditions, the testing situation can be accommodated for English learners. Extended time, large-print format, audio cassette recording, or changes in presentation format may provide English learners with access to the test content without compromising test security or integrity.

Test administrators are too often unclear about which accommodations to use, for whom, and under what conditions. Given the potential consequences of test results, Abedi, Hofstetter, and Lord (2004) caution against a one-size-fits-all approach. Empirical research is needed to determine what kinds of accommodations are effective.

# Language and Content Area Assessment

Teachers with a flexible repertoire of assessment strategies can design instruction to provide a range of evidence that English learners are advancing in English proficiency and accessing the core curriculum. In an integrated lesson format, each lesson combines language-development objectives aligned with the ELD standards, subject matter objectives aligned with content standards, and learning-strategy objectives designed to teach cognitive academic language proficiency and thinking skills.

## Combining Language and Content Standards and Learning-Strategy Objectives

Objectives are necessary to guide teaching. A lesson with a clear objective focuses the instruction by concentrating on a particular goal and guides the teacher to select those learning activities that accomplish the goal. Once objectives are clearly stated, the teacher selects material that will help students achieve those objectives.

**Assessing Content Objectives**  Figure 3.1 displays an example lesson with three types of objectives: content, language, and learning strategy. State agencies, district planners, and school officials have developed curricular maps matched to state standards for each content area. Each lesson contains content area objectives drawn from these standards, with assessment to match the objectives.

For example, in a grade 2 science lesson, the objective might be to learn about balance in nature by sequencing the life cycle of the butterfly. This objective addresses the following California life science standard: "Plants and animals have predictable life cycles. As a basis for understanding this concept: Students know the sequential stages of life cycles are different for different animals, such as butterflies, frogs, and mice" (California Department of Education, 2006b, n.p.). The assessment would be designed to determine whether the students understood this concept.

**Assessing Language-Development Objectives**  Each content area has specific language demands. The teacher considers the various tasks that language users must be able to perform in the different content areas (e.g., describing in a literature lesson, classifying in a science lesson, justifying in a mathematics lesson, etc.). In selecting the language objectives, the teacher reviews the target ELD levels of the students and selects objectives that are compatible with the language required in the content lesson. All four language modes (listening, speaking, reading, writing) should be included in the planning across the period of a week. Assessment for these would allow the teacher to "check off" these objectives for each student.

**Assessing Learning-Strategy Objectives**  Learning strategies help students learn *how* to learn. Chamot (2009) divided strategies into three areas: cognitive, metacognitive, and social-affective. Each lesson should teach students a skill that helps them learn better. Whether or not they learn this skill should be assessed like any other objective.

FIGURE 3.1    Liberty: Content, Language, and Learning-Strategy Objectives

**Social-Studies-Content Objectives**

The students will . . .

Examine the causes and course of the American Revolution and the contributions of South Carolinians

Identify and explain historical, geographic, social, and economic factors that have helped shape American democracy

Describe the means by which Americans can monitor and influence government

**English-Language-Development Objectives**

The students will . . .

Listen to, speak, read, and write about subject matter information

Gather information both orally and in writing

Select, connect, and explain information

**Learning-Strategy Objectives**

The students will . . .

Apply basic reading comprehension skills (skimming, previewing, reviewing text)

Take notes to record important information and aid their own learning

Determine and establish the conditions that help them become effective learners (when, where, how to study)

*Source:* Adapted from Majors (n.d.).

## English-Language-Development Assessments

Various types of informal and formal ELD assessments are used depending on the language skill involved. In the domain of reading instruction, for example, teachers employ a variety of assessment tools, including informal reading inventories, literacy skill checklists, running records, miscue analysis, guided observations, and portfolio assessment (Swartz et al., 2003). The goals of reading instruction, in general, are to expand word recognition, comprehension, and analytic skills.

The goals of writing are similar; vocabulary usage, organization of thought, and ability to master conventional usage in punctuation and grammar are paramount. To this end, assessments in writing balance three major areas: attention to sentence and paragraph structure and organization of ideas, originality and depth of thought, and mechanics (Swartz, Klein, & Shook, 2002).

Listening and speaking skills are the most difficult to assess because in the case of listening the skill is receptive and hard to measure. Often, however, a student's listening affects classroom behavior directly, in that a student with underdeveloped listening skills may misunderstand oral directions and appear distracted or unresponsive. To assess speaking skills, teachers can plan specifically for oral interchange between students or between teacher and student, using simple rubrics to record performance in such areas as pronunciation, fluency, and intelligibility.

## Interpreting the Results of Assessment

Using a three-level rubric, a teacher can scale a student's performance on any objective, including the skills stipulated by the ELD standards. The student may achieve a secure proficiency in the skill and can move on, may need more guided or independent practice, or may be unable to perform the skill even with assistance. In the last case, it might be necessary to revisit the same skill at a lower level of the ELD framework; a student may need to be regrouped with others at a lower proficiency level until the preceding level of skill is secure and the student is ready to advance.

**Need-Driven Classroom-Based Interventions**  Students who are not meeting the ELD standards may need individual interventions that can be performed in the regular classroom by the teacher. These include teaching the student with modified input, such as multimodalities (audio-recording a reading passage, using manipulatives, or increased primary-language instruction). Other resources might be offered to the learner, such as a simplified text, additional review, study outlines, computer-assisted skill drills, or the services of an instructional aide. These interventions modify and differentiate instruction to address individual learning needs. More modifications are described in a later section about special education intervention.

**Scaffolding Assessments**  Scaffolding means building a temporary structure to support instruction that is removed once learning takes place. Assessments are sometimes scaffolded to get students started or to help them focus on the desired outcome. At a physical level, this can mean supplying a map with the major rivers already drawn for a geography test or supplying a chart for $x$ and $y$ values on an algebraic graphing test. More commonly, test questions are scaffolded by underlining key terms, dividing a test question into subsections, or providing direct reference to prior knowledge. These are considered temporary aids, in that a student will not need such assistance every time.

# Special Issues in Assessment

A variety of associated issues surrounds the education of English learners. Some pertain to the skills and abilities of the individual learner, whereas other issues have their origin in larger social or political factors. These include the placement of English learners in special education as well as issues of under- and overachievement in schools.

## Academic and Learning Difficulties That English Learners May Experience

Because English learners and students with learning disabilities can experience similar difficulties, it may be a challenge to determine whether a learning impairment is due to the students' second-language-acquisition process or to an underlying learning disability that warrants a special education placement. Gopaul-McNicol and Thomas-Presswood (1998) noted the following possible factors that may cause English learners and culturally different students to resemble students with learning disabilities, possibly resulting in overreferral for special education.

**Sound–Symbol Relationships**    If an English learner's home language is nonalphabetic, he or she may have difficulty with alphabetic letters. If a student is not literate in L1, he or she may have difficulty connecting sounds with symbols.

**Receptive Language**    An English learner at the beginner level may experience difficulty following directions and understanding complex language.

**Metacognition**    English learners from a nonliterate background may lack literacy behaviors and strategies, such as predicting, planning, and self-monitoring while reading.

**Information Retention**    Lack of cognates between the first and second language may hinder memory.

**Motor Control**    Cultural differences and lack of previous education can influence motor performance such as graphomotor (pencil) skills.

**Social–Emotional Functioning**    English learners may experience academic frustration and low self-esteem. This may lead to self-defeating behaviors such as learned helplessness. Limited second-language skills may influence social skills, friendships, and teacher–student relationships.

**Attending and Focusing**    English learners may exhibit behavior such as distractibility, short attention span, impulsivity, or high motor level (e.g., finger tapping, excessive talking, fidgeting, inability to remain seated). These may stem from cognitive overload when immersed in a second language for a long period of time.

**Culture/Language Shock**    Students experiencing culture or language shock may show uneven performance, refuse to volunteer, fail to complete work, or seek constant attention and approval from the teacher. The emotional reactions to long-term acculturation stress may lead to withdrawal, anger, or a pervasive sense of sadness.

## Identification, Referral, and Early Intervention of English Learners with Special Needs

Classroom teachers, along with parents and other school-site personnel, are responsible for identifying English learners with special instructional needs. When a classroom teacher initially identifies a student who may need additional mediation, a phase of intensive focus begins that may or may not result in a placement in special education. The classroom teacher's primary concern is to determine whether a student's academic or behavioral difficulties reflect factors other than disabilities, including inappropriate or inadequate instruction.

**The Referral Process**   The school screen team, school-site assessment council, or otherwise-named entity is a school-site committee that bears responsibility for receiving and acting on an initial referral by the classroom teacher for a student who is in need of additional mediation in learning. The team reviews the classroom teacher's specific concerns about the student and makes suggestions for modifying the learning environment for the student within the regular classroom. This process of gathering data and implementing changes in the educational environment before testing is called the period of initial intervention.

How can the classroom teacher decide whether a student might have a disability requiring referral to special education? Friend and Bursuck (2002) offered these questions as a means to assist the decision-making process:

- What are specific examples of a student's needs that are as yet unmet in the regular classroom?
- Is there a chronic pattern that negatively affects learning? Or, conversely, does the difficulty follow no clear pattern?
- Is the student's unmet need becoming more serious as time passes?
- Is the student's functioning significantly different from that of classmates?

**Early Intervention**   The classroom teacher implements strategies over a period of time and documents the effect these innovations have on the student. If a student is not responsive to alternative instructional or behavioral interventions over a period of several weeks or months, there is more of a chance that a placement in special education will be necessary (García & Ortiz, 2004; Ortiz, 2002). A key to the diagnosis of language-related disorders is the presence of similar patterns in both the primary and the second languages. Poor oral language/vocabulary development and lack of comprehension in both languages often indicate learning disabilities.

In California, as in many states, to determine whether a student has a learning disability, educators must ascertain the presence of "a disorder in one or more of the basic psychological processes" that "is not the result of environmental, cultural, or economic disadvantage" (CA Regs, 56337[b]). Moreover, tests must be provided and administered in the primary language, by "someone who is competent in the oral and written skills of the individual's primary language and who has a knowledge and understanding of the cultural and ethnic background of the pupil" (CA Regs 3023[a]; Figueroa, 2006). These and other guidelines help to ensure that testing is not biased against English learners, overreferring them to special education placement.

**Continued Services during and after Placement**   Working directly with the student, the classroom teacher may tutor or test the child in the curricular material used in the classroom; chart daily measures of the child's performance to see whether skills are being mastered; consult with other teachers on instructional interventions; devise tests based on the classroom curriculum; and train older peers, parent volunteers, and teacher aides to work with the student as tutors.

If the evaluation process results in the recommendation of special education services, the classroom teacher may help to write the student's individual education program (IEP). Collaboration between the classroom teacher, special educators, parents, and the student is vital to the drafting and approval of an IEP that will result in academic success.

## Teaching Strategies for the CLD Special Learner

Modified instruction can accommodate different instructional needs within the classroom and foster learning across academic content areas. *Inclusion* is a term often used to describe the provision of instruction within the conventional or mainstream classroom for students with special needs or talents. Although primarily associated with the education of exceptional students, this term has also been used for the varying degrees of inclusion of CLD learners in the mainstream classroom.

The mainstream classroom of an included student is a rich, nonrestrictive setting for content instruction and language development activities. The three components of an exemplary program for CLD learners—comprehensible instruction in the content areas using primary language and SDAIE, language arts instruction in English, and heritage- (primary) language maintenance or development—are present.

The teacher makes every effort to help the student be "as dynamically a part of the class as any student that is perceived as routinely belonging to that class" (Florida Department of Education, 2003, n.p.). Overall, teaching for inclusion features practices that showcase learners' strong points and support the areas in which they may struggle. By using a variety of interactive strategies, teachers have ample opportunity to discover which methods and activities correspond to student success.

The task for the teacher becomes more complex as the increasingly varied needs of students—those who are mainstream (non-CLD/non–special education), mainstream–special education, CLD learner, CLD learner–special education—are mixed in the same classroom.

**TABLE 3.4**   Strategies for Additional Mediation of the Listening Process for Included Students

| Phase | Strategies |
|---|---|
| Before listening | ■ Directly instruct listening strategies.<br>■ Arrange information in short, logical, well-organized segments.<br>■ Demonstrate ways to pay attention.<br>■ Preview the content with questions that require critical thinking.<br>■ Establish a listening goal for the lesson.<br>■ Provide prompts indicating that the information about to be presented is important enough to remember or write down. |
| During listening | ■ Actively involve students in rehearsing, summarizing, and taking notes.<br>■ Use purposeful, curriculum-related listening activities.<br>■ Model listening behavior and furnish peer models.<br>■ Teach students to attend to teacher cues and nonverbal signs that denote important information.<br>■ Provide verbal, pictorial, or written prelistening organizers to cue students to important information.<br>■ Show students how to self-monitor their listening behavior with self-questioning techniques and visual imagery while listening. |
| After listening | ■ Discuss content. Use teacher questions and prompts to cue student response (e.g., "Tell me more").<br>■ Integrate other language arts and content activities with listening as a follow-up. |

*Source:* Adapted from Mandlebaum & Wilson (1989).

Such complexity would argue that an inclusive classroom be equipped with additional educational resources, such as teaching assistants, lower student-to-teacher ratio, and augmented budget for instructional materials. The chief resource in any classroom, however, is the breadth and variety of instructional strategies on which the experienced teacher can draw. The following sections suggest multiple strategies in the areas of listening skills, reading, and writing.

**Adapting Listening Tasks**   Techniques for teaching listening skills have been grouped in Table 3.4 into the three phases of the listening process: before listening, during listening, after listening.

**Adapting Reading Tasks**   Reading assignments for inclusion students listed in Table 3.5 follow the three-part division of the reading process (before reading, during reading, and after reading).

**Adapting Writing Tasks**   Writing is used for two main purposes in classrooms: to capture and demonstrate content knowledge (taking notes, writing answers on assignments or tests) and to express creativity. If the acquisition of content knowledge is the goal, students can often use a variety of alternatives to writing that avoid large amounts of written work (both in class and homework). In general, teachers of students with special needs in inclusive settings change the response mode to oral when appropriate (Smith, Polloway, Patton, & Dowdy, 2003).

**TABLE 3.5**   Strategies for Additional Mediation of the Reading Process for Included Students

| Phase | Strategies |
|---|---|
| Before reading | ■ Preview reading materials to assist students with establishing purpose, activating prior knowledge, budgeting time, and focusing attention.<br>■ Explain how new content to be learned relates to content previously learned.<br>■ Create vocabulary lists and teach these words before the lesson to ensure that students know these vocabulary words rather than just recognize them.<br>■ Ensure that readability levels of the textbooks and trade books used in class are commensurate with the students' language levels.<br>■ Locate lower-reading-level supplements on the same topic so that tasks can be adapted to be multilevel and multimaterial.<br>■ Rewrite material (or solicit staff or volunteers to do so) to simplify the reading level or provide chapter outlines or summaries.<br>■ Tape text reading or have it read orally to a student. Consider the use of peers, volunteers, and/or paraprofessionals in this process. |
| During reading | ■ Highlight key words, phrases, and concepts with outlines or study guides.<br>■ Reduce extraneous noise.<br>■ Use visual aids (e.g., charts and graphs) to supplement reading tasks. |
| After reading | ■ When discussing stories, paraphrase material to clarify content.<br>■ Encourage feedback from students to check for understanding.<br>■ Reteach vocabulary to ensure retention.<br>■ Provide the page numbers where specific answers can be found in a reading comprehension/content assignment.<br>■ Use brief individual conferences with students to verify comprehension. |

*Source:* Adapted from Smith, Polloway, Patton, & Dowdy (2003).

Overall, the classroom teacher with a wide repertoire of strategies for instructing English learners will be able to employ these techniques to augment mainstream instruction whenever necessary. One caution, however: Learning English is not a compensatory endeavor, not a handicap. English learners are doing on a daily basis what the average resident of the United States cannot do—function in two languages. When successful, it is an intellectual triumph.

Regardless of how valid, reliable, and practical an assessment may be, if it serves only the teachers' and the institution's goals, the students' language progress may not be promoted. Assessment must instead be an integral part of a learning environment that encourages students to acquire a second language as a means to fulfill personal and academic goals.

Go to the Topics Assessment and Students with Special Needs in the MyEducationLab (www.myeducationlab.com) for your course, where you can:

- Find learning outcomes for Assessment and Students with Special Needs along with the national standards that connect to these outcomes.
- Complete Assignments and Activities that can help you more deeply understand the chapter content.
- Apply and practice your understanding of the core teaching skills identified in the chapter with the Building Teaching Skills and Dispositions learning units.
- Examine challenging situations and cases presented in the IRIS Center Resources.
- Check your comprehension on the content covered in the chapter by going to the Study Plan in the Book Resources for your text. Here you will be able to take a chapter quiz, receive feedback on your answers, and then access Review, Practice, and Enrichment activities to enhance your understanding of chapter content.

Go to the Topic A+RISE in the MyEducationLab (www.myeducationlab.com) for your course. A+RISE® Standards2Strategy™ is an innovative and interactive online resource that offers new teachers in grades K–12 just-in-time, research-based instructional strategies that:

- Meet the linguistic needs of ELLs as they learn content
- Differentiate instruction for all grades and abilities
- Offer reading and writing techniques, cooperative learning, use of linguistic and nonlinguistic representations, scaffolding, teacher modeling, higher order thinking, and alternative classroom ELL assessment
- Provide support to help teachers be effective through the integration of listening, speaking, reading, and writing along with the content curriculum
- Improve student achievement
- Are aligned to Common Core Elementary Language Arts standards (for the literacy strategies) and to English language proficiency standards in WIDA, Texas, California, and Florida.

# 4

# Programs for English Learners

English learners enter schooling fluent in a primary language other than English, a proficiency that can function as a resource. In many parts of the world, including Canada, second-language instruction is considered either a widely accepted component of being well educated or a legal mandate in an officially bilingual country. Acquiring a second language is not easy, especially to the level of using that language to succeed in postsecondary education. English learners face that challenge daily.

A growing number of schools in the United States offer two-way immersion programs that help English learners develop academic competence in their heritage language while acquiring fluency and literacy in English—at the same time, native-English-speaking students develop speaking fluency and academic competence in the home language of the English learners. These programs showcase the idea that *multicompetent language use* (Cook, 1999, p. 190) is a valuable skill. Proficiency in multiple languages is also a career enhancement in the modern world of global commerce.

The classrooms of the United States are increasingly diverse, with students coming from many countries of the world. The challenge to any English-language development program is to cherish and preserve the rich cultural and linguistic heritage of the students as they acquire English.

This chapter addresses the history, legality, and design of program models that induct speakers of other languages into English instruction. Although most of these programs take place at the elementary level, an increasing number of students immigrate to the United States at the middle and high school levels, and programs must be designed to meet their needs as well. The program models presented in this chapter vary greatly on one key dimension—how much encouragement is offered to students to maintain their primary language and how much instructional support they receive to accomplish this.

# The History of Multilingual Competency in the United States

Bilingualism has existed in the United States since the colonial period, but over the more than two centuries of American history it has been alternately embraced and rejected. The immigrant languages and cultures in North America have enriched the lives of the people in American communities, yet periodic waves of language restrictionism have virtually eradicated the capacity of many U.S. residents to speak a foreign or second language, even those who are born into families with a heritage language other than English. For English learners, English-only schooling has often brought difficulties, cultural suppression, and discrimination even as English has been touted as the key to patriotism and success. This section traces the origin and development of, and support for, language services for English learners in the United States.

## Early Bilingualism in the United States

At the time of the nation's founding, at least twenty languages could be heard in the American colonies, including Dutch, French, German, and numerous Native-American languages. In 1664 at least eighteen colonial languages were spoken on Manhattan Island. Bilingualism was common among both the working and educated classes, and schools were established to preserve the linguistic heritage of new arrivals. The Continental Congress published many official documents in German and French as well as in English. German schools were operating as early as 1694 in Philadelphia, and by 1900 more than 4 percent of the United States' elementary school population was receiving instruction either partially or exclusively in German. In 1847, Louisiana authorized instruction in French, English, or both at the request of parents. The Territory of New Mexico authorized Spanish–English bilingual education in 1850 (Crawford, 1999). Table 4.1 surveys the early history of language use and policy in America.

Although there were several such pockets of acceptance for bilingual education, other areas of the country effectively restricted or even attempted to eradicate immigrant and minority languages. In 1879, the federal government forced Native-American children to attend off-reservation, English-only schools where they were punished for using their native language. In the East, as large numbers of Eastern Europeans immigrated, descendants of the English settlers began to harbor resentment against these newcomers. New waves of Mexican and Asian immigration in the West brought renewed fear of non-English influences (Crawford, 1999).

---

**Best Practice**   EARLY CHEROKEE LANGUAGE RIGHTS

Under an 1828 treaty, the U.S. government recognized the language rights of the Cherokee tribe. Eventually, the Cherokees established a twenty-one-school educational system that used the Cherokee syllabary to achieve a 90 percent literacy rate in the native language. About 350,000 Aniyunwiya (Cherokee) people currently live primarily in Oklahoma and North Carolina, and about 22,000 speak the language (which today is known as Tsalagi). (www.native-languages.org/cherokee.htm)

---

**TABLE 4.1**   Early History of Language Use and Policy in America

| Date | Event | Significance |
| --- | --- | --- |
| Pre-1492 | North America is rich in indigenous languages. | Linguistic diversity is a type of biodiversity, encoding millennia of information about the physical and social environment. |
| 16th century | Spain establishes missions in what is now California. | Spanish rulers decree the replacement of indigenous languages by Spanish. |
| 1781 | U.S. Articles of Confederation are written in English, French, and German. | Early acknowledgment of U.S. multilingualism on the part of the Founding Fathers. |
| 1800s | European Americans settle Western U.S. | Mexicans and Indians are excluded from Whites-only schools. |
| 1828 | U.S. government signs a treaty with Cherokee tribes. | The U.S. government recognizes the language rights of the Cherokee tribes. Eventually, a twenty-one-school educational system achieves a 90 percent literacy rate in Cherokee. |
| 1839 | Ohio adopts bilingual education. | Schools could operate in German and English by parental request. |
| 1848 | Mexican territory is annexed to the United States in the Treaty of Guadalupe Hidalgo. | Mexican residents of appropriated territory in what are now California, Arizona, New Mexico, Texas, Utah, and Nevada are promised the right to use Spanish in schools, courts of law, employment, and everyday life. |
| 1864 | The federal government forces Native-American children to attend off-reservation schools. | Schools are English-only. Native Americans are punished for using their native language. |
| 1888 | First antibilingual education legislation is passed. | Wisconsin and Illinois attempt to institute English-only schooling. |
| 1898 | U.S. wins Spanish–American War and colonizes Puerto Rico and the Philippines. | Public and private schools are forced to use English as the language of instruction. Submersion in English is a sustained policy in Puerto Rican schools until the 1950s. |

## The Struggles for Language Education Rights in the Twentieth Century

World War I brought anti-German hysteria, and various states began to criminalize the use of German in all areas of public life. Subsequently, fifteen states legislated English as the basic language of instruction. This repressive policy continued during World War II, when Japanese-language schools were closed. Until the late 1960s, "Spanish detention"—being kept after school for using Spanish—remained a formal punishment in the Rio Grande Valley of Texas, where using a language other than English as a medium of public instruction was a crime (Crawford, 1999).

Although the U.S. Supreme Court, in the *Meyer v. Nebraska* case (1923), extended the protection of the Constitution to everyday speech and prohibited coercive language restriction on the part of states, the "frenzy of Americanization" (Crawford, 1999) had fundamentally changed public attitudes toward learning in other languages. European immigrant groups felt strong pressures to assimilate, and bilingual instruction by the late 1930s was virtually eradicated throughout the United States. This assimilationist mentality worked best with northern European immigrants. For other language minorities, especially those with dark complexions, English-only schooling brought difficulties. Discrimination and cultural repression became associated with linguistic repression.

After World War II, writers began to speak of language-minority children as being "culturally deprived" and "linguistically disabled." The cultural deprivation theory pointed to such environmental factors as inadequate English-language skills, lower-class values, and parental failure to stress educational attainment. On the basis of their performance on IQ tests administered in English, a disproportionate number of English learners ended up in special classes for the educationally handicapped.

Bilingual education was reborn in the early 1960s in Dade County, Florida, as Cuban immigrants, fleeing the 1959 revolution, requested bilingual schooling for their children. The first program at the Coral Way Elementary School was open to both English and Spanish speakers. The objective was fluency and literacy in both languages. Subsequent evaluations of this bilingual program showed success both for English-speaking students in English and for Spanish-speaking students in Spanish and English. Hakuta (1986) reported that by 1974 there were 3,683 students in bilingual programs in the elementary schools nationwide and approximately 2,000 in the secondary schools.

## Legal and Legislative Mandates Supporting Language Education Rights

Progress in English-language development services in the United States has taken place on three fronts: cultural, legislative, and judicial. Culturally, the people of the United States have seemed to accept bilingualism when it has been economically useful and to reject it when immigrants were seen as a threat. Legislative and judicial mandates have reflected this ambivalence.

After the civil rights era, the provision of services for English learners has been viewed as a right. This is consonant with the Universal Declaration of Linguistic Rights signed in Barcelona in June 1996, the 1948 Universal Declaration of Human Rights, and the Declaration on the Rights of Persons Belonging to National, Ethnic, Religious and Linguistic Minorities of the General Assembly of the United Nations (1992).

**Lau v. Nichols**    In 1973 a group of non-English-speaking Chinese students sued San Francisco Unified School District officials, claiming that "sink or swim" instruction (denial of language development services) was a violation of their civil rights under Title VI of the Civil Rights Act of 1964. Lower federal courts had absolved the school district of any responsibility for minority children's "language deficiency." But a unanimous Supreme Court ruled as follows: "There is no equality of treatment merely by providing students with the same facilities, textbooks, teachers, and curriculum, for students who do not understand English are effectively foreclosed from any meaningful education"—essentially stating that imposing the requirement that a child must have basic skills in English before effectively participating in the educational program is "to make a mockery of public education" (414 U.S. 563).

Although *Lau v. Nichols* did not specify what type of program a school district must offer, the Chinese parents who sued the San Francisco Unified School District formed an advisory committee, and eventually a program emerged that satisfied the requirements set forth by the court.

The May 25 (1975) Memorandum from the Office for Civil Rights (also called the Lau Remedies) mandated that school districts with more than 5 percent national-origin minority children must offer special language instruction for students with a limited command of English. To be in compliance with *Lau v. Nichols,* the Lau Remedies are still used as the required elements in most states. They prohibit the assignment of students to classes for the handicapped on the basis of their English-language skills, disallow placing such students in vocational tracks instead of teaching them English, and mandate that administrators communicate with parents in a language they can understand.

Because the states reserve the right to dictate educational policy, services for English learners have depended on the vagaries of state law. When the U.S. Congress enacted legislation to begin Title VII of the Elementary and Secondary Education Act, federal funding became available for bilingual education programs. Almost simultaneously, the courts began to rule that students deprived of bilingual education must receive compensatory services. Together, the historical precedents, federal legislative initiatives, and judicial fiats combined to establish bilingual education in the United States (see Tables 4.2 and 4.3).

---

**Best Practice**   **INDIGENOUS LANGUAGE RIGHTS**

Times have changed for Native-American-language speakers. In the United States, 281,990 families speak an American-Indian home language (www.infoplease.com/ipa/A0192523. html). The most-spoken Native-American language is Navajo, with 150,000 speakers. In 1990 the U.S. Congress passed Public Law 101-477, which sustains the right of Native Americans to express themselves through the use of Native-American languages in any public proceeding, including publicly supported education programs. Among the goals of this law are the following:

- Preserve, protect, and promote the rights and freedom of Native Americans to use, practice, and develop Native-American languages
- Increase student success and performance
- Promote students' awareness and knowledge of their culture and history
- Enhance student and community pride

---

# Federal and State Requirements for ELD Services

Successive authorizations of the federal Elementary and Secondary Education Act in 1968, 1974, 1978, 1988, and 1989 incorporated federal recognition of the unique educational disadvantages faced by non-English-speaking students. In 1968, Congress authorized $7.5 million to finance seventy-six bilingual education projects serving 27,000 children. In 1974, Congress specifically linked equal educational opportunity to bilingual education, allowing Native-American and

**TABLE 4.2**  The Early Twentieth Century: Language Use and Policy Are Contested in the United States

| Date | Event | Significance |
|---|---|---|
| 1906 | Congress passes English requirement for naturalized citizenship. | First national English-language requirement |
| 1917–1918 | The governor of Iowa bans the use of any foreign language in public. Ohio passes legislation to remove all uses of German from the state's elementary schools. | With German speakers as the target, mobs raid schools and burn German textbooks. Subsequently, fifteen states legislate English as the basic language of instruction. |
| 1920s–1970s | Ku Klux Klan members in Maine, numbering 150,141 in 1925, burn crosses in hostility to French Americans. | French is forbidden to be spoken in schools in Maine. |
| 1923 | *Meyer v. Nebraska* | The Supreme Court bans an English-only law in a case brought by German Americans. |
| 1930 | *Del Rio Independent School District v. Salvatierra* | A Texas superior court finds that the Del Rio Independent school district cannot segregate Mexican students, but a higher court rules that the segregation is necessary to teach English to Mexican students. |
| 1931 | *Lemon Grove v. Álvarez* | A state superior court rules that school segregation is against the law in California. |
| 1936 | Massive IQ testing of Puerto Ricans in New York is used to justify widespread school placement of Spanish-speaking children two to three years below grade level. | Thousands of New York Puerto Ricans launch a campaign for bilingual education. |
| 1941 | Japanese-language schools are closed. | Japanese are incarcerated in internment camps with English-only schools. |
| 1946, 1947 | *Méndez v. Westminster School District* | The U.S. Ninth District Court applies the 14th Amendment to schools, insisting "schools must be open to all children . . . regardless of lineage." |
| 1961 | Immigrants fleeing the Cuban revolution demand Spanish-language schooling. | Dade County, Florida, implements Spanish–English bilingual education. |
| 1968 | 10,000 Chicanos boycott schools in Los Angeles demanding bilingual education and more Latino teachers; boycotts spread across U.S. | Leaders of Los Angeles boycott are arrested; two years later charges against them are declared unconstitutional. |

**TABLE 4.3**   Key Legislation and Court Cases in the Struggle for English Learners' Language Rights

| Date | Event | Significance |
| --- | --- | --- |
| 1964 | The Civil Rights Act: Title VI | Prohibits denial of equal access to education on the basis of race, color, national origin, or limited proficiency in English in the operation of a federally assisted program. Compliance is enforced through the United States Office for Civil Rights. |
| 1968 | ESEA Title VII offers funding for bilingual education programs. | First bilingual kindergarten in New York City; first bilingual education major at Brooklyn College. |
| Early 1970s | Bilingual programs reach only one out of every forty Mexican-American students in the Southwest. | Based on these data, the U.S. Office of Civil Rights begins enforcing compliance with judicial mandates. |
| 1972 | *Serna v. Portales Municipal Schools* | The first federal court enforcement of Title VI of the Civil Rights Act. A federal judge orders instruction in native language and culture as part of a desegregation plan. |
| 1973 | *Keyes v. School District No. 1, Denver, Colorado* | Latinos must be covered by *Brown v. Board of Education*—Mexicans cannot be labeled "White" and used to create falsely desegregated schools containing only Blacks and Latinos. |
| 1974 | The Equal Education Opportunities Act (EEOA) (U.S. Congress) | "No state shall deny equal educational opportunities to an individual on account of his or her race, color, sex, or national origin by the failure of an educational agency to take appropriate action to overcome language barriers that impede equal participation by its students in its instructional programs." |
| 1974 | *Lau v. Nichols* (414 U.S. 563) | U.S. Supreme Court establishes the right of students to differential treatment based on their language minority status, but it does not specify a particular instructional approach. |
| 1975 | Lau Remedies—guidelines from the U.S. Commissioner of Education | Standardized requirements for identification, testing, and placement into bilingual programs. Districts are told how to identify and evaluate children with limited English skills, what instructional treatments to use, when to transfer children to all-English classrooms, and what professional standards teachers need to meet. |
| 1977 | *Ríos v. Read* | A federal court rules that a bilingual program must include a cultural component. |

*(continued)*

**TABLE 4.3** Continued

| Date | Event | Significance |
|------|-------|-------------|
| 1981 | *Castañeda v. Pickard* | The Fifth Circuit Court tests the 1974 EEOA statute, outlining three criteria for programs serving EL students. District programs must be: (1) based on "sound educational theory," (2) "implemented effectively" through adequately trained personnel and sufficient resources, and (3) evaluated as effective in overcoming language barriers. Qualified bilingual teachers must be employed, and children are not to be placed on the basis of English-language achievement tests. |
| 1982 | *Plyler v. Doe* | The U.S. Supreme Court decides that a state's statute that denies school enrollment to children of illegal immigrants "violates the Equal Protection Clause of the Fourteenth Amendment." |
| 1987 | *Gómez v. Illinois State Board of Education* | State school boards can enforce state and federal compliance with EEOA regulations. Districts must properly serve students who are limited in English. |
| 1990 | Florida Consent Decree | A federal district court can mandate and monitor statewide teacher preparation and school districts' English learner education. |
| 1994 | California passes Proposition 187, which makes it illegal to provide public education to illegal immigrants. | Proposition is overturned in the courts because it violates *Plyler v. Doe.* |
| 1998 | California voters approve Unz Initiative Proposition 227 (ED Code 300-340). | Requires that K–12 instruction be overwhelmingly in English, restricting use of primary language as a means of instruction. Subsequent measures pass in Arizona and Massachusetts, but French speakers vote down similar initiative in Maine. |
| 2001 | No Child Left Behind Act, Title III | Federal funding is available to support schools in educating English learners. |
| 2004 | Individuals with Disabilities Education Improvement Act of 2004 (IDEA), Public Law 108-446 | Congress aligns education of children with disabilities with NCLB to mandate equity and accountability. |
| 2004 | *Williams et al. v. State of California et al.* | California schools must provide equitable access to textbooks, facilities, and teaching staffs, including teachers of English learners. |

*Note:* See also Crawford (2004, pp. 96–97) for expanded timeline, "Linguistic Diversity in America."

*Sources:* Cockcroft, 1995; Crawford, 1999; Wiese & García, 1998.

English-speaking children to enroll in bilingual education programs, and funding programs for teacher training, technical assistance for program development, and development and dissemination of instructional materials.

In 1978, Congress added to the definition of bilingual education, stipulating that instruction in English should "allow a child to achieve competence in the English language." Additionally, parents were included in program planning, and personnel in bilingual programs were to be proficient in the language of instruction and English. In 1988, Congress increased funding to state education agencies, placed a three-year limit on participation in transitional bilingual programs, and created fellowship programs for professional training. Developmental bilingual programs were expanded to maintain the native language of students in the reauthorization of 1989.

When the Elementary and Secondary Education Act of 1965 was amended and reauthorized in 1994, it was within the framework of Goals 2000, with the goal to "educate limited-English-proficient children and youth to meet the same rigorous standards for academic achievement expected of all children and youth" ([7102][b]). This emphasis on standards was the linchpin of the 2001 reauthorization, the No Child Left Behind Act, in which all schools are required to provide qualified teachers, and all students are required to pass standardized tests.

## No Child Left Behind

Under the No Child Left Behind Act, states must measure student progress on statewide achievement tests. Title III of this act, titled "Language Instruction for Limited English Proficient and Immigrant Students," proposes to measure the progress of English learners against common expectations for student academic achievement by aligning academic assessments, teacher preparation and training, curriculum, instructional materials, and state academic standards.

The purpose of Title III is to upgrade schooling for low-achieving children in the highest-poverty schools, including limited-English-proficient children. The goal is to hold schools, local educational agencies, and states accountable for improving the academic achievement of all students, potentially by closing underperforming schools or providing high-quality educational alternatives to students in such schools.

Because English learners must be tested annually after thirty months of schooling (with few exceptions), and because the continued existence of the school is predicated on annual improvement, English learners experience high-stakes pressure to test well. No second-language acquisition theory in existence makes the claim that the high anxiety of testing furthers language learning. Often, "teaching to the test" leaves little room for teaching English. NCLB, then, appears to be an unfortunate fit with what is known about effective second-language learning.

## The Florida Consent Decree

In 1990, a broad coalition of civil rights organizations involved in educational issues signed a consent decree giving the United States District Court, Southern District of Florida, the power to enforce an agreement with the Florida State Board of Education regarding the identification and provision of services to students whose native language is other than English. This remains the most extensive set of state mandates for the education of English learners.

The consent decree settlement terms mandate that six issues be addressed:

- *Identification and assessment.* National origin data of all students must be collected and retained in school districts, which must also form committees to oversee the assessment, placement, and reclassification of English learners.
- *Equal access to appropriate programming.* School districts must provide equal education opportunities for academic advancement and language support to English learners, including provisos for enhancing crosscultural understanding and self-esteem.
- *Equal access to appropriate categorical and other programming for limited-English-proficient (LEP) students.* Schools must provide programs for compensatory education, exceptional students, dropout prevention, student service, pre-kindergarten, immigrant students, Chapter 1, pre–first grade classes, home–school, and discipline.
- *Personnel.* Teachers must have various levels of ESOL endorsement.
- *Monitoring.* Procedures must be followed by the Florida Department of Education to determine the extent to which school districts comply with the requirements of the agreement.
- *Outcome measures.* Mechanisms must be instituted to assess whether student achievement is improved as a result of applying the implementation guidelines.

## Proposition 227 in California

In 1998, California, with a school enrollment of approximately 1.4 million limited-English-proficient children, passed Proposition 227, a measure rejecting bilingual education. The proposition stipulates that

> all children in California public schools shall be taught English by being taught in English. In particular, this shall require that all children be placed in English language classrooms. Children who are English learners shall be educated through sheltered English immersion during a temporary transition period not normally intended to exceed one year. . . . Once English learners have acquired a good working knowledge of English, they shall be transferred to English language mainstream classrooms. (California State Code of Regulations [CSCR], 1998, Article 2, 305)

Article 3, Provision 310 of the CSCR provided parents with waiver possibilities if their children met criteria spelled out in the law: "Under such parental waiver conditions, children may be transferred to classes where they are taught English and other subjects through bilingual education techniques or other generally recognized educational methodologies permitted by law." Before parents can ask for a waiver, however, a student must sit through thirty days of structured English immersion (SEI). Potentially one-ninth of a school year could pass before an English learner at the beginning level could comprehend instruction. Unfortunately, expecting children to learn English (along with academic subjects) in a single year flies in the face of contemporary research on language acquisition (Collier, 1987).

Empirical evidence is lacking that indicates any benefit to language-minority students from passage of Proposition 227. A summary of findings from ten studies conducted by research institutes and scholars affiliated with major California universities found that Proposition 227 had shown considerable disruption to the education of language-minority students with no demonstrable benefits in terms of improved teaching and learning conditions or academic achievement (García, 2000).

A study released by the University of California's Linguistic Minority Research Institute (Gándara, Maxwell-Jolly, García, Asato, Gutiérrez, Stritkus, & Curry, 2000) described the implementation of Proposition 227 in sixteen school districts and twenty-five schools throughout the state. The report documents wide variation in the ways school districts have interpreted 227's requirements. School districts with a strong English-only stance before passage showed a mean decrease in primary-language instruction from 17 percent in 1998 to 2 percent in 1999. In contrast, districts with strong primary-language instruction programs experienced only a 2 percent lower rate of Spanish use, from 33 to 31 percent, because parents applied for and were granted waivers.

Language census figures from the California Department of Education show that since Proposition 227 took effect in 1998, three out of five children this law was designed to help remain limited in English, even as the number of English learners statewide has grown nearly 14 percent, to 193,376. Annual redesignation rates remain basically unchanged. Almost one-half million children have been "mainstreamed" to regular classrooms where they receive little or no language support, even though they may still be in need of ELD services. At least 141,428 English learners remain in fully bilingual classrooms at parental request.

Unz's success in California in 1998 led him to fund subsequent propositions in Arizona and Massachusetts (2000) that were successful, as well as one in Colorado (2002) that was defeated. His national organization English for the Children continues to fund antibilingual education efforts (see Stensland, 2003).

## Williams et al. v. State of California et al.

In 2000, in a class action lawsuit, a group of plaintiffs, including Eliezer Williams, represented by the Mexican American Legal Defense and Educational Fund (MALDEF) sued the State of California, the California Department of Education, the California Board of Education, and the California Superintendent of Public Instruction on behalf of 75,000 public school students, alleging that substandard conditions in California schools were causing deprivation in violation of the equal protection clauses of the California Constitution. The lawsuit claimed that the students in question had suffered from poorly trained teachers, serious overcrowding, inadequate physical conditions for schooling (filthy bathrooms, leaky roofs, and nonfunctioning heating and cooling systems), and insufficient or outdated textbooks.

A settlement was reached requiring the State of California to pass legislation mandating that every school district provide a uniform process for complaints regarding insufficient instructional materials, unsafe or unhealthy facility conditions, and teacher vacancies and misassignments. Such a law was signed into effect in 2004. Funding was also provided for facilities repair, new instructional materials, upgraded education for teachers of English learners, and phasing out of multitrack schools in the lowest-performing schools. In return for these provisions, the plaintiffs in *Williams v. California* agreed not to initiate lawsuits for redress until a period of four years had elapsed.

This lawsuit should inaugurate a renewed emphasis on the preparation of teachers for classrooms of English learners, as well as improve the learning conditions in California's underperforming schools. For information on the impact of this case, see American Civil Liberties Union (ACLU) Foundation of Southern California (2007).

## What Is "Fully Qualified" under NCLB?

It is imperative that teachers are able to understand fundamental principles about second-language acquisition and to communicate, to some degree, with those students acquiring English. Therefore, for teachers to be fully qualified as required by the No Child Left Behind legislation, one might ask, "To be considered 'fully qualified' should teachers acquire at least a basic linguistic competency in the languages that students speak?"

The convenient and widely accepted mythology in the United States that a person can be well educated and remain monolingual is questionable with regard to being "fully qualified." The Hispanic population has become the largest minority in the United States, and educators who are able to augment their teaching using both second-language acquisition principles and Spanish-language skills are increasingly needed. Furthermore, teachers with linguistic competence can enhance the stature of the U.S. educational system in the eyes of the world, as U.S. citizens will no longer be viewed by linguistically multicompetent world citizens as being linguistically handicapped by monolingualism.

# The Politics of Bilingual Education

Perceptive teachers realize that the topic of provision of services for English learners is surrounded by political debate. Given the fact that few Americans engage in controversy about second-language acquisition, it is obvious that the underlying arguments for or against bilingual education probably have to do with attitudes about immigration and the role of language in public life. This controversy will continue as Spanish speakers surpass African Americans as the largest minority population in the United States. These arguments treat three main topics: the wisdom of supporting heritage-language proficiency, the role of the native English speaker in bilingual education, and the movement to establish governmental English-only policies. A fourth important aspect, Native-American language revitalization, is less controversial but no less important.

## Support for Heritage-Language Proficiency

Developmental bilingual programs are designed for students who enter schooling with a primary language other than English. The goals of developmental bilingual programs are maintenance and full development of the student's primary language; full proficiency in all aspects of English; grade-appropriate achievement in all domains of academic study; integration into all-English-language classrooms; and positive identification with both the culture of the primary- and the majority-language group (Cloud, Genesee, & Hamayan, 2000).

Monolingual English voters outnumber bilingual voters—for example, 61 percent of voters in California are White (presumably monolingual), whereas only 16 percent of voters are Hispanic despite making up 30 percent of the population. Changing the political climate from the current hostility to bilingual education will take a commitment on the part of English-only voters to foster heritage-language skills. Many heritage-language speakers enjoy and seek to preserve their primary language as a cultural and economic resource. Because Spanish is the third most widely spoken language in the world, Spanish–English bilingualism is a distinct competitive advantage in the local and global marketplace, a valuable asset not only for bilingual individuals but also for society as a whole.

## Support for Two-Way (Dual) Immersion

For parents of English speakers to start their child's second-language instruction in elementary school, they must seek to maintain or establish two-way immersion (TWI) language programs in conjunction with parents of language-minority students. In this model, English learners from a single language background are taught in the same classroom with approximately equal numbers of English-speaking students. Grade-level-approximate curriculum is provided in both languages. Speakers of each language develop proficiency in both their native and second language, achieve academically through and in two languages, and come to appreciate each other's language and culture (Lindholm, 1994).

One advocate of TWI found that this model promises "mutual learning, enrichment, and respect"; is "the best possible vehicle for integration of language minority students, since these students are grouped with English-speakers for natural and equal exchange of skills"; and is "particularly appealing because it not only enhances the prestige of the minority language but also offers a rich opportunity for expanding genuine bilingualism to the majority population" (Porter, 1990, p. 154). Cummins (2000a) argued that "a major advantage of two-way bilingual programs . . . is that they overcome segregation in a planned program that aims to enrich the learning opportunities of both minority- and majority-language students" (p. 142).

The politics of TWI are such that two distinct types of parents have sought and attained such programs in their communities. The first are the liberal, middle-class Whites who have seen the success of Canadian schools in promoting dual-language competence in English and French and have forged alliances with Spanish-speaking parents (for example, in Long Beach, California; Evanston, Illinois; and Alexandria, Virginia) or French-speaking parents (in the International School of Tucson French Program). The second group comprises parents who are not heritage speakers of a language but who want their children to regain the heritage language (for example, Spanish in Ontario-Montclair School District, California, or in San Antonio, Texas; Cantonese in San Francisco; or Navajo in Chinle, Arizona).

Parents of native-English-speaking children who advocate for the establishment of such a program for their children become advocates for language maintenance on the part of English learners. These parents see advantages in their children learning academic and social skills in two languages, and parents of English learners see that the home language is valued.

## English-Only Efforts

The politics of the U.S. English-only movement are driven by an assimilationist model in the belief that for many immigrants the ability to speak English is a necessity for access to the American middle class. However, as Mora (2002) noted, "this outdated image of the assimilation process ignores the multiple patterns of acculturation for different ethnic groups, many of whom enjoy and preserve their bilingualism as an important cultural and economic resource" (n.p.). Therefore, the idea that the majority should enforce monolingualism on a linguistic minority amounts to linguistic authoritarianism.

English-only bills in the U.S. Congress have repeatedly been defeated. Crawford (2006) described English-only efforts as the politics of fear:

> English Only has always been about fear. Fear of demographic and cultural change, as American communities are transformed by immigrants. Fear of strangers speaking Spanish in public places or posting business signs in Chinese. Fear among Anglos about losing their majority status and, with it, their political dominance. Fear of "the other." (n.p.)

Evidence has shown repeatedly that English learners are more successful when given a firm foundation in their primary language (c.f. Ramírez, 1992) and that bilingualism offers a cognitive advantage (Cummins, 1976). To insist that the United States revert to an outmoded model of monolingualism is to attempt to turn back the clock to an era of language restrictionism, a poor move in a world in which bilingual skills are in increasing demand.

## Language Revitalization

Many American Indian languages are undergoing revitalization, attempts to preserve endangered languages. Of the more than 800 Amerindian languages, including those in Central and South America, 500 are endangered or worse. In North America even relatively "healthy" languages such as Cherokee—spoken by 22,000 people—are threatened by low percentages of children learning the languages.

American Indian languages in the United States were deliberately destroyed as Indians were separated from their linguistic kin and resettled hundreds of miles away with individuals from other tribes who could not understand each other. Sending Indian children to boarding schools and punishing them for speaking their languages also caused linguistic devastation; for example, the percentage of Cherokee children being raised bilingually fell from 75 percent to 5 percent during the boarding-school-policy days. Other languages with fewer users died entirely. However, without such radical eradication policies, indigenous languages can persist for centuries. (In Paraguay, for example, more than 90 percent of the population is bilingual in Spanish and Guarani.)

Now that the Amerindian languages of North America are in such a precarious situation, simply leaving them alone will not diminish their extinction trends. However, languages can be revitalized by inspiring younger generations to take an interest and pride in ancestral languages and by providing learning opportunities for them. Navajo, for instance, was in steep decline until the 1940s, when the language was used by the Navajo code talkers to thwart the Germans and Japanese in World War II, causing its prestige to soar and numbers of users to increase steadily (Redish, 2001). Ironically, Indian casino gaming has furnished profits for tribes to pay for language classes, a hopeful trend toward language revitalization

# Empowerment Issues Related to English Learners

Despite the fact that research has shown the effectiveness of educational programs that support and develop a student's primary language, very few students have ever been fully served with bilingual education programs; for example, in California only 8 percent of students received bilingual education services before Proposition 227 (Mora, 2002). Therefore, one must ask, in a social climate that does not support primary-language programs for students, how can English learners nonetheless be supported? How can communities empower themselves to ensure that language-minority students receive educational equity?

One answer—equivalent to the real estate mantra "location, location, location"—is the political mantra "lawyers, lawyers, lawyers." MALDEF's victory in *Williams et al. v. State of California et al.* has provided school district–based means for families to submit grievances about poor facilities and resources. School authorities can also do much to create a positive affective environment for all students, communicating that school and the family are partners in education. They can respect parent program choices by encouraging parents to seek out primary-language maintenance programs and by staffing such programs in each neighborhood school rather than forcing families to bus their children to magnet programs.

Cummins (1989, 1996) contrasted educational practices that serve as *collaborative* relations of power with those that are *coercive*. Cummins cautioned that children who enter schools in which diversity is *not* affirmed soon perceive that their "difference" is not honored. Often English learners are not encouraged to think critically, to reflect, and to solve problems. This attitude on the part of teachers communicates a sense of reduced worth, resulting in poor motivation to achieve.

Pressuring students to conform to schooling practices that are unfair or discriminatory results in a loss of their identity as human beings. Teachers who are dedicated to social change must help students develop the confidence and motivation to succeed academically; they must also be aware of the ways in which spoken and unspoken language can encourage positive attitudes, building strong personal and social identities.

## Equity and Policy Issues Related to English Learners

Achieving high-quality education for English learners has been a centuries-long struggle in the United States. Judging from many measures (e.g., achievement gap, dropout rates, expulsion and detention rates, retention/promotion, tracking, access to AP classes, segregation, length of program, special education placements, gifted education placements, teacher qualifications, teacher retention, and funding and resources), the struggle is by no means over (Donato, 1997; Mora, 2000; Rumbaut, 1995).

Among the indicators that language-minority students have not done well in schools is the fact that nationally Latino students (30.3 percent of whom are limited-English-speaking) are behind their peers in grades 4 and 8, with more than 50 percent below the basic level in reading and math. Latino students are being taught by less qualified teachers, have less access to high-level rigorous classes, are enrolled in fewer college prep courses, and receive fewer state and local funds. More than 40 percent of the teachers teaching English-as-a-second language/bilingual classes are not certified to teach bilingual education or ESL (Gutiérrez & Rodríguez, 2005). Only 9.9 percent of Hispanics/Latinos have a college degree, and 48.5 percent do not have a high school diploma.

Statistics show poor progress as well for Cambodian students (56 percent of whom are limited-English-speaking); only 6 percent of this population have a college degree. Pacific Islanders, however, show a high college enrollment—35.4 percent (compared with 26.1 percent for Whites). Available data show that 31.3 percent of Chinese are not proficient in English, yet

46.3 percent have college degrees; 32.9 percent of Koreans are not proficient in English yet have a 43.6 percent rate of attaining a college degree (www.asian-nation.org).

There is no question that the public climate of support affects the supply of teachers with expertise in educating English learners. Gándara and colleagues (2000) found that between 1997–1998 and 1998–1999, the year of implementation of Proposition 227 in California, the number of credentialed bilingual teachers in California using their bilingual credential in a teaching assignment with language-minority students dropped by 32 percent. In 1998, 10,894 teacher candidates had bilingual certification; in 1999, that number was reduced to 5,670. The number of teacher candidates earning a credential with a crosscultural, language, and academic development (CLAD) endorsement, meanwhile, rose only 11 percent (Gándara et al., 2000). This does not bode well for staffing the classrooms of English learners, at least in California.

## Components of ELD Programs

In the widely varied climate of support from area to area in the United States, educational programs range from those that promote additive bilingualism to those that in effect eradicate primary-language proficiency. At the same time as learning English, the language-minority student must gain adequate access to academic content, so a comprehensive program must make

*Dual-language programs encourage students from two different languages to teach one another their languages.*

Lindfors Photography

provisions for both English and academic learning (and, ideally, a primary-language maintenance component to ensure content and language development in L1). The following sections offer a representative set of the main program types, with the acknowledgment that local implementations might result in a mix of program models or in outcomes that are not optimal.

## Immersion Bilingual Education

Immersion bilingual education provides academic and language instruction in two languages so students can become proficient in both languages—additive bilingualism. The term has come from program models in Canada where middle-class English-speaking children are instructed in French. In the United States, English-only submersion programs for English learners are sometimes mischaracterized as immersion. This misconception has led to confusion. Canadian immersion is not, and never has been, a monolingual program, because both English and French are incorporated into the programs as subjects and as the media of instruction. In addition, the social context of French immersion is the upper-middle class in Quebec Province, where both English and French have a high-language status for instructional purposes. In contrast, when English learners are submerged in mainstream English classes, instruction is not given in their home language, and they do not become biliterate and academically bilingual.

**U.S. Enrichment Immersion**   In the United States, a comparable social context to Canadian-style immersion is a program in which a foreign language is highly supported. This program model can be considered "enrichment immersion." This model is distinguished from foreign language programs in elementary schools (FLES) in that academic instruction may be delivered directly in a foreign language, and tutoring and travel abroad are often an integral part of the program.

**Dual-Language Development Programs (Additive Bilingualism)**   In two-way immersion classrooms (also called two-way maintenance bilingual classrooms), English learners from a single language background are grouped in the same classroom with approximately equal numbers of English-speaking students. Grade-level-approximate curriculum is provided in both languages. Speakers of each language develop proficiency in both their native and second language, achieve academically through and in two languages, and come to appreciate each other's languages and cultures (Lindholm, 1994). This enhances the status of the students' primary language, promoting self-esteem and increased cultural pride (Lindholm-Leary, 2000), leading to increased motivation.

Two-way immersion programs (TWI) had been implemented in 329 schools in the United States by 2006 (www.cal.org/twi/directory), with the number of schools growing yearly. Sites were located in twenty-nine states ranging from Alaska to Florida, with the largest numbers in California and New York. Nearly all schools (308) were Spanish–English in design, although other schools immersed students in Cantonese–English, Japanese–English, Navajo–English, Mandarin–English, and German–English. The grade levels served were predominantly K–6, but thirty-four of these schools were middle schools and nine were high schools.

Careful attention to a high-quality bilingual program in the context of primary-language maintenance is key to the success of dual immersion programs (Veeder & Tramutt, 2000). The

National Clearinghouse for English Language Acquisition has a wealth of information about two-way programs at www.ncela.gwu.edu, as does a website from the California Department of Education (www.cde.ca.gov/sp/el/ip/faq.asp).

---

### Best Practice  MANDARIN DUAL IMMERSION PROGRAM

The Cupertino Language Immersion Program (CLIP) is a K–8 education program located at R. I. Meyerholz Elementary (K–5) and Sam H. Lawson Middle School (6–8) in the Cupertino Union School District (CUSD), Cupertino, California. CLIP's goals are to develop biliteracy, enrich culturally, and achieve academic proficiency that meets or exceeds the district guidelines.

Mandarin was chosen as the target language, and in 1998 CLIP became the first public K–8 two-way Mandarin immersion program in California. In 2007, the first class of immersion students graduated from middle school. CUSD supports CLIP with teachers, facilities, and English curriculum; all aspects of the Mandarin curriculum are financed by grants and donations.

---

TWI is predicated on beginning literacy instruction for students in both languages. Reading in a foreign language above the level of emergent literacy takes place by using both literature and subject area content, following many of the same principles as reading in the native language. Time is given in class for reading so that students working in groups can facilitate one another's comprehension. To appeal to students' varied interests, all types of content are used (magazines, newspapers, plays, novels, stories, and poems), depending also on the proficiency level of students and the level of language studied. In this way, students are assured of receiving a challenging academic program in both languages.

Critics have alleged that TWI delays English learning and that these programs fail to teach English to English learners. Amselle (1999) argued, "dual immersion programs are really nothing more than Spanish immersion, with Hispanic children used as teaching tools for English-speaking children" (p. 8). Experts concede that the greatest challenge in two-way bilingual programs is to "reduce the gap" between the language abilities of the two groups (English learners and second-language learners [SLLs]). This gap appears when content classes in English are modified (slowed down) for English learners to "catch up," or when content delivery in the primary language is slowed for SLLs. Table 4.4 features program elements of two-way immersion programs.

---

### Best Practice  PROMOTING ADDITIVE BILINGUALISM

Skilled teachers help students build English proficiency on a strong first-language foundation by the following practices:

■ Encourage families to preserve the home language
■ Stock classroom libraries with books in the home language(s)
■ Welcome classroom visitors and volunteers who speak the home language and ask them to address the class about the importance of proficiency in two languages

**TABLE 4.4**   Program Components of Two-Way Immersion

| Program Elements | Program Features |
|---|---|
| Philosophy | Bilingualism as a resource |
| Goal | Additive bilingualism for English learners and native English speakers |
| Purpose | Cognitive academic language proficiency achieved through grade-level-appropriate instruction in both languages |
| Ideal Outcome | Additive bilingualism for English learners and native English speakers |
| Grade/Proficiency Level(s) | Usually begins in kindergarten, with cohort staying together throughout elementary or middle school |
| Placement Criteria | Parental exemption waiver |
| Exit Criteria | Parental choice |
| Program Length | Parent choice (usually K–6) |
| Class Composition | Ideally, 50/50 English native speaker and English learner |
| Language Components | English-language development and primary-language maintenance for English learners; English language arts (ELA) and primary-language-as-a-second-language instruction for native English speakers |
| Limitations | ELD and ELA must be taught separately, as must primary-language maintenance versus primary-language-as-a-second-language instruction for native English speakers, or both groups will be slowed in achievement in their native languages |

Not all primary-language maintenance programs are two-way immersion, but two-way immersion programs featuring native English speakers often enjoy more community support. The following vignette illustrates the public pressure faced by one such school that offers primary-language maintenance.

 **Classroom Glimpse**

### SEMILLAS DEL PUEBLO

A primary-language maintenance charter school in El Sereno (part of Los Angeles), Academia Semillas del Pueblo, found itself in the center of controversy when a local talk radio station and a conservative Internet blog made assertions that the school espoused a covert separatist ethos. Principal Minnie Ferguson said that despite low test scores, other measures of achievement are more encouraging, showing Semillas del Pueblo students advancing to English fluency at a greater rate than Los Angeles Unified students overall.

The Academia held an open house in June, during which groups of children in brightly colored red and yellow shirts sat in circles and played games as others listened intently to teachers reading history lessons in Spanish or sang songs in Mandarin. The curricular emphasis is on multicultural values, with enrollment in 2005–2006 that included White, Black, Latino, Asian-American, American-Indian, and native Hawai'ian or Pacific Islander children. (Rivera, 2006)

## Transitional Bilingual Education

Transitional bilingual education (TBE) programs support the use of students' home language in academic settings only during the period in which they are acquiring enough English proficiency to make the transition into English-only education. This supports a subtractive view of bilingualism, in effect requiring that English learners discontinue the use of their native language as they increase their fluency in English (Nieto, 2007). In these programs, students receive initial instruction in most, if not all, content areas in their home language while they are being taught English.

There are numerous problems with a TBE program. It may be perceived as a remedial program or another form of segregated, compensatory education. TBE rests on the common misconception that two or three years is sufficient time to learn a second language for schooling purposes, but in fact this is not long enough for students to build cognitive academic language proficiency (CALP) either in their native tongue or in English. As a consequence, they may not be able to carry out cognitively demanding tasks in English or their home language.

Another shortcoming of transitional bilingual education is the effect that English-only schooling has on home-language use. After transition to English, students frequently switch to English as their primary language of communication, and conversational fluency in the home language tends to erode. This retards rather than expedites academic progress in English, primarily because children and parents lose the benefit of a shared language for such purposes as homework help. For these and other reasons, TBE programs have not led to school success for many students (see Medina & Escamilla, 1992) (see Table 4.5).

It is misleading to think of transition as a brief phase in the life of a bilingual student that happens as they reach a certain grade. As Uribe and Nathenson-Mejia (2008) pointed out,

> Successful transition requires that the entire school have a specific infrastructure in which all the elements and personnel support ELL children in the changes they are facing. The teachers across grade levels and from all content and enrichment areas ensure that students have the cultural, language, and literacy development that helps them meet the academic standards and succeed as new participants in the school. (pp. 3–4)

## Structured English Immersion

In structured English immersion (SEI) programs students are taught solely in English supplemented with strategies designed to increase their understanding of the content. Teachers are not necessarily fluent in the L1 of the students. Many of the teaching techniques used for SEI programs were developed for multilingual, often urban, classes where there is not a single primary language shared by the learners and the use of L1 is not feasible.

SEI programs are designed to address the learning needs of English learners whose English is at the intermediate level of fluency or above. Unfortunately, this approach is too often used for beginning English learners. The chief element of "structure" built into these programs is the use of specially designed academic instruction in English (SDAIE), also called "sheltered instruction." SDAIE incorporates specific teaching modifications to make a lesson understandable to students.

**TABLE 4.5**   Program Components of Transitional Bilingual Education

| Program Elements | Program Features |
| --- | --- |
| Philosophy | Bilingualism as a bridge to English proficiency |
| Goal | Bilingualism for English learners only until replaced by English as the language of instruction |
| Purpose | Cognitive academic language proficiency achieved through grade-level-appropriate instruction in English |
| Ideal Outcome | Educational parity for English learners and native English speakers |
| Grade/Proficiency Level(s) | Usually K–2, from beginning through advanced proficiency |
| Placement Criteria | Parental exemption waiver |
| Exit Criteria | (See Chapter 3 on Reclassification) |
| Program Length | Usually three years (K–2) |
| Class Composition | Usually Spanish-speaking, but in California bilingual teachers have been certified in twenty languages |
| Language Components | Content instruction in the primary languages, combined with ELD instruction |
| Limitations | Lack of programmatic support after transition often leads to subtractive bilingualism |

English learners obtain access to core curriculum subjects when the content is modified using SDAIE, and thus they can maintain parity with native-English-speaking classmates. Even literature classes can be modified with SDAIE so that English learners are not relegated to ELD programs whose course credits may not be considered college preparatory in nature. SEI programs also have a key advantage in that all teachers are responsible for the education of English learners and must be knowledgeable about language development issues and techniques. However, even with an elaborate set of SDAIE techniques designed to augment verbal explanation, few experts would agree that a student subjected to SEI achieves the same level of comprehension that same student would reach if taught in the primary language.

Also missing in the SEI approach is the opportunity for additive bilingualism. The same drawbacks that can be identified in the TBE model also hold true for SEI programs: There is no development of the primary language, resulting in subtractive bilinguality (see Table 4.6). Moreover, as Lucas and Katz (1994) pointed out, the move toward English-only schooling disadvantages English learners and maintains the advantage of the socially powerful:

> This unspoken and unacknowledged political motivation for allowing instruction only in English is suspect. If all instruction is provided in English, students who are not fluent in English cannot hope to successfully compete with those who are. Thus, this situation perpetuates the power differences that already exist between native-born speakers of standard (middle-class) English and others. (p. 541)

**TABLE 4.6** Program Components of Structured English Immersion

| Program Elements | Program Features |
|---|---|
| Philosophy | Academic content acquisition is more important than primary-language maintenance |
| Goal | Primary-language use for English learners is acceptable only until replaced by English as the language of instruction |
| Purpose | Cognitive academic language proficiency can be achieved through grade-level-appropriate instruction in English |
| Ideal Outcome | Educational parity for English learners and native English speakers |
| Grade/Proficiency Level(s) | Possibility for all grades, all CELDT levels |
| Placement Criteria | CELDT score level of beginner through advanced |
| Exit Criteria | (See Chapter 3 on Reclassification) |
| Program Length | Varies depending on individual progress |
| Class Composition | Mixed CELDT levels |
| Language Components | Content instruction in SDAIE-enhanced English combined with ELD instruction |
| Limitations | Access to core academic content depends on SDAIE skills of teachers |

## Newcomer (Front-Loaded) English

The goal of newcomer programs is to foster in recent immigrants rapid English learning during the period of early acculturation (Short & Boyson, 2004). Newcomer centers, like Newcomer High School in San Francisco, are more common at the secondary level than in the elementary grades. Newcomer programs may be organized as centers, as separate programs in their own locations, or as programs within a school (Genesee, 1999).

The chief rationale for newcomer programs is that students must learn English before they can be educated in English. A second rationale is that students need social and emotional support during a time in which they may experience culture shock. A third reason is that there are not enough teachers for the number of English learners, so they must be grouped for educational services.

Programs vary in length; some are full day, whereas others are half-day or after school. Students may be enrolled for a year, four years, or only one semester (Short, 1998). The curriculum is designed to help students move into the regular language support program as soon as possible while helping them gain an understanding of U.S. schools and educational expectations. SDAIE techniques predominate in content classes, if offered. Increasingly, however, the newcomer model is called "front-loading." This means that only English-language development is offered, on an intensive basis, during the newcomer period, with students' having limited access to the core curriculum during this time.

However, research has cast doubt on the argument that students must learn English before they can be educated in English (Orfield & Lee, 2005). Major disadvantages of the newcomer approach are, first, the idea that newcomers should be separated from the mainstream

English-speaking population during their period of early adjustment. The U.S. Supreme Court, in the ruling *Brown v. Board of Education* (1954), decided that separate educational programs, however well meaning, are inherently unequal in implementation. The idea that immigrants should be educated separately—at any stage—promotes segregation in a nation whose school facilities are unfortunately increasingly ethnically separate (Orfield & Lee, 2005).

A second drawback is that the newcomer approach is based on subtractive bilingual education. Academic support in the primary language is seldom offered, much less primary-language development. It is probably helpful for students to receive counseling and other assistance to help with culture shock, but no amount of humanistic socioemotional "support" in English during students' adjustment period can realistically take the place of genuine support—receiving mediation in the primary language.

A third drawback is that content vocabulary cannot be learned effectively in a front-loaded manner because it is an integral part of learning content concepts. Unfortunately, students are inevitably slowed in their educational advancement when forced to halt academic learning until their English is developed to some arbitrary point. Moreover, if basic interpersonal skills take two years of exposure to English to develop, and cognitive academic language takes five or more years to develop (Cummins, 1981a; Hakuta, Butler, & Witt, 2000), then theoretically two to five years of "boot camp" English would be required, an inordinate amount of time for newcomers to be segregated. Thus, the newcomer, or front-loading, model is ill advised (see Table 4.7).

**TABLE 4.7**  Program Components of Newcomer (Front-Loaded) Programs

| Program Elements | Program Features |
| --- | --- |
| Philosophy | Intensive English is the key to English proficiency |
| Goal | Intensive English for English learners must take place before English can be used as the language of instruction |
| Purpose | Cognitive academic language proficiency can be achieved through grade-level-appropriate instruction in English |
| Ideal Outcome | English learners can participate in SDAIE-enhanced content instruction |
| Grade/Proficiency Level(s) | Newcomer programs are usually implemented in secondary schools, but front-loading can be done at any grade or level, beginning through intermediate proficiency |
| Placement Criteria | Varies—CELDT score level of beginner or early intermediate plus parental choice |
| Exit Criteria | (See Chapter 3 on Reclassification) |
| Program Length | Varies |
| Class Composition | Mixed CELDT levels |
| Language Components | Content instruction in SDAIE-enhanced English combined with ELD instruction |
| Limitations | Access to core academic content depends on SDAIE skills of teachers; segregative |

## English-Language-Development Programs

English is taught to English learners in a variety of ways, and studies have shown varying degrees of student success depending on the program model (Thomas & Collier, 1997). Whereas it may be true that extensive exposure to a high-quality English-language development program is a necessity, it is a fallacy to believe that total immersion in English is effective. When students are provided with a solid foundation in their primary language, faster English acquisition takes place. The following four models are the norm for teaching English to English learners.

**Pull-Out ELD**   When English learners must leave their home classroom and receive instruction in vocabulary, grammar, oral language, or spelling for separate half-hour to one-hour-a-day classes with a trained ELD teacher, they are said to be "pulled out." Such instruction rarely is integrated with the regular classroom program, and when students return to the home classroom, they usually are not instructed on curriculum they missed while they were gone. This lack only exacerbates an already difficult learning situation. Of the various program models, ELD pull-out is the most expensive to operate because it requires hiring an extra resource teacher (Chambers & Parrish, 1992).

Researchers who compared the instructional outcomes of a separate ELD oral language development instructional block at the kindergarten and first-grade levels found that teachers in a separate ELD period tended to be more efficient and focused on oral language objectives, but that the oral language instruction that ensued was no more focused on cognitive academic language than was a regular language arts class for English learners (Saunders, Foorman, & Carlson, 2006). Therefore, the particular opportunity was lost for developing CALP in a dedicated ELD period.

**ELD Class Period**   Although pull-out ELD is normally found at the elementary level, students in the secondary school often have separate ELD classes that help them with their English skills. Unfortunately, these classes often focus entirely on the English language and do not help students with their academic subjects. Moreover, in some school districts students who are placed in separate ELD classes at the high school level do not receive college-entrance-applicable credits for these classes. In other words, to be placed in an ELD class is to be denied the chance for college admission. This unfortunate policy is avoided if students are placed in SDAIE-enhanced high school English classes that do bear college-entry credit value.

**Content-Based ELD**   In content-based ELD classes, the ELD teacher collaborates with content area teachers to organize learning objectives around academic subjects in order to prepare students to master grade-level curricula (Ovando & Collier, 1998). Content-based ELD classes develop not only language proficiency but also content knowledge, cognitive strategies, and study skills. Learners receive comprehensible input in systematic, planned instruction that presents vocabulary, concepts, and structures required for mastery of the content (Snow, 1993). The content to be taught, general instructional goals, and time available for instruction are negotiated with the content teacher.

Learning English through content is a worldwide means of English instruction (Brinton & Master, 1997), whether for purposes of business, engineering, medicine, or science. It is most effective when content teachers take an interest in language development and ELD teachers take more responsibility for content.

**Universal Access to the Language Arts Curriculum**   As described in Chapter 3, the goal of ELD programs is for English learners to make the transition from the ELD standards to the standards outlined in the *Reading/Language Arts Framework* and the ELA standards so they can be instructed in a mainstream classroom. This is accomplished through implementing principles of Universal Instructional Design (UID).

With an augmented emphasis on learning styles and other learner differences, UID promotes access to information, resources, and tools for students with a wide range of abilities, disabilities, ethnic backgrounds, language skills, and learning styles. Burgstahler (2002) noted that "Universal Instructional Design principles . . . give each student meaningful access to the curriculum by assuring access to the environment as well as multiple means of representation, expression, and engagement" (p. 1).

Table 4.8 offers an overview of the principles of UID and some suggested applications of these principles in the education of English learners. UID does not imply that one universal strategy fits all but rather that a diversity of opportunities will work for many different students.

The recommended model for delivery of ELD is to integrate it with content instruction in a classroom in which the English learner has access to native speakers of English as language models. However, because the English learner is still acquiring basic English skills, ELD instruction cannot provide grade-level-appropriate content. To accomplish this, academic instruction and ELD must go hand in hand.

# English-Language Development and Academic Instruction

English learners can succeed in content area classes taught in English. If they can follow and understand a lesson, they can learn content material, and the content area instruction—if modified to include English-language development—becomes the means for acquiring English. Basically, specially designed academic instruction in English (SDAIE) addresses the following needs of English learners: (1) to learn grade-appropriate content, (2) to master English vocabulary and grammar, (3) to learn "academic" English, and (4) to develop strategies for learning how to learn.

## The SDAIE-Enhanced Content Classroom

Specially designed academic instruction in English (also called "sheltered content instruction"—see Echevarría and Graves, 2011) combines second-language-acquisition principles with those elements of quality teaching that make a lesson understandable to students. SDAIE is, ideally, one component in a program for English learners that includes ELD instruction, primary-language instruction in content areas (so that students continue at grade level as they learn English), and content-based ESL classes.

An SDAIE classroom has content objectives identical to those of a mainstream classroom in the same subject but, in addition, includes language and learning-strategy objectives. Instruction is modified for greater comprehensibility. The distinction between SDAIE and content-based ELD instruction is that SDAIE features content instruction taught by content

**TABLE 4.8**    Principles of Universal Instructional Design Applied to English Learners

| Principle | Definition | Application |
|---|---|---|
| Inclusiveness | A classroom climate that communicates respect for varying abilities | Use bilingual signage and materials; welcome and respect aides and assistants. |
| Physical access | Equipment and activities that minimize sustained physical effort, provide options for participation, and accommodate those with limited physical abilities | Furnish assistive technologies such as screen readers and online dictionaries to assist in translation; make online chatrooms available for students in two languages. |
| Delivery methods | Content is delivered in multiple modes so it is accessible to students with a wide range of abilities, interests, and previous experiences. | Provide a full range of audiovisual enhancement, including wireless headsets, captioned video, audiotaped read-along books, typed lecture notes, and study guides. |
| Information access | Use of simple, intuitive, and consistent formats | Ensure that information is both understandable and complete; reduce unnecessary complexity; highlight essential text; give clear criteria for tests and assignments. |
| Interaction | Accessible to everyone, without accommodation; use of multiple ways for students to participate | Set up both heterogeneous groups (across second-language ability levels) and homogeneous groups (same-language ability level); instruct students on how to secure a conversational turn. |
| Feedback | Effective prompting during an activity and constructive comments after the assignment is complete | Employ formative assessment for ongoing feedback. |
| Demonstration of knowledge | Provision for multiple ways students demonstrate knowledge—group work, demonstrations, portfolios, and presentations | Offer different modes to all students so that English learners are not the only ones with alternatives. |

*Source:* Adapted from Burgstahler (2002), Egbert (2004), and Strehorn (2001).

area teachers with English-language support. Content-based ELD, taught by ELD teachers, features the use of content area materials as texts for ELD lessons.

## A Model for SDAIE

A model for SDAIE originally developed at the Los Angeles Unified School District in 1993 had four components—content, connections, comprehensibility, and interaction. Often, however, teachers could be technically proficient in many of the SDAIE elements yet not be successful with English learners. Discussion and observation revealed that the teacher's attitude played such a critical part in the success of the class that it needed to be explicitly incorporated into the

Michael Newmann/PhotoEdit

*Depending on their assessed English level, students can participate in SDAIE-enhanced content lessons.*

model. Therefore, teacher attitude was added as an overarching component (see Figure 4.1). This model has been the foundation for the SIOP model (see Chapter 5).

Teachers often find that they do not use every aspect of the model in every lesson, but by working within the overall frame they are more assured of providing appropriate learning opportunities for their English learners. The following sections explain and illustrate each of the five SDAIE components.

**Teacher Attitude**  Teachers are no different from the rest of the population when faced with something new or different. Many recoil, dig in their heels, and refuse to change. But teachers have also chosen to work with people, and they frequently find delight and satisfaction in their students' work, behavior, and learning. It is this sense of delight that is important to capture in working with all learners, particularly English learners.

Three aspects characterize a successful attitude in working with second-language learners:

- Teachers believe that all students can learn.
- Teachers are willing to nurture language development.
- Teachers recognize that a person's self-concept is involved in his or her own language and that at times students need to use that language.

**FIGURE 4.1**    A Model of the Components of Successful SDAIE Instruction

**Teacher Attitude**

The teacher is open and willing to learn from
students.

**Content**

Lessons include subject, language, and learning-
strategy objectives.

Material is selected, adapted, and organized with
language learners in mind.

**Comprehensibility**

Lessons include explicit strategies that aid
understanding:

- Contextualization
- Modeling
- Teacher speech adjustment
- Frequent comprehension checks through
strategies and appropriate questioning
- Repetition and paraphrase

**Connections**

Curriculum is connected to students' background
and experiences.

**Interaction**

Students have frequent opportunities to

- Talk about lesson content
- Clarify concepts in their home language
- Represent learning through a variety of ways

---

**Best Practice**    POSITIVE TEACHER ATTITUDES

An ELD teacher observed and interviewed colleagues at her school. She discovered that
accomplished teachers set up effective learning environments for the English learners. They
understood the needs of their culturally and linguistically diverse students and created an
atmosphere in the classroom that helped newly arrived students integrate into the life of the
school. For example, they would pair each English learner with a buddy. They encouraged
friendships by asking a classmate to stay with the English learner at lunch. They provided
appropriate instruction for their English learners and applauded their successes. This environment helped relieve much of the beginners' anxiety. (Haynes, 2004)

---

**Content**    *Content objectives* are necessary to guide teaching. A lesson with a clear objective
focuses the instruction by concentrating on a particular goal and guides the teacher to select
learning activities that accomplish the goal. Teachers may have to be selective in choosing only
the most essential content standards to address in the time allotted.

---

**Best Practice**    ORGANIZING CONTENT FOR THE THEME
OF "ACCULTURATION"

Content materials for the social studies theme "acculturation" might include primary documents, personal histories, and literature. Students who research specific concepts related

to acculturation, such as immigration assimilation, culture shock, job opportunities, or naturalization, may find that each document features a unique voice. A government document presents a formal, official point of view, whereas a personal or family story conveys the subject from a different, more intimate perspective. In addition, numerous pieces of literature, such as Eve Bunting's *How Many Days to America?* (1988) or Laurence Yep's *Dragonwings* (1975), offer yet other points of view.

**Connections**   Students engage in learning when they recognize a connection between what they know and the learning experience. Therefore, a critical element of the SDAIE lesson is the deliberate plan on the teacher's part to elicit information from and help make connections for the students. This can be accomplished in several ways: through *bridging*—linking concepts and skills to student experiences or eliciting/using examples from students' lives—and by *schema building*—using scaffolding strategies to link new learning to old.

**Comprehensibility**   A key factor in learning is being able to understand. Through all phases of a lesson, the teacher ensures that students have plenty of clues to understanding. This is one of the aspects of SDAIE that makes it different from mainstream instruction. Teachers are aware that they need to present concepts in a variety of ways. They increase the comprehensibility of lessons in four ways: *contextualization* (strategies that augment speech and/or text through pictures, realia, dramatizations, etc.); *modeling* (demonstration of the skill or concept to be learned); *speech adjustment* (strategies to adjust speech from the customary native speech patterns); and *comprehension checks* (strategies to monitor listening and reading comprehension). Table 4.9 provides a list of both object and human resources that can help contextualize classroom content.

**Interaction**   The organization of discourse is important for language acquisition in content classes. In "teacher-fronted" classrooms (Harel, 1992), the teacher takes the central role in controlling the flow of information, and students compete for the teacher's attention and for permission to speak. More recent research (Gass, 2000), however, points to the role of the learner in negotiating, managing, even manipulating conversations to receive more comprehensible input. Instead of English learners being dependent on their ability to understand the teacher's explanations and directions, classrooms that feature flexible grouping patterns permit students to have greater access to the flow of information.

The teacher orchestrates tasks so that students use language in academic ways. Students are placed in different groups for different activities. Teachers themselves work with small groups to achieve specific instructional objectives (e.g., in literature response groups, as discussed in Chapter 7, or in instructional conversations, discussed in Chapters 1 and 6).

In planning for interaction in the SDAIE lesson, the teacher considers opportunities for students to talk about key concepts, expects that students may clarify the concepts in their primary language, and allows a variety of means through which students can demonstrate their understanding.

**TABLE 4.9**  Media, Realia, Manipulatives, and Human Resources to Contextualize Lessons

| Object Resources | Human Resources |
|---|---|
| Picture files | Cooperative groups |
| Maps and globes | Pairs |
| Charts and posters | Cross-age tutors |
| Printed material: | Heterogeneous groups |
|    Illustrated books | Community resource people |
|    Pamphlets | School resource people |
|    News articles | Parents |
|    Catalogs | Pen pals (adult and child) |
|    Magazines | Keypals |
| Puzzles | |
| Science equipment | |
| Manipulatives: | |
|    M&Ms | |
|    Buttons | |
|    Tongue depressors | |
|    Gummy bears | |
| Costumes | |
| Computer software | |
| Internet | |

 **Classroom Glimpse**

### INTERACTION

In one fifth-grade class, the students produced a news program with a U.S. Civil War setting. The program included the show's anchors; reporters in the field interviewing generals, soldiers, and citizens; a weather report; and reports on sports, economics, and political conditions. There were even commercial breaks. The students engaged in much research in order to be historically accurate, but enthusiasm was high as they shared their knowledge in a format they knew and understood. In addition, students were able to work in the area of their particular interest.

SDAIE offers English learners an important intermediate step between content instruction in the primary language, an environment in which they may not advance in English skills, and a "sink-or-swim" immersion, in which they may not learn key content-related concepts. In most effective instruction for English learners, ELD methods and SDAIE are used together to provide language development and achievement of core content standards for English learners, depending on the program model used and the specific needs of the students. SDAIE is covered in more depth in Chapter 5.

# Parental Rights and Communicating with Families

"Strong parent involvement is one factor that research has shown time and time again to have positive effects on academic achievement and school attitudes" (Ovando & Collier, 1998, p. 270). Yet, for various reasons on the part of both schools and communities, parent involvement has sometimes been an elusive goal. The growing number of English learners in the school system, however, clearly requires that efforts continue to establish communication, develop partnerships, and involve parents, families, and communities. Fortunately, over the past decade successful programs have been developed and various guidelines are available to help school personnel, parents, and communities work together to ensure parental rights, family involvement, successful programs, and school–community partnerships that benefit students.

## Parental Rights

Parents have numerous rights that educators must respect and honor in spite of the challenges they may present to the school. These include (1) the right of their children to a free, appropriate public education; (2) the right to receive information concerning education decisions and actions in the language parents comprehend; (3) the right to make informed decisions and to authorize consent before changes in educational placement occur; (4) the right to be included in discussions and plans concerning disciplinary action toward their children; (5) the right to appeal actions when they do not agree; and (6) the right to participate in meetings organized for public and parent information (Young & Helvie, 1996).

Parents have the right to choose in which language development program options their child will participate (e.g., waiver process) and have the right to be contacted about such rights in an appropriate and effective medium (e.g., bilingual phone calls, home visits, primary-language materials, videos). The *Williams et al. v. State of California et al.* remedies offer several mechanisms by which parents can exert more influence on school procedures.

A fundamental right that all parents have is support in school for the home language. To deny access to native-language literacy exploits minorities (Cummins, 1989). It is important that teachers help families understand the advantages that bilingualism provides to the individual, connecting students to their heritage culture; adding a cognitive dimension by expanding and deepening students' thinking; and, later in life, expanding career opportunities. Family support for bilingualism helps to establish expectations for high academic performance in two languages (Molina, Hanson, & Siegel, 1997). Chapter 9 continues this definition of family involvement.

## School–Community Partnerships

In addition to developing partnerships with parents, schools are reaching toward communities for help in educating all children. Community-based organizations (CBOs)—groups committed to helping people obtain health, education, and other basic human services—are assisting students in ways that go beyond traditional schooling. Adger (2000) found that school–CBO partnerships support students' academic achievement by working with parents and families, tutoring students in their first language, developing students' leadership skills and higher education goals, and providing information and support on issues such as health care, pregnancy, gang involvement, and so on.

Communities can foster a climate of support for English learners by featuring articles in local newspapers and newsletters about these students' achievements in the schools and prizes they have won, by sponsoring literature and art exhibitions that feature students' work, and by publishing their stories written in both languages. Students can be invited to the local library to offer their stories, books, and poetry to other students, again in both English and the primary language. In this way, support for bilingualism and bilingual education programs is orchestrated in the community at large. Working with families and communities is further detailed in Chapter 9.

# Teaching Collaboratively

Team teaching, peer tutoring, mentors, and bilingual paraprofessionals offer different means of supporting student learning. All individuals working with the teacher provide a challenge in planning activities and monitoring student achievement. Teachers who value the help provided by assistants and peers must be willing to invest time in both planning and supervising for such teamwork to be employed effectively.

## Teaching with Peers

Peer collaboration is "a style for direct interaction between at least two coequal parties voluntarily engaged in shared decision making as they work toward a common goal" (Friend & Cook, 1996, p. 6). This definition pinpoints several necessary principles: Professionals must treat one another as equals; collaboration is voluntary; a goal is mutually agreed on (that of finding the most effective instruction for the students under consideration); and responsibility is shared for participation, decision making, and resources, as well as accountability for outcomes. These are predicated on a collegial working environment of mutual respect and trust.

An ELD teacher who is a specialist can act as a helpful colleague with the classroom teacher, sharing expertise about L2 acquisition effects, lesson planning, or potential crosscultural misunderstandings. They collaborate to resolve conflicts, work with translators, and draw on community members for information, additional resources, and parental support. Some schools assign mentor teachers to work with beginning teachers, offering support and feedback.

## Working with Paraprofessionals

Paraprofessional educators may be instructional aides, volunteers from the parent community, tutors from other grades, high school students, or senior citizens and other community volunteers. Involving paraprofessionals requires careful organization to recruit skillful helpers and to use them effectively. Prudent planning is needed to maintain high-quality instruction and to ensure that assistants in the classroom feel valued.

A paraprofessional works alongside the teacher to assist in preparing materials, doing clerical work, monitoring small groups of students, giving tutorial help, or providing basic instruction under teacher supervision. The quasi-instructional duties, such as tutoring and assisting small groups of students, provide an extension of teacher expertise. It is the teacher's responsibility to see that the aide is effective in promoting student achievement and that students receive high-quality instruction.

Classroom teachers have responsibility for all instruction and classroom behavior. The tasks carried out by the aide should be planned by the teacher—paraprofessionals should not be expected to plan and prepare materials without teacher supervision. Instruction provided by the aide likewise is valid and important and should be considered as such by the students. Moreover, student achievement should not be evaluated solely by the paraprofessional; this is a responsibility of the classroom teacher.

Paraprofessionals should have a classroom space provided for their tutoring or group work. The number of students for which an aide is responsible may vary, from one-to-one tutoring to supervising the entire class while the teacher is involved in conferences or individual student contact. Should the aide be unavailable, the teacher must have backup plans so that the day's activities can be modified.

Often, paraprofessionals who are brought into the classroom to offer primary-language instruction share the students' cultural background. These individuals can provide valuable linguistic and emotional support for students as they learn English. On the other hand, such aides may subtly modify the teacher's educational intentions.

 **Classroom Glimpse**

### THE AIDE HAS HER OWN IDEAS

Mr. Burns, a fifth-grade teacher in a bilingual classroom, had a Cambodian aide, Sarit Moul, who was the mother of four students in the school. While working in cooperative groups, the students were expected to exchange ideas and information, as well as compose and deliver group reports. Mr. Burns began to notice that the Laotian students did not speak voluntarily but waited to be called on. In observing Ms. Moul work with these students, he found that she discouraged students from speaking unless they received permission to do so. In conferring with her, Mr. Burns discovered, to his chagrin, that she believed that speaking out undermined the teacher's authority. A compromise had to be negotiated that would encourage students to develop speaking proficiency.

**Box 4.1** Guidelines for Working with and Supervising a Paraprofessional Teaching Assistant

- Develop a daily schedule of activities.
- Inform your paraprofessional about your expectations of him or her.
- Demonstrate and verbally explain specific teaching tactics to be used for particular lessons and students.
- Be open to suggestions from the paraprofessional.
- Take time to observe the aide's performance, providing praise or corrective feedback for specific actions.
- Provide remedial attention for any documented weak areas and keep a record of effort spent working on these areas.
- Do not criticize the paraprofessional in front of the students.

*Source:* Adapted from Westling & Koorland (1988).

It is not easy to be a paraprofessional and to work under someone else's supervision. Making the aide feel part of the instructional team is an important aspect of morale. For this to happen, aides need to be engaged in meaningful work from which they can derive a sense of accomplishment and not be relegated to tedious and menial tasks. They need to be given clear directions and understand not only what is expected of them but also what is expected of the students. It is important that they participate in instructional planning and be involved in seeing certain activities through to closure. Aides are also a source of valuable feedback to the teacher on students' needs and accomplishments. For their efforts, paraprofessionals deserve appreciation, whether it is a spoken "thank you" and a pat on the back or an occasional gift or token of esteem. Box 4.1 provides guidelines for teachers who are working with a paraprofessional.

Many people feel that any tolerance of linguistic diversity undermines national unity. However, others hold the view of the United States as a "salad bowl," which features a mixture of distinct textures and tastes, instead of a "melting pot," in which cultural and linguistic diversity is melted into one collective culture and language. The best educational programs for English learners are explicitly bicultural as well so that students' native cultures and heritage languages can be fostered. With these programs in place, the United States will benefit from the rich language resources of all its people.

**myeducationlab**
The Power of Classroom Practice
www.myeducationlab.com

Go to the Topic Instructional Programs in the MyEducationLab (www.myeducationlab.com) for your course, where you can:

- Find learning outcomes for Instructional Programs along with the national standards that connect to these outcomes.
- Complete Assignments and Activities that can help you more deeply understand the chapter content.
- Apply and practice your understanding of the core teaching skills identified in the chapter with the Building Teaching Skills and Dispositions learning units.
- Examine challenging situations and cases presented in the IRIS Center Resources.
- Check your comprehension on the content covered in the chapter by going to the Study Plan in the Book Resources for your text. Here you will be able to take a chapter quiz, receive feedback on your answers, and then access Review, Practice, and Enrichment activities to enhance your understanding of chapter content.

**A+RISE**

Go to the Topic A+RISE in the MyEducationLab (www.myeducationlab.com) for your course. A+RISE® Standards2Strategy™ is an innovative and interactive online resource that offers new teachers in grades K–12 just-in-time, research-based instructional strategies that:

- Meet the linguistic needs of ELLs as they learn content
- Differentiate instruction for all grades and abilities
- Offer reading and writing techniques, cooperative learning, use of linguistic and nonlinguistic representations, scaffolding, teacher modeling, higher order thinking, and alternative classroom ELL assessment
- Provide support to help teachers be effective through the integration of listening, speaking, reading, and writing along with the content curriculum
- Improve student achievement
- Are aligned to Common Core Elementary Language Arts standards (for the literacy strategies) and to English language proficiency standards in WIDA, Texas, California, and Florida.

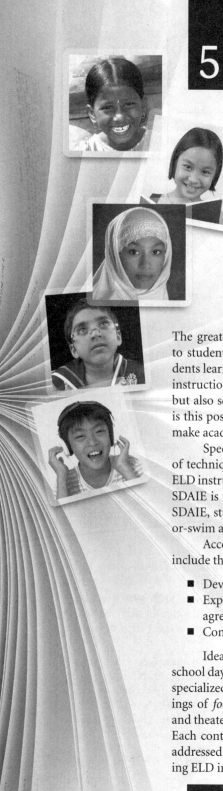

# 5

# English-Language Literacy Development, Lesson Planning, and Specially Designed Content Instruction in English

The greatest challenge in teaching today is to communicate content in English to students whose English is under development. Research has shown that students learn best in their primary language, but in most schools, primary-language instruction is not an option. Students today are expected to learn not only English but also science, mathematics, social studies, and other subjects in English. How is this possible? Instruction must be systematically modified so that teachers can make academic content more accessible to learners.

Specially designed academic instruction in English (SDAIE) comprises a set of techniques for adapting instruction for English learners. For English learners, ELD instruction is guided by a careful progression through the ELD standards, and SDAIE is used to make academic instruction comprehensible. Without ELD and SDAIE, students are mainstreamed without access to the curriculum—the sink-or-swim approach.

According to Gersten and Baker (2000), a high-quality ELD program should include three components:

- Development of proficiency and fluency in social and academic English
- Explicit instruction in grammar, including such formal aspects as tense agreement, use of plurals, and word order in sentences
- Content learning merged with English acquisition

Ideally, English-language development is not confined to one period of the school day but is instead a part of content area instruction. Each content area has a specialized knowledge base, vocabulary (consider, for example, the different meanings of *foot* in mathematics, biology, geography, furniture construction, poetry, and theater), and particular graphic and verbal means for organizing information. Each content area has standards guiding curriculum development that must be addressed along with ELD standards. Table 5.1 offers suggestions for implementing ELD in a variety of ways across the curriculum.

**TABLE 5.1**   Examples of English-Language Development in Content Areas

| Facet of Literacy Development | Examples |
| --- | --- |
| Creating a language-rich environment | Teachers can provide new experiences that arouse interest in and attention to a topic: field trips, guest speakers, fiction and nonfiction films, experiments, classroom discovery centers, music and songs, poetry and other literature, computer simulations, and so on. |
| Meaningful and purposeful activities | After students have had the opportunity to learn new literacy material in a meaningful way, they can transform that knowledge through other means, such as illustrating, dramatizing, creating songs, dancing, rewriting stories. Students can share their learning in a variety of ways—in learning centers; through dramatic, visual, or oral presentations; by staging a reader's theater; by developing slide, video, or computer-based audiovisual shows; or through maps and graphs. |
| Using standards-based thematic unit organization | After demonstrating the basic tools associated with mathematics (rulers, protractors, calculators, computers, etc.), the teacher provides students with a real-life opportunity to use them. Students are told that the classroom needs to be recarpeted. They first have to estimate the area, then check their estimates with the actual tools (using both standard and metric measuring instruments), and then use calculators to find the percentage of error in their estimates. This fits with ELD standards relating to negotiating/ initiating oral activities. |
| Selecting appropriate reading materials | Teachers can choose to have one primary content source or a package of content-related materials (chapters from various texts, video- and audiotapes, magazine and newspaper articles, encyclopedia entries, literary selections, Internet sources, software programs, etc.). Regardless of what is chosen, the teacher must consider two main criteria: Are the content objectives for the lesson adequately presented by the material? Is the material comprehensible to English learners? |
| Providing organized, systematic, explicit instruction in key skills | Students identify key words in mathematics problem solving and determine how other words are linked to the key words. For example, in the problem "The sum of two numbers is 77. If the first number is ten times the other, find the number," students need to know they are dealing with two different numbers (Dale & Cuevas, 1992). |
| Adapting instruction and materials for English learners | Some learners may need special textual material, such as excerpts taken from textbooks, advance organizers for the text that highlight the key topics and concepts in outline form, focus questions, concept maps, or tape-recorded text passages. |
| Integrating listening, speaking, reading, and writing | During the first week of the solar system unit, the names of the planets were tossed into a hat. Each of nine pairs of native-English-speaking and English-learning students selected one planet and developed a poster session about their planet based on resources in the school library. After each pair presented their planet, the teacher combined pairs into small groups. Each group was to create a tenth planet based on what they had learned and present that planet to the class. |

Using content area standards as the basis for content instruction combined with level-specific ELD standards ensures organized, systematic, explicit progress in language proficiency. A language-rich environment adds literacy to meaningful and purposeful instruction in key content knowledge and skills, integrating listening, speaking, reading, and writing with content objectives.

## Instructional Planning and Organization for ELD and SDAIE

When instruction is delivered in English and the student has not achieved advanced proficiency in English, a fundamental chasm undermines learning. This gulf between instruction and comprehension cannot be bridged by reducing the standards of expectation for the student—it must be overcome by adapting instruction to the student's second-language-acquisition level by using specially designed academic instruction in English (SDAIE). This chapter addresses pedagogy for English learners by focusing on SDAIE-enhanced curriculum design and lesson delivery, cognitive academic language proficiency, and use of learning strategies as core elements in teaching English-language development and content area knowledge.

SDAIE is an approach used in multilinguistic content classrooms to provide language support to students while they are learning academic subjects. This can take place either in mainstream classes made up of native English speakers mixed with non-native English speakers of intermediate proficiency or in classes consisting solely of non-native speakers who operate at similar English proficiency levels (Echevarría, Vogt, & Short, 2004).

Planning affords teachers the opportunity to adapt lessons for English learners so instruction is understandable and interactive. An SDAIE lesson plan follows a fairly predictable format. Box 5.1 describes the five main parts of the SDAIE lesson.

SDAIE combines second-language-acquisition principles with elements of quality teaching so students can improve listening, speaking, reading, and writing as they study an academic subject. SDAIE is the preferred method used by both middle and high schools when primary-language instruction is not available or is offered in only one primary language.

Instead of organizing this chapter by content area—treating only mathematics in its own section, for example—I have organized this material by the main parts of the SDAIE lesson. By viewing the same SDAIE principle across several content domains, it is easier to grasp the concept.

Careful planning and a well-organized classroom, combined with effective teaching, are keys to success for English learners. The cycle of instruction consists of the following five phases: (1) The teacher becomes familiar with the characteristics of the students (age, grade level, language-acquisition level); (2) the teacher plans instruction using state and local curriculum standards and textbooks as guides; (3) the teacher delivers instruction using formative assessment to monitor progress; (4) the teacher employs summative assessment to give grades and make information available about student progress; and (5) the teacher reflects.

This cycle is repeated throughout the school year. Based on assessment data, the teacher modifies instruction for the class as a whole or for individual students, groups and regroups students, and acquires additional resources as needed. Over this entire classroom-based cycle is the spector of standardized testing, which reports to the community at large, including federal,

**Box 5.1** Fundamental Elements of the SDAIE Lesson Plan

I. Setting objectives
   Content: Activity goals linked to grade-level standards
   English-language development:
      Speaking
      Listening
      Reading
      Writing
   Learning strategy: Augmenting long-term cognitive, metacognitive, or social-affective abilities
II. Preparing modified materials
III. Differentiated instruction
   Bridging: Accessing and building prior knowledge
   Appealing to diverse learning modalities
   Access to cognitive academic language
   SDAIE techniques
   Scaffolding: Temporary support for learning
   Guided and independent practice that promotes students' active language use
   Formative assessment and reteaching
IV. Summative assessment of objectives
V. Reflective pedagogy

state, and local authorities, sometimes with the threat of dire consequences to the school if expectations are not met. This is the contemporary context for planning and instructional delivery.

## Planning for Standards-Based ELD and Content Instruction

Lesson planning involves the careful design of content, language, and learning-strategy objectives and the selection, modification, and organization of materials and text that support those objectives. Objectives are necessary to guide teaching. A lesson with a clear objective focuses instruction by concentrating on a particular goal and guides the teacher to select those learning activities that accomplish the goal. Once objectives are clearly stated, the teacher selects materials that will help students achieve those objectives. Finally, assessment provides evidence that learning has, or has not, taken place.

**Considerations When Planning** Instructional planning takes the following factors into consideration:

### Knowledge about Students
- Cultures and home languages
- Prior knowledge of the content
- Interests
- Reading, writing, and oral skills

### Knowledge about the Content Area

- Standards that must be addressed
- What objectives will be set

### Knowledge about Language Development

- Literacy requirements of the content area
- Language objectives needed

### Knowledge about Students' Cognitive Development

- The learning strategies that students already have
- The learning strategies that will be useful in the lesson
- Ways to integrate the learning strategies (particularly critical thinking tasks) with students' cultural perspectives (Adapted from Quiocho & Ulanoff, 2009, p. 12)

**Objectives**   What is a lesson objective? The objective states, in behavioral terms, what the student will be capable of doing at the close of the lesson. Such verbs as *contrast, identify, list, summarize, compare, predict, survey,* and *outline* are specific, describing a behavior that can be measured or has a tangible product. In contrast, such verbs as *learn, look at, evaluate, think about, know, review,* and *become aware* are not specific or measurable. Moreover, some verbs do not specify a goal but merely a process or activity. Such terms as *listen to, reflect, practice,* and *work in groups* describe activities, not goals. Hence it is difficult to measure what is accomplished. In contrast, *draw, map, record data, plan,* or *punctuate* are terms that result in a product that can be assessed.

Knowledge and language cannot be separated—language is the brain's input device, whether verbal or figural (pictures, numbers, graphs). Content instruction (mathematics, social studies, literature, science, physical education, visual arts, music, and performance arts) takes place using language as the medium, so language objectives are an integral part of content instruction. To maintain grade-level content objectives and sustain academic expectations for achievement, both language and content objectives are included in SDAIE lessons. Moreover, the current emphasis on cognitive teaching mandates that learning-strategy objectives be included as well. This gives every SDAIE lesson a three-part focus.

- *Content objective.* Knowledge, skill, or disposition in a subject area or domain of communicative competence
- *Language-development objective.* Knowledge or skill in some facet of English
- *Learning-strategy objective.* Knowledge, skill, or learning strategy that teaches the student how to acquire or process information

Objectives can include more than one content area. Middle school as well as elementary school instruction increasingly features thematic units that integrate content areas. The teacher considers the various tasks that language users must be able to perform in the unit (listening, speaking, reading, writing) and makes provisions for students to learn the vocabulary and concepts needed in the discourse of the content areas involved.

**Objectives and Standards**　How are objectives chosen? Schools, school districts, or state agencies publish standards documents that spell out what students should know and be able to do. These furnish goals for each grade. A classroom teacher plans instruction using curriculum guides at the specific grade level. Units may be organized based on a theme or, if the course is text-driven, based on chapters in the text (instructional planning is presented in greater detail later in this chapter). Units or chapters are further divided into specific lessons containing the essential content area objectives. The classroom teacher is responsible for presenting the material in an understandable way, arranging for students to participate in learning activities, and then measuring the extent of the students' mastery of the material. Thus, instruction and assessment are linked.

The chosen objectives must be matched to specific performance that students will demonstrate. This is central to the contemporary focus on accountability because the specific performance expected of the student as a learning outcome can be directly linked to some standard for the performance. Together, these constitute *standards-based learning*.

A standard becomes useful to teachers only when they can identify when the standard has been met or progress is being made toward meeting it. Moreover, when schools communicate performance standards to students, students know what is considered important for them to accomplish, and they can judge where they stand in relation to the standard. Students must be prepared to receive targeted feedback in a way that encourages them to compare their work to specific standards. Assessment should provide information on what students already do well and pinpoint what they still need to learn; this provides information about aspects of instruction that need to be redesigned (Jametz, 1994).

**Content Standards**　Each content domain has standards suggested by the professional organization that represents expertise in the field, such as the National Council for the Social Studies, National Council of Teachers of Mathematics (NCTM), and National Association for Sport and Physical Education (NASPE). In turn, the state departments of education (such as the California Department of Education) incorporate these standards into state content standards, designed to define the knowledge, concepts, and skills that students should acquire at each grade level. These are in turn incorporated into curriculum frameworks (blueprints for implementing the content standards) that are then used by individual school districts to determine what instructors in each grade level should teach. When these goals are met, standardized testing should provide evidence that students are learning.

**Standards-Based Content Objectives**　The teacher first specifies learning goals using standards documents, usually in the form of school district curriculum programs. The teacher divides the overall goals for the year into units, then into specific lessons, and then into the content area objectives for each lesson.

Table 5.2 displays content domains, typical content standards topics, and matching objectives. The idea is to accomplish one content objective in one lesson.

In developing their sequence of content objectives, teachers want to keep two important questions in mind: (1) Have I reviewed the objectives for the year and organized them for thematic flow? (2) Have I considered the sequence of objectives and rearranged them, if necessary, putting more concrete concepts before more abstract ones (i.e., those that can be taught with hands-on materials, visuals, and demonstrations before those that are difficult to demonstrate or that require more oral or written skills)?

**TABLE 5.2**  Content Domains, Content Standards, Typical Topics, and Matching Objectives (Sources for standards are in parentheses)

| Content Domains | Content Standard | Typical Topic | Matching Objective |
|---|---|---|---|
| Mathematics | (Gr. 7) (Algebra and Functions). Students express quantitative relationships by using algebraic expressions, equations, inequalities, and graphs. (1) | Finding the unknown | Identify orally or in writing the pre-algebra concept of finding the unknown. |
| Social Studies | (Gr. 6) (World History and Geography: Ancient Civilizations). 6.2. Students analyze the geographic, political, economic, religious, and social structures of the early civilizations of Mesopotamia, Egypt, and Kush. (2) | Religion of Egypt | Identify Egyptian gods from tomb paintings. |
| Literature | (Gr. 11 & 12) (Literary Response and Analysis). 3.4. Analyze ways in which poets use imagery, personification, figures of speech, and sounds to evoke readers' emotions. (3) | Analyze poem | Analyze "We Real Cool" by Gwendolyn Brooks (Brooks, 1944) for plot, language, and theme. |
| Science | (Gr. 1) (Life Sciences). 2b. Students know both plants and animals need water, animals need food, and plants need light. (4) | Plants need light | Expose plants to different conditions of light to observe consequences. |
| Physical Education | (High school course 1, Standard 2). 2.7. Develop and implement a one-month personal physical fitness plan. (5) | Personal physical fitness | Compare two kinds of exercise that could become part of a one-month personal physical fitness plan. |
| Visual Arts | (Gr. 4) (Aesthetic Valuing). 4.3. Describe how using the language of the visual arts helps to clarify personal responses to works of art. (6) | Interpreting a painting | Compare personal responses to Picasso's *Las Meninas* with Renoir's *The Luncheon of the Boating Party at Bougival*. |
| Music | (Gr. 5) (Historical and Cultural Context). 3.2. Identify different or similar uses of musical elements in music from diverse cultures. (7) | Comparing music from different cultures | Contrast the use of drums in three cultural contexts: Brazil, Nigeria, and the United States. |
| Performance Arts | (Gr. 3) (Creative Expression). 2.2. Create for classmates simple scripts that demonstrate knowledge of basic blocking and stage areas. (8) | Staging a play | In groups, students will act out a scene from the Chinese fable *The Magic Sieve*. |

*Sources:* (1) California Department of Education (1997); (2) www.cde.ca.gov/be/st/ss/hstgrade6.asp; (3) www .cde.ca.gov/be/st/ss/enggrades11-12.asp (English Language Arts Content Standards); (4) www.cde.ca.gov/be/st/ss/ scgrade1.asp; (5) California Department of Education (2004a); (6) www.cde.ca.gov/be/st/ss/vagrade8.asp; (7) www .cde.ca.gov/be/st/ss/mugrade5.asp; (8) www.cde.ca.gov/be/st/ss/thgrade3.asp.

## Classroom Glimpse

### MATCHING AN OBJECTIVE TO A STANDARD

Emil Chantal's fourth-grade class read *Amelia's Road* (Altman, 1993) as a focal point for studying the regions of the state of California where certain crops grow. He based this lesson on History Social Science Content Standard 4.1: "Students demonstrate an understanding of the physical and human geographic features that define places and regions in California," specifically, 4.1.3: "Identify . . . and describe the various regions of California, including how their characteristics and physical environments (e.g., water, landforms, vegetation, climate) affect human activity," and 4.1.5: "Use maps, charts, and pictures to describe how communities in California vary in land use, vegetation, wildlife, climate, population density, architecture, services, and transportation."

The content objective for this lesson was "Using a map of California, link regions and crops to the plot of *Amelia's Road*."

Using a map of California's farm regions (http://score.rims.k12.ca.us/score_lessons/amelia_road/map.html), students located where Amelia was born, as well as the locations described in the book. On a study sheet, they also answered questions such as "What grew in the area in which Amelia went to school?"

**Language Standards**   The California English Language Development (ELD) Standards (California Department of Education, 1999) require that English learners develop proficiency in both the English language and the concepts and skills contained in the English language arts (ELA) content standards (California Department of Education, 1997). Like the ELA standards, the California ELD standards are organized in areas of reading, writing, and listening/speaking. The California English Language Development Test is aligned with the standards as a placement and achievement test. Using the ELD and ELA standards, teachers can work with students through a developmental framework that stipulates the requirements of each proficiency level.

## Classroom Glimpse

### LANGUAGE STANDARDS

In a content-based intermediate/advanced ELD high school social studies class, standards-based instruction was incorporated into the unit Exploring World Religions. Students created a word web journal to define religion; used reading passages and journals combined with discussions about religion; and read library and Internet research to identify important religious figures. Final portfolios were used to archive students' essays and other writings. Through the unit, note-taking skills, outlines, timelines, maps, games, and other knowledge technologies were incorporated into group research, oral presentations, paragraph writing, and grammar work. (Riles & Lenarcic, 2000)

**Content-Related Language-Development Objectives**   The language-development objectives of an SDAIE lesson are drawn from the ELD standards. Because students in a class are usually at various CELDT levels—even a single student usually scores at different CELDT levels on listening/

speaking, reading, and writing—the teacher plans for differentiated instruction by incorporating more than one level of language skill in each lesson. The language objective must also address the language needed to accomplish the content objective. In other words, if the lesson features a science laboratory objective, the language objective is integrated with laboratory activity—for example, making observations orally and recording data by writing in a lab manual.

*The CALLA Handbook* (Chamot, 2009) is a valuable resource for helping teachers understand the language demands of various disciplines. Each of the chief subjects—science, mathematics, social studies, and literature and composition—is the focus of a chapter in which the authors specifically address its language demands.

Table 5.3 illustrates the alignment of content and  language-development objectives for two ELD levels. This demonstrates differentiated instruction.

In reviewing language objectives, teachers should keep the following questions in mind:

- What is the concept load of the unit and what are the key concepts to demonstrate and illustrate?
- What are the structures and discourse of the discipline and are these included in the language objectives?
- Are all four language modes included in the planning (listening, speaking, reading, writing)?

 **Classroom Glimpse**

### PLANNING FOR SDAIE SCIENCE

In a sheltered (SDAIE) seventh-grade science class, students improve their English language skills while studying about the universe. The teacher's primary goal is for students to understand the content materials (in this case, about the origin of the universe). But she also spends some time helping students with language-related issues (e.g., academic vocabulary, reading skills) that pertain to the science unit they are studying. The exposure to higher-level language (through the content materials) and the explicit focus on language issues by the teacher set the stage for successful language acquisition. (Brinton, 2003, p. 203)

**Strategic Learning**   The cognitive revolution in learning turned the spotlight on how people transform, elaborate, store, and recover information. According to the cognitive view, people are active learners who initiate experiences, seek out information, and reorganize what they already know in order to achieve new insights, pursue goals, solve personally relevant problems, and attempt to make sense of the world (Bruner, 1986).

Cognitive training includes the use of learning strategies, study skills, memory enhancement, text-processing competencies, note taking, research techniques, test-taking abilities, problem solving, transfer, graphic organizers, and information processing tips, as well as learning the characteristics of the brain. A cognitivist view of learning means teaching students *how* to learn.

Teachers motivate students best when they provide course activities and projects that tap students' natural abilities and interests and develop their confidence in their ability to think. Teachers who ask thought-provoking questions and use concrete examples, activities, and demonstrations stimulate students' imaginations and develop their critical thinking skills.

**TABLE 5.3** Content and Language Objectives for Two ELD Levels in Two Content Areas (Sources for standards are in parentheses)

| Content Standard | Content Objective | Language Standards | Language- Development Objectives |
|---|---|---|---|
| *Life Sciences (Grade 1)* | | | |
| 2b. Students know both plants and animals need water, animals need food, and plants need light. (1) | Expose plants to different conditions of light to observe consequences. | (Beginning). Responds to simple directions and questions using physical actions. (Intermediate). Participates in instructional conversations using expanded vocabulary. | (Beginning). Working in a group, students will follow verbal directions to set up a plant light exposure experiment. (Intermediate). Students will discuss in a group how to set up an observation sheet for plant light exposure experiment. |
| *Physical Education (High School Course 1, Standard 2)* | | | |
| 2.7. Develop and implement a one-month personal physical fitness plan. (2) | Compare two kinds of exercise that could become part of a one-month personal physical fitness plan. | (Early Intermediate). Uses writing to convey meaning. (Early Advanced). Produces independent writing using consistent grammatical forms, mechanics, and word order. | (Early Intermediate). Students will list three reasons for and three reasons against two types of exercise for their personal fitness plan. (Early Advanced). Students will write a comparison paragraph giving three reasons for and three reasons against two types of exercise for their personal fitness plan. |

*Sources:* (1) California Department of Education (1997); (2) California Department of Education (2004a).

This includes metacognition in the form of cognitive self-knowledge (multiple intelligences, learning styles), goal setting, planning, self-monitoring, and self-evaluating.

**Learning-Strategy Objectives**   A cognitive lesson needs one or more learning-strategy objectives, which can be defined as the achievement or practice of direct or indirect strategies that facilitate acquiring new skills or information (Díaz-Rico, 2008). Learning strategies can be distinguished from content objectives by a simple test: Can the objective be applied outside the specific lesson? Is it a skill that can be used again and again as part of a learner's "mental toolkit"?

**Cognitive Academic Language Learning Approach (CALLA)**   Learning strategies are being recognized more and more as an integral part of teaching, an idea made explicit in Chamot's Cognitive Academic Language Learning Approach (CALLA) (2009). CALLA, designed for

## Best Practice  HELPING STUDENTS DEVELOP A PERSONAL SET OF LEARNING STRATEGIES

Teachers can help students become aware of, and acquire, learning strategies in the following ways:

- Modeling multiple ways to solve a problem
- Asking students to describe how they came up with an answer, solution, or process
- Being flexible and changing strategies if one approach does not achieve the desired result
- Praising the use of diverse strategies
- Offering systematic instruction in strategy use

(Adapted from Gregory & Kuzmich, 2005, p. 105)

English learners at the early intermediate to advanced levels of English-language proficiency, incorporates explicit teaching of learning strategies within academic subject areas. The CALLA model includes three components: topics from the major content subjects, the development of academic language skills, and explicit instruction in learning strategies for both content and language acquisition (Chamot, 2009).

The content topics, aligned with the all-English curriculum, are introduced gradually, emphasizing those that have extensive contextual supports or reduced language demands. The second component, academic language skills, includes all four language modes in daily content lessons. Students learn not just vocabulary and grammar but also important concepts and skills using academic language. In addition, they learn language functions important for specific curricular areas, such as analyzing, evaluating, justifying, and persuading.

The third—and central—component is instruction in learning strategies, which are divided into three major categories: *metacognitive, cognitive,* and *social-affective.* The metacognitive strategies help students to plan, monitor, and evaluate their learning processes. Teachers help students learn to preview the main concepts in material to be learned, plan the key ideas that must be expressed orally or in writing, decide in advance what specific information must be attended to, check comprehension during listening or reading, and judge how well learning has been accomplished when the lesson is completed.

 **Classroom Glimpse**

### THINK-ALOUDS AS METACOGNITION

Mrs. Barr, a first-grade teacher, verbalizes her thoughts aloud to show students how she experiences reading comprehension. "I always model a think-aloud before asking anything from students," she says. Then students try it with a partner before sharing their thoughts with the whole group. Finally she asks students to write down what they are thinking, so she can assess how they use this metacognitive strategy.

(Adapted from Herrera, Pérez, & Escamilla, 2010, p. 142)

Cognitive strategies include using reference materials resourcefully; taking effective notes; summarizing material adequately; applying rules of induction or inference; remembering information using visual images, auditory representation, or elaboration of associations to new knowledge; transferring prior skills to assist comprehension; and grouping new concepts, words, or terms understandably. Social-affective strategies teach how to elicit needed clarification, how to work cooperatively with peers in problem solving, and how to use mental techniques or self-talk to reduce anxiety and increase a sense of personal competency.

 **Classroom Glimpse**

### LEARNING-STRATEGY OBJECTIVES

The high school ELD classroom just got three new computers. Mrs. O'Dale knew that several students had computers at home, but nevertheless she wanted to make sure that all the students had basic word-processing skills. Before beginning a unit on autobiography, she identified a set of skills that are useful in word processing. In addition to such content objectives as identifying a topic, including descriptive details, and using time sequence connectors, each lesson in the writing unit would have an objective relating to word processing, beginning with saving and retrieving files, moving text within a file, and spellchecking. Thus, the acquisition of computer skills became learning-strategy objectives.

Skillful lesson planning includes integrating content, learning-strategy, and language-development objectives. A unit on bacteria would include a learning-strategy objective on the use of microscopes and a language objective relating to writing a brief summary (of laboratory observations). In contrast, a social studies lesson would use the reading selection as content but a comprehension-enhancing technique such as "using a cause-and-effect organizer" as a learning strategy.

 **Classroom Glimpse**

### INTEGRATING THREE TYPES OF OBJECTIVES

The Most Beautiful Place in the World is an instructional unit based on the book by the same title (Cameron, 1988) about a young boy in Guatemala who longs to attend school and learn to read (Levine, 2000). Levine found that the Spanish words, foods, and other cultural aspects incorporated in the novel were particularly appropriate for her students, who were all from Spanish-speaking families. The unit also integrated social studies curricular goals as students studied map locations, compass directions, and cultural comparisons.

## Teaching with SDAIE Strategies

English learners need support to enable them to successfully complete tasks that require academic language proficiency. SDAIE means a curriculum that teaches content first and English second. Bell (2002) explained the rationale for such classes at the high school level:

Students, parents, teacher, and counselors were concerned when we proposed [SDAIE] classes because they felt they might not match the curriculum, and they might affect acceptance into four-year colleges and universities. We explained that our English language development classes would focus on English language acquisition at the student's proficiency level. The SDAIE classes would focus on teaching the same curriculum as the regular courses, with added support materials.

My students were so relieved to be in these classes. They have struggled with lowered self-esteem from lowered grades in previous years. In English 10, they learn the themes, symbols, and plot of important literature. In history they learn the key events, the important political concepts, and key people from the time period. They can understand and keep up with the materials, getting grades that reflect their knowledge in the SDAIE classroom. (p. 15)

SDAIE strategies include increasing the use of cooperative learning, activating connections to students' previous knowledge, differentiating instruction to meet the needs of students with varying learning styles, promoting cognitive academic language proficiency, modifying instructional delivery without simplification, furnishing scaffolding (temporary support for instruction), providing graphic organizers, and providing assessment to promote learning and reflection. These strategies are addressed in the following pages, followed by examples in such content areas as language arts, social studies, math, science, music, and visual and performing arts.

Lesson plans in science using the Sheltered Instruction Observation Protocol (SIOP) model for SDAIE can be found in Short, Vogt, and Echevarría (2011). SIOP plans for mathematics are found in Echevarría, Vogt, and Short (2010).

## Cooperative Learning

Many teachers include opportunities for discussion about key concepts, ensuring that students have numerous conversational partners and occasions to interact with the content of lessons. A noncompetitive environment can be established through cooperative learning activities, both formally and informally structured. Heterogeneous groups encourage language development as students talk about learning experiences with one another.

Material presented in a mainstream class may be difficult for English learners if the topics are cognitively complex and highly language dependent. Using cooperative learning, English learners have increased opportunities to verify their comprehension by receiving explanations from their peers and sharing prior knowledge. This helps them clarify and familiarize themselves with the lesson content.

Probably more was written on cooperative and collaborative learning in the last twenty years of the twentieth century than in all the previous history of education. David and Robert Johnson (c.f. Johnson, Johnson, & Holubec, 1993), Robert Slavin (1991), and others advocated the use of cooperative learning for elementary students. Others documented the success of cooperative learning with elementary school English learners (c.f. Cohen, 1994; Johns, 1992; Johnson & Johnson, 1994; Kessler, Quinn, & Fathman, 1992) as well as with secondary school ELD students (Faltis, 1993).

**Benefits to English Learners**   Small-group learning provides English learners with a rich discourse environment and multiple opportunities for face-to-face interaction. This is particularly necessary when students must exchange information about academic content and procedures. When students are collaborating in small groups, they have substantially more chances to practice language—without worrying about whether their production is exactly right. This lowers their anxiety and lets them concentrate on the content of learning. They can hear and say key words and phrases and repeat them in a variety of ways until they feel comfortable with their language mastery (Faltis, 2001). Cooperative grouping also increases the possibility that English learners will feel a part of the culture of the classroom as a whole.

**Guidelines for Cooperative Learning**   Developing cooperative skills requires a focus in the classroom on communication and teamwork. Kluge (1999) emphasized the following elements:

- *Positive interdependence:* Members of a group depend on one another, and no one is exploited or left out.
- *Face-to-face interaction:* Students work in proximity to one another.
- *Individual accountability:* Each group member bears full responsibility for the work performed by the group.
- *Social skills training:* The teacher explicitly explains and models the kind of communication and cooperation that is desired.
- *Group processing:* The teacher makes time for reflection on how the group is working together and helps the group set goals for improvement. (n.p.)

Table 5.4 summarizes the instructional use of cooperative learning with English learners. This information represents a synthesis of tips and guidelines from Bassano and Christison (1995), Cantlon (1991), and Kagan (1998, 1999). (Sources are identified with number keys.)

Even under the best of circumstances, cooperative learning has its challenges. Even though many educators seize on the advantages of having English learners help one another in class, this should not become the default strategy for classroom cooperative learning. Cohen

*Cooperative learning helps to build a sense of community in the classroom.*

Myrleen Ferguson Cate/PhotoEdit

**TABLE 5.4** Instructional Use of Cooperative Learning

| Component of Cooperative Learning | Explanation or Example |
| --- | --- |
| Definition | "An approach to education and a repertoire of teaching strategies based on the philosophy that students can learn effectively in small groups. Cooperative learning restructures the traditional classroom into small, carefully planned learning groups to provide opportunities for all students to work together and to learn from one another." (Source: 5, p. 3) |
| Rationales for using cooperative learning | Practice speaking and listening. <br> Share information. <br> Create things together. <br> Learn democratic processes. <br> Practice negotiating and compromising. (Source: 1, p. 29) <br> Develop leadership, communication, decision-making, and conflict management skills. (Source: 2) <br> Promote real-world team skills. <br> **T**ogether **E**veryone **A**chieves **M**ore (TEAM)! <br> Builds positive interpersonal relations. <br> Transcends differences (cliques). (Source: 4) |
| Roles in teams | Language Monitor, Task Monitor, Timekeeper, Secretary, Clarifier, Encourager, Reporter. (Source: 1, page 29) <br> Materials Monitor, Quiet Captain. (Source: 3) |
| Optimal team size | For initial start-up, dyads (teams of two) are most successful. (Source: 2) <br> If teams of three are necessary, have them sit side by side. (Source: 2) <br> Teams of four are ideal, small enough for active participation and split evenly for pair work. (Source: 3) |
| Frequency of use of cooperative structures | Minimum of three times a week; but simple structures (pair/share) can be used more often. (Source: 2) |
| Room and seating arrangements | Partners should sit side by side. If students are in fours, provide two sets of materials. No student's back should be to the teacher. (Source: 2) |
| Role of the teacher | Source of task; arranger of materials; accountable authority; partner in learning. (Source: 1) |
| Team composition | Heterogeneous (mixed gender, ethnicity, ability); teacher-assigned, long term; this is preferable. (Source: 3) <br> To form heterogeneous ability groups, list students in ability from high to low (1–28), divide into quartiles, then form one group from 1, 8, 15, 22; next group 2, 9, 16, 23, etc. (Avoids highest grouped with lowest.) <br> Random (randomly mixed ability, etc.); breaks up the monotony; short term. (Source: 3) <br> Random teams may be a problem if all high achieving are in one group, or two students create mutual discipline problems. (Source: 2) <br> Random grouping: Use colored marbles or slips with group numbers in a jar; group students by month of birth; count off around class. (Source: 1) |

*(continued)*

**TABLE 5.4**    Continued

| Component of Cooperative Learning | Explanation or Example |
|---|---|
| Team management | Inform students how much time is allotted to task; have an agreed signal to stop working (clap pattern, ringing a bell, countdown, etc.). (Source: 2) |
| Rationale statement | Teacher explains why work is done in a team, what the benefits are, and what behavior is expected. (Source: 2) |
| Necessary group skills | Forming into groups quickly.<br>Participating with muted voices.<br>Establishing turn-taking routines.<br>Involving more hesitant members in group processes. (Source: 1) |
| Trust building/bonding | Rapport building; discuss favorite foods, hobbies, likes, dislikes.<br>Nonacademic fun activities: games, puzzles.<br>Academic tasks: partner reading, checking homework together (staple papers together, teachers correct top paper). (Source: 2) |
| Teaching social skills | Teacher models behavior: quiet voices, taking turns, everyone participating, encouraging partner, signal to stop. (Source: 2) |
| Appreciation statements by peers at debriefing | "(Name), you helped the team by ____."<br>"(____), you did a great job of ____."<br>"(____), I appreciated it when you ____."<br>"(____), you are very good at ____." (Source: 2) |
| Clarification statements by peers | "I don't understand."<br>"Excuse me?"<br>"Speak more slowly, please."<br>"Okay?" (Source: 1, p. 29) |
| Procedural statements by peers | "It's my/your/his/her turn."<br>"Quickly! We have four minutes."<br>"You first, then me." (Source: 1, p. 29) |
| Peers asking for/offering help | "Are you finished?"<br>"I need help."<br>"Do you need help?" (Source: 1, p. 29) |
| Individual accountability | Students have progress conferences with instructor.<br>Groups are rated by teacher using monitoring chart.<br>Groups monitor themselves periodically using rating charts. (Source: 1) |
| Rewards (nonmaterial); avoid message that reward involves escape from work (extra recess) | Elementary: Happygrams, applause, display group work, AV treat, play a special game.<br>Middle/high school: library passes, computer time, daily announcements recognition, newsletter recognition, display work, special privileges, team picture displayed. (Source: 2) |
| Feedback | At the close of activity, teammates write on 3" × 5" card: "Which question/problem gave you difficulty?" "Give examples of what you might do differently next time." "List ways in which your partners helped the team to reach its goal." (Source: 2) |

*Sources:* (1) Bassano & Christison (1995); (2) Cantlon (1991); (3) Kagan (1998); (4) Kagan (1999); (5) Coehlo, Winer, & Olsen (1989).

(1994) found barriers to successful group work, including "undesirable domination on the part of some students, and nonparticipation and withdrawal on the part of others" (p. 26). As Beaumont (1999) noted, the quality of collaborative learning varies with the maturity of students, and "often peer assistance did not provide sufficient support for students whose academic success depended on additional instructional interventions" (p. 235). Table 5.5 offers tactics for teachers to address barriers to successful cooperative learning.

Many types of tasks have been designed that feature cooperative structures. These range from simply pairing students for discussion to more elaborate setups requiring extensive time for preparation and monitoring. Table 5.6 presents a few cooperative structures and tasks. (Sources are identified with number keys.)

The jigsaw model of cooperative learning is particularly useful in that students are individually accountable for learning their own material and for sharing their information effectively with other group members. In the jigsaw method, each member (A, B, C, or D) of each base team (I, II, III, or IV) attends an expert group session (all the As huddle together) to study one aspect or section of the topic and thus has one piece of the knowledge puzzle (hence the name "Jigsaw"). Then the individuals return to their base team to share what they have learned.

**TABLE 5.5**   Challenges to Cooperative Learning and Tactics to Meet Them

| Challenge | Tactics for Teachers |
|---|---|
| Students cannot get along. | Keep activities short and simple while students are learning how to work together.<br>Group students wisely; place a socially immature student with two who are more mature.<br>Teach social skills and review regularly. |
| Student prefers to work alone. | Provide encouragement by emphasizing importance of working in a group, giving examples from teacher's work.<br>Give bonus points to class for working well together.<br>Provide individual work occasionally as "safety valve." |
| Student is unmotivated. | Use interest inventory to discover student's likes and dislikes.<br>Ask previous teachers what works for the student.<br>Give student a role in the group in which he or she will succeed. |
| Student cannot keep up with others. | Let student prepare some part of task prior to group work.<br>Provide a modified worksheet for slow student.<br>Provide an alternate way for student to perform. |
| Group finishes before others. | Provide an extension or enrichment task that extends the activity.<br>Two groups who finish first can compare their products. |
| Group finishes last. | See if task can be modified so all groups will finish together.<br>Teacher or member of early-finishing group can spend some time to help slow group.<br>Let individuals take home tasks. |
| Too much noise. | Monitor groups and commend those who are quiet and on task.<br>Use a standard signal for noise such as blinking room lights.<br>Assign a member of each group as noise control. |

*Source:* Ellis & Whalen, 1992.

**TABLE 5.6** Sample Cooperative Learning Activities

| Name of Activity | Description of Activity |
| --- | --- |
| Relay | Four students learn a skill; they teach it to four others; eight teach it to eight more, until everyone knows it. (Source: 1) |
| Group Memory | In groups of six, give each group a line to memorize. Group members receive extra credit if everyone can say it when time is up. (Source: 1) |
| Listen Please (also called Information Gap) | In this paired activity, student A has words on various cards and student B has a matching set of picture cards. Listening to the description on a card, student B must pick out the matching card. (Source: 1) |
| Sequencing Task | Students put a cut-up sequence in correct order. Example: scrambled dialogue from a phone call to a friend. (Source: 1) |
| Scavenger Hunt | With a stack of newspapers, group finds one of each: some good news, some bad news, weather map, letter to editor, overseas news, etc. (Source: 1) |
| Round Robin | Each person does a problem (using one color ink) and then passes paper to next team member, who does the next problem. Teacher corrects one sheet. (Source: 2) |
| Jigsaw | Students receive number and letter (Ex.: I–IV, A–D). Base teams: I, II, III, IVs. Students exit base team; all As group to study one aspect, etc., then return to base team to share expertise. (Source: 2) |
| Numbered Heads Together | Each student in the group has a number (1–4); students huddle to make sure all can respond, then a number is called and that student responds. (Source: 3) |
| Rotating Review | Students visit wall charts; each chart has different review question; they write answers, then rotate to next chart. (Source: 3) If they agree with what is already written, they mark with asterisk. |
| Send-a-Problem | Groups create problems that are sent around the class for other teams to solve. (Source: 3) |
| Pairs Compare | Pairs come up with ideas to solve a problem. When pairs are through, two pairs make a team of four and compare ideas, generating more ideas. (Source: 4) |
| 4S Brainstorming | While brainstorming solutions to an open-ended prompt, team members take one of four roles: Speed Sergeant: Encourages many responses quickly; Sultan of Silly: Tries to come up with silly ideas; Synergy Guru: Helps members build on one another's ideas; and Sergeant Support: Encourages all ideas, suspends judgment. (Source: 4) |
| Group Memory | Students write everything they know about a topic they plan to study, including unanswered questions that come to them. In groups of three, they read the paper to the group, and everybody adds ideas to their list. The group compiles unanswered questions and turns in a Group Memory Sheet. (Source: 5) |
| Partner Prediction | Teacher preidentifies places in a literature story where the students can stop and predict what happens next. They share predictions with a partner. They must then share aloud what the partner predicts. |

**TABLE 5.6**   Continued

| Name of Activity | Description of Activity |
| --- | --- |
| 2/4 Question Some More | Teacher identifies key points in a read-aloud story. Partners talk about the story so far, then discuss what questions occur to them. They share these in a team of four, then with the class. (Source: 5) |
| Panel of Experts | Students read selected passages, taking notes of possible comprehension questions. In a group, students agree on four questions. One group in the room forms a panel, and others question them. Play continues until panel gets two right or one wrong; then questioning group becomes panel. (Source: 5) |
| Picture Dialogue | Before reading, teacher displays a picture from the book or sets a mental image using words. Working in pairs, students take character A or B and write a dialogue that characters say to each other. They read them aloud. (Source: 5) |

*Sources:* (1) Bassano & Christison (1995); (2) Cantlon (1991); (3) Kagan (1998); (4) Kagan (1999); (5) Whisler & Williams (1990).

The ultimate learning goal is for each member of the base team to have the whole set of information, so each member must communicate what has been learned in the expert group.

 **Classroom Glimpse**

### JIGSAW COOPERATIVE LEARNING

In one use of the jigsaw model, intermediate ELD students studied the use of persuasion in advertising by looking at three different types of ads in three expert groups and completing worksheets with questions such as "How is the ad trying to persuade you? Is it using reason, an appeal to the emotions, or an appeal to a feeling of right or wrong? Is the advertisement effective? Why or why not?" Returning to their base group, group members described the ad they studied and completed a second worksheet summarizing the types and effectiveness of persuasion used in various ads. Students then worked cooperatively to write their own ads. (Weatherly, 1999, p. 79)

## Activating Connections to Students' Previous Knowledge

In the teaching context, prior knowledge refers to what students bring with them that can be tapped and built on during the lesson, consisting of students' existing concepts, understandings, and relevant experiences. These ideas may include misconceptions, so some "unlearning" may have to take place. Also, some prior knowledge may be based on experiences and conceptualizations of the students' home cultures that are beyond the teacher's experience.

Brain-based theory postulates that learners are engaged when the brain is able to create meaning by blending knowledge from previous experiences with concepts from present experiences. Effective teachers thus orchestrate meaning by making connections, instead of leaving this to chance. These connections can be made by establishing links to students' lives and their previous academic knowledge and then by anchoring previous knowledge to new ideas and concepts.

**Best Practice** TAPPING INTO PREVIOUS KNOWLEDGE

The following strategies elicit information from students and help the teacher understand the extent of students' understanding:

- Brainstorming
- K-W-L (What do I *know*? What do I *want* to learn? What have I *learned*?)
- Mind maps
- Pretests
- Questionnaires
- Interviews

If students have little prior knowledge about the topic at hand, teachers can help them build schema or schemata—that is, construct a framework of concepts that shows the relationships between old and new learning and how they are connected. Semantic mapping and webs are ways of presenting concepts to show their relationships. After a brainstorming session, the teacher and students could organize their ideas into a semantic map, with the main idea in the center of the chalkboard and associated or connected ideas as branches from the main idea. Alternatively, a teacher could be more directive in creating a map by writing the central topic and branching out from it with several major subtopics. Students could provide information that the teacher then writes into the appropriate category.

## Classroom Glimpse

### BUILDING SCHEMATA

Mrs. Figueroa read *Cloudy with a Chance of Meatballs* (Barrett, 1978) to her second-grade students. Using a concept map with the words "junk food" in the center, they brainstormed on the following questions: "What is junk food?" "What junk food can you think of?" and "What is in junk food that our bodies don't need?" Students then grouped in pairs to write an adventure story with junk food as the villain.

An anticipation guide can help to determine the extent of students' prior knowledge. As a prelearning exercise, students receive five to ten statements presented in written or oral form, which they judge as true or false. Reviewing the same statements after teaching can help students clarify any misunderstandings they might have had initially.

## Classroom Glimpse

### ANTICIPATION GUIDE FOR EARTHQUAKE UNIT

Ellen Wexford's sixth-grade earth science class was about to begin a unit on earthquakes. She knew from experience that despite being residents of an earthquake-prone region, her students held many misconceptions about tectonic activity. So she constructed an anticipation guide that would be useful to her and her students. She chose items that would correlate with the core knowledge they would need for the unit. Included was the statement, "California might break off from the continent because of a large earthquake." By the end of the unit, she hoped that students would be able to give a reason-based response, choosing "False!" (Adapted from Fisher & Frey, 2009, pp. 43–47)

## Differentiating Instruction to Meet Students' Learning Style Diversity

**Appealing to Diverse Learning Modalities**   The nature of teaching requires some kind of standardization and grouping because class sizes are usually too large to treat each student in a unique manner. The reality in U.S. classrooms, however, is that students are increasingly heterogeneous in an array of ways beyond language: religion; mainstreamed students with disabilities; race/ethnicity (one-third of the U.S. school population is non-White; see Marlowe & Page [1999]); and mobility (43 million people in the United States move every year; see Hodgkinson [1998]). The challenge is clear: How can curriculum, instruction, and assessment be responsive to this learner diversity?

The use of learning styles is based on a few basic hypotheses: (1) that every learner—and teacher—has a learning style preference; (2) that all styles are equally valid, although the educational context may value some more than others; (3) that learning about one's preferences, and acquiring styles other than one's preference, may assist students in learning; and (4) that learning strategies are linked to learning styles (Reid, 1995). Teachers can reduce the complexity of the learning style typologies by surveying various systems, analyzing themselves, and settling on one or two systems that both explain individual differences and offer a relatively easy way to accommodate instruction to learner differences.

In the typical classroom, some modification may be made that takes learning styles into account. If students as a group are both competitive and dependent, for example, assignments that enhance other characteristics (such as collaborative and independent learning) might be developed. Teachers can use a variety of learning activities to accommodate distinct learning styles. Students' awareness of their learning style preferences constitutes a metacognitive strategy. Once aware of their own preferences, students can use this knowledge to support their learning.

A comprehensive source for the incorporation of learning styles into second-language acquisition instruction is Reid's (1995) *Learning Styles in the ESL/EFL Classroom,* a compendium of articles on research and practice in this area. The book features various inventories of learning styles; suggestions for learners with visual, auditory, and haptic preferences; and a look at crosscultural implications.

Teachers can incorporate learning styles into instruction in the following ways:

- Diagnose one's own learning style preferences to understand oneself as a teacher.
- Settle on one or two systems that help create awareness of students' learning style diversity.
- Find a way to add variety to instructional plans that makes a difference on this set of preferences.

**Best Practice** LEARNING CENTERS FOR DIFFERENTIATED INSTRUCTION

Centers can be used in any content class to provide intentional experiences that allow students to learn in diverse ways, such as the following examples of centers that can be used at the secondary level:

- *Poet's corner.* Using different types of verse as models, students can work alone or with partners to read or create poetry.
- *Technology center.* Students can write and publish their own stories, using Inspiration software that displays the sequence of events in the story.
- *Storyboards.* Students can create storyboard pictures, with text underneath to tell the story.
- *Cool stuff.* Using interesting materials such as gel pens and paper with interesting borders, students can create ads for books they write or have read. (Adapted from Gregory & Kuzmich, 2005, p. 195)

**Using Realia, Manipulatives, and Hands-On Materials**   Student learning activities should develop students' interactive language but not disadvantage an English learner. Collaborative problem-solving teams include member roles that provide a variety of input and output modalities to balance the English skills and nonverbal talents of students. English learners can benefit from the use of media, realia, science equipment, diagrams, models, experiments, manipulatives, and other modalities that make language more comprehensible and that expand the means and modes by which they receive and express information.

## Promoting Cognitive Academic Language Proficiency

Cummins (1979, 1980) has posited two different yet related language skills: basic interpersonal communication skills (BICS) and cognitive academic language proficiency (CALP). BICS involves those language skills and functions that allow students in school to communicate in everyday social contexts that are similar to those of the home: to perform classroom chores, chat with peers, or consume instructional media as they do television shows at home.

BICS is *context embedded* because participants can provide feedback to one another, the situation itself provides cues that further understanding, and factors apart from the linguistic code can furnish meaning. In contrast, CALP, as the name implies, is the language needed to perform abstract and decontextualized school tasks successfully. Students must rely primarily on language to attain meaning. For English learners, BICS has been found to approach native-like levels within two years of exposure to English, but five or more years may be required for minority students to match native speakers in CALP (Collier, 1987; Cummins, 1981a; Hakuta, Butler, & Witt, 2000). Students need skills in both kinds of language.

Because CALP provides few concrete cues to assist comprehension, Cummins (1984) calls CALP *context-reduced* communication. CALP also involves systematic thought processes, the cognitive toolbox needed to categorize, compare, analyze, and accommodate new experiences and is therefore key to acquiring the in-depth knowledge needed in a complex modern society.

CALP requires growing beyond the simple *use* of language to the more complex ability to *think and talk about* language—metalinguistic awareness (Scarcella & Rumberger, 2000). Precise differentiation of word meaning and the ability to decode complicated sentences demand from students a gradual understanding of the cultural and social uses of the language to which they are exposed. CALP is not gained solely from school or solely from the home—one reinforces the other. However, CALP is highly dependent on the assistance of teachers because, for the most part, CALP is learned in school.

Some teachers confuse CALP and BICS as correct versus incorrect usage of English. CALP is *not* just hypergrammatical BICS. Teachers can help students to acquire CALP by analyzing the conceptual and critical thinking requirements of the grade-level curriculum *and* taking the time to ensure that all students are explicitly taught such requirements. Good teachers use CALP with their students; but excellent teachers ensure that students can use CALP themselves.

Without this explicit attention to teaching CALP, one of three outcomes is all too common. First, students who come to school already having acquired CALP as a benefit of a privileged home environment may outshine English learners. Second, the curriculum for English learners may be watered down due to the assumption that those who lack CALP cannot perform academically at a high cognitive level. Third, students lacking CALP in English are not able to participate knowledgeably and are often confined to a skills-based, direct instruction approach that does not encourage a constructivist learning environment.

Academic materials that incorporate CALP teach not only content but also the cognitive skills to acquire content. *High Point* (Schifini, Short, & Tinajero, 2002) makes CALP explicit by listing CALP terminology to be covered in each unit. For example, Level C Unit 4 Theme 1 (A Fork in the Road) presents words such as *choice, decision, advantages, disadvantages, pros,* and *cons* to accomplish the academic function of "justifying" (p. 223). Level C Unit 5 Theme 2 (Moving Forward) offers CALP terms such as *responsible, avoid, accept,* and *solve a problem;*

*Pictures and hands-on activities help students to gain basic interpersonal communicative skills as well as academic language.*

Will Hart/PhotoEdit

subsequent vocabulary work teaches *denotation, connotation, thesaurus, substitute,* and *synonym.* Thus, *High Point* is an exemplar of a CALP-equipped curriculum.

The complexity of CALP can be captured by examination of the five Cs: communication, conceptualization, critical thinking, context, and culture (see Table 5.7). Many of the skills that are a part of CALP are refinements of basic interpersonal communication skills (BICS), whereas others are more exclusively school-centered.

 **Classroom Glimpse**

### DEVELOPING CALP

Mrs. Álvarez found in her second-grade structured English immersion class that, although the students were fairly fluent in English when chatting with one another, they lacked the vocabulary to perform on academic tasks. When she gave instructions or briefly reviewed concepts, the students appeared lost. She became aware that students needed to move along the continuum from their everyday English usage to more abstract academic language.

The class was studying the ocean. Mrs. Álvarez set up learning centers with shells, dried seaweed, fish fossils, and other ocean objects. The instructions for these centers featured patterned, predictable language tied to the concrete objects, with words such as *group, shape,* and *size.* Gradually Mrs. Álvarez tape-recorded more complex and abstract instructions for use in the learning centers, such as *classify, arrange,* and *attribute.* This progression and integration of activities helped the children move along the continuum from BICS to CALP.

## Modifying Instructional Delivery without Simplification

Teachers must ensure that students understand what is said in the classroom. Teachers in SDAIE classrooms devote particular attention to four communication strategies: *language contextualization, teacher's speech modification, repetition and paraphrase,* and *use of patterned language.*

**Language Contextualization**   Teaching should be focused on the context of the immediate task, augmenting vocabulary with gestures, pictures, realia, and so forth to convey instructions or key words and concepts. This provides a rich visual and/or kinesthetic (e.g., through drama and skits) environment. Verbal markers are used to organize the lesson, such as *note this* to denote importance, or *now, first, second,* and *last* to mark a sequence. To help with directions, teachers can determine the ten most frequently used verbal markers and teach these through mini-total physical response (TPR)-type lessons. The teacher might also learn how to say simple directions in the students' language(s).

**Teacher's Speech Modification**   To be understandable to those who do not speak or understand English well, the teacher must adjust speech from the customary native speech patterns. This takes place at many linguistic levels—phonological (precise articulation); syntactic (shorter sentences, with subject–verb–object word order); semantic (more concrete, basic vocabulary; fewer idioms); pragmatic (frequent and longer pauses; slower delivery; and exaggerated intonation, especially placing more stress on important new concepts); and discourse (self-repetition; main idea easily recognized and supporting information following immediately). Teachers in SDAIE classrooms also speak less in the classroom, encouraging students to talk. There is much

**TABLE 5.7**   Components of Cognitive Academic Language Proficiency (CALP)

| Component | Explanation |
|---|---|
| Communication | Reading: Increases speed; masters a variety of genres in fiction (poetry, short story) and nonfiction (encyclopedias, magazines, Internet sources).<br>Listening: Follows verbal instructions; interprets nuances of intonation (e.g., in cases of teacher disciplinary warnings); solicits, and benefits from, help of peers.<br>Speaking: Gives oral presentations, answers correctly in class, and reads aloud smoothly.<br>Writing: Uses conventions such as spelling, punctuation, report formats. |
| Conceptualization | Concepts become abstract and are expressed in longer words with more general meaning (*rain* becomes *precipitation*).<br>Concepts fit into larger theories (*precipitation* cycle).<br>Concepts fit into hierarchies (rain → precipitation cycle → weather systems → climate).<br>Concepts are finely differentiated from similar concepts: (*sleet* from *hail*, *typhoons* from *hurricanes*).<br>Conceptual relations become important (opposites, subsets, causality, correlation). |
| Critical thinking | Uses graphic organizers to represent the structure of thought.<br>Uses textual structures (outlines, paragraphing, titles, main idea).<br>Reads between the lines (inference).<br>Detects bias; separates fact from opinion; tests validity of sources. |
| Context | Nonverbal: Uses appropriate gestures; interprets nonverbal signs accurately.<br>Formality: Behaves formally when required to do so.<br>Participation structures: Fits in smoothly to classroom and schoolwide groups and procedures. |
| Culture | Draws on background knowledge.<br>Uses social-class markers, such as "manners."<br>Moves smoothly between home and school.<br>Marshals parental support for school achievement.<br>Deploys primary-language resources when required.<br>Maintains uninterrupted primary-culture profile ("fits in" to neighborhood social structures). |

evidence indicating that teachers should reduce teacher talking time (TTT) while teaching and increase the amount of student talking time (STT). As Harmer (2007) pointed out,

> Overuse of TTT is inappropriate because the more a teacher talks, the less chance there is for students to practice their own speaking—and it is students who need the practice, not the teacher. If the teacher talks and talks, the students will have less time for other things, too, such as reading and writing. For these reasons, a good teacher maximizes STT and minimizes TTT. (p. 38)

As students become more proficient in English, teachers again adjust their speech, this time increasing speed and complexity. Ultimately, English learners will need to function in an all-English-medium classroom; therefore, over time, SDAIE teachers need to reduce the speech modification scaffolds they use to accommodate their students' evolving proficiency. Table 5.8 summarizes the modifications teachers can make in speech and instructional delivery to make their teaching more comprehensible.

**Repetition and Paraphrase**   Verbal repetition can be employed to increase comprehensibility (for example, using the same type of directions throughout various lessons), as can organizational repetition (lessons that occur at specific times, lessons with clearly marked verbal and nonverbal boundaries, such as "Now it's time to . . . ," or the use of specific locations for specific content). Concepts are presented numerous times through various means. Elaboration, in which the teacher supplies redundant information through repetition and paraphrase, may also prove effective.

**Use of Patterned Language**   It is helpful for teachers to signal the beginnings and endings of lessons clearly, using stock phrases (e.g., "Math time is over. Put away your books"). Procedures and classroom routines should be predictable so that English learners do not feel they have to be ever-vigilant for a change in rules. This reduces stress and gives students a feeling of security.

Although SDAIE teaching involves presentation of subject matter in English, opportunities are available throughout the lesson for students to clarify their understanding using their primary language, supplemented whenever possible by primary-language resources (print, electronic, personnel) that can help students with key concepts.

The scope of this book does not permit an exhaustive discussion of SDAIE. For an excellent in-depth treatment, refer to *Making Content Comprehensible for English Language Learners: The SIOP Model* (Echevarría, Vogt, & Short, 2004).

**Explanation of Concepts in the Primary Language**   In SDAIE classrooms, students are afforded opportunities to learn and clarify concepts in their own language. When possible, the teacher offers primary-language resources (print, electronic, personnel) that can help students with key concepts. Although SDAIE teaching involves presenting subject matter in English, teachers continue to provide opportunities throughout the lesson for students to clarify their understanding using the primary language.

Recourse to the primary language is still a controversial issue, and many teachers shy away from it on the mistaken belief that primary-language use detracts from developing English proficiency. However, research continues to show that when students are able to employ their first language, they make more academic gains in both content and language than if they are prohibited from using it (Collier, 1995).

**Clarification Checks**   Teachers monitor listening and reading comprehension at intervals to gain a sense of the students' ability to understand. The teacher might pause to ask a question requiring a simple response, such as "Show me how you are going to begin your work," or ask individual students to restate the instruction using their own words.

Questions at the literal level are designed simply to check whether students understand directions, details, or procedures. During formal presentations, teachers often use strategies such as asking students to "vote" on their understanding of what has been said by a show of hands. This helps to maintain interest and check for understanding. Depending on student

**TABLE 5.8**   Teachers' Language Modification in SDAIE

| Type of Modification | Definition | Example |
|---|---|---|
| Precise articulation | Increased attention to enunciation so that consonants and vowels in words are understandable | "Trade your *homework* with the person *beside* you." |
| Use of gestures | Showing with hands what is to be done | Make a swapping gesture with papers to act out "trading homework." |
| Intonation | Increased stress on important concepts | "The number of *correct* answers goes at the top of the page." |
| Simplified syntax | Shorter sentences, with subject-verb-object word order | "Mark the papers. Give them back." |
| Semantic clarity | More concrete, basic vocabulary; fewer idioms | "Turn in your work. I mean, give me your homework." |
| Pragmatic distinctness | Frequent and longer pauses; slightly slower delivery | "Check the chemicals . . . Check the list . . . Be sure your team has all the chemicals for your experiment." |
| Use of discourse markers | Careful use of transition words, emphasis, and sequence markers | "Note this" to denote importance, or "now," "first," "second," and "last" to mark a sequence. |
| Use of organizational markers | Clearly indicating change of activity | "It's time for recess . . . Put away your books." |
| More structured discourse | Main idea easily recognized and supporting information following immediately | "Today we are learning about mole weight. . . . I will show you how to calculate mole weight to make the correct solution." |
| Use of clarification checks | Stopping instruction to ask students if they understand; monitoring students' comprehension | "Hold your thumb up in front of your chest if you understand how to use the formula for acceleration." |
| Soliciting written input | Having students write questions on index cards | "I have a card here asking for another explanation of longitude degrees and minutes. OK . . ." |
| Repetition | Revisiting key vocabulary terms | "*Precipitation* means overall rain or snowfall; we are going to study the precipitation cycle." |
| Use of mini-TPR lessons to preteach key terms | Acting out terms to increase understandability | " 'On the other hand' ": Carlos, stand over here, and Elena, stand here—you are 'on one hand,' he *is* 'on the other hand.'" |
| Use of primary language | Saying simple directions in the students' language(s) | "*tsai jher,* over here, *tsai nar,* over there" (Mandarin). |

response, teachers may need to rephrase questions and information if the students do not initially understand.

**Using Questions to Promote Reflection**   Effective questioning techniques can probe for students' abilities to infer and evaluate. Teachers need to be patient when asking questions—to wait for students to understand the question before calling on individuals. Even after nominating a student to answer, wait-time is necessary to allow an English learner to compose and deliver a response. He or she may know the answer but need a little more processing time to say it in English.

Effective mediational questions—those that promote reflection—focus on the process of thought rather than on low-level details. The following questions or requests provoke thought:

- Tell me how you did that.
- What do you think the problem is?
- What's another way we might approach this?
- What do you think would happen if . . . ?
- What might you do next? (Adapted from Costa & Garmston, 2002)

Students need to be encouraged by teachers to engage in active oral participation in class. Zwiers (2008) suggested five kinds of prompts to urge students to elaborate their talk. First, teachers should *prompt further thinking* using phrases like "You're on to something important. Keep going" or "You're on the right track. Tell us more." Students can be asked to *justify their responses:* "That's a probable answer. How did you get to that answer?" or "What evidence do you have to support that claim?"

Teachers can *ask for a report* on an investigation by saying, "Describe your result," or "What do you think caused that to happen?" *To see other points of view,* students can be asked, "If you were in that person's shoes, what would you have done?" or "Would you have reacted like that? Why or why not?" Finally, to prompt students to *consider consequences,* one might say, "What if she had not done that?" or "How can we apply this in real life?" Open-ended questions like these elicit a greater balance between the amount of student talk and teacher talk.

Skilled questioning using a linguistic hierarchy of question types helps teachers ascertain students' understanding. For students in the "silent period," questions elicit a nonverbal response—a head movement, pointing, or manipulation of materials. Once students begin to speak, they can choose the correct word or phrase to demonstrate understanding of either/or questions: "Does the water expand or contract to form ice?" "Did Russians come to California from the west or the north?" Once students are more comfortable producing language, *wh-* questions are used: "What is happening to the water?" "Which countries sent explorers to California?" "What was the purpose of their exploration?" Skillful teachers can ask questions requiring critical or creative thinking even at the beginning level; students at advanced English levels are not the only ones capable of inferential thinking.

## Scaffolding: Temporary Support for Learning

In education, scaffolding is used to help the learner construct knowledge (Berk & Winsler, 1995). During scaffolding, the teacher helps to focus the learner's attention on relevant parts of the task by asking key questions that help to determine the zone of proximal development for that student on the particular task. Questions and verbalizations give students the opportunity to think and talk about what they must do.

Dividing the task into smaller, manageable subcomponents and sensitively withdrawing assistance when it is no longer required furthers success (Díaz, Neal, & Vachio, 1991). The teacher who uses scaffolding skillfully does so in a form of dynamic assessment, evaluating and teaching at the same time. Table 5.9 presents scaffolding strategies in various content areas.

## Providing Graphic Organizers

Another way to scaffold is to make verbal information visual. Graphic organizers are visual frames used to represent and organize information—"a diagram showing how concepts are related" (McKenna & Robinson, 1997, p. 117). Many kinds of graphic organizers can also be used to help students focus their thoughts and reactions—for example, as they read a literature selection. Because graphic organizers balance visual with verbal representation, they can help to make visible the conceptual structures that underlie content. This helps students make models for understanding ideas and outcomes.

Graphic organizers are particularly useful in content instruction. With mind maps or other information organizers, students can interact with the concepts presented in various content areas in a way that supplements verbal text (Flynn, 1995). Thus, English learners can access core content even when their reading skills are weak. This results in greater student engagement in their learning.

Graphic organizers have at least three major applications. First, *representative/explanatory* organizers are used to increase content understanding, either by building background

**TABLE 5.9** Scaffolding Strategies for Use in Content Areas

| Scaffolding Strategy | Description of Use in the Content Class |
| --- | --- |
| Previewing vocabulary | Before beginning a social studies lesson, students in pairs skim the chapter and look up definitions in the glossary. |
| Prereading activities | Students make collages with pictures of vegetables cut from magazines before reading in the health book about the vitamins found in common foods. |
| Language experience approach | After performing a laboratory experiment, students interview one another and write down a report of the experiment results. |
| Interactive journals | Students describe personal exercise goals and write daily results in a journal; their peer "personal trainer" reads and provides feedback and encouragement. |
| Shared reading | Students "buddy read" encyclopedia entries as they write a group science research report. |
| Learning logs | In a mathematics center, students make entries into a group log as they try to solve a weekly puzzle. |
| Process writing | Students working on a monthlong family history project share their rough drafts with family members to gain input before final revision. |

knowledge before students read a text or synthesizing new information that is gained from a text. Second, *generative* organizers promote ideas related to content. Students can talk or write about the information presented on a chart. Third, *evaluative* organizers help explain content. Figure 5.1 shows examples of these three types.

    A *sequential organizer* is an explanatory diagram that shows items in order, such as parts of a book, a letter, or an essay; events in a story plot; or steps in written directions (Kagan, 1998, 1999). Figure 5.2 shows a sequential organizer used to list the beginning, middle, and end of a story. Figure 5.3 shows the problem–solution chain in a Native-American "coyote" story. If the events repeat, a cycle graph might be used. A sequence can be a cartoon, a picture strip, or a timeline.

---

**FIGURE 5.1**    Three Types of Graphic Organizers

| **Representative/Explanatory** | **Generative** | **Evaluative** |
|---|---|---|
| ▪ Sequential | ▪ Concept development | ▪ Grade scale |
| ▪ Compare/contrast circles | ▪ Mind map | ▪ Likert scale |
| ▪ T-chart | ▪ Spider map | |
| ▪ Comparison chart | ▪ K-W-L | |
| ▪ Embedded | | |
| ▪ Whole/part | | |
| ▪ Cause/effect | | |
| ▪ Classification | | |

---

**FIGURE 5.2**    Sample Sequential Organizer: Story Sequence Chart

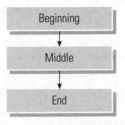

**FIGURE 5.3**    Sample Sequential Organizer: Problems and Solutions in a Story

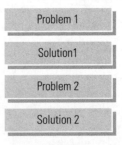

**FIGURE 5.4**   Sample Compare/ Contrast (Venn) Diagram Used for the Questions "How Are Two Things Alike? How Are They Different?"

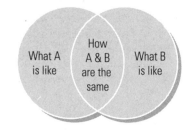

**FIGURE 5.5**   Sample T-Chart: Comparison of Same and Different

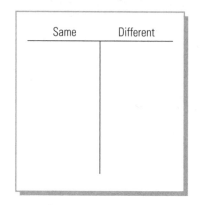

*Compare/contrast organizers* can be used to compare characters in the same story or in different stories, types of correspondence (business versus friendly letters), or genres of reading (fiction versus nonfiction). Visually, comparison charts can be of various types: compare/ contrast circles (Venn diagram, see Figure 5.4), T-charts (see Figure 5.5), or comparison charts (see Figure 5.6).

Other *relational organizers* can show information that is embedded (see Figure 5.7), whole/part (see Figure 5.8), or cause/effect (see Figure 5.9).

*Classification organizers* are used to create hierarchies (Figure 5.10), matrixes (Figure 5.11), or other concept relations that show specific structures. Figure 5.12 shows a two-dimensional plot; Figure 5.13 demonstrates an alternative way to display a hierarchy.

**FIGURE 5.6**   Sample Comparison Chart Showing Comparison by Attributes

### Comparison of Civilizations

|  | *Egypt* | *United States* |
|---|---|---|
| Duration | More than 4000 years | About 400 years |
| Political structure | Towns united by centralized government | Hierarchy: towns, counties, states, federal government |
| Religion | Pharaonic, later Islam | Predominantly Protestant Christian, then Catholic Christian, then Jewish, Islam, other |

etc.

**FIGURE 5.7**  Sample Relational Organizer Showing Embedded Concepts (Teacher's Phenomenal Field of Personal Relations in the Role of Teacher)

**FIGURE 5.8**  Sample Relational Organizer Showing Whole/Part (Parts of the Atom)

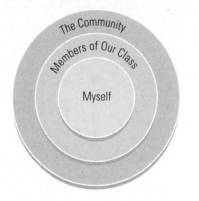

| Atom | Nucleus | Protons |
| | | Neutrons |
| | Electrons | |

---

**Best Practice    A CLASSIFICATION TASK**

Students can practice a classification graphic organizer by sorting a list of recyclable items: newspapers, soda bottles, soup cans, shampoo containers, office paper, clean aluminum foil, junk mail, a shoe box, plastic water bottles, and so on. (Let them make their own categories.)

(Adapted from Bonesteel, Gargagliano, & Lambert, 2010, p. 169)

---

*Concept development organizers* are used to brainstorm. They do not display information that is already related. The K-W-L chart is used to introduce a theme, a lesson, or a reading. It can help generate interest in a topic and support students in using their prior knowledge as they read. Students can enter K (what we Know) and W (what we Want to know) in advance, reserving L (what we Learned) for the end of the unit or lesson (see Figure 5.14). The mind map is basically a circle showing the topic in the center, with lines or other connectors around it that tie students' ideas to the topic (see Figures 5.15 and 5.16).

*Evaluation organizers* show degree of positivity (Kagan, 1998). These can be grade scales (A to F); Likert scales (from 1 = strongly disagree to 7 = strongly agree); rubric scales (needs work→ satisfactory→ good→ excellent); or they can comprise two boxes ("I like/agree with" versus "I dislike/disagree with") or three boxes (plus/maybe/minus).

Once students and teachers become familiar with graphic organizers, they are a help to English learners in grasping basic concepts without dependence on language as the sole source of understanding. An excellent source is Parks and Black's *Organizing Thinking: Graphic Organizers* (1990).

**FIGURE 5.9** Sample Relational Organizer Showing Cause/Effect (Possible Causes of Lightbulb Nonfunctioning)

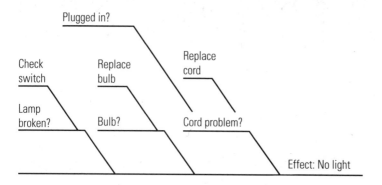

**FIGURE 5.10** Sample Classification Chart Showing Main Ideas

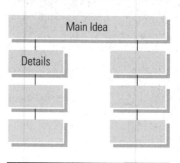

**FIGURE 5.11** Sample Classification Chart Showing a Matrix

|  | Boys | Girls | Totals |
|---|---|---|---|
| Blue-eyed | 4 | 7 | 11 |
| Brown-eyed | 13 | 10 | 23 |
| Totals | 17 | 17 | 34 |

**FIGURE 5.12** Sample Classification Chart Showing Dimensions (Learning Styles)

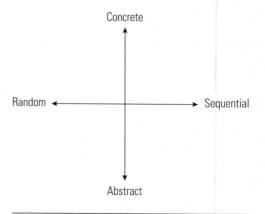

 **Classroom Glimpse**

### TUTORING WITH GRAPHIC ORGANIZERS

Semantic mapping proved to be a successful approach for three English learners, two boys ages five and nine and their sister, age ten, whom Judy was tutoring. The children had chosen "Halloween" as an interesting topic to explore as a way to increase their vocabulary in English. Starting with words they knew in English (skeleton, witch), Judy wrote the words on chart paper, which the children copied in their notebooks. The children gave other words in Spanish, and Judy found the English equivalents and wrote them too. (Continued)

> Using a fresh piece of chart paper, Judy asked the students how the list of words could be grouped into categories. The activity continued until the words had been grouped into the categories Animals, Monsters, and Trick-or-Treat. Judy followed up this activity by reading a book on Halloween, *Rotten Ralph's Trick or Treat*. When they came to a word on the chart, Judy pointed it out for reinforcement. (Brisk & Harrington, 2000, pp. 71–72)

## Using Assessment to Promote Learning and Reflection

**Formative Assessment and Reteaching**   As students are learning, the teacher can help them maintain momentum and solve ongoing problems through a process of formative assessment

**FIGURE 5.13**   Sample Classification Chart Showing Hierarchy

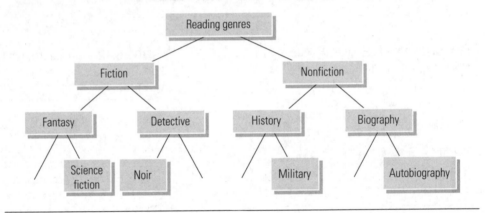

**FIGURE 5.14**   Sample Concept Development Chart: K-W-L

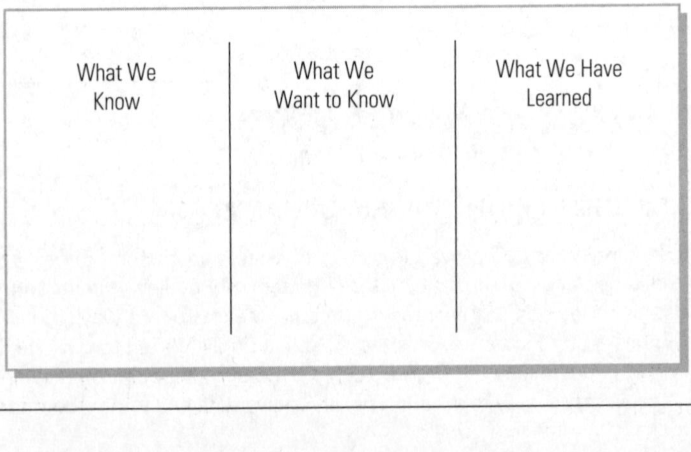

| What We Know | What We Want to Know | What We Have Learned |
| --- | --- | --- |
| | | |

**FIGURE 5.15**   Sample Concept Development Chart: Mind Map or Idea Web

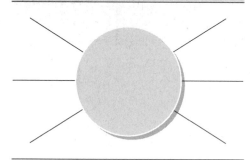

**FIGURE 5.16**   Sample Concept Development Chart: Character Trait Web

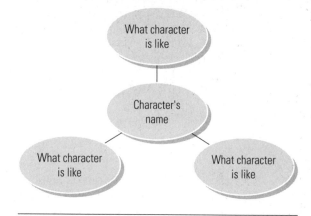

involving progress checks, which helps students to evaluate their efforts in the light of their goals and stay on track. The teacher may require formal weekly progress reports, ask for partial products at predetermined times, or set deadlines for circulation of rough drafts. Formative evaluation can permit much valuable ongoing readjustment of the learning process.

Teachers exercise patience in helping students monitor and adjust their learning to meet the desired performance standards; vanquish students' habits of sloth or procrastination, if these are a problem; conquer the students' lack of faith in themselves by providing encouragement, structure, and guidelines; overcome students' impatient desire to improve instantly, as they perhaps try and fail several times before succeeding; help students accept the disappointment of failure if there is some aspect of a complex problem that eludes solution; or make themselves available during students' basic struggle to use English as a means of expression.

Not all learning is successful. Sometimes problems that are worth addressing are beyond comprehension, and sometimes problems that are comprehensible are simply not interesting. Most teachers do everything possible to facilitate successful learning. But, in the last analysis, it is not the teacher's job to rescue students from disappointment or failure; these are a part of authentic learning. Sometimes metalearning—the wisdom about learning—comes after the learning has been attempted, in a process of reflection and hindsight.

**Summative Assessment, Culminating Performance, and Metalearning**   A final performance on a certain day—such as a play with other students as audience or an exhibit for parents— helps students understand the real world of promise and fulfillment. Despite the satisfaction these culminating events offer, the substance of assessment remains with the content standards that have been achieved. Peer evaluation, self-evaluation, and teacher evaluation together garner the final evidence: Was the learning successful? What was learned about the content? What was learned about the process? And most excitingly, what is still not known? What remains to be discovered?

**Box 5.2**   Critical Reflection in Lesson Planning

- What were the strengths in the lesson?
- Were content, learning, and language objectives clearly stated to students?
- Were students, including English learners, engaged in the lesson?
- How many opportunities were provided for English-language development?
- What evidence do I have to demonstrate that lesson adaptations for English learners were adequate?
- Which evidence demonstrated learning by English learners?
- Which opportunities allowed students to self-assess and be responsible for their own learning?
- What areas require changes for lesson improvement?

*Source:* Balderrama & Díaz-Rico (2006).

**Reflective Pedagogy**   Pausing to reflect is the final step in lesson delivery; it occurs at the end of instruction for English learners and in turn reactivates the cycle of teaching and planning. Some questions teachers may use to frame critical contemplation of their teaching are listed in Box 5.2.

# Effective Resource Use in ELD and SDAIE

A key to success in the SDAIE classroom is the provision of resource-rich teaching to expand the modalities in which English learners can receive information. But which materials? And how to select them?

## Selecting and Using Appropriate Materials

Choosing the right genre is one way to help English learners develop their conceptual and linguistic schemata. The literature curriculum, for example, can be a planned sequence that begins with familiar structures of folktales and myths and then uses these as a bridge to more complex works of literature. Myths and folktales from many cultures are now commonly available in high-quality editions with vibrant illustrations. Students can move from these folktales and myths to selected short stories by authors of many cultural backgrounds, then to portions of a longer work, and finally to entire works.

  **Classroom Glimpse**

### A VARIETY OF MATERIALS

William Pruitt (2000, pp. 31–49) describes how his students move from studying different versions of a folktale to studying other kinds of tales.

One of the goals of the story unit is for students to examine how the same story may differ as it appears in different perspectives, media, and cultures, and to compare and contrast these forms. Over the course of the two-week unit, we read and compare and contrast an original (translated) version of "Beauty and the Beast," a poem entitled "Beauty and the Beast," and three video versions of the story. Once students have gained experience with this folktale and understand the pattern of activities, we move to other texts that have film adaptations, for example, *Tuck Everlasting* (Babbitt, 1976).

Materials used in the classroom are most accessible when they match the age, language ability, and prior content knowledge of the students. Materials in the primary language can supplement content delivery in English. In fact, with a rich theme, materials from around the world can be featured in instruction.

**Best Practice**    **MATERIALS FOR A RICH THEME**

A good example of an application of a rich theme is "Tool Use" (*Into English*, Level C, pp. 58–71). Students identify, graph, and discuss their use of tools; they can investigate what tools are found at home or at their parents' workplaces; they can explore tools used for everyday life such as in cooking; they can brainstorm new uses for tools and learn the names of common academic tools. This unit can incorporate crosscultural study (Chinese abacus) and total physical response (a game of charades acting out tool use). Classroom visitors can discuss the tools they use in their work. (Tinajero & Schifini, 1997)

Selecting materials involves an initial choice by the teacher whether to have one main content source or a package of content-related materials (chapters from various texts, video- and audiotapes, magazine and newspaper articles, encyclopedia entries, literary selections, Internet sources, software programs, etc.). Regardless of what is chosen, the teacher must consider two criteria: Are the content objectives for the lesson adequately presented by the material? Is the material comprehensible to English learners?

The following list enumerates items to consider when selecting materials:

- The information is accurate, up-to-date, and thorough.
- The tasks required of students are appropriate to the discipline and promote critical thinking.
- The text is clearly organized and engaging, with attractive print and layout features that assist students' comprehension.
- The text appeals to a variety of learning styles.
- Sources represented in the text include various literary genres (e.g., narrative, descriptive, analytic).
- The language of the text is straightforward, without complex syntactic patterns, idioms, or excessive jargon.
- New content vocabulary is clearly defined within the text or in a glossary.
- Diagrams, graphs, and charts are clearly labeled and complement and clarify the text.

Content area teachers must also use primary-language resources, such as dictionaries, books, software programs, Internet sites, encyclopedias, textbooks, and illustrated charts as well as people resources, such as cross-age tutors, parents, and community volunteers, in helping students to understand concepts. English learners in the content class are continually exposed to new content material and often find primary-language sources helpful.

## Modifying Materials for Linguistic Accessibility

The teacher selects, modifies, and organizes text material to accommodate the needs of English learners. In modifying text, the goal is to improve comprehensibility through such means as providing study guides or defining new content vocabulary by showing definitions pictorially. Other modifications that may be necessary to help English learners comprehend connected discourse include the following approaches:

- Supply an advance organizer for the text that highlights the key topics and concepts in outline form, as focus questions, or as concept maps.
- Change the modality from written to oral. By reading aloud, the teacher can also model the process of posing questions while reading to show prediction strategies used when working with text (see the discussion of directed reading–thinking activity in Chapter 7).
- Selected passages can be tape-recorded for students to listen to as they read along in the text.
- By working in groups, students can share their notes and help one another complete missing parts or correct misunderstood concepts.

These adaptations increase readability. As students' language proficiency increases, so should the complexity of their reading material. The goal is to move students toward the ability to work with unmodified texts (Richard-Amato & Snow, 1992).

## Culturally Appealing Materials

Multicultural materials are a rich source of language and content area learning, including books and other print media, visual aids, props, realia, manipulatives, materials that access other modalities, and human resources. Students may be able to bring in pictures, poems, dances, proverbs, or games; new ways to do math problems; or maps that show a different perspective than that given in the textbook. Shen's Books (www.shens.com) carries a wide selection of multicultural materials that include such themes as multicultural Cinderella stories and other fables; music around the world; foods of the world; immigrant life, adoption, and interracial families; Arabic and Islamic culture; Southeast Asia; and alphabets around the world.

The Internet is also a rich source of multicultural content. Students can search for their own primary-language materials. However, it's possible that the teacher who does not speak or read the primary language of the student may not be able to screen for inappropriate content. However, family or community members might be able to assist in finding educationally relevant content.

Sources for multicultural viewpoints and materials for various curriculum areas are presented in Table 5.10.

**TABLE 5.10**   Multicultural Materials: Sources for the Content Areas

| Content Area | Suggested Material |
| --- | --- |
| Mathematics | *Multicultural Mathematics: A More Inclusive Mathematics.* Accessed May 24, 2010, from www.ericdigests.org/1996-1/more.htm. |
| Social Studies | Multicultural history and social studies sites. Accessed May 24, 2010, from www .edchange.org/multicultural/sites/history.html. |
| Literature | *Multicultural Children's Literature.* Accessed May 24, 2010, from www .multiculturalchildrenslit.com. |
| Science | *Multicultural Science and Math Connections: Middle School Projects and Activities.* Accessed May 24, 2010, from http://fermat.nap.edu/html/rtmss/5.72.html. |

## Technological Resources to Enhance Instruction

Computer-assisted instruction (CAI) has been used in classrooms since the earliest days of word processing (late 1970s), with large-scale tutoring systems available in the 1980s that enabled the individual user to attempt repeated answers and receive error feedback without public embarrassment. Computer-mediated communication (CMC) and more sophisticated computer-simulated learning environments have come into use in the twenty-first century (see Bitter, Pierson, & Burvikovs, 2004; Herring, 1996).

**Tools for Instruction and Communication**   The digital revolution is changing the way people learn (Murray, 2000). Websites offer lesson plans, quizzes, chatrooms, and bulletin boards that allow the learner to sample English idioms, prepare for standardized tests, or connect with English learners in other parts of the world. Many teachers have access to Internet hookups in the classroom. Students can interact with others meaningfully, writing informal e-mails with "keypals" in different areas of the world or using writing-based chatrooms online in real time (Warschauer, 1995).

The instant communication available through the Internet connects students with other parts of the world, with speakers of English, and with rich sources of information. The World Wide Web delivers authentic materials, including texts, images, sound recordings, videoclips, virtual reality worlds, and dynamic, interactive presentations. Students can listen to live radio stations from around the world or hear prerecorded broadcasts of music, news, sports, and weather (LeLoup & Ponterio, 2000). Search engines (e.g., Google, Yahoo!, Bing) help the student find authentic materials on classroom, group, or individual research topics.

Today's teachers are educated to maximize the instructional and communicative use of the Internet, CD-ROM-based software, and other CMC tools, including audio and video production using computers, although in the process, older non-computer-based tools of multimedia production are falling by the wayside (see Herrell, 2000, pp. 134–138, for tips on the use of a variety of multimedia formats, including camcorder and overhead projector). Some teachers are also skilled in using computer-managed instruction (CMI) techniques such as grade book programs and database management.

Michael Newmann/PhotoEdit

*Students who are literate in their native language can use the computer to access primary-language content information as they learn English.*

**Computers Support Learning** Word processing supports the formal writing process by allowing students to electronically organize, draft, revise, edit, and publish their work. Students can develop oral skills by using presentation or authoring software to create professional-looking oral presentations, and they can apply both aural and oral skills in Web-enabled telephone conversations.

Software available for ELD includes traditional drill-and-practice programs focusing on vocabulary or grammar; tutorials; games; simulations that present students with real-life situations in the language and culture they are learning; productivity tools, such as word processing, databases, spreadsheets, graphics, and desktop publishing (DTP); and presentation or authoring programs. Material from encyclopedias and even *National Geographic* is available on CD-ROM and DVD formats.

The computer is a powerful learning tool that requires the teacher to organize, plan, teach, and monitor. Egbert and Hanson-Smith (1999) found that computer technology can provide students with the means to control their own learning, to construct meaning, and to evaluate and monitor their own performance.

Although language learning has long consisted of face-to-face interaction between teachers and students in the same physical location, new virtual learning environments have been made possible by the development of widespread, rapid Internet access. During virtual learning, students can participate when they choose (many events do not take place simultaneously) and where they choose (students can "log on" from home, from a neighborhood Internet-enabled café, or from a self-access computer lab at school). Software such as Skype enables users to see one another while learning, but even so, it is difficult to replicate the immediacy of real-life presence. Virtual learning is made possible by up-to-date software and hardware and fast, reliable Internet connections; but it is made effective in the same way that learning has always been effective—by expert teaching and motivated, receptive learners.

---

**Best Practice**   TIPS FOR ONLINE TEACHING

When designing Web-based virtual environments, some aspects are important to remember:

- Students often need mentoring in addition to academic content; in their minds, the two are intertwined to the extent that learners want to see that course assignments are part of a "bigger picture" of real-world applicability.
- Students may not be computer-savvy to the same degree. Computer-based delivery should require middle-of-the-road abilities, not expecting an extreme degree of expertise but not boring those who are accomplished "net-denizens."
- One cannot take for granted that students know their way around online educational software. They may need an orientation module before content delivery. Some students may need the instructor specifically to take them step-by-step through the software, with explicit modeling of what is required.
- Students often want "instant" turnaround and feedback on assignments. Instructors must balance these demands with a responsive yet controlled rhythm of communication in order to accustom students to regular patterns of reinforcement.
- Students often want a high degree of interactivity and communication not only with the course instructor but with other students in the class, using both synchronous (simultaneous) and asynchronous (delayed) delivery.
- There should be some mechanism for mediating communication issues that arise between students if they are engaged in peer communication online.

---

## Examples of SDAIE in the Content Domains

When the planning for instructional objectives aligned with content standards has been completed, consideration then moves to the needs of the English learner. The following sections address the issue of making instruction meaningful to the learner using various facets of SDAIE.

### Bridging: Accessing Prior Knowledge and Building Schemata

All learning builds on what has been previously learned, because the brain uses schemata to think. When exposed to new information, students access what is already known to them. If little prior knowledge exists, the teacher must supply background knowledge so that instruction can make sense.

**Best Practice** WAYS "INTO" LITERATURE

Before reading a work of literature, the teacher can employ various ways to access prior knowledge:

- *Anticipation/reaction guides.* A short list of statements with which students agree or disagree
- *Pictures, art, movies.* Visual cues to build a feeling for the setting
- *Physical objects.* Items relating to the reading selection that students identify and discuss
- *Selected read-alouds.* Passages that pique students' interest in the selection

**Assessing What Is Known** Before teaching, one must assess students' prior knowledge of the concepts and vocabulary that will be presented in the lesson in order to establish a starting point for the lesson, help students to review and stabilize their background information, and avoid spending instructional time on what is already known. Assessments can include a quick written pretest, informal survey, show of hands, pair/share (students discuss in pairs, then tell the whole class), teacher-led oral review, or a student quickwrite of some key points.

Sometimes what is already known is a mishmash of media images and hearsay that must be clarified. At other times, students may not be familiar with, or may disagree with, commonly held beliefs of the mainstream culture.

> [S]tudents bring much more background knowledge to the study of history than we sometimes credit them with. History is, after all, not confined to historians. The media also interpret historical events. . . . [T]here are also persistent historical myths and legends held dear by parts of the larger culture—Betsy Ross sewing the first flag, Columbus discovering a new world, and so forth. For some students, these images are comforting; others may feel excluded by the popular culture's mythologies. (Levstik & Barton, 2001, p. 25)

**Best Practice** SOME QUESTIONS TO ASK BEFORE BEGINNING

Sometimes students can write down their prior knowledge. Before beginning a new topic, students can interview each other in pairs to ask the following questions:

- Have you ever read or heard anything about this topic?
- Can you tell me about a similar topic that you think will help us learn about this one?
- If you were a reporter and could talk to someone about this topic, who would you seek out? (Adapted from Fisher, Brozo, Frey, & Ivey, 2007)

**Building Background Schemata** Teachers can provide new experiences that arouse interest in and draw attention to a topic, including field trips, guest speakers, fiction and nonfiction films, experiments, classroom discovery centers, music and songs, poetry and other literature, and computer simulations. To deepen these experiences, the teacher can guide the students to talk and write about them.

 **Classroom Glimpse**

### INTEREST-GENERATING QUESTIONS

Mr. Gruen, a seventh-grade science teacher, wrote the following statement on the board: "It's only a matter of time before the earth will be hit by a large object from space." He then asked students to find a partner and think of three questions they would most like answered about this statement. Afterward, he gathered the questions and wrote them on the board, placing a star next to the ones that were similar so students could see common themes of interest. This is part of a larger sequence known as Student Questions for Purposeful Learning (SQPL) (Ediger & Pavlik, 1999; Guthrie & Wigfield, 2000). (Adapted from Fisher et al., 2007, p. 113)

 **Classroom Glimpse**

### NEW EXPERIENCES TO BUILD BACKGROUND KNOWLEDGE

The firsthand experiences of a field trip piqued the interest of Dorothy Taylor's students in Virginia history and prepared them for the unit she had planned about colonial America.

In the fall, all of the fourth-grade classes in the school went on a field trip to Jamestown, Virginia. The children returned from their trip eager to talk about what they had learned. The field trip and students' enthusiasm were a perfect introduction to the social studies unit on the hardships faced by the Jamestown colonists. The students shared with one another what they knew about Jamestown and colonial America and added to their knowledge and vocabulary by reading and watching a video. (Taylor, 2000, pp. 53–55)

Teachers who are familiar with the background of the students can elicit beliefs, observations, and questions using students' everyday knowledge and cultural patterns.

**Best Practice**   THE CHECHE KONNEN SCIENCE PROJECT

Case studies in classrooms with low-income students from African-American, Haitian, and Latino backgrounds found ways that students deployed "sense-making practices—deep questions, vigorous argumentation, situated guesswork, embedded imagining, multiple perspectives, and innovative uses of everyday words" (Lee, 2005, p. 504)—to construct new meanings that were productive bridges to scientific practices. The teachers in the Cheche Konnen project tapped students' linguistic and cultural experiences to link their prior experiences to instruction, letting students draw on the forms of reasoning they employ in their daily lives as intellectual resources in science learning (Rosebery, Warren, & Conant, 1992; Warren, Ballenger, Ogonowski, Rosebery, & Hudicourt-Barnes, 2001).

**Contextualization** When students are asked to learn a new concept, the use of materials, resources, and activities can provide contextualization. The verbal presentation of a lesson is supplemented by manipulatives, realia, media, and visual backup as teachers write key words and concepts on the chalkboard or butcher paper and use graphs, pictures, maps, and other physical props to communicate. By presenting concepts numerous times through various means and in a rich visual, auditory (for example, software programs and Internet sources that offer sounds and experiences), and kinesthetic (drama and skits, "gallery" walks) environment, teachers provide lessons that also appeal to students' different learning styles.

Teachers can contextualize mathematics instruction by having sports fans calculate batting average, points per game, or average speed; students who shop with their parents can help to keep purchases within budget by determining the best-priced item. Many activities in mathematics lend themselves to multicultural reference. Systems of numeration and measurements that originated in ancient civilizations (e.g., Egyptian, Inca, Aztec, Maya) can be explored and contrasted (Hatfield, Edwards, Bitter, & Morrow, 2004). Many countries around the world use the metric system, and English learners may have expertise in this system that they could share.

 **Classroom Glimpse**

### CULTURAL CONTEXTUALIZATION

Linda Arieto, a Puerto-Rican American who grew up in a low-income community in the Bronx, shared a great deal in terms of language, culture, race, and class background with her students at Peter Towns Elementary. She was skillful using and responding to multiple varieties of language familiar to her students, such as Puerto-Rican Spanish, Puerto-Rican English, Black English vernacular, and Standard English. In the area of mathematics, she consistently found and applied lessons in the text that made sense to her students' cultural backgrounds and urban experiences. She used dominoes as math manipulatives, for example, because they correspond to a game that is popular in Caribbean culture. (Remillar & Cahnmann, 2005, pp. 178–179)

One example of contextualization is the effort to organize science instruction around common themes (e.g., nature of matter or magnetic energy) or societal issues (e.g., water pollution, drug addiction) to increase the relevance of scientific knowledge to students' lives. This makes science more approachable, allowing for more understanding and reflection, and permits key vocabulary to be used again and again.

## Vocabulary Preteaching

Building vocabulary concept by concept is integral to content teaching. Not all vocabulary is learned when it is pretaught; it can be presented before a lesson, but it must also be repeated again and again during the lesson as well as afterward, for purposes of long-term memory.

Several strategies are central to vocabulary retention. To encourage *visual cueing*, teachers can post important concepts on the bulletin board throughout a unit, offer key terms in test questions to be used in short-answer responses, color or highlight new words, or try to connect concrete images with terms. Teachers cue *episodic memory* by having students role-play the meanings of key terms, demonstrate or model new ideas, or create semantic maps, posters, or collages to make key ideas more memorable. To promote *verbal rehearsal*, teachers can praise the use of key terms during student discussions, require important words to be used during oral presentations, or use a pointer to refer to central concepts during lectures (Gregory & Kuzmich, 2005).

## Best Practice   VOCABULARY DEVELOPMENT ACROSS PROFICIENCY LEVELS

Instructors of English learners should not assume that all vocabulary instruction must be concrete. Each particular word calls for a unique balance of concrete (real objects, meaningful movement [TPR], modeling, actual experience), symbolic (pictures, charts, icons, maps, models, graphic organizers), or abstract representation (verbal-only explanations orally or in print). Boyd-Batstone (2006) recommends a three-part checklist to judge the best way to teach or depict a new word: (1) Can a real object or experience be used? (2) Is a visual model useful? (3) Can an abstract term be "unpacked" (using word origin, related roots, cognates, primary-language translation, or metaphors)?

 **Classroom Glimpse**

### TEACHING THE WORD *METAMORPHOSIS*

Ny Ha took considerable care to teach her third-grade students the term *metamorphosis*. She brought in a fishbowl with tadpoles and students observed and recorded the change of life cycle. She provided numerous picture books as well as computer programs that showed sequential pictures. Students created semantic maps of the concept. They made life cycle collages. They looked at models of caterpillars undergoing change. They used Kidspiration to generate mind maps using pictorial clip art. In the end, Ny thinks they "got it"! (Adapted from Boyd-Batstone, 2006)

## Strategic Teaching Using Multimodalities

Students can be provided with cognitively engaging input (both oral and written) in ways that appeal to their learning styles and preferences. Many students need to see, hear, smell, touch, and feel knowledge all at the same time!

 **Classroom Glimpse**

### SUPPLEMENTING THE VERBAL PRESENTATION

In a middle school life science class, Ms. Chen teaches about flowers by referring students to the explanation in the text (paragraph form), to a diagram of a flower in the text (graphic form), to a wall chart with a different flower (pictorial form), to a text glossary entry (dictionary form), and to actual flowers that students can examine. Through these numerous media, the concepts "petal," "stamen," "pistil," and "sepal" are understood and provide a basis for future study about life-forms. The teacher's task here is to ensure that these multiple sources are organized to communicate clearly and distinguish each concept.

## Access to Cognitive Academic Language Across the Content Areas

Each academic subject makes distinct demands on the student. For example, mathematics uses discourse that is unlike natural language. Readers may find confusing the tendency to interrupt for the inclusion of formulae. Such texts require a reading rate adjustment because they must be read more slowly and require multiple readings. Charts and graphs are an integral part of the text, not a supplement, and technical language has precise meaning. Besides the key words and phrases heard in lesson presentations, there are also key direction words that students need to know, such as *analyze, compare, contrast, define, describe, discuss, explain, evaluate, illustrate, justify, state,* and *summarize.*

**The Language of Mathematics** Language difficulties for English learners lie in vocabulary, syntax, semantics, and discourse. Vocabulary in mathematics includes technical words such as *numerator, divisor,* and *exponent.* Words such as *regroup, factor,* and *table* have a meaning different from everyday usage. Two or more mathematical concepts may combine to form a different concept: *line segment, cross multiply.* A variety of terms can signal the same mathematical operation: *Add, and, plus, sum, combine,* and *increased by* all represent addition (Dale & Cuevas, 1992). Sentence structures may involve complex syntax: "____ is to ____ as ____ is to ____" and "____ is percent of ____." Statements must be translated into logical symbols before problems can be completed, posing additional linguistic difficulty.

Problems with meaning (semantics) occur when natural language becomes the language of mathematics. For example, in the problem "Five times a number is two more than ten times the number," students must recognize that "a number" and "the number" refer to the same quantity.

Abbreviations and other math symbols may need to be interpreted. For example, *ft* for foot or the use of the apostrophe may be confusing for students, especially those who were previously educated in the metric system. Vocabulary charts that include the use of abbreviations and symbols can be placed around the classroom to help students remember. Teachers must be aware of these language differences and mediate the transition in learning a new language to express mathematical concepts.

 **Classroom Glimpse**

### EMBODYING THE LANGUAGE OF RATIO

In a lesson on fractions, Mr. Goodall asked three students to come to the front of the class for a demonstration. One student measured the height and arm spread of a second student while the third student wrote the measurements on the board. The students used these numbers to express the relationships both as a ratio and as a percentage. (Adapted from Weiss & Pasley, 2004, p. 25)

**The Language of Science** The four major language areas (vocabulary, syntax, semantics, discourse features) detailed in the section on mathematics are also relevant for science. Students not only have to learn scientific definitions, but they must also learn complex syntactic structures, which include passive voice, multiple embeddings, and long noun phrases (Pérez & Torres-Guzmán, 2002).

A number of types of text structures are common in science content materials. The *cause/effect* structure links reasons with results or actions with their consequences. The *compare/contrast* structure examines the similarities and differences between concepts. The *time-order* structure shows a sequential relationship over the passage of time (Pérez & Torres-Guzmán, 2002). To assist in their comprehension, students can receive special training in following written instructions for procedures or experiments.

English-language development must be an objective in all science instruction. Teachers should review vocabulary terms to be used in a lesson before beginning, including the names of equipment and activities that will be used; scientific definitions of some common words (e.g., *energy, speed, work*); and new content words (e.g., *acceleration, inertia*). Students need to be taught text processing techniques (how to take notes, how to reread text for answers to study questions, how to interpret charts and picture captions) and then held to a high level of recall about the information they read (Anderson & Gunderson, 2004). To assist their learning of scientific language, students can receive special training in following written instructions for procedures or experiments and in using glossaries.

**Best Practice**   DEVELOPING SCIENTIFIC LANGUAGE

- Provide appropriate contexts for new vocabulary, syntactic structures, and discourse patterns. Isolated lists or exercises do not appear to facilitate language acquisition.
- Engage students in hands-on activities in which they discuss concepts in a genuine communicative context.
- Promote activities in which students actively debate with one another about the truth of a hypothesis or the meaning of data gathered.

(Adapted from Carrasquillo & Rodríguez, 2002; Kessler et al., 1992)

**The Language of Social Studies**   Because history itself has taken place in many languages, a strong social studies curriculum builds on dual-language skills. Students can use communication skills in two languages to gather oral histories from their families and communities. Their own family histories can teach them firsthand about complex historical issues. For more information about oral history projects, read "Junior Historians: Doing Oral History with ESL and Bilingual Students" (Olmedo, 1993).

As a discipline, social studies is concept-rich in ideas that may be difficult to depict in visuals. Student interaction is necessary for concept acquisition and subsequent application in different situations. Inquiry skills that are used first in the classroom and then in the community help students practice what they are learning in authentic situations (Sunal & Haas, 2005).

**The Language of Music**   Music is a universal language. All cultures make music, expressing their cultural heritage in the particular sounds they make. However, music has its own language that requires specific understanding before an individual can become a proficient performer. For example, words such as *jazz, pitch, atonality,* and *folk music* are important technical concepts specific to music; if not taught within the proper context, they may pose a challenge for many English learners.

Music can also be used to teach concepts in other content domains. A first-grade lesson teaches opposites through music. Students listen to a story about opposites, which they then discuss before seeking opposites in music, using the books *Elmo's Big Lift and Look Book* and *Pooh Popping Opposites* and the music tapes *Down on Grandpa's Farm* and *Lullaby and Goodnight.* After a warm-up in which the teacher asks students, "What are opposites?" and "How do we find them?" the teacher reads books that illustrate the concept, asking students for some more examples and stating some pairs that are not opposites. Then the teacher plays tapes of songs that show opposites: fast/slow, number of instruments or people singing, etc.). For assessment, students listen to two more tape selections and write the opposites found (Graves, 1996).

**Language in the Visual Arts**    Artists have specific ways of doing art, and there is a language to express those ways. Part of an effective visual arts education involves exposing students to appropriate language that describes artistic expression and creates a common language in the community of artists. Accomplished teaching, particularly with English learners, requires explicit teaching of words such as *movement, medium,* or *organic.* Art lends itself to contextualization of terms but still demands careful and skillful teaching to connect language and art.

## Scaffolded Content Instruction

Each content domain has particular ways of presenting content, including differences between elementary and secondary methods. Scaffolded teaching approaches support learning in various content areas at both elementary and secondary levels.

**Elementary Mathematics**    Adapting math instruction for English learners takes many forms. Table 5.11 shows how math centers set up to teach multiplication in the mainstream classroom can be adapted for English learners.

**Secondary Mathematics: The Three-Phase Pattern**    Many mathematics teachers follow a three-phase pattern. The first phase involves the introduction, demonstration, and explanation of the concept or strategy by the teacher, followed by an interactive questioning segment, in which the teacher establishes how well students are grasping the concept. The second phase involves guided practice, in which students make the transition from "teacher regulation" to student "self-regulation" (Belmont, 1989). Supporting techniques can include coaching, prompting, cueing, and monitoring student performance. The third phase allows students to work independently. If students are having difficulty during independent practice, they can receive more guided practice.

Further research in secondary mathematics teaching suggests the importance of making short- and long-term goals clear, as well as explaining to students the usefulness of each mathematical concept. Projects are very effective, although long projects need to be used with discretion. Table 5.12 shows additional strategic approaches for teaching mathematics to English learners.

**TABLE 5.11**   Adapting Math Centers for English Learners: Multiplication Station Activities

| Unadapted Center | Suggested Adaptations |
| --- | --- |
| 1. In Shopping Spree, students make purchases from a list of items, spending exactly $25 for their combination of items. | Directions can be in pictorial form. |
| 2. In Circles and Stars, students use dice to play a multiplication game. The roll of the first die determines the number of circles the student will draw. The second roll, using a different colored die, indicates the number of stars the student should draw in each circle. The student then writes a number sentence that reflects the roll of the dice and the product (the total number of stars drawn). | A peer or older tutor can be stationed at the center to explain directions in L1. |
| 3. In Comparison Game, students use a deck of cards from which the face cards have been removed. Aces are equal to one. Students draw two cards each and use the numbers to create a multiplication number sentence and the product of the two numbers. A "more or less" spinner is used to determine which student's product wins for each round. | A pair of students can observe while another pair plays until they get the idea. |

*Source:* Adapted from http://mathforum.org/t2t/message.taco?thread=5024&message=4.

**TABLE 5.12**   Mathematics Teaching Strategies for English Learners

| Teaching Strategy | Description |
| --- | --- |
| Encourage exploration. | Plan activities that facilitate explorations and investigations of mathematical concepts, nurture students' curiosity, and stimulate creativity. |
| Use manipulatives. | Manipulatives help make abstract concepts concrete. |
| Use real-world problem-solving activities. | Using mathematics as it applies to daily life and to solve real-life problems makes it interesting and meaningful. |
| Encourage oral and written expression. | Mathematics requires specific language and CALP, and students should be provided opportunities to practice and express their mathematical knowledge orally and in writing. |
| Offer an enriched curriculum and challenging activities. | Mathematics is a discipline with its own CALP characterized by specific experiences and abilities involving inquiry, problem solving, and higher thinking. |
| Use a variety of problem-solving experiences. | Teachers should plan challenges that stimulate higher-order thinking and problem solving and that are nonroutine and open-ended. For example, provide math problems that may have various correct solutions and answers, problems with multiple interpretations, and answers that can be represented in multiple ways. |

*Source:* Balderrama & Díaz-Rico (2006).

**Elementary Science**   The important idea in science instruction is to adopt a problem-solving approach featuring questions that are both comprehensible and interesting. Students can be assisted to solve problems in science by developing a personal set of learning strategies. Teachers can help students describe the thinking they use to come up with solutions and praise innovative techniques they apply. Students can share their processes with one another, resulting in multiple ways of approaching a problem. Teachers can also discuss with students the biographies of famous scientists, showing the perseverance it took to solve the problems they addressed.

**Secondary Science**    Alternative means of representing information is important in secondary science instruction. T-charts and other graphic organizers are ways to train students to translate verbal information from texts and lectures into mental structures for purposes of memorization as well as understanding. Pictures are important sources of information, whether from texts or supplementary sources. In summary, any method of noting and organizing details or creating and testing hypotheses furthers the goals of science inquiry.

**Elementary Literature**    Many graphic organizers are available for use in scaffolding literature instruction: character trait charts, sequence-of-events outlines, cause-and-effect diagrams, setting description maps, and so forth. One key method of scaffolding literature that can be used in other content areas is the *cognitive apprentice model*. Children learn to read from teachers, but they also learn from teachers to enjoy reading. Teachers can model why they like certain genres, why a certain turn of phrase is delightful, why a plot is compelling, and so forth. Students then become the apprentices of teachers' thinking about literature—an apprenticeship in literature appreciation.

**Secondary Literature**    Building on the love of reading that is the foundation of elementary instruction, students at the secondary level must balance consumption with production. It is one thing to read poetry and entirely another to write it, to struggle firsthand with the freshness of images, the discipline of meter, the lure of rhyme. To appreciate literature, one must be willing to dive in, to create and re-create in the leading genres of the day. Therefore, scaffolding literature is intrinsically bound up with creative production of language.

Integral to production of language is scaffolded creativity in the primary language. Students who create in two languages are addressing a peer audience that appreciates the effort. Even students with a primary language not understood by peers can share the poetic sound and meaning (in translation). All creativity stimulates the common underlying proficiency that makes language a human treasure.

### Classroom Glimpse

**PRIMARY-LANGUAGE POETRY**

Judith Casey (2004) encourages students to share native language with classmates during a poetry activity, in which students bring in and read aloud a poem in their L1. On Poetry Day, the atmosphere of the class is charged. No one knows exactly what to expect, but the students are excited. Amazingly, hearing one another read in their L1 lets the students see each other in a new light. The class is forever changed as students recognize the value, contributions, and abilities of their classmates. (pp. 51–52)

**Elementary Social Studies**    Scaffolded social studies starts with the timeline and the map as the basic graphic organizers. Students need a firm understanding of when and where events took place. Any mental device is useful that helps students visualize when and where. If the computer program Google Earth can be displayed from the computer screen onto a large surface at the beginning of each lesson, students can start "zoomed in" at their own school and then "zoom out" to the picture of the earth in space, move the map to the location of the day's lesson in history or geography, and then "zoom in" to locate any feature under discussion. This grounds students in their own place before making the transition to another.

**Secondary History/Social Science**   The reading load in secondary history often needs to be scaffolded. Bradley and Bradley (2004, n.p.) offered several useful methods to help students monitor their comprehension during reading.

- *Analyzing captions.* Look at the picture captions and ask, "How does this tie into the reading?"
- *Turning subheads into questions.* By rephrasing a subheading into a question, readers are able to predict upcoming content.
- *Making margin notes.* Using small sticky notes, students write new vocabulary words they encounter—even words not in the content glossary.

A useful scaffolding technique for secondary social studies, the question–answer relationships (QAR) model (Raphael, 1986), describes four kinds of questions: Right There (direct quote from the text), Think and Search (the answer must be inferred from several text passages), Author and You (text integrated with personal experience), and On Your Own (drawn from personal experiences). Each question requires a different set of text processing or thinking resources. This method can be taught in one lesson, and thereafter students can learn to classify questions and locate answers independently.

---

**Best Practice**   **TEACHING NOTE-TAKING SKILLS**

Better note takers produce greater academic achievement in middle and high school (Faber, Morris, & Lieberman, 2000). Here are tips on taking better notes:

- Date and title notes at the top of the page.
- Split the page: Keep lecture notes on the left side and organizational and summary notes on the right side.
- Skip lines to show change of topic.
- Apply the same organization as the lecturer to number subpoints or mark details.
- Use underlining, circling, or highlighting to indicate important ideas. (Adapted from Stahl, King, & Henk, 1991)

---

 **Classroom Glimpse**

---

**COLLABORATION IN MIDDLE SCHOOL SOCIAL STUDIES**

At Gerona Middle School (pseudonym) in a medium-sized California agricultural town, more than half of the students are English learners, some from migrant labor families. The majority of students are academically underprepared according to their scores on standardized tests.

In a recent unit about the Crusades, students wrote expository essays in which they described, justified, and persuaded. At the end of each group activity and each unit, students wrote a final essay, making connections between their group activities and the central theme of the unit. Content area and language arts teachers coordinated interdisciplinary responsibility for this writing, in what is known as sustained-content instruction. (Adapted from Bunch, Abram, Lotan, & Valdés, 2001)

## Guided and Independent Practice That Promotes Students' Active Language Use

**Guided Practice**    Teachers working in mixed-ability classrooms can plan group activities that help students in different ways. Students can work in homogeneous groups when the goal of the activity is accuracy and in heterogeneous groups when the goal is fluency. For example, to develop accuracy, first-grade students can listen to a reading of the Chinese folktale "The Magic Sieve." A group of beginning students can retell the story using pictures and then talk about the pictures. Intermediate students can retell the story to the teacher or a cross-age tutor. The teacher writes their story for them, and then students can reread, illustrate, and rearrange the story from sentence strips. A group of more proficient students can create a new group story.

At the secondary level, as students work in class, teachers can use various strategies to guide their learning. Groups of students can work together to create visual summaries or chapter reviews of textbook content. Specific students can each take on the persona of a literary character or historic personage and provide background for other students' questions throughout the reading. Charts, graphs, pictures, and symbols can trace the development of images, ideas, and themes.

### Best Practice    GUIDED PRACTICE IN READING LITERATURE

Scaffolded activities help students as they work with text. Reading aloud as students follow along can give them an opportunity to hear a proficient reader, get a sense of the format and story line, and listen to the teacher think aloud about the reading. In the think-aloud, teachers can model how they monitor a sequence of events, identify foreshadowing and flashback, visualize a setting, analyze character and motive, comprehend mood and theme, and recognize irony and symbolism. To help students develop a sense of inflection, pronunciation, rhythm, and stress, a commercial tape recording of a work of literature can be obtained for listening and review, or native-English-speaking students or adult volunteers may be willing to make a recording.

**Maintaining the First Language in Guided Practice**    Students can be encouraged to use and develop their native language during guided practice. Aides and tutors can help explain difficult passages and guide students in summarizing their understanding. Native-language books, magazines, films, and other materials relating to the topic or theme of the lesson can support and even augment students' learning. They can also maintain reading logs or journals in their native language.

**Independent Practice**   Computers and other resources can be used to extend practice in various content domains. Many English learners are unfamiliar with the basic tools associated with mathematics (rulers, protractors, calculators, computers, etc.) (Buchanan & Helman, 1997). After demonstrating each, teachers can provide students with real-life opportunities to use them. For example, students are told that the playground needs to be repaved. They first have to estimate the area, then check their estimates with the actual tools (using both standard and metric measuring instruments, as they will not know which system the parking company uses), and then use calculators to find the percentage of error in their estimates. Computer programs can also help to provide estimates and calculations.

**Best Practice**   INDEPENDENT REACTIONS TO WORKS OF LITERATURE

- Authentic written responses encourage students to reflect on the piece of literature and to express their interpretations to an audience beyond the classroom.
- Students write poems and share them with other classes or parents at a Poetry Night.
- Student journalists write reviews of literature works for the school or classroom newspaper or act as movie critics and review the film version of a text studied in class. They can then compare the differences and draw conclusions about the pros and cons of the different media.
- Students write letters to authors to express their reactions to the story or to pen pals recommending certain pieces of literature.
- Favorite parts of selections can be rewritten as a play and enacted for other classes as a way to encourage other students to read that piece of literature.
- Students can plan a mock television game show and devise various formats that include ideas from the literature studied.

**Best Practice**   INDEPENDENT QUESTIONING STRATEGIES

"Question swap" (Gregory & Kuzmich, 2005) is a useful device for helping students personalize social studies. For any given topic, students write out two questions each (with answers) and then swap one question with the first partner, each writing out answers. The questioners then do the same with the second question. This process restructures information from verbal input to mental schemata. The questions are the scaffold. The teacher should gather up the questions and answers at the end and skim quickly to clear up any misrepresentation.

## Resources for Independent Practice

Across the content areas, teachers can help make resources available for students as they approach learning tasks autonomously. This helps students take responsibility for their own learning.

 **Classroom Glimpse**

### USING MULTIPLE RESOURCES FOR INDEPENDENT RESEARCH

Students studying a fifth-grade unit on settlement of the West can examine the legal issues involved in the Treaty of Guadalupe-Hidalgo, compare the various cultures that came into contact in the Southwest, delve into the history of land grant titles, and pursue many more issues of interest. Through filmstrips, films, videos, computer simulations, literature, nonfiction texts, and oral discussions, students develop conceptual knowledge. Such a unit incorporates history, geography, sociology, economics, values, information-seeking skills, group participation, and perhaps dramatic talents as students act out the signing of treaties and other cultural events.

**Math Resources for Elementary English Learners**    Almost all math programs at the primary level are supported by sets of manipulative materials; however, manipulatives are not a magic substitute for intensive, multimodal instruction that ensures all students acquire mathematics concepts at every stage. The World Wide Web is a vast source of problems, contests, enrichment, and teacher resources to supplement classroom instruction.

Family Math is a program that focuses on families learning mathematics together in support of the elementary math curriculum. Adults and children come to Family Math classes together once a week for several weeks, doing activities in small groups, with two or three families working together. As a follow-up, family members use inexpensive materials found in the home (bottle caps, toothpicks, coins) to practice ideas that were presented in class. The website www.techteachers.com/mathweb/familymath/index.htm offers resources for Family Math activities.

**Math Resources for Secondary English Learners**    The Internet provides numerous sites that are both resources for teachers and opportunities for students to practice mathematical skills. Table 5.13 features several websites recommended by some of the mathematics teachers with whom I work, including their descriptions of how these sites help them in working with English learners.

**Internet Social Studies Resources for English Learners**    Classroom teachers can combine the enormous range of materials from the Internet with other instructional resources and methods. Field trips via the Internet include visiting the White House (www.whitehouse.gov), exhibitions of African and pre-Columbian Native-American art (www.nmai.si.edu), or the Egyptian pyramids (www.pbs.org/wgbh/nova/pyramid). Many of the virtual field trip sites are designed specifically for education, featuring lesson plans and interactive student activities (see www

**TABLE 5.13** Websites for Teaching Secondary Mathematics to English Learners

| Website | Description |
|---------|-------------|
| http://matti.usu.edu/nlvm/nav/vlibrary.html | Provides manipulatives as a visual demonstration of concepts taking place in the class. The graph is an excellent tool; one can graph several lines on the same Cartesian plane and see the variations made by changing a coefficient. |
| www.purplemath.com/modules/translat.htm | Translates word problems into algebraic expressions. When English learners are faced with word problems, it is rarely one word that gives them problems, but more often a phrase. That phrase is usually the key to setting up the problem. The website provides a step-by-step account of how to set up these problems. |

*Source:* Balderrama & Díaz-Rico (2006).

.internet4classrooms.com). Students can also create their own virtual field trips of local historical sites, or even of their school. Table 5.14 offers selected websites for teaching secondary social studies to English learners.

 **Classroom Glimpse**

### A HISTORIC WEBSITE

Ms. Rosie Beccera Davies's third-grade class at Washington Elementary School in Montebello, California, made a historical website for their community, beginning with the Gabrielino (Tongva) Indians, and including many local historical sites.

**Science Resources outside of the School**   The school science program often extends beyond the walls of the school to the resources of the community. Teachers can work with local

**TABLE 5.14** Websites for Teaching Secondary Social Studies to English Learners

| Website | Description |
|---------|-------------|
| www.DiscoverySchool.com | An excellent supplement to world history videos. The site offers vocabulary words and terms used in the video, rubrics, and a list of additional resources. |
| http://atozteacherstuff.com | Contains many ELD lessons specifically designed for all content areas, especially for English learners in U.S. history and government. |
| www/eduref.org/Virtual/Lessons | An easy to use site, containing social studies lessons for English learners. |

personnel, such as those at science-rich centers (museums, industries, universities, etc.), to plan for the use of exhibits and educational programs that enhance the study of a particular topic. In addition, the physical environment in and around the school can be used as a living laboratory for the study of natural phenomena in project-based and service-learning activities.

**Resources for Music**   When adapting music lessons for English learners, primary-language music audiotapes are available through Shen's Books at www.shens.com, including tapes in Spanish, Hmong, Vietnamese, Cambodian, Korean, Japanese, and Mandarin, as well as tapes from cultures other than the native cultures of the students.

Technology is increasingly an important resource in music education. A powerful application for music education is the use of computers, allowing students to improvise, make arrangements, and access vast libraries of recorded music. When instruments are connected to electronic instruments and computers, they can be used to record, transcribe, and even permit practice performances.

Musical and cultural resources abound in all communities, and skillful music educators tap into these resources by working with parents, churches, and other civic organizations. Local musicians, professionals, music faculty at local universities, family members, and students at colleges and universities can conduct sessions and workshops in conjunction with the regular instructional program.

## Formative Assessment and Reteaching Content

The hands-on nature of problem solving in science can naturally align with performance-based assessment. By performing actual science activities, students are actively demonstrating the skills for which assessment holds them responsible. The use of formative assessment involves teachers in the role of offering guidance and feedback so the given skills can be accomplished.

 **Classroom Glimpse**

### CHECKING EXIT COMPREHENSION IN SCIENCE

Mr. Petersen uses exit slips as a strategy just before students leave their middle school science class. He provides a preprinted prompt, such as "I'm still not clear about . . . ," to help students pinpoint what is still fuzzy for them about the day's lesson. Students can reflect on what they have just learned, show their thinking process, and prepare for continued learning on the topic. Teachers can use this information to select what to revisit, elaborate, or expand on in the next lesson. (Adapted from Fisher et al., 2007)

## Summative Assessment of Content Lessons

Multiple strategies can be used to assess students' mastery of language objectives and grade-level content objectives across diverse content domains.

**Assessment in Mathematics**   Although traditional assessment in mathematics focuses on the mastery of algorithms, many alternative forms can be used to measure mathematical thinking and problem solving. Authentic assessment allows the teacher to evaluate mathematics understanding while students are actively engaged in such learning activities as running a school store or simulating trade on the stock market. Assessments should allow for differences in understanding, creativity, and accomplishment. Flexible expectations permit different pacing for students with basic versus advanced math skills.

---

**Best Practice**   ALTERNATIVE MEANS OF DEMONSTRATING MATH KNOWLEDGE

Students can use various methods to show math learning:

- Produce or find three different drawings for the number $x$.
- Write three story problems that have the number $x$ as an answer.
- Make up a pattern and explain it.
- Interview ten people to find out the favorite ice cream flavors and then invent a way to show this information to the class.

*Source:* Adapted from Rowan & Bourne (1994).

---

**Assessment in Visual and Performing Arts**   Instruction and assessment go hand in hand in the visual and performing arts. The teacher and the artist interact and collaborate in ongoing feedback, with self-monitoring and self-assessment being a part of the daily experience. Portfolios are very common assessment tools used by artists in the performing arts because they track individual growth. They can help high school students, for example, apply for college entrance to an art institute or for employment in the visual arts.

Student exhibitions are also a way that teachers can create safe opportunities for assessment, whereby peers and other adults give feedback on completed works or works-in-progress. These exhibitions can take place in the classroom, and rubrics can be developed by the class to evaluate basic elements in a work.

---

**Best Practice**   ASSESSMENT AS MUSICAL PERFORMANCE

Showcasing musical talent by means of group and individual performance is a time-honored assessment of musical involvement. The excitement of performance and the responsibility of individuals toward their peers and audience teach maturity and poise. Bridging cultural gaps by offering music in many languages helps to involve the families and community in preparing for, attending, and enjoying concerts.

---

**Assessment in Social Studies**   Assessment of all students must be equitable in a social studies program. English learners can show proficiency in multiple ways: portfolios, performance

Nancy Sheehan Photography

*Members of the community can share cultural activities such as music and art with students.*

assessments, written reports, role-plays, and research projects. When high-stakes educational decisions for individual students are made, the decisions should be based on a variety of assessments, rather than on a single test score. Assessments of students in social studies should be designed and used to further the goal of educating students to be active citizens in a democratic society (see Chapter 3 for more on assessment).

Table 5.15 presents strategies for adapting curricula in secondary school social studies. Similar strategies may apply in other content areas. These strategies represent a sample of SDAIE methods.

## Instructional Needs beyond the Classroom

To be successful in their academic courses, English learners often need assistance from organizations and volunteers outside of the classroom. This assistance can come from academic summer programs, additional instructional services such as after-school programs and peer tutoring, and Dial-a-Teacher for homework help in English and in the primary language. Support in the affective domain may include special home visits by released time teachers, counselors, or outreach workers and informal counseling by teachers. Monitoring of academic progress by counselors also helps to encourage students with language needs.

**TABLE 5.15**   Strategies for Adapting Curricula in Secondary Social Studies

| Strategy | How It Helps |
| --- | --- |
| Identify similarities and differences | Helps students compare, create metaphors, and use analogies (comparing the U.S. Cabinet to a school can clarify the concept of analogy); builds vocabulary, comprehension. |
| Historical investigation | Gives students an active role in understanding history and allows them to pursue a question using strategies that work for them; focuses on students' interests; allows students flexibility; encourages self-monitoring of progress. |
| Inventions | Inventions are/have been an important part of U.S. history; students are able to demonstrate comprehension, knowledge, and creativity within a historical framework while reliving history. |
| Role-playing | Adolescents are quite dramatic and like to be in "someone else's shoes"; students learn about others' perspectives while using language, gestures, and body language to show their understanding. |
| Group work | Collaborative projects or assignments help students to solve problems together as they hear and use history-related CALP in a low-anxiety environment; structured group work addresses status issues so that "everyone participates, no one dominates" and English learners have chances to talk. |
| Decision making | This provides for contemplation and discussion of concepts central to many historical issues; provides students a chance to hear and use language to make decisions. |
| "What if" stories | Help students use language to create hypothetical predictions about history: for example, what if Columbus had not sailed to America? |
| Puzzles, riddles | Students see representations of historical concepts in different formats that engage and incorporate multiple intelligences. |
| Explanations with concrete referents | Help students understand abstract concepts. |
| Alternative representation formats | Different ways of presenting facts; for example, graphic organizers, maps, tables, charts, and graphs can reduce verbiage and identify key concepts in a lesson; this also models the different means historians use to gather evidence. |
| Summarizing and note taking | An important skill of historians; allows students to make sense of extensive text and lecture by listening for key words and identifying relevant information. |
| Preteach assignments | Helps students anticipate key concepts before reading assignment. |
| Prepare for exams | Teacher can model how to use textbook features such as chapter goals and overviews, summaries, and glossaries; this also helps students self-monitor comprehension and progress. |
| Provide learning, reading, and study support | Helps students process text and use language to voice their ideas; puts them in role of experts. Teachers arrange jigsaw groups to read text, assigning students to groups and making groups of students experts on specific portions of reading; students read and discuss together; teacher reviews and addresses specific issues with the entire class. |
| Word association | Vocabulary enrichment; teaching students to hear a word and associate it with an image helps comprehension and retention. |
| Listen for specific information | Teaches students explicitly what is important in a lecture, text, or historical document; students use teacher-created graphic organizers or fill-in-the-blank lecture notes. |

**Best Practice**    **MEETING INSTRUCTIONAL NEEDS BEYOND THE CLASSROOM**

Escalante and Dirmann (1990) explicated the main components of the Garfield High School advanced placement (AP) calculus course in which Escalante achieved outstanding success in preparing Hispanic students to pass the AP calculus examination. Escalante's success was not due solely to outstanding classroom teaching; he was the organizer of a broad effort to promote student success. In his classroom, he set the parameters: He made achievement a game for the students, the "opponent" being the Educational Testing Service's examination; he coached students to hold up under the pressure of the contest and work hard to win; and he held students accountable for attendance and productivity. But beyond this work in the classroom was the needed community support.

Community individuals and organizations donated copiers, computers, transportation, and souvenirs such as special caps and team jackets. Parents became involved in a campaign against drug use. This helped Escalante emphasize proper conduct, respect, and value for education. Past graduates served as models of achievement. They gave pep talks to students and acted as hosts in visits to high-tech labs. The support from these other individuals combined to give students more help and encouragement than could be provided by the classroom teacher alone. Students saw concentrated, caring, motivated effort directed toward them—something they had rarely before experienced. The results were dramatized in the unforgettable feature film *Stand and Deliver*.

## Teacher Commitment

Although technological tools and techniques for ELD and content area teaching are changing rapidly, what remains constant is the need for English learners to receive high-quality instruction that permits them access to the cognitive academic language they need for school success. Teachers who are dedicated to student achievement are key.

In SDAIE classrooms, it is not only the students who are learning. Successful teachers themselves are open, not only *willing* to learn but also *expecting* to learn.

English-language development and content learning go hand in hand in classrooms that support high-quality instruction for English learners. These classrooms feature multiple modalities for instruction and a rich mix of stimulating materials and linguistic interaction. Most of all, classrooms that foster high achievement have teachers who are committed to enriching language and promoting a high level of content learning using SDAIE to make instruction comprehensible and meaningful.

**A+RISE**

Go to the Topics Building Background Knowledge, Content Area Learning, Instructional Strategies, and Differentiating Instruction in the MyEducationLab (www.myeducationlab.com) for your course, where you can:

- Find learning outcomes for Building Background Knowledge, Content Area Learning, Instructional Strategies, and Differentiating Instruction along with the national standards that connect to these outcomes.
- Complete Assignments and Activities that can help you more deeply understand the chapter content.
- Apply and practice your understanding of the core teaching skills identified in the chapter with the Building Teaching Skills and Dispositions learning units.
- Examine challenging situations and cases presented in the IRIS Center Resources.
- Check your comprehension on the content covered in the chapter by going to the Study Plan in the Book Resources for your text. Here you will be able to take a chapter quiz, receive feedback on your answers, and then access Review, Practice, and Enrichment activities to enhance your understanding of chapter content.

Go to the Topic A+RISE in the MyEducationLab (www.myeducationlab.com) for your course. A+RISE® Standards2Strategy™ is an innovative and interactive online resource that offers new teachers in grades K–12 just-in-time, research-based instructional strategies that:

- Meet the linguistic needs of ELLs as they learn content
- Differentiate instruction for all grades and abilities
- Offer reading and writing techniques, cooperative learning, use of linguistic and nonlinguistic representations, scaffolding, teacher modeling, higher order thinking, and alternative classroom ELL assessment
- Provide support to help teachers be effective through the integration of listening, speaking, reading, and writing along with the content curriculum
- Improve student achievement
- Are aligned to Common Core Elementary Language Arts standards (for the literacy strategies) and to English language proficiency standards in WIDA, Texas, California, and Florida.

# 6

# English-Language Oracy Development

Oracy in English—learning to speak and listen—makes it possible for students to succeed in school. English learners already know a great deal about using oral language in their primary language. They know how to share their thoughts and opinions with others and how to use language strategically to get what they want, be recognized, take turns, and so forth. Bourdieu (1977) called this knowledge "linguistic capital," a part of the resources that English learners bring to schooling.

Of course, if English learners acquire a dialect characteristic of the middle class and are backed by a houseful of cultural tools such as atlases, encyclopedias, magazines, and other reference materials, the oral language they use is even more valuable as linguistic capital. The knowledge about life coded in the L1 is worth quite a lot, however, if the teacher views this knowledge as a resource that can be used to promote academic success. Oracy that is directly connected to the community strengthens an individual's cultural capital. Children's intellectual development is built on verbal interaction in the first language. According to Vygotsky (1981), children learn to engage in higher-level thinking by first listening and speaking. This has profound implications for the education of English learners: The more that students use language within the social context of the classroom, the better they will learn how to think. Teaching strategies provide imaginative ways to use oral language to further develop students' intellects. The following sections discuss ways to teach English oracy.

## The Focus on Communicative Interaction

English-language development is a specialty that is essential for English learners, who must improve their English while learning grade-level academic content. ELD includes speaking/oral language development and listening, reading (both content area reading and literature), and writing. To develop learners' English, teachers need an array of strategies.

Current research emphasizes that meaningful and purposeful communicative interactions (both oral and written) promote learners' English-language development and content area learning. Second, the language that is *learned* takes precedence over the language that is *taught*. Assessment plays a key role in documenting what is actually learned. Finally, the learner's interlanguage is the basis for instruction. Empirical teaching takes note of learners' needs and instruction is planned accordingly. Each of these ideas is explored in turn.

## What Is Communicative Competence?

In 1972, Hymes introduced the term *communicative competence* to emphasize the idea that the *use* of language in a social setting is the key to language performance. Current theories of language have moved away from a grammatical view of language to the more inclusive concept of language for communicative purposes. The competent speaker is recognized as one who knows when, where, and how to use language appropriately.

Canale (1983) identified four components of communicative competence. *Grammatical competence* focuses on the skills and knowledge necessary to speak and write accurately. *Sociolinguistic competence* involves knowing how to produce and understand language in different social contexts, taking into consideration such factors as the status of participants and the purposes and conventions of interaction. *Discourse competence* is the ability to combine and connect utterances (spoken) and sentences (written) into a meaningful whole. *Strategic competence* helps the language user repair breakdowns in communication and enhance the effectiveness of communication.

 **Classroom Glimpse**

### DISCOURSE COMPETENCE IN KINDERGARTEN STUDENTS

An example of discourse competence can be seen in the following conversation between two kindergarten boys, one a native English speaker and the other an English learner. Rolando responds appropriately (though not kindly) to Andrew's request and adds information about his decision at the proper moment. This conversation shows that Rolando has discourse competence.

> **Andrew:** Can I play?
> **Rolando:** No.
> **Andrew:** There're only three people here.
> **Rolando:** Kevin went to the bathroom.
> **Andrew:** Can I take his place 'til he comes back?
> **Rolando:** You're not playing.

## The Cognitive Perspective

Current language teaching is being shaped by several important ideas. First, the shift toward a cognitive paradigm means that *learning* has taken precedence over *teaching*. What the student learns is the important outcome of the teaching–learning process, not what the teacher teaches. Second, learning is maximized when it matches what takes place naturally in the brain. Third, thematic integration across content areas unifies the language processes of reading, writing, speaking, listening, thinking, and acting. Therefore, current perspectives on second-language learning align with brain-compatible instruction.

The cognitive perspective emphasizes assessment as the way to ensure that learning has taken place. Additionally, one sees the strong push to develop students' CALP as a cognitive focus. Last, the emphasis on acquisition of cognitive tools—learning strategies—as a key part of each lesson is a cognitive perspective. The idea of cognitive tools plays an increasing role in current understanding of oracy as well as literacy (Egan & Gajdamaschko, 2003).

## An Interlanguage Perspective

Learners of a second language have only one starting point: their primary language. Therefore, every understanding they have of the second language is filtered through their existing knowledge. As they become more familiar with the second language (in this case, English), they move toward learning that builds on their new knowledge base. Until they have that new knowledge, however, the language they produce is a hybrid form, an interlanguage (Selinker, 1972, 1991). The term *interlanguage* means that the communication produced by a person learning a second language will have the quality of intermediacy; it is a transitional phenomenon that may or may not develop into proficiency in the target language.

Interlanguage theory asserts that the learner's language should be viewed as creative and rule governed. An ELD curriculum that elicits creative response allows the learner to show the current state of his or her interlanguage. The view that learners have intermediary language modes that are not flawed misrepresentations of English, but rather are natural, creative expressions of the learner's innate language "genius," offers a refreshing opportunity for teachers to view second-language learning in a positive light.

Second, the errors that the learner makes (systematic errors that show a pattern of thinking, not random mistakes) are a necessary part of the learning process and provide a source of information for the teacher. Thus, the learner's interlanguage (and no two learners' interlanguages are identical) is the foundation for ELD teaching that respects and delights in individual creativity, channeled through the ELD standards.

Contemporary English-language development teaching is woven of three parts—the emphasis on communication, the need to develop the learner's cognitive academic language, and support for the learner's developmental interlanguage. These theoretical trends are amalgamated into a solid foundation for English-language oracy development.

## Basic Interpersonal Communication Skills

A newcomer to the English language needs to learn basic interpersonal communication skills (BICS) that permit adjustment to the routines of schooling and the comforts of peer interaction. The importance of BICS is that students can begin to understand and communicate with their teacher, develop and fine-tune their interpersonal skills, and start to overcome culture shock. School-age children use BICS to communicate basic needs to others or to share informal social interactions with peers. The focus in BICS is on getting across a message, with little regard for sentence structure and word choice.

Cummins (1984) called BICS *context embedded* because factors apart from the linguistic code can furnish meaning. For example, one student asks another for an eraser: "Mine's gone. You got one?" The student points to the pencil eraser and beckons for a loan. The item itself, rather than the language, provides the context. Other cues that add meaning to BICS in this situation are the tone of voice (requesting) and the "give me" gesture.

**Time to Attainment of BICS**    Fluency in BICS often leads students, parents, or other adults to assume that the child has mastered English. In a poll taken in 2000, 86 percent of children ages five to seventeen whose home language was Spanish reported that they spoke English "well" or "very well," and 90 percent of youths whose home language was Asian or Pacific Islander reported that they spoke English "well" or "very well" (U.S. Census Bureau, 2001c). However, students who might appear to be fluent enough in English to survive in an all-English classroom may in fact have significant gaps in the development of academic aspects of English.

**Helping Students Acquire BICS**    Teachers can encourage newcomers' acquisition of basic social language in several ways. First, pairing a new student with a bilingual buddy who speaks the same primary language as well as English eases the pain of culture shock. Seating newcomers so that they can be involved with other pupils and participate with other students can help to keep the new students alert and interactive.

A "Newcomer Handbook" is helpful during the earliest stages of BICS acquisition. Students can help to create this orientation guide, with sections that might feature simple school rules and procedures, English phrases to use for various social functions (asking for help, volunteering for class jobs, etc.), advice for homework help, and a map of the school with bilingual labels.

Cooperative tasks of all kinds provide opportunities for students to speak with one another. Cooperative groups with mixed abilities, in which students are assigned well-defined roles, permit some measure of participation with certain duties that do not require high level of verbal ability in English. Box 6.1 summarizes ways to help students develop BICS in the classroom.

**BICS Combined with Cognitive Language**    Throughout the school years, oral language activities need to balance an oracy focus on informal classroom discussions with specific training in conversations that are stimulating and thought provoking, with carefully sequenced instruction of academic vocabulary and thinking skills. It is these goals for which the Instructional Conversation (IC) discourse format is designed (see the section on IC that follows in this chapter).

## Listening

Although listening may be seen as a "receptive" skill, it is by no means passive. According to the sociocognitive approach to learning, listening is an act of constructing meaning. Listeners draw on their store of background knowledge and their expectation of the message to be conveyed as they actively comprehend a conversation or oral presentation. The role of the teacher is to set up situations in which students can develop their own purposes and goals for listening,

**Box 6.1**   Ways to Develop Basic Interpersonal Communication Skills (BICS) in the Classroom

Encourage friendships between English-speaking students and newcomers.
- Classroom grouping is linguistically heterogeneous.
- Playground activities are structured for heterogeneity.
- Students may work on group projects and make new friends.
- Encourage parents to make friends (perhaps in after-school clubs).
- Younger siblings may be included.

Use flexible grouping for academic work.
- Students are exposed to a variety of linguistic models.
- If one speaker dominates the group, variety will give others a chance to be heard.
- Students can speak with others who speak more or less fluently.
- Structure groups so that everyone talks, including through presentations.

Project-based learning allows students to discuss plans together.
- Projects may permit different intelligences to shine.
- English learners may be strong contributors in nonverbal ways (e.g., drawing).
- Projects promote collaboration and sharing.

Cross-age tutoring encourages language growth.
- Students gain fluency by reading to younger children.
- Older students can read to younger students who need language models.
- Older students can supervise classroom learning centers.
- Cross-age combinations can be useful (sixth grader + third grader + two kindergartners).

Instructional conversations can help develop students' speaking skills.
- When the teacher is a conversant, conversations are more academic.
- The teacher is the best model for thinking skills.
- A skilled conversation leader can draw out shy speakers.
- The conversation models literate, intellectual behavior.

Interviews can encourage English use at home.
- A variety of survey formats are available.
- Students can survey friends and neighbors.
- Writing up the results or graphing allows students to practice other skills.

acquire the English that is most useful in their daily lives, feel a sense of purpose, and engage in real communication. Over 40 percent of daily communication time is spent listening (Burley-Allen, 1995), and teachers are becoming more aware that listening skills should be taught, rather than assuming that the skill develops itself.

Listening can be divided into conversational listening and academic listening (Long, 1987). For purposes of simplification, listening activities are discussed here under the categories of listening for beginning comprehension, listening to repeat, listening to understand, and listening for communication.

## Listening for Beginning Comprehension

At the beginning level of language acquisition, the ELD objectives focus on demonstrating comprehension through active participation. During the initial "silent period," learners actively listen as they segment the sound stream, absorb intonation patterns, and become comfortable with English. They demonstrate comprehension through nonverbal means. With this methodology, academic subjects can be included.

Listening is for the purpose of comprehension. For example, students can view a poster of animals in a barn. The teacher might ask a student in the beginning stage, "Are people *safe* around these tame animals?" (pointing to the sheep, cat, and calf). A nod as a response to the word *safe* indicates comprehension. The teacher could ask a student who is in the beginning stage, "Which odors do you like?" (pointing to the Sense of Smell poster). The student can show comprehension by pointing.

A "listening area" can be set up in which English learners can listen to books on tape, with picture books or models provided to support understanding of what is heard. Two such stations might be set up side by side so students can share this listening experience with a friend. It might be comforting to a child if the person recording the tape speaks English with the same accent heard in the primary-language community.

## Listening to Repeat

At the early intermediate stage, the ELD standards indicate a student should be able to "participate in recitation, singing, and dramatics." For example, teachers use poems, nursery rhymes, and songs to introduce rhyming words, asking students to fill in the blanks at the ends of lines. In addition, teachers can read aloud books containing wordplay, alliteration, or tongue twisters, encouraging students to talk about how the author manipulates words. Other listening activities could include listening for focal stress or for syllables (Kozyrev, 1998). Such activities help students hear the language and develop phonemic awareness.

Jones (2007) recommended some teacher-led "repeat after me" listening and speaking practice:

> Some students may feel that repeating in chorus is childish and beneath them, but it's an effective way of helping them to get their tongues around new phrases and expressions so that they can say them easily and comfortably.... A question like *What are we supposed to do?* needs to be mastered as a whole phrase, not as six separate words. It may take several repetitions for students to manage this. Repeating phrases in chorus helps students to copy the rhythm of each phrase and say it again and again without inhibition. (p. 23)

Chants provide rhythmic presentations of the sentence intonation patterns of English. "The rhythm, stress, and intonation pattern of the chant should be an *exact* replica of what the student would hear from a native speaker in natural conversation" (Graham, 1992, p. 3). Graham (1988) has put fairy tales into jazz chant form, giving younger and less proficient students the opportunity to work with longer texts.

Actions can accompany songs, chants, and poems. It is easy to make up simple hand, arm, or body movements. To the poem "Here Is the Beehive," one first-grade teacher made up a series of hand motions: "Here is the beehive, where are the bees? / Hidden away where nobody sees. / Watch and you'll see them come out of the hive, One, two, three, four, five / Bzzzzz" (close fingers into a fist, hold it up, open it up one finger at a time, wave fingers in the air) (Linse, 2006).

## Listening to Understand: The Task Approach

Students are asked to demonstrate comprehension by performing tasks such as writing the proper response or selecting the proper answer. To be successful, they must listen carefully. Typical classroom tasks include listening to an audiotape and completing true/false exercises based on the content, listening to a prerecorded speech and circling vocabulary items on a list, and listening to a lecture and completing an outline of the notes. Students may be asked to listen for the main idea, for specific information, for synonyms, or for vocabulary in context. Teachers in content classes in which English learners are mainstreamed especially need to attend to the listening skills of these students to make sure they are understanding the content.

To enhance listening for understanding, students listen to stories and information, responding appropriately using both verbal and nonverbal responses; they listen for implied meaning and for main ideas, details, and sequences, applying knowledge of vocabulary, idiomatic expressions, discourse markers, organization, and tone to further their understanding.

 **Classroom Glimpse**

### LISTENING FOR UNDERSTANDING

Daniela Panferov's eighth-grade ELD class invited the artist Yi Kai to their class to talk about his art training in mainland China and the group to which he belongs, Global Harmony Through Arts. Mrs. Panferov and students discuss the topic of the upcoming talk and brainstorm questions and comments the students might like to ask or make. During the talk, students listen for answers to their questions. The talk is tape-recorded and the tape subsequently put into a listening center. Students are able to relisten, making note of ideas they may have missed. (Sholley, 2006)

## Listening for Communication

One emphasis at the early advanced and advanced levels is listening for communication: developing students' abilities to communicate fluently and accurately by integrating listening, speaking, and pronunciation practice, as well as developing skills in anticipating questions, understanding suggestions, and note taking. In the communicative approach, once listeners are beyond the initial stage, interviews are often used to augment listening skills. Listening can also be used in problem-solving situations by means of riddles, logic puzzles, and brainteasers as well as more traditional mathematical problems. Listening, far from being a mere receptive skill, can be successfully combined with other language modes as part of an integrated approach to English acquisition. Table 6.1 provides sample listening comprehension activities within each ELD level.

**TABLE 6.1**   Activities for Listening Comprehension by ELD Level

| Level | Example Listening Activity |
| --- | --- |
| Beginning | Hearing sound patterns:<br>  Rhyming poems<br>  Songs<br>  Couplets<br>  Comprehending narratives<br>  Read-aloud stories<br>  Small-group sharing-time anecdotes |
| Early Intermediate | Hearing sound patterns:<br>  Tongue twisters<br>  Jingles<br>  Jazz chants<br>  Alliterative poems and books<br>Listening to sentences:<br>  Dialogues<br>  Skits<br>  Open-ended sentences<br>  Conversation starters<br>Playing games:<br>  Twenty questions<br>  Pictionary<br>  Password |
| Intermediate | Listening to answer factual questions orally or in writing:<br>  Dialogues<br>  Talks<br>  Arguments<br>Listening to discourse:<br>  Books on tape<br>  Classroom dramatics, plays<br>  Instructional conversations |
| Early Advanced | Listening to make notes:<br>  Class lectures<br>  Taped content readings<br>  Movies and computer files<br>Cooperative problem-solving activities:<br>  Group work<br>  Logic puzzles<br>  Brainteasers |
| Advanced | Listening to make notes:<br>  Guest lecturers<br>  Whole-class presentations<br>Cooperative problem-solving activities:<br>  Riddles<br>  Logic puzzles<br>  Brainteasers |

*Source:* Adapted from Díaz-Rico & Weed (2010).

## The Listening Process

**Before Listening**   Explicit instruction in listening can be organized as "before," "during," and "after listening" in a similar fashion as in reading instruction (see Chapter 3). Prelistening tasks can include a preview of vocabulary, a brief chat to assess schemata and prior knowledge, a cue to the type of text organization expected (such as chronological order), or attention to a map that cues a spatial setting for the listening task. Unit 5, Chapter 1 ("The American Civil War") of Dunkel and Lim's *Intermediate Listening Comprehension* (1994) offers a prelistening preparation task defining *civil war,* introducing key vocabulary, and previewing the text structure of causal explanation. At a more advanced level, Dunkel, Pialorsi, and Kozyrev's *Advanced Listening Comprehension* (1996) presents a preview of the content of the listening tasks and also a lengthy outline to assist the listener in previewing the textual organization of the excerpt.

**During Listening**   Students can follow an outline as they listen or take notes cued by a set of questions or by using idea maps, outlines, paragraphs, or lists. They can listen several times, with slightly different purposes: for detection of transition words, key content terms, the main idea, supporting details, or the attitude of the speaker.

If the teacher feels the need to lecture, a helpful strategy for English learners is to have the lesson videotaped while students simply listen to the lecture, concentrating on understanding and writing down only questions or parts of the lecture they do not understand. Later, the videotape is played and the teacher and several students take notes on the board. The teacher can model the type of outline that indicates the main ideas and supporting details. After a few minutes, the videotape is stopped and the discussion then highlights various note-taking strategies and provides new strategies. This activity can be used on a periodic basis to enhance students' ability to comprehend lectures and take effective notes (Adamson, 1993).

**After Listening**   Many kinds of activities can follow up a listening task. Students can write, discuss, read, draw, or act out their interpretation of the content. They can attend to the linguistic aspects of what they have heard by completing worksheets on word meaning, idiomatic usage, formal versus informal English, words that compare/contrast, or words that introduce causal statements. The focus can be on cultural aspects of the reading, content applications across the disciplines, or critical thinking, including problem solving.

The postlistening time offers the most authentic activities—most conversation takes place after listeners have shared a talk, movie, or similar event. The postlistening phase can

 **Classroom Glimpse**

### LISTENING TO A RECORDING

Mr. Geller's American history class is going to listen to a recording of F. D. Roosevelt's radio fireside chats. Here is what he will say:

- Before listening: "Today we are going to listen to President Roosevelt address the nation. What do you think he might talk about? Why does a president talk directly to the people?"

- During listening: "While you listen to the program, try to listen for the main idea. Also, try to listen for the emotional tone."
- After listening: "Let's group into threes. In your group, complete these two tasks. *Summarize* the talk. *Describe* the emotional tone."

host critical conversation on the main ideas and a genuine sharing of opinions. This is one of the pleasures of real conversation (Miller, 2004).

**Authentic Tasks in and out of the Real World**    An effective listening curriculum exposes students to a variety of speakers, for a variety of tasks, on a variety of topics, for a variety of purposes. The test of real listening skill is going out into the real world. Students can be encouraged to interview classmates and community members; attend movies, plays, and concerts; participate in hobby groups; or work in community service. In these situations, listeners must bring a relatively sophisticated set of understandings to bear: what to expect from the speaker, the setting in time and place, the topic, the genre of the text, and the co-text, or accompanying clues to meaning (Morley, 1999).

Despite the complexity of listening tasks and the emphasis on communicative approaches, however, listening is only half the work—one must also learn to speak.

# Speaking, Communication Skills, and the ELD Standards

Speaking involves a number of complex skills and strategies. In spoken discourse, words must not only be strung together in proper grammatical sequence, but they must also make sense in form, meaning, purpose, and function. Part of the role of the teacher is to help students assimilate and produce discourse not only for the purpose of basic interpersonal communication (informal) but also for the comprehension and production of cognitive academic language (formal). In addition, the teacher provides opportunities for students to express themselves in the wide range of language functions.

The emphasis on communicative methodology mandates that teachers try to get English learners to talk. In K–12 classrooms in U.S. schools, large numbers of English learners are mainstreamed into contexts that render them silent. Language learners develop best when they have opportunities to interact (Wells, 1998). It is therefore vital that teachers help students develop their speaking abilities.

## Speaking in the ELD Standards

Listening and speaking are the only skills assessed on the CELDT during kindergarten and first grade. The emphasis in speaking at the early intermediate level is on asking and answering questions and making simple statements, retelling stories, and participating in classroom oral language events; consistent use of correct grammar and intonation are not expected. At the intermediate level, the expectation is for English learners to use English sounds and grammar more consistently and expand vocabulary as they continue to ask and answer questions, retell stories, and participate in conversations. At early advanced and advanced levels, students are expected to produce academic language, with more precise vocabulary, details, and concepts across a range of tasks, using nativelike English. Clearly these goals require extensive oral practice.

## Developing Oral Language

Morgan (1992) offers a host of ways that teachers can develop oral language in the classroom. An encouraging classroom climate helps students to feel confident, to be able to speak freely and make mistakes, and to believe that their way of speaking is respected and their opinions taken seriously. A noncompetitive atmosphere encourages sharing ideas through interaction, especially at a dedicated sharing time every day. A "productively talkative" work environment is not so noisy that a timid child feels overwhelmed. However, even in a "normally noisy" class, a shy student may need a "home corner" where he or she can listen to tapes in the primary language or engage in nonverbal play in which English is not necessary. This allows rest from the stress of foreign language immersion.

Fluency is the most important speaking skill. Jones (2007) defined *fluency* as follows:

> Fluency doesn't mean speaking really fast without hesitating. It's being able to express yourself despite gaps in your knowledge, despite the mistakes you're making, despite not knowing all the vocabulary you might need. . . . The opposite of fluency is being tongue-tied and embarrassed when speaking English—or not speaking at all. Fluency means speaking slowly and clearly, not speaking fast and unclearly. Fluency depends on knowing more vocabulary and on confidence—and on not worrying about losing face by making mistakes. Another component of fluency is being able to articulate easily and comprehensively. (p. 18)

---

**Best Practice**   STRATEGIES TO DEVELOP STUDENTS' SPEAKING SKILLS

- Academic opportunities for talking and working together range from low structure (work-related chitchat) to highly structured (for example, each person in a cooperative group is responsible for one section of an oral report).
- Listening to students with enthusiasm and interest communicates that their thoughts are valued.
- A pocket chart with slots for every student can be filled with a paper flower after they have spoken at sharing time, with no student receiving a second turn until everyone has had a chance to volunteer a personal anecdote.
- Make sure a quiet area is available where a child can "escape" English for a while.

---

**Situations for Speaking**   Students need opportunities to talk in natural interactional contexts and for a variety of purposes: to establish and maintain social relationships; to express reactions; to give and seek information; to solve problems, discuss ideas, or teach and learn a skill; to entertain or play with language; or to display achievement. In addition, students need to learn to interact with a variety of conversational partners: students, the teacher, other adults at school, cross-age peers, guests, and so on.

Speaking reinforces listening comprehension. The content or SDAIE teacher, to ensure comprehension, needs to solicit feedback from students about the course content. To find out who is comprehending the material, the teacher must ask. If no one asks questions, the teacher finds other ways to check for understanding. Cooperative speaking activities are a part of every SDAIE lesson. Some instructors stop for a pair/share break every so often, so each student can ask a partner one question.

---

**Best Practice**    SUSTAINING A CONVERSATION BY ASKING OPEN-ENDED QUESTIONS

Asking open-ended questions helps to involve others in a conversation. Open-ended questions (those not answerable by yes or no or one-word responses) encourage the other person in a conversation to give more information—for example, "Do you like living in this area?"

(Adapted from Matthews, 1994, pp. 34–36)

---

If structured public speaking is important in the content of the class, students are given a tight outline and timetable for each presentation. The teacher might invite students to meet outside of class before the presentation to rehearse. Other students can help by participating in a peer-scoring rubric in which content is emphasized over understandability.

It is wise not to surprise students with requests for extemporaneous talk because few individuals shine at extemporaneous speaking. Speaking activities that include a planning phase often draw forth from students a more complex response. This helps students by "stretching their interlanguage" (Folse, 2006, p. 49) in that they can take the time to find the language that expresses their ideas more fully. Having students write down their ideas—with a minimum length for the preparatory notes—can improve the number of participants in a discussion and help discussants to speak more clearly, with more elaborate sentences.

---

**Best Practice**    SHOW AND TELL

Students can learn to improve the familiar oral format "Show and Tell" by using standard expressions that fit into a familiar format.

> **Topic:** *This is* . . . a postcard of the Golden Gate Bridge.
> **Personal slant:** *We went* to San Francisco . . .
> **Description of object:**
> > **(present)** The bridge **is** almost two miles long . . .
> > **(past)** It **was** completed in 1937.
> **Closing:** *So,* it was my favorite part of the trip.

(Adapted from LeBeau & Harrington, 2003, p. 76)

---

## Classroom Glimpse

### CREATING CONVERSATION-FRIENDLY ENVIRONMENTS

The kindergarten teacher transformed her room into a rain forest by putting artificial trees in the center, arranging several live plants and a small inflatable plastic pool underneath them, putting more live plants in the water-filled pool, hanging photographs of the rain forest throughout the room, placing area rugs near the display, and posting a question in large letters: "Why are rain forests important?" Whole-group instruction occurred early in the morning, before lunch, and at the end of the school day. At other times, students worked in small groups on the area rugs.

A high school teacher, for the Civil War unit, displayed flags of the period and a Confederate uniform crafted by the students, involved students in a letter-writing project imagining they were Confederate solders writing home during the war, and grouped the desks into clusters, each one representing a regiment of soldiers or a home community. (Adapted from Zacarian, 2005)

**Resources for Spoken Discourse**   Opportunities for oral discourse range from carefully constructed activities to those that are completely student generated. Several kinds of speaking activities can be included in daily lessons, including problem solving in small groups, practicing persuasive or entertaining speeches, role-plays, interviews, chain stories, talks, problems, and discussions (c.f. Zelman, 1996). *Discussion Starters* (Folse, 1996) offers speaking activities that build oral fluency using exercises specifically designed for group participation. The discussion prompts are based on role-play, "finish-the-story" situations, problems that can be solved only if members of a group work together, and real court cases for groups to play "judge."

Table 6.2 organizes representative oral activities into the three categories suggested by Allen and Vallette (1977). These categories range from tightly structured on the left to freely constructed on the right.

One discussion topic featured in LeBeau and Harrington (2003) is "Designing a Menu for the International Students' Welcoming Party." What could be served at a multinational, multicultural party that welcomes students from thirty different countries to the Newcomer High School? What menu can include food to satisfy everyone? What criteria can be used to choose dishes? Is cost a factor? Are there some foods that some people cannot eat? What foods would be unusual or interesting for people to try? To enrich the discussion, can conversants describe food from their culture that they might like to share with others?

### Best Practice   PRACTICING FLUENCY BY MAKING A RECORDING

1. Working individually or with a partner, students plan a three-minute presentation (perhaps explaining a grade-level-appropriate proverb—see www.englishclub.com/ref/Sayings).
2. Using a tape recorder or audio-recording computer software such as Audacity (http://audacity.sourceforge.net), students make a recording (working from notes, but *not* reading from a script).

3. Students listen to themselves, checking for a smooth, natural, conversational tone, and for adequate volume and clarity.
4. Students record again, and submit a peer or self-evaluation to the teacher, comparing versions 1 and 2.

(Adapted from Mathews, 1994, p. 78)

**Teaching Pronunciation** English learners need proficiency in the English sound system. Pronunciation involves the correct articulation of the individual sounds of English as well as the proper stress and pitch within syllables, words, and phrases. Longer stretches of speech require correct intonation patterns. Accurate pronunciation, including phoneme production, stress, pitch, and prosody, is one of the most difficult features of learning a second language. Native speakers acquire the phonology of their native language by listening to and producing speech. The same is true to some degree in a second language, but by using audiolingual methods (see Chapter 2) there is a role for such phonemic drills as minimum pair work (*bit/pit, hill/hail, dog/dock*). Beyond word-level pronunciation, students can practice sentence-level intonation.

However, the goal of teaching English pronunciation is not necessarily to make second-language speakers sound like native speakers of English. Some English learners do not wish to have a nativelike pronunciation but prefer to retain an accent that indicates their first-language roots and allows them to be identified with their ethnic community. Still others may wish to integrate actively into the mainstream culture and therefore are motivated to try to attain a

**TABLE 6.2** Formats for Oral Practice in the ELD Classroom

| Guided Practice | Communicative Practice | Free Conversation |
| --- | --- | --- |
| Formulaic exchanges | Simulations | Discussion groups |
| Greetings | Guessing games | Debates |
| Congratulations | Group puzzles | Panel discussions |
| Apologies | Rank-order problems | Group picture story |
| Leave taking | Values continuum | Socializing |
| Dialogues | Categories of preference | Storytelling/retelling |
| Mini-conversations | Opinion polls | Discussions of: |
| Role-plays | Survey taking | Films |
| Skits | Interviews | Shared experiences |
| Oral descriptions | Brainstorming | Literature |
| Strip stories | News reports | |
| Oral games | Research reports | |
| | Storytelling | |

*Source:* Díaz-Rico & Weed (2010).

native accent in English. Teachers need to recognize these individual goals and enable learners to achieve pronunciation that does not detract from their ability to communicate.

---

**Best Practice**   **PRONUNCIATION SELF-CORRECTION**

The teacher can encourage pronunciation self-correction in the following ways:

- Writing overheard utterances on the board (without identifying the student) for the class as a whole to practice
- Pointing to a wall chart with typically mispronounced items (for example, the pronunciation of -*ed* and -*s* endings, *r*/*l* errors, basic word stress rules, and sentence intonations)
- Offering students pronunciation software that has a recording feature so students can receive feedback (Goodwin, Brinton, & Celce-Murcia, 1994)

---

Students' attempts to reproduce correct word stress, sentence rhythm, and intonation may improve by exposure to native-speaker models. The teacher's role, in this case, is to create a nonthreatening environment that stimulates and interests students enough that they participate actively in producing speech. Teachers may also take a more direct role in improving pronunciation. Clarification checks can be interjected politely when communication is impaired. Teacher correction or sentence completion can be given after the teacher has allowed ample wait-time. Older students might be given the task of comparing speech sounds in their native language with sounds in English in order to better understand a contrastive difference. Even though pronunciation practice is essential, teachers should not stigmatize English learners or require them to repeat phrases aloud in front of other students. Pronunciation practice should be private.

---

**Best Practice**   **A GAME FOR STRESS AND SENTENCE INTONATION**

Working in pairs, students receive a card containing a dialogue. In pairs, student A mimics the stress and intonation of one of the sentences on the card using nonsense syllables. Student B tries to guess which is the target sentence (Cogan, 1999). Another game for practicing stress is Stress Clapping. A student comes to the front of the room, pulls a sentence written on a folded overhead transparency strip out of a box, and displays the sentence on the overhead projector (sentences are taken from song lyrics, poems, or limericks). The student must read the sentence aloud and clap each time there is a stressed word. The student's team receives a point for each stressed word correctly identified (Mahoney, 1999b).

---

Teachers can help students practice intonation by leading choral reading, one clause at a time, repeated once. This differs from a regular read-aloud because the explicit purpose here is to practice prosody. Learners may benefit from looking at a chart representing a normal sentence curve. As a declarative sentence is read aloud, the teacher—or a lead student—traces the progression of the intonation pattern across the curve. A question would require a different demonstration curve. This helps English learners listen for and replicate the desired prosody. Table 6.3 offers activities to teach intonation in English.

**TABLE 6.3**    Activities to Teach Intonation in English

| Name of Activity | Description | Language-Acquisition Level |
| --- | --- | --- |
| Consonant Memory | One student completes a sentence with a target consonant sound. The next student repeats the sentence and adds another word containing the same sound. ("I went on vacation and packed a dog [doll, dish].") | Beginning, Early Intermediate |
| Plural Practice Bragging | Students make up closets full of clothes, refrigerators full of food, or garages full of vehicles. ("I have twelve cars and ten bicycles.") | Beginning, Early Intermediate |
| Three Verb Tag | Prepare lists of three past-tense verbs at a time, one of which has a different ending sound (*baked, cleaned, cooked*—answer is *cleaned*). See how many "odd" verbs each student can "tag." | Beginning to Intermediate |
| Yes/No Interview | Students formulate questions to ask one another that are answered by brief affirmative or negative sentences. ("Do you like school?" "Yes, I like it a lot.") | Early Intermediate, Intermediate |
| Tongue Twister | Students make up their own tongue twisters using words from the dictionary with the target consonant in the initial position. | Early Intermediate to Advanced |
| Found a Dog | Students write fake ads about finding a dog that contain two or three sentences. Each student gets a turn reading aloud his or her dog description. | Early Intermediate to Advanced |
| Contraction Interview | Students interview each other for five facts. When they present these facts about their partner aloud to the class, they must use three contractions. ("He's on a soccer team.") | Early Intermediate to Advanced |

*Source:* Adapted from Dale & Poms (2005).

---

**Best Practice**    FOCUS ON BLENDS

Between the end of one word and the beginning of the next word, there are three kinds of blends.

1. Consonant plus vowel: *box office*
2. Consonant plus same consonant: *music class*
3. Consonant plus different consonant: *hit music*

Students can practice these blends using the list below.

| | | | |
| --- | --- | --- | --- |
| rock **s**tar | devote**d f**ans | talen**t sh**ow | mo**sh p**it |
| acousti**c g**uitar | har**d r**ock | roc**k c**oncert | hi**t s**ong |
| blue**s m**usic | mi**c s**tand | pin**k C**adillac | golde**n o**ldie |

Teachers who overemphasize exact pronunciation when learners are in the early stages of learning English may hinder the innovative spirit of risk-taking that is preferable when a learner is trying to achieve fluency. Teaching intonation through fun activities such as chants and songs brings enjoyment to language learning. On the other hand, at higher levels of proficiency it is essential to provide the learner with corrective feedback.

If an older learner has serious accent issues—to the point of unintelligibility—computer software such as that available from Auralog (www.auralog.com) can provide individualized tutoring. Such pronunciation software is excellent for the specific, repetitious drills needed to develop a more native-sounding accent. Many such programs allow the user to record speech and then compare the recording with a norm; some even show a graphic representation of the speech tone for purposes of comparison. Students can work in privacy at a listening center or in a computer laboratory.

 **Classroom Glimpse**

### COMPUTER-ASSISTED ENGLISH PRONUNCIATION PRACTICE

To practice pronunciation for his ELD class, Abdul uses software that enables him to click on a word or sentence to hear it repeatedly, look up a meaning, see a related picture or video-clip, or read a related text. He can also listen to a sentence, compare his voice to a computer model of the correct response, and have the computer judge the accuracy of his attempts.

Learners of English can look for phonological cues in word structure only when the pronunciation is regular. For example, knowing the pronunciation for *bad* will help with *had, Dad, pad,* and *fad,* but not with *wad.* Still, many phonics-based reading approaches carefully control the learner's exposure to vocabulary, focusing on words that are phonetically regular during the learner's early reading phase. This can lead to some contrived text, such as Learning Pyramid's *Miss Nell Fell in the Well* (Whitman, 1994). One solution would be to balance the use of controlled readers with read-aloud texts that expose the learner to a broader range of phonemes during listening comprehension.

To ensure that adequate attention is paid to developing pronunciation skills, two principles to keep in mind when evaluating ELD programs are the following: First, does the program offer the teacher an ample set of tools to explain, practice, and review pronunciation in a structured way? Second, does the program balance texts based on strict sound–symbol correspondence with texts that expose the reader or listener to a naturally occurring set of phonemes, a set that mirrors the distribution of phonemes in everyday speech?

## The Speaking Process

Strategic speaking involves a combination of cognitive, social, and emotional factors. Table 6.4 offers a compendium of strategies to enhance English learners' oral presentations.

**Before Speaking**   Prespeaking activities warm the students to the topic and activate or provide some prior knowledge. In Kehe and Kehe's (1998) Unit 11 ("Your Hometown and

**TABLE 6.4**    Some Strategies Useful for English Learners in Speaking

| Phase of the Speaking Process | Sample Strategies for English Learners |
|---|---|
| Before speaking | Lower anxiety by taking a few deep breaths, visualizing success, repeating positive self-talk phrases. |
| | Review the purpose of the talk; ask for clarification if unsure of goal. |
| | Activate background knowledge; make associations with similar situations. |
| | Predict what will happen and what language is needed; practice difficult vocabulary in advance. |
| | Plan the talk, using an outline, rehearsing with a partner if it is a joint presentation. |
| While speaking | Ask for clarification or help if necessary. |
| | Concentrate on the task, avoiding distractions. |
| | Stay involved with others; negotiate meaning with listeners. |
| | Monitor speech, paying attention to vocabulary, grammar, and pronunciation; try new words; back up and fix mistakes if necessary. |
| | Compensate for vocabulary shortcomings by using cognates, synonyms, gestures, or guesses; simplify message if necessary; base talk on information about which speaker has some prior knowledge. |
| After speaking | Self-reward with positive affirmations. |
| | Evaluate accomplishment, reviewing goals and strategies, asking for feedback and tuning in to the reactions of others. |
| | Identify problem areas, looking up grammar and vocabulary that were troublesome. |
| | Make a plan for improvement, noting strategies of classmates or instructor's suggestions. |
| | Ask for help or correction from more proficient speakers. |
| | Keep a learning log, writing down reflections, strategies, reactions, and outcomes. |

*Source:* Adapted from Alcaya, Lybeck, Mougel, & Weaver (1995).

Childhood Home"), students write their answers to several questions about their hometown before beginning the discussion. In Huizenga and Thomas-Ruzic's (1992) *All Talk,* Unit 13 ("Pick Your Perfect Vacation"), students warm up to the task of interviewing a partner by circling new words in vacation ads. These activities help students practice vocabulary and survey the content terrain before speaking.

Students can prepare for an impromptu speech on the subject of a news story by watching the evening news on television, listening to a news radio station, reading a newspaper or newsmagazine such as *Time* or *Newsweek,* or talking to people outside of class about selected issues. Students who must prepare for a formal public presentation need a more structured approach, with an attention-getting opener, a preview of what will be said, a substantive main body of the speech, a summary of the main points, and a memorable conclusion. An outline helps the student keep the presentation on topic. Rehearsal in advance of delivery—whether aloud to oneself, onto an audio- or videotape, or before a critical audience—helps students pace the delivery, create a natural tone, and practice difficult pronunciation (Wong, 1998).

**While Speaking**   Teachers working in mixed-ability classrooms can plan group activities that help students in different ways. Students can work in homogeneous groups when the goal of the activity is accuracy and in heterogeneous groups when the goal is fluency.

---

**Best Practice**   **STORY RETELLING AT FOUR ELD LEVELS**

First-grade students at the beginning ELD level can listen to a reading of "The Three Little Pigs" and recite the wolf's "I'll blow your house down!" along with the reader. A group of early intermediate students can retell the story using pictures and then talk about the pictures. Intermediate students can retell the story to the teacher or a cross-age tutor who can write their story for them, and then students can reread, illustrate, and rearrange the story from sentence strips. Early advanced English learners can create a new ending for the story.

---

Informal class discussions are a low-key way to practice speaking. While speaking, a student makes eye contact with listeners and adjusts the volume to an appropriate distance between the speakers. A speaker usually does not use notes when chatting with a classmate, but sometimes such notes are available from a previous brainstorming session. Turns are usually shared in small groups, and one person does not monopolize discussion.

Students making a public speech or academic presentation require a more formal approach, with a neat public appearance that shows respect for the situation and audience. Visual aids in the form of charts or overhead projections help listeners to see as well as hear the presentation. Memorizing the presentation is not advisable, for it may lead to a stiff and forced delivery. Stance should be facing the audience, with hands and feet appearing calm and under control (Wong, 1998).

Correction while a person is speaking is seldom appropriate. If the teacher makes such corrections, the speaker may become tense and less fluent or creative. If the speaker is genuinely unable to be understood, the teacher can be honest about it. However, it impedes communication if the teacher expects an imperfect sentence to be repeated correctly. Reformulation is the best alternative; if the teacher hears an incorrect utterance, a similar sentence can be repeated to the student naturally and in the context of the conversation without embarrassing the student (Bartram & Walton, 1994).

Oral presentations can be assessed using *holistic scoring*, with a three-level score (good/excellent/superior) based on content (clear purpose, vivid and relevant supporting details), organization (well-structured introduction, body, and conclusion), and delivery (skillful verbal and nonverbal language, with clear, appropriate, and fluent speech). Alternatively, *analytic scoring* gives point values to each aspect of content, organization, and delivery, and the speaker receives as a grade the sum of the points for each aspect (see Chaney & Burk [1998] for examples of each type of scoring).

Spencer Grant/PhotoEdit

*English learners can use drama as an extension activity to practice speaking.*

**After Speaking**    Many kinds of activities can follow up a speaking task. As in the listening task, students can write, discuss, read, draw, or act out their interpretation of the content, attending to the linguistic or cultural aspects of what they have heard. For the most part, oral discussion is a vital part of any other task and should be developed as a top priority. When students have been outside the classroom on a service-learning project, debriefing is needed so that students can reflect on and share with one another what they have learned.

---

**Best Practice**    ASSESSING A PRESENTATION

Use the following categories to assess a student's oral presentation (+ = good, ✓ = satisfactory, – = needs more practice):

- *Content.* Fulfilled assignment; developed topic adequately, within time limit; appropriate topic for level of audience
- *Delivery.* Maintained eye contact with listeners; spoke naturally, loudly, and clearly; appropriate posture, movements, and gestures; used notes effectively

- *Fluency.* Clear pronunciation; accurate use of vocabulary and grammar, without too much repetition or hesitation
- *Organization.* Effective introduction, logic, coherence, and conclusion (Adapted from Matthews, 1994, p. 209)

**Speaking Games and Tasks**   Table 6.5 describes three kinds of tasks by ELD level that enhance listening and speaking. The game-style format reduces speaking anxiety.

**Oral Discourse and the Instructional Conversation**   Contemporary educators have sought discussion formats that engage students in critical thinking and intellectually productive social interaction. In the instructional conversation (IC), the instructor functions as "thinker-leader" while encouraging voluntary oral participation. The IC model developed by Goldenberg and Gallimore (1991) has both instructional and conversational elements. The most important instructional element is the thematic focus. Themes are drawn from text that participants read in common before beginning the conversation. A good theme is one that is flexible and grows out of the ideas of the participants, without being superimposed by the leader. This flexibility creates shared responsibility for the discussion by the participants.

The conversation elements include aspects that defuse anxiety and promote interaction. It is helpful, for example, to talk while seated in a circle of chairs, which facilitates eye contact and allows individuals equal access to turns. Disagreement and difference of opinion are protected; part of the challenging atmosphere is for students to find a way to evaluate one another's viewpoints. In the IC format, turns are voluntary—no one is called on to speak. Grammar is not corrected. Group members talk with one another in everyday English on topics that elicit opinions without necessarily requiring expertise or prior knowledge.

To support the conversational elements of the IC, the thinker-leader asks open-ended questions, responds positively to student ideas, and weaves ideas that are volunteered by class members into the instructional content. A tone of challenging, nonthreatening, intellectual give-and-take promotes critical thinking and speaking. As one student speaks, others listen. Teachers might offer lunch-hour discussions with interested students on a voluntary basis on selected topics of interest to students.

**Oracy and Web 2.0**   Web 2.0 is a term for media tools that help the user to share information and collaborate using the World Wide Web. English learners join Web-based communities, participate in social networking sites, share audio podcasts and videos, and use wikis and blogs in audio formats to enhance their oral skills. Computer-mediated communication (CMC) tools enable students to speak with one another directly over Skype and other Voice-over-Internet-Protocol (VoIP) technologies using oral chatrooms and other forms of synchronous (immediate connection) and asynchronous (delayed or audio-recorded formats) modes. These tools have the potential to augment students' desire to practice speaking and listening in their second language.

**Media Literacy**   Critical media analysis is an excellent way to stimulate English learners' listening and speaking skills. Being able to sort out information and critically research, analyze, and understand media are becoming more and more important. *Media literacy* has been used as an umbrella term for the analysis of Internet information, computers, art, graphics, images,

**TABLE 6.5**  Three Activities for Listening and Speaking

| Name of Activity | ELD Level | Directions for the Teacher |
|---|---|---|
| Shadow Tableaux | Beginning | Pass around a bag and have each student put in a small personal object. Spread these out on an overhead projector so only their shadow can be seen. Have students work in pairs to name all the objects. (Mahoney, 1999a) |
| Give Me a Word That . . . | Early Intermediate | Students form three groups (A, B, C). Prepare index cards (one for each student) with vocabulary questions starting with the phrase, "Give me . . ." For example, "Give me a word that dances . . ." (*ballerina, Usher*)<br><br>A word that runs (*runner, river*)<br><br>A blue word (*sky*)<br><br>A cold word (*ice, winter*)<br><br>Student A reads a word; group B has 30 seconds to give an answer; if not, group C can answer. Whichever is correct wins that round. (Mansour, 1999) |
| Headline News | Intermediate | Cut out interesting headlines and their corresponding photographs from newspapers. Cut the headlines in half (do not split word phrases). Paste the beginnings and endings of the headlines onto index cards. Students in group A receive photographs, group B, headline beginnings, and group C, headline endings. Students move around the room, asking one another (not showing) the content of their card. The first set to identify its three parts wins the game. (Hetherton, 1999) |

text, advertising, and so forth. From a critical perspective, students can respond to questions such as "What media do you watch? Is there a 'best' way to get your information? Do advertising techniques have an impact on you or someone you know? How accurate is the content? What biases can be spotted?" (see www.medialit.org).

 **Classroom Glimpse**

### CONNECTING ORACY TO THE COMMUNITY

Each student in Nora Bryce's ELD class created a short presentation about some aspect of his or her native culture. They practiced giving the presentations to one another during class. As "cultural ambassadors," various students went with Nora in pairs to a local breakfast Kiwanis meeting once a month before school. The Kiwanis members became so interested in the students' presentations that they devoted their fundraising activity to awarding college scholarships to class members. In this way, community connections enhanced the students' cultural capital and vice versa.

Speaking and listening are ends in themselves and do not always have to be linked to reading and writing. But such links, both planned and unplanned, demonstrate that language is a whole, and proficiency in one skill mutually reinforces others.

In summary, current approaches to oracy instruction vary in emphasis, but the best teaching supports the following principles: (1) Oracy begins with BICS but should also include the development of oral academic language; (2) listening activities are important across a range of skill levels and academic tasks; (3) ELD standards should be included in all listening and speaking lesson plans; (4) the design of the classroom should support ways in which English learners can converse for both social and instructional purposes; (5) both listening and speaking instruction follow a process of preparation, teaching and practice, and follow-up; (6) new forms of Web-based media are available to enhance oral skills; and (7) oracy activities can connect to, and serve, the community at large.

**PEARSON myeducationlab**
The Power of Classroom Practice
www.myeducationlab.com

Go to the Topic Listening and Speaking in the MyEducationLab (www.myeducationlab.com) for your course, where you can:

- Find learning outcomes for Listening and Speaking along with the national standards that connect to these outcomes.
- Complete Assignments and Activities that can help you more deeply understand the chapter content.
- Apply and practice your understanding of the core teaching skills identified in the chapter with the Building Teaching Skills and Dispositions learning units.
- Examine challenging situations and cases presented in the IRIS Center Resources.
- Check your comprehension on the content covered in the chapter by going to the Study Plan in the Book Resources for your text. Here you will be able to take a chapter quiz, receive feedback on your answers, and then access Review, Practice, and Enrichment activities to enhance your understanding of chapter content.

**A+RISE**

Go to the Topic A+RISE in the MyEducationLab (www.myeducationlab.com) for your course. A+RISE® Standards2Strategy™ is an innovative and interactive online resource that offers new teachers in grades K–12 just-in-time, research-based instructional strategies that:

- Meet the linguistic needs of ELLs as they learn content
- Differentiate instruction for all grades and abilities
- Offer reading and writing techniques, cooperative learning, use of linguistic and nonlinguistic representations, scaffolding, teacher modeling, higher order thinking, and alternative classroom ELL assessment
- Provide support to help teachers be effective through the integration of listening, speaking, reading, and writing along with the content curriculum
- Improve student achievement
- Are aligned to Common Core Elementary Language Arts standards (for the literacy strategies) and to English language proficiency standards in WIDA, Texas, California, and Florida.

# 7

# English-Language Literacy Development

Literacy instruction is a crucial aspect of K–12 schooling in the United States. The topic of how best to instruct English learners has been a part of the debates over the best ways to help students learn to read and read to learn (see Wolfe & Poynor [2001] for a discussion of the politics of reading instruction). However, a complicating factor that is sometimes not considered by reading researchers is the varying background experiences that English learners bring to the reading task. California TESOL (CATESOL, 1998) provided the following five classifications for English learners that help teachers understand the differences in English learners according to their literacy background:

- Young learners (K–3) whose beginning literacy instruction is in their primary language
- Young learners (K–3) acquiring initial literacy in English because they do not have access to primary-language reading instruction
- Older learners with grade-level primary-language literacy who are beginning to develop literacy in English
- Older learners with limited formal schooling in their home country
- Older learners with inconsistent school history and limited development of either the primary language or English (p. 1)

This complex terrain, with English learners coming from a wide range of backgrounds and achieving a wide range of scores on the CELDT, suggests it is unlikely that a one-size-fits-all approach to reading instruction will be suitable. Instead, a differentiated instruction model is necessary.

# Connections among Oracy, Literacy, and Social Functions

How do speaking and listening connect to reading and writing? Vygotsky (1981) believed that children learn to engage in higher-level thinking by learning first how to communicate. The more students can use language in the classroom environment, the more they will learn. The language that students bring from home is the foundation not only for the language used at school but also for the process of learning itself. Thus, both English proficiency and learning in the content areas are furthered by a solid base of primary-language proficiency.

Writing and reading, like speech, are social acts. This means that the natural sociability of children in their first language is the foundation for their intellectual development. This chapter presents ways in which literacy and oracy develop within a social context and are enhanced by strategic teaching of language functions. Students need opportunities to engage with English in natural interactional contexts and for a variety of purposes: to establish and maintain social relationships; to express reactions; to give and seek information; to solve problems, discuss ideas, or teach and learn a skill; to entertain or play with language; or to display achievement.

While teaching, observant educators take note of what activities "light a fire" in learners and take care to balance students' receptive and productive skills within a learning environment that respects culture, human interests, and imagination.

## English for Empowerment

Teachers of English must become aware that language is inextricably joined with cultural identity and social differences, and the individual's relationship to institutions and sociocultural contexts affects opportunities for oracy and literacy. As Peim (1993) puts it, it is not the case that any activity in class simply and directly enhances language development. Direct connections to the community and to the circulation of power (Foucault, 1980) strengthen the chance that an individual's oracy and literacy efforts will actually enhance his or her social and cultural prospects in life.

Banks (1991) set empowerment in the context of personal and social change:

> A curriculum designed to empower students must be transformative in nature and help students to develop the knowledge, skills, and values needed to become social critics who can make reflective decisions and implement their decisions in effective personal, social, political, and economic action. (p. 131)

However, Wink (2000) cautioned that the verb *empower* should not be used with a direct object, because it is patronizing to believe that one can empower someone else.

Take the contrasting examples of two parent newsletters sent home by a school. The first newsletter is part of the school's open house packet distributed with about six other papers, some of which are in Spanish. The newsletter is a word-for-word primary-language translation of the reverse side, a letter to English-speaking parents. There are no illustrations—merely a page consisting of ten paragraphs, each explaining a different homework tip. This newsletter assumes that the parents welcome the advice of the school authorities and that the parents' role is to help the students complete the assignments sent home by the teachers.

In contrast, another teacher works with students to write Homework Help manuals, six-page "little books" composed by students themselves in cooperative groups. Each group decides on a title for their book and brainstorms the book's content. Will it be in both Spanish and English? Will it include recommendations of a special place to study at home? Will it mention adequate lighting? Will it discuss how to deal with the distractions of television or of siblings? Will it advise students how to solicit help from parents? Each group adds the ideas that the members choose. When the books are ready, the teacher asks each student to take the book home, discuss it with the family, and then come back to class with feedback about whether the suggestions are apt, plus additional ideas.

Looking at these two products, which would benefit students more? Which is more likely to be a focal point for discussion at home? One must admit that the student product is more likely to influence attitudes and behavior toward studying than the administrator's version, no matter the difference in expertise. Moreover, what social functions of language were involved in the student project (interpersonal, representational, heuristic)? In the process of creating the manual, the students naturally used speaking and listening together with reading and writing. This is an example of a transformative literacy that served an institutional purpose.

## An Integrated Approach to Oracy and Literacy

The idea that speaking and listening must precede literacy is outdated. Oral language proficiency promotes literacy and vice versa. Most people are visual learners—memory of a new word, for example, is enhanced when the word can be seen as well as heard. So an integrated approach to English language arts (Pappas, Kiefer, & Levstik, 2006) is recommended, not only at the elementary level but also for content area instruction at the secondary level. Speaking and listening should be combined with reading and writing, and content instructors should integrate the teaching of English with subject matter instruction.

To integrate oracy with literacy, English learners need environments that help them to meet the social, emotional, cognitive, and linguistic demands of learning. Students need a positive *emotional setting,* a climate of trust and respect. Teachers can encourage students to respect the language of their peers and can model respectful listening when students speak. Students need a flexible *physical setting* for interaction: round or rectangular tables, clusters of desks, workstations, and centers. In addition, classrooms need to contain *things to talk about:* nature displays, flags, maps, artifacts, a variety of print material, and a challenging, interesting curriculum. Finally, students need *frequent opportunities to interact:* flexible grouping that allows work with a variety of classmates, cross-age tutors, the teacher, aides, volunteers, other adults at school, guests, and so on (Dudley-Marling & Searle, 1991).

Speaking can be integrated with literacy and oracy activities in many ways (Morgan, 1992). Students can listen to the sharing-time stories of others and use these as starting points for their own "adventures." Inviting community elders to tell stories in class provides rich stimuli, and when the visitors are gone, the students can finish these stories to continue the entertainment or write other stories in response. Older students can write response comments to their peers' oral presentations, share notes from class lectures with a group, or create group research reports. Negotiating, co-creating, responding, and giving presentations help to integrate speaking, listening, reading, and writing.

## Reading First in the Primary Language

Study after study has demonstrated that the degree of children's native-language proficiency is a strong predictor of their progress in ELD. Hurrying young children into reading in English without adequate preparation in their own language is counterproductive. The report of the National Research Council (Snow, Burns, & Griffin, 1998) recommended that language-minority children who arrive at school with no proficiency in English but speaking a language for which there are instructional guides, learning materials, and locally available proficient teachers should be taught how to read in their native language while acquiring oral proficiency in English and subsequently taught to extend their skills to reading in English.

**Personal Factors Affecting Literacy Development in English**   Similar factors influence literacy in English as those that affect second-language acquisition in general (see Chapter 2). An understanding of these factors can help teachers support students' process of learning to read in English.

**Primary-Language Literacy Level**   The more advanced the native-language competency, the more rapid the progress made in English, providing the student is motivated and the social context is supportive. Each year of schooling adds sophistication. In the early grades, a child with concepts about print in the first language has an advantage (including the ideas that print carries a message; that books are organized with a cover, title, and author and are held in a certain way for reading; that reading in English flows in a particular and consistent direction, left to right and top to bottom; that printed language consists of letters, words, sentences, punctuation marks, and case markers—upper- and lowercase, title case, etc.). Successful beginning readers build on their emergent literacy that starts before formal schooling.

In later grades, students who have learned in their primary language how discourse works have an advantage. For example, they can scan text for key ideas or specific details, they can read picture captions to interpret visual information, and they can use text aids such as the table of contents or a glossary. In addition to concepts about print and basic literacy skills, students bring a wealth of reading strategies. Most important, however, is *metastrategic knowledge*—being able to choose the right strategy for the task from a repertoire of strategies. In addition, students with oracy skills can use their listening and speaking productively in understanding task directions, asking clarifying questions, or displaying knowledge in response to the teacher's questions.

For the most part, primary-language literacy means that the student is familiar with the culture of schooling, including the need to sit still and focus, to follow classroom procedures, and to use pragmatic skills such as manners to act as a productive member of the class. Having the intellectual self-discipline instilled by schooling accompanied by literacy skills in the primary language bodes well for success in English literacy.

**Transfer of Primary-Language Literacy**   Language transfer occurs when the comprehension or production of a second language is influenced by the way the first language has been acquired (Odlin, 1989). Sometimes learners use rules from their first language that are not applicable to the second (*negative transfer*). As an illustration, Natheson-Mejia (1989) describes substitutions that Spanish speakers make when writing in English. These include *es* for /s/ as in *estop,* *d* for /t/ or /th/ as in *broder, ch* for /sh/ as in *chort, j* for /h/ as in *jelper,* and *g* for /w/ as in *sogen* (*sewing*).

What transfers from the first language? Training in literacy enhances *phonological awareness,* the ability to distinguish units of speech. The capacity to focus on syllables and words is a foundational reading skill, which helps students read and in turn is advanced as they read. Moreover, *phonemic awareness* is a key factor that distinguishes good from poor readers (Stanovich, 1986); this is the ability to work with phonemes—to separate phonemes; to add, delete, or substitute phonemes in words; and to blend or split syllables.

Students can also transfer sensorimotor skills (eye–hand coordination, fine muscle control, spatial and directional skills, visual perception and memory); auditory skills (auditory perception, memory, discrimination, and sequencing); common features of writing systems (alphabets, punctuation rules); comprehension strategies (finding the main idea, inferring, predicting, use of cueing systems); study skills (taking notes, using reference sources); habits and attitudes (self-esteem, task persistence, focus) (Cloud et al., 2000); the structure of language (speech–print relationships, concepts such as syllable, word, sentence, paragraph); and knowledge about the reading process (Thonis, 1983).

Aside from the preceding skills, students can transfer direct linguistic content. Of course, names for concrete objects in the first language must be relearned, but a few cognates can transfer from Spanish to English (cognates are words in two languages that look alike and have the same or similar meaning; see Garrison [1990]; Nagy, García, Durgunoglu, & Hancin-Bhatt [1993]). Recognizing a similar word with a similar meaning makes learning new vocabulary easier. Even more important than concrete nouns and cognates are abstract concepts that can transfer. Students have to learn such concepts as proofreading or photosynthesis only once; they can then transfer that knowledge into the second language. The more concepts stored in the first language, the more enabled the student during ELD.

In addition to language labels, phonological awareness, and discourse skills, students can transfer *metalinguistic awareness*—knowledge about the structural properties of language, including sounds, words, grammar, and functions (Gombert, 1992), or the ability to use language as a tool, to step outside of the use of language to think about the language itself. Metalinguistic awareness may develop during middle childhood as the child learns to think about the linguistic system (Tunmer, Herriman, & Nesdale, 1988). Another view is that metalinguistic awareness is a result of schooling, particularly of learning to read. Metalinguistic ability is a function of age—to a point—and students vary in this ability. Bilingual individuals outperform monolinguals on tasks requiring metalinguistic abilities (Hamers & Blanc, 1989). To summarize best practice in promoting metalinguistic awareness, knowledge, and skills, Table 7.1 divides these into four components and prescribes practices that enhance these components.

Teachers can transform language transfer into a learning strategy by helping students become aware of ways in which they can draw from prior knowledge of how language works to make English easier. Explicit attention to transfer, both in teacher attitude (welcoming dual-language use, understanding code-switching, providing support for literacy in multiple languages, and honoring primary languages) and in specific strategies, will help students build second-language acquisition on a firm foundation of first-language proficiency.

**TABLE 7.1**    Practices That Promote Metalinguistic Awareness

| Component of Metalinguistic Awareness | Definition | Suggestions to the Teacher to Enhance Awareness |
|---|---|---|
| Metaphonological | Identifying the phonological components in linguistic units and intentionally manipulating them | ■ Teach sound–symbol connection (phonics). ■ Teach word segmentation into syllables and onset-rime awareness (the idea that rhymes occur when the ending phonemes are the same sounds, even when beginning phonemes vary). |
| Metasyntactic | The ability to reason consciously about the syntactic aspects of language and to exercise intentional control over the application of grammatical rules | ■ Have students make good/bad judgments on the correct form of sentences. |
| Metapragmatic | Concern with the awareness or knowledge one has about the relationships that obtain between the linguistic system and the context in which the language is embedded | ■ Help students judge the adequacy of messages and their context. ■ Point out ironic, sarcastic, humorous, and polite forms of language. |
| Metasemantic | Refers both to the ability to recognize the language system as a conventional and arbitrary code and the ability to manipulate words or more extensive signifying elements, without the signified correspondents being automatically affected by this | ■ Teach students about word denotation and connotation. ■ Expand vocabulary of synonyms and antonyms. ■ Help students find cognates between languages. |

*Source:* Gombert, 1992, p. 15; Gombert, 1992, p. 39; Gombert, 1992, p. 63; Pratt & Nesdale, 1984, p. 105.

**Level of English-Language Proficiency**    English learners enter U.S. schools from diverse backgrounds. Some are balanced bilinguals, literate in two languages; others are limited bilinguals, with oracy and literacy skills more developed in one language than the other. Others are monolingual and literate only in their native language; still others are monolingual yet preliterate. This creates a complex situation for instructors and requires differentiated instruction. Careful assessment is needed so that the teacher is aware of the various skill levels (speaking/listening, reading, writing) of each student, and flexible grouping is required to advance each student differentially in his or her strong and weak skills.

A student's CELDT score, combined with other measures of proficiency such as teacher observation and reading assessment, determines the appropriate level of instruction for that student. Table 7.2 displays English-language development objectives for listening and reading comprehension at five CELDT levels. The complexity of the standards increases gradually as expectations increase for language proficiency.

**TABLE 7.2**  Expectations for Listening and Reading Comprehension at Five CELDT Levels

| CELDT Level | Listening Comprehension | Reading Comprehension |
|---|---|---|
| Beginning | Responds to simple directions and questions using physical actions | Responds orally to stories read aloud by answering factual comprehension questions using one- or two-word responses |
| Early Intermediate | Asks/answers questions and makes statements using phrases or simple sentences | Responds to stories read aloud by answering factual comprehension questions using phrases or simple sentences |
| Intermediate | Asks/answers instructional questions using simple sentences | Uses simple sentences to respond to stories by answering factual comprehension questions in the language experience approach (LEA) and guided reading |
| Early Advanced | Comprehends detailed information with minimal contextual clues on unfamiliar topics | Restates facts and details from content area texts |
| Advanced | Identifies orally and in writing key details and concepts from information/stories on unfamiliar topics | Locates and uses text features such as title, table of contents, chapter headings, diagrams, and index |

A student's CELDT level in grade 2 and beyond is represented as three scores: listening/speaking, reading, and writing. Because of individual differences, students will have mixed skill proficiency levels; one person may be at the early advanced level in speaking/listening, the intermediate level in reading, and early intermediate level in writing. Each proficiency requires distinct objectives.

It would be relatively easy to plan instruction if students at a grade level were homogeneous in English ability, but that is seldom the case. More frequently, English learners with four or five levels of proficiency are mixed in the same class. Therefore, planning must accommodate twenty to thirty students at up to five CELDT levels, with many students at mixed levels. How is this possible?

The answer is differentiated instruction that develops students at two CELDT levels at a time. If a lesson is geared to accomplish writing objectives at the early intermediate and early advanced levels, the beginning-level students may listen while the early intermediate students read aloud what they have written; intermediate and advanced writers may act as peer tutors. In this way, students can participate in lessons although their particular objectives are not addressed on that day.

## ELD and ELA Standards in Reading

The California English Language Development Standards correspond to the California English Language Arts Standards in reading. The same categories are used so that as English learners progress, their skills are developed in the categories that will be used for evaluation in the mainstream class. These categories are as follows: Reading Word Analysis, Reading Fluency and Systematic Vocabulary Development, and Reading Literary Response and Analysis. Although the subskills that make up these categories become progressively more challenging across the five ELD levels, even at the beginning level students are exposed to literature and asked to respond ("Listens to a story and responds orally or in drawings").

The chief difficulty in teaching reading to English learners is that for native English speakers, reading is a matter of recognizing on paper the meaning that already exists in oral language. Those who do not understand English, however, must first learn the language before decoding its written form.

The difficulty, then, is that when working with English learners, teachers have to teach English as they teach how to read English. Most teachers of reading are aware that students do not understand everything they read—even native English speakers need to acquire vocabulary as well as the thinking skills (comprehension, inference) that accompany literacy. English learners need to learn thousands more words just to reach the starting point of the linguistic knowledge that native speakers learned before starting school. This catch-up must take place at school. ELD reading and ELA reading fundamentally differ in that there is a double burden on the English learner. Therefore, the ELD standards precede the mainstream ELA standards.

## Foundations of Literacy

### Purposes for Reading

During the advent of the era of television, critics asked, "Is reading dead?" With the advent and proliferation of the Internet, people are asking the same question as they see young people inundated with images and sounds that flout classic print conventions. At the same time, however, more individuals are expected to be literate than ever before, as employment in modern technology requires advanced reading and writing skills.

However, in the midst of calls for enhanced literacy to benefit the workplace, Corley (2003) cautioned that this functionalist approach ignores the need for critical literacy: "The practice of helping learners make sense of what they are learning by grounding it in the context of their daily lives and reflecting on their individual experiences, with an eye toward social action" (p. 1). McLaren (1995) called for media studies to be a central focus of school curricula so that learners can be educated beyond a functional literacy that serves the purpose of the school but perhaps not the purpose of the individual (Barton, Hamilton, & Ivanič, 2000).

The search for reading strategies that fit the generic learner quickly runs afoul not only of current calls for situated literacy but also of the impossibility of finding a "best" method. Certainly, contextual and instructional variation complicates matters. Older learners need different reading instruction than do children, learners' prior schooling creates diverse starting points for instruction, and learners' goals deviate from official policy mandates. In spite of these shortcomings, it is clear that instruction in reading can be applied situationally and experimentally until some wisdom is reached about best practices for the particular context and learners.

Most people learn new skills in an integrated way, starting from the need to learn for some purpose. May and Rizzardi (2002) emphasize that most learners read and write because they see others doing it—reading directions, newspapers, or road signs for information, or reading novels, just to pass the time. However, many English learners do not see their families reading or writing. Therefore, it takes a leap of imagination for them to see themselves as readers. It is important, then, that the classroom as a community become a place in which reading is enjoyable. A context of shared enjoyment is the key to making literacy an everyday part of life.

One reading expert summarizes the issues that characterize current thinking about the teaching of reading:

> One thing that we know is that reading is a complex act. It seems easy once you know how to do it, but reading requires the coordination of a number of processes: knowing letters and sounds, spelling patterns, the meaning of words being read, how collections of words combine to form phrases and longer pieces of text and how to apply what you know in order to understand what you read. A reading program that ignores any of these is unlikely to be successful. "Back to basics" fans like to trumpet the fact that "phonics works." But they're only partly right. Phonics in a vacuum—in the absence of purpose and meaning, in other words, interesting things to read and hear and talk about—won't help children learn to read well. (Goldenberg, 2001, B11)

 **Classroom Glimpse**

### A PURPOSE FOR READING

The SAIL program, a grades 1–6 reading intervention program in Montgomery County, Maryland, was designed to deliver meaning-centered instruction to the lowest-achieving students. Rather than looking for deficits in these students, in effect blaming them for not reading, educators developed an integrated-skills, strategies-based program. Before having students read, teachers probed for personal commitment by asking each student, "Why do you want to become a better reader?" Answers varied: "I want to read to my little brother," "I want to get smart," or "I want to be an astronaut." These are places to begin—to find the fit between curriculum and personal aspirations. (Bergman & Schuder, 1993)

## Standards-Based Reading Instruction

Basal readers on the market reflect the current emphasis on standards-based instruction. For example, *Launch into Reading, Level I* (Heinle & Heinle, 2002), an ELD reader, refers to the specific California English Language Arts Standard to which each lesson is connected. Lesson 13, "Flowers (A Poem by E. Greenfield)" addresses Reading Standard 6, 3.4, "Define how tone or meaning is conveyed in poetry." Follow-up exercises ask students to use a continuum scale to rank "five ways you can learn about people's feelings and ideas" (short story, poem, magazine or newspaper article, movie or TV program, and conversation), which addresses Reading Standard 2, 2.7, "Interpret information from diagrams and charts."

Later in the lesson, students are asked to find the rhyming words in the poem "Flowers" (Reading Standard 1, 1.6, "Create and state a series of rhyming words") and then work with a partner to interpret a poem (Writing Standard 6, 2.4, "Write responses to literature: Organize the interpretation around several clear ideas, premises or images"). All teaching materials, including the teacher's resource book, the student workbook, and the student reading book, contain explicit references to standards on each page.

## Transfer of Reading Skills

Students who are already literate in their first language have many useful reading skills that transfer directly into the second language. These include the ability to decode a word by sight, to sound out more difficult words, to use context clues, to read text in a certain direction, to skim or scan as necessary to find information, to use cues such as the title and pictures to help create meaning, to identify the main idea when reading, to use story-sequence skills, to predict or anticipate story outcomes, to read critically, to understand characters and plot events, to distinguish between fact and opinion, and to connect causes with effects (Cloud et al., 2000). These do not have to be retaught as reading skills progress.

## Developing Word Analysis Skills

What characterizes literacy instruction for English learners? The natural developmental processes that children undergo in learning their first language (oral and written) also occur in second-language acquisition (oral and written). For reading, these processes include using knowledge of *sound–symbol relationships* (graphophonics), *word order and grammar* (syntax), and *meaning* (semantics) to predict and confirm meaning, as well as using background knowledge about the text's topic and structure along with linguistic knowledge and reading strategies to make an interpretation (Peregoy & Boyle, 2005). The following sections specifically detail the major tenets of current reading pedagogy and practice.

**Emergent Literacy**   A key insight of emergent literacy theory is that children learning to read already understand quite a bit about print. Most young children have had much exposure to print in the culture at large and may have engaged in various informal kinds of reading. Even homes without books often have magazines and the ubiquitous advertising on television, which includes product names. Therefore, it is the teacher's job to build on these nascent skills so students can "grow into reading."

Emergent literacy involves a combination of components. Emergent readers must learn the following skills:

- Drawing on their prior knowledge of the world to connect the printed word with its semiotic meaning (for example, the red octagonal sign at a street corner means "stop")
- Enhancing their phonemic awareness by linking sounds with symbols
- Recognizing a set of sight words that are not phonetically predictable (*the* is not "ta-ha-ay")
- Acquiring reading behaviors, such as handling books and focusing on text
- Participating in a culture of reading for enjoyment and sharing their pleasure in reading with others, borrowing and returning books to the class library, and working in the company of others to acquire meaning from books

**Concepts about Print**   Students need a foundation of basic ideas about print. They may already intuit some of these, or they may need schooling to gain these concepts. This knowledge involves practice with print (see www.ncrel.org/sdrs/areas/issues/content/cntareas/reading/li1lk11.htm).

- Where to begin writing or reading, going from left to right.
- Where to go after the end of the line (return sweep).
- The print, not the picture, carries the message.
- Word-by-word pointing (one-to-one correspondence).
- Concept of a letter, word, sentence.
- Concept of first and last part (of the word, sentence, story).
- Letter order in words is important.
- There are first and last letters in words.
- Upper- and lowercase letters have purpose.
- Different punctuation marks have meaning.

Other authors have called this *skill with print,* which includes the preceding concepts listed with a few additional insights (Gunning, 2005):

- Language is divided into words.
- Words can be written down.
- Space separates written words.
- Sentences begin with capital letters and end with punctuation.
- A book is read from front to back.
- Reading goes left to right and top to bottom.
- Words, not pictures, are read.
- A book has a title, an author, and sometimes an illustrator.

---

**Best Practice**    **FOSTERING EMERGENT LITERACY IN CHILDREN**

- Provide an accessible, appealing literacy environment with attractive reading and writing materials.
- Classroom reading materials should include extra copies of books read aloud by the teacher or books by the same author, commercial books, student-written books, comic or cartoon books (with words), magazines, encyclopedias, and bilingual, age-appropriate dictionaries.
- Encourage children to role-play or playact reading and writing activities.
- Incorporate shared book experiences using Big Books or enlarged text.
- Follow up shared reading with independent reading, small-group review of the Big Book, or work with language skills such as phonics.
- Bolster reading with chanting or singing based on reading the lyrics together.

(Adapted from Gunning, 2005)

---

**Phonemic and Morphemic Awareness**    The ability to hear and manipulate sounds in words is called *phonemic awareness.* The basic insight is that spoken language consists of identifiable units—utterances are composed of spoken words, which in turn consist of syllables, which in turn have distinct sound units (Chard, Pikulski, & Templeton, n.d.). Phonemic awareness is an auditory skill and does not involve words in print. The following are phonemic awareness exercises:

- Blending: What word am I trying to say? Ppppppiiiiiiin.
- Segmentation (first sound isolation): What is the first sound in *pin*?
- Segmentation (last sound isolation): What is the last sound in *pin*?
- Segmentation (complete): What are all the sounds you hear in *pin*?

---

**Best Practice** ACTIVITIES TO HELP LEARNERS DEVELOP
PHONEMIC AWARENESS

- *Wordplay* (What is left if I take away the *b* in *bright*? *right*)
- *Rhyming games* (One, two, buckle your shoe)
- *Nursery rhymes* (Jack and Jill went up the hill)
- *Picture books with rhymes*

---

*Morphemic awareness* is the understanding that the smallest elements of meaning contained in words play a role in word recognition. Readers advance in skill when they can combine their knowledge of spelling and meaning patterns with sound–symbol correspondence (Ehri, 1997). Both of these concepts are taught explicitly in direct approaches to reading.

**Vocabulary and Concept Development**    The prior knowledge most useful for reading is largely word knowledge (vocabulary). This is the chief hurdle faced by English learners because reading a word successfully depends on knowing the word in the first place. Once students start to read, vocabulary acquisition accelerates because general comprehension of a text allows readers to predict and infer meaning of unknown words they encounter. The teacher's job is to help students develop background knowledge through the use of other books, oral discussion, exposure to media, or pictures or other visual prompts, combined with text, in order to build schemata—that is, construct a framework of concepts that shows the relationships of old and new learning and how they are connected.

**Decoding**    Incomplete or inaccurate decoding limits comprehension—decoding is essential to reading. Students with phonemic awareness can use this skill in phonics instruction as they come to understand that there is an orderly relationship between written letters and speech sounds. Attempting to read an unfamiliar word is a process of trying to connect the letter with its sound and then to affirm the meaning from the context.

Using *sight words* (those that do not conform to phonetic rules—about 10 percent of English written words), the learner relies on visual memory to match sound with writing. Using *phonics,* the learner explicitly constructs the sound–symbol connection. Each of these techniques has its place in learning basic words. Lists of sight words can be obtained from reading texts. These include frequently used words with nonpredictable spelling, such as *the, might, could,* and so forth. Phonics can be taught using the synthetic method (bottom up), with students learning phonemes in isolation, then learning to blend them, and finally seeing them in the context of words. Or students can learn using the analytic method, beginning first with contrasting words that contain the target phonemes and then having students generate similar words. The analytic method is illustrated in Box 7.1.

**Box 7.1** Teaching Reading via the Analytic Method of Phonics

1. *Planning.* Make a list of easy words that includes the target phonic element, for example the digraph /sh/: *cash, crash, mash, dish, fish,* and so forth. Write simple, meaningful sentences for each one, or a little story, if possible, that contains the words. Find pages in a common reading book that has these or other *sh*- words, including /sh/ as a final sound.
2. *Teaching.* Read the sentences aloud to the students in a smooth and informal fashion. Have the students echo-read the sentences—repeating after the teacher, then repeating each underlined target word after the teacher, looking to see what sound the words have in common.
3. *Guided practice.* Students each produce the target sound and look again at the letters that make the sound. Have students say other words with the same sound. Students choral-read the sentences and then take turns reading them aloud.

*Source:* May & Rizzardi (2002, p. 177).

Books designed for phonics instruction as much as possible use words with a regular sound–symbol correspondence. This does not always lend itself to engaging prose. Because English as a language has changed in sound–symbol correspondence in the 550 years since the printing press was first used, its basic, everyday prose often features the most irregular, least phonics-amenable words. Unfortunately, then, in English, sometimes the more interesting the text, the less phonics-friendly the words.

The International Reading Association finds that phonics is an important part of a beginning reading program but states explicitly that phonics instruction needs to be embedded in a total reading/language arts program (International Reading Association, 1997). Today, teachers introduce phonics through mini-lessons and gamelike activities such as making words and word sorts rather than by having students mark letters and words on worksheets.

Unfortunately, commercial phonics products such as "decodable" books are designed to provide structured reading practice, but the content is often contrived and the sentences sound unnatural. As Herrera, Pérez, and Escamilla (2010) pointed out, the story lines can be less than compelling: "Three bees got in a cab. Three bees wish to see Cat. Three bees will give Cat a gift" (from Lee, 2001, p. 61). (Nothing here to motivate reading!)

On the other hand, Mole's adventure in *The Wind in the Willows* (Grahame, 1983) begins, "The Mole has been working very hard all morning long, spring-cleaning his little home—first with brooms, then with a pail of whitewash, till he had dust in his throat and spots on his black fur" (p. 4) (I don't know about you, but I have a lot of questions already. How does one clean a mole's tunnel with brooms? How did Mole get the whitewash? Did Mole have spots already?) There is nothing like real literature, even if it is not strictly "phonical"!

**From Letter to Word Recognition** Written English is based on the alphabetic principle, and children need to understand that sounds correspond to letters. Prereading activities help to develop visual discrimination, including such tasks as matching pictures and patterns, sequencing story cards in a meaningful order, and matching uppercase letters to lowercase letters. Teaching letters phonetically takes place in a sequence. First, alphabet cards introduce the name of each consonant letter and the sound it makes. Matching objects and pictures to letters helps learners to identify initial sounds. Ending sounds can be treated in a similar way. Then short vowels are introduced, usually in the order *a, i, o, u,* and *e;* this is followed by the short vowels blended with consonants. Simple stories featuring short vowels help students find early success with reading. Long vowels and vowel blends are taught next, followed by digraphs (consonants which together make a single sound, like /th/).

However, reading based on phonetic awareness alone may not be the best approach for English learners (Flood, Lapp, Tinajero, & Hurley, 1997). Hamayan (1994) cites four reasons why structural approaches (phonics based and grammar based) are not sufficient to meet the needs of preliterate English learners: (1) They do not meet the learner's need to acquire an understanding of the functional aspects of literacy; (2) literacy is forced to emerge in an unnatural way and in an artificial form; (3) a focus on form without a functional context makes learning abstract, meaningless, and difficult; and (4) literacy becomes a boring chore.

Teachers of English learners are encouraged to provide students with rich language experiences, including wordplay, which lead them to understanding sound–symbol correspondences. During and after read-alouds, for example, teachers point out specific sound and letter patterns that occurred in the texts. According to Peregoy and Boyle (2005), specific instruction in sound–symbol correspondence emerges best through students' own writing. Their invented or temporary spelling represents "an important step on the way to conventional spelling while providing individualized phonics practice that will assist both reading and writing development" (p. 153).

## Developing Reading Fluency

The ability to decode rapidly, accurately, and efficiently is known as fluency. The *Literacy Dictionary* (Harris & Hodges, 1995) defines *fluency* as "freedom from word-identification problems that might hinder comprehension in silent reading or the expression of ideas in oral reading" (p. 85). Because human beings have limited attention capacity, decoding words needs to become so automatic that it can be accomplished with minimal active attention. This theory of automaticity (Laberge & Samuels, 1974) posits that if a reader has to devote sizable attention to decoding, insufficient attention will be available for that constructive, critical reading comprehension. Chard and colleagues (n.d.) put it this way: "Although fluent decoding is not sufficient for high levels of reading comprehension, it is definitely a prerequisite for comprehension" (n.p.).

Through careful attention to print in sequential decoding, readers begin to notice that patterns of letters, such as -*ing* and -*ike*, occur in many words. Helping them focus on these patterns and recognize these repeated patterns in words can help readers to process or "chunk" the letters as a single unit. When readers are able to do this, they are able to more rapidly identify and process words during reading, increasing fluency.

One would like to believe that extensive use of context cues makes reading more fluent, as the reader does not have to pause to define an unfamiliar word. However, even if a reader correctly identifies a word using context, there is no guarantee the word will be recognized the next time it is encountered in print. Without the letter-sound connection, the contextual advantage is lost. If a reader can decode a word using other skills, context can provide a useful "check" or confirmation of the word—but only after the word has been tentatively decoded.

**Reading Aloud** A learner's specific approach to decoding can be analyzed by listening to him or her read aloud. When attempting a sentence with an unknown word, various readers use distinct strategies. One type of reader uses *semantic knowledge*. If the sentence reads, "Joey pushed open the door of the haunted . . . ," a reader might guess that the next word is not *hose*, because the meaning would not make sense. Another type of reader might use *syntactic knowledge* in the sentence "Joey drives a small . . ." to reject the word *care* as the wrong choice for that part of the sentence. Still a third type of reader might use *orthographic shape* in the sentence "Joey drove a load of trees to the paper mill," knowing that the words *pap* and *paperwork* look wrong. A single reader might use these three types of meaning-making equally often, or the teacher might detect a preference for one type of decoding. Interventions would be designed accordingly (Newman, 1985).

**Seeking Meaning** The need to understand is natural to the mind. The goal of the reading instructor is for students to come away from a reading passage with meaning. Because the reader constructs this meaning, there will always be some imperfect match between the meaning as intended and the meaning as attained by each reader. The richest of text evokes the most fundamentally meaningful, yet passionate and idiosyncratic response. Anything less is reductionistic—to be doomed to accept the exact understandings of others rather than to glory in our own, however unique. This is the chief reason for the existence of literature.

**Systematic Vocabulary Development** Throughout one's schooling, acquiring vocabulary is a constant. One important research question that remains unresolved concerns whether adequate vocabulary in a second language can be acquired through reading (Nagy, 1997) or is more likely to result from some kind of direct instruction (Zimmerman, 1997). What is the minimal number of recognition vocabulary words needed to facilitate reading comprehension? One study suggests that 3,000 words (in word families) are needed (Laufer, 1989). Part of the problem with acquiring vocabulary is that word learning takes place in increments; although a single encounter with a word may provide some learning, even 100 encounters may not spark in an English learner the native speaker's complex knowledge of the word and the way it is used in the culture. The real problem is achieving adequate, in-depth exposure to content-related vocabulary.

New vocabulary words can be introduced before a reading lesson, or meaning can be inferred from context during reading. Explicit work with new vocabulary words, though, is usually reserved for the after-reading phase. Students can study words by means of the *word element approach*, isolating roots, prefixes, and suffixes and using word families to expand a new word into its host of relations (e.g., the words *biology, sociology,* and *psychology* are relatives of *anthropology*). Or students can practice *specific vocabulary-acquisition strategies,* such as inferring from context (finding synonyms in apposition, making use of a subsequent list of examples of a new word, or using a dictionary).

Students can practice *acquiring technical words* by using a glossary, sidebar, chart, or graphs. Worksheets or other kinds of practice can help students recognize meaning. Students can practice *word formation* through compounding (*room + mate = roommate*), blending (*motor hotel = motel*), and making acronyms (*self-contained underwater breathing apparatus = scuba*). However, moving a new word from students' acquisition vocabulary (used in reading or listening) to their production vocabulary (used in writing or speaking) requires far more guided practice.

In terms of how many and what type of words a person needs to learn, Richards (2008) described vocabulary learning as "involving acquisition of a core vocabulary that is common to different domains, genres, and text types. In addition, learners build up a more specialized vocabulary related to their own needs and fields of interest, whether these be academic, occupational, or social" (p. 12).

As students transition from the structured vocabulary that characterizes the beginning and intermediate states of English acquisition in school, they need strategies to deal with new words that they encounter independently. Moras (2001) suggested such strategies as guided discovery (directing learners to guess word meanings correctly), contextual guesswork (helping students to use cues such as parts of speech to infer the function of a word in a sentence), and dictionary use (to look up not only definitions but also pronunciation, grammar, style, and register).

Students can find suggestions and restrictions on which words can go with which in a helpful resource such as the *Oxford Collocations Dictionary*. Online collocation tools like the Compleat Lexical Tutor (www.lextutor.ca) can help students learn which words and expressions in English are used most often (frequency), in which situations certain words are used (context), which words are found together (collocation), and how words are used grammatically and strategically. McCarthy (2004) and O'Keefe, McCarthy, and Carter (2007) are good sources for learning to use computerized language databases to teach vocabulary.

Additionally, McCarten (2007) recommended presenting vocabulary to students in multiple modalities, including pictures, sounds, stories, conversations, webpages, and so on, with topics relevant to students' interests; vocabulary learning should be personal and enjoyable. Learners need to hear, see, and say new words again and again, while being encouraged to notice, use, and reuse new words in their everyday life. Along with basic word usage, academic vocabulary is learned strategically, as an important part of the content objectives in every discipline.

---

**Best Practice**   **PRETEACHING CRITICAL VOCABULARY**

Vocabulary acquisition is an important part of the content objectives in an instructional plan. Here are a few ways to share key terms:

- In pairs, students examine new words, looking for primary-language cognates, component morphemes, and associated terms.
- A picture glossary keeps key terms fresh through the lesson.
- In pairs, students create graphic organizers for each term, including meanings (denotations), analysis of word subparts (morphemes), or word associations (connotations). (Adapted from Quiocho and Ulanoff, 2009, pp. 12, 116)

---

**Contextual Redefinition**   Learning to use context to increase comprehension while reading is an important skill of proficient readers. Contextual redefinition shows students the importance of context in gaining meaning. This is a useful learning strategy for beginning, below-grade-level, and above-grade-level readers because the context can be used to define terms they may not know and encourage them to use prior knowledge to find meaning even when there are no dictionaries readily available.

The teacher can select a few essential words students will encounter in the text, present these in isolation, and then have students offer suggestions about their meaning. The teacher can then provide a context for each of the words, with clues of definition. Students offer suggestions about the meanings and work in groups to consult dictionaries. This activity builds reading, writing, comprehension, listening, and speaking skills; encourages a natural and holistic view of language learning; and provides multiple opportunities for English learners to use and hear language in a variety of settings.

## Reading Processes

**Before Reading**   "Into" activities activate students' prior knowledge by drawing from their past experiences or help students develop background knowledge through new experiences. Films, texts, field trips, visual aids, and graphic organizers can clarify meaning and help students anticipate the work. Brainstorming ideas about a topic is one way to activate prior knowledge. Some teachers have students make predictions about the content of a story. Students can discuss what happened later in the book to confirm or disprove their original predictions.

Background knowledge can be activated or developed through classroom activities that include all of the language processes. Two such activities are brainstorming and K-W-L (What do I **K**now? What do I **W**ant to learn? What have I **L**earned?). Asking, "What do I know?" allows students to place new knowledge in the context of their own episodic memories and existing concepts.

During brainstorming and K-W-L, all ideas should be accepted. Once ideas are exhausted, the students and teacher together can organize the list, grouping and selecting appropriate category labels to create a beginning model from which they can work and learn.

K-W-L not only taps into what students already know but also draws from their interest and curiosity. After listing everything they know about a topic, students then tell the teacher what they would like to learn. The chart is kept up throughout the duration of the unit, and students refer to it from time to time. When the unit is completed, they return to the chart and talk about what they have learned. By starting each topic or unit with an activity that actively engages students in reviewing their own experiences relevant to the topic, the teacher gains valuable insights.

**During Reading**   "Through" activities help students as they work with the text. Reading aloud is a useful strategy that gives the students an opportunity to hear a proficient reader, to get a sense of the format and story line, and to listen to the teacher "think aloud" about the reading. In the think-aloud, teachers can model how they monitor a sequence of events, identify foreshadowing and flashbacks, visualize a setting, analyze character and motive, comprehend mood and theme, and recognize irony and symbols.

Teachers may find that English-language literature does not elicit the same responses from English learners as from native English speakers. By selecting materials judiciously, slowing the pace slightly, portioning work into manageable chunks, and increasing the depth of each lesson, the teacher can ensure that English learners have a fulfilling experience with literature.

Students can perform the actual reading through a variety of methods. Table 7.3 offers some reading methods for in-class use across a variety of grade levels.

| TABLE 7.3 | In-Class Reading Methods for English Learners |
|---|---|
| **Method** | **Description** |
| Page and paragraph | Teacher or fluent reader reads a page and then English learner reads a paragraph; finally, group discusses what has been read. |
| Equal portions | Students work in pairs and each reads aloud the same amount of text. |
| Silent with support | Students read silently in pairs and can ask each other for help with a difficult word or phrase. |
| Choral reading | Passage is divided into sections, and various parts of the audience read various sections. |
| Radio reading | One student reads while others close their books and listen. After reading, the reader can question each student about what was read. |
| Repeated reading | Students read silently a book that has been read aloud, or independently reread books of their choice. |
| Interactive read-aloud | Students can join in on repetitious parts or take parts of a dialogue. |
| Echo reading | For rhythmic text, students echo or repeat lines. |
| Cloze reading | When reading Big Books, teacher covers certain words and students try to guess word in context. |
| Nonprint media support | Students can follow along with a taped version of the book. |

*Source:* Hadaway, Vardell, & Young (2002).

To sustain students' interest in a longer work of literature, class time can be used to review the narrative to date and discuss students' understanding of the assigned reading. A preview of the next reading can feature interesting aspects of the new passage. In *Literature in the Language Classroom,* Collie and Slater (1987) suggested ways a teacher can structure literature homework:

- *Gap summary.* A technique in which the teacher provides an almost-complete and simply phrased description of the main points of the section assigned for home reading. Gaps are usually key words or expressions that only a reading of the passage can reveal.
- *Character diary.* An ongoing record of what each character is feeling that helps students step within the character.
- *What's missing.* An exercise encouraging students to make inferences about missing aspects of the story: What were the characters like at school? What were their favorite subjects? Did they have friends? Were they close to their parents?
- *Story mapping.* A way for students to use a graphic organizer to follow the events in the plot. Younger students can chart "What Happens Next." Older students can explore categories such as Characters, Intent, Opposition, and Resolution.

**After Reading**   "Beyond" activities are designed to extend the students' appreciation of literature, usually in another medium.

**Box 7.2**  Strategies by ELD Level of Student for Use Before, During, and After Reading

| Before, During, and After Reading | Students' ELD Level as Measured by CELDT | | | |
|---|---|---|---|---|
| | *Beginning* | *Early Intermediate  Intermediate* | | *Early Advanced  Advanced* |
| Before Reading | *Visual and kinesthetic prompts:* Pictures, art, movies, physical objects relating to the reading selection that students identify and discuss. | *Anticipation/reaction guides:* A short list of statements to which students agree or disagree. | | *Selected read-alouds:* Passages that pique students' interest in the selection. |
| During Reading | *Read-along tapes:* Tapes encourage slower readers, allow absent students to catch up, and provide auditory input for students. | *Image/theme development:* Charts, graphs, pictures, and symbols can trace the development of images, ideas, and themes. | | *Visual summaries:* Groups of students create chapter reviews, character analyses, or problem–solutions on overhead transparencies. |
| After Reading | *Character review:* Specific students become a character and provide background for other students' questions about the reading. | *Critic:* "Journalists" write reviews of literature works for the school or classroom newspaper or act as movie critics and review the film version of a text studied in class. They can then compare the differences and draw conclusions about the pros and cons of the different media. | | *Genre switch:* Favorite parts of selections can be rewritten as a play and enacted for other classes as a way to encourage other students to read that piece of literature; students can plan a mock television show and devise various formats that include ideas from the literature studied. For example, a game show host can ask contestants to answer questions or to act as characters or objects in the story. |

- Poems can be written and shared with other classes or parents at a Poetry Night.
- Reviews of literature works can be written for the school or classroom newspaper.
- Letters to authors or to pen pals encourage students to express their reactions to certain pieces of literature.
- Students can be movie critics and view the film representation of a text studied in class, comparing the differences and discussing the pros and cons of the two media.
- Favorite parts of selections can be rewritten as a play and enacted for other classes.
- Using reminder sheets, students in pairs can restate to each other various parts of what they have read (cued retelling).
- Students can plan a mock television show—for example, a game show—in which a host asks contestants to answer questions or to act as characters or objects in the story.

One instructor started an ESL book club, with special bookmarks and regular meeting times (ESL Meet), at which students presented book reviews or recommended books to one another. About six to ten students attended the meetings, with about twenty-five to thirty active club members (Suresh, 2003).

## Developing Reading Comprehension

Comprehension is the key to meaning. Readers generally form some initial hypothesis about the content or main idea of a book or a reading passage based on their expectations, previous knowledge of genre, or other clues such as the title or first sentence. Reading further, the reader modifies the initial prediction (Gunning, 2005). Getting the gist of a reading passage is the most important skill a reader can develop, because getting the main idea makes further reading more purposeful, facilitates recall, and helps to make sense of the supporting details.

 **Classroom Glimpse**

### DAILY READING INTERVENTIONS

Based on observations during the previous school year of those children who had made unexpected progress in reading skills, Mrs. Greaver-Pohzehl, a second-grade teacher, devised a new program involving the use of volunteers and a take-home reading program.

In the classroom, the students received daily directed, guided reading instruction with the teacher or a classroom aide to introduce and discuss new texts and build comprehension. Parent volunteers, trained to offer appropriate prompts for struggling readers, provided additional daily opportunities for children to reread texts for fluency, practice spelling words, and develop phonemic awareness through games and activities. Each child received a tape recorder and checked out books to read or tapes to listen to at home with a parent.

By the end of the year every child in the program made progress—all of them advanced at least two reading divisions on the district's literacy scale; demonstrated a greater range of reading and writing skills; developed a stronger, more fluent voice while reading; and showed positive attitudes toward reading and writing. (Greaver & Hedberg, 2001)

**Teaching of Reading Matched to Proficiency Levels**  Teaching reading to English learners implies that reading activities can be matched to the language-proficiency level of the student. Omaggio (1986) provided strategies that she considers appropriate for several proficiency levels. As shown in the box, these separate beginning from intermediate and advanced levels.

**Best Practice**  READING STRATEGIES FOR STUDENTS AT DIFFERENT LEVELS OF PROFICIENCY

*Novice:* anticipating/predicting, skimming, scanning, extracting specific information, contextual guessing, prereading activities, simple fill-in-the-blanks

*Intermediate/Advanced:* Comprehension checks, guessing from context, clue searching, making inferences, scrambled stories, extracting specific information, skimming, scanning, paraphrasing, note taking/outlining, passage completion, understanding idioms, learning discourse structures, comprehending linking words. (Omaggio, 1986, pp. 153–155)

**Strategies When Comprehension Fails**   Too often, students do not know what to do when they cannot comprehend a text. Table 7.4 presents several strategies that are useful when comprehension fails.

Each of these strategies can be developed using a variety of reading selections. When introducing a new comprehension strategy, the teacher explains when the strategy is useful, models the process, and then gives the students guided practice.

**TABLE 7.4**   Strategies That Readers Can Use When Comprehension Fails

| Strategy | Description |
| --- | --- |
| Rereading: Text-based answers | *Text-based* means one can skim the text and find the answer. (1) |
| "Right there" answers | Answer is easily found in the book. (2) |
| "Think and search" answers | Reader needs to put together different parts of the reading to obtain a solution. (2) |
| Rereading: Reader-based answers | *Reader based* means the reader must infer the answer: Look for clues from text. (1) |
| "Author and you" answer | Solution lies in a combination of what is in the story plus the reader's experience. (2) |
| "On my own" answers | Answer comes from one's own experience. (2) |
| Visual imagery | Before rereading, students discuss what pictures come to mind. Younger children can draw these pictures, and older children can use verbal description. Ask students to form mental images while rereading. (3) |
| Think-aloud | Students self-monitor comprehension by asking, "Does this make sense?" as they read. What question can they ask that will help them focus on what they need in order for it to make sense? (1) |
| Suspending judgment | Read ahead when a new concept is not well explained, seeking information to develop clarity. (1) |
| Reciprocal teaching | Students predict, summarize, ask questions, and suspend judgment, using these techniques with one another. (4) |
| Mine, yours, and ours | Students make individual summaries and compare with a partner, then write a joint paragraph outlining their similarities and differences. (5) |
| Summary pairs | Students read aloud to each other and summarize what they have read. (5) |
| Shrinking stories | Students write their own versions of a passage in 25 words or less. (6) |
| Simply put | Students rewrite a selection so that students two or three years younger might understand it. (6) |

*Sources:* (1) Barr & Johnson (1997); (2) Raphael (1986); (3) Gamrel & Bales (1986); (4) Palinscar & Brown (1984); (5) Lipton & Hubble (1997); (6) Suid & Lincoln (1992).

**Text Genres**    Readers must become familiar with the features, structures, and rhetorical devices of different types of texts, such as narrative, descriptive, and analytic. For example, a government document presents a formal, official point of view, whereas a personal or family story conveys the subject from a different, more intimate perspective. Even samples from the same type of content—storytelling, for example—feature various genres, such as folktales, myths, legends, and autobiographies. Scientific writing includes varied genres—peer-reviewed academic journals, "high-brow" general magazines (e.g., *Nature*), popular magazines (e.g., *Wired*), science fiction, and even comic books. Students need to be taught text processing techniques (how to take notes, how to reread text for answers to study questions, how to read charts and picture captions) and then held to a high level of recall about the information they read (Anderson & Gunderson, 2004).

*Multicultural literature* helps students see life from a variety of points of view, compare cultures on different aspects of life, and view their own culture represented in the curriculum. Anthologies of multicultural literature provide a wealth of materials, some grouped thematically (see Harris, 1997; Monroe, 1999). *Multicultural Voices in Contemporary Literature* (Day, 1994) presents thirty-nine authors and illustrators from twenty different cultures. A follow-up book, *Latina and Latino Voices in Literature for Children and Teenagers* (Day, 1997), has biographies of thirty-eight authors, with synopses of their work, as well as an extensive list of resources for books in English on Latino themes. Day (2003) is a follow-up extending the Latina and Latino theme.

**Grade-Level-Appropriate Texts**    Students read at grade level for schooling purposes, but they can also read below grade level for entertainment and above grade level with assistance. Many classrooms have "leveled" books so that frustration can be allayed. However, mentoring is essential to help students grow.

Several sources are available that suggest *age-level-appropriate reading material.* Public libraries have detailed reference books that list thousands of children's books, including the Caldecott and Newbery Medal books. Sometimes a school will send out a list of recommended books to every family. At one school, fourth graders prepared their own list of books and duplicated it for every child in the school. Generally speaking, children respect the teacher's recommendations, but if a recommended book is not grade-level appropriate, the young reader may become discouraged.

**Critical Thinking**    An important aspect of schooling in a democracy is the ability to think for oneself—to analyze ideas, separate fact from opinion, support opinions from reading, make inferences, and solve problems. Critical thinking can create self-understanding because a person might approach significant issues in life differently with the acquisition of analytic skills.

Thinking skills are an important part of reading comprehension. Distinguishing fact and opinion, identifying cause and effect, using a text to draw conclusions and make inferences, and evaluating the credibility of text are among the skills incorporated into high-quality reading lessons. The four-volume set *Critical Thinking Handbook* (grades K–3, 4–6, 7–9, and high school) presents lesson plans that have been remodeled to include critical thinking strategies (available from the Center for Critical Thinking at Sonoma State University, online at www .sonoma.edu/cthink).

**Creative Thinking and Risk Taking**    Creativity is a part of cognition and should not be confined to music and art classes. During problem solving and project-based learning, for example, once the requirements of a problem or project have been surveyed and the goals determined, creative thinking can be applied to generate possible solutions. Creative thinking can be used in every reading lesson to generate alternatives and to expand the point of view of reading comprehension: What if the main character were female rather than male? What if the book were set in the seventeenth century rather than in the modern era? What if the setting were Thailand rather than the United States? Can we imagine a different outcome?

This focus opens the door to a fertile terrain, the imaginary, a world in which possibilities are unlimited and constraints of reality do not pinch. In addition, use of the imaginary can stimulate scholars to explore other cultures and other times in history, as well as nonhuman worlds, such as in science fiction, myths, or animal tales.

The genre of brain puzzles is also mentally stimulating. Books of such puzzles can be found at major bookstores and are fun to use to keep young brains alert.

Both critical and creative thinking are integral parts of the human mind that enrich any part of the curriculum. Thinking is the key to the creation of meaning, during which children learn to react not just in response to the immediate, real world before them, but also in accord with their internal world, the world of ideas. Channeling the power of thought is an important part of language education in the context of cognitive development.

**Language Experience Approach**    A language development activity that encourages students to respond to events in their own words is the language experience approach (LEA). As a student tells a story or relates an event, the teacher writes it down and reads it back so that students can eventually read the text for themselves. Because the students are providing their own phrases and sentences, they find the text relevant and interesting and generally have little trouble reading it. The importance of LEA in developing the language of English learners cannot be overemphasized.

- By having students express themselves orally, LEA connects them to their own experiences and activities.
- LEA reinforces the notion that sounds can be transcribed into specific symbols and that those symbols can then be used to re-create the ideas expressed.
- LEA provides texts for specific lessons on vocabulary, grammar, writing conventions, structure, and more.

 **Classroom Glimpse**

**USING LEA AFTER READING**

Sixth-grade teacher Laura Bowen tells how she used LEA to help reinforce key concepts after her students read about the Qin dynasty.

After finishing the lesson on the Qin dynasty, I had my class brainstorm key ideas. I wrote their points on the board and then asked them to tell a story about a fictional family of three living during that era. The only restriction was that they had to keep in mind the key points. Their story follows:

> Chang, Li, and their son, Wei, lived during the Qin dynasty. Li was excited because Chang was able to buy the family some land. A few days later, Chang was taken by the emperor to go build the Great Wall. Li and Wei were sad. They did not like the emperor, because he had strict laws and punishments. Chang died on the long walk to the Great Wall. Li and Wei grew crops so they could survive. They hoped a new and better emperor would come and overthrow the mean one.

After the class finished their story, they read it aloud many times. This experience helped them to personalize history.

**Directed Reading–Thinking Activity**   Students need to understand that proficient readers actively work with text by making predictions as they read. Directed reading–thinking activity (DR–TA) is a teacher-guided activity that leads students through the prediction process until they are able to do it on their own. The teacher asks students to make predictions and then read to confirm or disconfirm their ideas. The key to successful DR–TA lessons is for students to update their ideas as new information is revealed.

## Developing Literary Response and Analysis Skills

Students of literature need to acquire a set of literary response skills in order to fully appreciate fiction, nonfiction, and other creative work. Literary criticism consists of analysis of plot, character, theme, and creative language use. These skills are described and levels provided in the ELD and ELA frameworks.

To help develop a community of readers and encourage students to understand the richness of the literacy experience, teachers engage them in literature response groups. After having read a piece of literature, the teacher and a small group meet to discuss the piece. Each student is given an opportunity to express ideas about the story before a general discussion begins. The teacher listens and, after each student has had a turn, opens the discussion with a thought-provoking question.

As points are made, the teacher guides the students to deeper understandings by, for example, asking them to support their point with words from the text and asking what words or devices the author used to invoke a mood, establish a setting, describe a character, move the plot along, and so on.

 **Classroom Glimpse**

### A LITERATURE RESPONSE GROUP

Teacher Christina Dotts describes how literature response groups worked in her second-grade classroom. The students had read Tomi dePaola's *Now One Foot, Now the Other* (1981).

In planning this lesson, I was a bit apprehensive about the students' overall reaction to this type of discussion. However, I found that they enjoyed discussing the story in a more intimate setting as opposed to a whole-class discussion. These second graders were indeed up to the challenge of using higher-order thinking skills. One of my objectives was for the students to verbalize their thoughts and convey meaning. They needed practice in doing so. I discovered my students had definite ideas about major issues—illness, hospitals, family members, working, being responsible, and being good friends. Their concerns were very important in their lives, and this piece of literature and forum for discussion provided an opportunity for them to talk about these concerns. Students felt proud to lead discussions and exercise their leadership skills.

## Secondary-Level Content Reading

Reading in the content areas in high school was addressed according to specific disciplines in Chapter 5. There are also fundamental generic reading adaptations that teachers of English learners can make in their planning and instruction (see Box 7.3).

Despite the success of approaches based on social constructionism, a generation of students is being taught how to read through a series of controlled, behaviorally based lessons. Such programs as Reading Mastery, Open Court, and Direct Instruction employ teacher-centered methods in step-by-step curricula that follow highly structured, interactive scripts (Groves, 2001). Reading Mastery requires students to be grouped in precisely measured skill levels, and Open Court expects teachers to follow an exact script verbatim day by day to reinforce skills. Only time will tell if the students taught in this manner learn to read both for academics and for enjoyment. Groves makes the point that middle-class gifted students are not taught in such a prescriptive manner. It may be that being taught to read in this didactic manner is yet another social-class marker in the United States.

### Best Practice    AN UNCONVENTIONAL ASSIGNMENT

The following instructions for an open-ended assignment can be adapted to a variety of units:

You have read a complex work of literature in Shakespeare's *Julius Caesar*. To show what you have learned through your engagement with this play, create an interpretive text in any form of your choice: collage, painting, poetry, music, drama, sculpture, performance art, or other textual form. Furthermore, you may use different forms within forms—that is, you can include a gravestone with an epitaph, a haiku, a song, an encyclopedia entry, a movie review, and so on, keeping in mind that it should in some way depict your understanding of the play's characters, Roman history, or how some aspects of the play have helped you to learn something about yourself and your world. You may produce this individually or with a group of five or less. You will have two class periods to work on it, with the rest of the preparation taking place outside of class. You must prepare a three- to five-minute presentation of your text to the class in which you explain its significance and your understanding of the play. (Adapted from Smagorinsky, 2008, pp. 91–92)

**Box 7.3**   Generic Reading Adaptations for English Learners at the Secondary Level

- Use read-alouds.
- Create a print-rich environment.
- Accommodate students' interests and backgrounds.
- Read, read, read.
- Employ systematic, varied strategies for recognizing words.
- Offer a variety of reading methods to raise interest.
- Integrate language activities.
- Activate students' prior knowledge.
- Provide authentic purpose, materials, and audiences in the development of oracy and literacy.
- Construct, examine, and extend meaning.
- Furnish explicit instruction of what, when, and why.
- Present opportunities for students to take control of the reading process.

# Writing and the English Learner

Hand in hand with reading goes writing, no longer considered an activity that can be postponed until English learners speak fluently: "Child ESL learners, early in their development of English, can write English and can do so for various purposes" (Hudelson, 1984, p. 221). Writing in English is not only a key to academic success but also an outlet for self-expression.

Although much has been written about the writing process, it is more accurate to use the term *writing processes.* Most writers do not simply draft, revise, edit, and publish. Instead, the process is recursive, with much travel back and forth from drafting to redrafting, from editing to redrafting, from revising to redrafting, and so forth. Many teachers teach a five-step writing process, but in reality, in a classroom with a rich learning environment, students are in various stages simultaneously. If teachers honor the reality of the learning process, rather than try to impose a lockstep system, the mind stays engaged throughout the struggle to "write down" and clarify thinking.

## Generation 1.5 and College Writing

Students who are still in the process of acquiring English are entering colleges and universities at an unprecedented rate. The good news is that English learners are being encouraged to pursue higher education. The bad news is that few are ready to perform college-level work. In the California State University system of twenty-two campuses, for example, 46 percent of the 36,655 first-year students who enrolled in the fall of 2001 failed the English Placement Test and therefore could not enroll in English 101 (Tresaugue, 2002). Why are so many students unprepared for college writing?

Many first-year college students are Generation 1.5 students, U.S.-educated English-language learners who immigrated to the United States while they were in elementary or high school or who were born in the United States but grew up speaking a language other than English at home. These students are diverse in terms of their prior educational experience, native- and English-language proficiency, language dominance, and academic literacy. They have learning needs that differ from other English learners and can benefit from targeted intervention in academic writing and other skills.

Students' prior academic work and social situations may hamper their ability to participate in discourse at the university level. To become insiders in the world of academic culture, students must learn to write essays that express their personal values, experiences, knowledge, and questions. In this way, students can discover an "enlarging horizon that every discourse can open to [their] view" and "gradually enter the community of 'knowers' while retaining their own voice" (Spellmeyer, 1989, p. 274).

## Writing as a Social Construction

Writing is no longer seen as a lone pursuit of the individual. A sociocultural approach to writing holds that individuals engage in literacy for specific purposes, in specific contexts, and as participants in specific communities. Writers learn from one another as they take part in the larger community. Farr (1994) studied the motivation of a group of Mexican immigrants in Chicago. The motivation for many students to improve their writing is not so much internal or intrinsic, but rather lies embedded in the social context in which the writing takes place.

Rodby (1999) described case studies of ELD students who were more or less able to draw on multiple and overlapping systems of support from work, home, church, clubs, peer interactions, faculty, and social/cultural systems to revise their writing in a pre-first-year English class. These students are examples of the way their social contexts influenced their literacy behavior, which in turn influenced their academic potential. Therefore, interventions to improve their writing must be sensitive to context and culture.

## Stages of Writing Development for Young English Learners

Writing behavior on the part of children who are native speakers of English reflects a series of developmental stages, starting with *scribbling and drawing*. Then, at the *prephonemic* stage, the writer uses real letters, but the meaning stands for whole ideas. Moving on to the *early phonemic* stage, the writer uses letters—usually consonants—to stand for words, and at the *letter-naming* stage, vowels may accompany the consonants in an attempt to approximate phonemic sequences. As the writer goes through a *transitional* phase in moving toward *conventional* spelling, the child uses "invented" or "temporary" spelling to convey meaning. If children are held to correct spelling, they write much less (Hadaway, Vardell, & Young, 2002).

The actual spelling that children write is a fascinating indicator of their thinking and their emotions, as well as their progress in learning conventional forms. Kress (2000) looked at one child's form, *dided* ("died"), and speculates that the child is struggling with overregularization of past tense, while another child, Emily, prints the upper case *E* with four horizontal strokes, perhaps an indication that this letter carries extra signification as the first letter of her name. Emergent spelling, whether it stems from first- or second-language acquisition, is a rich source of knowledge about intellectual and interlanguage development.

Beginning English learners usually enter English in the transitional phase; that is, they generally catch on to the sound–symbol principle of the alphabet, even if their own language is ideographic. The more similar their home language alphabet is to the English alphabet, the more easily their writing skills will transfer to English. Word banks can be a rich source of vocabulary building; students can collect words on index cards to alphabetize, classify, or illustrate, or nominate them for Word of the Week contests (Lipton & Hubble, 1997). Beginning students can engage in interactive journal writing with their teacher, or complete simple frame sentences such as "I like _____ because _____." They can copy words and sentences, or they can make their own books by copying and illustrating simple books (Hadaway et al., 2002).

Intermediate English learners increase their vocabulary as they attempt more complex sentences while writing. They can try their hand at various genres of personal and expressive writing, such as letter writing, as well as various types of academic writing such as note taking, short essays, and lists. Exercises in sentence combining help English learners extend the length and variety of their writing. Students at this level of English acquisition are struggling with the correct forms of plural nouns, pronouns, verb tenses, and subject–verb agreement. Many errors are at the sentence level, such as the correct use of adverb and adjective phrases and clauses, sentence fragments and run-on constructions, and collocation errors (inaccurate verb + preposition combinations) (Leki, 1992).

Advanced English learners write responses to many academic assignments, such as personal or literary essays and written work on worksheets, laboratory manuals, and test questions. Their writing may feature many of the issues with which native speakers struggle, such as topic focus, parallel sentence structure, and paragraph cohesion.

## The Importance of Writing in the Native Language

Some teachers discourage the use of a student's native language when writing, in the mistaken belief that drawing on their first language is a sign of interference with English. However, this is an example of the powerful difference between first and final drafts; one would hope that the unique voice of the writer is preserved in the polished version if the outcome is to be totally in English. However, Fu (2009) makes a persuasive case for the usefulness of code-switching when English learners write:

> Code-switching is not only a necessary transitional state, but a useful strategy in promoting the growth of their English writing. When ELLs try to write in English, their thinking is often blocked due to their limited vocabulary. Code-switching can serve as a borrowing strategy by using the native language to fill in the English words they don't know, so they can continue their thinking process. (p. 49)

Many writers code-switch to express their emotions and identify. As one writer explains,

> With two ways to say everything I'm hardly at a disadvantage. How I speak Spanish and English is a reflection of the culture I live everyday. And unless there's something wrong with my almost bilingual and very bicultural life, then there's nothing wrong with combining the two languages I grew up with. Yo hablaré en dos idioms as long as I can think in two. (Figueroa, 2004, p. 286)

## Handwriting in English

The era has passed when handwriting was neglected. All students, but particularly English learners with primary languages that are nonalphabetic, need to learn the basics of letter formation, letter size and proportion, spacing, slant, alignment, and line quality (Barbe, Wasylyk, Hackney, & Braun, 1984). Letters are best learned when sorted by shape, with the line letters first (l, t, i, L, T, I, E, F, H), followed by angle (k, v, w, x, y, z, A, K, M, N, V, W, X, Y, Z); circle/line (o, a, b, d, p, q, O, Q); open circle (c, e, C, G); line/half-circle (B, D, P, R); curved (h, m, n, u, U); partial curve (f, r, j, g, J); and S-curve (s, S). TPR can be used to link physical actions with demonstrated commands to orient students to the forms of letters (Boyd-Batstone, 2006).

## Writing Genres and Prompts

Almost all writing can be divided into narrative and expository genres. Both of these modes rely on description using visual images and observations to make details come alive for the reader.

**Writing Narrative Prose**   Fiction is a "narrative or story about imaginary events, characters, and setting, made to seem real through description" (Houston, 2004, p. 130). Narratives usually proceed in a sequential recounting of events called the *plot*. Writers can create fiction out of personal experience; events presented in true-to-life form are considered biography or auto-biography. Narratives of place are also personal in quality, evoking the writer's experience of detail and mood.

*Prompts* are questions or opening sentences of an essay given to writers to provoke content. How many college admission prompts are versions of "Describe an experience that shows one of your important personal qualities"? What narrative prompts have in common is evocation of personal experience. What makes a narrative outstanding is the unique response to a prompt. This quality of uniqueness argues for prompts that are not too prescriptive but leave room for an imaginative response. Contemporary writing does not hold the narrative to a strictly linear plot but meshes time with memory in more fluid ways.

Consider, for example, the mystery called forth by Ian Frazier's opening sentence to his essay entitled "Hungry Minds; Tales from a Chelsea Soup Kitchen" (*The New Yorker*, 26 May 2008). With this opening, the mind of the reader races ahead to uncover more information:

> The Church of the Holy Apostles, at the corner of Twenty-eighth Street and Ninth Avenue in Manhattan, is a church only two-sevenths of the time.

**Writing Expository Prose**   Structured formats are more common in writing that persuades, describes a process, presents two sides of an issue, or explains cause and effect (Oshima & Hogue, 2006). To follow the argument, the reader must have a carefully sequenced set of facts and background information, tied together with attention to sequence and logic connectors. The short research paper is an example of this genre (Boardman, 2009). Although narrative writing depends on chronological prepositions, conjunctions, and transition words (*at first, after that, later on*), expository essays require more logical phrases (*as a result, for instance, in that case, because of*). Even small words such as *then* and *thus* have distinct meanings, making the job of the writing teacher one of clarifying students' thinking as well as improving their prose styling.

## The Writing Workshop

In the workshop environment, students are free to talk with one another as they write. English learners can draw on other students, not just the teacher, as a resource, and can in turn use their own experiences to enrich their writing and that of their peers. The teacher's role, then, becomes that of facilitator and listener.

Writing can be fun if students write collaboratively. Students can brainstorm and share ideas and then write these ideas in a list form that resembles poetry. One useful convention is the phrase "I used to _____ but now _____." Once the story is completed, it can be copied onto a chart and used for reading practice. This is a version of the language experience approach that connects students to their own experiences and activities by having them express themselves orally.

Students may enjoy writing buddy journals, a kind of diary in which a pair of students write back and forth to each other (Bromley, 1989). The teacher models this by suggesting sample topics and perhaps putting a daily journal entry on the board: "Today I feel excited about the field trip. I got up extra early to find something to pack in my lunch!" (The buddy journals are not as private as a teacher–student dialogue journal might be, because every two weeks or so the students change buddies, and the new buddies have access to previous entries.)

The process approach to writing involves several stages: the planning or prewriting stage, the writing stage, and the feedback/editing stage.

**The Writing Process: Prewriting**   During *prewriting*, students are involved in oral language experiences that develop their need and desire to write. These activities may include talking and listening about shared experiences, reading literature, brainstorming, or creating role-playing or other fantasy activities. Mind mapping encourages students to generate and organize their ideas graphically on chart paper or on the chalkboard. Some classes may use *Inspiration*, a computer program that facilitates idea generation.

The prewriting phase helps to generate, incubate, explore, test, and integrate ideas. Most writers find it often helps to talk about a topic, bouncing ideas off others, benefiting from the questions others ask as they shape and explore ideas. Not only does this help students build a representation of the topic about which they are writing, but also the challenges, prompts, and questions from collaborators help to fashion a working representation of the assignment or task (Flower, 1994).

Some writers experience prolonged silent periods, whereas others report heightened emotional states or sudden bursts of productivity. The best writing springs from creative sources within the person that may manifest as the individual becomes "distracted, preoccupied, or temperamental. If new ideas are bubbling, the individual may become restless, excitable, emphatic even, while lack of manifest progress may result in gloom and despondency" (Smith, 1982, p. 126). The most profound education reaches deep into the individual, and in reaching deeply, evokes emotional reaction. Teachers who respect this passion sympathize with its companion emotions. The alternative? Apathy.

**The Writing Process: Drafting**   The drafting stage involves quickly capturing ideas. There may be several false starts, changes of mind, and search for more ideas. Writers do the best they can in spelling, vocabulary, and syntax, without a concern for accuracy. This is followed by revision. Students share and discuss the content and clarity of their writing, drawing on the teacher as a resource for advice and support. This helps students to expand their thinking and communicate more expressively before editing perfects the form and grammar.

A *word wall* or *word bank* is useful for English learners, providing a visual representation of words they may need to draw on while writing. For example, a pictorial word wall for a unit on fairy tales might include matched pictures and the printed words *queen, king, castle, crown,* and other words that a writer might need to use. This helps English learners to be more fluent as they draft their ideas.

**Self-Correction and Revision**   Writers face similar problems as they draft. Gregory and Kuzmich (2005) suggest that the following components can be used for student self-assessment:

> *Ideas:* Is my message clear? Do I know enough about my topic? Did I try hard to make it interesting?

> *Organization:* Does the paper have a good beginning? Are things told in a logical order? Does the paper end well?

> *Conventions:* Are there paragraphs? Are words spelled correctly? Did I use appropriate capitalization and punctuation?

> *Voice:* Does the writing sound like me? Are the thoughts clear to the reader? Will the reader be interested?

**Feedback through Peer Response and Writing Conferences**   Students can give one another feedback through formal "sharing" meetings, organized by the teacher, in which students read their work and ask peers for comments; or they can be informal, student-initiated interactions. Peer response can be more valuable than teacher feedback in helping writers analyze their own drafts (Reid, 1993). To be useful, peer responding must be modeled and taught as part of the writing process from the beginning so that students are aware of writing for their peers as well as for the teacher.

One way to shape peer response is to provide students with a peer review sheet that is specifically designed for the writing prompt or the evaluation criteria for the final paper (Campbell, 1998). These might include the following:

- Is the title specific, related to the central idea?
- Does the introductory paragraph preview the entire paper?
- Is the thesis clearly stated? Does it tie the ideas together?
- Are paragraphs logically organized? Are claims supported by evidence?
- Is there a clear differentiation between writer's ideas and those of other authors?
- Is there a concluding paragraph discussing the significance of the ideas?
- Is there appropriate grammar and usage?

Peer response to writing is not editing. It should include feedback about the content, point of view, and tone of the work. This helps students focus on the communicative content of the writing and draws them together in a more respectful sharing of the messages they intend.

Individual writing conferences with the teacher are interviews in which the teacher listens to each student talk about the work in progress, commenting and asking questions to help the student organize and focus the writing. This questioning also helps the teacher understand the student's topic and focus. Ideally, the tone of the conference makes it clear that the writer is in charge. The writer speaks first to set the agenda and communicate the intended meaning. The teacher may then query specific sections ("What is the main point of this part?") and offer suggestions as alternatives.

**The Writing Process: Editing**   Editing takes place after the message is intact, to "fix up" errors or mistakes in usage and spelling. Students who learn to self-edit can examine their own writing critically and improve it. The teacher's proofreading is beneficial only if the students can use it to improve their own writing.

If a perfected version is not necessary, students may archive their rough drafts in a portfolio, without rewriting. If, however, the writing is published or publicly shared, and students are to achieve the pride of authorship, accuracy in such areas as spelling is more warranted.

**Error Correction**   In the early stages of writing English, fluency is a much more vital goal than accuracy. With English learners, the teacher must consider the level of their general language proficiency before decisions about error correction can be made. Law and Eckes (2000) suggested that with younger children and newcomers, one should encourage expression of ideas without correcting grammar. Writers should be rewarded for their courage in trying new formats and more complicated sentence syntax, with encouragement for risk taking. Error correction is a process in which attention is paid to the communication of meaning and the learner is guided toward self-correction.

Proofreading marks should be simple and consistent. Moreover, teachers may wish to use *restrictive correcting*, a focus on only a few types of errors at one time (Bartram & Walton, 1994, p. 80). Some instructors set certain standards of submission before accepting a paper, such as requiring that a word-processed paper be electronically spellchecked. Each instructor of writing sets his or her own level of importance to what Houston (2004) called the "cosmetic" aspects of writing—the level of error correction that creates "optimum readability" (Houston, 2004, p. 227). When the emphasis is on ideas, the first draft may actually be more important than the final version. The reverse may be true when student writing is displayed on PTA Night.

**Publishing**   Ways of publishing can vary: A play is performed, a story is bound into a book for circulation in the class library, a poem is read aloud, an essay is posted on a bulletin board, a video is made of a student reading aloud, a class newspaper is circulated to the community. Desktop publishing software has made more readily accessible the look of professional typesetting and layout, usually using a simple page layout computer program combined with a word processor. When printed, the class newspaper can circulate to the school and community.

## Issues with ESL Writing

*Selecting a topic* can sometimes be a concern for English learners. Not all writers find a topic of a personal nature, such as childhood experiences, particularly fruitful for generating ideas. Being familiar with a topic is no guarantee of writing ease. Just because a topic is popular with native English speakers is no guarantee that the topic will enable English learners.

*Establishing a tone* may be difficult for English learners, especially at the young adult level. Tones to avoid are flippancy (disrespectful levity), sarcasm (contemptuous remarks), sentimentality (shallow feeling), self-righteousness (taking on a special claim to virtue), belligerence (trying to bully the reader into agreement), and apology ("poor little me") (Packer & Timpane, 1997).

*Issues of plagiarism* may be difficult to convey. Students may feel pressure to help others by letting them copy, they may have different "rules" about using others' work in their own cultures, or they may simply work together in a way that results in identical copies of student work. At a deeper level, however, plagiarism may occur because English learners feel coerced into writing in English, either due to social, academic, or economic demands on their lives, or to feeling a lack of ownership over English (Pennycook, 1998). The best solution to the problem of plagiarism is to give students support and accurate feedback at various stages in their writing, offering specific guidelines and training in using "textual borrowing" strategies (Bloch, 2001, p. 246; see also Barks & Watts, 2001).

*The use of dictionaries and the library* are two areas in which English learners may need guidance and direction. Many students rely on bilingual dictionaries, which in their brevity do not always supply accurate translations. Teaching dictionary skills explicitly can be of great help to students, especially those whose first language is written in the same alphabet as English (see Feuerstein & Schcolnik [1995], for an example of such instruction). International students sometimes rely on pocket translating devices, which do not always supply accurate translations.

English learners may not be familiar with the use of a library, especially if such resources are not available in their native culture. Students more familiar with libraries may simply need special training about the library's features, such as the electronic card catalog. In other cases, students who may have come to rely on the libraries within their own families, if they are among the elite, or who may never have had occasion to use a library will require more help in learning to navigate its resources. Table 7.5 summarizes adaptations in writing for English learners.

## Writing in the Age of the Internet

Writing in a Web 2.0 environment requires a change in assumptions and procedures from writing in the past. According to Knobel and Lankshear (2006), a different approach is needed, one that "inevitably involves networks, collaboration, and shared visions of how knowledge is made and distributed differently in digital space" (p. 80). In other words, digital writing is not just writing using technology instead of paper and pencil, but rather is about designs of meaning that may employ aural, spatial, and gestural modalities as well as visual.

Digital writing differs from traditional writing in other respects too; the audience is potentially vast, and the information offered is obtained from an ever-expanding multiplicity of sources. Writers must access, organize, and process more information than ever before, in multiple new forms of visual and vocally enhanced communication, including blogs, YouTube videos, wikis, and webinars, to name but a few. For example, bloggers use cyberspace to "reflect on their own ideas, comment on other blogs, and synthesize their readings from other sources . . . utilizing the full capacity of blogs as a literacy practice, not just replicating traditional practices in an online space" (Hicks, 2009, p. 16).

**TABLE 7.5**    Adaptations in Writing for English Learners

| Writing Strategies | Description |
|---|---|
| Write. Write. Write. | Provide students with a wide variety of opportunities to write and share their writing. |
| | Write in all subject areas. |
| | Encourage students to use and practice writing across the curriculum. |
| Invite authentic writing. | Set up tasks that have real purpose and real audiences. |
| Offer examples of good writing. | Furnish access to a variety of written materials and examples of good writing. |
| | Make the expression of thoughts and ideas the primary goal, with correctness of form secondary. |
| Model writing as a process. | Writing is developmental and takes time; steps in writing are made visible and practiced. |
| Schedule writing conferences. | Confer individually with students on a regular basis to enhance students' self-assessment of their own writing skills and their understanding of the processes. |
| Teach students "how to write." | Present explicit instruction, often in the form of mini-lessons, demonstrating what students are expected to do in their writing. |
| Allow time to learn supportive skills. | Reinforce writing skills such as prewriting, planning, drafting, revising, and editing on a daily basis; establish a routine for these behaviors and encourage students to use their own strategies, move naturally between states, and work at their own pace. |
| Provide clear criteria for evaluation. | Foster independence and responsibility by providing criteria (e.g., rubrics, exemplars) students can use to evaluate their own writing. |
| Include contextual instruction in grammar. | Grammar is taught within the context of writing, not in isolation, and also emphasizes strategies consistent with individual learner needs. |
| Use the inquiry method. | Create structured assignments based on inquiry to help students produce writing that expands strategy use, accommodates a variety of purposes and audiences, and addresses increasingly complex topics. |
| Develop writing portfolios. | Establish portfolios to monitor and evaluate students' writing abilities in different genres and to provide students with greater responsibility for their progress as writers through self-assessment of their own work. |
| Involve students in the evaluation process. | Students are held accountable for their own growth and employ multiple measures to assess literacy skills. |

 **Classroom Glimpse**

### A CLASS WIKI ON CENSORSHIP

In a high-school-level lesson plan regarding activity about censorship, Sara Beauchamps-Hicks designed a wiki page that encompasses a number of tasks: Students visit various websites, view multimedia on the topic, discuss what they have found, and add content to their group's wiki. Classroom groups use Google Docs to create a shared text that all group members can edit. Beauchamps-Hicks guides students through the research process, encouraging them to develop new ideas about censorship. Her goal is for students to grow as digital writers who produce their own texts rather than just consume information. (Hicks, 2009, p. 17)

# The Role of Grammar

Following Chomsky's lead, linguists envision grammar as a set of rules that human beings unconsciously know and use. They believe that human beings, once exposed to the language(s) of their environment, have an innate ability to understand and produce sentences they have never before heard, because the mind has the capacity to internalize and construct language rules that help native speakers determine whether a group of words forms a sentence in their language.

If application of the rules of sentence formation is largely unconscious, what role does explicit teaching of grammar play? There are two ways to think about this. First, linguists are not clear on how first- and second-language acquisition of grammar differ. Krashen's acquisition hypothesis (see Chapter 2) claimed that second-language syntax was acquired in the same order as that of the first language, but it is not clear if the same internal brain mechanisms are involved (for a discussion of this issue, see Gass & Selinker [2008]). Moreover, if second-language acquisition follows different brain pathways (and in most people's subjective experience, this is true, learning a second language is more difficult than learning the first, which is why more people are not bilingual), then there is a role for explicit teaching of grammar.

Krashen (2003) has a few current words to say on this topic:

> I do not think that grammar teaching should be at the core of curriculum, but there are good reasons for including it. First, grammar teaching can be an excellent introduction to the study of linguistics, which has obvious value, e.g., the study of universals, language change, and dialects. Second, even with massive reading, complete acquisition of the conventions of writing may not take place.... [T]hese gaps are typically small and rarely interfere with the clarity of the message. Conscious knowledge of grammar rules can help fill at least some of these gaps, and can be used in the editing stage of the composing process, after ideas are on the page. (n.p.)

Another author has a slightly different view:

> In determining how much grammar to teach explicitly, how much accuracy to demand, and at what stages and in what contexts: one size does not fit all. Teachers must juggle three important elements: (1) the goal of instruction/time for instruction, (2) the structure of the target language, and (3) the style of the learner. (Robin, 2006, n.p.)

Robin goes on to explain that grammar has a larger role to play in second-language acquisition if the learner intends to achieve advanced proficiency, if the language has highly difficult morphology, or if a highly structured environment fits the learner's cognitive style. One might argue that the older and more disciplined the learner, the larger a role explicit instruction in grammar could play.

## Benefits of Explicit Instruction of Language

Second-language acquisition, as a domain of learning, is difficult. To attain linguistic and cultural proficiency requires precise control of meaning, careful attunement to intonation, and mastery of behavioral subtlety. Explicit instruction usually means direct instruction (with goals, activities, and assessment strictly determined by the teacher or other authorities) combined with precise error correction or other overt feedback.

The earliest type of language teaching was grammar-translation pedagogy, in which the instructor explained the meaning of vocabulary words and the structure of sentences, and students' access to the target language was limited to a carefully controlled curriculum. The strengths of this methodology are that those skilled in traditional school behaviors—memorization and rote learning—receive good grades. Moreover, the explaining and translating involve the first language—little of this instruction takes place directly in the target language. Therefore, students are more likely to find the explanations and translations comprehensible.

Drawbacks to this direct instruction include limited independent language acquisition, minimal access to the target language and culture, and little social interaction with target-language speakers. Speaking and listening—the foundations of the brain's acquisition of language—are restricted, and oral proficiency is seldom achieved. Grammar-focused lessons that are not communicatively based can also be boring, cumbersome, and difficult for students.

Explicit teaching may be required when some basic feature of English is so illogical or dissimilar to the L1 that it is not easily understood, even in context. Aspects of English grammar that may offer exceptional challenge to English learners include use of word order, determiners (*this, that, these, those, a, an, the*), prepositions (*in, on, at, by, for, from, of*), auxiliaries (*do, be, have*), conjunctions (*but, so, however, therefore, though, although*), interrogatives, intensifiers (*some, any, few, more, too*), and distinctions among modal verbs (*can, could, would, should, may, might, must*). Phrasal verbs (*look over, pick up*) also present considerable difficulty to Spanish speakers learning communicative English.

 **Classroom Glimpse**

### EXPLICIT FEEDBACK DURING READING TUTORING

The following exchange during the tutoring of reading shows explicit teaching of the sound–symbol connection in English:

> **Pedro:** Miscle?
> **Tutor:** /mus/ . . .
> **Pedro:** /muskl/
> **Tutor:** *Muscle* has what is called silent /c/; you see it but you don't pronounce it. *Muscle* without /c/ sounds like /musl/.
> **Pedro:** Muscle.

## The Role of Feedback in Explicit Teaching

Feedback is essential to the knowledge and performance of any new skill, usually involving explicit error correction, but it can also mean indirect hints. A teacher's job is to understand the conditions under which feedback works best. For example, a teacher needs to know that students benefit from the time teachers spend providing extensive responses on writing. But what is known about feedback in language learning? Under what conditions are the different forms effective for particular learners? The answers to such questions would enable teachers to predict which responses are likely to work best.

Feedback is integrated differently into different types of practice. For example, communicative activities are usually low in feedback as long as participants are understandable; grammar instruction tends to invite right/wrong correction; and oral presentations produce feedback on clarity, organization, and audibility. Modality of language (e.g., written, oral, computer-mediated) influences the type of feedback—people are usually more anxious about feedback on their oral performances than on their written products, and most people are not at all upset about feedback received during computerized tutoring.

Although research on feedback is still underway, some general principles are well known, such as the idea that highly anxious learners need positive as well as corrective feedback. To date, there has been scarce research on the characteristics of learners that enable them to learn from feedback. This is a promising avenue for further investigation. Whatever research is carried out on this subject should be combined with formative assessment, as feedback can be considered a kind of formative assessment.

---

**Best Practice**    ERROR CORRECTION GUIDELINES

Systematic errors, such as Chinese learners' omissions of past-tense declensions in verbs ("Yesterday he drinks"), are a window into the learner's thinking. A thoughtful awareness of error is the best teacher. The more language is produced, the more errors are made, the more learning can occur. The goal is to have the learner produce as much language as possible and create awareness about errors.

At the beginning ELD level, learners need to listen to and look at language but not be required to produce it in public, where errors are an embarrassment. Individual or paired practice is useful, including high-interest activities with lots of visuals, controlled vocabulary, and simple sentence structures.

At the early intermediate and intermediate levels, high-interest activities in which errors do not impede the communication of meaning are useful. Tasks are structured to accomplish focused growth in measurable ways, balanced by language activities in which the learner is interested and successful.

At the early advanced and advanced levels, error correction focuses on learner self-correction, balanced by targeted teacher feedback. Emphasis is equal across grammatical, strategic, sociolinguistic, and discourse functions.

---

Because assessment is such an important part of the contemporary emphasis on learning, error correction and formative assessment as feedback are featured in the discussions that follow on the teaching of each specific modality (listening/speaking, reading, and writing).

## The Supplemental Role of Implicit Learning

In addition to explicit instruction, implicit learning has a role in second-language acquisition. By providing grammar in context in an implicit manner, we can expose students to substantial doses of grammar study without alienating them from the learning of English. One can teach short grammar-based sessions, immediately followed by additional function-based lessons in which the new grammar or structure is applied in context, and trust that the brain will absorb the grammar point while communication takes place.

Current studies have combined explicit and implicit instruction under the term *focus-on-form* approach. Gascoigne (2002) discussed the arguments for and against explicit teaching of grammar and suggested the use of such methods as boldfacing target grammar forms in a text, raising the learner's consciousness about forms through various noticing activities, and careful choice of activities that involve correcting language forms.

## Teaching Grammar

Teachers are often uncertain about what features of grammar to include in language teaching. Savage, Bitterlin, and Price (2010) look at grammar teaching from several perspectives:

- Grammar teaching needs to be connected closely to social functions of language—the language that people need to function in their daily lives.
- The focus should be on forms that are used routinely and are necessary to convey meaning. The verb tenses of present, past, and future, for example, are essential for people to establish conversation, whereas other tenses like the past perfect (*I had eaten before I left*) are less common and therefore less important.
- Grammar instruction in an academic context is most useful for success in school. Error correction that takes place indirectly, in the context of school assignments, is easier for the learner to accept and does not threaten one's self-confidence as might overt oral grammar correction.

Grammar is taught explicitly by using a grammar book that presents systematic reference and explains grammar points with a suitable degree of accuracy. An example is Byrd and Benson's *Problem-Solution: A Reference for ESL Writers* (1994), an excellent resource that covers grammar points with clear explanation and examples.

A focus on correct usage and sentence structure—including spelling, capitalization, and punctuation—is important for English learners, although this should not be taken to the extreme. Often, mainstream teachers base their estimation of students' academic potential on a few key features of written production—namely, the look of writing, such as legible handwriting, correct spelling of basic words, and well-formed sentences. Therefore, as students write—for purposes of critical thinking, reaction to literature, or project-based learning—some products of their writing should be taken to the final, corrected draft stage.

**Working with Syntax**    Awareness of sentence structure can be enhanced by having students work creatively with sentences. They can *expand* sentences by adding details to a simple sentence ("I went home for lunch" becomes "I skipped home with my mama's tortilla at the tip of my tongue"). They can *link* sentences by taking an element from a simple sentence and using it to create an image-rich subsequent sentence ("My cat brought me a lizard in her mouth." [The idea = something about the lizard] "I couldn't tell if that lizard was dead or just pretending"). They can *rearrange* sentences by moving internal phrases to the opening slot ("Lisa drives her tricycle out front to meet Papa when he comes home from work"/"When Papa comes home from work . . .").

**Working with Parts of Speech**    Students who are familiar with parts of speech can make better use of dictionaries to improve their writing. Table 7.6 displays commonly used terms. For a more explicit definition of these terms one might consult a grammar book.

**Writing for Grammar**    Writing tasks can incorporate correct usage. One example is a tongue-in-cheek book that students produced about points of interest in the surrounding neighbor-

**TABLE 7.6**   Parts of Speech

| Part of Speech | Example |
| --- | --- |
| noun | concrete (if countable, can form plurals): *apple, apples* |
| | abstract (often takes no plural): *happiness* |
| noun phrase (often composed of article, adjective, and noun) | *the long road* |
| pronoun | personal (*I, you*) |
| | interrogative (*who, which*) |
| | relative (*whomever*) |
| adjective | *helpful, charming* |
| verb | dynamic: *jump, seem* |
| | stative: *am, are* |
| | auxiliary: *have been* (helping) |
| verb phrase (verb plus auxiliary, verb plus adverb or adverb phrase) | *have been running* |
| | *running away from home* |
| adverb | *slowly* |
| adverbial phrase | *at work* |
| | *along the highway* |
| preposition | *on, under, beside* |
| determiner | (definite article) *the* |
| | (indefinite article) *a* |
| | possessive (*his, our*) |
| | demonstrative (*that, this*) |
| | quantifier (*some, any*) |
| conjunction | *and, but* |

hoods, *The Homegirls' Guide to South Seventh Street.* Key stores, names of streets, and even car brands were correctly capitalized. For a class meal, another group collected recipes from home that featured the imperative form of the verb ("Slice cucumbers thinly") (Shoemaker & Polycarpou, 1993). Thus, correct usage and grammar can be an integral part of learning activities. Correct usage such as punctuation, capitalization, and paragraph structure is emphasized in the context of composition, allowing grammar to be taught in an integrated way, which includes a special focus on difficult features when necessary.

## Content-Based English-Language Development

Content literacy is "the ability to use reading and writing for the acquisition of new content in a given discipline" (McKenna & Robinson, 1997, p. 8). In content-based instruction (CBI) ELD classrooms, ELD educators, in collaboration with content teachers, organize learning objectives around academic subjects to prepare students to master grade-level curricula. This is a supplement to the students' English class.

Content literacy is more than "having knowledge" in a particular discipline; it represents skills needed to acquire knowledge of content and make it easier for the student to read and write in the discipline. This literacy is content specific; an individual who can read and write about science may not be able to do so in mathematics. However, being able to think clearly, understand key concepts, and express oneself are cognitive skills that do generalize across disciplines, so efforts to promote content literacy in one subject can positively affect learning in other subjects.

CBI-ELD classes develop not only language proficiency but also content knowledge, cognitive strategies, and study skills. Teachers familiarize students with the difference in the style and structure of texts and the type of vocabulary featured in the particular discipline. Reference might be made to background knowledge restricted to that discipline (Addison, 1988), along with abstract, specialized, and difficult vocabulary.

## Collaboration and Reciprocity

Content-based instruction can be of great benefit if content instructors and language teachers work together to provide comprehensible input to the learner, as well as to design tasks that are both understandable and important. Systematic, planned instruction must present vocabulary, concepts, and structures that are required for mastery of the content. Whether an *adjunct* model—having the language teacher assist in content teaching by providing additional contact and support (Snow & Brinton, 1988)—or a *collaborative* model—with the ELD teacher co-teaching the content course—is chosen, providing English instruction coupled with content-specific instruction increases the likelihood of academic success.

Is the collaboration between ELD and content instructors reciprocal? If ELD teachers teach content, then the content teachers should also include language-development objectives along with content objectives. If this is not the case, then content-based ELD unfortunately positions ELD teachers as adjunct content instructors, which leads instructors of other disciplines to believe that ELD is not a content domain in its own right. This tends to undermine the professional status of ELD. The collaboration with content instructors should be two way, with both types of classes having language and content objectives.

## CBI-ELD: Lesson Planning

In CBI-ELD, the content to be taught, general instructional goals, and time available for instruction are negotiated with the content teacher. One important factor in the success of CBI-ELD is the ELD teacher's past experiences in teaching similar content or ability to transfer knowledge gained from teaching similar concepts in other disciplines.

Five types of reading lesson plans are commonly used in content-based ESL (McKenna & Robinson, 1997). Table 7.7 describes the five lesson types in detail.

TESOL, Inc. has published a series of four volumes (*Integrating the ESL Standards into Classroom Practice* [Agor, 2000; Irujo, 2000; Samway, 2000; and Smallwood, 2000]) that demonstrate CBI-ELD.

**TABLE 7.7** Types of Reading Lesson Plans in ELD Content-Based Instruction

| Lesson Plan Type | Directions to Teacher |
|---|---|
| **Directed Reading Activity**<br>Advantages:<br>■ Flexible, purposeful<br>Disadvantage:<br>■ May be too teacher-directed | Establish readiness for reading, relating to students' prior knowledge and preteaching vocabulary or specialized skills (maps or charts, etc.).<br>Set purposes for reading (analyze goals and communicate these goals to students).<br>Arrange for students to read silently.<br>Discuss the reading.<br>Extend students' understanding by using supplementary materials or by assigning a writing task. |
| **Directed Reading–Thinking Activity**<br>Advantages:<br>■ Emphasizes the reading–thinking connection<br>■ Encourages students to set own purposes<br>Disadvantage:<br>■ Not well suited to new or unfamiliar material | Help students set purposes for reading; check students' prior knowledge, preteaching concepts if necessary; encourage students to predict content using cues.<br>Facilitate reasoning as students read.<br>Help students test their predictions, locating and discussing bases for conclusions. |
| **K-W-L** (what students *know*, *want* to learn, and *learn*)<br>Advantages:<br>■ Activates prior knowledge<br>■ Establishes group purposes<br>Disadvantage:<br>■ Not well suited to unfamiliar material | Brainstorm with students to elicit prior knowledge of the topic, then discuss, grouping ideas into subtopics.<br>Select subtopics of interest based on what they need to know; have students write out their interests.<br>Assess what was learned by the reading. |
| **Explicit Teaching**<br>Advantage:<br>■ Permits clear-cut, sequential planning<br>Disadvantages:<br>■ May encourage overreliance on teacher for direction<br>■ Literacy activities may be avoided when planning | Create readiness by a positive introduction and by communicating objectives clearly.<br>Teach concepts directly, checking for understanding, reteaching if needed.<br>Provide opportunities for guided and independent practice. |
| **Listen-Read-Discuss**<br>Advantage:<br>■ Effective with low-ability readers<br>Disadvantages:<br>■ Does not appear to encourage voluntary reading<br>■ May encourage overreliance on teacher for direction<br>■ Highly teacher-directed | Present complete text through lecture and demonstration.<br>Give students a chance to read the material silently.<br>Conduct a discussion of the selection. |

*Source:* McKenna & Robinson (1997).

# Literacy in the Cyber Age

Internet tools can extend literacy activities into the "real" world and provide English learners with opportunities to practice reading and writing from their own homes or from local libraries. Students can work individually or with others to create blog entries or comment on others' work, to share information or chat on social networking sites, to "surf" the Net for content relating to their hobbies or interests, or just to practice reading and writing anonymously in cyberspace. Literacy takes on a whole new meaning when each user can access, consume, develop, edit, and share—whether during class or beyond the school day.

## Possibilities for Alternative Literacies

Although much has been made of the role of technology in new forms of literacy, Jiménez (2003) explored an "ecologies of literacy" perspective in asking the question "What forms of literacy serve the English learner community?" He pointed to "syncretic literacy" practices, in which students fuse their in-school and out-of-school literacies to create usable forms of literacy for their daily lives. Students who must serve as language brokers for their families in navigating rental/lease agreements, income tax forms, and telephone/utility bills in English must address their own and their families' short- and long-term goals using a combination of native-language and English oracy and literacy skills. González, Moll, and Amanti (2005) employed the term "funds of knowledge" to capture the information access and language skills that communities use and need if they are to survive and prosper into subsequent generations.

Fisher and Frey (2009) caution that the digital age has brought speed at the expense of thoughtfulness. This is a thought-provoking coda to a chapter on reading and writing for English learners.

> The new literacies of the digital world allow people to locate, create, and disseminate information at breathtaking speed. Yet this accelerated pace can come at a cost to critical literacy. As it becomes increasingly easier to post to a blog, add to a wiki space, or upload a video, the temporal speed that naturally occurred with slower modes has vanished. And with it, lingering over ideas and taking on other viewpoints have evaporated as well. (pp. 137–138)

Although many forms of literacy delivery are changing from print to electronic media, the importance of reading proficiency in the lives of English learners has not changed. Television and the Internet deliver a wide variety of entertainment to the home, tempting many young people from the rigors of homework; yet the individual must learn to marshal books, study materials, media literacy, and other forms of information in the service of academic achievement. Teachers who teach study skills and other literacy strategies systematically can help English learners to read and write across a variety of genres using a variety of media. The forms of media may change dramatically in the years ahead; the need for literacy—including biliteracy—will remain as the greatest challenge facing English learners.

Go to the Topic Reading and Writing in the MyEducationLab (www.myeducationlab.com) for your course, where you can:

- Find learning outcomes for Reading and Writing along with the national standards that connect to these outcomes.
- Complete Assignments and Activities that can help you more deeply understand the chapter content.
- Apply and practice your understanding of the core teaching skills identified in the chapter with the Building Teaching Skills and Dispositions learning units.
- Examine challenging situations and cases presented in the IRIS Center Resources.
- Check your comprehension on the content covered in the chapter by going to the Study Plan in the Book Resources for your text. Here you will be able to take a chapter quiz, receive feedback on your answers, and then access Review, Practice, and Enrichment activities to enhance your understanding of chapter content.

## A+RISE

Go to the Topic A+RISE in the MyEducationLab (www.myeducationlab.com) for your course. A+RISE® Standards2Strategy™ is an innovative and interactive online resource that offers new teachers in grades K–12 just-in-time, research-based instructional strategies that:

- Meet the linguistic needs of ELLs as they learn content
- Differentiate instruction for all grades and abilities
- Offer reading and writing techniques, cooperative learning, use of linguistic and nonlinguistic representations, scaffolding, teacher modeling, higher order thinking, and alternative classroom ELL assessment
- Provide support to help teachers be effective through the integration of listening, speaking, reading, and writing along with the content curriculum
- Improve student achievement
- Are aligned to Common Core Elementary Language Arts standards (for the literacy strategies) and to English language proficiency standards in WIDA, Texas, California, and Florida.

# 8

# Culture and Cultural Diversity and Their Relationship to Academic Achievement

## Cultural Concepts and Perspectives

People used to think of culture as Culture, as in "highbrow" activities such as going to the opera or symphony, or as Exotic Culture, such as viewing a display of African masks. But culture is more than performing traditional rites or crafting ritual objects. Culture, though largely invisible, influences the way people think, talk, and act—the very way people see the world.

Cultural patterns are especially evident in schools because home and school are the chief sites where the young are acculturated. If we accept the organization, teaching and learning styles, and curricula of the schools as natural and right, we may not realize that these patterns are cultural; they seem natural and right only to the members of the culture who created them. As children of nondominant cultures enter the schools, however, they may find the organization, teaching and learning styles, and curricula to be alien, incomprehensible, and exclusionary.

Fortunately, teachers can learn to see clearly the key role of culture in teaching and learning. They can incorporate culture into classroom activities in superficial ways—as a group of artifacts (baskets, masks, distinctive clothing), as celebrations of holidays (Cinco de Mayo, Martin Luther King Jr. Day), or as a laundry list of stereotypes and insensitivities to be avoided. These ways of dealing with culture are limiting but useful as a starting point.

However, teachers can also gain a more insightful view of culture and cultural processes and use this understanding to move beyond the superficial. To be knowledgeable as an intercultural educator is to understand that observable cultural items are but one aspect of the cultural web—the intricate pattern that weaves and binds a people together. Knowing that culture provides the lens through which people view the world, teachers can look at the "what" of a culture—the artifacts, celebrations, traits, and facts—and ask "why?" Knowledge of the deeper elements of culture—beyond aspects such as food, clothing, holidays, and celebrations—can give teachers a crosscultural perspective that allows them to educate students to the fullest extent possible.

## What Is Culture?

Does a fish understand water? Do people understand their own culture? Teachers are responsible for helping to pass on cultural knowledge through the schooling process. Can teachers step outside their own culture long enough to see how it operates and to understand its effects on culturally diverse students? A way to begin is to define culture.

**Defining Culture**    The term *culture* is used in many ways. It can refer to activities such as art, drama, and ballet or to items such as pop music, mass media entertainment, and comic books. The term *culture* can be applied to distinctive groups in society, such as adolescents and their culture. It can be a general term for a society, such as the "French culture." Such uses do not, however, define what a culture is. As a field of study, culture is conceptualized in various ways (see Table 8.1).

The definitions in Table 8.1 have common factors but they vary in emphasis. Early cultural theorists emphasize the way an individual is immersed in culture, even unknowingly; whereas postmodern definitions (see Grossberg, 1988, and Fraser & Nicholson, 1988) make the point that the individual plays an active role in shaping his or her cultural ambiance, and must continually remake a cultural identity (using language and power) to adapt to shifting circumstances. The following definition of culture combines the ideas in Table 8.1 with other contemporary notions:

> Culture is the explicit and implicit patterns for living, the dynamic system of commonly agreed-upon symbols and meanings, the deep structure of knowledge, belief, art, morals, law, customs, behaviors, traditions, and/or habits that are shared and make up the total way of life of a people, as negotiated by individuals in the process of constructing a personal identity.
>
> To understand culture, one must look beyond the obvious to understand how values, codes, beliefs and social relations are continually being reshaped by shifting parameters of place, identity, history, and power. Rather than individuals being excluded for differing from cultural norms, people with dissonant, flexible, complex, and hybrid racial and ethnic identities struggle to generate new meanings within accommodating contexts as they use experimentation and creativity to rework existing configurations of knowledge and power and thus extend the possibilities of being human, even in the face of an uncertain outcome. (Díaz-Rico, 2008, pp. 271–272)

The important idea is that culture involves both observable behaviors and intangibles such as beliefs and values, rhythms, rules, and roles. The concept of culture has evolved over the last fifty years away from the idea of culture as an invisible, patterning force to that of culture as an active tension between the social "shortcuts" that make consensual society possible and the contributions and construction that each individual creates while living in society. To mix metaphors, culture is not only the filter through which people see the world but also the raw dough from which each person fashions a life that is individual and satisfying.

Because culture is all-inclusive, it includes multiple aspects of life. Snow (1996) listed a host of components (see Table 8.2).

**TABLE 8.1**   Definitions of Culture

| Definition | Source |
|---|---|
| The sum total of a way of life of a people; patterns experienced by individuals as normal ways of acting, feeling, and being. | Hall (1959) |
| That complex whole that includes knowledge, belief, art, morals, law, and custom, and any other capabilities acquired by humans as members of society. | Tylor (in Pearson, 1974) |
| A dynamic system of symbols and meanings that involves an ongoing, dialectic process in which past experience influences meaning, which in turn affects future experience, which in turn affects subsequent meaning, and so on. | Robinson (1985) |
| Mental constructs in three basic categories: *shared knowledge* (information known in common by members of the group), *shared views* (beliefs and values shared by members of a group), and *shared patterns* (habits and norms in the ways members of a group organize their behavior, interaction, and communication). | Snow (1996) |
| Partial solutions to previous problems that humans create in joint mediated activity; the social inheritance embodied in artifacts and material constituents of culture as well as in practices and ideal symbolic forms; semi-organized hodgepodge of human inheritance. Culture is exteriorized mind and mind is interiorized culture. | Cole (1998) |
| Frames (nationality, gender, ethnicity, religion) carried by each individual that are internalized, individuated, and emerge in interactions. | Smith, Paige, & Steglitz (1998) |
| People are never merely passively subordinated, never totally manipulated, never entirely incorporated. People are engaged in struggles with, within, and sometimes against real tendentious forces and determinations in their efforts to appropriate what they are given. Consequently, their relations to particular practices and texts are complex and contradictory. . . . If people's lives are never merely determined by the dominant position, and if their subordination is always complex and active, understanding culture requires us to look at how practices are actively inserted at particular sites of everyday life and how particular articulations empower and disempower their audiences. | Grossberg (1988, pp. 169–170) |
| [T]he social bond is a weave of crisscrossing threads of discursive practices, no single one of which runs continuously throughout the whole. Individuals are the nodes or "posts" where such practices intersect and, so, they participate in many simultaneously. It follows that social identities are complex and heterogeneous. | Fraser & Nicholson (1988, pp. 88–89) |

## Key Concepts about Culture

To understand culture, one cannot simply total a list of traits—there is wholeness about cultures, with various aspects overlapping and integrated with other aspects. Cultures cannot be taught merely by examining external features such as art and artifacts, although those may be a useful starting point. Even traveling to a country may not engender a deeper understanding of that country's culture(s). To understand a culture, one must examine the living patterns and values of the people living in that culture. Despite the aspects of diverse cultures that may seem unique, cultures have various elements in common.

**Culture Is Universal**   Everyone in the world belongs to one or more cultures. Each culture provides organized ways to carry out and interpret such experiences as serving food, speaking

**TABLE 8.2** Components of Culture

| Component | Example | Component | Example |
|---|---|---|---|
| Daily life | Animals | Interacting | Chatting |
| | Clothing | | Eating |
| | Daily schedule | | Drinking |
| | Food | | Gift giving |
| | Games | | Language learning |
| | Hobbies | | Parties |
| | Housing | | Politeness |
| | Hygiene | | Problem solving |
| | Jobs | Society | Business |
| | Medical care | | Cities |
| | Plants | | Economy |
| | Recreation | | Education |
| | Shopping | | Farming |
| | Space | | Industry |
| | Sports | | Government and politics |
| | Time | | Languages and dialects |
| | Traffic and transport | | Law and order |
| | Travel | | Science |
| The cycle of life | Birth | | Social problems |
| | Children | The nation | Holidays |
| | Dating/mating | | Geography |
| | Marriage | | History |
| | Divorce | | Famous people |
| | Friends | | National issues |
| | Old age | | Stereotypes |
| | Funerals | Creative arts | Arts |
| | Rites of passage | | Entertainment |
| Values | Philosophy | | Literature |
| | Religion | | Music |
| | Beliefs | | Television |

*Source:* Snow, D. (1996). *More than a native speaker.* Alexandria, VA: TESOL.

to children, marrying, and so forth. Because humans have similar needs, cultures must meet these needs, albeit in diverse ways.

**Culture Simplifies Living**   Social behaviors and customs offer structure to daily life that minimizes interpersonal stress. Cultural patterns are routines that free humans from endless negotiation about each detail of living. Culture helps to unify a society by providing a common base of communication and social customs.

**Culture Is Learned in a Process of Deep Conditioning**   Cultural patterns are absorbed unconsciously from birth, as well as explicitly taught by other members. The fact that cultural patterns are deep makes it difficult for the members of a given culture to see their own culture as learned behavior.

**Culture Is Demonstrated in Values**    Every culture holds some beliefs and behaviors to be more desirable than others, whether about nature, human character, material possessions, or other aspects of the human condition. Those members of the culture who exemplify these values are rewarded with prestige or approval.

**Culture Is Expressed Both Verbally and Nonverbally**    Although language and culture are closely identified, nonverbal components of culture can be just as powerful in communicating cultural beliefs, behaviors, and values. Images, gestures, and emotions are as culturally conditioned as words. In the classroom, teachers may misunderstand a student's intent if nonverbal communication is misinterpreted.

 **Classroom Glimpse**

### NONVERBAL MISCOMMUNICATION

Ming was taught at home to sit quietly when she was finished with a task and wait for her mother to praise her. As a newcomer in the third grade, she waited quietly when finished with her reading assignment. Mrs. Wakefield expected Ming to take out a book to read or to begin another assignment when she completed her work. She made a mental note: "Ming lacks initiative."

**Societies Represent a Mix of Cultures**    The patterns that dominate a society form the *macroculture* of that society. Within the macroculture, a variety of *microcultures* (subcultures) coexist, distinguished by characteristics such as gender, socioeconomic status, ethnicity, geographical location, social identification, and language use.

Generational experiences can cause the formation of microcultures. For example, the children of Vietnamese who immigrated to the United States after the Vietnam War often became native speakers of English, although their parents often spoke little English. This separated the two generations by language. Similarly, Mexicans who migrate to the United States may find that their children born in the United States do not consider themselves Mexicans but instead identify with other terms such as *Chicano*.

**Most Societies Have a Mainstream Culture**    The term *mainstream culture* refers to those individuals or groups who share values of the dominant macroculture. In the United States, the macroculture's traditions and cultural patterns—the mainstream culture—have largely been determined by European Americans who constitute the middle class. Mainstream American culture is characterized by the following values (Gollnick & Chinn, 2002):

- Individualism and privacy
- Independence and self-reliance

---

**DID YOU KNOW?**

### GENERATIONS OF JAPANESE IMMIGRANTS

The first generation of Japanese immigrants, who often referred to themselves as *issei* or first generation, came to the United States starting about 1900. These were, for the most part, young men who worked as agricultural laborers or skilled craftsmen. Often seen as a threat by European Americans, these immigrants were often the targets of discrimination. This prejudice came to a head after the attack by the Japanese on Pearl Harbor in 1941, when the *issei* were divested of their property and removed to relocation camps. After the war, their children, the *nisei* generation, assumed a low ethnic profile, perhaps as a response to the treatment of their parents. (Leathers, 1967)

- Equality
- Ambition and industriousness
- Competitiveness
- Appreciation of the good life
- Perception that humans are separate from, and superior to, nature

**Culture Is Both Dynamic and Persistent** Some features of human cultures are flexible and responsive to change, and other features last thousands of years without changing. Values and customs relating to birth, marriage, medicine, education, and death seem to be the most persistent, for humans seem to be deeply reluctant to alter those cultural elements that influence labor and delivery, marital happiness, health, life success, and eternal rest.

**Culture Is a Mix of Rational and Nonrational Elements** Much as individuals living in western European post-Enlightenment societies may believe that reason should govern human behavior, many cultural patterns are passed on through habit rather than reason. People who bring a real tree into their houses in December—despite the mess it creates—do so because of centuries-old Yule customs. Similarly, carving a face on a hollow pumpkin or hiding colored eggs are hardly rational activities. Other customs persist because they provide workable solutions to persistent problems, such as assigning postal numbers to houses on a street.

**Cultures Represent Different Values** The fact that each culture possesses its own particular traditions, values, and ideals means that each culture of a society judges right from wrong in a different way. Actions can be judged only in relation to the cultural setting in which they occur. This point of view has been called *cultural relativism*. In general, the primary values of human nature are universal—for example, few societies condone murder. However, sanctions relating to actions may differ. The Native-American cultures of California before contact with Europeans were peace loving to such an extent that someone who took the life of another would be ostracized by the tribe. In contrast, the U.S. macroculture deems it acceptable for soldiers to kill in the context of war.

 **Classroom Glimpse**

### CLASHING VALUES ABOUT READING FICTION

Jerome Harvey gave out library prizes in the sixth grade for ROAR (Required Outside Additional Reading). Students competed with one another to see how many pages they could read and report during the contest period. Min-Yi Chen, one of the outstanding readers in class, ranked near the bottom in number of pages. Mr. Harvey brought this up with the Chens at the fall parent–teacher conference. "Well," said Mr. Chen, "Reading of stories is a waste of time—we expect her to go to summer math camp, and the entrance exam is in January. She will be working two or three hours per night on that." Mr. Harvey wonders if he should quit urging Min-Yi to read on her own.

**Culture Affects People's Attitudes toward Schooling** Educational aspiration affects the attitude people have toward schooling, what future job or profession they desire, the importance parents ascribe to education, and how much investment in education they are willing to make. The son of blue-collar workers, for example, might not value a college education because his parents, who have not attained such an education, have nevertheless prospered, whereas the daughter of a recent low-wage immigrant may work industriously in school to pursue higher education and a well-paid job. Cultural values also affect the extent to which families are involved in their children's schooling and the forms this involvement takes. Family involvement is discussed in Chapter 9.

---

**Best Practice**   WORKING WITH ASPIRATIONS ABOUT SCHOOLING

In working with English learners, teachers will want to know the following:

- What educational level does the family and community desire for the student?
- What understanding do family members have about the connection between educational level attained and career aspiration?
- What link does the family make between current effort and career aspiration?

---

**Culture Governs the Way People Learn**   Any learning that takes place is built on previous learning. Students have absorbed the basic patterns of living in the context of their families. They have acquired the verbal and nonverbal behaviors appropriate for their gender and age and have observed their family members in various occupations and activities. They have seen community members cooperating to learn in a variety of methods and modes. Their families have given them a feeling for music and art and have shown them what is beautiful and what is not. Finally, they have learned to use language in the context of their homes and communities, and they can express their needs, desires, and delights.

The culture that students bring from the home is the foundation for their learning in school. Although certain communities exist in relative poverty—that is, they are not equipped with middle-class resources—poverty should not be equated with cultural deprivation. Every community's culture incorporates vast knowledge about successful living. Teachers can use this cultural knowledge to organize students' learning in schools.

Culture appears to influence the way individuals select strategies and approach learning (Shade & New, 1993). For example, students who live in a farming community may have sensitive and subtle knowledge about weather patterns, and this may predispose students to value study in the classroom that helps them better understand natural processes such as climate. These students may prefer a kinesthetic style that builds on the same kind of learning that has made it possible for them to sense subtleties of weather. In a similar manner, Mexican-American children from traditional families who are encouraged to view themselves as an integral part of the family may prefer social learning activities.

Acting and performing are the focus of learning for many African-American children. Children observe other individuals to determine appropriate behavior and to appreciate the performance of others. In this case, observing and listening culminates in an individual's performance before others (Heath, 1999). In contrast, reading and writing may be primary learning modes for other cultures. Traditionally educated Asian students equate the printed page with learning and often use reading and writing to reinforce understanding. Despite these varying approaches, all cultures lay out the basic design for learning for their members.

*[handwritten margin note: cultural ethno relativism centrism]*

**Ethnocentrism versus Cultural Relativism**    Individuals who grow up within a macroculture and never leave it may act on the assumption that their values are the norm. When encountering other cultures, they may be unable or unwilling to recognize that alternative beliefs and behaviors are legitimate within the larger society. Paige (1999) defined this ethnocentrism as how "people unconsciously experience their own cultures as central to reality. They therefore avoid the idea of cultural difference as an implicit or explicit threat to the reality of their own cultural experience" (p. 22).

In contrast, people who accept cultural relativism recognize that all behavior exists in a cultural context, including their own. They understand the limitation this places on their experience, and they therefore seek out cultural diversity as a way of understanding others and enriching their own experience of reality (Paige, 1999). When people adopt a culturally relative point of view, they are able to accept that a different culture might have different operating rules, and they are willing to see that in a neutral way, without having to judge their own culture as inferior or superior by comparison.

**Cultural Relativism versus Ethical Relativism**    Accepting the fact that a person from another culture may have different values does not mean that from a culturally relative point of view one must always agree with the values of a different culture—some cultural differences may be judged negatively—but the judgment is not ethnocentric in the sense of denying that such a difference could occur. Cultural relativism is not the same as ethical relativism—saying "cultures have different values" is not the same as saying "morally and ethically, anything goes" (all behavior is acceptable in all contexts). One does not have to abandon one's own cultural values to appreciate the idea that not all cultures share the same values.

**Cultural Pluralism**    The idea that a society can contain a variety of cultures is a pluralist viewpoint. There are two kinds of pluralist models—*pluralist preservation* holds that a society should preserve all cultures intact, with diversity and unity as equal values, whereas *pluralistic integration* is the belief that a society should have consensus about core civic values. Both these positions contrast with the idea that a society should be composed of a monoculture, with all diversity assimilated (the "melting pot" model) (National Center for Culturally Responsive Educational Systems, 2006).

Individually, some people are *bicultural,* able to shift their cultural frames of reference and intentionally change their behavior to communicate more effectively when in a different culture. However, just because people are raised in two cultures does not necessarily give them the ability to understand themselves or to generalize cultural empathy to a third culture.

Even in a society in which members of diverse cultural groups have equal opportunities for success, and in which cultural similarities and differences are valued, ethnic group identity differences may lead to intergroup conflict. A dynamic relationship between ethnic groups is inevitable; each society must find healthy ways to mediate conflict. The strength of a healthy society is founded on a basic willingness to work together to resolve conflicts. Schools can actively try to foster interaction and integration among different groups. Integration creates the conditions for cultural pluralism.

**Cultural Congruence**    In U.S. schools, the contact of cultures occurs daily. Students from families whose cultural values are similar to those of the European-American mainstream culture may be relatively advantaged in schools, such as children from those Asian cultures who are taught that students sit quietly and attentively—behavior that is rewarded in most classrooms. In contrast, African-American students who learn at home to project their personalities and call attention to their individual attributes (Gay, 1975) may be punished for acting out. The congruence or lack thereof between mainstream and minority cultures has lasting effects on students.

Teachers, who have the responsibility to educate students from diverse cultures, find it relatively easy to help students whose values, beliefs, and behaviors are congruent with U.S. schooling but often find it difficult to work with others. The teacher who can find a common ground with diverse students will promote their further education. Relationships between individuals or groups of different cultures are built through commitment, enjoyment of diversity, and a willingness to communicate. The teacher, acting as intercultural educator, accepts and promotes cultural content in the classroom as a valid and vital component of the instructional process and helps students to achieve within the cultural context of the school.

 **Classroom Glimpse**

### SCHOOLING IN VIETNAM

American schools may be a shock for children—and for parents—who have immigrated from Vietnam. In Vietnam children go to school six days a week for about four hours. In addition to academic subjects, they also are taught traditional manners and customs, including respect for their elders, family, and community. Most school days begin with the teacher calling on students to stand and answer a question; this also comprises the final assessment on Saturday. Students sit together and chant during lessons. Most schools have no playground equipment or extracurricular activities. (Accessed on May 19, 2010, from www.pocanticohills.org/vietnam/vietnam.htm)

**The Impact of Physical Geography on Cultural Practices**   A social group must develop the knowledge, ideas, and skills it needs to survive in the kind of environment the group inhabits. The geographical environment or physical habitat challenges the group to adapt to or modify the world to meet its needs. When the Native Americans were the sole inhabitants of the North American continent, a wide variety of cultures existed, a necessary response to the variety in the environment. The Iroquois were a village people who lived surrounded by tall wooden palisades. The Chumash, in contrast, had a leisurely seashore existence on the California coast where fishing was plentiful and the climate moderate. Still a third group, the Plains Indians, were a nomadic people who followed the bison. Each group's culture was adapted for success in its own specific environment.

Classrooms constitute physical environments. These environments have an associated culture. In a room in which the desks are in straight lines facing forward, participants are acculturated to listen as individuals and to respond when spoken to by the teacher. This may be a difficult environment for a young Pueblo child whose learning takes place largely in the communal courtyards outside comfortable adobe dwellings and who is taught traditional recipes by a mother or grandmother or the secrets of tribal lore in an underground kiva by the men of the village. The physical environments in which learning takes place vary widely from one culture to another.

**Intragroup and Intergroup Cultural Differences**    Even among individuals from the same general cultural background, there are intragroup differences that affect their worldviews. Some student populations have very different cultures despite a shared ethnic background. Such is the case at Montebello High School in the Los Angeles area:

> Students at Montebello . . . may look to outsiders as a mostly homogeneous population—93 percent Latino, 70 percent low-income—but the 2,974 Latino students are split between those who are connected to their recent immigrant roots and those who are more Americanized. On the "TJ" (for Tijuana) side of the campus, students speak Spanish, take ESL classes, and participate in soccer, *folklorico* dancing, and the Spanish club. On the other side of campus, students speak mostly English, play football and basketball, and participate in student government. The two groups are not [mutually] hostile . . . but, as senior Lucia Rios says, "it's like two countries." The difference in values between the two groups stems from their families' values—the recent immigrants are focused on economic survival and do not have the cash to pay for extracurricular activities. . . . Another difference is musical taste (soccer players listen to Spanish music in the locker room, whereas football players listen to heavy metal and rap). (Hayasaki, 2004, pp. A1, A36–A37)

In the preceding example, the immigrants who had arrived within the last three to five years still referred to Mexico as home. Most of these students were monolingual in Spanish, with varying levels of English proficiency. In contrast, the U.S.-born Mexican-American students were English speakers—although they had Mexican last names, they were strongly acculturated into mainstream U.S. values and manifested few overt Mexican cultural symbols. Each of these groups could be considered a microculture within the larger microculture of people of Mexican descent living within the United States.

In this case, social identification and language usage, as well as dress, were the markers of the distinct microcultures. As immigrants enter American life, they make conscious or unconscious choices about which aspects of their culture to preserve and which to modify. These decisions are a response to cultural contact.

## Looking at Culture from the Inside Out

**External Elements of Culture**    External elements of culture (e.g., shelter, clothing, food, arts and literature, religious structures, government, technology, language) are relatively easily identified as cultural markers. Certainly young immigrant children would feel comfortable if external elements of their home culture were prominently displayed in the classroom or school. A display of Mexican-style paper cutouts as decoration in a classroom, for example, usually would be viewed in a positive way and not as a token of superficial cultural appropriation.

Indeed, external elements of culture are visible and obvious, to the extent that these are often used as symbols of cultural diversity. How many times does a printed flyer for a Chinese guest speaker have to display a bamboo border before this becomes hackneyed? These visible markers are "ethnic," as in "ethnic food." When one goes out for "ethnic food," does one eat roast beef and potatoes—quintessentially British food? When these external symbols are marked only for minorities, the mainstream culture thinks of itself as "culturally neutral," whereas those displaying external elements of microcultures are considered "ethnic." Thus, European-American culture is maintained as the norm.

**Internal Elements of Culture**    Internal elements of culture (e.g., values, customs, worldview, mores, beliefs and expectations, rites and rituals, patterns of nonverbal communication, social

*Bringing the students' culture into the classroom can motivate students to value their heritage.*

roles and status, gender roles, family structure, patterns of work and leisure) are harder to identify as cultural markers because they are intangible. Yet these can be as persistent and emotionally loaded as external symbols such as flags or religious icons. In fact, behaviors and attitudes that are misinterpreted can be considered potentially more damaging than misunderstandings about overt symbols, especially with people from cultures that are skilled in reading subtle behavior signals.

 **Classroom Glimpse**

### CAN'T YOU TELL I'M BORED?

In an English-language development class with beginning middle school English learners, Iris Schaffer pointed to a picture with birds on a tree. "Is this a bird or a tree?" she asked. "How many leaves are there on the ground? What is the color of the leaves?"

From the student's facial expressions and voice tones, a visitor noted that they were bored and showed little interest in learning. To be asked these types of questions at their age could be insulting. The question was, why didn't the teacher know the students were bored? Were their behaviors and attitudes too subtle for the teacher to read? Was she unable to decipher these internal elements of culture? (Adapted from Fu, 2004, pp. 9–10)

## Cultural Diversity: Historical and Contemporary Perspectives

The rhetoric seeking to explain school failure of minority children has changed over the years. Because racial explanations have largely failed—although even as late as the turn of the twenty-first century, several psychologists tried to resurrect racial inferiority theory—there have been attempts to find other explanations based more on cultural than racial differences.

**From Racial Inferiority to Cultural Inferiority**    After Binet's research on intelligence at the turn of the twentieth century, researchers became convinced that inherited racial differences were an explanation for the differential success of students. This became a rationale for unequal school facilities. The genetic inferiority argument, now discredited, assumes that certain populations do not possess the appropriate genes for high intellectual performance.

After the 1954 *Brown v. Board of Education* decision officially signaled the end of segregated schools, the continued lack of school achievement on the part of racial minorities in the United States was attributed not to racial differences but to the fact that families originating in poor, working-class, urban areas were holders of a culture that was inherently inferior (Josephs, 2004). This was a *cultural deprivation* or *cultural deficit* model—essentially, it blamed the poor for the lack of resources in the home. Conveniently, it could be used to blame cultural minorities as well as racial minorities.

**Cultural Incompatibility Theory**    The next theory, *cultural incompatibility* or *cultural mismatch,* denied the implication of an inherent inferiority in minority cultures but posited that the difference in home culture versus school culture was one of the reasons minority students do poorly (Irvine, 1990). The cultural mismatch perspective maintains that cultures vary and that some of the skills learned in one culture may transfer to a second, but that other skills will be of little value or, worse, interfere with assimilation to the new culture.

Cultural mismatch was quickly generalized from its origin in race theory to all cultural differences, including those involving language. Furthermore, unlike cultural deprivation theory, it placed no explicit value judgment on the culture of either the school or the home, merely stating that when teachers and students do not share the same culture, the different cultural behaviors performed by the other are open to misinterpretation because neither party realizes they may be operating on different cultural codes.

The concept that minority students experience a cultural dissonance between their home and school culture is well documented (Heath, 1999). Unfortunately, this theory has left the onus on teachers to change conditions within the classroom to accommodate the students' cultures, which has proved to be difficult when students from many cultures are schooled in the same room. The result has been "business as usual," with the culture of the schools remaining intact along with the expectation that the culture of the home will change.

**The Contextual Interaction Model**    Another explanation posits that achievement is a function of the interaction between two cultures. The contextual interaction model states the values of each are not static but instead adapt to one another when contact occurs. This is the origin of the idea that teachers should accommodate instruction to students as they acculturate.

**Issues of Power and Status**    In classrooms during the monolingual era, students spoke one language or remained silent. The institution controlled the goals and purposes of students' second-language acquisition. There was no question who had the power—the teacher, the authorities, and the language sanctioned by the school (see Darder, 1991; McCarty, 2005).

As for theories of cultural incompatibility, in retrospect these were too narrowly focused on the student, the school, and the home, ignoring the larger issue of inequity of resources in society. The "cure" for school failure in the cultural dissonance model was to align the cultures of the home and school more congruently—and because teachers and schools could not accomplish that mission in the short time allotted for teacher multicultural education, the burden was put again to the families to assimilate more rapidly. Hence the classic emphasis put on the individual to transcend his or her social class.

As soon as the limitations of this liberalist model became apparent, a conservative administration instituted rigorous testing, setting into motion the specter of failure not only for individuals but also for entire schools in minority communities. This distracted schools from the mission of cultural congruence and left the issues unresolved, emphasizing instead standardized testing.

**The Impact of Ethnic Politics**   In the postmodern shift, power circulates, just as dual-language acquisition circulates power between peoples and among cultures. Instead of the pretense that power is nonnegotiable, unavailable, and neutral, communities sought to gain the power to speak, to use a public voice for their self-determined ends. This resulted in the movement toward charter schools, by which families can choose to exit the public schools. Over 2,200 charter schools now operate in many poor and working-class communities, educating over 750,000 children nationwide (Center for Educational Reform, 2000).

Some charter schools have done a better job than the public schools of fostering ethnic pride. One student from a small middle school in Oakland, California, put it this way:

> It was just really like a community setting . . . like we were learning at home . . . with a bunch of our friends. They had really nice teachers who were, you know, mostly Chicano and Chicana. . . . We could relate to them. They know your culture, your background. [They] talk to your parents and your parents trust them. It's like a family. (Wexler & Huerta, 2002, p. 100)

The pursuit of local schools that reflect the values of the parent community has led to serious alternatives to the dream of the public school that can educate all children with equity under one roof. Many advocates of charter schools no longer believe that the children of diversity can wrest a high-quality education from neighborhood schools that are underfunded and mediocre. The notion of empowerment has taken many ethnic communities down the path of separatism (Fuller, 2003). Overall, charter schools have proven to be of mixed success.

## Political and Socioeconomic Factors Affecting English Learners and Their Families

By the year 2010, one of every three Americans will be African American, Hispanic American, or Asian American. This represents a dramatic change from the image of the United States throughout its history. Immigration, together with differing birthrates among various populations, is responsible for this demographic shift. Along with the change in racial and ethnic composition has come a dramatic change in the languages spoken in the United States as well as the languages heard in U.S. schools.

These changing demographics are seen as positive or negative depending on one's point of view. Some economists have found that immigrants contribute considerably to the national economy by filling low-wage jobs, spurring investment and job creation, revitalizing once-decaying communities, and paying billions annually in taxes. Unfortunately, the money generated from federal taxes is not returned to the local communities most affected by immigration to pay for schools, hospitals, and social services needed by newcomers (Shuit & McConnell, 1992). The resultant stress on these services may cause residents to view newcomers negatively.

In the midst of changing demographics in the United States, immigrants and economically disadvantaged minorities within the country face such challenges as voting and citizenship status; family income, employment, and educational attainment; housing; and health care availability.

**Culture and Gender Issues**   Parents of English learners often work long hours outside the home, and some families simply are unable to dedicate time each evening to help students complete school assignments. Many young people find themselves working long hours outside the home to help support the family or take care of siblings while parents work double shifts. The role of surrogate caretaker often falls disproportionately on young women, compromising their academic potential. Some immigrant families favor the academic success of sons over daughters, to the dismay of teachers in the United States who espouse equality of opportunity for women. This issue may be more acute as high school students contemplate attending college.

Other issues have emerged as immigrants enter U.S. schools from ever more diverse cultures. Some girls from traditional cultures are forbidden by their families to wear physical education attire that reveals bare legs. Male exchange students from Muslim cultures may be uncomfortable working in a mixed-gender cooperative learning group in the classroom. Parents who have adopted children from the People's Republic of China may request heritage-language services from the local school district. Multiple issues of language and culture complicate schooling for English learners.

**Poverty among Minority Groups**   A key difficulty for many minorities is poverty. Almost one-quarter (24 percent) of African Americans and over one-fifth (22 percent) of Hispanic Americans live in poverty (U.S. Census Bureau, 2004). Worse, Blacks and Hispanics are even more likely not to be simply poor, but to be *extremely* poor—with incomes under half the poverty level of Whites. In fact, at 16.1 percent, the share of the Black population that is extremely poor is over four times that of non-Hispanic Whites (3.7 percent) and well above that of Hispanics (10.5 percent) (Henwood, 1997).

Poverty hits minority children particularly hard. In 2003, 12.9 million children in the United States lived below the poverty line, and more than one out of every six American children (17.6 percent) were poor. In numbers, 4.2 million poor children are non-Hispanic White, 3.9 million are Black, and 4.1 million are Hispanic. However, the proportion of minority children who are poor is higher: 34.1 percent of Black children, 29.0 percent of Latino children, 12.5 percent of Asian children, and 9.8 percent of non-Hispanic White children.

Poverty does not mean merely inadequate income; rather, it engenders a host of issues, including underemployment, insufficient income and jobs with limited opportunity, homelessness, lack of health insurance, inadequate education, and poor nutrition. Poor children are at least twice as likely as non-poor children to suffer stunted growth or lead poisoning or to be kept back in school. They score significantly lower on reading, math, and vocabulary tests when compared with similar non-poor children (Children's Defense Fund, 2005). However, not all poverty can be linked to these difficulties; some minorities continue in poverty because of social and political factors in the country at large, such as racism and discrimination.

Poverty affects the ability of the family to devote resources to educational effort and stacks the deck against minority student success. Demographic trends ensure that this will be a continuing problem in the United States. Almost three-quarters (74.0 percent) of the Hispanic population are under thirty-five years of age, compared with a little more than half (51.7 percent) of the non-Hispanic White population. The average Hispanic female is well within childbearing age, and Hispanic children constitute the largest growing school population. Therefore, the educational achievement of Hispanic children is of particular concern.

## Educational Issues Involving English Learners beyond the Classroom

What obligation does a community have toward non-English-speaking children? When education is the only means of achieving social mobility for the children of immigrants, these young people must be given the tools necessary to participate in the community at large. When school dropout rates exceed 50 percent among minority populations, it seems evident that the schools are not providing an adequate avenue of advancement. Clearly, some English learners do succeed: Asian-American students are overwhelmingly represented in college attendance, whereas Hispanics are underrepresented.

Individual states are addressing the obligation to educate all students by adhering to content standards documents, written by mandate of the 2001 No Child Left Behind legislation. Nevertheless, children continue to receive different treatment in the public schools. The structure of schooling creates equity problems, all the way from segregative tracking procedures to the day-to-day operation of classrooms, in which some students' voices are heard while others are silenced. These structural components of schools must be addressed lest the belief continue that achievement problems reside solely within students.

In schools, underachievement, the "overachievement" myth, segregation, overreferral to special education, lack of access to the core curricula, and little support for the home language are key concerns. These phenomena may occur because of the ways in which schools and classrooms promote unequal classroom experiences for students. In response to the perception that some students underachieve or overachieve or drop out or are pushed out, schools have designed various mechanisms to help students succeed. Some of these have been successful, others problematic.

The economy of the United States in the future will rest more on Asian-American and Hispanic-American workers than at present. As a consequence, the education of these populations will become increasingly important. Consider that in 2000, 38.8 percent of students enrolled in public elementary and secondary schools were minorities—an increase of 30 percent from 1986, largely due to the growth in the Hispanic population (National Center for Education Statistics [NCES], 2002).

Of these minorities, 87.6 percent of Asian Americans have a high school degree and 49.8 percent have bachelor degrees. In contrast, only 57 percent of Hispanics have high school diplomas and 11.4 percent have college degrees, whereas 85 percent of non-Hispanic Whites, on the other hand, have high school diplomas and over a quarter (27.6 percent) have bachelor degrees (U.S. Census Bureau, 2004). With these numbers, the extent of the problem becomes clearer.

**Underachievement—Retention, Placement, and Promotion Policies**  Unfortunately, some students are at risk of retention due to underachievement almost immediately on entering school. In 1995, of the 13.7 percent of children who spoke a language other than English in the home, one student in ten (10 percent) was retained at least one grade. (The same percentage was also true for children who speak English at home.) However, retention rates for English learners differed according to language: Spanish, 10.4 percent; other European, 4.3 percent; Asian, 2.4 percent; other, 6.6 percent (NCES, 2000). Thus, Spanish-speaking students are much more at risk of school failure than Asians. On the other side of the coin, students are also differentially distributed in advanced placement courses, a type of "in-house" promotion.

*Tracking* offers very different types of instruction depending on students' placement in academic or general education courses. To justify this, educators have argued that tracking is a realistic, efficient response to an increasingly diverse student population. However, tracking has been found to be a major contributor to the continuing gaps in achievement between minorities and European Americans (Oakes, 1985, 1992).

**Underachievement—ELD as Compensatory Education**    The impetus behind the success of the original Bilingual Education Act was that language-minority students needed compensatory education to remediate linguistic "deficiencies." However, compensatory programs are often reduced in scope, content, and pace, and students are not challenged enough, nor given enough of the curriculum to be able to move to mainstream classes.

The view that ELD is compensatory education is all too common. As a part of ELD programs, a portion of the instructional day is usually reserved for ELD instruction. Too often the ELD instruction is given by teaching assistants who have not had professional preparation in ELD teaching, and the instruction has consisted of skill-and-drill worksheets and other decontextualized methods.

*Inclusion* of English learners in mainstream classrooms and challenging educational programs is now the trend. In a study of good educational practice for LEP students, researchers found numerous schools that have successfully been educating English learners to high standards (McLeod, 1995). In these schools, programs for English learners were an integral part of the whole school program, neither conceptually nor physically separate from the rest of the school.

> The exemplary schools have devised creative ways to both include LEP students centrally in the educational program and meet their needs for language instruction and modified curriculum. Programs for LEP students are so carefully crafted and intertwined with the school's other offerings that it is impossible in many cases to point to "the LEP program" and describe it apart from the general program. (McLeod, 1995, p. 4)

Several reform efforts have attempted to dismantle some of the compensatory education and tracking programs previously practiced in schools. These have included accelerated schools, cooperative learning, restructured schools, and "untracking." A particularly noteworthy high school program is Advancement Via Individual Determination (AVID). This "untracking" program places low-achieving students (who are primarily from low-income and ethnic or language-minority backgrounds) in the same college preparatory academic program as high-achieving students (who are primarily from middle- or upper-middle-income and "Anglo" backgrounds) (Mehan & Hubbard, 1999).

**Underachievement—Dropping Out of High School**    An unfortunate and direct result of being schooled in an unfamiliar language is that some students begin falling behind their expected grade levels, putting them at risk eventually. Students who repeat at least one grade are more likely to drop out of school. Every year across the country, a dangerously high percentage of students—disproportionately poor and minority—disappear from the educational pipeline before graduating from high school. Nationally, only about 68 percent of all students who enter ninth grade will graduate "on time" with regular diplomas in twelfth grade.

Whereas the graduation rate for White students is 75 percent, only approximately half of Latino students earn regular diplomas alongside their classmates. Even though California reports a robust overall graduation rate of 86.9 percent, researchers at the Harvard Civil Rights Project have claimed that this figure dramatically underestimates the actual numbers of dropouts and that graduation rates in individual districts and schools—particularly those with high minority concentrations—remain at crisis-level proportions.

Recent research reveals disturbing dropout rates for minorities in the United States. For the predominantly Latino populations in New York City and Houston school districts, the graduation rates are 38 and 40 percent, respectively, and lower still for the predominantly Black districts of Oakland (30.4%), Atlanta (39.6%), Cleveland (30%), and Columbus (34.4%) (Orfield, Losen, Wald, & Swanson, 2004). These data suggest that students of color will be underrepresented in higher education for years to come.

An independent study by Dr. Julie Mendoza of the University of California All Campus Consortium on Research for Diversity (UC/ACCORD) finds that in the Los Angeles Unified School District (LAUSD) the exodus of Los Angeles youth from school is especially pronounced between grades 9 and 10; only 48 percent of Black and Latino students who start ninth grade complete grade 12. Of the Black and Latino youth who complete high school in LAUSD, only one in five has met the curriculum requirements to qualify for admission to a four-year public university in California (Losen & Wald, 2005).

An important marketplace repercussion from dropout statistics is the differential rate of employment of these two groups: Sixty-one percent of high school dropouts are in the labor force versus 80 percent of graduates who were not in college (Kaufman, Alt, & Chapman, 2004).

 **Classroom Glimpse**

### SEGREGATION AND DROPPING OUT

The predominantly Puerto-Rican community in North Philadelphia is located in an economically depressed part of the city that is plagued by many of the problems of low-income urban neighborhoods across the United States. Latinos make up between 85 and 99 percent of the total student population in this community, and the Latino dropout rate is disproportionately high in the district. According to a Harvard University report that examined issues of racial justice in the United States, such segregation of Latinos in poorly performing schools in low-income neighborhoods is relatively common across the nation. In fact, it is pervasive in cities in the Northeast (Harvard Civil Rights Project, online at www.civilrightsproject.harvard.edu/research/reseg03/resegregation03.php). (Freeman, 2004, p. 88)

Noting the alarmingly high percentage of Hispanic dropouts, U.S. Secretary of Education Richard W. Riley in 1995 initiated a special project to study issues related to the problem. In its final report, *No More Excuses*, the Hispanic Dropout Project (1998) explicated the continuing stereotypes, myths, and excuses that surround Hispanic-American youth and their families:

What we saw and what people told us confirmed what well-established research has also found: Popular stereotypes—which would place the blame for school dropout on Hispanic students, their families, and language background, and that would allow people to shrug their shoulders as if to say that that was an enormous, insoluble problem or one that would go away by itself—are just plain wrong. (p. 3)

The Hispanic Dropout Project (1998) found that teachers may make one of two choices that undermine minority students' school achievement: either to blame the students and their families for school failure or to excuse the students' poor performance, citing factors such as low socioeconomic status or lack of English proficiency. This latter attitude, although well meaning, is particularly harmful as it does not allow students access to cognitively demanding instruction (Lockwood, 2000).

The three recommendations the Hispanic Dropout Project (1998) report made for teachers are consistent with the principles, concepts, and strategies outlined in this text: (1) Provide high-quality curriculum and instruction—methods and strategies presented in Part II of this book; (2) become knowledgeable about students and their families, as discussed in Part III; and (3) receive high-quality professional development—an ongoing task for which this entire text can be an impetus. The online *Transforming Education for Hispanic Youth: Exemplary Practices, Programs, and Schools* (Lockwood & Secada, 1999) provides more in-depth information about, and examples of, exemplary schools for Hispanic-American youth.

**Underachievement–Difficulties in Higher Education**    Several measures of achievement reveal discrepancies in the achievement of Whites in comparison with ethnic minorities. Ethnic minority groups, except for Asian Americans, attain lower levels of higher education. Of college students in 1996, Latinos represented 11.7 percent of community college students and only 5.7 percent in four-year institutions. In 2001, of the 62 percent of high school graduates who attended college, 54.6 percent were White and only 5.6 percent were of Hispanic origin (National Center for Education Statistics [NCES], 2005).

As of 2003, young Blacks and Hispanics (ages eighteen to twenty-four) participated in postsecondary education at a lower rate than Whites: Blacks at 26 percent, Hispanics at 22 percent, compared to 38 percent for Whites. Participation rates for Hispanic young men have declined since 1974 (NCES, 2005). Only about one in six Latinos who attend college ultimately graduates (Thernstrom & Thernstrom, 2003). Low educational levels have resulted in poor subsequent incomes and a lower likelihood of attaining high-prestige occupations.

In an encouraging note, Hispanic students represent the largest and fastest-growing minority group taking the SAT and now account for 13.5 percent (206,584) of all SAT takers compared to 7.8 percent (94,677) ten years ago, showing that the number of Hispanics taking the test has more than doubled between 1999 and 2009 (College Board, 2009).

**Underachievement–Difficulties Attaining Management Status**    Hispanic Americans represent only a small number of faculty members and administrators in higher education; they hold 3.3 percent of such positions (NCES, 2003). Whether due to English-language limitations or other structural problems in society, Latino men hold only 0.7 percent of top management positions in U.S. society, and Latinas only 0.1 percent (Cockcroft, 1995). As of 2007, only four CEOs of Fortune 500 companies were Latino, and these may have included Spaniards or other non-U.S. minorities (Cole, 2007). There were also only four Black men and one Black woman in CEO positions.

It is unclear whether underachievement is the real problem, which may instead be racism—even ethnic minorities who achieve in school may not be able to attain positions of responsibility in society. It is equally unclear to what extent English proficiency—or lack of it—is linked to underachievement and discrimination.

**The "Overachievement" Myth**   A pernicious view ascribes exceptional achievement to a specific group—Asian Americans. The term *model minority* has been coined for Asian Americans, connoting a supergroup whose members have succeeded in U.S. society despite a long history of racial oppression. Asian-American students are seen as academic superstars who win academic distinction and are overrepresented in elite institutions of higher education (Suzuki, 1989).

This stereotype plays out in at least two ways with equally damaging results. First, ascribing a "whiz kid" image to students can mask their individual needs and problems and lead the teacher to assume a student needs little or no help. This may ultimately lead to neglect, isolation, delinquency, or inadequate preparation for the labor market among these students (Feng, 1994).

Second, lumping all Asian Americans together into this stereotype ignores the different cultural, language, economic, and immigration statuses of the various groups and severely limits those most in need of help. Among Southeast Asian students, the Khmer and the Lao tend to have a grade point average (GPA) below that of White majority students, whereas Vietnamese, Chinese-Vietnamese, Japanese, Korean, Chinese, and Hmong students tend to achieve well above this GPA level (Trueba, Cheng, & Ima, 1993).

---

**Best Practice**   COUNTERING THE MODEL MINORITY MYTH

To avoid reenacting the model minority myth in the classroom:

- Treat students as individuals.
- Do not ascribe high or low expectations based on national origin or ethnicity.
- Recognize that Asian/Pacific Island-American students speak different languages and come from different cultural areas.
- Take time to learn about the languages and cultures of students to appreciate their differences. (Nash, 1991)

---

"Asian-American Children: What Teachers Should Know" (Feng, 1994) provides general information about Asian-American students and a list of practices to help teachers become more knowledgeable about Asian cultures. Equally helpful is O'Connor's (2004) "Understanding Discrimination against Asian Americans."

**Segregated Schools**   Although during the 1970s and 1980s districts were working at desegregating their schools, the 1990s witnessed an increasing number of court cases that released districts from these efforts (Weiler, 1998). Inequity follows segregation. In a study in the Boston metro area, "97 percent of the schools with less than a tenth white students faced concentrated poverty compared to 1 percent of the schools with less than a tenth minority students" (Orfield & Lee, 2005, n.p.). In addition, segregation makes it difficult for English learners to be grouped with native speakers of English during the school day.

Minority students typically live in racially isolated neighborhoods and are more likely to attend segregated schools. Over one-third of Hispanic students (38 percent) and Black students (37 percent) attended schools with minority enrollments of 90 to 100 percent. Seventy-seven percent of Hispanics and 71 percent of Blacks were enrolled in schools where minorities constitute 50 percent or more of the population.

Therefore, nearly a half-century after *Brown v. Board of Education,* a student who is Black, Latino, or Native American remains much less likely to succeed in school. A major factor is a disparity of resources—inner-city schools with large minority populations have been found to have higher percentages of first-year teachers, greater enrollments, fewer library resources, and less in-school parental involvement, all characteristics that have been shown to relate to school success (U.S. Government Accounting Office, 2002).

 **Classroom Glimpse**

### HIGH SCHOOL APARTHEID?

Marshall Cox teaches tenth-grade world cultures in a Los Angeles high school. The high school is situated in a neighborhood that is mixed Hispanic and African-American families and has a science magnet program that attracts high-achieving science students from various other parts of the city. The science students, mostly Asian and European Americans, socialize with their own groups during school and at lunch, as do students of the other ethnicities. Even in his world cultures classes, which are not specific to the regular or magnet program, students from the two programs attend classes at separate times. As part of his responsibilities as a world cultures teacher, Marshall would like to see students from the various ethnicities communicate interculturally more often. Should he try to be proactive? If so, what can he do?

**Overreferral to Special Education**     Referrals and placements in special education have been disproportionate for culturally and linguistically different students. Various explanations have been offered for this overreferral: language problems, poor school progress, academic or cognitive difficulties, low level of acculturation, inadequate assessment, or special learning problems (Malavé, 1991). Biased assessment can result in negative evaluation of English learners, especially when tests are given in English to students without sufficient exposure to it, include language or concepts that favor the middle-class native English speaker, or are predicated on models of cultural deprivation or other deficit models (Valenzuela & Baca, 2004).

**Access to Core Curricula**     Access to the core curriculum is essential for English learners to make adequate progress in school. This means that ELD activities cannot stand in the way of other academic subjects. A student who is pulled out of the class to receive ESL services, for example, cannot miss social studies class. Nor can a student who arrives in a large urban high school without adequate English proficiency be denied an appropriate mathematics curriculum. Meeting the needs of English learners with SDAIE instruction is a challenge that must be addressed.

Issues of race and class are compounded by ideas about language in U.S. schools. For example, compared to White and Asian students, Latino students are less likely to be placed in education tracks with rigorous curricula that prepare them for college (Haycock, Jerald, & Huang, 2001). Researchers have pointed out that in spite of multiple initiatives addressing the lack of school success by Hispanics during the 1990s, the achievement gap for Hispanic students is still very much an issue. Hinojosa, Robles-Piña, and Edmonson (2009) commented, "Although the disparity between Hispanic student achievement and that of White and Asian students has been an area of concern for both policy makers and educators for a number of years, the improvement in this area has been minimal" (p. 3).

**Little Support for the First Language**   In U.S. schools, second-language and foreign language learning are neglected in the core curriculum, unlike, for example, in European schools, in which many elementary children are given foreign language classes. U.S. students who are already proficient in a heritage language bring a rich resource to academia that is being tapped now only in two-way immersion programs. Foreign language in the elementary school (FLES) is an academic subject in the United States in elite schools (private schools in New York and Washington, D.C., for example), where French (or, less commonly, Japanese) is offered, as well as in privileged environments such as the wealthy suburbs of New York, Boston, San Francisco, and Minneapolis and in university towns such as Chapel Hill, North Carolina, and Austin, Texas.

Yet the urban school districts that do not support maintenance programs in heritage languages are causing students to lose the very language resources that are difficult to reestablish as foreign languages at the high school level. Access to the core curriculum is the right of all learners—and in the case of English learners, that core curriculum should include language classes in the heritage as well as perhaps a third language.

The issues just outlined offer some examples of the complexity involved in educating students of diverse primary languages and cultures. The current emphasis on standards heightens the tensions inherent in such a project. On the positive side, students have a right to a high standard of rich, challenging instruction no matter what linguistic and cultural resources they bring to schooling. On the other hand, the emphasis on high standards must be matched with allocation of funds so that teachers are given the resources they need to accomplish these lofty goals.

The conclusion is inescapable: The educational system of the United States has been fundamentally weak in serving the fastest growing school-age populations. Today's minority students are entering school with significantly different social and economic backgrounds from those of previous student populations and therefore require educators to modify their teaching approaches to ensure that these students have access to the American dream.

These issues involving the education of English learners will not be resolved solely through the efforts of individual teachers, but require a determined effort on the part of educators as a social movement to reverse discriminatory educational policies and achieve full funding for the educational services that English learners deserve. This will require reversal of the damaging educational politics of neoliberalism over the past twenty years (Anyon, 1994).

# Cultural Contact

Since the 1980s, an unprecedented flow of immigrants and refugees has entered the United States. One of the impacts of this immigration is that many school districts not only have students speaking three or more languages in a single classroom, but they also have students who speak the same non-English language but who come from different cultures. School officials have found, for example, that many immigrants from Central America do not follow the same pattern of school performance as Mexican-American students. These demographic issues provoke the question of whether we can understand how to increase the school success of all students by studying the process of cultural contact.

As immigrants enter American life, they make conscious or unconscious choices about which aspects of their culture to preserve and which to modify, and these decisions affect learning. The contact between the home culture and the school culture influences schooling. The immigrant culture can be swallowed up (*assimilation*), immigrants can adapt to the dominant culture (*acculturation*), both may adapt to each other (*accommodation*), or they may coexist (*pluralism* or *biculturalism*). Contact between cultures is often fraught with misunderstanding, but it can also be positive and enriching. Means of mediation or resolution must be found to help students benefit from one another's cultural knowledge as well as alleviate cultural conflict.

## Fears about Cultural Adaptation

Pryor (2002) captured the nature of immigrant parents' concerns about their children's adjustment to life in the United States:

> In the United States, some immigrant parents live in fear that their children will be corrupted by what they believe to be the materialistic and individualistic dominant culture, become alienated from their families, and fall prey to drugs and promiscuity. One Jordanian mother stated, "I tell my son (who is 8 years old) not to use the restroom in school. I tell him it is because he might catch germs there that he could bring home, and make the whole family ill. I really am afraid he may get drugs from other kids in the restroom." (p. 187)

Many immigrant parents are overwhelmed with personal, financial, and work-related problems; they may miss their homelands and family members abroad and have few resources to which to turn for help. They struggle to maintain their dignity in the face of humiliation, frustration, and loneliness. In the process of coming to terms with life in a foreign country, they may be at odds with the assimilation or acculturation processes their children are experiencing, causing family conflict.

## Processes of Cultural Contact

**Assimilation**    *Cultural assimilation* is the process by which individuals adopt the behaviors, values, beliefs, and lifestyle of the dominant culture, neglecting or abandoning their own culture in the process. *Structural assimilation* is participation in the social, political, and economic institutions and organizations of mainstream society. It is structural assimilation that has been problematic for many immigrants, especially for groups other than White Protestant immigrants from northern and western Europe.

Individuals may make a choice concerning their degree of cultural assimilation. However, the dominant society determines the extent of structural assimilation. These two related but different concepts have important consequences in classrooms. Teachers may be striving to have students assimilate but be blind to the fact that some of their students will not succeed because of attitudes and structures of the dominant society.

**Acculturation**    When individuals *acculturate*, they adapt to a second culture without necessarily giving up their first culture. It is an additive process in which individuals' rights to participate in their own heritage are preserved (Finnan, 1987). Schools are the primary places in which children of various cultures learn about the mainstream culture. According to Cortés (1993):

Acculturation . . . should be a primary goal of education. Schools have an obligation to help students acculturate because additive acculturation contributes to individual empowerment and expanded life choices. But schools should not seek subtractive assimilation, which can lead to personal and cultural disempowerment by eroding students' multicultural abilities to function effectively both within the mainstream and within their own ethnic milieus. Although assimilation is acceptable, it should be regarded as a student's choice and not as something for the school to impose. (p. 4)

**Accommodation**   A two-way process, *accommodation* involves adaptations by members of the mainstream culture in response to a minority culture, who in turn accept some cultural change in adapting to the mainstream. Thus, accommodation is a mutual process. To make accommodation a viable alternative in schools, teachers need to demonstrate that they are receptive to learning from the diverse cultures in their midst.

 **Classroom Glimpse**

## ACCOMMODATING STUDENTS' CULTURE

[I]n non-[American]-Indian classes students are given opportunities to ask the teacher questions in front of the class, and do so. Indian students are given fewer opportunities for this because when they do have the opportunity, they don't use it. Rather, the teacher of Indians allows more periods in which she is available for individual students to approach her alone and ask their questions where no one else can hear them. (Philips, 1972, p. 383)

**Biculturalism**   Being able to function successfully in two cultures constitutes biculturalism. Darder (1991) defined *biculturalism* as

a process wherein individuals learn to function in two distinct sociocultural environments: their primary culture, and that of the dominant mainstream culture of the society in which they live. It represents the process by which bicultural human beings mediate between the dominant discourse of educational institutions and the realities they must face as members of subordinate cultures. (pp. 48–49)

Everyone is to some extent bicultural. At a minimum level, everyone who works outside the home functions daily in two cultures—personal (home) and professional (work). For some individuals, the distance between the cultures of work and home are almost indistinguishable, whereas for others the separation is great. For example, Native-American children who were sent to Bureau of Indian Affairs boarding schools often experienced great difficulties in adjusting to the disparate cultures of home and school.

What is it like to be bicultural in the United States? Bicultural people are sometimes viewed with distrust. Even parents may feel threatened by their bicultural children. Appalachian families who moved to large cities to obtain work often pressured their children to maintain an agrarian, preindustrial lifestyle, a culture that is in many ways inconsistent with urban environments (Pasternak, 1994). Similarly, families from rural Mexico may seek to maintain traditional values even as their children adopt behaviors from the macroculture. The process of becoming bicultural is not without stress, especially for students who are expected to internalize dissimilar, perhaps conflicting values.

## Psychological and Social–Emotional Issues Involving Cultural Contact

**Phases of Acculturation**    Reactions to a new culture vary, but there are distinct stages of emotional ups and downs in the process of experiencing a different culture: Typical emotions and behaviors begin with elation or excitement, move to anxiety or disorientation, and culminate in some degree of adjustment (Levine & Adelman, 1982). Students go through these same emotional stages, with varied intensity depending on the degree of similarity between home and school cultures, the individual child, and the teacher.

The first state, *euphoria* or the *honeymoon period,* may result from the excitement of and fascination with the customs, foods, and sights of the new culture. The next stage, *culture shock* or *cultural fatigue,* may follow as the newcomer is increasingly frustrated by disorienting cultural cues. Deprivation of the familiar may cause a loss of self-esteem, depression, anger, or withdrawal. The severity of this shock will vary as a function of the personality of the individual, the emotional support available, and the perceived or actual differences between the two cultures (see Box 8.1).

The final stage, *adjustment* or *adaptation* to the new culture, can take months or years. Ideally, the newcomer borrows habits, customs, and characteristics from the new culture, resulting in a feeling of comfort in negotiating everyday activities such as going to school and shopping. On the other hand, individuals who do not adjust may feel lonely, frustrated, and repulsed by aspects of the new culture. Eventually, successful adaptation results in newcomers being able to actively express themselves and to create a full range of meaning in the situation.

In the classroom, students may show culture shock as withdrawal, depression, or anger. Mental fatigue may result from continually straining to comprehend the new culture. Individuals may need time to process personal and emotional as well as academic experiences. The teacher must take great care to not belittle or reject a student who is experiencing culture shock.

## Resolving Problems of Cultural Contact

Students experiencing cultural conflict may meet racism and anti-immigration sentiment and behaviors ranging from subtle innuendos to verbal abuse and threats, even physical violence. Schools are crucial to the resolution of hate crime because the young are perpetrators and the schools are staging grounds. Policies, curricula, and antiracism programs are needed to moderate conflicts when cultures come into contact.

**The Culturally Receptive School**    In general, research suggests that substantive changes in attitudes, behaviors, and achievement occur only when the entire school adopts a multicultural

**Box 8.1**    Example of Concept: Language and Culture Shock

Zacarian (2004) related the story of one student experiencing language and culture shock and the effect it had on his personality: "One student, whom I'll call Jin, shared some powerful feelings with his classmates. Through his tutor, he stated that he had been very popular in China, made friends easily, and loved to be with his friends. However, after a few weeks of attempting to ask short questions in English and not being able to understand the responses he received he had found it increasingly painful and frustrating to try to speak English. 'From being popular and having a lot of friends,' Jin stated through his translator, 'to being silenced by my lack of English is terrible for me.'" (pp. 12–13) atmosphere. In such schools, all students learn to understand cultures different from their own. Minority students do not internalize negativity about their culture and customs. Cooperative learning groups and programs that allow interaction between students of diverse backgrounds usually result in fewer incidents of name-calling and ethnic slurs as well as in improved academic achievement (Nieto, 2007).

When the languages and cultures of students are highly evident in their schools and teachers refer to them explicitly, they gain status. Schools that convey the message that all cultures are of value—by displaying explicit welcome signs in many languages, by attempts to involve parents, by a deliberate curriculum of inclusion, and by using affirmative action to promote hiring of a diverse faculty—help to maintain an atmosphere that reduces interethnic conflict.

**Strategies for Conflict Resolution**   If interethnic conflict occurs, taking immediate, proactive steps to resolve the conflict is necessary. The Conflict Resolution Network online at www .crnhq.org/twelveskills.html recommends a twelve-skill approach. Table 8.3 presents a scenario requiring conflict resolution in which the twelve skills are applied.

---

**Best Practice**   CONFLICT RESOLUTION IN NEW JERSEY

Real estate development in the West Windsor–Plainsboro School District in the 1980s and 1990s brought a diverse population into one rural area. Increasing incidents of racial unrest in the schools and in the community at large caused school administrators to begin a program of conflict resolution in K–12 classrooms with the following components:

- A peacemaking program at the elementary level to teach children how to solve problems without resorting to aggression
- Training for middle school students in facilitating positive human relations
- A ninth-grade elective course in conflict resolution
- An elective course for students in grades 11 and 12 to prepare student mediators for a peer-mediation center
- An annual "human relations" retreat for student leaders and teachers that encouraged frank conversations about interpersonal and race relations
- A planned welcome program for newcomers at the school to overcome feelings of isolation
- A minority recruitment program for teachers
- Elimination of watered-down, nonrigorous academic courses in lieu of challenging courses, accompanied by a tutoring program for academically underprepared high school students

Within three years, the number of incidences of vandalism, violence, and substance abuse in the school district was reduced considerably. The people of West Windsor and Plainsboro "accomplished much in their quest to rise out of the degradation of bigotry" (Bandlow, 2002, pp. 91–92; also Prothrow-Smith, 1994).

---

Explicit training for elementary students in negotiation and mediation procedures has proved effective in managing conflict, especially when such programs focus on safely expressing feelings, taking the perspective of the other, and providing the rationale for diverse points

**TABLE 8.3** Applying the Twelve-Skill Approach to Interethnic Conflict

Scenario: A group of four White girls in tenth grade had been making fun of Irena and three of her friends, all of whom were U.S.-born Mexican Americans. One afternoon Irena missed her bus home from high school, and the four girls surrounded her when she was putting books in her locker. One girl shoved a book out of the stack in her hands. Irena shoved her back. Just then, a teacher came around the corner and took Irena to the office for discipline. The assistant principal, Ms. Nava, interviewed Irena to gain some background on the situation. Rather than dealing with Irena in isolation, Ms. Nava waited until the next day, called all eight of the girls into her office, and applied the twelve-skill approach to conflict resolution.

| Skill | Application of Skills to Scenario |
|---|---|
| 1. The win–win approach: Identify attitude shifts to respect all parties' needs. | Ms. Nava asked each girl to write down what the ideal outcome of the situation would be. Three of the girls had written "respect." Ms. Nava decided to use this as a win–win theme. |
| 2. Creative response: Transform problems into creative opportunities. | Each girl was asked to write the name of an adult who respected her and how she knew it was genuine respect. |
| 3. Empathy: Develop communication tools to build rapport. Use listening to clarify understanding. | In turn, each girl described what she had written. The other girls had to listen, using eye contact to show attentiveness. |
| 4. Appropriate assertiveness: Apply strategies to attack the problem, not the person. | Ms. Nava offered an opportunity for members of the group to join the school's Conflict Resolution Task Force. She also warned the group that another incident between them would result in suspension. |
| 5. Cooperative power: Eliminate "power over" to build "power with" others. | Each girl was paired with a girl from the "other side" (cross-group pair) to brainstorm ways in which teens show respect for one another. |
| 6. Managing emotions: Express fear, anger, hurt, and frustration wisely to effect change. | Ms. Nava then asked Irena and the girl who had pushed her book to tell their sides of the incident without name-calling. |
| 7. Willingness to resolve: Name personal issues that cloud the picture. | Each girl was asked to name one underlying issue between the groups that this incident represented. |
| 8. Mapping the conflict: Define the issues needed to chart common needs and concerns. | Ms. Nava mapped the issues by writing them on a wall chart as they were brought forth. |
| 9. Development of options: Design creative solutions together. | Still in the cross-group pairs from step 5, each pair was asked to design a solution for one of the issues mapped. |
| 10. Introduction to negotiation: Plan and apply effective strategies to reach agreement. | Ms. Nava called the girls into her office for a second day. They reviewed the solutions that were designed and made a group plan for improved behavior. |
| 11. Introduction to mediation: Help conflicting parties move toward solutions. | Each cross-group pair generated two ideas for repair if the above plan failed. |
| 12. Broadening perspectives: Evaluate the problem in its broader context. | The eight girls were asked whether racial conflict occurred outside their group. Ms. Nava asked for discussion: Were the same issues they generated in this conflict responsible for other conflicts? |

Source: Adapted from www.crnhq.org.

of view (Johnson, Johnson, Dudley, & Acikgoz, 1994). Especially critical is the role of a mediator in establishing and maintaining a balance of power between two parties in a dispute, protecting the weaker party from intimidation, and ensuring that both parties have a stake in the process and the outcome of mediation.

Perhaps the best way to prevent conflict is to include a variety of cultural content and make sure the school recognizes and values cultural diversity. If conflict does occur, however, there are means to prevent its escalation. Teachers should be aware of conflict resolution techniques before they are actually needed.

---

**Best Practice**   RESOLVING CONFLICTS IN THE CLASSROOM

- To defuse a problem:
  - ✓ Talk to students privately, encouraging the sharing of perceptions on volatile issues.
  - ✓ Communicate expectations that students will be able to resolve their differences.

- If confrontation occurs:
  - ✓ Resolve to be calm in the face of verbalized anger and hostility.
  - ✓ Set aside a brief period for verbal expression.
  - ✓ Allow students to vent feelings as a group.
  - ✓ Do not tolerate violence or personal attacks.

---

Programs that teach about "group differences," involve exhortation or mere verbal learning, or are designed merely to "reduce prejudice" are usually not effective, because to achieve a long-term change in attitudes, a change in behavior must come first. Schools that are committed to increasing intercultural communication can make cultural contact a positive experience for everyone involved.

## Cultural Diversity in the United States

### The Demographics of Change

Throughout the United States, 47 million people (18 percent of the population) speak a language other than English at home (U.S. Census Bureau, 2003). In the 2000 census, almost 23 million people in the United States reported that they *do not* speak English well. Although the largest percentage of non–English speakers (37 percent) lives in the West, English learners and their families are increasingly living in places such as the Midwest (9 percent) and the South (15 percent) that have not previously needed to hire English-language development (ELD) teachers. The majority of English learners in the United States are Spanish-speaking (28.1 million); this represents an increase of 62 percent over the decade 1990–2000.

Again according to the 2000 census, almost 3 million school-age children spoke Spanish as a native language—more than three-quarters (76.9 percent) of English learners in schools. No other native language exceeded 3 percent. The five most common languages after Spanish were Vietnamese (2.4 percent), Hmong (1.8 percent), Korean (1.2 percent), Arabic (1.2 percent), and Haitian Creole (1.1 percent) (Hopstock & Stephenson, 2003).

California had the largest population percentage of non-English-language speakers, followed by New Mexico, Texas, New York, Hawai'i, Arizona, and New Jersey (see Table 8.4). Other states—Florida (3.5 million), Illinois (2.2 million), and Massachusetts (1.1 million)—also have large populations of non-English-language speakers. The largest percentage increase from 1990 to 2000 occurred in Nevada, where the number increased by 193 percent. In California, English learners increased 44 percent in the decade 1992–2002.

The National Clearinghouse for English Language Acquisition and Language Instruction Educational Programs (NCELA) put the number of children of school age with a home language other than English at 9,779,766—one of every six children. Of these language-minority students, almost half (or 4,747,763) do not yet have sufficient proficiency in English to be able to succeed academically in traditional all-English-medium classrooms (NCELA, 2004). Los Angeles Unified School District leads all other school districts in the nation in the number of English learners (299,232 in 2002–2003), the number of languages (56), and the percent of total enrollment (40 percent), followed by New York City, Dade County in Florida, Chicago, Houston, Dallas, San Diego, and Long Beach, California. In 2004, California led the states in need for English learner services at the K–12 level with a school enrollment of approximately 1.6 million English learners (California Department of Education, 2004b).

These population demographics indicate that all states need to provide services for English learners, with the need greatest in California, New Mexico, New York, and Texas, serving Hispanics or Asian/Pacific Islanders. The linguistic and cultural variety of English learners suggests that more and more teachers use ELD strategies and methods to serve as intercultural and interlinguistic educators—those who can reach out to learners from a variety of backgrounds and offer effective learning experiences.

## Migration and Immigration in the United States

The United States has historically been a nation of immigrants, but the nature and causes of immigration have changed over time. The earliest settlers to the east coast of North America

**TABLE 8.4**   States with the Highest Percent of Population Speaking a Language Other Than English

| State | Population of Non-English-Language Speakers (in millions) | Percent of the State's Population |
|---|---|---|
| California | 12.4 | 39.5 |
| New Mexico | 0.5 | 36.5 |
| Texas | 6.0 | 31.2 |
| New York | 5.0 | 28.0 |
| Hawai'i | 0.3 | 26.6 |
| Arizona | 1.2 | 25.9 |
| New Jersey | 2.0 | 25.5 |

came from England and Holland, whereas those to the south and west came mainly from Spain. In the early eighteenth century, these settlers were joined by involuntary immigrants—slaves from Africa. The social upheavals and overpopulation that characterized nineteenth-century Europe and Asia brought more than 14 million immigrants to the United States in the forty-year period between 1860 and 1900. Immigration from the Pacific Rim countries was constrained by severe immigration restrictions until the last decades of the twentieth century.

However, imperialistic policies of the United States, primarily the conquest of the Philippines, Puerto Rico, Hawai'i, and the Pacific Islands, caused large influxes of these populations throughout the twentieth century. The wars in Southeast Asia and Central America in the 1970s and 1980s led to increased emigration from these areas. In the 1990s, immigrants arrived from all over the world. In 2000, 40 percent of all legal immigrants came from just five countries—Mexico, China, the Philippines, India, and Vietnam (Migration Policy Institute, 2004).

Immigrants have come to the United States for a variety of reasons: the desire for adventure and economic gain in a new world, the need to flee religious and political persecution, or as a result of forcible abduction. Factors involve both attractive forces (pull) and expulsive forces (push). Later, U.S. foreign policy created connections with populations abroad that pulled certain groups to the United States. For example, the conquest of the Philippines at the turn of the century eventually resulted in significant Philippine immigration to the United States.

Immigration laws responded to both push and pull factors throughout the nineteenth and twentieth centuries, at times curtailing emigration from specific regions and at other times allowing increased immigration. Once in the United States, both immigrants and natives have historically been restless populations. Much of the history of the United States consists of the migration of groups from one part of the country to another.

## Contemporary Causes of Migration and Immigration

Migration is an international phenomenon. Throughout the world, populations are dislocated by war, famine, civil strife, economic change, persecution, and other factors. The United States has been a magnet for immigrants seeking greater opportunity and economic stability. Politics and religion as well as economics provide reasons for emigration. U.S. domestic and foreign policies affect the way in which groups of foreigners are accepted. Changes in immigration policy, such as amnesty, affect the number of immigrants who enter the country each year.

**Economic Factors**   The great disparity in the standard of living attainable in the United States compared to that of many developing countries makes immigration attractive. Self-advancement is uppermost in the minds of many immigrants and acts as a strong incentive despite the economic exploitation often endured by immigrants (e.g., lower wages, exclusion from desirable jobs). Immigrants may bring with them unique skills. On the whole, however, the economy of the United States does not have an unlimited capacity to employ immigrants in specialized niches.

Immigration policy has corresponded with the cycles of boom and bust in the U.S. economy. The Chinese Exclusion Act of 1882 stopped immigration from China to the United States because of the concern that Chinese labor would flood the market. The labor shortage in the western United States that resulted from excluding the Chinese had the effect of welcoming

Japanese immigrants who were good farm laborers. Later, during the Great Depression of the 1930s, with a vast labor surplus in the United States, the U.S. Congress severely restricted Philippine immigration, and policies were initiated to "repatriate" Mexicans back across the border.

When World War II transformed the labor surplus of the 1930s into a severe worker shortage, the United States and Mexico established the Bracero Program, a bilateral agreement allowing Mexicans to cross the border to work on U.S. farms and railroads. However, despite the economic attractiveness of the United States, now, as then, most newcomers to this society experience a period of economic hardship (see Box 8.2).

**Political Factors**     Repression, civil war, and change in government create a push for emigration from foreign countries, whereas political factors within the United States produce a climate of acceptance for some political refugees and not for others. After the Vietnam War, many refugees were displaced in Southeast Asia. Some sense of responsibility for their plight caused the U.S. government to accept many of these people into the United States, such as Cambodians who cooperated with the U.S. military: 6,300 Khmer in 1975; 10,000 Cambodians in 1979; and 60,000 Cambodians between 1980 and 1982 (Gillett, 1989a). In the 1980s, civil war caused the displacement of 600,000 Salvadorans, nearly 200,000 of whom were admitted to the United States through the Deferred Enforced Departure program (Gillett, 1989b).

Other populations, such as Haitians claiming political persecution, have been turned away from U.S. borders. U.S. policy did not consider them to be victims of political repression but rather of economic hardship—a fine distinction, in many cases, and here one might suspect that racial issues in the United States make it more difficult for them to immigrate. It would seem, then, that the grounds for political asylum—race, religion, nationality, membership in a particular social group, political opinion—can be clouded by confounding factors.

Religion complicates the political picture; many eastern European Jews, forced to emigrate because of anti-Semitic pogroms in the nineteenth century, came to the United States in great numbers. Unfortunately, during the 1930s and 1940s, Jews persecuted by Nazis were not free to emigrate or were not accepted as immigrants and were killed. Under the communist regime in the former USSR, Russian Jews were allowed to emigrate in small numbers and were accepted into the United States. Current immigration policies permit refugees to be accepted on the basis of religion if the applicant can prove that persecution comes from the government or is motivated by the government.

In sum, people are pushed to the United States because of political instability or unfavorable political policies in their home countries. Political conditions within the United States affect whether immigrants are accepted or denied.

**Family Unification**     The risks associated with travel to the New World have made immigration a male-dominated activity since the early settlement of North America. For example, today's

**Box 8.2**  Find Out More about Economic Factors

The site US Immigration Facts (www.rapidimmigration.com/usa/1_eng_immigration_facts.html) provides general facts about recent U.S. immigration and then discusses immigrant entrepreneurs and economic characteristics of immigrants.

Mexican immigrant population consists largely of young men who have come to the United States without their families to work. However, once settled, immigrants seek to bring family members. Thus, a primary motivation for many applications to the Bureau of Citizenship and Immigration Services (BCIS) in the Department of Homeland Security is family unification.

**Migration within the United States**   Today, many immigrants are sponsored by special-interest groups such as churches and civic organizations that invite them to reside in the local community. Once here, however, some groups find conditions too foreign to their former lives and eventually make a *secondary migration* to another part of the United States. For example, a group of Hmong families sponsored by Lutheran charities spent two years in the severe winter climate of the Minneapolis area before resettling in California. Hispanics, on the other hand, are migrating from cities in the Southwest, New York, and Miami toward destinations in the Midwest and middle South (Wilson, 1984). California, which had attracted 33 percent of these immigrants, recently has only received 22 percent (Migration Policy Institute, 2004).

For newly arriving immigrants, historical patterns are also changing. See the following Did You Know box.

---DID YOU KNOW?---

**HISPANIC MIGRATION**

Although Hispanics are the most urbanized ethnic/racial group in the United States (90 percent living in metropolitan areas in 2000), the nonmetro Hispanic population is now the most rapidly growing demographic group in rural and small-town America. By 2000, half of all nonmetro Hispanics lived outside traditional Southwest cities. Many of these Hispanics are newly arrived undocumented young men from rural, depressed areas of Mexico. In spite of their relatively low education levels and weak English skills, employment rates exceeded those of all other nonmetro Hispanics and non-Hispanic Whites. (Kandel & Cromartie, 2004)

**U.S. Immigration Laws and Policies**   Economic cycles in the United States have affected immigration policies, liberalizing them when workers were needed and restricting access when jobs were scarce. These restrictive immigration policies were often justified using overtly racist arguments.

The immigration laws of the 1920s (the National Origins Acts of 1924 and 1929) banned most Asian immigration and established quotas that favored northwestern European immigrants. The quota system, however, did not apply to Mexico and the rest of the Western Hemisphere. In 1943, Congress symbolically ended the Asian exclusion policy by granting ethnic Chinese a token quota of 100 immigrants a year. The Philippines and Japan received similar tiny quotas after the war.

The Immigration and Nationality Act Amendments of 1965 brought about vast changes in immigration policy by abolishing the national origins quota system and replacing it with a seven-category preference system for allocating immigrant visas, a system that emphasizes family ties and occupation. Although there is a per-country limit for these preference immigrants, certain countries are "oversubscribed" and hopefuls are on long waiting lists (People's Republic of China, India, Mexico, and the Philippines). An additional provision in the 1965 act was the diversity immigrant category, in which 55,000 immigrant visas can be awarded each fiscal year to permit immigration opportunities for persons from countries other than the principal sources of current immigration to the United States.

Immigration is a political and social "hot button" in the United States. Many conservative leaders in Congress have voiced their opposition to immigration reform measures that would feature pathways to citizenship and guest worker programs. Other leaders believe that immigration policy reform is necessary to stabilize border security and provide economic security (see Box 8.3).

**Legal Status**   Many immigrants are *documented*—legal residents who have entered the United States officially and live under the protection of legal immigration status. Some of these are officially designated *refugees,* with transitional support services and assistance provided by the U.S. government, including most immigrants from Cambodia, Laos, Vietnam, and Thailand. *Undocumented* immigrants are residents without any official status, who often live in fear of being identified and deported.

Being in the United States illegally brings increased instability, fear, and insecurity to school-age children because they and their families are living without the protection, social services, and assistance available to most immigrants. With the passage of the Immigration Reform and Control Act in 1986, however, undocumented children are legally entitled to public education.

**Resources Available to Immigrants**   The Emergency Immigrant Education Program (EIEP) (No Child Left Behind, Title III, subpart 4) provides assistance to school districts whose enrollment is affected by immigrants. The purpose of the program is to offer high-quality instruction to immigrant children and youth, helping them with their transition into U.S. society and supporting their efforts to meet the demands of challenging academic content and student academic achievement standards (NCLB, sec. 3241).

In addition, the immigrant communities themselves have networks of linguistic, financial, and social support, such as the extensive Taiwanese communities of the San Gabriel Valley in Southern California, the Afghan community in the San Francisco Bay area, and the Arab communities of Michigan. These communities have primary-language activities throughout the year, as well as hosting websites for the immigrant community.

## The Cultural and Linguistic Challenges of Diversity

No other country in the world faces a diversity challenge as great as that of the United States. At any given time, almost one-fifth of the population speaks another language, with issues of primary-language maintenance and loss. New refugees are suffering culture shock, undocumented immigrants are living in fear of apprehension, and other nonresidents are seeking support networks and services. Worse, many immigrants face bias and discrimination.

**Box 8.3**   Find Out More about Immigration Legislation

"Executive Summary: U.S. Immigration: A Legislative History" (www.rapidimmigration .com/usa/1_eng_immigration_history.html) contains a bulleted listing of U.S. immigration legislation from 1790 to President George W. Bush's proposed immigration reform, as well as pie charts of countries of origin during various periods and graphs of the U.S. foreign-born population.

**Issues of Bias and Discrimination in the United States**   If diversity is recognized as a strength, educators will "avoid basing decisions about learners on inaccurate or stereotypical generalizations" (Manning, 2002, p. 207). Misperceptions about diversity often stem from prejudice, which can be diffused when various groups interact and come to know one another more deeply. But discrimination also stems from fear; dominant groups are afraid to lose power, and they benefit from the disadvantage of the subordinated.

The United States is a diverse country, with vast disparities among its residents in social class, age, gender, occupation, education level, geographic isolation, race, U.S.-born versus immigrant status, sexual orientation, and handicapping condition. As long as schools privilege some students and subordinate others based not on an individual's gifts and talents but on external social factors, schools will not represent level playing fields.

**The Dynamics of Prejudice**   One factor that inhibits intercultural communication is prejudice, which takes various forms: excessive pride in one's own ethnic heritage, country, or culture so that others are viewed negatively; ethnocentrism, in which the world revolves around oneself and one's own culture; prejudice against members of a certain racial group; and stereotypes that label all or most members of a group. All humans are prejudiced to some degree, but it is when people act on those prejudices that discriminatory practices and inequalities result.

A closer look at various forms of prejudice, such as racism and stereotyping, as well as resulting discriminatory practice, can lead to an understanding of these issues. Teachers can then be in a position to adopt educational methods that are most likely to reduce prejudice.

**Racism**   The view that one race is superior to another is racism. For example, one sixteenth-century justification for genocide in the New World stated that Native Americans were not human. Racism can also involve cultural ideas that the traditions, beliefs, language, artifacts, music, and art of other cultures are inferior. On the basis of such concepts, racists justify discriminating against or scapegoating other groups. Racism may be expressed in hate crimes, which are public expressions of hostility directed at specific groups or individuals (harassment, scrawling graffiti on people's homes, burning crosses on lawns, etc.) or, at the extreme, assaults and murder directed toward minorities.

*Youth at the Edge,* a report by the Southern Poverty Law Center (1999), described a frustrated, marginally employed, and poorly educated underclass of disenchanted youth in the United States who are susceptible to hate groups and seek out scapegoats to harass such as immigrants, particularly those of color. The availability of information on the Internet has unfortunately encouraged sites that foment racial hatred. Schools are often prime sites in which hate crimes are committed. This fact underscores the urgency of educators' efforts to understand and combat racism.

**Stereotypes**   Often resulting from racist beliefs, stereotypes are preconceived and oversimplified generalizations about a particular group, race, or gender. The danger of stereotyping is that people are not considered as individuals but are categorized with all other members of a group. A person might believe that a racial group has a global trait and subsequently everyone from that group is judged in this stereotypical way. Conversely, a person might judge an entire group on the basis of an experience with a single individual. Whether positive or negative, a stereotype results in a distorted perspective.

Classroom Glimpse

## EDUCATING AGAINST A STEREOTYPE

Mrs. Abboushi, a third-grade teacher, discovers that her students hold many misconceptions about the Arab people. To present an accurate and more rounded view of the Arab world, she has students read *Ibrahim* (Sales, 1989), *The Day of Ahmed's Secret* (Heide & Gilliland, 1990), and *Nadia, the Willful* (Alexander, 1983).

After reading and interactively discussing the books, students are divided into groups. Each group is assigned a different book. Students prepare a Cultural Feature Analysis chart that includes the cultural features, setting, character and traits, family relationships, and message of their book. Groups share their information and Mrs. Abboushi records the information on a large summary chart. During the follow-up discussion, students discover that not all Arabs live the same way, dress the same way, or look the same way. They recognize the merging of traditional and modern worlds and the variability in living conditions, customs and values, architecture, clothing, and modes of transportation (Diamond & Moore, 1995, pp. 229–230).

**Teaching against Racism**   Students and teachers alike must raise awareness of racism in the attempt to achieve racial equality and justice. Actively listening to students in open discussion about racism, prejudice, and stereotyping can increase teachers' understanding of how students perceive and are affected by these concepts. School curricula can be used to help students be aware of the existence and impact of racism. Science and health teachers can debunk myths surrounding the concept of race. Content area teachers can help students develop skills in detecting bias.

## Best Practice   ANTIRACIST ACTIVITIES AND DISCUSSION TOPICS

- Understand the origins of racism and why people hold racial prejudices and stereotypes.
- Learn to identify racist images in the language and illustrations of books, films, television, news media, and advertising.
- Be able to detect current examples of racism in the immediate community and society as a whole.
- Seek specific ways of developing positive interracial contact experiences.
- Extend the fight against racism into a broader fight for universal human rights and respect for human dignity.

*Source:* Adapted from Bennett (2003, pp. 370–373).

**Programs to Combat Prejudice and Racism**   The Southern Poverty Law Center distributes *Teaching Tolerance* magazine, a free resource sent to over 600,000 educators twice a year that provides antibias strategies for K–12 teachers. Carnuccio (2004) describes the Tolerance.org website, a Web project of the Southern Poverty Law Center (available at www.splcenter.org), as an "extremely informative resource."

The project has done an excellent job of collecting and disseminating information on the advantages of diversity. . . . *Planet Tolerance* has stories for children to read and listen to and games for them to play. Teens can find ideas on how to bring diverse groups together in their schools. Teachers' pages feature articles, films and books to order, lesson ideas, and a forum in which to share ideas with other teachers. *101 Tools for Tolerance* suggests a variety of ideas for community, workplace, school, and home settings. *Parenting for Tolerance* offers ways for parents to guide their children to develop into tolerant adults. (p. 59)

**Institutional Racism**    Classroom teaching that aims at detecting and reducing racism may be a futile exercise when the institution itself—the school—promotes racism through its policies and practices, such as underreferral of minority students to programs for gifted students or failing to hire minority teachers in classrooms where children are predominantly of minority background. There may be no intent to discriminate on the part of an institution such as a school; however, interactions with minority students may reflect unquestioned negative assumptions about the abilities or participation of these students.

Teachers do not have to look far to encounter educational practices that are imbued with racial, ethnic, and class privilege. How does one identify institutional racism? One way is to profile the racial and ethnic composition of school staff, of academic "tracks," and of school activities. The following questions help to clarify the issue of institutional racism:

- Do the racial demographics of the teaching staff match those of the students?
- As English learners come to school, do they meet only maintenance personnel and cafeteria workers who speak their language?
- Does the school offer English learners equal access to an academic curriculum, including classes for the gifted and talented?
- Does the school provide equality in resources to support and enrich learning for all students?
- Do school clubs recruit effectively from all races and cultures of the student body, or are English learners segregated into "culture" clubs while native speakers of English staff the more high-status activities such as the school yearbook, newspaper, and student leadership clubs?
- Are family members of all students provided equal opportunities for involvement in school-level activities, or is the only parent organization available designed for middle-class parents who are English literate and have flexible work schedules that enable them to participate in school functions and fundraisers during the school day?

**Classism**    In the United States, racism is compounded by classism, discrimination against the poor. Although this classism is often directed against linguistic and cultural minorities—in the American imagination, a typical poor person is urban, black, and young—portraying poverty that way makes it easier to stigmatize the poor (Henwood, 1997).

Classism has engendered its own stereotype against poor European Americans—for example, the stereotyped White indigent who is called, among other things, "white trash" ("the white trash stereotype serves as a useful way of blaming the poor for being poor") (Wray & Newitz, 1997, p. 1). Poor Whites, who outnumber poor minorities, may bear the brunt of a castelike status in the United States (Ogbu, 1978) as much as do linguistic and cultural minorities.

**Discrimination**    Discrimination refers to actions that limit the social, political, or economic opportunities of particular race, language, culture, gender, and/or social-class groups and legitimize the unequal distribution of power and resources. Blatant, legally sanctioned discrimination may be a thing of the past, but de facto segregation continues—most students of color are still found in substandard schools, taught by faculty who have less experience and academic preparation, do not share the ethnic background of their students, and may not interact well with these students (Ortiz, 1988). These teachers may communicate low expectations to minority students.

In the past, those in power often used physical force to discriminate. Those who did not go along were physically punished for speaking their native language or adhering to their own cultural or ethnic customs. With the spread of literacy, discrimination took the form of internalized shame and guilt, leading minorities to become ashamed of their parents and origins. Skutnabb-Kangas (1981) cited a variety of examples of this *symbolic-structural violence* against minority students in Swedish and Norwegian schools:

> The headmaster said, "You have a name which is difficult for us Swedes to pronounce. Can't we change it?" "Well, I suppose I'd better change it," I thought. (p. 316)

> I love my parents and I respect them but what they are and everything they know counts for nothing. (p. 317)

Students experiencing racism and anti-immigration sentiment from peers in their environment, together with the increasing involvement of young adults on and off campus in supporting prejudice, is a disturbing trend on today's campuses. Policies, curricula, and antiracism programs are needed to prevent and control hate crimes. Hand in hand with sanctions for such negative behavior, students need training in intercultural communication.

**Fighting for Fairness and Equal Opportunity**    Schools in the United States have not been level playing fields for those of nonmainstream cultures. Teachers can remedy this in both academic and extracurricular areas. According to Manning (2002), teachers should

> consider that all learners deserve, ethically and legally, equal access to curricular activities (e.g., higher-level mathematics and science subjects) and opportunities to participate in all athletic activities (e.g., rather than assuming all students of one race will play on the basketball team and all students of another race will play on the tennis or golfing teams). (p. 207)

Cultural fairness can extend to the social and interpersonal lives of students, those daily details and microinteractions that also fall within the domain of culture. Teachers who invest time in getting to know their students, as individuals as well as cultural beings, address issues of fairness through a personal commitment to equality of treatment and opportunity.

# Intercultural Communication

Exchange that takes place between individuals of different cultures is known as *intercultural communication*. Channels of communication are verbal and nonverbal.

## Cultural Diversity in Nonverbal Communication

Nonverbal communication is just as important as verbal interaction; however, educators are oriented toward verbal means of expression and less likely to accord importance to "silent language." However, more than 65 percent of the social meaning of a typical two-person exchange is carried by nonverbal cues (Birdwhistell, 1974). Physical appearance is an important dimension of the nonverbal code during initial encounters. Body movements, gestures, and facial expressions can enhance a message or constitute a message in itself. *Paralanguage,* the nonverbal elements of the voice, is a primary aspect of speech that can affirm or belie a verbal message. *Proxemics,* the communication of interpersonal distance, varies widely across cultures. Last but not least, *olfactics*—the study of interpersonal communication by means of smell—constitutes a factor that is powerful yet often overlooked.

**Body Language**   The way one holds and positions oneself—one's body language—is a significant way a teacher communicates authority in the classroom. To become the focus of attention, a teacher stands in front of the room; by passing from desk to desk while students are working, he or she communicates individual attention to students' needs. In turn, students convey that they are paying attention with eyes up front; if they act industrious (busily writing or quietly reading a book), they are often seen as more effective academically. Thus, body language helps to shape and maintain one's image in the eyes of others.

In a parent conference, however, cultural differences in body language may impede communication. In traditional cultures, a guest is formally ushered into the classroom and not merely waved in with a flick of the hand. Parents from a culture that offers elaborate respect for the teacher may become uncomfortable if the teacher slouches, moves his or her chair too intimately toward the parent, or otherwise compromises the formal nature of the interchange. In contrast, welcoming body language enhances communication.

**Gestures and Facial Expressions**   Expressive motions or actions made with hands, arms, head, or even the whole body are culturally based signs that are often misunderstood. "Yes" is generally signaled by a nod of the head, but in some cultures a shake of the head means "yes." This can be particularly unnerving for teachers if they constantly interpret the students' head-shakes as rejection rather than affirmation. Facial expressions are also easily misinterpreted. Through the use of eyebrows, eyes, cheeks, nose, lips, tongue, and chin, people nonverbally signal any number of emotions, opinions, and moods. Although some facial expressions of happiness, sadness, anger, fear, surprise, disgust, and interest appear to be universal across cultures, other expressions are learned.

**Eye Contact**   Another communication device that is highly variable and frequently misunderstood is eye contact. Both insufficient and excessive eye contact create feelings of unease. Generally, children in European-American culture are taught to look people in the eye when addressing them. In some cultures, however, children learn that respect is conveyed by looking down when addressed, and a teacher may incorrectly interpret a student's downcast eyes as an admission of guilt. The teacher may need to explain to the student that in English the rules of address call for different behavior.

**Distance between Speakers**   Personal space is an aspect of social customs that differs according to cultural experience. Personal space varies: In some cultures, individuals touch one another frequently and maintain high degrees of physical contact; in other cultures, touch and proximity cause feelings of tension and embarrassment. The following incident and thousands of others that may be unpredictable, puzzling, uncomfortable, or even threatening occur in situations in which cultural groups come into contact.

### PERSONAL SPACE

"Teacher," Maria said to me as the students went out for recess. "Yes, Maria?" I smiled at this lively Venezuelan student and we launched into conversation. The contents of this talk are now lost on me, but not the actions. For as we talked, we slowly moved, she forward, me backward, until I was jammed up against the chalkboard. And there I remained for the rest of the conversation, feeling more and more agitated. She was simply too close.

Because I knew the different cultural norms under which Maria and I were operating—the fact that the requirement for space between interlocutors is greater for me as a North American than for her as a South American—I did not ascribe any negative or aggressive tendencies to her. But knowing the norm difference did not lessen my anxiety. What it afforded me was the knowledge that we were behaving differently and that such differences were normal for our respective groups. (Kathryn Weed quoted in Díaz-Rico & Weed, 2010, p. 264)

**Best Practice**   ACCOMMODATING DIFFERENT CONCEPTS OF PERSONAL SPACE

- If students from the same culture (one with a close personal space) and gender have a high degree of physical contact and neither seems bothered by this, the teacher does not have to intervene.
- The wise teacher accords the same personal space to students no matter what their culture (e.g., does not touch minority students more or less than mainstream students).
- Students from affluent families should not bring more "stuff" to put in or on their desks than the average student.

## Cultural Diversity in Verbal Communication

Whether oral or written, verbal communication constitutes the other half of intercultural interaction. Aside from first- and second-language differences, a world of patterns and practices surrounds oral and written expression.

**Diversity in Oral Discourse**   In learning a second language, students (and teachers) often focus on the form. Frequently ignored are the ways in which that second language is used (see the section on pragmatics in Chapter 1). The culture that underlies each language prescribes distinct patterns and conventions about when, where, and how to use the language. Heath's (1999) *Ways with Words* noted that children in "Trackton," an isolated African-American community in the South, were encouraged to engage in spontaneous verbal play, rich with metaphor, simile, and allusion. In contrast, the children of "Roadville," a lower-middle-class European-American community in the South, employed language in more restricted ways, perhaps because of habits encouraged by a fundamentalist religious culture.

Using language to satisfy material needs, control the behavior of others, get along with others, express one's personality, find out about the world, create an imaginative world, or communicate information seems to be universal among language users. How these social functions are accomplished, however, varies greatly among cultures. For example, when accidentally bumping someone, Americans, Japanese, Koreans, and Filipinos would say, "Excuse me" or "Pardon me." The Chinese, however, would give an apologetic look. Within a family, Hispanics often say "thank you" nonverbally for acts of service, whereas European-American children are taught that a spoken "thank you" is necessary, especially to a family member.

**The Role of Silence**   People throughout the world employ silence in communicating. Silence can in fact speak loudly and eloquently. The silence of a parent in front of a guilty child is more powerful than any ranting or raving. As with other language uses, however, silence differs dramatically across cultures. In the U.S. mainstream culture, silence is interpreted as expressing embarrassment, regret, obligation, criticism, or sorrow (Wayne in Ishii & Bruneau, 1991). In Asian cultures, silence is a token of respect. Particularly in the presence of the elderly, being quiet honors their wisdom and expertise. Silence can also be a marker of personal power. In many Eastern cultures, women view their silent role as a symbol of control and self-respect. In many Native-American cultures, silence is used to create and communicate rapport in ways that language cannot.

 **Classroom Glimpse**

### THE ROLE OF SILENCE

In a research project that took place in several Oglala Sioux classrooms, a central factor involved the withdrawal of the Sioux students. Teachers were faced with unexpectedly intense, sometimes embarrassingly long periods of silence. They cajoled, commanded, badgered, and pleaded with students, receiving an inevitable monosyllabic or nonverbal response. Yet outside the classroom, these children were noisy, bold, and insatiably curious. The lack of verbal response from students frustrated teachers. The solution? The teachers involved themselves in the daily life of the community and reduced the isolation of the school from the values of the community. They went so far as to locate classrooms in community buildings. In a different context, students were more willing participants. (Dumont, 1972)

**The Nature of Questions**   Intercultural differences exist in asking and answering questions. In middle-class European-American culture, children are exposed early on to their parents' questioning. While taking a walk, for example, a mother will ask, "See the squirrel?" and later, "Is that a squirrel? Where did that squirrel go?" It is obvious to both parent and child that the adult knows the answer to these questions. The questions are asked to stimulate conversation and to train children to focus attention and display knowledge. In the Inuit culture, on the other hand, adults do not question children or call their attention to objects and events in order to name them (Crago, 1993).

Responses to questioning differ across cultures as well. Students from non-Western cultures may be reluctant to attempt an answer to a question if they do not feel they can answer absolutely correctly. These students may not share the European-American value of answering questions to the best of their ability regardless of whether that "best" answer is absolutely correct.

**Discourse Styles**   Cultures may differ in ways that influence conversations: the words or phrases that open and close conversations, how people take turns, or the way messages are repaired to make them understandable. Those who have traveled to a foreign country recognize that a small interaction such as answering the telephone may have widely varying sequences across cultures. Sometimes callers give immediate self-identification, sometimes not; sometimes greetings are followed with "how are you" sequences. Deviations from these routines may be cause to terminate a conversation in the earliest stages. Differences in discourse customs may be stressful for second-language learners.

 **Classroom Glimpse**

### CLASSROOM DISCOURSE PATTERNS

Discourse in the classroom can be organized to involve children positively—in ways that are culturally compatible. A group of Hawai'ian children, with the help of an encouraging and participating adult, produced group discourse that was co-narrated, complex, lively, imaginative, and well connected. Group work featured twenty-minute discussions of text in which the teacher and students mutually participated in overlapping, volunteered speech and in joint narration (Au & Jordan, 1981). In contrast, Navajo children in a discussion group patterned their discourse after the adults of their culture. Each Navajo student spoke for an extended period with a fully expressed statement, and other students waited courteously until a clear end was communicated. Then another took a similar turn. In both communities, children tended to connect discourse with peers rather than with the teacher functioning as a central "switchboard." If the teacher acted as a central director, students often responded with silence. (Tharp, 1989)

--- **DID YOU KNOW?** ---

### HOW STUDENTS TELL YOU THEY DON'T UNDERSTAND

Arabic (men): *Mish fahem*

Arabic (women): *Mish fahmeh*

Armenian: *Yes chem huskenur*

Chinese (Cantonese): *Ngoh m-ming*

Chinese (Mandarin): *Wo bu dung*

Persian: *Man ne'me fah'mam*

Japanese: *Wakarimasen*

Korean: *Juh-neun eehae-haji mot haget-ssum-nida*

Russian: *Ya nye ponimayu*

Spanish: *No comprendo*

Vietnamese: *Toi khong hieu*

In addition to ways to say "I don't understand" in 230 languages, J. Runner's webpage has translations in many languages for the following phrases: "Hello, how are you?," "Welcome," "Good-bye," "Please," "Thank you," "What is your name?," "My name is . . . ," "Do you speak English?," "Yes," and "No." There is also a link to Internet language resources; see www.elite.net/~runner/jennifers/understa.htm.

*Source:* Runner (2000).

**Oral versus Written Language**   In studying oral societies, researchers have noted that the structure and content of messages tend to be narrative, situational, and oriented toward activity or deeds, although abstract ideas such as moral values are often implicit. In contrast, the style represented by literacy is conceptual rather than situational. Words are separate from the social context of deeds and events, and ideas can be extracted from written texts. In an oral society, learning takes place in groups because narration must have an audience. This contrasts with a literate society, in which reading and writing can be solitary experiences. Separation from the group appears to be one of the burdens of literacy. In an oral society, much reliance is placed on memory, as this is the principal means of preserving practices and traditions (Ong, 1982).

**Cultural Differences in Written Discourse**   Oracy is the foundation of languages. Written expression is a later development. In fact, of the thousands of reported languages in use, only seventy-eight have a written literature (Edmonson, 1971). Research has suggested that acquiring literacy involves more than learning to read and write. Thinking patterns, perception, cultural values, communication style, and social organization can be affected by literacy.

Many features of written language have to be learned in school. The style of argumentation, the use of voice and formality level, and the organizational structure employed in writing are unique to each culture. This is a part of acquiring cognitive academic language proficiency.

## Strategies for Intercultural Communication in the School and Classroom

Communicating with students from other cultures is more than learning a few phrases in the second language and expecting the students and families to stretch more than halfway. Much can be done to adapt one's communication styles and habits to make others more comfortable and to get one's message across.

**Teaching Styles**   The way teachers are taught to teach is a reflection of the expectations of U.S. culture. Teachers raised in a mainstream culture have elements of that culture embedded in their personal teaching approach. Some of these elements may need to be modified to meet the needs of students from other cultures. As a beginning step, a teacher can examine his or her teaching style to evaluate whether, for example, it is student-centered or subject-centered or whether students are encouraged to work alone or cooperatively.

Even in monocultural classrooms, the teacher's style is more in accordance with some students than with others. Flexibility becomes a key to reaching more students. In a multicultural classroom, this flexibility is even more crucial. With knowledge of various teaching styles, a teacher can examine his or her own style, observe students' reactions to that approach, ask questions about a teacher's expected role and function in the community, and modify teaching style as necessary for different situations.

**Teacher–Student Interactions**   The teacher–student interaction is culturally mandated in general ways, although individuals may vary. Students who have immigrated may bring with them varying notions of teacher–student interactions. For example, in some cultures, learning takes place in an absolutely quiet classroom where the teacher is in complete control and authority is never questioned. In other cultures, students talk among themselves and are able to engage with teachers in cooperative planning. Attitudes toward authority, teacher–student relationships, and teacher expectations of student achievement vary widely. Yet the heart of the educational process is in the interaction between teacher and student. This determines the quality of education the student receives.

Differences in the culture of the teacher and the student may cause miscommunication. Language and word choice are other factors making intercultural communication challenging. Words that may seem harmless in one context may have a subculture connotation. Teachers have to be equally careful both to use appropriate terms of address and reference when communicating with students and to be aware of terms used in the classroom that might have an incendiary effect.

## Best Practice   ENCOURAGING POSITIVE RELATIONSHIPS

Although it may appear daunting to be able to accommodate the various teacher–student relations represented by different cultural groups in a classroom, there are several ways teachers can improve rapport with their students:

- Express care and respect equally to all students.
- Openly communicate acceptance of students and be accessible to them.
- In classroom discussions and in private, encourage students to talk about their lives, feelings (including the sometimes tragic details), and expectations for learning.
- Understand that you are not only helping students academically but also that you may be helping families adjust. (Lemberger, 1999)

**Power and Authority**   Most students expect power and authority to be vested in the teacher, and teachers expect respect from students. Respect is communicated verbally and nonverbally and is vulnerable to cultural misunderstanding. In the United States, respect is shown to teachers by looking at them, but in some cultures looking at the teacher is a sign of disrespect. Moreover, students are expected to raise their hands in North American classrooms if they wish to ask or answer a question. Vietnamese culture, on the other hand, does not have a way for students to signal a desire to talk to a teacher; students speak only after the teacher has spoken to them (Andersen & Powell, 1991).

## Best Practice   UNDERSTANDING BEHAVIORS RELATED TO POWER AND AUTHORITY

- Seek alternative explanations to unexpected behavior rather than interpreting the behavior according to your own cultural framework.
- Ask "Why is this behavior occurring?" Rather than "What is the matter with this child?" (Cushner, 1999, p. 75)

## Teaching Intercultural Communication

Students are often fascinated by cultural difference. Because this content is not on standardized tests, teachers may be reluctant to spend time on such a topic. However, the "teachable moment" occurs whenever a cultural difference is relevant to a classroom occurrence.

Multicultural literature and other facets of a multicultural curriculum are useful ways to teach about culture. Practicing intercultural communication skills—listening and speaking in a culturally sensitive way—is a daily occurrence.

A classroom bulletin board display area may be put to good use throughout the school year, with one half devoted to cultural artifacts, language, numbering systems, and other external elements of culture. The other half might display key ideas about culture such as ideas about personal space, nonverbal language, and other concepts that students can acquire. This keeps the issue of cultural diversity open and available as food for thought.

# Investigating Ourselves as Cultural Beings

Teachers who function as intercultural educators acquire a sense of the difficulties faced by English learners. However, many prospective teachers initially are unaware of their own cultural values and behaviors and how these might be at odds with the home cultures of students.

The most powerful means of learning about culture is studying about ourselves and our own culture. Those who are willing to engage in self-assessment activities are often richly rewarded with a deeper understanding of their professional and personal lives. The goal of such assessment is to enable prospective teachers to sustain intercultural contact, foster culturally responsive pedagogy, and develop the skills of advocacy for, and appreciation of, English learners. Understanding ourselves builds the foundation for understanding others.

## The Personal Dimension

For intercultural educators, self-reflection is vital. By examining their own attitudes, beliefs, and culturally derived beliefs and behaviors, teachers begin to discover what has influenced their value systems. Villegas and Lucas (2002) summarized this self-reflection in seven components (see Table 8.5).

## Cultural Self-Study

Self-study is a powerful tool for understanding culture. A way to begin a culture inquiry is by investigating one's personal name. For example, ask, "Where did I get my name? Who am I named for? In which culture did the name originate? What does the name mean?" Continue the self-examination by reviewing favorite cultural customs, such as holiday traditions, home decor, and favorite recipes.

More difficult self-examination questions address the mainstream U.S. values of individual freedom, self-reliance, competition, individualism, and hard work. One can consider

**TABLE 8.5** Components of the Personal Dimension of Intercultural Education

| Component | Description |
| --- | --- |
| Engage in reflective thinking and writing. | Awareness of one's actions, interactions, beliefs, and motivations—such as racism—can catalyze behavioral change. |
| Explore personal and family histories by interviewing family members. | Exploring early cultural experiences can help teachers better relate to individuals with different backgrounds. |
| Acknowledge group membership. | Teachers who acknowledge their affiliation with various groups in society can assess how this influences views of and relationships with other groups. |
| Learn about the experiences of diverse groups by reading or personal interaction. | Learning about the histories of diverse groups—from their perspectives—highlights value differences. |
| Visit or read about successful teachers. | Successful teachers of children from diverse backgrounds serve as exemplary role models. |
| Appreciate diversity. | Seeing difference as the norm in society reduces ethnocentrism. |
| Participate in reforming schools. | Teachers can help reform monocultural institutions. |

*Source:* Adapted from Villegas & Lucas (2002).

the following questions: If someone in authority tells me to do something, do I move quickly or slowly? If someone says, "Do you need any help?" do I usually say, "No, thanks. I can do it myself"? Am I comfortable promoting myself (for example, talking about my achievements in a performance review)? Do I prefer to work by myself or on a team? Do I like to associate with high achievers and avoid spending much time with people who do not work hard?

These and other introspective questions help to pinpoint cultural attitudes (see Box 8.4). Without a firm knowledge of one's own beliefs and behaviors, it is difficult to contrast the cultural behaviors of others. However, the self-examination process is challenging and ongoing. It is difficult to observe one's own culture.

## Participating in Growth Relationships

Self-study is only one means of attaining self-knowledge. Teachers who form relationships with individuals whose backgrounds differ from their own, whether teacher colleagues or community members, can benefit from honest feedback and discussions that help to expand self-awareness. Intercultural educators are not free from making mistakes when dealing with students, family and community members, and colleagues whose cultures differ from their own. The only lasting error is not learning from these missteps or misunderstandings.

**Box 8.4**   Cultural Self-Study: Self-Exploration Questions

- Describe yourself as a preschool child. Were you compliant, curious, adventuresome, goody-goody, physically active, nature loving? Have you observed your parents with other children? Do they encourage open-ended exploration, or would they prefer children to play quietly with approved toys? Do they encourage initiative?
- What was the knowledge environment like in your home? What type of reading did your father and mother do? Was there a time when the members of the family had discussions about current events or ideas and issues? How much dissent was tolerated from parental viewpoints? Were children encouraged to question the status quo? What was it like to learn to talk and think in your family?
- What kind of a grade school pupil were you? What is your best memory from elementary school? What was your favorite teacher like? Were you an avid reader? How would you characterize your cognitive style and learning style preferences? Was the school you attended ethnically diverse? What about your secondary school experience? Did you have a diverse group of friends in high school?
- What is your ethnic group? What symbols or traditions did you participate in that derived from this group? What do you like about your ethnic identity? Is there a time now when your group celebrates its traditions together? What was the neighborhood or community like in which you grew up?
- What was your experience with ethnic diversity? What were your first images of race or color? Was there a time in your life when you sought out diverse contacts to expand your experience?
- What contact do you have now with people of dissimilar racial or ethnic backgrounds? How would you characterize your desire to learn more? Given your learning style preferences, how would you go about this?

Exploring culture and cultural diversity is a lifelong endeavor. Many people experience this only after retirement, in traveling around the world as tourists. How lucky intercultural educators are, to be exposed to cultural diversity on a daily basis and have the opportunity to learn intercultural communication as they teach!

Go to the Topic Cultural and Linguistic Diversity in the MyEducationLab (www.myeducationlab.com) for your course, where you can:

- Find learning outcomes for Cultural and Linguistic Diversity along with the national standards that connect to these outcomes.
- Complete Assignments and Activities that can help you more deeply understand the chapter content.
- Apply and practice your understanding of the core teaching skills identified in the chapter with the Building Teaching Skills and Dispositions learning units.
- Examine challenging situations and cases presented in the IRIS Center Resources.
- Check your comprehension on the content covered in the chapter by going to the Study Plan in the Book Resources for your text. Here you will be able to take a chapter quiz, receive feedback on your answers, and then access Review, Practice, and Enrichment activities to enhance your understanding of chapter content.

Go to the Topic A+RISE in the MyEducationLab (www.myeducationlab.com) for your course. A+RISE® Standards2Strategy™ is an innovative and interactive online resource that offers new teachers in grades K–12 just-in-time, research-based instructional strategies that:

- Meet the linguistic needs of ELLs as they learn content
- Differentiate instruction for all grades and abilities
- Offer reading and writing techniques, cooperative learning, use of linguistic and nonlinguistic representations, scaffolding, teacher modeling, higher order thinking, and alternative classroom ELL assessment
- Provide support to help teachers be effective through the integration of listening, speaking, reading, and writing along with the content curriculum
- Improve student achievement
- Are aligned to Common Core Elementary Language Arts standards (for the literacy strategies) and to English language proficiency standards in WIDA, Texas, California, and Florida.

# 9

# Culturally Inclusive
# Instruction

## The Role of Culture in the Classroom and School

Culture influences every aspect of school life. Becoming an intercultural educator requires not only specific knowledge about the culture(s) of the students but also general knowledge about how to use that knowledge appropriately in specific contexts. Students from a nonmainstream culture are acquiring a mainstream classroom culture that may differ markedly from their home culture. Intercultural educators who understand students' cultures design instruction to meet children's learning needs.

### Acknowledging Students' Differences

Imagine a classroom of thirty students, each with just one unique fact, value, or belief included in the more than fifty categories presented in Table 8.2 ("Components of Culture"). Yet this dizzying array of uniqueness is only the tip of the iceberg, because within each of these categories individuals can differ. Take, for example, the category "food" under "daily life" in Table 8.2. Each student in a classroom of thirty knows a lot about food. What they know, however, depends largely on what they eat every day.

Culture includes diversity in values, social customs, rituals, work and leisure activities, health and educational practices, and many other aspects of life. Each of these can affect schooling, as we will discuss, including ways that teachers can respond to these differences in adapting instruction.

## The Alignment of Home and School

Teachers who are members of the mainstream culture and have an accommodating vision of cultural diversity recognize that they need to adapt culturally to CLD students, just as these individuals, in turn, accept some cultural change as they adapt to the mainstream. In this mutual process, teachers who model receptiveness to learning from the diverse cultures in their midst help students to see this diversity as a resource.

All the influences that contribute to the cultural profile of the family and community affect the students' reactions to classroom practices. Students whose home culture is consistent with the beliefs and practices of the school are generally more successful in school. However, different cultures organize individual and community behavior in radically different ways—ways that, on the surface, may not seem compatible with school practices and beliefs. To understand these differences is to be able to mediate for the students by helping them bridge relevant differences between the home and the school cultures.

Cultural accommodation is a two-way exchange. Obviously, a single teacher cannot change the culture of an entire school; similarly, families cannot change the deep structure of their values solely for the sake of their children's school success. Flexibility and awareness of cultural differences go a long way toward supporting students and defusing misunderstanding.

## The Value System of the Teacher and Cultural Accommodation

Because culture plays such an important role in the classroom and the school, the degree to which home and school are congruent can affect the student's learning and achievement. Some of this congruence—this alignment of the cultures of home and school—depends on what teachers see as important. Because over 80 percent of teachers represent mainstream culture, the following information contrasts U.S. mainstream values with those that might differ.

**What Are Values?**   Values are "beliefs about how one ought or ought not to behave or about some end state of existence worth or not worth attaining" (Bennett, 2003, p. 64). Values are particularly important to people when they educate their young, because education is a primary means of transmitting cultural knowledge. Parents in minority communities are often vitally interested in their children's education even though they may not be highly visible at school functions.

**Values about Time**   Cultures cause people to lead very different daily lives. These customs are paced and structured by deep habits of using time and space. For example, *time* is organized in culturally specific ways.

 **Classroom Glimpse**

### CULTURAL CONCEPTIONS ABOUT TIME

Adela, a Mexican-American first-grade girl, arrived at school about twenty minutes late every day. Her teacher was at first irritated and gradually exasperated. In a parent conference, Adela's mother explained that braiding her daughter's hair each morning was an important time for the two of them to be together, even if it meant being slightly late to school. This family time presented a values conflict with the school's time norm.

Other conflicts may arise when teachers demand abrupt endings to activities in which children are deeply engaged or when events are scheduled in a strict sequence. In fact, schools in the United States are often paced very strictly by clock time, whereas family life in various cultures is not regulated in the same manner. Moreover, teachers often equate speed of performance with intelligence, and standardized tests are often a test of rapidity. Many teachers find themselves in the role of "time mediator"—helping the class adhere to the school's time schedule while working with individual students to help them meet their learning needs within the time allotted.

---

**Best Practice**   **ACCOMMODATING TO DIFFERENT CONCEPTS OF TIME AND WORK RHYTHMS**

- Provide students with choices about their work time and observe how time spent on various subjects accords with students' aptitudes and interests.
- If a student is a slow worker, analyze the work rhythms. Slow yet methodically accurate work deserves respect, but slow and disorganized work may require a peer helper.
- If students are chronically late to school, ask the counselor to meet with the responsible family member to discuss a change in morning routines.

---

**Values about Space**   Another aspect about which values differ according to cultural experience is the concept and experience of space. Just as attitudes toward personal space vary among cultures, a cultural sense of space influences in which rooms and buildings people feel comfortable. Large cavernous classrooms may be overwhelming to students whose family activities are carried out in intimate spaces. The organization of the space in the classroom sends messages to students, such as how free they are to move about the classroom and how much of the classroom they "own." Both the expectations of the students and the needs of the teacher can be negotiated to provide a classroom setting in which space is shared.

---

 **Classroom Glimpse**

**DISCOMFORT IN THE CLASSROOM SPACE**

The classroom . . . was terribly huge and smelled of medicine like the village clinic I feared so much. Those fluorescent light tubes made an eerie drone. Our confinement to rows of desks was another unnatural demand made on our active little bodies. . . . We all went home for lunch since we lived a short walk from the school. It took coaxing, and sometimes bribing, to get me to return and complete the remainder of the school day. (Suina, 1985, n.p.)

---

**Values about Dress and Appearance**   Sometimes values are about externals, such as dress and personal appearance. For example, a third-grade girl wearing makeup is communicating a message that some teachers may consider an inappropriate indicator of premature sexuality, although makeup on a young girl may be acceptable in some cultures.

**Best Practice**  CULTURALLY INFLUENCED SCHOOL DRESS CODES

- Boys and men in some cultures (rural Mexico, for example) wear hats. Classrooms need to have a place for these hats during class time and provision for wearing the hats during recess.
- Schools that forbid "gang attire" yet permit privileged students to wear student council insignia (sweaters with embroidered names, for instance) should forbid clique-related attire for all.
- A family–school council with representatives from various cultures should be responsible for reviewing the school dress code on a yearly basis to see if it meets the needs of various cultures.

**Rites, Rituals, and Ceremonies**  Each culture incorporates expectations about the proper means for carrying out formal events. School ceremonies—for example, assemblies that begin with formal markers such as the Pledge of Allegiance and a flag salute—should have nonstigmatizing alternatives for those whose culture does not permit participation.

Rituals in some elementary classrooms in the United States are relatively informal. For example, students can enter freely before school and take their seats or go to a reading corner or activity center. Students from other cultures may find this confusing if they are accustomed to lining up in the courtyard, being formally greeted by the principal or head teacher, and then dismissed in their lines to enter their respective classrooms.

A traditional Hawai'ian custom involved students chanting outside the classroom door and listening for the teacher's welcome chant from within. In U.S. classrooms, a bell normally rings to start the school day, but individual class periods at the elementary level are not usually set off by formal signals to cue transitions.

**Best Practice**  ACCOMMODATING SCHOOL RITUALS

- Teachers might welcome newcomers with a brief explanation of the degree of formality expected of students.
- School seasonal celebrations are increasingly devoid of political and religious content. The school may, however, permit school clubs to honor events with extracurricular rituals.
- Teachers might observe colleagues from different cultures to view the rituals of family–teacher conferences and adapt their behavior accordingly to address families' cultural expectations.
- Greeting and welcome behaviors during parent conferences vary across cultures. The sensitive teacher understands how parents expect to be greeted and incorporates some of these behaviors in the exchange.

**Values about Work and Leisure**  Crosscultural variation in work and leisure activities is a frequently discussed value difference. Many members of mainstream U.S. culture value work over play; that is, one's status is directly related to one's productivity, salary, or job description. Play, rather than being an end in itself, is often used in ways that reinforce the status achieved through work. For example, teachers may meet informally at someone's home to bake holiday dishes, co-workers form bowling leagues, and alumni enjoy tailgate parties before attending football games; one's work status governs who is invited to attend these events.

Young people in the mainstream U.S. culture, particularly those in the middle class, are trained to use specific tools of play, and their time is structured to attain skills (e.g., organized sports, music lessons). In contrast, other cultures do not afford children structured time to play but instead expect children to engage in adult-type labor at work or in the home. In still other cultures, such as that of the Hopi Nation in Arizona, children's playtime is relatively unstructured, and parents do not interfere with play. Cultures also vary in the typical work and play activities expected of girls and of boys. All these values have obvious influence on the ways children work and play at school (Schultz & Theophano, 1987).

In work and play groups, the orientation may be individual or group. The United States is widely regarded as a society in which the individual is paramount. This individualism often pits students against one another for achievement. In contrast, many Mexican immigrants from rural communities have group-oriented values and put the needs of the community before individual achievement. Families may, for example, routinely pull children from school to attend funerals of neighbors in the community; in mainstream U.S. society, however, children would miss school only for the funerals of family members.

——————————— DID YOU KNOW? ———————————

**COOPERATION AND COMPETITION IN JAPAN**

In Japan, individuals compete fiercely for admission to prestigious universities, but accompanying this individual competitiveness is a sense that one must establish oneself within a group. Competition in the Japanese classroom is not realized in the same way as in U.S. schools; being singled out for attention or praise by teachers may result in embarrassment. (Furey, 1986)

**Best Practice**   ACCOMMODATING DIVERSE IDEAS ABOUT WORK AND PLAY

- Many high school students arrange class schedules in order to work part time. If a student appears chronically tired, a family–teacher conference may be needed to review priorities.
- Many students are overcommitted to extracurricular activities. If grades suffer, students may be well advised to reduce activities to regain an academic focus.
- Out-of-school play activities should not be organized at the school site, such as passing out birthday party invitations that exclude some students.

**Values about Medicine, Health, and Hygiene**   Health and medicine practices involve deep-seated beliefs because the stakes are high: life and death. Each culture has certain beliefs about sickness and health, beliefs that influence the interactions in health care settings. Students may have problems—war trauma, culture shock, poverty, addiction, family violence, crime—that their culture treats in particular culturally acceptable ways. When students come to school with health issues, teachers need to react in culturally compatible ways.

Miscommunication and noncooperation can result when teachers and the family view health and disease differently (Witte, 1991). For example, community health practices, such as the Cambodian tradition of coining (in which a coin is dipped in oil and then rubbed on a sick person's back, chest, and neck), can be misinterpreted by school officials who, seeing marks on the child, swiftly call Child Protective Services.

 **Classroom Glimpse**

### EXOTIC FAMILY HEALTH PRACTICE?

One of Ka's uncles called to explain that his nephew was sick and would miss school another two days. Lenny had read that the Hmong were animists and believed sickness was often caused by evil spirits who lured the soul from the body. Getting well sometimes required an animal sacrifice and a healing ceremony with a shaman who found and returned the runaway soul. Lenny wished the boy well and then asked about the nature and course of Ka's illness, fully expecting the evil spirit, animal sacrifice, and shaman scenarios. "Strep throat," answered the uncle, "but we went to the hospital and got antibiotics." (Cary, 2000, p. 19)

**Best Practice** HEALTH AND HYGIENE PRACTICES

- Families who send sick children to school or, conversely, keep children home at the slightest ache may benefit from a conference with the school nurse.
- All students can profit from explicit instruction in home and school hygiene.

**Values about Economics, Law, Politics, and Religion**  The institutions that support and govern family and community life have an influence on behavior and beliefs. The economic institutions of the United States are diverse, ranging from small business enterprises to large corporate or government agencies. These institutions influence daily life in the United States by means of a complex infrastructure. The families of English learners may fit in anywhere along this continuum.

Interwoven into this rich cultural-economic-political-legal texture are religious beliefs and practices. In the United States, religious practices are heavily embedded but formally bounded—people argue over Christmas trees in public schools but there is almost universal acceptance of increased consumer spending at the close of the calendar year. Religious beliefs underlie other cultures even more fundamentally.

Immigrants with Confucian religious and philosophical beliefs, for example, subscribe to values that mandate a highly ordered society and family through the maintenance of proper social relationships. In Islamic traditions, the Koran prescribes proper social relationships and roles for members of society. When immigrants with these religious beliefs encounter the largely secular U.S. institutions, the result may be that customs and cultural patterns are challenged, fade away, or cause conflict within the family (Chung, 1989).

---

**Best Practice** ACCOMMODATING ECONOMIC, LEGAL, POLITICAL, AND RELIGIOUS PRACTICES

- On a rotating basis, teachers could be paid to supervise after-school homework sessions for students whose parents are working multiple jobs.
- Schools can legally resist any attempts to identify families whose immigration status is undocumented.
- Schools should not tolerate messages of political partisanship.
- Permission for religious garb or appearance (e.g., Islamic head scarves, Sikh ritual knives, Hassidic dress) should be a part of the school dress code.

---

**Values and Expectations about Education** In the past, educational systems were designed to pass on cultural knowledge and traditions, which constituted much the same learning that parents taught their children. Students come to school steeped in the learning practices of their own family and community. However, many of the organizational and teaching practices of the school may not support the type of learning to which students are accustomed.

For example, Indochinese students expect to listen, watch, and imitate. They may be reluctant to ask questions or volunteer answers and may be embarrassed to ask for the teacher's help or reluctant to participate in individual demonstrations of a skill or project. For immigrant children with previous schooling, experience in U.S. classrooms may engender severe conflicts. Teachers who can accommodate these students' proclivities can gradually introduce student-centered practices while supporting an initial dependence on the teacher's direction.

--- **DID YOU KNOW?** ---

**OVERCOMING PASSIVITY**

Polynesian students newly arrived from the South Pacific may have experienced classroom learning as a relatively passive activity. They expect teachers to give explicit instruction about what to learn and how to learn it. When these students arrive in the United States and encounter teachers who value creativity and student-centered learning, they may appear passive as they wait to be told what to do. (Funaki & Burnett, 1993)

**Best Practice** ACCOMMODATING CULTURALLY BASED
EDUCATIONAL EXPECTATIONS

Teachers who seek to understand the value of education within the community can do the
following:

- Invite classroom guests from the community to share methods for teaching and learning that are used in the home (e.g., modeling and imitation, didactic stories and proverbs, direct verbal instruction).
- Pair children from cultures that expect passive responses to teachers (observing only) with more participatory peers to help the former learn to ask questions and volunteer.
- In communities with a high dropout rate, support the systematic efforts of school counselors and administrators to help families accommodate their beliefs to a more proactive support for school completion and higher education.

**Values about Roles and Status**    Cultures differ in the roles people play in society and the status accorded to these roles. For example, in the Vietnamese culture, profoundly influenced by Confucianism, authority figures are ranked in the following manner: The father ranks below the teacher, who ranks only below the king (Chung, 1989). Such a high status is not accorded to teachers in U.S. society, where, instead, medical doctors enjoy this type of prestige. Such factors as gender, social class, age, occupation, and education level influence the manner in which status is accorded to various roles. Students' perceptions about the roles possible for them in their culture affect their school performance.

**Values about Gender**    In many cultures, gender is related to social roles in a similar way. Anthropologists have found men to be in control of political and military matters in all known cultures. Young boys tend to be more physically and verbally aggressive and to seek dominance more than girls do. Traditionally, women have had the primary responsibility for child-rearing, with associated tasks, manners, and responsibilities. Immigrants to the United States often come from cultures in which men and women have rigid and highly differentiated gender roles. The gender equality that is an ostensible goal in U.S. classrooms may be difficult for students of these cultures.

 **Classroom Glimpse**

### TO MENTOR OR NOT TO MENTOR?

Chad is a journalism teacher in a large urban high school and the advisor of the school newspaper. Khalia is a young woman who enrolled in a beginning journalism class as a junior. Although English was not her first language, she showed unusual ability and creativity in writing the stories to which she was assigned. Chad routinely advises students on their vocational choice, writes letters of recommendation for them when they apply to college, and encourages those who want to further their education. Khalia has confided in him that her parents have discouraged her from attending college. Khalia does not want to marry immediately after high school and has asked Chad's help in applying to college. Should Chad help Khalia?

---

**Best Practice**   GENDER-ROLE EXPECTATIONS

- Monitor tasks performed by boys and girls to ensure they are the same.
- Make sure that boys and girls perform equal leadership roles in cooperative groups.
- If families in a given community provide little support for the scholastic achievement of girls, a systematic effort on the part of school counselors and administrators may be needed to help families accommodate their beliefs to a more proactive support for women.

---

**Values about Social Class**   Stratification by social class differs across cultures. Cultures that are rigidly stratified, such as India's caste system, differ from cultures that are not as rigid or that, in some cases, border on the anarchic, such as continuously war-torn countries. The belief that education can enhance economic status is widespread in the dominant culture of the United States, but individuals in other cultures may not have similar beliefs.

In general, individuals and families at the upper socioeconomic levels are able to exert power by sitting on college, university, and local school boards and thus determining who receives benefits and rewards through schooling. However, middle-class values are those that are generally incorporated in the culture of schooling. The social-class values that children learn in their homes largely influence not only their belief in schooling but also their routines and habits in the classroom.

---

**Best Practice**   ACCOMMODATING THE INFLUENCE OF SOCIAL CLASS ON SCHOOLING

- Students who are extremely poor or homeless may need help from the teacher to store possessions at school.
- A teacher who receives an expensive gift should consult the school district's ethics policies.
- A high grade on a school assignment or project should not depend on extensive family financial resources.

---

**Values about Age-Appropriate Activities**   Age interacts with culture, socioeconomic status, gender, and other factors to influence an individual's behavior and attitudes. In various cultures, expectations about appropriate activities for children and the purpose of those activities differ. Middle-class European Americans expect children to spend much of their time playing and attending school rather than performing tasks similar to those of adults. Cree Indian children, on the other hand, are expected from an early age to learn adult roles, including contributing food to the family. Parents may criticize schools for involving children in tasks that are not related to their future participation in Cree society (Sindell, 1988).

Cultures also differ in their criteria for moving through the various (culturally defined) life cycle changes. An important stage in any culture is the move into adulthood, but the age at which this occurs and the criteria necessary for attaining adulthood vary according to what adulthood means in a particular culture. Rural, traditional families in many countries expect young men and women to be socially mature when they enter high school, whereas other families, for example, middle-class families in Taiwan, expect a much longer period of adolescence.

---

### Best Practice   ACCOMMODATING BELIEFS ABOUT AGE-APPROPRIATE ACTIVITIES

- Child labor laws in the United States forbid students from working for pay before a given age. However, few laws govern children working in family businesses. If a child appears chronically tired, the school counselor may need to discuss the child's involvement in a family business with a responsible family member.
- Cultural groups in which girls are expected to marry and have children at the age of fifteen or sixteen (e.g., Hmong) may need access to alternative schools.
- If a student misses school because of obligations to accompany family members to social services to act as a translator or to stay at home as a babysitter, the school counselor may be able to intervene to help families find other resources.

---

**Values about Occupations**   In the United States, occupation very often determines income, which in turn is a chief determinant of prestige in the culture. Other cultures, however, may attribute prestige to those with inherited status or to those who have a religious function in the culture. Prestige is one factor in occupational choices. Other factors can include cultural acceptance of the occupation, educational requirements, gender, and attainability. Students therefore may not see all occupations as desirable or even available to them and may have mixed views about the role education plays in their future occupations.

Some cultural groups in the United States are engaged in a voluntary way of life that does not require public schooling (e.g., the Amish). Other groups may not be adequately rewarded in the United States for school success but expect to be rewarded elsewhere (e.g., children of diplomats and short-term residents who expect to return to their home country). Still other groups may be involuntarily incorporated into U.S. society and relegated to menial occupations and ways of life that do not reward and require school success (e.g., Hispanics in the Southwest). As a result, they may not apply academic effort (Ogbu & Matute-Bianchi, 1986).

---

### Best Practice   ACCOMMODATING OCCUPATIONAL ASPIRATIONS

- At all grade levels, school subjects should be connected with future vocations.
- Role models from minority communities can visit the classroom to recount stories of their success. Successful professionals and businesspeople can visit and explain how cultural diversity is supported in their place of work.
- Teachers should make available at every grade an extensive set of books on occupations and their requirements and discuss these with students.

---

**Values about Child-Rearing**   The ways in which families raise their children have significant implications for schools. Factors such as who takes care of children, how much supervision they receive, how much freedom they have, who speaks to them and how often, and what they are expected to do affect students' behavior on entering schools. Many of the misunderstandings that occur between teachers and students arise because of different expectations about behavior, and these different expectations stem from early, ingrained child-rearing practices.

Because the largest group of English learners in California is of Mexican ancestry, teachers who take the time to learn about child-rearing practices among Mexican immigrants can help students adjust to schooling practices in the United States. An excellent source for this cultural study is *Crossing Cultural Borders* (Delgado-Gaitan & Trueba, 1991).

**Food Preferences and Practices** As the numbers of school-provided breakfasts and lunches increase, food preferences are an important consideration. Furthermore, teachers who are knowledgeable about students' dietary practices can incorporate their students' background knowledge into health and nutrition instruction.

Besides customs of what and when to eat, eating habits vary widely across cultures, and "good" manners at the table in some cultures are inappropriate or rude in others. For example, the Indochinese consider burping, lip smacking, and soup slurping to be common behaviors during meals, even complimentary to hosts. Cultural relativity is not, however, an excuse for poor or unhygienic eating, and teachers do need to teach students the behaviors that are considered good food manners in the U.S. mainstream context.

---

**Best Practice** DEALING WITH FOOD PREFERENCES

- In addition to knowing in general what foods are eaten at home, teachers will want to find out about students' favorite foods, taboo foods, and typical foods.
- Eating lunch with students, even on a by-invitation basis, can provide the opportunity to learn about students' habits.
- If a student's eating habits alienate peers, the teacher may need to discuss appropriate behaviors.

---

**Valuing Humanities and the Arts** In many cultures, crafts performed at home—such as food preparation, sewing and weaving, carpentry, home building and decoration, and religious and ritual artistry for holy days and holidays—are an important part of the culture that is transmitted within the home. Parents also provide an important means of access to the humanities and the visual and performing arts of their cultures. The classroom teacher can foster an appreciation of the works of art, architecture, music, and dance that have been achieved by students' native cultures by drawing on the resources of the community and then sharing these with all members of the classroom.

**Cooperation versus Competition** Many cultures emphasize cooperation over competition. Traditional U.S. classrooms mirror middle-class European-American values of competition: Students are expected to do their own work; are rewarded publicly through star charts, posted grades, and academic honors; and are admonished to do their individual best. In the Cree Indian culture, however, children are raised in a cooperative atmosphere, with siblings, parents, and other kin sharing food as well as labor (Sindell, 1988). In the Mexican-American culture, interdependence is strength; individuals have a commitment to others, and all decisions are made together. Those who are successful have a responsibility to others to help them succeed.

A classroom structured to maximize learning through cooperation can help students extend their cultural predilection for interdependence. However, this interdependence does not devalue the uniqueness of the individual. The Mexican culture values *individualismo*, the affirmation of an individual's intrinsic worth and uniqueness aside from any successful actions or grand position in society (deUnamuno, 1925). A workable synthesis of individualism versus interdependence would come from classroom activities that are carried out as a group but that affirm the unique gifts of each individual student.

## Adapting to Students' Culturally Supported Facilitating or Limiting Attitudes and Abilities

A skilled intercultural educator recognizes that each culture supports distinct attitudes, values, and abilities that may either facilitate or limit learning in U.S. public schools. For example, the cultures of Japan, China, and Korea, which promote high academic achievement, may foster facilitating behaviors such as the ability to listen and follow directions, attitudes favoring education and respect for teachers and authorities, ideas of discipline as guidance, and high-achievement motivation. However, other culturally supported traits may hinder adjustment to the U.S. school, such as lack of previous participation in discussions; little experience with independent thinking; strong preference for conformity, which inhibits divergent thinking; and distinct sex-role differentiation, with males more dominant.

Mexican-American cultural values encourage cooperation, affectionate and demonstrative parental relationships, children's assumption of mature social responsibilities such as child care and translating family matters from English to Spanish, and eagerness to try out new ideas. All of these values facilitate classroom success. On the other hand, such attitudes as depreciating education after high school, especially for women; explicit sex-role stereotyping favoring limited vocational roles for women; emphasis of family over the achievement and life goals of children; and dislike of competition may work against classroom practices and hinder school success (Clark, 1983).

Accommodating school routines is a schoolwide responsibility that is furthered when the principal sets the tone of appreciation and support for cultural diversity. Much can also be done by individual teachers in the classroom to set high standards of achievement that students and family members can support.

# Educating Students about Diversity

Both mainstream students and CLD students benefit from education about diversity, not only cultural diversity but also diversity in ability, gender preference, and human nature in general. This engenders pride in cultural identity, expands the students' perspectives, and adds cultural insight, information, and experiences to the curriculum.

Cultural content is an important part of education; it is a means by which students come to understand their own culture(s) as well as the mainstream U.S. culture. As Curtain and Dahlberg (2010) commented,

The interests and developmental levels of the students in the class must guide the choice of cultural information selected for instruction. . . . Children penetrate a new culture through meaningful experiences with cultural practices and cultural phenomena that are appropriate to their age level, their interests, and the classroom setting. (p. 259)

## Global and Multicultural Education

ELD teachers, as well as mainstream teachers who teach English learners, can bring a global and multicultural perspective to their classes.

Language teachers, like teachers in all other areas of the curriculum, have a responsibility to plan lessons with sensitivity to the racial and ethnic diversity present in their classrooms and in the world in which their students live. . . . [Students] can learn to value the points of view of many others whose life experiences are different from their own. (Curtain & Dahlberg, 2010, p. 276)

Table 9.1 lists some cultural activities that Curtain and Dahlberg recommended for adding cultural content to the curriculum.

There is a clear distinction between multiculturalism and globalism, although both are important features of the school curriculum: "Globalism emphasizes the cultures and peoples of other lands, and multiculturalism deals with ethnic diversity within the United States" (Ukpokodu, 2002, pp. 7–8).

**TABLE 9.1** Sample Cultural Activities for Multicultural Education

| Activity | Suggested Implementation |
|---|---|
| Visitors and guest speakers | Guests can share their experiences on a variety of topics, using visuals, slides, and hands-on materials. |
| Folk dances, singing games, and other kinds of games | Many cultures can be represented; cultural informants can help. |
| Field trips | Students can visit neighborhoods, restaurants, museums, or stores that feature cultural materials. |
| Show-and-tell | Students can bring items from home to share with the class. |
| Read fables, folktales, or legends | Read in translation or have a visitor read in another language. |
| Read books about other cultures | Age-appropriate fiction or nonfiction books can be obtained with the help of the school or public librarian. |
| Crosscultural e-mail contacts | Students can exchange cultural information and get to know peers from other lands. |
| Magazine subscriptions | Authentic cultural materials—written for adults or young people—give insight about the lifestyles and interests of others. |

*Source:* Curtain & Dahlberg (2010).

—————————————— DID YOU KNOW? ——————————————

**STUDYING CULTURES HERE AND THERE**

James Banks explained the difference between studying the cultures of other countries and studying the cultures within the United States. For example, according to Banks, many teachers implement a unit on the country of Japan but avoid teaching about Japanese internment in the United States during World War II. (Brandt, 1994)

## The Multicultural Curriculum: From Additive to Transformative

The goal of multicultural education is to help students "develop cross-cultural competence within the American national culture, with their own subculture and within and across different subsocieties and cultures" (Banks, 1994, p. 9). Banks introduced a model of multicultural education that has proved to be a useful way of assessing the approach taken in pedagogy and curricula. The model has four levels, represented in Table 9.2 with a critique of strengths and shortcomings taken from Jenks, Lee, and Kanpol (2002).

**TABLE 9.2**  Banks's Levels of Multicultural Education, with Critique

| Level | Description | Strengths | Shortcomings |
|---|---|---|---|
| Contributions | Emphasizes what minority groups have contributed to society (examples: International Food Day, bulletin board display for Black History Month). | Attempts to sensitize the majority White culture to some understanding of minority groups' history. | May amount to "cosmetic" multiculturalism in which no discussion takes place about issues of power and disenfranchisement. |
| Additive | Adding material to the curriculum to address what has been omitted (reading *The Color Purple* in English class). | Adds to a fuller coverage of the American experience, when sufficient curricular time is allotted. | May be an insincere effort if dealt with superficially. |
| Transformative | An expanded perspective is taken that deals with issues of historic, ethnic, cultural, and linguistic injustice and equality as a part of the American experience. | Students learn to be reflective and develop a critical perspective. | Incorporates the fallacy that discussion alone changes society. |
| Social Action | Extension of the transformative approach to add students' research/action projects to initiate change in society. | Students learn to question the status quo and the commitment of the dominant culture to equality and social justice. | Middle-class communities may not accept the teacher's role, considering it as provoking students to "radical" positions. |

*Sources:* Model based on Banks (1994); strengths and shortcomings based on Jenks, Lee, & Kanpol (2002).

Similar to Banks's superficial-to-transformative continuum is that of Morey and Kilano (1997). Their three-level framework for incorporating diversity identifies as "exclusive" the stereotypical focus on external aspects of diversity (what they called the four *f*'s: food, folklore, fun, and fashion); as "inclusive" the addition of diversity into a curriculum that, although enriched, fundamentally has the same structure; and as "transformed" the curriculum that is built on diverse perspectives, equity in participation, and critical problem solving. Thus, it is clear that pouring new wine (diversity) into old bottles (teacher-centered, one-size-fits-all instruction) is not transformative.

 **Classroom Glimpse**

### TRANSFORMATIVE MULTICULTURAL EDUCATION

Christensen (2000) described how her students were moved to action:

> One year our students responded to a negative newspaper article, about how parents feared to send their children to our school, by organizing a march and rally to "tell the truth about Jefferson to the press." During the Columbus quincentenary, my students organized a teach-in about Columbus for classes at Jefferson. Of course, these "spontaneous uprisings" only work if teachers are willing to give over class time for the students to organize, and if they've highlighted times when people in history resisted injustice, making it clear that solidarity and courage are values to be prized in daily life, not just praised in the abstract and put on the shelf. (pp. 8–9)

## Validating Students' Cultural Identity

"An affirming attitude toward students from culturally diverse backgrounds significantly impacts their learning, belief in self, and overall academic performance" (Villegas & Lucas, 2002, p. 23). Cultural identity—that is, having a positive self-concept or evaluation of oneself and one's culture—promotes self-esteem. Students who feel proud of their successes and abilities, self-knowledge, and self-expression, and who have enhanced images of self, family, and culture, are better learners.

Of course, the most powerful sense of self-esteem is the result not solely of one's beliefs about oneself but also of successful learning experiences. Practices of schooling that damage self-esteem, such as tracking and competitive grading, undermine authentic cooperation and a sense of accomplishment on the part of English learners.

**Classroom Practices That Validate Identity**  Siccone (1995) described the activity Name Interviews in which students work in pairs using a teacher-provided questionnaire: "What do you like about your name? Who named you? Were you named for someone? Are there members of your family who have the same name?" This activity can be adapted for both elementary and secondary classrooms. Díaz-Rico (2004) suggested that interested teachers might ask students to provide initial information about cultural customs in their homes, perhaps pertaining to birthdays or holidays. Through observations, shared conversations during lunchtime or before or after school, and group participation, teachers can gain understanding about various individuals and their cultures.

Educators who form relationships with parents can talk about the students' perception of their own identity. Teachers can also ask students to interview their parents about common topics such as work, interests, and family history and then add a reflective element about their relationship and identification with these aspects of their parents' lives.

---

**Best Practice**   **CULTURAL CONTENT PROMOTES SCHOOL ENGAGEMENT**

In a study of 600 middle and high school teachers in Hawai'i, Takayama and Ledward (2009) found that school engagement was higher on the part of students whose teachers drew upon the concepts of *'ohana* (family), *kaiaulu* (community), and *olelo* (Haiwaiian language) to create culturally relevant content, contexts, and assessments during classroom learning. School engagement includes "emotional engagement (students' feelings about teachers, other students, and school in general); behavioral engagement (inferred through positive conduct and adherence to rules); and cognitive engagement (willingness to exert effort in learning)." (Takayama & Ledward, 2009, p. 1)

---

**Instructional Materials That Validate Identity**   Classroom texts are available that offer literature and anecdotal readings aimed at the enhancement of identity and self-esteem. *Identities: Readings from Contemporary Culture* (Raimes, 1996) includes readings grouped into chapters titled "Name," "Appearance, Age, and Abilities," "Ethnic Affiliation and Class," "Family Ties," and so forth. The readings contain authentic text and may be best used in middle or high school classes.

Multicultural literature can enhance cultural and ethnic identity, but this is not always the case. In 1976 a committee of Asian-American book reviewers formed the Asian-American Children's Book Project under the aegis of the Council for Interracial Books for Children. Their main objective was to evaluate books and identify those that could be used effectively in educational programs.

When they had evaluated a total of sixty-four books related to Asian-American issues or characters, they concluded that most of the existing literature was "racist, sexist, and elitist and that the image of Asian Americans present [in the books] is grossly misleading" (Aoki, 1992, p. 133). The criticism was that these books depicted "Orientals" as slant-eyed, black-haired, quietly subservient people living lives far removed from those of mainstream Americans. The challenge, then, is to represent ethnic characters in a more realistic way.

A book that is useful for a comparison of Asian cultural values with those of mainstream American culture is Kim's (2001) *The Yin and Yang of American Culture.* This book presents a view of American culture—its virtues and vices—from an Eastern perspective and may stimulate discussion on the part of students. *Exploring Culturally Diverse Literature for Children and Adolescents* (Henderson & May, 2005) helps readers understand how stories are tied to specific cultural and sociopolitical histories.

## Promoting Mutual Respect among Students

The ways in which we organize classroom life should make children feel significant and cared about—by the teacher and by one another. Unless students feel emotionally and physically safe, they will be reluctant to share real thoughts and feelings. Classroom life should, to the greatest extent possible, prefigure the kind of democratic and just society we envision and thus contribute to building that society. Together, students and teachers can create a "community of conscience," as educators Asa Hillard and George Pine call it (Christensen, 2000, p. 18). Mutual respect is promoted when teachers listen as much as they speak, when students can build on their personal and cultural strengths, when the curriculum includes multiple points of view, and when students are given the chance to genuinely talk to one another about topics that concern them. The instructional conversation is a discourse format that encourages in-depth conversation, a lost art in today's world (see Chapters 1 and 6).

## Learning about Students' Cultures

Teachers can use printed, electronic, and video materials, books, and magazines to learn about other cultures. However, the richest source of information is local—the life of the community. Students, parents, and community members can provide insights about values, attitudes, and habits. One method of learning about students and their families, ethnographic study, has proved useful in illuminating the ways that students' experiences in the home and community compare with the culture of the schools.

### Ethnographic Techniques

Ethnography is an inquiry process that seeks to provide cultural explanations for behavior and attitudes. Culture is described from the insider's point of view, as the classroom teacher becomes not only an observer of the students' cultures but also an active participant (Erickson, 1977; Mehan, 1981; Robinson, 1985). Parents and community members, as well as students, become sources for the gradual growth of understanding on the part of the teacher.

For the classroom teacher, ethnography involves gathering data in order to understand two distinct cultures: the culture of the students' communities and the culture of the classroom. To understand the home and community environment, teachers may observe and participate in community life, interview community members, and visit students' homes. To understand the school culture, teachers may observe in a variety of classrooms, have visitors observe in their own classroom, audio- and videotape classroom interaction, and interview other teachers and administrators.

**Observations**  Ideally, initial observations of other cultures must be carried out with the perspective that one is seeing the culture from the point of view of a complete outsider. Of course, when observing interactions and behaviors in another culture, one always uses the frame of reference supplied by one's own culture. This stance gradually changes as one adopts an ethnographic perspective.

Observers need to be descriptive and objective and make explicit their own attitudes and values in order to overcome hidden sources of bias. This requires practice and, ideally, some training. However, the classroom teacher can begin to observe and participate in the students' culture, writing up field notes after participating and perhaps summing up the insights gained in an ongoing diary that can be shared with colleagues. Such observation can document children's use of language within the community; etiquettes of speaking, listening, writing, greeting, and getting or giving information; values and aspirations; and norms of communication.

When analyzing the culture of the classroom, teachers might look at classroom management and routines; affective factors (students' attitudes toward activities, teachers' attitudes toward students); classroom talk in general; and nonverbal behaviors and communication. In addition to the raw data of behavior, the thoughts and intentions of the participants can also be documented.

**Interviews**    Interviews can be divided into two types: structured and unstructured. Structured interviews use a set of predetermined questions to gain specific kinds of information. Unstructured interviews are more like conversations in that they can range over a wide variety of topics, many of which the interviewer would not necessarily have anticipated. As an outsider learning about a new culture, the classroom teacher would be better served initially by using an unstructured interview, beginning with general questions and being guided in follow-up questions by the interviewees' responses. The result of the initial interview may in turn provide a structure for learning more about the culture during a second interview or conversation. A very readable book about ethnography and interviewing is *The Professional Stranger: An Informal Introduction to Ethnography* (Agar, 1980).

**Home Visits**    Home visits are one of the best ways in which teachers can learn what is familiar and important to their students. The home visit can be a social call or a brief report on the student's progress that enhances rapport with students and parents. Scheduling an appointment ahead of time is a courtesy that some cultures may require and provides a means for the teacher to ascertain if home visits are welcome. The visit should be short (twenty to thirty minutes) and the conversation positive, especially about the student's schoolwork. Viewing the child in the context of the home provides a look at the parent–child interaction, the resources of the home, and the child's role in the family.

 **Classroom Glimpse**

### A HOME VISIT

Hughes describes the result of one home visit:

> Years ago a child named Nai persuaded her parents to let me visit them. Many people lived in the small apartment. One of the men spoke a little English as I tried a few Mien phrases that drew chuckles and good will. I ate with them. Recently a community college student dropped in at our school. "Nai!" I cried, delighted. . . . "How's your family?" "They OK." "I enjoyed my visit with them," I said. She smiled. "My parents . . . they talk still about 'that teacher,' they call you." (Hughes, 2004, p. 10)

## Students as Sources of Information

Students generally provide teachers with their initial contact with other cultures. Through observations, one-on-one interaction, and group participatory processes, teachers gain understanding about various individuals and their cultural repertoires. Teachers who are good listeners offer students time for shared conversations by lingering after school or opening the classroom during lunchtime. Questionnaires and interest surveys are also useful. Cary (2000) called this information about students their "outside story": "The outside story unfolds away from school and is built from a thousand and one experiences hooked to home and home country culture—family structure, language, communication patterns, social behavior, values, spirituality, and worldview" (p. 20).

Cary's *Working with Second Language Learners: Answers to Teachers' Top Ten Questions* (2000) details one teacher's exploration of the culture and homeland of a Hmong student, Ka Xiong. Lenny Rossovich, the teacher of the new fifth grader, used every resource from a school encyclopedia, websites (including the Hmong homepage [see Table 9.3]), the local library, and one of Ka's uncles to learn more about the Hmong culture. Lenny even took a few Hmong language lessons on the Web. Lenny's adventure toward understanding his student is an engrossing model.

## Families as Sources of Information

Family members can be sources of information in much the same way as their children. Rather than scheduling one or two formal conferences, PTA open house events, and gala performances, the school might encourage family participation by opening the library once a week after school. This offers a predictable time during which family members and teachers can casually meet and chat. Families can also be the source for information that can form the basis for classroom writing. Using the language experience approach, teachers can ask students to interview their family members about common topics such as work, interests, and family history. In this way, students and family members together can supply knowledge about community life.

## Community Members as Sources of Information

Community members are an equally rich source of cultural knowledge. Much can be learned about a community by walking or driving through it, or stopping to make a purchase in local stores and markets. Teachers may ask older students to act as tour guides. During these visits, the people of the neighborhood can be sources of knowledge about housing, spaces where children and teenagers play, places where adults gather, and sources of food, furniture, and services.

Through community representatives, teachers can begin to know about important living patterns of a community. A respected elder can provide information about the family and which members constitute a family. A religious leader can explain the importance of religion in community life. Teachers can also attend local ceremonies and activities to learn more about community dynamics.

## The Internet as an Information Source about Cultures

Websites proliferate that introduce the curious to other cultures. Webcrawler programs assist the user to explore cultural content using key word prompts. Table 9.3 lists websites with information about cultures commonly represented in U.S. schools.

# Culturally Inclusive Learning Environments

Culturally responsive accommodations help teachers maintain culturally inclusive learning environments. But what characteristics of classroom and school environments facilitate culturally responsive accommodations to diverse communities?

**TABLE 9.3** Websites Featuring Cultures Found in U.S. Schools

| Culture | Website |
|---|---|
| Armenia | www.loc.gov/rr/international/amed/armenia/resources/armenia-culture.html |
| Cambodia | http://ethnomed.org/culture/cambodian |
| China | http://chineseculture.about.com |
| Eritrea | http://ethnomed.org/culture/eritrean/eritrean-cultural-profile |
| Hmong | www.hmongnet.org |
| India | www.culturopedia.com |
| Iran | www.iranvision.com |
| Japan | www.japan-zone.com/culture/index.shtml |
| Laos | www.laoheritagefoundation.org |
| Mexico | www.infoplease.com/ipa/A0107779.html |
| Philippines | http://pinas.dlsu.edu.ph/culture/culture.html |
| Russia | www.goehner.com/russinfo.htm |
| Somalia | http://news.bbc.co.uk/2/hi/africa/country_profiles/1072592.stm |
| South Korea | www.korea.net/index.do |
| Tonga | www.answers.com/topic/culture-of-tonga |
| Ukraine | www.infoukes.com/culture |
| Vietnam | http://ethnomed.org/cultures/vietnamese/ vietnamese_cp.html |

## What Is a Culturally Supportive Classroom?

A variety of factors contribute to classroom and school environments that support cultural diversity and student achievement. The most important feature of these classrooms is the expectation of high achievement from English learners while supporting them culturally, intellectually, and emotionally toward the attainment of this goal. Communicating these expectations requires specific educational programs that draw attention to the hidden curriculum of the school, quality of interaction between teachers and students, diverse learning styles, the use of the community as a resource, and a commitment to democratic ideals in the classroom (Gollnick & Chinn, 2002). Such factors as culturally accommodating schooling, supporting students' culture(s) and language(s), and conflict resolution have already been discussed. High expectations, active student learning, and use of critical thinking and critical consciousness are explored in turn, followed by ways to involve the family and community.

**High Expectations for All Students** Expectations for student achievement are also a feature of culturally responsive schooling. Teachers need to challenge students to strive for excellence as defined by their potential. Teachers tread a fine line between expecting too much of their students, causing frustration on students' part through stress and overwork, and expecting too little by watering down the curriculum, leading to boredom and low academic achievement.

Many students' abilities are underestimated because their second-language skills do not adequately convey their talents. Sometimes unfamiliarity with the students' culture compounds the language barrier. Ongoing formative assessment, combined with a sensitive awareness of students' needs and a willingness to be flexible, help the teacher monitor and adjust the instructional level to students' abilities.

Teachers' behavior varies with the level of expectation held about the students. Students of whom much is expected are given more frequent cues and prompts to respond to, asked more and harder questions, given a longer time to respond, encouraged to provide more elaborate answers, and interrupted less often (Good & Brophy, 1984). Teachers tend to be encouraging toward students for whom they have high expectations. They smile at these students more often and show greater warmth through nonverbal responses such as leaning toward the students and nodding their head as students speak (Woolfolk & Brooks, 1985).

Students' responses to teacher expectations seem to be highly influenced by cultural background and home discourse patterns. Sato (1982) found that Asian students initiated classroom discourse less often than English learners from other countries. Some cultures encourage students to set internal standards of worth, and peer pressure also devalues dependence on teachers for approval; therefore students are less apt to participate in classroom discourse.

**Motivating Students to Become Active Participants in Their Learning** Learner autonomy is a key element of constructivist learning, in which teachers help students to construct new knowledge, providing scaffolds between what students already know and what they need to learn. Autonomy is the learner's ability and willingness to study due to internal volition. Learner autonomy is the basis for self-managed, self-motivated instruction. More than a preference or strategy by the learner, autonomy must be supported in a systematic way by the teacher and curriculum for the learner to benefit, but it is at risk in the climate of coercive adherence to standardized test scores as the sole criterion of effective instruction. Certainly, in democratic schooling, there is a place for choice in topics and freedom to voice divergent views (Giroux & McLaren, 1996).

**Encouraging Students to Think Critically and Become Socially and Politically Conscious**
"Sociocultural consciousness means understanding that one's way of thinking, behaving, and being is influenced by race, ethnicity, social class, and language" (Kea, Campbell-Whatley, & Richards, 2004, p. 4). Students as well as teachers need to have clarity of vision about their sociocultural identities and their role in the institutions that maintain social and economic distinctions based on social class and skin color.

Political and social consciousness is hard-won. It requires teachers to offer students a forum in which to discuss social and political events without partisan rancor, to investigate issues in the national and local press that are open to multiple perspectives, and to find a way to support students' voices about their lives and feelings. Bulletin boards on which student writing can be posted, weekly current event discussions, and class newsletters are projects that can encourage autonomous student thinking, writing, and discussion.

An important aspect of schooling in a democracy is the ability to think for oneself, analyze ideas, separate fact from opinion, support opinions from reading, make inferences, and solve problems. The ability to think critically can enhance self-understanding and help students approach significant issues in life with analytic skills. Critical thinking includes the ability to look for underlying assumptions in statements, to detect bias, to identify illogical connections between ideas, and to recognize attempts to influence opinion by means of propaganda. These skills are fundamental to the clear thinking required of autonomous citizens in a democracy.

# Family and Community Involvement

Family and community involvement supports and encourages students and provides opportunities for families and educators to work together in educating students. Families need to become involved in different settings and at different levels of the educational process. Family members can help teachers establish a genuine respect for their children and the strengths they bring to the classroom. They can work with their own children at home or serve on school committees. Collaborative involvement in school restructuring includes family and community members who help set goals and allocate resources.

## Value Differences in Family and Community Support for Schooling

Family involvement in the school is influenced by cultural beliefs. The U.S. system was developed from small, relatively homogeneous local schools with considerable community and parental control. The pattern of community and parental involvement continues today with school boards, PTAs, and parent volunteers in the schools. This pattern is not universal outside the United States. For example, in traditional Cambodia, village families who sent their children to schools in cities had no means of involving themselves in the school (Ouk, Huffman, & Lewis, 1988).

In cultures in which teachers are accorded high status, parents may consider it improper to discuss educational matters or bring up issues that concern their children. Other factors that make family involvement difficult are school procedures such as restrictive scheduling for family–teacher conferences and notification of parents that students' siblings are not welcome at school for conferences and other events. These procedures tend to divide families and exclude parents. School staff members can involve the community by talking with parents and community liaisons to work out procedures that are compatible with cultural practices.

**Issues in Family Involvement** Schools grappling with how to increase parental involvement have encountered many of the same issues. Ovando and Collier (1998, pp. 301–309) organized these issues around five areas: language, survival and family structure, educational background and values, knowledge about education and beliefs about learning, and power and status. From each area arise questions that serve as guides for school personnel as they build collaborations with parents. These questions, and some strategies that address these issues, are presented in Table 9.4.

## Myths about Families and Other Communication Barriers

Often teachers think that families of English learners are not interested in what happens in schools because they are not visible at parent meetings or traditional parent–school activities. However, surveys of parents show that an overwhelming number express interest in being

**TABLE 9.4**   Strategies for Teachers Based on Questions Regarding Parent–School Relationships

| Area of Concern | Questions | Strategies for Teachers |
|---|---|---|
| Language | How does educators' language (jargon?) affect home–school communication? | Translate jargon into plain English and then into the home language. |
| | Do community members support using the home language in school? | Advocate use of the home language in all communication with families. |
| Family structure | How do the struggles of day-to-day survival affect the home–school partnership? | Arrange conferences at convenient times for working families. |
| | How does family structure affect the relationship? | Speak about "families" rather than "parents." Honor all types of families. |
| Educational background, attitudes toward schooling | Do school expectations match the parents' educational backgrounds? | Discover the parents' aspirations for their children. The school and family should agree on high standards. |
| | What do educators assume about the attitudes of parents toward schooling? | Communicate with families honestly and positively. |
| Knowledge and beliefs about education | How do parents learn about school culture, their role in U.S. schools, and the specific methods being used in their child's classroom? | Incorporate family education events, family literacy classes, primary-language written and oral information, formal and informal teacher–family talks, and family tutoring training. |
| Power and status | How does the inherent inequality of the educator–layperson relationship affect the partnership? | Try to have a "family space" at the school. Parents should be informed and involved in decisions. |
| | Do programs for parents convey a message of cultural deficiency? | The funds-of-knowledge approach affirms and respects the knowledge of the home. |
| | To what degree are language-minority community members a part of the school in instructional and administrative positions? | Bilingual speakers are considered respected assets for the school as well as the classroom. |

*Source:* Adapted from Ovando & Collier (1998, pp. 301–309).

involved in school events, activities, and decisions. At the same time, they report that they are often not consulted about the type of involvement, scheduling of activities, or location of events. These reports show that the so-called lack of interest myth that circulates in low-achieving schools may be due to poor communication between home and school.

## Enhancing Home–School Communication

If the teacher does not speak the same language as the family, nonverbal messages assume an increased importance. Teachers who meet family members informally as they arrive to drop off their child, at a classroom open house, or during other school events should strive to demonstrate "warm" body language rather than cold. Teachers can show respect toward family members by, for example, rising as visitors enter the room, greeting guests at the door, and accompanying them to the door when they leave.

Any notes, letters, or newsletters sent home need to be translated into the home language. If communication sent home is positive, there is more chance it will be read. Many teachers establish a positive communication pattern by sending a consistent stream of "happy grams" describing what a student has done well. However, if a student has a problem in class, communication between home and school must be consistent and sustained. Any program of home–school communication is first based on having established a rapport with parents in person.

Teachers have modified a wide range of classroom behaviors through the use of school-to-home notes. The most effective notes focus on the improvement of academic productivity, such as the amount or quality of completed classwork or homework. In contrast, a focus on disruptiveness does not cause an improvement in academic performance (Kelley, 1990).

## Family–Teacher Conferences

Preparation for meetings with families enhances success. The concerned teacher makes sure that scheduled times are convenient for family members and prepares a portfolio of the student's successes. The conference might begin with a limited amount of small talk, especially if there has been a recent notable family event. Then the teacher reviews the student's performance, using the portfolio or other evidence of student work. Showing an anonymous example of a grade-level performance may make it easier for family members to put their child's performance in perspective. Listening to family members helps the teacher get a more complete view of the child. If a plan for improvement needs to be drawn up, specific steps are outlined, as well as a time in the near future to compare notes on the child's progress.

**The Use of an Interpreter** Having a translator facilitate parent conferences shows respect for the home language of families. During the conference, the interpreter usually translates the client's words as closely as possible to give a sense of the client's concepts, emotional state, and other important information. Despite the language difference, the teacher can watch nonverbal, affective responses and extend communication by observing facial expressions, voice intonations, and body movements.

**Tracking Contact with the Family** All family contact should be documented in an activity log, including date, subject, and parents' reactions. In this way, a record is available to see what communication efforts have been made.

**Three-Way Conferences** Including the student in the family–teacher conference invites family members into a dialogue about their child's schooling. Students can use this opportunity to demonstrate what they know, share their accomplishments, and set new learning goals. Teachers act as guides by clarifying ideas and issues and responding to specific questions (Davies, Cameron, Politano, & Gregory, 1992). In this way, students are encouraged to follow through on their self-regulated learning.

## How Families Can Assist in a Child's Learning

Schools that have a take-home library of print- and media-based materials encourage learning activities outside of school. In a dual-language setting, families can work with their children in either language.

**If the Family Is Not Supportive**   Families may not support learning in two languages. For example, Watahomigie (1995) described parents' negative reaction on the Hualapai Indian reservation in Peach Springs, Arizona, when educators proposed that schools establish a Hualapai–English bilingual program. The parents had been told for over 100 years that the native language was unimportant, and they did not believe that such instruction would benefit their children. A high-tech approach was eventually successful, built on efforts to convince parents of its value.

**Family Literacy Projects**   In Fresno, California, the Hmong Literacy Project was initiated by parents to help students appreciate their cultural roots, preserve oral history, and maintain the culture through written records. Parents asked for literacy lessons in Hmong (a language that has been written for only about thirty years) and in English. The program helped families to develop not only literacy skills but also skills in math and computers, which then allowed them to help their children academically. The Hmong Parents Newsletter increased communication between the school and the community, leading to greater parent participation in school activities (Kang, Kuehn, & Herrell, 1996).

## Internet Resources for Family Involvement

Websites are available that feature various models of family involvement: www.extension.umn .edu/ParentEducation/SchoolSuccess.html, www.rci.rutgers.edu/~cfis/, www.ed.gov/pubs/ Fam Involve/index.html, www.ncpie.org, and www.ericdigests.org/1999-1/father.html.

## A Model of Home–School Relationships

Faltis (2001) provided a four-level sequence for home–school relationships based on an earlier model proposed by Rasinski and Fredericks (1989). Although teachers may not be able to reach the highest level of parental involvement at a particular school site, the model presents an overall view of the possibilities. This reciprocal process is summarized in Table 9.5.

Box 9.1 offers a host of tactics for involving parents in learning, ranging from providing information to learning from them about their views on education. These suggestions are drawn from Jones (1991) and Díaz-Rico and Weed (2010), among other sources, including Fredericks and Rasinski (1990). Rather than include a separate list of suggestions from each source, I have amalgamated them in categories.

## Family Members as Cultural Mediators

Family members play an important role as "brokers" or go-betweens who can mediate between the school and the home to solve cultural problems and create effective home–school relations (Arvizu, 1992).

**TABLE 9.5** A Two-Way Parent–School Involvement Model

| Level of Involvement | Description of Activity |
|---|---|
| I. Teacher–parent contact | The teacher learns about parents' daily experiences and initiates positive home–school contact and dialogue by chatting, making home visits, talking with community workers, and arranging for after-school homework help or tutoring to promote students' success. |
| II. Sharing information in the home about schooling | The teacher keeps the parents informed (in the home language, if possible) about important school and community events and meetings, changes in school schedules, help available from community-based organizations, and sources of academic support, using such means as student-produced newsletters, personal notes, telephone calls, and other notices. |
| III. Participation at home and school | Parents, caregivers, and other concerned adults are welcomed and encouraged to come to class and to attend school meetings and social events. Parents may linger in the morning to watch reading and writing take place, or to see a little poetry reading, especially if it takes place in the home language. Students may be assigned to find out about knowledge their families have about planting, banking, and so on, and then teachers can find a way to use and elaborate on this information in class. |
| IV. Parental empowerment in curricular decisions | After the success of the previous three levels, teachers support parents who become involved as colleagues in professional activities and decisions. Some parents form advisory committees, start community tutoring centers, and find multiple means to influence school policy and support academic learning outside of the classroom. The role of the teacher is to encourage and work with parents to make these possible. |

*Source:* Faltis 2001).

 **Classroom Glimpse**

### A PARENT FOSTERS CULTURAL PRIDE

One Chinese-American parent successfully intervened in a school situation to the benefit of her daughter and her classmates.

> After my daughter was teased by her peers because of her Chinese name, I gave a presentation to her class on the origin of Chinese names, the naming of children in China, and Chinese calligraphy. My daughter has had no more problems about her name. What is more, she no longer complains about her unusual name, and she is proud of her cultural heritage. (Yao, 1988, p. 224)

Whether parents are willing to come to school is largely dependent on their attitude toward school, a result in part of the parents' own experiences. This attitude is also a result of the extent to which they are made welcome by the schools. Invitational barriers can exclude parents as well as students. On the other hand, teachers who are willing to reach out to parents and actively solicit information from them about their children and their hopes for their children's schooling are rewarded with a richer understanding of students' potential.

**Box 9.1**  Strategies to Involve Parents in Schooling

**Providing Information**

- Informally chat with parents as they pick up their child after school.
- Use the telephone as an instrument of good news.
- Videotape programs for parents.
- Operate a parent hot line.
- Encourage parent-to-parent communication.
- Hold parent workshops on helping their children with reading skills.
- Offer materials in the home language.
- Provide bilingual handouts that describe programs available through the school.
- Make available a list of parental rights under the Bilingual Education Act.
- Send home personal handwritten notes, using a translator if necessary.
- Send home notes when students are doing well.
- Create parent–student handbooks.
- Have students write classroom newsletters.
- Welcome new families with packets delivered to the home.

**Ways to Showcase English Learners**

- Enter students in poetry, essay, or art contests or exhibits sponsored by community or professional organizations.
- Offer to train students how to read aloud at libraries or children's centers.
- Encourage dual-language proficiency as a mark of prestige in school.

**Ways to Bring Parents to School**

- Encourage parents to come to class to make crafts with students or to discuss culture, calligraphy, or family history.
- Find out if parent conferences or meetings conflict with work schedules.
- Ensure that siblings are welcome at parent conferences or meetings.
- Provide babysitting services for parent conferences.
- Maintain a friendly school office.
- Establish an explicit open-door policy so parents will know they are welcome; include welcoming signs in primary language.
- Suggest specific ways parents can help to promote achievement.
- Help parents to obtain remedial help if necessary in a timely way.
- Make meetings into social events, with food, dramatic, or musical performances if time permits.
- Hold student–teacher–family breakfasts once a month.
- Schedule primary-language speakers at school events.
- Recognize parents for involvement at award ceremonies, send thank-you notes, and speak positively of parents to their child.

**What Teachers Can Learn from Parents**

- Ideas of better ways to communicate.
- A richer understanding of the student's role(s) in the family.
- The hopes that parents have for schooling.
- Students' hobbies, interests, and strengths.

*(continued)*

**Box 9.1**   Continued

### Homework Tips for Parents (adapted from Jones, 1991)
- Set aside a family quiet time when each person has homework or other activities to do that demand concentration.
- Have a regular means for finding out what assignments to expect.
- Make sure there is a place set aside for homework; provide paper, pencils, adequate lighting, etc.
- Check with the child to see if he or she understands the assignment. If needed, work through a problem. Have someone to call for help if necessary.
- Check the completed assignment with the child.
- Praise the work or offer constructive improvements.

### Workshops and Parent Support Groups (adapted from Jones, 1991)
- Make-it-and-take it workshops to construct home learning materials
- Family Learning Center—school library or computer center is open several nights a week with learning activities for all ages
- Learning Fairs—single-topic sessions held in the evening
- Parent support groups hosted by community members
- Family Room—a room at school set aside for families to drop in and participate in informal activities, play with toys, and talk with other parents
- Child and adolescent development talks
- Special topic workshops on reading, math, study skills, self-esteem, etc.

## The Home–School Connection

Parents and older siblings can be encouraged to work with preschool and school-age children in a variety of activities. Teachers can encourage home language with children in ways that build underlying cognitive skills. Family members can sit with the child to look at a book, pointing to pictures and asking questions; they can read a few lines and let the child fill in the rest, or let the child retell a familiar story. Children can listen to adults discuss something or observe reading and writing in the primary language. Schools can assist communities with implementing literacy or cultural classes or producing a community primary-language newspaper. The school can also educate students and parents on the benefits of learning the home language of the parents and can find ways to make dual-language proficiency a means of gaining prestige at school (Ouk et al., 1988).

 **Classroom Glimpse**

### THE PUBLISHING PARTY

One teacher describes the success of a nonfiction Publishing Party hosted by the students. Parents and many extended family members came, as did neighbors and youth organization leaders with whom the students were involved. At various places around the room, reports were visible with yellow comment sheets. Visitors could sit at a desk or table, read, and comment on what they had read.

*Families and community volunteers can provide tutoring and language enrichment.*

Language was not a barrier. Many parents encouraged their children to read to them in English and translate the stories into the native language. They were proud of the English their child had learned and proud that the child remembered the native language well enough to translate. . . . Everywhere I looked, I saw proud children beaming as they showed their work off to the people they cared about and who cared about them. (Cho Bassoff, 2004, para. 9, 10)

## Involving the Family and Community in School Governance

Encouraging parents to participate in school activities is vital. The extra step of sending parents letters, reports, and notices in their home language helps to build rapport and extend a welcome to the school. These language policies constitute the daily message that home languages are important and valued. Parents can receive the message that they are valued in many ways:

- Representative parent committees can advise and consent on school practices that involve English learners.
- School facilities can be made available for meetings of community groups.
- Frequent attendance at school board meetings sends the message that officials are monitored by those who support English learners' achievement.
- Running for a seat on the school board brings power directly to the community.

This chapter has emphasized the important role that teachers can play in learning about their students' communities and cultures and in reducing the culture shock between home and school by working actively toward the creation of culturally compatible instruction. The best way for a teacher to understand culture is first to understand himself or herself and the extent to which U.S. mainstream cultural values are explicitly or implicitly enforced during instruction. A teacher who understands his or her own teaching and learning styles can then ask to what extent each student is similar or dissimilar. This goes a long way toward understanding and honoring individual differences. The key for the intercultural educator is to be sensitive, flexible, and open.

The teacher can then use direct personal observation of social behavior to construct an image of students' cultures from the perspective of the members of those cultures. This understanding can be used to organize classroom activities in ways that are comfortable and promote learning. Thus, an understanding of cultural diversity leads to engagement in the struggle for equity and then to a commitment to promoting educational achievement for all students.

## PEARSON myeducationlab
**The Power of Classroom Practice**
www.myeducationlab.com

Go to the Topic Cultural and Linguistic Diversity in the MyEducationLab (www.myeducationlab.com) for your course, where you can:

- Find learning outcomes for Cultural and Linguistic Diversity along with the national standards that connect to these outcomes.
- Complete Assignments and Activities that can help you more deeply understand the chapter content.
- Apply and practice your understanding of the core teaching skills identified in the chapter with the Building Teaching Skills and Dispositions learning units.
- Examine challenging situations and cases presented in the IRIS Center Resources.
- Check your comprehension on the content covered in the chapter by going to the Study Plan in the Book Resources for your text. Here you will be able to take a chapter quiz, receive feedback on your answers, and then access Review, Practice, and Enrichment activities to enhance your understanding of chapter content.

## A+RISE

Go to the Topic A+RISE in the MyEducationLab (www.myeducationlab.com) for your course. A+RISE® Standards2Strategy™ is an innovative and interactive online resource that offers new teachers in grades K–12 just-in-time, research-based instructional strategies that:

- Meet the linguistic needs of ELLs as they learn content
- Differentiate instruction for all grades and abilities
- Offer reading and writing techniques, cooperative learning, use of linguistic and nonlinguistic representations, scaffolding, teacher modeling, higher order thinking, and alternative classroom ELL assessment
- Provide support to help teachers be effective through the integration of listening, speaking, reading, and writing along with the content curriculum
- Improve student achievement
- Are aligned to Common Core Elementary Language Arts standards (for the literacy strategies) and to English language proficiency standards in WIDA, Texas, California, and Florida.

# BIBLIOGRAPHY

Abedi, J. (2004). The No Child Left Behind Act and English language learners: Assessment and accountability issues. *Educational Researcher, 33*(1), 4–14.

Abedi, J., Hofstetter, C. H., & Lord, C. (2004). Assessment accommodations for English language learners: Implications for policy-based empirical research. *Review of Educational Research, 74*(1), 1–28.

Adamson, H. D. (1993). *Academic competence.* New York: Longman.

Addison, A. (1988, November). Comprehensible textbooks in science for the nonnative English-speaker: Evidence from discourse analysis. *The CATESOL Journal, 1*(1), 49–66.

Adger, C. (2000). *School/community partnerships to support language minority student success* (Research Brief No. 5) Santa Cruz, CA: Center for Research on Education, Diversity and Excellence. Retrieved July 7, 2006, from www.crede.org/products/print/research_briefs/rb5.shtml

Agar, M. (1980). *The professional stranger: An informal introduction to ethnography.* Orlando, FL: Academic Press.

Agor, B. (Ed.). (2000). *Integrating the ESL standards into classroom practice: Grades 9–12.* Alexandria, VA: Teachers of English to Speakers of Other Languages (TESOL).

Airasian, P. W. (2005). *Classroom assessment: Concepts and applications* (5th ed.). New York: McGraw-Hill.

Alcaya, C., Lybeck, K., Mougel, P., & Weaver, S. (1995). *Some strategies useful for speaking a foreign language.* Unpublished manuscript, University of Minnesota.

Alexander, S. (1983). *Nadia, the willful.* New York: Dial.

Allen, E., & Vallette, R. (1977). *Classroom techniques: Foreign languages and English as a second language.* San Diego, CA: Harcourt Brace Jovanovich.

Altman, L. J. (1993). *Amelia's road.* New York: Lee and Low Books.

American Civil Liberties Union (ACLU) Foundation of Southern California. (2007). *Williams v. California: The statewide impact of two years of implementation.* Los Angeles: Author.

Amselle, J. (1999). Dual immersion delays English. *American Language Review, 3*(5), 8.

Andersen, J., & Powell, R. (1991). Intercultural communication and the classroom. In L. Samovar & R. Porter (Eds.), *Intercultural communication: A reader* (6th ed.). Belmont, CA: Wadsworth.

Anderson, J., & Gunderson, L. (2004). *You don't read a science book, you study it: An exploration of cultural concepts of reading.* Retrieved July 24, 2006, from www.reading online.org/electronic/elec_index.asp?HREF=anderson/index.html

Anyon, J. (1994). The retreat of Marxism and socialist feminism: Postmodern and poststructural theories in education. *Curriculum Inquiry, 24,* 115–133.

Aoki, E. (1992). Turning the page: Asian Pacific American children's literature. In V. J. Harris (Ed.), *Teaching multicultural literature in grades K–8.* Norwood, MA: Christopher-Gordon Publishers.

Arvizu, S. (1992). Home-school linkages: A cross-cultural approach to parent participation. In M. Saravia-Shore & S. Arvizu (Eds.), *Cross-cultural literacy: Ethnographies of communication in multiethnic classrooms.* New York: Garland.

Asher, J. (1982). *Learning another language through actions: The complete teachers' guidebook.* Los Gatos, CA: Sky Oaks.

*Asian nation: Asian American history, demographics, & issues.* Retrieved April 14, 2010, from www.asian-nation.org

Au, K., & Jordan, C. (1981). Teaching reading to Hawaiian children: Finding a culturally appropriate solution. In H. Trueba, G. Guthrie, & K. Au (Eds.), *Culture and the bilingual classroom: Studies in classroom ethnography.* Rowley, MA: Newbury House.

Babbitt, N. (1976). *Tuck everlasting.* New York: Bantam Books.

Baker, C. (1993). *Foundations of bilingual education and bilingualism.* Clevedon, UK: Multilingual Matters.

Balderrama, M. V., & Díaz-Rico, L. T. (2006). *Teacher performance expectations for educating English learners.* Boston: Allyn & Bacon.

Bandlow, R. (2002). Suburban bigotry: A descent into racism & struggle for redemption. In F. Schultz (Ed.), *Annual editions: Multicultural education 2002–2003* (pp. 90–93). Guilford, CT: McGraw-Hill/Dushkin.

Banks, J. (1991). A curriculum for empowerment, action, and change. In C. Sleeter (Ed.), *Empowerment through multicultural education.* Albany: State University of New York Press.

Banks, J. (1994). *An introduction to multicultural education.* Boston: Allyn & Bacon.

Barbe, W. B., Wasylyk, T. M., Hackney, C. S., & Braun, L. A. (1984). *Zaner-Bloser creative growth in handwriting (grades K–8).* Columbus, OH: Zaner-Bloser.

Barks, D., & Watts, P. (2001). Textual borrowing strategies for graduate-level ESL students. In D. Belcher and

A. Hirvela (Eds.), *Linking literacies: Perspectives on L2 reading-writing connections* (pp. 246–267). Ann Arbor: The University of Michigan Press.

Barr, R., & Johnson, B. (1997). *Teaching reading and writing in elementary classrooms* (2nd ed.). New York: Longman.

Barrett, J. (1978). *Cloudy with a chance of meatballs.* New York: Scholastic Books.

Bartolomé, L. I. (1994). Beyond the methods fetish: Toward a humanizing pedagogy. *Harvard Educational Review, 64*(2), 173–194.

Barton, D., Hamilton, M., & Ivanič, R. (2000). Introduction. In D. Barton, M. Hamilton, & R. Ivanič (Eds.), *Situated literacies* (pp. 1–15). London and New York: Routledge.

Bartram, M., & Walton, R. (1994). *Correction: A positive approach to language mistakes.* Hove, UK: Language Teaching Publications.

Bassano, S., & Christison, M. A. (1995). *Community spirit: A practical guide to collaborative language learning.* San Francisco: Alta Book Center.

Beaumont, C. J. (1999). Dilemmas of peer assistance in a bilingual full inclusion classroom. *The Elementary School Journal, 99*(3), 233–234.

Bell, C. (2002). Secondary level report—Explaining SDAIE to colleagues. *CATESOL News, 34*(3), 15.

Belmont, J. M. (1989). Cognitive strategies and strategic learning: The socioinstructional approach. *American Psychologist, 44,* 142–148.

Bembridge, T. (1992). A MAP for reading assessment. *Educational Leadership, 49*(8), 46–48.

Bennett, C. (2003). *Comprehensive multicultural education: Theory and practice* (5th ed.). Boston: Allyn & Bacon.

Bergman, J. L., & Schuder, T. (1993). Teaching at-risk students to read strategically. *Educational Leadership, 50*(54), 19–23.

Berk, L. E., & Winsler, A. (1995). *Scaffolding children's learning: Vygotsky and early childhood education.* Washington, DC: National Association for the Education of Young Children.

Birdwhistell, R. (1974). The language of the body: The natural environment of words. In A. Silverstein (Ed.), *Human communication: Theoretical explorations.* Hillsdale, NJ: Erlbaum.

Bitter, G., Pierson, M., & Burvikovs, A. (2004). *Using technology in the classroom* (6th ed.). Boston: Allyn & Bacon.

Blair, R. W. (Ed.). (1982). *Innovative approaches to language teaching.* Boston: Heinle & Heinle.

Bloch, J. (2001). Plagiarism and the ESL student: From printed to electronic texts. In D. Belcher & A. Hirvela (Eds.), *Linking literacies: Perspectives on L2 reading-writing connections* (pp. 209–228). Ann Arbor: The University of Michigan Press.

Block, C. C., & Israel, S. E. (2005). *Reading first and beyond.* Thousand Oaks, CA: Corwin Press.

Boardman, C. A. (2009). *Writing to communicate: Essays and the short research paper.* White Plains, NY: Pearson Longman.

Bonesteel, L., Gargagliano, A., & Lambert, J. (2010). *Future: English for results.* White Plains, NY: Longman.

Bosher, S. (1997). Language and cultural identity: A study of Hmong students at the postsecondary level. *TESOL Quarterly, 31*(3), 593–603.

Bourdieu, P. (with Passeron, J.). (1977). *Reproduction in society, education, and culture.* Los Angeles: Sage.

Boyd-Batstone, P. (2006). *Differentiated early literacy for English language learners: Practical strategies.* Boston: Pearson.

Bradley, K. S., & Bradley, J. A. (2004). *Scaffolding academic learning for second language learners.* Retrieved July 31, 2006, from http://iteslj.org/Articles/Bradley-Scaffolding

Brandt, R. (1994). On educating for diversity: A conversation with James A. Banks. *Educational Leadership, 51,* 28–31.

Brend, R. M. (1975). Male-female intonation patterns in American English. In B. Thorne & N. Henley (Eds.), *Language and sex: Differences and dominance.* Rowley, MA: Newbury House.

Brinton, D. (2003). Content-based instruction. In D. Nunan (Ed.), *Practical English language teaching.* New York: McGraw-Hill.

Brinton, D., & Master, P. (Eds.). (1997). *New ways in content-based instruction.* Alexandria, VA: Teachers of English to Speakers of Other Languages (TESOL).

Brisk, M. E., & Harrington, M. M. (2000). *Literacy and bilingualism.* Mahwah, NJ: Erlbaum.

Bromberg, M., Liebb, J., & Traiger, A. (2005). *504 absolutely essential words* (5th ed.). Hauppage, NY: Barron's.

Bromley, K. D. (1989). Buddy journals make the reading-writing connection. *The Reading Teacher, 43*(2), 122–129.

Brooks, G. (1944). *Selected poems.* New York: Harper & Row.

Brown, D. (1987). *Principles of language learning and teaching* (2nd ed.). Englewood Cliffs, NJ: Prentice Hall.

Brown, D. (2000). *Principles of language learning and teaching* (4th ed.). Englewood Cliffs, NJ: Prentice Hall.

Bruner, J. (1986). *Actual minds, possible worlds.* Cambridge, MA: Harvard University Press.

Brutt-Griffler, J., & Samimy, K. K. (1999). Revisiting the colonial in the postcolonial: Critical praxis for the non-native-English-speaking teachers in a TESOL program. *TESOL Quarterly, 33*(3), 413–431.

Buchanan, K., & Helman, M. (1997). Reforming mathematics instruction for ESL literacy students. *ERIC Digest.*

Retrieved Oct. 15, 2004, from www.cal.org/resources/digest/buchan01.html

Bunch, G. C., Abram, P. L., Lotan, R. A., & Valdés, G. (2001). Beyond sheltered instruction: Rethinking conditions for academic language development. *TESOL Journal, 10*(2/3), 28–33.

Bunting, E. (1988). *How many days to America?* New York: Clarion.

Burgstahler, S. (2002). *Universal design of instruction.* Retrieved July 7, 2006, from www.washington.edu/doit/Brochures/Academics/instruction.html

Burley-Allen, M. (1995). *Listening: The forgotten skill.* New York: John Wiley & Sons.

Burns, M. S., Griffin, P., & Snow, C. E. (Eds.). (1999). *Starting out right: A guide to promoting children's reading success.* Washington, DC: National Academies Press.

Byrd, P., & Benson, B. (1994). *Problem-solution: A reference for ESL writers.* Boston: Heinle & Heinle.

Caine, R. N., Caine, G., McClintic, C., & Klimek, K. (2004). *Brain/mind learning principles in action: The fieldbook for making connections, teaching, and the human brain.* Thousand Oaks, CA: Sage.

California Department of Education. (1997). *English/language arts standards.* Sacramento: Author. Retrieved July 18, 2006, from www.cde.ca.gov/be/st/ss/engmain.asp

California Department of Education. (1999). *English language development standards.* Sacramento: Author. Retrieved www.cde.ca.gov/statetests/eld/eld_grd_span.pdf

California Department of Education. (2004a). *English learner students.* Retrieved August 4, 2006, from www.cde.ca.gov/re/pn/fb/yr04english.asp

California Department of Education. (2004b). *Physical education model content standards for California public schools.* Sacramento: Author.

California Department of Education. (2006a). *English learners in California: Frequently asked questions.* Retrieved April 14, 2010, from www.cde.ca.gov/sp/el/er/documents/elfaq.doc

California Department of Education (CDE). (2006b). *The science content standards for kindergarten through grade five.* Retrieved August 4, 2006, from www.cde.ca.gov/re/pn/fd/sci-frame-dwnld.asp

California Department of Education. (2007). *Reading/language arts framework for California public schools.* Sacramento: Author. Retrieved July 18, 2006, from www.cde.ca.gov/ci/rl/cf/index.asp

California Department of Education (CDE). (2008). *Number of English learners by language.* Retrieved August 24, 2010, from http://data1.cde.ca.gov/dataquest/LEPbyLang1.asp

California Department of Education. (2009). *English-language development standards for California public schools for kindergarten through grade twelve.* Retrieved August 20, 2010, from www.cde.ca.gov/be/st/ss/documents/englangdevstnd.pdf

California Department of Education, Educational Demographics Unit. (2010). *2009–10 English learners, instructional settings and services.* Retrieved August 17, 2010, from http://dq.cde.ca.gov/dataquest/ElP2_State.asp?RptYear=2009-10&RptType=ELPart2_1a

Cameron, A. (1988). *The most beautiful place in the world.* New York: Random House.

Campbell, C. (1998). *Teaching second language writing: Interacting with text.* Pacific Grove, CA: Heinle & Heinle.

Canale, M. (1983). From communicative competence to communicative language pedagogy. In J. Richards & R. Schmidt (Eds.), *Language and communication.* New York: Longman.

Cantlon, T. L. (1991). *Structuring the classroom successfully for cooperative team learning.* Portland, OR: Prestige Publishers.

Carnuccio, L. M. (2004). Cybersites. *Essential Teacher, 1*(3), 59.

Carrasquillo, A., & Rodríguez, V. (2002). *Language minority students in the mainstream classroom.* Clevedon, UK: Multilingual Matters.

Cary, S. (2000). *Working with second language learners: Answers to teachers' top ten questions.* Portsmouth, NH: Heinemann.

Casey, J. (2004). A place for first language in the ESOL classroom. *Essential Teacher, 1*(4), 50–52.

CATESOL. (1998). *CATESOL position statement on literacy instruction for English language learners, grades K–12.* Retrieved July 24, 2006, from www.catesol.org/literacy.html

Celce-Murcia, M., & Olshtain, E. (2001). *Discourse and context in language teaching.* Cambridge, UK: Cambridge University Press.

Center for Educational Reform. (2000). *National charter school directory* (7th ed.). Washington, DC: Author.

Chambers, J., & Parrish, T. (1992). *Meeting the challenge of diversity: An evaluation of programs for pupils with limited proficiency in English: Vol. 4. Cost of programs and services for LEP students.* Berkeley, CA: BW Associates.

Chamot, A. U. (2009). *The CALLA handbook.* Boston: Pearson.

Chandler, D. (2005). *Semiotics for beginners.* Retrieved June 27, 2006, from www.aber.ac.uk/media/Documents/S4B/semiotic.html

Chaney, A. L., & Burk, T. L. (1998). *Teaching oral communication in grades K–8.* Boston: Allyn & Bacon.

Chard, D. J., Pikulski, J. J., & Templeton, S. (n.d.). *From phonemic awareness to fluency: Effective decoding instruction in a research-based reading program.* Retrieved July 24, 2006, from www.eduplace.com/state/pdf/author/chard_pik_temp.pdf

Cheng, L. (1987). English communicative competence of language minority children: Assessment and treatment of language "impaired" preschoolers. In H. Trueba (Ed.), *Success or failure? Learning and the language minority student.* Boston: Heinle & Heinle.

Chesterfield, R., & Chesterfield, K. (1985). Natural order in children's use of second language learning strategies. *Applied Linguistics, 6,* 45–59.

Children's Defense Fund. (2005). *The state of America's children.* Retrieved August 2, 2006, from http://cdf.convio.net/site/PageServer?pagename=research_publications

Cho Bassoff, T. (2004). Compleat Links: Three steps toward a strong home-school connection. *Essential Teacher, 1*(4). Retrieved August 3, 2006, from www.tesol.org/s_tesol/sec_document.asp?CID=65&DID=2586

Chomsky, N. (1959). Review of B. F. Skinner "Verbal Behavior." *Language, 35,* 26–58.

Christensen, L. (2000). *Reading, writing, rising up: Teaching about social justice and the power of the written word.* Milwaukee, WI: Rethinking Schools.

Chung, H. (1989). *Working with Vietnamese high school students.* San Francisco: New Faces of Liberty/SFSC.

Cipollone, N., Keiser, S. H., & Vasishth, S. (1998). *Language files* (7th ed.). Columbus: Ohio State University Press.

Clark, B. (1983). *Growing up gifted: Developing the potential of children at home and at school* (2nd ed.). Columbus, OH: Merrill.

Cloud, N., Genesee, F., & Hamayan, E. (2000). *Dual language instruction.* Boston: Heinle & Heinle.

Cockcroft, J. D. (1995). *Latinos in the struggle for equal education.* Danbury, CT: Franklin Watts.

Coehlo, E., Winer, L., & Olsen, J. W.-B. (1989). *All sides of the issue: Activities for cooperative jigsaw groups.* Hayward, CA: Alemany Press.

Cogan, D. (1999). What am I saying? In N. Shameem & M. Tickoo (Eds.), *New ways in using communicative games* (pp. 22–23). Alexandria, VA: Teachers of English to Speakers of Other Languages (TESOL).

Cohen, E. (1994). *Designing groupwork: Strategies for the heterogeneous classroom.* New York: Teachers College Press.

Cohn, D., & Bahrampour, T. (2006, May 10). Of U.S. children under 5, nearly half are minorities. *Washington Post,* A01.

Cole, K. (2003, March). *Negotiating intersubjectivity in the classroom: Mutual socialization to classroom conversations.* Presentation at the American Association for Applied Linguistics annual conference, Arlington, VA.

Cole, M. (1998). *Cultural psychology: Can it help us think about diversity?* Presentation at the annual meeting of the American Educational Research Association, San Diego, CA.

Cole, Y. (2007). *Why are so few CEOs people of color and women?* Retrieved May 20, 2010, from www.diversityinc.com/content/1757/article/2696/?Why_Are_So_Few_CEOs_People_of_Color_and_Women

College Board. (2009). *2009 college-bound seniors are most diverse group ever to take SAT® as more minority students prepare for higher education.* Retrieved May 20, 2010, from www.collegeboard.com/press/releases/206201.html

Collie, J., & Slater, S. (1987). *Literature in the language classroom.* Cambridge, UK: Cambridge University Press.

Collier, V. (1987). Age and rate of acquisition of second language for academic purposes. *TESOL Quarterly, 21*(4), 617–641.

Collier, V. P. (1995). Acquiring a second language for school. *Directions in Language & Education, National Clearinghouse for Bilingual Education, 1*(4). Retrieved July 7, 2006, from www.ncela.gwu.edu/pubs/directions/04.htm

Contra Costa County Office of Education. (2006). *Curriculum and instruction: Standards implementation.* Retrieved August 4, 2006, from www.cccoe.k12.ca.us/edsvcs/assessment.html

Cook, V. (1999). Going beyond the native speaker in language teaching. *TESOL Quarterly, 33*(2), 185–209.

Corley, M. A. (2003). *Poverty, racism, and literacy.* ERIC Digest No. 243. ERIC Clearinghouse on Adult, Career, and Vocational Education.

Cortés, C. (1993). Acculturation, assimilation, and "adducation." *BEOutreach, 4*(1), 3–5.

Costa, A. L., & Garmston, R. J. (2002). *Cognitive coaching: A foundation for renaissance schools* (2nd ed.). Norwood, MA: Christopher-Gordon.

Crago, M. (1993). Communicative interaction and second language acquisition: An Inuit example. *TESOL Quarterly, 26*(3), 487–506.

Crawford, J. (1999). *Bilingual education: History, politics, theory, and practice* (4th ed.). Los Angeles: Bilingual Educational Services.

Crawford, J. (2004). *Educating English learners: Language diversity in the classroom* (5th ed.). Los Angeles: Bilingual Educational Services.

Crawford, J. (2006). *National language amendment: Political blunder by Republicans.* Retrieved July 6, 2006, from http://ourworld.compuserve.com/homepages/JWCrawford

Cummins, J. (1976). The influence of bilingualism on cognitive growth: A synthesis of research findings and explanatory hypothesis. *Working Papers on Bilingualism, 9,* 1–43.

Cummins, J. (1979). Linguistic interdependence and the educational development of bilingual children. *Review of Educational Research, 49*(2), 222–251.

Cummins, J. (1980). The cross-lingual dimensions of language proficiency: Implications for bilingual education and the optimal age issue. *TESOL Quarterly, 14*(2), 175–187.

Cummins, J. (1981a). Age on arrival and immigrant second language learning in Canada: A reassessment. *Applied Linguistics, 2*(2), 132–149.

Cummins, J. (1981b). The role of primary language development in promoting educational success for language minority students. In *Schooling and language minority students: A theoretical framework.* Sacramento: California State Department of Education.

Cummins, J. (1984). *Bilingualism and special education: Issues in assessment and pedagogy.* San Diego, CA: College-Hill.

Cummins, J. (1989). *Empowering minority students.* Sacramento: California Association for Bilingual Education.

Cummins, J. (1996). *Negotiating identities: Education for empowerment in a diverse society.* Los Angeles: California Association for Bilingual Education.

Cummins, J. (2000). Beyond adversarial discourse: Searching for common ground in the education of bilingual students. In P. McLaren & C. J. Ovando (Eds.), *The politics of multiculturalism and bilingual education* (pp. 126–147). Boston: McGraw-Hill.

Cummins, J. (2010). *Biliteracy, empowerment, and transformative pedagogy.* Retrieved April 16, 2010, from www.iteachilearn.com/cummins/biliteratempowerment.html

Curtain, H., & Dahlberg, C. A. (2010). *Language and children—Making the match: New languages for young learners, grades K–8* (4th ed.). Boston: Allyn & Bacon.

Cushner, K. (1999). *Human diversity in action.* Boston: McGraw-Hill.

Dale, P., & Poms, L. (2005). *English pronunciation made simple.* White Plains, NY: Pearson/Longman.

Dale, T., & Cuevas, G. (1992). Integrating mathematics and language learning. In P. Richard-Amato & M. Snow (Eds.), *The multicultural classroom.* White Plains, NY: Longman.

Daloğlu, A. (2005). Reducing learning burden in academic vocabulary development. *Teachers of English to Speakers of Other Languages EFLIS Newsletter, 5*(1).

Danesi, M. (1985). *A guide to puzzles and games in second language pedagogy.* Toronto, Canada: Ontario Institute for Studies in Education.

Darder, A. (1991). *Culture and power in the classroom.* New York: Bergin and Garvey.

Davies, A., Cameron, C., Politano, C., & Gregory, K. (1992). *Together is better: Collaborative assessment, evaluation, and reporting.* Winnipeg, Canada: Peguis.

Day, F. A. (1994). *Multicultural voices in contemporary literature: A resource for teachers.* Portsmouth, NH: Heinemann.

Day, F. A. (1997). *Latina and Latino voices in literature for children and teenagers.* Portsmouth, NH: Heinemann.

Day, F. A. (2003). *Latina and Latino voices in literature: Lives and works.* Westport, CT: Greenwood Publishers.

de Boinod, A. J. (2006). *The meaning of tingo.* New York: Penguin.

DeGeorge, G. (1987–1988, Winter). *Assessment and placement of language minority students: Procedures for mainstreaming* (NCBE Occasional Papers No. 3). Retrieved March 23, 2005, from www.ncela.gwu.edu/pubs/classics/focus/03mainstream.htm

Delgado-Gaitan, C., & Trueba, H. (1991). *Crossing cultural borders: Education for immigrant families in America.* London: Falmer Press.

dePaola, T. (1981). *Now one foot, now the other.* New York: G. P. Putnam's Sons.

deUnamuno, M. (1925). *Essays and soliloquies.* New York: Knopf.

Diamond, B., & Moore, M. (1995). *Multicultural literacy.* White Plains, NY: Longman.

Díaz, R. M., Neal, C. J., & Vachio, A. (1991). Maternal teaching in the zone of proximal development: A comparison of low- and high-risk dyads. *Merrill-Palmer Quarterly, 37,* 83–108.

Díaz-Rico, L. T. (2004). *Teaching English learners: Strategies and methods.* Boston: Allyn & Bacon.

Díaz-Rico, L. T. (2008). *Strategies for teaching English learners.* Boston: Pearson.

Díaz-Rico, L. T., & Dullien, S. (2004). *Semiotics and people watching.* Presentation, California Teachers of English to Speakers of Other Languages regional conference, Los Angeles.

Díaz-Rico, L. T., & Weed, K. Z. (2010). *Crosscultural, language, and academic development handbook* (4th ed.). Boston: Allyn & Bacon.

Dicker, S. (1992). Societal views of bilingualism and language learning. *TESOL: Applied Linguistics Interest Section Newsletter, 14*(1), 1, 4.

Dillon, S. (2009). *Report envisions shortage of teachers as retirements escalate.* Retrieved April 14, 2010, from www.nytimes.com/2009/04/07/education/07teacher.html

Donato, R. (1997). *The other struggle for equal schools: Mexican Americans during the Civil Rights Era.* New York: State University of New York Press.

Dudley-Marling, C., & Searle, D. (1991). *When students have time to talk.* Portsmouth, NH: Heinemann.

Dumont, R. (1972). Learning English and how to be silent: Studies in Sioux and Cherokee classrooms. In C. Cazden, V. John, & D. Hymes (Eds.), *Functions of language in the classroom.* New York: Teachers College Press.

Dunkel, P., & Lim, P. L. (1994). *Intermediate listening comprehension: Understanding and recalling spoken English.* Boston: Heinle & Heinle.

Dunkel, P. A., Pialorsi, F., & Kozyrev, J. (1996). *Advanced listening comprehension: Developing aural and notetaking skills.* Boston: Heinle & Heinle.

Echevarría, J., & Graves, A. (2011). *Sheltered content instruction: Teaching English learners with diverse abilities* (4th ed.). Boston: Pearson.

Echevarría, J., Vogt, M. E., & Short, D. (2004). *Making content comprehensible for English language learners: The SIOP model* (2nd ed.). Boston: Allyn & Bacon.

Echevarría, J., Vogt, M., & Short, D. J. (2010). *The SIOP model for teaching mathematics to English learners.* Boston: Pearson.

EdData. (2008). *Comparing California.* Retrieved April 19, 2010, from www.ed-data.k12.ca.us/articles/article.asp?title=california%20comparison#demographics

Ediger, A., & Pavlik, C. (1999). *Reading connections: Skills and strategies for purposeful reading.* New York: Oxford University Press.

Edmonson, M. (1971). *Lore: An introduction to the science of fiction.* New York: Holt, Rinehart and Winston.

Egan, K., & Gajdamaschko, N. (2003). Some cognitive tools of literacy. In A. Kozulin, B. Gindis, V. S. Ageyev, & S. M. Miller (Eds.), *Vygotsky's educational theory in cultural context* (pp. 83–98). Cambridge, UK: Cambridge University Press.

Egbert, J. (2004). Access to knowledge: Implications of Universal Design for CALL environments. *CALL_EJ Online, 5*(2). Retrieved July 7, 2006, from www.tell.is.ritsumei.ac.jp/callejonline/journal/5-2/egbert.html

Egbert, J., & Hanson-Smith, E. (1999). *CALL environments: Research, practice, and critical issues.* Alexandria, VA: Teachers of English to Speakers of Other Languages (TESOL).

Ehri, L. (1997). Learning to read and learning to spell are one and the same, almost. In C. Perfetti, L. Rieben, & M. Fayol (Eds.), *Learning to spell: Research, theory, and practice across languages* (pp. 237–269). Mahwah, NJ: Erlbaum.

Ellis, S. S., & Whalen, S. F. (1992). Keys to cooperative learning: 35 ways to keep kids responsible, challenged, and most of all, cooperative. *Instructor, 101*(6), 34–37.

Erickson, F. (1977). Some approaches to inquiry in school-community ethnography. *Anthropology and Education Quarterly, 8*(2), 58–69.

Escalante, J., & Dirmann, J. (1990). The Jaime Escalante math program. *Journal of Negro Education, 59*(3), 407–423.

Faber, J. E., Morris, J. D., & Lieberman, M. G. (2000). The effect of note taking on ninth grade students' comprehension. *Reading Psychology, 21,* 257–270.

Faltis, C. (1993). Critical issues in the use of sheltered content instruction in high school bilingual programs. *Peabody Journal of Education, 69*(1), 136–151.

Faltis, C. (2001). *Joinfostering* (3rd ed.). Upper Saddle River, NJ: Prentice Hall.

Farr, M. (1994). En los dos idiomas: Literacy practices among Chicago Mexicanos. In B. Moss (Ed.), *Literacy across communities* (pp. 1–9). Cresskill, NJ: Hampton Press.

Feng, J. (1994). *Asian-American children: What teachers should know.* ERIC Digest ED369577. Urbana, IL: Clearinghouse on Elementary and Early Childhood Education. Retrieved from August 20, 2010, from www.ericdigest.org/1994/teacher.htm

Feuerstein, T., & Schcolnik, M. (1995). *Enhancing reading comprehension in the language learning classroom.* San Francisco: Alta Book Center.

Figueroa, A. (2004). Speaking Spanglish. In O. S. Ana (Ed.), *Tongue-tied: The lives of multicultural children in public education* (pp. 284–286). New York: Rowman & Littlefield.

Figueroa, R. A. (2006). The diagnosis of LD in English learners: Is it nondiscriminatory? *Journal of Learning Disabilities, 39*(3), 206–214.

Finnan, C. (1987). The influence of the ethnic community on the adjustment of Vietnamese refugees. In G. & L. Spindler (Eds.), *Interpretive ethnography of education: At home and abroad.* Hillsdale, NJ: Erlbaum.

Fisher, D., Brozo, W. G., Frey, N., & Ivey, G. (2007). *50 content area strategies for adolescent literacy.* Upper Saddle River, NJ: Merrill/Prentice Hall.

Fisher, D., & Frey, N. (2009). *Background knowledge: The missing piece of the comprehension puzzle.* Portsmouth, NH: Heinemann.

Flood, J., Lapp, D., Tinajero, J., & Hurley, S. (1997). Literacy instruction for students acquiring English: Moving beyond the immersion debate. *The Reading Teacher, 50*(4), 356–358.

Florida Department of Education. (2003). *Inclusion as an instructional model for LEP students.* Retrieved February 10, 2005, from www.firn.edu/doe/omsle/tapinclu.htm

Flower, L. (1994). *The construction of negotiated meaning: A social cognitive theory of writing.* Carbondale and Edwardsville: Southern Illinois University Press.

Flynn, K. (1995). *Graphic organizers . . . helping kids think visually.* Cypress, CA: Creative Thinking Press.

Flynt, E. S., & Cooter, R. B. (1999). *The English-Español reading inventory for the classroom.* Upper Saddle River, NJ: Merrill/Prentice Hall.

Folse, K. S. (1996). *Discussion starters.* Ann Arbor: The University of Michigan Press.

Folse, K. S. (2006). *The art of teaching speaking.* Ann Arbor: The University of Michigan Press.

Fosnot, C. T. (1989). *Enquiring teachers, enquiring learners: A constructivist approach for teaching.* New York: Teachers College Press.

Foucault, M. (1979). *Discipline and punish: The birth of the prison.* New York: Vintage Books.

Foucault, M. (1980). *Power/knowledge: Selected interviews and other writings 1971–1977.* New York: Pantheon Books.

Fraser, N., & Nicholson, L. (1988). Social criticism without philosophy: An encounter between feminism and postmodernism. In A. Ross (Ed.), *Universal abandon? The politics of postmodernism* (pp. 83–94). Minneapolis: University of Minnesota Press.

Fredericks, A. D., & Rasinski, T. V. (1990). Increasing parental involvement: A key to student achievement. *The Reading Teacher, 43*(6), 424–425.

Freeman, R. (2004). *Building on community bilingualism.* Philadelphia: Caslon.

Freire, P. (1970). *Pedagogy of the oppressed.* New York: Seabury Press.

Friend, M., & Bursuck, W. D. (2002). *Including students with special needs: A practical guide for classroom teachers.* Boston: Allyn & Bacon.

Friend, M., & Cook, L. (1996). *Interactions: Collaboration skills for school professionals.* White Plains, NY: Longman.

From the Classroom. (1991). Teachers seek a fair and meaningful assessment process to measure LEP students' progress. *Teacher Designed Learning, 2*(1), 1, 3.

Fu, D. (2004). Teaching ELL students in regular classrooms at the secondary level. *Voices from the Middle, 11*(4), 8–15.

Fu, D. (2009). *Writing between languages: How English language learners make the transition to fluency.* Portsmouth, NH: Heinemann.

Fuller, B. (2003). Educational policy under cultural pluralism. *Educational Researcher, 32*(9), 15–24.

Funaki, I., & Burnett, K. (1993). *When educational systems collide: Teaching and learning with Polynesian students.* Presentation at the Association of Teacher Educators annual conference, Los Angeles.

Furey, P. (1986). A framework for cross-cultural analysis of teaching methods. In P. Byrd (Ed.), *Teaching across cultures in the university ESL program.* Washington, DC: National Association of Foreign Student Advisors.

Gamrel, L. B., & Bales, R. J. (1986). Mental imagery and the comprehension-monitoring performance of fourth- and fifth-grade poor readers. *Reading Research Quarterly, 21,* 454–464.

Gándara, P. (1997). *Review of research on instruction of limited English proficient students.* Davis: University of California, Linguistic Minority Research Institute.

Gándara, P., Maxwell-Jolly, J., García, E., Asato, J., Gutiérrez, K., Stritkus, T., & Curry, J. (2000). *The initial impact of Proposition 227 on the instruction of English learn-ers.* Davis: University of California Linguistic Minority Research Center.

Gaouette, N. (2006, May 10). Latinos boost U.S. population. *Los Angeles Times,* A04.

García, E. (2000). *The best of times and the worst of times: Proposition 227 aftermath in California.* Tenth Annual Bilingual Education Institute, Arizona State University West, Phoenix.

García, S. B., & Ortiz, A. A. (2004). *Preventing disproportionate representation: Culturally and linguistically responsive prereferral interventions.* National Center for Culturally Responsive Educational Systems. Retrieved August 4, 2006, from www.nccrest.org/publications.html

Gardner, H. (1983). *Frames of mind: The theory of multiple intelligences.* New York: Basic Books.

Gardner, R., & Lambert, W. (1972). *Attitudes and motivation in second language learning.* Rowley, MA: Newbury House.

Garrison, D. (1990). Inductive strategies for teaching Spanish-English cognates. *Hispania, 73*(2), 508–512.

Gascoigne, C. (2002). *The debate on grammar in second language acquisition: Past, present, and future.* Lewiston, NY: Edwin Mellen Press.

Gass, S. (2000). *Interaction in classroom discourse.* Presentation at the Teachers of English to Speakers of Other Languages annual meeting, Vancouver, Canada.

Gass, S., & Selinker, L. (2008). *Second language acquisition: An introductory course* (3rd ed.). New York: Routledge.

Gay, G. (1975, October). Cultural differences important in education of Black children. *Momentum,* 30–32.

Genesee, F. (Ed.). (1999). *Program alternatives for linguistically diverse students.* Santa Cruz, CA: Center for Research on Education, Diversity & Excellence. Retrieved August 20, 2010, from http://gse.berkeley.edu/research/credearchive/products/print/eprs/epr1.shtml

Gersten, R., & Baker, S. (2000). What we know about effective instructional practices for English-language learners. *Exceptional Children, 66*(4), 454–470.

Gillen, J. (2003). *The language of children.* London and New York: Routledge.

Gillett, P. (1989a). *Cambodian refugees: An introduction to their history and culture.* San Francisco: New Faces of Liberty/SFSC.

Gillett, P. (1989b). *El Salvador: A country in crisis.* San Francisco: New Faces of Liberty/SFSC.

Giroux, H. (1983). Theories of reproduction and resistance in the new sociology of education: A critical appraisal. *Harvard Educational Review, 53,* 257–293.

Giroux, H., & McLaren, P. (1996). Teacher education and the politics of engagement: The case for democratic schooling. *Harvard Educational Review, 56*(3), 213–238.

Giroux, H. A. (1988). *Teachers as intellectuals: Toward a pedagogy of critical learning.* New York: Bergin & Garvey.

Glaser, S., & Brown, C. (1993). *Portfolios and beyond: Collaborative assessment in reading and writing.* Norwood, MA: Christopher-Gordon.

Goldenberg, C. (2001, January 25). These steps can help us teach Johnny to read. *Los Angeles Times,* B11.

Goldenberg, C., & Gallimore, R. (1991). Changing teaching takes more than a one-shot workshop. *Educational Leadership, 49*(3), 69–72.

Gollnick, D. M., & Chinn, P. C. (2002). *Multicultural education in a pluralistic society* (6th ed.). Upper Saddle River, NJ: Merrill Prentice Hall.

Gombert, J. E. (1992). *Metalinguistic development.* Chicago: The University of Chicago Press.

González, N. E., Moll, L., & Amanti, C. (Eds.). (2005). *Funds of knowledge: Theorizing practices in households, communities, and classrooms.* Mahwah, NJ: Erlbaum.

Good, T., & Brophy, J. (1984). *Looking in classrooms* (3rd ed.). New York: Harper and Row.

Goodman, K. (1986). *What's whole in whole language?* Portsmouth, NH: Heinemann.

Goodwin, J., Brinton, D., & Celce-Murcia, M. (1994). Pronunciation assessment in the ESL/EFL curriculum. In J. Morley (Ed.), *Pronunciation pedagogy theory: New views, new directions.* Alexandria, VA: Teachers of English to Speakers of Other Languages (TESOL).

Gopaul-McNicol, S., & Thomas-Presswood, T. (1998). *Working with linguistically and culturally different children.* Boston: Allyn & Bacon.

Gottlieb, M. (1995). Nurturing student learning through portfolios. *TESOL Journal, 5*(1), 12–14.

Graham, C. (1988). *Jazz chant fairy tales.* New York: Oxford University Press.

Graham, C. (1992). *Singing, chanting, telling tales.* Englewood Cliffs, NJ: Regents/Prentice Hall.

Grahame, K. (1983). *The wind in the willows.* New York: Simon & Schuster Children's Publishing.

Grasha, A. F. (1990). Using traditional versus naturalistic approaches to assess learning styles in college teaching. *Journal on Excellence in College Teaching, 1,* 23–38.

Graves, K. (1996). *Teaching opposites through music: Lesson plan.* Retrieved August 20, 2010, from www.lessonplanspage.com/MusicOpposites.htm

Greaver, M., & Hedberg, K. (2001). *Daily reading interventions to help targeted ESL and non-ESL students.* Retrieved July 24, 2006, from www.fcps.k12.va.us/DeerParkES/TchrResearch.html

Gregory, G. (2003). *Differentiating instructional strategies in practice: Training, implementation, and supervision.* Thousand Oaks, CA: Corwin.

Gregory, G. H., & Kuzmich, L. (2005). *Differentiated literacy strategies for student growth and achievement in grades 7–12.* Thousand Oaks, CA: Corwin.

Grognet, A., Jameson, J., Franco, L., & Derrick-Mescua, M. (2000). *Enhancing English language learning in elementary classrooms study guide.* McHenry, IL: Center for Applied Linguistics and Delta Systems.

Grossberg, L. (1988). Putting the pop back into postmodernism. In A. Ross (Ed.), *Universal abandon? The politics of postmodernism* (pp. 167–190). Minneapolis: University of Minnesota Press.

Groves, M. (2000, January 26). Vast majority of state's schools lag in new index. *Los Angeles Times,* A1, A14.

Groves, M. (2001, August 20). "Direct instruction" paying off. *Los Angeles Times,* B1, B8.

Gunning, T. G. (2005). *Creating literacy: Instruction for all students* (5th ed.). Boston: Allyn & Bacon.

Guthrie, J., & Wigfield, A. (2002). Engagement and motivation in reading. In M. Kamil, P. Mosenthal, P. D. Pearson, & R. Barr (Eds.), *Handbook of reading research* (Vol. 3, pp. 403–422). Mahwah, NJ: Erlbaum.

Gutiérrez, A. S., & Rodríguez, A. P. (2005). *Latino student success (K–20): Local community culture and context.* Spring 2005 Colloquium of the Maryland Institute for Minority Achievement and Urban Education, Baltimore.

Hadaway, N. L., Vardell, S. M., & Young, T. A. (2002). *Literature-based instruction with English language learners, K–12.* Boston: Allyn & Bacon.

Hafernik, J. J., Messerschmitt, D. S., & Vandrick, S. (2002). *Ethical issues for ESL faculty.* Mahwah, NJ: Erlbaum.

Hakuta, K. (1986). *Mirror of language.* New York: Basic Books.

Hakuta, K., Butler, Y. G., & Witt, D. (2000). *How long does it take English learners to attain proficiency?* (Policy Report 2000–1). Santa Barbara: University of California Linguistic Minority Research Institute.

Haley, M. H. (2010). *Brain-compatible differentiated instruction for English language learners.* Boston: Pearson.

Hall, E. (1959). *The silent language.* New York: Anchor Books.

Halliday, M. (1975). *Learning how to mean: Explorations in the development of language.* London: Edward Arnold.

Halliday, M. (1978). *Language as a social semiotic.* Baltimore: University Park Press.

Hamayan, E. (1994). Language development of low-literacy students. In F. Genesee (Ed.), *Educating second language children.* Cambridge, UK: Cambridge University Press.

Hamers, J. F., & Blanc, M. A. H. (1989). *Bilinguality and bilingualism.* Cambridge, UK: Cambridge University Press.

Han, Z. (2004). *Fossilization in adult second language acquisition.* Clevedon, UK: Multilingual Matters.

Hancock, C. (1994). Alternative assessment and second language study: What and why? *ERIC Digest.* Retrieved August 20, 2010, from www.cal.org/resources/digest/hancoc01.html

Harel, Y. (1992). Teacher talk in the cooperative learning classroom. In C. Kessler (Ed.), *Cooperative language learning.* Englewood Cliffs, NJ: Prentice Hall.

Harmer, J. (2007). *How to teach English.* Harlow, UK: Longman.

Harris, T. L., & Hodges, R. E. (1995). *The literacy dictionary: The vocabulary of reading and writing.* Newark, DE: International Reading Association.

Harris, V. (1997). *Teaching multicultural literature in grades K–8.* Norwood, MA: Christopher-Gordon.

Hatfield, M. M., Edwards, M. T., Bitter, G., & Morrow, J. (2004). *Mathematics methods for elementary and middle school teachers.* Hoboken, NJ: John Wiley & Sons.

Hayasaki, E. (2004, December 3). Cultural divide on campus. *Los Angeles Times,* A1, A36, A37.

Haycock, K., Jerald, C., & Huang, S. (2001). *Thinking K–16, closing the gap: Done in a decade.* Washington, DC: The Education Trust.

Haynes, J. (2004). What effective classroom teachers do. *Essential Teacher, 1*(5), 6–7.

Heath, S. B. (1999). *Ways with words: Language, life and work in communities and classrooms* (2nd ed.). Cambridge, UK: Cambridge University Press.

Heide, F., & Gilliland, J. (1990). *The day of Ahmed's secret.* New York: Lothrop, Lee, & Shepard.

Heilman, A. W. (2002). *Phonics in proper perspective.* Upper Saddle River, NJ: Merrill Prentice Hall.

Heinle & Heinle. (2002). *Launch into reading, Level I: Teacher's resource book.* Boston: Author.

Henderson, D., & May, J. (2005). *Exploring culturally diverse literature for children and adolescents.* Boston: Pearson.

Henwood, D. (1997). Trash-o-nomics. In M. Wray, M. Newitz, & A. Newitz (Eds.), *White trash: Race and class in America* (pp. 177–191). New York and London: Routledge.

Herrell, A. L. (2000). *Fifty strategies for teaching English language learners.* Upper Saddle River, NJ, and Columbus, OH: Merrill Prentice Hall.

Herrera, S. G., Murry, K. G., & Cabral, R. M. (2007). *Assessment accommodations for classroom teachers of culturally and linguistically diverse students.* Boston: Pearson.

Herrera, S. G., Perez, D. R., & Escamilla, K. (2010). *Teaching reading to English language learners: Differentiated literacies.* Boston: Pearson.

Herring, S. (1996). *Computer-mediated communication: Linguistic, social, and cross-cultural perspectives.* Amsterdam/Philadelphia: John Benjamins Publishing.

Hetherton, G. (1999). Headline news. In N. Shameem & M. Tickoo (Eds.), *New ways in using communicative games* (pp. 67–68). Alexandria, VA: Teachers of English to Speakers of Other Languages (TESOL).

Hicks, T. (2009). *The digital writing workshop.* Portsmouth, NH: Heinemann.

Hinojosa, R., Robles-Piña, R. A., & Edmondson, S. (2009). Gender differences in placement, support, and participation in early school programs for urban Hispanic students in advanced placement courses. *Advancing Women in Leadership Journal, 29*(8), 1–11.

Hispanic Dropout Project. (1998). *No more excuses: The final report of the Hispanic Dropout Project.* Washington, DC: U.S. Department of Education, Office of the Under Secretary. Retrieved August 20, 2010, from http://eric.ed .gov /ERICWebPortal/search/detailmini.jsp?_nfpb=true &_&ERICExtSearch_SearchValue_0=ED461447&ERIC ExtSearch_SearchType_0=no&accno=ED461447

Hodgkinson, H. L. (1998). Demographics of diversity for the 21st century. *The Education Digest, 64*(1), 4–7.

Hopstock, P. J., & Stephenson, T. (2003). *Descriptive study of services to LEP students and LEP students with disabilities.* Washington, DC: U.S. Department of Education. Retrieved August 4, 2006, from www.ncela.gwu .edu/resabout/research/descriptivestudyfiles/native_ languages1.pdf

Horwitz, E., Horwitz, M., & Cope, J. (1991). Foreign language classroom anxiety. In E. Horwitz & D. Young (Eds.), *Language anxiety: From theory and research to classroom implications* (pp. 27–36). Englewood Cliffs, NJ: Prentice Hall.

Houston, G. (2004). *How writing works.* Boston: Pearson.

Hudelson, S. (1984). Kan yu ret an rayt in Ingles: Children become literate in English as a second language. *TESOL Quarterly, 18,* 221–238.

Hughes, J. (2004). On bridge making. *Essential Teacher, 1*(1).

Huizenga, J., & Thomas-Ruzic, M. (1992). *All talk: Problem solving for new students of English.* Boston: Heinle & Heinle.

Huntley, H. (2006). *Essential academic vocabulary: Mastering the complete academic word list.* Boston: Houghton Mifflin.

Hymes, D. (1972). On communicative competence. In J. Pride & J. Holmes (Eds.), *Sociolinguistics.* Harmondsworth, UK: Penguin.

International Reading Association. (1997). *The role of phonics in reading instruction: A position statement of the International Reading Association.* Newark, DE: Author.

Irujo, S. (1998). *Teaching bilingual children: Beliefs and behaviors.* Cambridge, MA: Heinle & Heinle.

Irujo, S. (Ed.). (2000). *Integrating the ESL standards into classroom practice: Grades 6–8.* Alexandria, VA: Teachers of English to Speakers of Other Languages (TESOL).

Irvine, J. J. (1990). *Black students and school failure.* Westport, CT: Greenwood Press.

Ishii, S., & Bruneau, T. (1991). Silence and silences in cross-cultural perspective: Japan and the United States. In L.

Samovar & R. Porter (Eds.), *Intercultural communication: A reader* (6th ed.). Belmont, CA: Wadsworth.

Jametz, K. (1994). Making sure that assessment improves performance. *Educational Leadership, 51*(6), 55–57.

Jenks, C., Lee, J. O., & Kanpol, B. (2002). Approaches to multicultural education in preservice teacher education: Philosophical frameworks and models for teaching. In F. Schultz (Ed.), *Annual editions: Multicultural education 2002–2003* (pp. 20–28). Guilford, CT: McGraw-Hill/Dushkin.

Jensen, E. (1998). *Teaching with the brain in mind.* Alexandria, VA: Association for Supervision and Curriculum Development.

Jiménez, R. T. (2003). Literacy and Latino students in the United States: Some considerations, questions, and new directions. *Reading Research Quarterly, 38*(1), 122–128.

Johns, K. (1992). Mainstreaming language minority students through cooperative grouping. *The Journal of Educational Issues of Language Minority Students, 11,* Boise, ID: Boise State University Press.

Johnson, D. W., & Johnson, R. (1994). Cooperative learning in second language classes. *The Language Teacher, 18,* 4–7.

Johnson, D. W., Johnson, R., & Holubec, E. (1993). *Circles of learning: Cooperation in the classroom* (3rd ed.). Edina, MN: Interaction Book Company.

Johnson, D. W., & Johnson, R. T. (1995). Why violence prevention programs don't work—And what does. *Educational Leadership, 52*(5), 63–68.

Johnson, D. W., Johnson, R. T., Dudley, B., & Acikgoz, K. (1994). Effects of conflict resolution training on elementary school students. *The Journal of Social Psychology, 134*(6), 803–817.

Jones, L. (2007). *The student-centered classroom.* New York: Cambridge University Press.

Jones, L. T. (1991). *Strategies for involving parents in their children's education.* Bloomington, IN: Phi Delta Kappa Educational Foundation.

Jordan, C., Tharp, R., & Baird-Vogt, L. (1992). "Just open the door": Cultural compatibility and classroom rapport. In M. Saravia-Shore & S. Arvizu (Eds.), *Cross-cultural literacy.* New York and London: Garland.

Josephs, K. M. (2004). *African American language styles in Afrocentric schools.* Retrieved August 1, 2006, from www.swarthmore.edu/SocSci/Linguistics/papers/2004/josephs.doc

Jussim, L. (1986). Self-fulfilling prophecies: A theoretical and integrative review. *Psychological Review, 93,* 429–445.

Kagan, S. (1998). *Cooperative learning smart card.* Kagan Cooperative Learning. Retrieved from www.kagan online.com/catalog/SmartCards.php#TTB

Kagan, S. (1999). *Teambuilding smart card.* Kagan Cooperative Learning. Retrieved from www.kaganonline.com/catalog/SmartCards.php#TTB

Kame'enui, E. J., & Simmons, D. C. (2000). *Planning and evaluation tool for effective schoolwide reading programs.* Eugene, OR: Institute for the Development of Educational Achievement.

Kandel, W., & Cromartie, J. (2004). *New patterns of Hispanic settlement in rural America.* Retrieved January 16, 2005, from www.ers.usda.gov/publications/rdrr99

Kang, H. W., Kuehn, P., & Herrell, A. (1996). *The Hmong literacy project: Parents working to preserve the past and ensure the future.* Retrieved July 7, 2006, from www.ncela.gwu.edu/pubs/jeilms/vol16/jeilms1602.htm

Kaufman, P., Alt, M. N., & Chapman, C. (2004). *Dropout rates in the United States: 2001* (NCES 2005-046). U.S. Department of Education. National Center for Education Statistics. Washington, DC: U.S. Government Printing Office. Retrieved August 4, 2006, from www.nces.ed.gov/pubs/205/2005046.pdf

Kea, C., Campbell-Whatley, G. D., & Richards, H. V. (2004). *Becoming culturally responsive educators: Rethinking teacher education pedagogy.* National Center for Culturally Responsive Educational Systems. Retrieved January 29, 2005, from www.nccrest.org/publications.html

Kealey, J., & Inness, D. (1997). *Shenanigames: Grammar-focused interactive ESL/EFL activities and games.* Brattleboro, VT: Prolingua.

Keefe, M. W. (1987). *Learning style theory and practice.* Reston, VA: National Association of Secondary School Principals.

Kehe, D., & Kehe, P. D. (1998). *Discussion strategies.* Brattleboro, VT: Prolingua Associates.

Kelley, M. L. (1990). *School-home notes: Promoting children's classroom success.* New York: Guilford Press.

Kessler, C., Quinn, M., & Fathman, A. (1992). Science and cooperative learning for LEP students. In C. Kessler (Ed.), *Cooperative language learning* (pp. 65–83). Englewood Cliffs, NJ: Regents/Prentice Hall.

Kim, E. Y. (2001). *The yin and yang of American culture.* Yarmouth, ME: Intercultural Press.

Kluge, D. (1999). *A brief introduction to cooperative learning.* ERIC Document Service (ED437840). Retrieved August 4, 2006, from www.eric.ed.gov

Knobel, M., & Lankshear, C. (2006). Profiles and perspective: Discussing new literacies. *Language Arts, 84*(1), 78–86.

Kozyrev, J. R. (1998). *Talk it up! Oral communication for the real world.* Boston: Houghton Mifflin.

Krashen, S. (1981). Bilingual education and second language acquisition theory. In *Schooling and language minority students: A theoretical framework.* Los Angeles: Evaluation, Dissemination and Assessment Center, California State University, Los Angeles.

Krashen, S. (1982). *Principles and practice in second language acquisition.* Oxford, UK: Pergamon.

Krashen, S. (1985). *The input hypothesis: Issues and implications.* New York: Longman.

Krashen, S. (2003). *Explorations in language acquisition and language use: The Taipei lectures.* Portsmouth, NH: Heinemann. Quote retrieved July 20, 2006, from www.coas.uncc.edu/linguistics/courses/6163/should_we_teach_grammar.htm

Krashen, S., & Terrell, T. (1983). *The natural approach: Language acquisition in the classroom.* Oxford, UK: Pergamon.

Kress, G. (2000). *Early spelling: Between convention and creativity.* London and New York: Routledge.

Kress, G. R., & Van Leeuwen, T. (1995). *Reading images: The grammar of visual design.* London: Routledge.

Laberge, D., & Samuels, S. J. (1974). Toward a theory of automatic information processing in reading. *Cognitive Psychology, 6,* 293–323.

Laufer, B. (1989). What percentage of text-lexis is essential for comprehension? In C. Lauren & M. Nordman (Eds.), *Special language: From humans thinking to thinking machines* (pp. 316–323). Clevedon, UK: Multilingual Matters.

Laufer, B., & Paribakht, S. (1998). The relationship between passive and active vocabularies: Effects of language learning contexts. *Language Learning, 48,* 365–391.

Lave, J., & Wenger, E. (1991). *Situated learning: Legitimate peripheral participation.* New York: Cambridge University Press.

Law, B., & Eckes, M. (2000). *The more-than-just-surviving handbook* (2nd ed.). Winnipeg, Canada: Peguis.

Leathers, N. (1967). *The Japanese in America.* Minneapolis, MN: Lerner Publications.

LeBeau, C., & Harrington, D. (2003). *Getting ready for speech.* Medford, OR: Language Solutions.

LeCompte, M. (1981). The Procrustean bed: Public schools, management systems, and minority students. In H. Trueba, G. Guthrie, & K. Au (Eds.), *Culture and the bilingual classroom: Studies in classroom ethnography.* Rowley, MA: Newbury House.

Lee, B. J. (2001). Cat and his pals. In *McGraw-Hill Reading: Phonics practice reader 1.* New York: McGraw-Hill.

Lee, O. (2005). Science education with English language learners: Synthesis and research agenda. *Review of Educational Research, 75*(4), 491–530.

Leistyna, P., Woodrum, A., & Sherblom, S. (Eds.). (1996). Glossary. In P. Leistyna, A. Woodrum, & S. A. Sherblom (Eds.), *Breaking free: The transformative power of critical pedagogy* (pp. 301–331). *Harvard Educational Review* Reprint Series #27. Cambridge, MA: Harvard University Press.

Leki, I. (1992). *Understanding ESL writers.* Portsmouth, NH: Boynton/Cook.

LeLoup, J., & Ponterio, R. (2000). *Enhancing authentic language learning experiences through Internet technology.* Retrieved August 20, 2010, from www.cal.org/resources/digest/0002enhancing.html

Lemberger, N. (1999). Factors affecting language development from the perspectives of four bilingual teachers. In I. Heath & C. Serrano (Eds.), *Annual editions: Teaching English as a second language* (2nd ed.). Guilford, CT: Dushkin/McGraw-Hill.

Lenneberg, E. (1967). *Biological foundations of language.* New York: John Wiley & Sons.

LePage, R. B., & Tabouret-Keller, A. (1985). *Acts of identity: Creole-based approaches to language and ethnicity.* Cambridge, UK: Cambridge University Press.

Levine, D., & Adelman, M. (1982). *Beyond language: Intercultural communication for English as a second language.* Englewood Cliffs, NJ: Prentice Hall.

Levine, L. N. (2000). The most beautiful place in the world. In K. D. Samway (Ed.), *Integrating the ESL standards into classroom practice: Grades 3–5* (pp. 109–131). Alexandria, VA: Teachers of English to Speakers of Other Languages (TESOL).

Levstik, L. S., & Barton, K. C. (2001). *Doing history: Investigating with children in elementary and middle schools* (2nd ed.). Mahwah, NJ: Erlbaum.

Lewis, G., & Bedson, G. (1999). *Games for children.* Oxford, UK: Oxford University Press.

Lewis, M. (1997). *New ways in teaching adults.* Alexandria, VA: Teachers of English to Speakers of Other Languages (TESOL).

Lindholm, K. (1994). Promoting positive cross-cultural attitudes and perceived competence in culturally and linguistically diverse classrooms. In R. A. DeVillar, C. Faltis, & J. Cummins (Eds.), *Cultural diversity in schools: From rhetoric to practice* (pp. 189–206). Albany: State University of New York Press.

Lindholm-Leary, K. (2000). *Biliteracy for a global society: An idea book on dual language education.* Washington, DC: National Clearinghouse for Bilingual Education.

Linn, R. L. (2000). Assessments and accountability. *Educational Researcher, 29*(2), 4–26.

Linn, R. L., & Miller, M. D. (2005). *Measurement and assessment in teaching* (9th ed.). Upper Saddle River, NJ: Prentice-Hall.

Linse, C. (2006). Using favorite songs and poems with young learners. *English Teaching Forum, 44*(2), 38–40.

Lippi-Green, R. (1997). *English with an accent.* London and New York: Routledge.

Lipton, L., & Hubble, D. (1997). *More than 50 ways to learner-centered literacy.* Arlington Heights, IL: Skylight Professional Development.

Lockwood, A. T. (2000). *Transforming education for Hispanic youth: Broad recommendations for teachers and program staff.* Washington, DC: National Clearinghouse for Bilingual Education. Retrieved January 28, 2005, from www .ncela.gwu.edu/pubs/issuebriefs/ib4.html

Lockwood, A. T., & Secada, W. G. (1999). *Transforming education for Hispanic youth: Exemplary practices, programs, and schools. NCELA Resource Collection Series, 12.* Retrieved August 3, 2006, from www.ncela.gwu.edu/ pubs/resource/hispanicyouth/hdp.htm

Long, M. (1980). *Input, interaction, and language acquisition.* Unpublished doctoral dissertation, University of California, Los Angeles.

Long, M. H. (1987). Listening comprehension: Approach, design, procedure. In M. H. Long & J. C. Richards (Eds.), *Methodology in TESOL: A book of readings* (pp. 161–176). New York: Newbury House.

Losen, D., & Wald, J. (2005). *Confronting the graduation rate crisis in California* (Final Report). Cambridge, MA: Harvard Civil Rights Project.

Lu, M. L. (2000). *Language development in the early years* (ERIC, Digest No. 154). Bloomington, IN: ERIC Clearinghouse on Reading, English, and Communication.

Lucas, T., & Katz, A. (1994). Reframing the debate: The roles of native languages in English-only programs for language minority students. *TESOL Quarterly, 28*(3), 537–561.

Lucas, T., & Wagner, S. (1999). Facilitating secondary English language learners' transition into the mainstream. *TESOL Journal, 8*(4), 6–13.

Lyons, C. A., & Clay, M. M. (2003). *Teaching struggling readers: How to use brain-based research to maximize learning.* Portsmouth, NH: Heinemann.

McCarten, J. (2007). *Teaching vocabulary: Lessons from the corpus, lessons for the classroom.* Cambridge, UK: Cambridge University Press.

McCarthy, M. (2004). *Touchstone: From corpus to course book.* Cambridge, UK: Cambridge University Press.

McCarty, T. L. (Ed.). (2005). *Language, literacy, and power in schooling.* Mahwah, NJ: Erlbaum.

Maciejewski, T. (2003). *Pragmatics.* Retrieved August 4, 2006, from www.lisle.dupage.k12.il.us/maciejewski/social.htm

McKenna, M. C., & Robinson, R. D. (1997). *Teaching through text: A content literacy approach to content area reading* (2nd ed.). New York: Longman.

McLaren, P. (1995). Critical multiculturalism, media literacy, and the politics of representation. In J. Frederickson (Ed.), *Reclaiming our voices: Bilingual education, critical pedagogy, and praxis* (pp. 99–138). Ontario, CA: California Association for Bilingual Education.

McLeod, B. (1995). *School reform & student diversity: Lessons learned—Educating students from diverse linguistic and cultural backgrounds.* Retrieved January 28, 2005, from www.ncela.gwu.edu/pubs/ncrcdsll/srsd/school org.htm

Maculaitis, J. (1988). *The complete ESL/EFL resource book: Strategies, activities, and units for the classroom.* Lincolnwood, IL: National Textbook Company.

Mahoney, D. (1999a). Shadow tableaux. In N. Shameem & M. Tickoo (Eds.), *New ways in using communicative games* (pp. 13–14). Alexandria, VA: Teachers of English to Speakers of Other Languages (TESOL).

Mahoney, D. (1999b). Stress clapping. In N. Shameem & M. Tickoo (Eds.), *New ways in using communicative games* (pp. 20–21). Alexandria, VA: Teachers of English to Speakers of Other Languages (TESOL).

Majors, P. (n.d.). *Charleston County School District, Charleston, SC, sample standards-based lesson plan.* Retrieved August 4, 2006, from www.cal.org/eslstandards/ Charleston.html

Malavé, L. (1991). Conceptual framework to design a programme intervention for culturally and linguistically different handicapped students. In L. Malavé & G. Duquette (Eds.), *Language, culture and cognition* (pp. 176–189). Clevedon, UK: Multilingual Matters.

Mandlebaum, L. H., & Wilson, R. (1989). Teaching listening skills in the special education classroom. *Academic Therapy, 24,* 451–452.

Manning, M. L. (2002). Understanding diversity, accepting others: Realities and directions. In F. Schultz, (Ed.), *Annual editions: Multicultural education 2002/2003.* Guilford, CT: McGraw-Hill/Dushkin.

Mansour, W. (1999). Give me a word that . . . In N. Shameem & M. Tickoo (Eds.), *New ways in using communicative games* (pp. 103–104). Alexandria, VA: Teachers of English to Speakers of Other Languages (TESOL).

Marinova-Todd, S., Marshall, D., & Snow, C. (2000). Three misconceptions about age and L2 learning. *TESOL Quarterly, 34*(1), 9–34.

Marlowe, B. A., & Page, M. L. (1999). Making the most of the classroom mosaic: A constructivist perspective. *Multicultural Education, 6*(4), 19–21.

Marton, W. (1994). The antipedagogical aspects of Krashen's theory of second language acquisition. In R. Barasch & C. James (Eds.), *Beyond the monitor model.* Boston: Heinle & Heinle.

Marzano, R. J. (1994). Lessons from the field about outcome-based performance assessments. *Educational Leadership, 51*(6), 44–50.

Matthews, C. (1994). *Speaking solutions.* White Plains, NY: Longman.

May, F. B., & Rizzardi, L. (2002). *Reading as communication* (6th ed.). Upper Saddle River, NJ: Merrill Prentice Hall.

Medina, M., Jr., & Escamilla, K. (1992). Evaluation of transitional and maintenance bilingual programs. *Urban Education, 27*(3), 263–290.

Mehan, H. (1979). *Learning lessons.* Cambridge, MA: Harvard University Press.

Mehan, H. (1981). Ethnography of bilingual education. In H. Trueba, G. Guthrie, & K. Au (Eds.), *Culture and the bilingual classroom: Studies in classroom ethnography.* Rowley, MA: Newbury House.

Mehan, H., Hubbard, L., Lintz, A., & Villavueva, I. (1994). *Tracking untracking: The consequences of placing low track students in high track classes.* Santa Cruz, CA: The National Center for Research on Cultural Diversity & Second Language Learning. Retrieved August 20, 2010, from http://gse.berkeley.edu/research/credearchive/research/tier/rb3.shtml

Mehrabian, A. (1968). Communication without words. *Psychology Today, 2*(9), 52–55.

Menken, K. (2000). *What are the critical issues in wide-scale assessment of English language learners?* (ED 450595). Washington, DC: National Clearinghouse for Bilingual Education.

Migration Policy Institute. (2004). *A new century: Immigration and the US.* Retrieved January 15, 2005, from www.migrationinformation.org/Profiles/display.cfm?ID=6

Miller, G. (1985). Nonverbal communication. In V. Clark, P. Eschholz, & A. Rosa (Eds.), *Language: Introductory readings* (4th ed.). New York: St. Martin's Press.

Miller, L. (2004). *Developing listening skills with authentic materials.* Retrieved July 21, 2006, from www.eslmag.com/modules.php?name=News&file=article&sid=20

Miller, W. H. (1995). *Alternative assessment techniques for reading and writing.* West Nyack, NJ: The Center for Applied Research in Education.

Molina, H., Hanson, R. A., & Siegel, D. F. (1997). *Empowering the second-language classroom: Putting the parts together.* San Francisco: Caddo Gap Press.

Monroe, S. (1999). Multicultural children's literature: Canon of the future. Reprinted in *Annual editions 99/00: Teaching English as a second language.* Guilford, CO: Dushkin/McGraw-Hill.

Mora, J. K. (2000). Staying the course in times of change: Preparing teachers for linguistically diverse classrooms. *Journal of Teacher Education, 51*(5), 345–357.

Mora, J. K. (2002). *Proposition 227's second anniversary: Triumph or travesty?* Retrieved June 30, 2006, from http://coe.sdsu.edu/people/jmora/Prop227/227YearTwo.htm

Moras, S. (2001). *Teaching vocabulary to advanced students: A lexical approach.* Retrieved May 11, 2010, from www3.telus.net/linguisticsissues/teachingvocabulary.html

Morey, A., & Kilano, M. (1997). *Multicultural course transformation in higher education: A broader truth.* Boston: Allyn & Bacon.

Morgan, R. (1992). Distinctive voices—Developing oral language in multilingual classrooms. In P. Pinsent (Ed.), *Language, culture, and young children* (pp. 37–46). London: David Fulton Publisher.

Morley, J. (1999). Current perspectives on improving aural comprehension. *ESL Magazine, 2*(1), 16–19.

Moskowitz, G. (1978). *Caring and sharing in the foreign language classroom.* Cambridge, MA: Newbury House.

Murray, D. E. (2000). Protean communication: The language of computer-mediated communication. *TESOL Quarterly, 34*(3), 397–421.

Nagy, W. E. (1997). On the role of context in first- and second-language vocabulary learning. In N. Schmitt & M. McCarthy (Eds.), *Vocabulary: Description, acquisition, pedagogy* (pp. 64–83). Cambridge, UK: Cambridge University Press.

Nagy, W. E., García, G. E., Durgunoglu, A., & Hancin-Bhatt, B. (1993). Spanish-English bilingual students' use of cognates in English reading. *Bilingual Research Journal, 18,* 83–97.

Nash, P. (1991). ESL and the myth of the model minority. In S. Benesch (Ed.), *ESL in America.* Portsmouth, NH: Boynton/Cook.

Natheson-Mejia, S. (1989). Writing in a second language. *Language Arts, 66*(5), 516–526.

Nation, I. S. P. (1990). *Teaching and learning vocabulary.* New York: Newbury House.

Nation, P. (1994). *New ways in teaching vocabulary.* Alexandria, VA: Teachers of English to Speakers of Other Languages (TESOL).

National Center for Culturally Responsive Educational Systems (2006). *Cultural pluralism.* Retrieved July 31, 2006, from http://nccrest.edreform.net/subject/culturalpluralism

National Center for Education Statistics (NCES). (2000). *NAEP 1999 trends in academic progress: Three decades of student performance.* Washington, DC: U.S. Department of Education.

National Center for Education Statistics (NCES). (2002). *Percentage distribution of enrollment in public elementary and secondary schools, by race/ethnicity and state: Fall 1986 and fall 2000.* Retrieved August 3, 2005, from http://nces.ed.gov/programs/digest/d02/dt042.asp

National Center for Education Statistics (NCES). (2003). *Employees in degree-granting institutions, by race/ethnicity, primary occupation, sex, employment status, and control and type of institution: Fall 2001.* Retrieved March 20, 2005, from http://nces.ed.gov/programs/digest/d03/tables/dt228.asp

National Center for Education Statistics (NCES). (2005). *Postsecondary participation rates by sex and race/ethnicity: 1974–2003.* Washington, DC: Author.

National Clearinghouse for English Language Acquisition and Language Instruction Educational Programs (NCELA). (2004). *ELLs and the No Child Left Behind*

*Act*. Retrieved August 2, 2006, from www.ncela.gwu.edu/about/lieps/ 5ellnclb.html

National Clearinghouse for English Language Acquisition & Language Instruction Educational Programs (NCELA). (2008). *How has the English language learner (ELL) population changed in recent years?* Retrieved April 14, 2010, from www.ncela.gwu.edu/files/rcd/BE021773/How_has_the_limited_English.pdf

National Commission on Teaching and America's Future. (2002). *Teacher shortage question unraveled: NCTAF challenges the nation to address the teacher retention crisis.* Washington, DC: Author.

National Education Association. (1975). *Code of ethics of the education profession.* Washington, DC: Author.

National High School Center. (2009). *Educating English language learners at the high school level: A coherent approach to district- and school-level support* (ED 507 622). Washington, DC: American Institutes for Research.

Nelson-Barber, S. (1999). A better education for every child: The dilemma for teachers of culturally and linguistically diverse students. In Mid-continent Research for Education and Learning (McREL) (Ed.), *Including culturally and linguistically diverse students in standards-based reform: A report on McREL's Diversity Roundtable I* (pp. 3–22). Aurora, CO: Author.

Nemmer-Fanta, M. (2002). Accommodations and modifications for English language learners. In *Serving English language learners with disabilities: A resource manual for Illinois educators.* Retrieved February 9, 2005, from www.isbe.state.il.us/speced/bilingualmanual2002.htm

Nero, S. J. (1997). English is my native language . . . or so I believe. *TESOL Quarterly, 31*(3), 585–593.

Newman, J. M. (1985). What about reading? In J. M. Newman (Ed.), *Whole language: Theory in use* (pp. 99–100). Portsmouth, NH: Heinemann.

Nieto, S. (2007). *Affirming diversity* (5th ed.). New York: Longman.

No Child Left Behind (NCLB). (2001). Title III, Part A, Sec. 3102. Purposes (1). Retrieved August 4, 2006, from www.ncela.gwu.edu/about/lieps/5_ellnclb.html

Oakes, J. (1985). *Keeping track: How schools structure inequality.* New Haven, CT: Yale University Press.

Oakes, J. (1992). Can tracking research inform practice? Technical, normative, and political considerations. *Educational Researcher, 21*(4), 12–21.

O'Barr, W. M., & Atkins, B. K. (1980). Women's language or powerless language. In S. McConnell-Ginet, R. Borker, & N. Furman (Eds.), *Women and language in literature and society* (pp. 93–110). New York: Praeger.

O'Connor, T. (2004). *Understanding discrimination against Asian-Americans.* Retrieved August 4, 2006, from http://faculty.ncwc.edu/toconnor/soc/355lect10.htm

Odlin, T. (1989). *Language transfer: Cross-linguistic influence in language learning.* Cambridge, UK: Cambridge University Press.

Ogbu, J. (1978). *Minority education and caste: The American system in crosscultural perspective.* New York: Academic Press.

Ogbu, J., & Matute-Bianchi, M. (1986). Understanding sociocultural factors: Knowledge, identity, and school adjustment. In Evaluation, Dissemination and Assessment Center, California State University, Los Angeles (Ed.), *Beyond language: Social and cultural factors in schooling language minority students.* Los Angeles: Author.

O'Keefe, A. M., McCarthy, M. J., & Carter, R. A. (2007). *From corpus to classroom.* Cambridge, UK: Cambridge University Press.

Olmedo, I. M. (1993, Summer). Junior historians: Doing oral history with ESL and bilingual students. *TESOL Journal, 2*(4), 7–9.

Omaggio, A. (1978). *Games and simulations in the foreign language classroom.* Washington, DC: Center for Applied Linguistics.

Omaggio, A. C. (1986). *Teaching language in context.* Boston: Heinle & Heinle.

O'Malley, J. M., & Pierce, L. V. (1996). *Authentic assessment for English language learners.* Menlo Park, CA: Addison-Wesley.

Ong, W. (1982). *Orality and literacy.* London: Methuen.

Orfield, G., Losen, D., Wald, J., & Swanson, C. (2004). *Losing our future: How minority youth are being left behind by the graduation rate crisis.* Harvard Education Publishing Group. (ERIC Document Reproduction Service No. ED 489177)

Orfield, T., & Lee, C. (2005). *Why segregation matters: Poverty and educational inequality.* Retrieved August 6, 2006, from www.civilrightsproject.harvard.edu/research/deseg/deseg05.php

Ortiz, A. A. (2002). Prevention of school failure and early intervention for English language learners. In A. J. Artiles & A. A. Ortiz (Eds.), *English language learners with special education needs: Identification, assessment, and instruction* (pp. 31–63). Washington, DC: Center for Applied Linguistics and Delta Systems.

Ortiz, F. (1988). Hispanic-American children's experiences in classrooms: A comparison between Hispanic and non-Hispanic children. In L. Weis (Ed.), *Class, race, and gender in American education.* Albany: State University of New York Press.

Oshima, A., & Hogue, A. (2006). *Writing academic English* (4th ed.). White Plains, NY: Pearson Longman.

Ouk, M., Huffman, F., & Lewis, J. (1988). *Handbook for teaching Khmer-speaking students.* Sacramento, CA: Spilman Printing.

Ovando, C., & Collier, V. (1998). *Bilingual and ESL classrooms: Teaching in multicultural contexts.* Boston: McGraw-Hill.

Oyama, S. (1976). A sensitive period for the acquisition of nonnative phonological system. *Journal of Psycholinguistic Research, 5,* 261–284.

Packer, N. H., & Timpane, J. (1997). *Writing worth reading: The critical process* (3rd ed.). Boston: Bedford Books.

Paige, R. M. (1999). Theoretical foundations of intercultural training and applications to the teaching of culture. In R. M. Paige, D. L. Lange, & Y. A. Yershova (Eds.), *Culture as the core: Integrating culture into the language curriculum* (pp. 21–29). Minneapolis: Center for Advanced Research on Language Acquisition, University of Minnesota.

Palinscar, A. S., & Brown, A. L. (1984). Reciprocal teaching of comprehension-fostering and comprehension-monitoring activities. *Cognition and Instruction, 1,* 117–175.

Pappas, C. C., Kiefer, B. Z., & Levstik, L. S. (2006). *An integrated language perspective in the elementary school* (4th ed.). Boston: Allyn & Bacon.

Parks, S., & Black, H. (1990). *Organizing thinking: Graphic organizers.* Pacific Grove, CA: Critical Thinking Press & Software.

Pasternak, J. (1994, March 29). Bias blights life outside Appalachia. *Los Angeles Times,* A1, A16.

Pearson, R. (1974). *Introduction to anthropology.* New York: Holt, Rinehart and Winston.

Peim, N. (1993). *Critical theory and the English teacher.* London and New York: Routledge.

Pennycook, A. (1998). Text, ownership, memory, and plagiarism. In V. Zamel & R. Spack (Eds.), *Negotiating academic literacies: Teaching and learning across languages and cultures* (pp. 265–292). Mahwah, NJ: Erlbaum.

Peregoy, S., & Boyle, O. (2005). *Reading, writing, and learning in ESL* (4th ed.). Boston: Pearson.

Pérez, B., & Torres-Guzmán, M. (2002). *Learning in two worlds* (3rd ed.). New York: Longman.

Philips, S. (1972). Participant structures and communicative competence: Warm Springs children in community and classroom. In C. Cazden, V. John, & D. Hymes (Eds.), *Functions of language in the classroom.* New York: Teachers College Press.

Phillips, J. (1978). College of, by and for Navajo Indians. *Chronicle of Higher Education, 15,* 10–12.

Phipps, R. (2010). When testprep goes too far. *Language, 9*(8), 19.

Pinnell, G. S. (1985). Ways to look at the functions of children's language. In A. Jaggar & M. Smith-Burke (Eds.), *Observing the language learner.* Newark, DE: International Reading Association.

Porter, C. (2010). English is not enough. *Chronicle of Higher Education, 56*(32), 64.

Porter, R. (1990). *Forked tongue: The politics of bilingual education.* New York: Basic Books.

Pratt, C., & Nesdale, A. R. (1984). Pragmatic awareness in children. In W. E. Tunmer, C. Pratt, & M. L. Herriman (Eds.), *Metalinguistic awareness in children* (pp. 105–125). Berlin: Springer Verlag.

Pridham, F. (2001). *The language of conversation.* New York and London: Routledge.

Prothrow-Smith, D. (1994, April). Building violence prevention into the classroom. *The School Administrator, 8*(12), 8–12.

Pruitt, W. (2000). Using story to compare, conclude, and identify. In B. Agor (Ed.), *Integrating the ESL standards into classroom practice: Grades 9–12* (pp. 31–49). Alexandria, VA: Teachers of English to Speakers of Other Languages (TESOL).

Pryor, C. B. (2002). New immigrants and refugees in American schools: Multiple voices. In F. Schultz (Ed.), *Annual editions: Multicultural education 2002/2003* (pp. 185–193). Guilford, CT: McGraw-Hill/Dushkin.

Quiocho, A. L., & Ulanoff, S. H. (2009). *Differentiated literacy instruction for English language learners.* Boston: Pearson.

Raimes, A. (Ed.). (1996). *Identities: Readings from contemporary culture.* Boston: Houghton Mifflin.

Ramírez, J. (1992, Winter/Spring). Executive summary, final report: Longitudinal study of structured English immersion strategy, early-exit and late-exit transitional bilingual education programs for language-minority children. *Bilingual Research Journal, 16*(1&2), 1–62.

Raphael, T. E. (1986). Teaching question answer relationships, revisited. *The Reading Teacher, 39,* 516–523.

Rasinski, T., & Fredericks, A. (1989). Dimensions of parent involvement. *The Reading Teacher, 43*(2), 180–182.

Redish, L. (2001). *Native languages of the Americas: Endangered language revitalization and revival.* Retrieved April 28, 2010, from www.native-languages.org/revive.htm

Reid, J. M. (1993). *Teaching ESL writing.* Englewood Cliffs, NJ: Prentice Hall Regents.

Reid, J. M. (1995). Preface. In J. Reid (Ed.), *Learning styles in the ESL/EFL classroom* (pp. viii–xvii). Boston: Heinle & Heinle.

Remillar, J. T., & Cahnmann, M. (2005). Researching mathematics teaching in bilingual-bicultural classrooms. In T. L. McCarty (Ed.), *Language, literacy, and power in schooling* (pp. 169–187). Mahwah, NJ: Erlbaum.

Richard-Amato, P. (2003). *Making it happen* (3rd ed.). White Plains, NY: Longman.

Richard-Amato, P., & Snow, M. (1992). Strategies for content-area teachers. In P. Richard-Amato & M. Snow (Eds.), *The multicultural classroom.* White Plains, NY: Longman.

Richards, J. C. (2008). *Moving beyond the plateau: From intermediate to advanced levels in language learning.* New York: Cambridge University Press.

Riles, G. B., & Lenarcic, C. (2000). Exploring world religions. In B. Agor (Ed.), *Integrating the ESL standards into classroom practice: Grades 9–12* (pp. 1–29). Alexandria, VA: Teachers of English to Speakers of Other Languages (TESOL).

Rivera, C. (2006, June 9). Charter school fights back. *Los Angeles Times.* Retrieved July 7, 2006, from www.latimes.com/news/local/lame-charter9jun09,1,4660030.story?ctrack=1&cset=true

Robin, R. (2006). *Should we teach grammar?* Retrieved July 20, 2006, from www.coas.uncc.edu/linguistics/courses/6163/should_we_teach_grammar.htm

Robinson, G. (1985). *Crosscultural understanding.* New York: Pergamon Institute of English.

Rodby, J. (1999). Contingent literacy: The social construction of writing for nonnative English-speaking college freshman. In L. Harklau, K. M. Losey, & M. Siegal (Eds.), *Generation 1.5 meets college composition: Issues in the teaching of writing to U.S.-educated learners of ESL* (pp. 45–60). Mahwah, NJ: Erlbaum.

Rose, C. (1987). *Accelerated learning.* New York: Dell.

Rosebery, A. S., Warren, B., & Conant, F. R. (1992). Appropriating scientific discourse: Finding from language minority classrooms. *Journal of the Learning Sciences, 21,* 61–94.

Rowan, T., & Bourne, B. (1994). *Thinking like mathematics.* Portsmouth, NH: Heinemann.

Rumbaut, R. G. (1995). The new Californians: Comparative research findings on the education progress of immigrant children. In R. G. Rumbaut & W. A. Cornelius, *California's immigrant children: Theory, research, and implications for educational policy* (pp. 17–70). San Diego: University of California, San Diego Center for U.S.-Mexican Studies.

Runner, J. (2000). *"I don't understand" in over 230 languages.* Retrieved August 2, 2006, from www.elite.net/~runner/jennifers/understa.htm

Sales, F. (1989). *Ibrahim.* New York: Lippincott.

Samway, K. D. (Ed.). (2000). *Integrating the ESL standards into classroom practice: Grades 3–5.* Alexandria, VA: Teachers of English to Speakers of Other Languages (TESOL).

Santa Ana, O. (2004). Giving voice to the silenced. *Language, 3*(8), 15–17.

Sato, C. (1982). Ethnic styles in classroom discourse. In M. Hines and W. Rutherford (Eds.), *On TESOL '81.* Washington, DC: Teachers of English to Speakers of Other Languages (TESOL).

Saunders, W. M., Foorman, B. R., & Carlson, C. D. (2006). Is a separate block of time for oral English language development in programs for English learners needed? *The Elementary School Journal, 107*(2), 181–198.

Savage, K. L., Bitterlin, G., & Price, D. (2010). *Grammar matters: Teaching grammar in Adult ESL programs.* New York: Cambridge Press.

Scarcella, R. (1990). *Teaching language minority students in the multicultural classroom.* Englewood Cliffs, NJ: Prentice Hall.

Scarcella, R., & Rumberger, R. W. (2000). Academic English key to long-term success in school. *University of California Linguistic Minority Research Institute Newsletter, 9*(4), 1–2.

Schifini, A., Short, D., & Tinajero, J. V. (2002). *High point.* Carmel, CA: Hampton-Brown.

Schultz, J., & Theophano, J. (1987). Saving place and marking time: Some aspects of the social lives of three-year-old children. In H. Trueba (Ed.), *Success or failure?* Cambridge, MA: Newbury House Publishers.

Schumann, J. (1978). The acculturation model for second-language acquisition. In R. Gringas (Ed.), *Second language acquisition and foreign language teaching.* Washington, DC: Center for Applied Linguistics.

Schumann, J. (1994). Emotion and cognition in second language acquisition. *Studies in Second Language Acquisition, 16,* 231–242.

Scollon, R., & Scollon, S. W. (2003). *Discourses in place: Language in the material world.* London and New York: Routledge.

Selinker, L. (1972). Interlanguage. *IRAL, 10*(3), 209–231.

Selinker, L. (1991). Along the way: Interlanguage systems in second language acquisition. In L. Malavé & G. Duquette (Eds.), *Language, culture and cognition.* Clevedon, UK: Multilingual Matters.

Shade, B., & New, C. (1993). Cultural influences on learning: Teaching implications. In J. Banks & C. Banks (Eds.), *Multicultural education: Issues and perspectives.* Boston: Allyn & Bacon.

Shaffer, D. R. (1999). *Developmental psychology: Childhood & adolescence* (5th ed.). Pacific Grove, CA: Brooks Cole Publishing Company.

Shoemaker, C., & Polycarpou, S. (1993). *Write ideas: A beginning writing text.* Boston: Heinle & Heinle.

Sholley, D. (2006, July 20). Two cultures, one unique talent. *The Sun-San Bernardino County,* U1–U2.

Short, D. (1998). Secondary newcomer programs: Helping recent immigrants prepare for school success. *ERIC Digest.* Retrieved January 28, 2005, from http://searcheric.org/scripts/seget2.asp?db=ericft&want=http://searcheric.org/ericdc/ED419385.htm

Short, D. J., & Boyson, B. A. (2004). *Creating access: Language and academic programs for secondary school newcomers.* Santa Cruz, CA: Center for Research on Education, Diversity & Excellence.

Short, D. J., Vogt, M., & Echevarría, J. (2011). *The SIOP model for teaching science to English learners.* Boston: Pearson.

Shuit, D., & McConnell, P. (1992, January 6). Calculating the impact of California's immigrants. *Los Angeles Times,* A1, A19.

Siccone, F. (1995). *Celebrating diversity: Building self-esteem in today's multicultural classrooms.* Boston: Allyn & Bacon.

SIL International. (2000). *Geographic distribution of living languages, 2000.* Retrieved May 17, 2006, from www.ethnologue.com/ethno_docs/distribution.asp

Silver, H. F., Strong, R. W., & Perini, M. J. (2000). *So each may learn: Integrating learning styles and multiple intelligences.* Alexandria, VA: Association for Supervision and Curriculum Development.

Sindell, P. (1988). Some discontinuities in the enculturation of Mistassini Cree children. In J. Wurzel (Ed.), *Toward multiculturalism.* Yarmouth, ME: Intercultural Press.

Singleton, D. M., & Ryan, L. (2004). *Language acquisition: The age factor.* Clevedon, UK: Multilingual Matters.

Skutnabb-Kangas, T. (1981). *Bilingualism or not: The education of minorities* (L. Malmberg & D. Crane, Trans.). Clevedon, UK: Multilingual Matters.

Slavin, R. E. (1991). A synthesis of research on cooperative learning. *Educational Leadership, 48,* 71–82.

Smagorinsky, P. (2008). *Teaching English by design.* Portsmouth, NH: Heinemann.

Smallwood, B. A. (Ed.). (2000). *Integrating the ESL standards into classroom practice: Grades Pre-K–2.* Alexandria, VA: Teachers of English to Speakers of Other Languages (TESOL).

Smilkstein, R. (2002). *We're born to learn: Using the brain's natural learning process to create today's curriculum.* Thousand Oaks, CA: Sage Publications.

Smith, F. (1982). *Writing and the writer.* New York: Holt, Rinehart, & Winston.

Smith, F. (1983). *Essays into literacy.* Portsmouth, NH: Heinemann.

Smith, S. L., Paige, R. M., & Steglitz, I. (1998). Theoretical foundations of intercultural training and applications to the teaching of culture. In D. L. Lange, C. A. Klee, R. M. Paige, & Y. A. Yershova (Eds.), *Culture as the core: Interdisciplinary perspectives on culture teaching and learning in the language curriculum* (pp. 53–91). Minneapolis: Center for Advanced Research on Language Acquisition, University of Minnesota.

Smith, T. E. C., Polloway, E. A., Patton, J. R., & Dowdy, C. A. (2003). *Teaching children with special needs in inclusive settings* (4th ed.). Boston: Allyn & Bacon.

Snow, C., & Hoefnagel-Hoehle, M. (1978). The critical period for language acquisition: Evidence from second language learning. *Child Development, 49,* 1114–1118.

Snow, C. E., Burns, S. M., & Griffin, P. (Eds.). (1998). *Preventing reading difficulties in young children.* Washington, DC: National Academies Press.

Snow, D. (1996). *More than a native speaker.* Alexandria, VA: Teachers of English to Speakers of Other Languages (TESOL).

Snow, M. A. (1993). Discipline-based foreign language teaching: Implications from ESL/EFL. In M. Krueger & F. Ryan (Eds.), *Language and content: Discipline- and content-based approaches to language study* (pp. 37–56). Lexington, MA: D.C. Heath.

Snow, M. A., & Brinton, D. M. (1988). Content-based language instruction: Investigating the effectiveness of the adjunct model. *TESOL Quarterly, 22*(3), 201–217.

Sonbuchner, G. M. (1991). *How to take advantage of your learning styles.* Syracuse, NY: New Readers Press.

Sousa, D. A. (2005). *How the brain learns to read.* Thousand Oaks, CA: Corwin.

Southern Poverty Law Center. (1999). *Youth at the edge.* Montgomery, AL: Author. Retrieved August 2, 2006, from www.splcenter.org/intel/intelreport/article.jsp?aid=302

Spears, R. A. (1992). *Common American phrases.* Lincolnwood, IL: National Textbook Company.

Spellmeyer, K. (1989). A common ground: The essay in the academy. *College English, 51,* 262–276.

Spinelli, E. (1994). *English grammar for students of Spanish* (3rd ed.). Ann Arbor, MI: The Olivia and Hill Press.

Spohrer, K. (2009). *Teaching NLP in the classroom.* London: Continuum International.

Spring, J. (2001). *The new Mandarin society? Testing on the fast track.* Retrieved July 31, 2006, from www.mhhe.com/socscience/education/spring/commentary.mhtml

Stahl, N. A., King, J. R., & Henk, W. A. (1991). Enhancing students' notetaking through training and evaluation. *Journal of Reading, 34*(8), 614–622.

Stanovich, K. (1986). Matthew effects in reading: Some consequences in individual differences in the acquisition of literacy. *Reading Research Quarterly, 21,* 360–407.

Stensland, L. (2003). *The Unz initiatives and the dangers of direct democracy.* Retrieved April 27, 2010, from www.oberlin.edu/library/friends/research.awards/STENSLAND.pdf

Strehorn, K. (2001). The application of Universal Instructional Design to ESL teaching. *Internet TESL Journal.* Retrieved July 7, 2006, from http://iteslj.org/Techniques/Strehorn-UID.html

Suid, M., & Lincoln, W. (1992). *Ten-minute whole language warm-ups.* Palo Alto, CA: Monday Morning Books.

Suina, J. (1985). . . . And then I went to school. *New Mexico Journal of Reading, 5*(2). Retrieved August 24, 2010, from www.ndsg.org/jsuina/index.html

Sunal, C. S., & Haas, M. E. (2005). *Social studies for elementary and middle grades: A constructivist approach.* Boston: Allyn & Bacon.

Suresh, B. (2003). Get 'em hooked on books—Start an ESL book club. *CATESOL News, 30*(2), 14.

Suzuki, B. (1989, November/December). Asian Americans as the "model minority." *Change, 21,* 12–19.

Swartz, S., Klein, A. F., & Shook, R. E. (2002). *Interactive writing & interactive editing: Making connections between writing and reading.* Carlsbad, CA: Dominie Press.

Swartz, S. L., Shook, R. E., Klein, A. F., Moon, C., Bunnell, K., Belt, M., & Huntley, C. (2003). *Guided reading and literacy centers.* Carlsbad, CA: Dominie Press.

Takahashi, E., Austin, T., & Morimoto, Y. (2000). Social interaction and language development in an FLES classroom. In J. K. Hall & L. S. Verplaetse (Eds.), *Second and foreign language learning through classroom interaction* (pp. 139–162). Mahwah, NJ: Erlbaum.

Takayama, B., & Ledward, B. (2009). *Hawaiian cultural influences in education (NCIE): School engagement among Hawaiian students.* Honolulu, HI: Kamehameha Schools Research & Evaluation Division.

Tannen, D. (2001). *Discourse analysis.* In Linguistic Society of America, "Fields of Linguistics." Retrieved August 20, 2010, from http://www.lsadc.org/info/ling-fields-discourse.cfm

Taylor, B. P. (1987). Teaching ESL: Incorporating a communicative student-centered component. In M. Long & J. C. Richards (Eds.), *Methodology of TESOL* (pp. 45–58). Rowley, MA: Newbury House.

Taylor, D. (2000). Facing hardships: Jamestown and colonial life. In K. Samway (Ed.), *Integrating the ESL standards into classroom practice* (pp. 53–55). Alexandria, VA: Teachers of English to Speakers of Other Languages (TESOL).

*Texas English as a second language standards.* Retrieved April 19, 2010, from www.sbec.state.tx.us/sbeconline/standtest/standards/allesl.pdf

Tharp, R. (1989). Culturally compatible education: A formula for designing effective classrooms. In H. Trueba, G. Spindler, & L. Spindler (Eds.), *What do anthropologists have to say about dropouts?* New York: Falmer Press.

Tharp, R., & Gallimore, R. (1991). *The instructional conversation: Teaching and learning in social activity.* Washington, DC: National Center for Research on Cultural Diversity and Second Language Learning.

Thernstrom, A., & Thernstrom, S. (2003). *No excuses: Closing the racial gap in learning.* New York: Simon & Schuster.

Thomas, W., & Collier, V. (1997). *School effectiveness for language minority students.* Retrieved August 4, 2006, from www.ncela.gwu.edu/pubs/resource/effectiveness

Thonis, E. (1983). *The English-Spanish connection.* Los Angeles: Santillana.

Tinajero, J. V., & Schifini, A. (1997). *Into English.* Carmel, CA: Hampton-Brown.

Tresaugue, M. (2002, January 31). Back to the basics. *Riverside Press-Enterprise,* A1, A8.

Trueba, H. (1989). *Raising silent voices.* Boston: Heinle & Heinle.

Trueba, H., Cheng, L., & Ima, K. (1993). *Myth or reality: Adaptive strategies of Asian Americans in California.* Washington, DC: Falmer Press.

Tunmer, W. E., Herriman, M. L., & Nesdale, A. R. (1988). Metalinguistic abilities and beginning reading. *Reading Research Quarterly, 23*(2), 134–158.

Ukpokodu, N. (2002). Multiculturalism vs. globalism. In F. Schultz (Ed.), *Annual editions: Multicultural education 2002–2003* (pp. 7–10). Guilford, CT: McGraw-Hill/Dushkin.

Uribe, M., & Nathenson-Mejia, S. (2008). *Literacy essentials for English language learners.* New York: Teachers College Press.

U.S. Census Bureau. (2000). *Hispanic population in the United States: Population characteristics.* Retrieved August 4, 2006, from www.census.gov/population/www/socdemo/hispanic/ho00.html

U.S. Census Bureau. (2001). *Census 2000 supplementary survey.* Washington, DC: Author.

U.S. Census Bureau. (2003). *Language use, English ability, and linguistic isolation for the population 5 years and over by state, 2000* (Summary File 3, Tables P19, PCT13, and PCT14). Washington, DC: Author.

U.S. Census Bureau. (2004). *Educational attainment in the U.S.: 2003.* Retrieved August 2, 2006, from www.census.gov/population/www/socdemo/educ-attn.html

U.S. Census Bureau (2006). *Hispanics in the United States.* Retrieved August 20, 2010, from www.census.gov/population/www/socdemo/hispanic.html

U.S. Census Bureau. (2007). *The American community—Asians: 2004.* Retrieved August 20, 2010, from www.census.gov/population/www/socdemo/race/reports-wkpaers.html

U.S. Government Accounting Office. (2002). *Per-pupil spending differences between selected inner city and suburban schools varied by metropolitan area.* Retrieved August 2, 2006, from www.gao.gov/new.items/d03234.pdf

*U.S. immigration history in your own language.* (2010). Retrieved on August 24, 2010, from www.rapidimmigration.com/usa/1_eng_immigration_history.html

Valenzuela, A. (2004). *Leaving children behind: How "Texas-style" accountability fails Latino youth.* New York: State University of New York Press.

Valenzuela, J. S., & Baca, L. (2004). Procedures and techniques for assessing the bilingual exceptional child. In L. M. Baca & H. T. Cervantes (Eds.), *The bilingual special education interface* (4th ed., pp. 184–203). Upper Saddle River, NJ: Pearson Merrill/Prentice Hall.

Veeder, K., & Tramutt, J. (2000). Strengthening literacy in both languages. In N. Cloud, F. Genesee, & E. Hamayan (Eds.), *Dual language instruction.* Boston: Heinle & Heinle.

Verdugo Hills High School. (2004). *Redesignated students.* Retrieved August 24, 2010, from www.lausd.k12.ca.us/Verdugo_HS/classes/esl/redes.htm

Villegas, A. M., & Lucas, T. (2002). Preparing culturally responsive teachers: Rethinking the curriculum. *Journal of Teacher Education, 53*(1), 20–32.

Vogt, M., Echevarría, J., & Short, D. L. (2010). *The SIOP model for teaching English-language arts to English learners.* Boston: Pearson.

Vygotsky, L. (1981). The genesis of higher mental functions. In J. V. Wertsch (Ed.), *The concept of activity in Soviet psychology.* Armonk, NY: Sharpe.

Wallraff, B. (2000). What global language? *The Atlantic Monthly, 286*(5), 52–66.

Walqui, A. (1999). Assessment of culturally and linguistically diverse students: Considerations for the 21st century. In Mid-continent Research for Education and Learning (McREL) (Ed.), *Including culturally and linguistically diverse students in standards-based reform: A report on McREL's Diversity Roundtable I* (pp. 55–84). Aurora, CO: Author. Retrieved August 20, 2010, www.mcrel.org/topics/productDetail.asp?topicsID=3&productID=56

Ward, A. W., & Murray-Ward, M. (1999). *Assessment in the classroom.* Belmont, CA: Wadsworth.

Warren, B., Ballenger, C., Ogonowski, M., Rosebery, A., & Hudicourt-Barnes, J. (2001). Rethinking diversity in learning science: The logic of everyday language. *Journal of Research in Science Teaching, 38*(5), 529–552.

Warschauer, M. (1995). *E-mail for English teaching.* Alexandria, VA: Teachers of English to Speakers of Other Languages (TESOL).

Warschauer, M., Shetzer, H., & Meloni, C. (2000). *Internet for English teaching.* Alexandria, VA: Teachers of English to Speakers of Other Languages (TESOL).

Watahomigie, L. (1995). The power of American Indian parents and communities. *Bilingual Research Journal, 19*(1), 99–115.

Weatherly, S. D. (1999). I'll buy it! In R. E. Larimer & L. Schleicher (Eds.), *New ways in using authentic materials in the classroom* (pp. 73–80). Alexandria, VA: Teachers of English to Speakers of Other Languages (TESOL).

Weaver, C. (1988). *Reading process and practice.* Portsmouth, NH: Heinemann.

Weber, E. (2005). *MI strategies in the classroom and beyond.* Boston: Pearson.

Weiler, J. (1998). Recent changes in school desegregation. *ERIC Digest* (ED 419029). Clearinghouse on Urban Education. Retrieved August 4, 2006, from www.ericfacility.net/ericdigests/ed419029.htm

Weiss, I. R., & Pasley, J. D. (2004, February). What is high-quality instruction? *Educational Leadership, 61*(5), 24–28.

Wells, C. G. (1981). *Learning through interaction: The study of language development.* Cambridge, UK: Cambridge University Press.

Wells, G. (1998). Using the tool-kit of discourse in the activity of learning and teaching. In G. Wells (Ed.), *Dialogic inquiry* (pp. 231–266). Cambridge, UK: Cambridge University Press.

Wells, G., & Chang-Wells, G. L. (1992). *Constructing knowledge together: Classrooms as centers of inquiry and literacy.* Portsmouth, NH: Heinemann.

Westling, D. L., & Koorland, M. A. (1988). *The special educator's handbook.* Boston: Allyn & Bacon.

Wexler, E., & Huerta, K. (2002). An empowering spirit is not enough: A Latino charter school struggles for leadership. In B. Fuller (Ed.), *Inside charter schools: The paradox of radical decentralizaion* (pp. 98–123). Cambridge, MA: Harvard University Press.

Whisler, N., & Williams, J. (1990). *Literature and cooperative learning: Pathway to literacy.* Sacramento, CA: Literature Co-op.

Whitman, E. L. (1994). *Miss Nell fell in the well.* Kissimmee, FL: Learning Pyramid.

Wiese, A. M., & García, E. (1998). The Bilingual Education Act: Language minority students and equal educational opportunity. *Bilingual Research Journal, 22*(1). Retrieved June 21, 2005, from http://brj.asu.edu/v221/articles/art1.html

Wiggins, G. P., & McTighe, J. (1998). *Understanding by design.* Alexandria, VA: Association for Supervision and Curriculum Development.

Wilson, W. (1984). The urban underclass. In L. Dunbar (Ed.), *Minority report.* New York: Pantheon Books.

Wilton, D. (2003). *How many words are there in the English language?* Retrieved May 19, 2006, from www.wordorigins.org/number.htm

Wink, J. (2000). *Critical pedagogy: Notes from the real world.* New York: Addison-Wesley.

Witte, K. (1991). The role of culture in health and disease. In L. Samovar & R. Porter (Eds.), *Intercultural communication: A reader* (6th ed.). Belmont, CA: Wadsworth.

Wolfe, P., & Poynor, L. (2001). Politics and the pendulum: An alternative understanding of the case of whole language as educational innovation. *Educational Researcher, 30*(1), 15–20.

Wolfram, W. (1991). *Dialects and American English.* Englewood Cliffs, NJ: Prentice Hall.

Wolfram, W. (1995). Reexamining dialect in TESOL. *TESOL Matters, 5*(2), 1, 22.

Wong, M. S. (1998). *You said it! Listening/speaking strategies and activities.* New York: St. Martin's Press.

Woolfolk, A. (2003). *Educational psychology* (9th ed.). Boston: Allyn & Bacon.

Woolfolk, A., & Brooks, D. (1985). The influence of teachers' nonverbal behaviors on students' perceptions and performance. *Elementary School Journal, 85,* 514–528.

Wray, M., & Newitz, A. (1997). *White trash: Race and class in America.* New York and London: Routledge.

Wright, W. E., & Li, X. (2006). Catching up in math? The case of newly-arrived Cambodian students in a Texas intermediate school. *TABE Journal, 9*(1), 1–22.

Yao, E. (1988). Working effectively with Asian immigrant parents. *Phi Delta Kappan, 70*(3), 223–225.

Yep, L. (1975). *Dragonwings.* New York: Harper and Row.

Young, M., & Helvie, S. (1996). Parent power: A positive link to school success. *Journal of Educational Issues of Language Minority Students, 16.* Retrieved July 7, 2006, from www.ncela.gwu.edu/pubs/jeilms/vol16/jeilms1611.htm

Zacarian, D. (2004). I was lost before the end of the first minute. *Essential Teacher, 1*(3), 11–13.

Zacarian, D. (2005). Rainforests and parking lots. *Essential Teacher, 2*(1), 10–11.

Zacarian, D. (2006). Testing, testing. *Essential Teacher, 3*(2), 10–12.

Zelman, N. (1996). *Conversational inspirations: Over 2000 conversation topics.* Battleboro, VT: Pro Lingua Associates.

Zimmerman, C. (1997). Do reading and interactive vocabulary instruction make a difference? An empirical study. *TESOL Quarterly, 31*(1), 121–140.

Zwiers, J. (2008). *Building academic language: Essential practices for content classrooms.* San Francisco: Jossey-Bass.